THE
HISTORY
OF THE
Celtic
PEOPLE

THE
HISTORY
OF THE
Celtic
PEOPLE

HENRI HUBERT

BRACKEN BOOKS
LONDON

Originally published 1934 as
The Rise of the Celts and *The Greatness and
Decline of the Celts* by Henri Hubert.

This edition published in 1992 by Bracken Books,
an imprint of Studio Editions Ltd.,
Princess House, 50 Eastcastle Street,
London, W1N 7AP.

Printed and bound in Finland.

ISBN 1 85170 952 5

PUBLISHER'S NOTE

The History of the Celtic People is a facsimile reprint of
Henri Hubert's two volumes, *The Rise of the Celts* and *The
Greatness and Decline of the Celts*, which were first
published in English in 1934. The publishers wish to point
out that the original page numbering has been retained for
each book, with the exception of the bibliography, which
initially appeared in both volumes, but has only been
incorporated at the end of this edition. Book II, *The
Greatness and Decline of the Celts*, begins on page
number 317.

BOOK
I

THE
RISE
OF THE
Celts

HENRI HUBERT

CONTENTS

ix

x

CONTENTS

PART TWO

PLATES

ILLUSTRATIONS IN THE TEXT

xi

PLATES

MAPS

FOREWORD

THE EXPANSION OF THE CELTS

WITH the Celts a very important factor enters into the history of civilization, and a much-expected work appears in this series—expected for the subject's sake and for the author's.

About this racial group, and the capital part which it played in European history, it was known that the best-informed scholar, whose knowledge was both widest and most profoundly thought out, was Henri Hubert. Now Hubert died four years ago, and many despaired of ever seeing the work announced under his name.

It appears, with a long and grievous story behind it. "The main part of the work," in Hubert's own words, was done in 1914 (his letter of the 15th June, 1915). After the unavoidable interruption of the war—during which he did valued work chiefly with the Ministry of Armament—he hastened to pick up the threads, and on the 5th January, 1923, he wrote to me: "To-day I wrote the last line of my last chapter." He added: "Now I have to take up the whole thing again, to cut, patch together, and check." Various circumstances—a cruel loss, family concerns, and ill-health which gradually grew worse— delayed this work of revision, which he was carrying on at the same time as he was preparing his book on the Germans. In July, August, and October, 1925, he sent me news which was at once reassuring and saddening. "I am at work. I progress slowly but surely. I was kept in bed all May. I am gradually climbing up the hill . . . My work progresses steadily, but in very adverse circumstances. I have got rid of all my lectures. You can therefore count on me to the full extent of my will. But it seems that an evil fortune dogs me, and I do not know what it still has in store for me." On the 9th October, 1926, he again reassured me. "All intensive work upsets me, whatever it is. But I have done a little work, all the same, and I shall be able to do more. I cannot tell you when I shall have finished. It would be absurd. But it cannot be long now."

On Wednesday, the 18th May, 1927, he was once again telling me how his task had progressed, and concluded, " It is obviously not easy to write the history of the Celts to-day. But that is done. It is chiefly mechanical work which remains." On Thursday, the 26th, a note from our common friend, Marcel Mauss, told me that he had just died of a heart attack. And Mauss added a detail which was very affecting for me : " The manuscript of the Celts was on his table ; he had been working at it on Tuesday."

Three devoted friends undertook to prepare the manuscript for publication. For four years they have in turn given up to this duty all the time which they could afford. One of them, in pages which you will read later, tells the exact share of each. That this work should appear, representing Hubert's scientific testament and giving an idea of his knowledge and his talents to a large public which was not reached by his learned treatises, is a great satisfaction to all his friends. But that it should appear after his death, and that he should not reap the harvest of success and esteem which he may not have sought, but had at least slowly earned, is a great grief to those who had grown attached both to the scholar and thinker and to the man—the man of heart, the man of taste, the rare and most attractive personality.

From his youth onwards Hubert had won many strong friendships. One of the close intimates of his years at the École Normale has told how far his ability rose above the lessons which he was doing at that time, how much more mature he was than his fellows, being already " sure of his vocation and his methods ". Another chosen brother has related his life— too short, but so full of work and thought.[1] The beginnings, the achievement of ancient or primitive peoples, both of an intellectual and of a material kind—languages, categories of thought, religions, arts, tools—were what gradually came to compel his interest, which was at once very wide and very penetrating. Much travel, including a voyage round the world which enabled him to see various types of man and to become acquainted with the chief institutes and museums of ethnography, prehistory, and archæology, brought him and kept him in touch with the realities of mankind, past and present. His mind was thereby enriched and stimulated. Work on the Semitic religions,

---

[1] *Marcel Drouin*, in Annuaire de l'Association amicale des anciens élèves de l'École normale supérieure, 1929, *pp.* 45–51.

a class in the history of the primitive religions of Europe at the École des Hautes-Études, a class in national archæology at the École du Louvre, Celtic research connected with his post as Keeper at the Saint-Germain Museum, active collaboration on the Année sociologique, *were the expression of his keenness to know and to understand. Hubert was a historian in the strongest sense of the word. His whole career was inspired by the spirit of synthesis. He was a born collaborator for this series, and he was one of the first to promise me his whole-hearted assistance.*

When I published Marcel Granet's Chinese Civilization *and announced a second volume,* Chinese Thought, *I justified the division into two volumes and declared that there was no intention of making it a precedent. On the whole, it is better, in conducting a series on a very large scale, to avoid definite statements and over-absolute principles. The manuscript handed to me by Hubert's friend amounted, with the illustrations and the usual additional matter, to seven or eight hundred pages of type. It would have been inconvenient to offer such a compact volume and one so unlike the others in size. On the other hand, it was impossible, after all the reductions which Hubert had either made himself or allowed for,[1] to cut any more out of a work which is so valuable in every respect.*

What Hubert conceived, and has been the first to carry out, is a history of all the Celts, a picture of every part of the Celtic world. From the most distant origins to which we can in the present state of our knowledge go back, to the last submergences or survivals, he embraces the whole of Celticism, with incomparable knowledge and a sympathy which does not blind him, but rather gives him vision. This wealth of material, fortunately, was of a nature to be divided without difficulty into two volumes of about the same size.[2]

The present volume tells of the Celtic world down to the La Tène period, that is to the second Iron Age. The second will treat of the three phases of that period, and, after a picture of

[1] *See the Note by Marcel Mauss.*
[2] *The second part of the work, on the movements of the Celtic peoples, which contained twelve long chapters, fairly logically falls into three divisions—Celtic expansion to the La Tène period (second part of the first volume), Celtic expansion in the La Tène period, and the end of the Celtic world (first and second parts of the second volume).*

*the decline of the Celts, it will describe the essential features of
their civilization.   There we shall see them more and more
appearing as a factor in the history of the world, and more
particularly in Roman history, until at last they are incorporated
in the Empire.*[1]

*In accordance with the principle which we have adopted
of placing human groups in our general scheme at the moment
when their activities visibly enter into the great stream of
historical evolution, we have placed the* Celts *in the Roman
section, before the formation of the Empire* [2] *; but it was desirable
at this point to look backwards, to show what the Celts were,
whence they came, and what they did in the obscure times of
their life as barbarians.   These questions are exactly what this
present volume covers, so far as it is possible to answer them at
all.   It links up with the works of J. de Morgan on* Prehistoric
Man *and Eugène Pittard on* Race and History, *and, in general,
it comes as a completion to all those which, in this first section,
have dealt with the great movements of mankind and the peopling
of the earth.*

*In this volume, then, we have to do with barbarians, not
in the ancient sense of* βάρβαρος, barbarus *"foreign to Greece
or Rome" (for we do not regard the Egyptians and Persians
as barbarians), but in the sense of peoples incompletely stabilized
and civilized, of masses in process of moving and changing.*[3]
*We are dealing with barbarians whom the Greeks and Romans
doubtless knew, but knew very little at first, and about whom the
ancients, in their writings, give us information which at first
is very vague or disputable.*[4]   *There are human groups which,
as we know, came only very late into the ken of "civilized men".
How, then, are we at this day to come to know that protohistoric
Europe, which lay on the borders of a Mediterranean Europe
already rich in history?   How, in particular, are we to know
those Celts and Germans, who were to play such a great part one
day in the Roman Empire, the former strengthening it and the
latter overthrowing it?   How are we to know them, save from*

---

[1] *See V. Chapot,* The Roman Empire, *in this series, pp.* 293 *ff.*
[2] *We had a glimpse of them in Homo,* Primitive Italy, *in this series,*
pp. 165 *ff.*
[3] *See Lot,* The End of the Ancient World, *Foreword, p. xiii, n.* 3.
[4] *" A great part of ancient ethnology has come down to us in the form of
fables and myths through the epic or lyric poets and the polygraphers "* (p. 299).

*what they themselves tell us, gathering up the only evidence
which survives of their racial personality and their doings—
linguistic facts and archæological facts ?*

*Hubert in the first part of this volume has laid stress on the
methods which he uses to determine, to isolate, the Celtic element,
to know " what the Celts were ".*

*Without excluding anthropology,[1] he carefully limits its
rôle. " One must not resort to that inexhaustible source of error
and contradictions, save with great moderation and in a very
critical spirit ; it must not be forgotten that peoples and races,
being different things, do not necessarily coincide, and, in fact,
never coincide exactly." [2] The Celts " are not a race " ; it is
the name of a people or of a group of peoples, and that group is
an aggregate of anthropological types.*

*It is, then, the ethnography of the Celts that Hubert endeavours
to constitute, by studying the surviving traces of their civilization.
If the history of civilization as a whole is something quite other
than ethnography, and, as I believe, requires to be clearly
differentiated from it,[3] we must recognize that the various
civilizations, when their special characteristics are studied,
" represent and distinguish peoples." And, for civilizations
which have " left their remnants in the ground ", it is largely
archæology that, finding in them " legitimate indications of
vanished peoples ", " brings together the scattered data of their
ethnography " (p. 80). There is, in Hubert's words, an
archæological* ethnography *(p. 129). Once again we note, as
J. de Morgan, Pittard, Moret, and yet others have given us
occasion to do, the marvellous range of that militant history
which burrows in the ground and reconstructs the past with
documents of stone and metal, or recreates life from fossil
skeletons.[4] And we must lay weight on Hubert's appeal when*

[1] *" Every group of men living together forms a physical, social, and moral
unit "* (p. 21). *Anthropological study is at the foundation.*

[2] p. 31 ; *cf. pp.* 28, 32, *and Pittard,* Race and History, passim.
Cf. M. Boule, Les Hommes fossiles, p. 320 : *the word " Celtic " means to
some a language, to others a special civilization ; it is often used as a synonym
for Gallic ; in the mind of some writers, it represents the fair, tall, long-headed
type of the North ; others say that it should be applied to a dark, short, round-
headed type from the Central Plateau or the Alps. " The best thing for
anthropologists to do is to leave the word to archæologists and historians."*

[3] *See, among the publications of the Centre International de Synthèse,*
Civilisation : le mot et l'idée, 1930 ; *and, in the* Revue de Synthèse, *June,*
1931, p. 195, " Ethnographie et ethnologie," *a draft of an article for the*
Vocabulaire historique.

[4] *On this subject, see* Revue de Synthèse, Dec., 1931.

he asks for more intense activity (for exploration is still singularly incomplete), and wishes that, instead of the chance which usually directs archæological discoveries, there may be more and more methodical and certain exploitation of these material records.[1]

Secondly there is a linguistic ethnography *(p. 33). If the study of speech belongs to the history of civilization, languages are facts of civilization which count among " the most typical or most apparent " of such facts, among " the clearest and truest " characteristics of peoples (p. 33). Perhaps the greatest achievement of Hubert, that complete historian, has been to make such extensive and original use of European philology of which he had a vast knowledge. " Nothing else could take the place of this kind of information. That is why," he says, " we must spend some time in examining the Celtic languages and their affinities " (p. 34). And he shows that one of the most valuable achievements of philology has been to compare the remains of Celtic supplied by names of places and people and a few inscriptions with the Celtic languages which are still spoken. " The unity of the Celtic languages is plain. There were very close similarities between them, such as did not exist between any of them and any other language " (p. 42). In general, the study of the island Celts, which is almost always left to the philologists, seems to Hubert to be indispensable to a knowledge of " Celticness " ; for there are deep strata of the past which can be reached through their literature.*

Hubert's effort to utilize both kinds of evidence and to make the combination of them fruitful is truly admirable. It is conducted with exemplary caution, with " the sternest and most austere method " (p. 17). " It is, of course, true," he says, " that phonetic facts, like archæological, have no absolute racial significance." Often delicate interpretation is called for (pp. 132, 144). " I am inclined to think, without being quite sure " (p. 31)—phrases of the kind constantly fall from that ingenious but prudent pen.

There are, however, objects, forms of tombs, manners of speech, which allow us to classify the Celts as Indo-Europeans, to place them among the Europeans, to distinguish them from the Græco-Latins, Germans, and Balto-Slavs, to contrast them with the Iberians and Ligurians, to determine the Celtic world

---

[1] *p. 81 and the following volume, pt. i, chaps. i, v.*

*and its boundaries. Hubert clearly brings out the racial unity
of the Celts; it may not be anthropological, but " common life
produced a kind of unification of physical types in a sort of
habitus common to all " (p. 32). He perceives diversity within
the unity, but reduces that diversity to a division into four
groups—Goidels, Picts, Brythons (including the Gauls), and
Belgæ.*

*There are in this preliminary essay in Celtic ethnography
two points on which especial weight should be laid : Hubert's
indications on the Goidels and those on the relations of the Celts
and the Germans, in which he touches on the subject of the volume
which he has devoted to this last people.*

*Neither archæologists nor historians distinguish, at any
rate clearly enough, between the two groups of Celts, the Brythons
of the Continent and Britain and the Goidels of Ireland and
Scotland, " who had advanced furthest west of the Celts "
(p. 137). By an extremely ingenious demonstration Hubert
establishes an important fact—that the Goidelic group broke
off at a very early date (pp. 138–9, 169). By an equally convincing
demonstration he reveals the close contact which subsisted
between Germans and Celts, and the influence exerted by Celtic
culture on Germanic, extending, indeed, beyond the Germans
to the Balto-Slavs and Finns (p. 68). This influence is manifest
in linguistic and material borrowings. " The Celts seem to have
been for long ages the schoolmasters of the Germanic peoples."
The facts adduced by Hubert and the conclusions which he draws
from them conflict curiously with the theories of the rôle of
Germanentum which have inspired so many modern German
books. If, as seems to have been the case, there were intimate
relations, phenomena of " reception " and even of intermingling, and if the Celts appeared as the preponderant
people, we must, at the least, regard this as one of those cases
of contamination and racial fusion which have been for the
good of mankind.[1]*

*The same archæological and linguistic facts which first
enable Hubert, by collecting them all together, to describe
Celticism as a whole, afterwards enable him, by setting them in
their proper place and time, " to find out whence the Celts came,*

---

[1] *pp. 67–8, 224; cf. pp. 64 ff., 156, 182, and second volume, pt. i,
ch. iv, and pt. iii, ch. i.*

*where they went, how they expanded, and where they stopped—
in short, to trace their history " (p. 131).[1]*

*So, taking as his starting-point the Indo-European unity
of which he sees signs in the East (pp. 75–6), he follows the
group as it breaks off into what will long be its habitat, the
centre of Europe, the future Germany—for the Rhine is Celtic
and the Danube, too (pp. 148–152). Before the first millennium
before Christ, he sees the Goidels breaking off, and the Italici,
and then the Picts. Beginning in the Bronze Age, this expansion
goes on in the first Iron Age, in what is known as the Hallstatt
period, and a homogeneous civilization extends, down to the
fifth century, over Western Germany, Upper Austria, Switzerland, Lorraine, Franche-Comté, and Burgundy. And beyond
that domain the Celtic drive will reach to the British Isles
and Italy and Spain, to go on, as we shall see in the next volume,
through the La Tène period ; so, by the absorption of borrowed
elements into the culture of Hallstatt, it will help to make the
civilization of the new period.*

*This history of Celtic expansion, the migrations, the settle-
ments, the daring advances of smaller bodies in every direction,
the contacts and conflicts with various peoples, need not be
repeated here in its complex detail ; what I wish to do, rather,
is to emphasize the marvellously vivid and picturesque manner
in which Hubert has described it.*

*Imagination is a dangerous thing when it lets itself go on
insufficient evidence ; but, as I have often said, it plays
a legitimate part when it comes in to crown a long piece of
analysis, when it is inspired by a wealth of learning, when it
completes and vivifies a synthesis by a sort of spontaneous
generation of images which have arisen to the inward eye. Here,
precisely, is the great historian's gift of recreating ; he is, as
he has been called, " the seer of the past."*

*Now a man who for many years has handled the weapons,
helmets, shields, brooches, and torques of his Celts, who has
looked into their tumuli and seen, not only objects, but skulls
and skeletons (grandiaque effossis mirabitur ossa sepulcris—
Hubert himself quotes Virgil's line somewhere), although
historical discipline and critical sense restrain and govern his
imagination, cannot help picturing all that past in which he has
lived in spirit.*

---

[1] *See p. 139 for certain hypotheses on which this work is based.*

" One may try to imagine "—" We can form a fairly true picture "—" I imagine "—such are the phrases which continually express that effort, or, rather, that achievement of the imagination. As a result of following, on the ground or on the map,[1] the migrations of archæological and linguistic forms, and of observing all those human footprints, he comes to see the groups themselves migrating, settling, advancing, and receding. In this volume, and in the second, in which he follows the Gauls and the Galatians on their epic inroads, you will find pictures of great power. Hubert sees, and he makes you see.

Between the North Sea and Switzerland, the Meuse and the Oder, there was a population, not very dense, very mobile, partly pastoral and partly agricultural (and therefore attracted and held for some time by good land), intermingled with warlike tribes, hunters, fishers, and brigands, who were attracted by forests and hills or rivers (pp. 180–1). " We must not imagine these prehistoric peoples as keeping strictly within neat frontiers " (p. 186), and we must not imagine them as being always unmixed, " divided racially into clearly defined watertight compartments." It was amid diffusion and interspersion in the " racial hotchpotch " of Western Germany that " those Celtic societies came into being, round which the whole population finally crystallized " and a " single civilization of their own " was built up (pp. 157, 182, 241). But it was not until the Bronze Age that the Celts were numerous and homogeneous enough to go and found huge settlements at a distance. For we must distinguish migrations in mass, the movements of " the great hordes which periodically descended on the good lands of Europe ; sometimes shy, sometimes raging, laden with baggage and loot . . . sometimes led by chiefs of astonishing clearness of mind, sometimes seeming to be guided by chance and instinct "[2] from the forays of daring bands of adventurers and fortune-seekers (p. 217) ; the sea is a " great road " (p. 200) favourable to this latter kind of incursion. So the " vagabondage " of the Celts took many forms ; and small bands often went before or after the great masses, social units and more or less composite groups of social units.

Once the great Celtic migrations had started they continued

---

[1] *He is always cautious : " When one starts pricking out routes on a map, one is too easily led into imagining movements and directions " (p. 143).*
[2] *Next volume, pt. i, chap. iv. Cf. Homo, loc. cit.*

*in successive waves. It seems that each wave, " exactly following
its predecessors and tending to spread on the top of them, went
as far as it could, until it was forced to stop " (p. 229) ; and as
each left a deposit, each altered the racial structure and the
domain of the Celtic world. Hubert sees Goidels, Picts, Brythons,
and Belgæ spreading out in turn ; he traces the routes by which
they went ; he pictures, in the Hallstatt period, " the warriors,
with shaven faces (they took their razors with them into their
graves), long, broad iron swords with heavy conical pommels
and wooden sheaths, seldom wearing helmets . . . seldom having
breastplates, and carrying round shields " (p. 256).*

*When Hubert comes to the invasions of the second and first
centuries, for which we have literary evidence, he finds in the
contemporary accounts details and features which seem to him
to have a retrospective interest outside the period with which
they deal. Thus Cæsar's story of the last migration of the
Continental Celts—the Helvetii and Boii—gives, he says,
" a very vivid picture, and certainly an idea of the very typical
fashion in which the great migrations were prepared and took
place, of the conditions, the objects, the collective phantoms
which rose up, the pow-wows in which the programme was
settled, and the start organized." [1] All through his work, to
give strength and precision to the picture called up by the vestiges
of the past, he takes inspiration from the " model " offered by
the last invasions ; they have supplied him with a* transposable
image.[2]

*But outside the movements of the Celtic peoples, the image
which Hubert gives of them is equally transposable. We are
indebted to him for a better idea, in general, of all those
phenomena of migration which are one of the most characteristic
and most interesting aspects of the early history of mankind.
At the beginning of the Bronze Age and at the beginning of the
Iron Age there were movements on a huge scale, which went
beyond the confines of the Celtic world. And in prehistory as in
protohistory there were periods of unrest, in which " demographic
laws ", " general facts in the history of civilization," produced
great movements of the masses of mankind (pp. 138, 263).*

*The expressions which I have just quoted would be sufficient
to show that Hubert does not give merely the transposable* image.
The very intensity of his vision makes his understanding of the

---

[1] *Next volume, pt. i, chap. i.*   [2] *Ibid.*

*phenomenon more natural and surer. So he makes one under-
stand at the same time as he makes one see ; in his work one can
glean sober but suggestive remarks on the general causes of
migrations. Their causes, like the ways in which they were
carried out, vary greatly.*

*There are physical causes. Changes in climate create
vacancies and new attractions ; cold and abundant rain drive
the population to a more favoured region. Sudden cataclysms
produce the same effect ; the Celts soon found that it was useless
to advance, arms in hand, against high tides or floods.*[1]

*There are social causes, economic or political. Increase of
the population leads to a search for better soil or a wider field
of activity. And the progress of political institutions may have
a similar result.*[2]

*There are moral causes. Here the love of adventure, the
" desire for room ", play an obvious part, and the charm of
the unknown is only surpassed by the attraction of the lands of
civilization.*

*There are technical causes. It is plain that inventions in
the matter of navigation, the possession of bronze tools, and then
of iron, and progress in wagon-building and armament helped
in various ways to make peoples more mobile and more
enterprising.*[3] *M. Boule has observed that from Neolithic times
onwards, " thanks to the development of his crafts, man freed
himself much more easily from physical circumstances " ;
" his migrations in mass," he adds, " now depended almost
entirely on his own will or on that of his leaders "* [4]—*let us say,
on social and logical causes.*

*But we must not omit, among the contingent and persistent
causes of migrations, the effect which an initial movement has
on the neighbouring peoples, or those met on the way by direct
attack, or by rubbing shoulders, and, in general, by " setting
free to move or encouraging to follow ".*[5] *That, too, contributes
to the " tremendous commotion " of the times of great migrations.*

*So in Hubert's work, while the study of primitive man on
the move is continued, what was suggested by other volumes in*

[1] *See pp. 141, 188, 260–1, 263, and the next volume, pt. i, chap. iv.*
[2] *Ibid.*
[3] *See pp. 188, 263.*
[4] Les Hommes fossiles, *p. 321.*
[5] *pp. 262–3 ; next volume, pt. i, chap. iv.*

this section about the essence of the phenomenon of migration is confirmed or completed.[1]

The degree of social organization reached by the Celts, and the culture which they spread over the top of that of the megaliths and the pile-villages, will be shown expressly in the next volume. There I shall lay stress on their character and on the part which they have played in the making of France. Here I shall make only one more remark, or, rather, I shall repeat what has already been said elsewhere.[2] *We sometimes hear of a Celtic Empire and also of a Ligurian Empire and an Indo-European Empire.*[3] *In all three cases, like Hubert, I consider the term improper.*[4] *There can be no empire without political unity, central power, domination intended and carried into effect. Unity of racial character and unity of civilization do not necessarily imply the existence of an empire. And it was because they could not create one by themselves that the Celts rallied, without much resistance, to the imperial idea which animated Rome in her conquests.*[5]

HENRI BERR.

(Owing to the death of M. Hubert before the publication of this work, the French text contained a certain number of errors. Many of these have been corrected in this English edition, but in the circumstances it has not been possible to check all references.—Trs.)

[1] *Cf. F. Hertz, " Die Wanderungen : ihre Typen und ihre geschichtliche Bedeutung," in* Kölner Vierteljahrshefte für Soziologie, 1929, i, p. 36. *I have previously distinguished migration and invasion. Migration is when the mass moves on to free ground or among non-sedentary populations ; invasion is when it comes among settled populations* (Race and History, Foreword, p. xiii). *On* conquest, colonization, emigration, *and* nomadism, *see* Forewords *to* Prehistoric Man, A Geographical Introduction to History, From Tribe to Empire, Israël, *and* The End of the Ancient World.
[2] *See Homo,* Primitive Italy, Foreword, *p. ix.*
[3] *See e.g. A Grenier, in an excellent little book,* Les Gaulois, *pp. 27, 29, 35–6, 38, 49, 83.*
[4] *" Nothing in the prehistoric archæology of the Celtic world or the Ligurian world gives the least suggestion of an empire, even in the nature of the Aztec Empire "* (p. 145).
[5] *See next volume, pt. iii, chap. ii.*

NOTE

By Marcel Mauss

*T*HIS work is the last which Henri Hubert expressly prepared for printing. He had promised it to M. Berr long before the War.[1]

He had worked long at it. He had lectured on the subject twice in his class of Celtic Archæology at the École du Louvre. He did so a third time in two years, in 1923–4 and 1924–5. We have the complete draft of these courses.

All that remained to be done was to give it the form of a book. Two-thirds of this task was done when Hubert died. The manuscript was in almost perfect condition, notes included, down to the end of the second part (the chapter on the Celts of the Danube).[2] Beyond that point the executors of Hubert's wishes had only his course of lectures, which, it is true, was in an admirable state. The illustrations were almost entirely arranged.

It was our duty to make good the promise which he had made to our friend M. Berr. With the lectures, we have finished the book. For that there were three of us co-operating.

It was only right that M. P. Lantier, Hubert's successor at Saint-Germain and one of the men whom he had trained in archæology, should draw up the text of what was lacking in the second part of the book.[3] Here the lectures are in excellent condition. I myself have dealt with one chapter (second volume, Part II, Chapter I).

The third part of the book, that which treats of the social life and civilization of the Celts,[4] has a different history. It had formed the subject of a very long course, lasting a year. But the present work, although published in two volumes, would have been too long for this series if Hubert had published without alteration the admirable matter which he had prepared with this intention. To come into line with the instructions of the director

---

[1] Together with another on the Germans, which, we hope, will appear shortly, with the aid of M. Janse.
[2] Second volume, pt. i, chap. ii.
[3] Second volume, pts. i and ii.
[4] Second volume, pt. iii.

and editors of the series, he had promised to summarize it in two chapters. In his place we have ventured, as we were bound to do, to fulfil this undertaking. For that purpose we have attempted the barbarous task of condensing into a few pages the matter of a large book. But, using only sentences taken from Hubert's own text, and being authorized to abridge sometimes by his own notes, we are sure that we have never been untrue to his ideas, to his manner of expressing himself and proving his case. In this work M. Jean Marx, another pupil, historian and Celticist, has taken on most of the chapters. M. Lantier has written the summary of the lectures condensed in the paragraphs concerning the crafts and arts of the Celts.

The chapter of Conclusions alone is rather patchy, since we had several versions to choose from.

We hope elsewhere to publish in full in another volume in Hubert's name, this Course in the Descriptive Sociology of the Celts of which we here give only the fundamental idea.

M. Vendryès, who was a friend of Hubert, and from whom Hubert took lessons in Celtic, has revised the text and the proof-sheets of the chapters on language. His great authority guarantees the value of this part of the work.

In over thirty years of friendly collaboration Henri Hubert had satisfied himself that I was a faithful depositary of his ideas, and that I knew the secrets of his style well enough to be a conscientious editor of those parts of his work which had not been published and could be published. I have therefore assumed the responsibility for this book.

But it is fair to say that my part has chiefly consisted in associating myself with the work of Hubert's two posthumous collaborators. Both, in addition to the labour of bringing the book out, have seen to it that it included all information received down to 1930. Moreover, M. Lantier has checked all Hubert's references, added his own, and adapted them to the bibliographical methods of the series. He has also perfected and completed the illustrative material for which Hubert had provided.

The good things, then, which will be found here are Hubert's and theirs ; any mistakes which I have left in are mine. They are certainly not the doing of Henri Hubert. I sincerely believe that they will not be many, compared with the size and the learning of a work like this. If we have been so daring as to expose ourselves to the risk of making them, it was to save the rest from oblivion.

Pie factum est.

To this note, which I owed to the reader, I may be allowed to add some scientific considerations regarding facts and method.

First as to method. Hubert would, no doubt, have explained somewhere the methods of archæology and ethnographic history which he followed and perfected from year to year in the immense work which he did as Keeper at the Museum of National Antiquities at Saint-Germain. Being no lover of adjectives, he would not have expatiated on their excellence, but he would certainly have explained their principles. I merely ask the reader to pay attention to them. I must tell him that this work, like the forthcoming book on the Germans, and all Hubert's courses in prehistory, formed part of an ethnographic history of Europe and mankind which he had in view. And I may permit myself, being myself a sociologist and ethnologist, as Hubert was, to emphasize the agreement of history, so understood in this book, with the other branches of learning on which Hubert left his mark—sociology and prehistoric archæology. There is no opposition between these branches of knowledge, in Hubert's mind, or in the facts, or in logic, neither for us nor for anyone, in the case of a complete account of human events such as is attempted here.

There is another consideration, of facts this time. One must feel how completely some of Hubert's fundamental ideas, historical ideas regarding the origins of the Celts, have been justified. Our friend was not a man to glory when the facts confirmed hypotheses which he had put forward. For one thing, as you will see, he offers very few hypotheses. It was not that he was not capable of inventing many, and those very just. But he made it a strict rule never to formulate one prematurely. In this matter he showed a delicate and scrupulous modesty. In the expression of his personal beliefs in history, he always came far short of his conviction of their truth. Those who are experts in these matters will see clearly that he accepted very few of the orthodox assumptions which, often without foundation, make the texture of almost all our current knowledge of the Celtic world. He recognized none as valid and reasonable until he had tested it himself; he used his criticism on himself, and never offered anything as certain except facts.

Yet this strict method led him to the most distant truths. I may justifiably extol the excellence of his reasoning, and call attention to the brilliant confirmation which some of his leading ideas on the early homes of the Celts and their contacts with other civilizations have received from recent discoveries. I am speaking of the great number of works which have revived the question, since the discoveries of Winckler and the decipherment of inscriptions by Hrozny, Forrer, and others threw new light on the languages of Asia Minor and Hither Asia, commonly classed together as Hittite, and since we obtained a clear notion of the archæology of the civilizations—very mixed in origin, but fairly uniform—of the whole area in which those languages were spoken for nearly a thousand years. This new knowledge led M. Meillet [1] and others to conceive in a new fashion, no longer only linguistic, but historical, clear, probable, and proved (by the best of all proofs, that of the document, written or otherwise, found in situ), something which they had not previously been able to conceive with the same definiteness— the antiquity, the kinship, and even the certain contacts of the two groups of languages, Italo-Celtic and Indo-Iranian, and their relations with this Hittite group. So, to-day, we no longer suppose; we are beginning to know when and where things happened, if nothing more.

At the end of his life Henri Hubert was fully acquainted with all this new material in history, archæology, and historical philology, which was beginning to accumulate, even if order and clarity were not brought into it until after his death. In any case, he knew that it agreed with what he had written here of the very early breaking-off of the first Goidelic branch and the contact, direct and indirect, which the Celts had had and maintained with the East, the Near East and even further countries.[2] And he knew that he himself contributed to these researches by remarking on the almost Celtic character of the torques and bracelets of Byblos and the tombs of Kutaïs.[3] He only suggested

[1] "*Essai de chronologie des langues indo-européennes,*" in Bull. de la Soc. de Linguistique, 1931, xxxii, pp. 1 ff.

[2] "*La Numeration sexagésimale en Europe à l'âge du Bronze,*" in l'Anthropologie, xxx, 1920, pp. 578–580; L'Origine des Aryens (*with reference to the American excavations in Turkestan*), ibid., xxi, 1910, pp. 519–528.

[3] "*De quelques objets de bronze trouvés à Byblos,*" in Syria, i, 1925, pp. 16–29.

these connections, without any emphasis. Let me say outright that he always believed in them, and that they lay at the bottom of his oral teaching.

The recent discoveries would have led him on to further discoveries yet. On this point he had unique knowledge. He had the double competence of a Celticist and an Assyriologist. And what an archæologist he was ! He stood at a point where history and archæology met, and he could survey the whole question.

It was worth while to note here the historical value of his general theories. And I shall be forgiven the melancholy pleasure which I take in saying here what a discoverer we have lost.

M. M.

INTRODUCTION

I

THE BARBARIANS

THE European borders of the Græco-Roman world were inhabited by barbarians, some of whom have earned a place in history. There were the Scythians in the east, the Iberians and Ligurians in the west, and the Thracians, Illyrians, Germans, and Celts in the centre. Classical authors took the trouble to write down their names, and some inquired with curiosity into their life and manners. Mediterranean merchants visited them, and may have penetrated among the very remotest, in search of amber, tin, furs, and slaves. Barbarians appeared in Greek and Italian cities as slaves or travellers. There were certainly some among them who were prophets of civilization, and some were cited as models of wisdom.

As Greece and Italy expanded, the nearest of these barbarians were absorbed by them. Others, later, appearing on the horizon like a hurricane, waged furious war on Greece and Rome. In any case, they entered into various kinds of relations with classical civilization and with the Roman Empire, which became its base, and thereby were to some extent incorporated in that civilization and with it helped to make the civilization of the future.

We shall attempt to draw a historical outline for the best-known of these peoples, the Celts and the Germans. Some of the others will come into the story incidentally. Those not mentioned in this history of the Celts, nor in that of the Germans, nor in previous volumes of this series dealing with Greece and Rome, belong to the domain of prehistoric archæology.

II

THE CELTS AND THE GREEKS

This is what the Greek writers tell us of their advance. We are given two dates which enable us to judge from the

Greek point of view: one by the Hesiodic poems, and the other by the historian Ephoros who lived in the second half of the fourth century before Christ. The former suppose that there is in the north-west of the " world " a great Ligurian region ; the latter imagines a great Celtic region.

At the time when the Hesiodic poems were written the Ligurians were one of the three great peoples which dwelt at the ends of the world known to the Greeks :—

> Αἰθίοπάς τε Λίγυς τε ἰδὲ Σκύθας ἱππημολγούς.

This line in the *Catalogues* (fr. 132)[1] must date from the beginning of the sixth century. A hundred years later the first Greek historian, Hecatæos of Miletos, in his *Europe* talks of a Celtic part of this Liguria ; the lexicographer Stephanos of Byzantion quotes the *Europe* when speaking of Marseilles, which, like Hecatæos, he describes as " a city in the Ligystic country, near the Celtic country ". Hecatæos also mentioned a Celtic city named Nyrax, which cannot be identified.[2] Marseilles had been founded by Phocæan settlers about 600, a century before.

What exactly was the extent of this Ligystic country ? There is an old *periplus*, or account of a voyage, perhaps written by a Marseilles man and probably at the end of the sixth century, which, after being refashioned several times, has come down to us in a Latin verse translation from the pen of one Rufus Festus Avienus,[3] a person of consular rank who fancied himself as a man of letters. According to this account, the Ligurians had once extended as far as the North Sea, but had been driven back to the Alps by the Celts.[4] But the peoples mentioned in the *Ora Maritima* of Avienus as dwelling near the Lake of Geneva bear names which have disappeared from geographical literature,[5] and when, later than the original *periplus*, Aristotle speaks in his *Meteorologica*[6] of the Perte du Rhône at Bellegarde, he still places it in Liguria, περὶ τὴν Λιγυστικήν. Was this information out of date?

---

[1] In Strabo, vii, 3, 7. "Ethiopians and Ligyans and mare-milking Scythians." Cf. d'Arbois de Jubainville, **CCXLVIII**, xii, *passim*.

[2] Stephanos, s.v. ; for Narbonne, see Dottin, **CCCXXII**, p. 298. E. Philipon, in **DXVI**, p. 121, rejects the other passages from Hecatæos, in allegiance to his theory regarding the relative positions of the Ligurians and the Iberians, whom he places in the Marseilles district.

[3] 130–145.   [4] 637–640.   [5] 674–6.   [6] i, 13.

There was a time when the southern limits of the Celts lay there. Apollonios of Rhodes, who used the earlier geographers conscientiously, describes, in his Book IV, the Argonauts going up the Rhone, which they reached by way of the Po, and being tossed by storms on the Swiss lakes, under the Hercynian Mountains, which extend into the midst of the country of the Celts.[1] In the time of Herodotos, whose information was far more up-to-date, the Celts were separated from the Mediterranean not only by the Ligurians but by the Sigynnes. These latter occupied the country inland from the Veneti on the Adriatic side.[2] But their name was also to be found near Marseilles. "The Ligyes," says Herodotos, "dwelling in the heights above Marseilles, call small traders 'Sigynnes'." There was not one people, but a whole succession of peoples, between the Celts and the inhabitants of the Mediterranean coast, and these peoples practised a prosperous trade, as excavations bear witness. As late as about 350 that valuable geographical document, the *Periplus* attributed to Scylax of Caryanda, makes no mention of Celts on the coasts of the Western Mediterranean, and yet they were already very near.

Long before, they had come into contact on the Atlantic coast with mariners of Tartessus, who had eventually spoken of them to the people of Marseilles. The old *periplus* which Avienus translated mentioned them as being on the shores of the North Sea, from which they had driven the Ligurians.[3] It designated Brittany, and also Spain, by the name of Œstrymnis,[4] in which we may perhaps see the name of the Osismii or the Ostiæi, who still occupied Finistère in Cæsar's day. At the beginning of the fifth century Herodotos mentions them as being south of the Pyrenees, and probably on the Ocean. "The Danube," he says, "starts from the country of the Celts and the city of Pyrene, and flows all through Europe, which it divides in two. Now the Celts are outside the Pillars of Heracles, and march with the Cynesii, who are the westernmost people of Europe "[5]; and, indeed, Cape St. Vincent was in their territory.

[1] *Argon.*, 627–647. The (probably late) author of the *Orphic Argonautica* likewise takes the Argonauts through the country of the Celts, and even to Ireland (l. 161).   [2] v, 9.   [3] Avien., 130–145.   [4] Avien., 91 ff., 152–5.
[5] ii, 33 ; iv, 49. Aristotle, in *Meteorologica*, i, 13, 19, repeats Herodotos's mistake about the sources of the Danube.

The first Greek who was in a position to give more definite and circumstantial information about the Celts of the Ocean was a traveller of Marseilles named Pytheas.[1] Unfortunately his account of his voyage, *Of the Ocean*, was severely mishandled by erudite persons, like Polybios and Strabo, for whose critical spirit it was too much. He was a strange individual, no doubt, but he knew as much of mathematics and astronomy as anyone of his time, and he had the spirit of the explorer. He embarked twice with a few companions in Phœnician vessels, and sailed from Spain to Britain, to distant Thule, and eastwards to Denmark, perhaps further. He saw the sea icebound, and days which lasted twenty-four hours. He came across the Osismii at the end of Finistère. He knew the Celtic name of the Isle of Ushant, " Uxisama," [2] that of Kent, " Cantion," [3] and also the name by which Britain was to be henceforth always called, " the Prettanic Isles," which superseded its Ligurian or Iberian name of Albion.[4] Pytheas lived in the fourth century. Some decades after his time the Sicilian historian Timæos stated that the rivers which flow into the Atlantic went through the Celtic country.[5]

So the Greeks knew that the Celts had arrived on the coasts of the western seas before 600 B.C. and on the Atlantic seaboard of Spain before 500, and that those of them whom we now call the Brythons had reached Britain and Brittany and occupied the whole of the Gallic coast of the Ocean before 300. By that time they had at last come down on to the Mediterranean, but only within the last few decades. On the whole, it was on the Atlantic side that the Celts first came into direct contact with the Mediterranean mariner. Behind Pytheas lay a long past of seafaring—Ægean, Mycenæan, and Tartessian—in the course of which Northern Europe had received much of Mediterranean civilization. The navigators of the West knew the Celts, the names of their countries and of their peoples ; things on the Celtic coast were familiar to them and, so far as the Greeks were concerned,

[1] D'Arbois, **CCXLVIII**, xii, pp. 63 ff. ; Müllenhoff, **CCCLXII**, i, pp. 327 ff. ; Jullian, **CCCXLVII**, i, pp. 415 ff. ; A. Blazquez, in **XXXVI**, Jan.–Mar., 1913.
[2] Loth in **CXL**, x, p. 352.
[3] Strabo, i, 4, 3 ; Rhys, **CCXXX**, p. 22 ; Irish *céte*, market.
[4] E. Philipon, **CCCLXI**, pp. 294 ff.
[5] Fr. 36, in Plutarch, *De Plac. Phil.*, iii, 17, 2.

could be brought into the domain of Greek legend,[1] whereas, hidden behind misty mountains, the Celts of the Continent were still something mysterious and remote. No doubt the mariners of that time could keep their discoveries secret. There were, too, catastrophes in the Mediterranean world in which local traditions were lost. Nevertheless, a writer who about 150 B.C. could say that the discovery of the countries on the Great Ocean was quite recent [2] was displaying lamentable ignorance. But the great majority of the Greeks were no wiser. Meanwhile, the whole interior of the Celtic region and the movements of the Celts remained quite unknown to the mass of Greeks and Romans until Cæsar conquered Gaul.[3]

In the Mediterranean region, on the other hand, the Celts advanced rapidly from the fourth century onwards. One fine day the Greeks, or rather the Macedonians, found themselves face to face with their military organization to the north of the Balkans. This was in the time of Alexander, in 335 B.C. Alexander, in the course of an expedition against the Getæ, was receiving the representatives of the Danubian peoples. " Some, too, came," says Arrian,[4] " from the Celts established on the Ionic Gulf." Alexander received them amicably. This was the occasion on which he asked them, at a feast, what they feared most in the world. " That the sky should fall on our heads," is their alleged reply. The scene was described, so Strabo assures us,[5] by Ptolemy, son of Lagos, who added that the Celts of the Adriatic coast ($\tau o \dot{v} s$ $\pi \epsilon \rho \dot{\iota}$ $\tau \dot{\eta} \nu$ $\, ' A \delta \rho \iota a \nu$) had entered into bonds of friendship and hospitality with him.

If these Celts who came to Alexander really lived on the Adriatic, they came from the Italian coast of that sea.[6] The story of the events which had brought them thither had already reached Greece. In his *Life of Camillus* Plutarch quotes a curious passage from Heracleides Ponticos,

---

[1] e.g., the legend of Geryon. Cf. Reinach, **CCCLXXII**, pp. 121, 177 ; **CCCLXXIV**, i, p. 244.
[2] Polybios, iii, 37–8. For Greek ignorance of geography, see Bertrand and Reinach, **DXLII**, p. 4. Cf. Xenophon, *Cyr.*, 2.
[3] Cicero, Ep. clxi.
[4] *Anab.*, i, 4, 6.
[5] vii, 3, 8.
[6] The *Periplus* of Scylax (18–19) speaks of Celts on the Adriatic as early as 350.

a philosopher of the fourth century. " Heracleides," he says, " relates in his *Treatise on the Soul* that news came to Pontus, simultaneously with the event, that an army from the land of the Hyperboreians had taken a Greek city named Rome, situated near the Great Sea." [1] He was astonished at the speed with which the news had travelled, and it seems to have created some excitement. It was a kind of cataclysm, and one could not foretell how far-reaching it might be ; and it is plain that the world of the Greek cities of Italy, no longer at their best in military power, was alarmed.

The events which followed the fall of Rome brought the Celts into more direct contact with the Greeks, but lacked the sensational effect of the capture of Rome and the legendary glamour of the meeting with Alexander. After Rome was delivered, the Celts had returned and gone past it. In 367 they were in Apulia. In the previous year Dionysios I of Syracuse, having treated with them, took a band of them into his service and sent them to the aid of the Macedonians against the Thebans.[2] This was really the first occasion on which the Greeks as a whole came into contact with the Celts.

Just about this time the historian Ephoros substituted the Celts for the Ligurians among the three great peoples on the circumference of the world, and assigned to them the whole north-west of Europe as far as the borders of the Scythians.[3]

Some years after the appearance of the Celts at the camp of Alexander, in 310, a sudden disaster fell on the Antariatae, a great Illyrian people living north of the Veneti. They started fleeing *en masse*. There was talk of plagues, of lands ravaged by invasive mice.[4] It was a great Celtic incursion, led by a chief named Molistomos. The flying Antariatae came up against the Macedonians, who defeated them and then settled them down. But the collapse of the Antariatae was like the breaking of a dike. Celtic bands invaded Greece and looted Delphi. They did not stop until they reached Asia Minor, where they founded Galatia. Others went on along the coast of the Black Sea to the Sea of Azov. There the ancient geographers place the extreme limit of their advance.

[1] xxii, 2–3.
[2] Justin, xx, 4, 9 ; Xen., *Hell.*, vii, 1, 20, 31 ; Diod., xv, 70.
[3] Fr. 38 ; Strabo, iv, 46 ; Diod., v, 25, 4 ; 32, 1.
[4] Appian, *Illyrica*, 4.

At the same time others were at last coming, through the midst of Iberians and Ligurians, to the shores of the Gulf of Lions, where Hannibal found them established in 218.[1] Later the conquest of the Province, followed by that of Gaul, brought them into the orbit of a Mediterranean empire. Then they found someone to write about them in Poseidonios, who visited them as Pytheas had done their ancestors, but was happy in inspiring more confidence than his predecessor.

From this survey we see that the rise of the Celts, from their first appearance on the Greek horizon, was extremely rapid. For in three hundred years they attained the height of their power. Also we see that it occurred at the same time as that of the Latins and shortly after that of the Greeks, for the Celts entered into Greek history after that history had begun.

III

CELTIC MIGRATIONS AND THEIR DIRECTION

But we see something else : that the Celts whom the amber-traders encountered on their journeys up the Rhone and Danube, and the coasting vessels found again on the low shores of the North Sea, must have belonged to a people which came originally from Central Europe, gaining ground westwards at the expense of the Ligurians and Iberians, and had its first centre of gravity towards the east of the region which it occupied when it attained its greatest extension. A map of their present location gives quite a different picture.[2] It is in the very west of Europe, in the islands and peninsulas, in the Finistères and Land's Ends in fact (Map 1), that the Celtic languages are still spoken—in Ireland, in the Isle of Man, in Wales, in the north of Scotland and the neighbouring isles, and in the tip of Brittany west of a line drawn from Morbihan to Saint-Brieuc. Cornish was spoken in Cornwall down into the eighteenth century.

Which is the truer picture ? Did Celticism survive in

---

[1] Schulten, **DXIX**, i, p. 96. The Celts are said to have been reported on the shore of Provence in the time of Timæos, who wrote about 260, for the following passage in Polybios (xii, 28a) is ascribed to him : πολυπραγμονῆσαι τὰ Λιγύων ἔθη καὶ Κελτῶν, ἅμα δὲ τούτοις Ἰβήρων.

[2] Ripley, **CCCLXXVIII**, p. 23.

the western end of its domain because it was most firmly
established there, or because it was driven there ?   Is it not
in these parts that we should look for the main mass of the
Celts, their origin, and their purest type ?   Is it not an abuse
and a faulty interpretation of a collection of historical texts

MAP 1.   The Movement of the Celts and their Present Habitat.   (W. Z.
Ripley, *The Races of Europe*, p. 313.)

to look elsewhere ? Here, at the beginning of a story bristling with contradictions, is a first conflict.

The impression given by the map of to-day could be confirmed by traditions and facts. Livy regarded Gaul as the centre of the Celts and the starting-point of their migrations. Cæsar asserts that the institution of the Druids originated in Britain. When the Roman Empire declined bands of Irishmen came as adventurers to Gaul and as settlers to Britain ; the kingdom of Scotland was their most lasting foundation. The Celts of Britain were not behindhand ; they colonized Armorica, which they made into what we call Brittany.

But these are untrue traditions or mere individual facts. In the main the Celts, after advancing to the west of Europe, retreated in the same direction. If we look carefully at the map we shall see that the districts where they are found are refuges. The Celts came to a stop there at the sea, clinging to the rocks. Beyond the sea was their next world. They stayed on the shore, waiting for the ferry, like the dead in Procopios. One of the nicest stories in the collection of epic and mythical tales which forms the Welsh Mabinogion [1] relates the adventures of a Roman emperor, Macsen Wledig, who, having fallen asleep while hunting and dreamed of a wonderful princess, set out to seek her, and found her in Britain. She was called Elen Lluyddawg, " Leader of Hosts." The emperor married her, and with her he raised Britain to its greatest power and glory. But Rome had forgotten him, and he had to reconquer it. Britain sent forth hosts which never came back, and the army of Elen Lluyddawg dwells in Llydaw, or Litavia, the country of the dead. Apart from the few facts of purely local significance mentioned above, none but phantom armies or armies of romance— like that of Arthur, who likewise conquered Gaul and Italy and Rome—ever went out from the British Isles to occupy the lands to which the Celtic name is attached. What now remains of the Celts, in the west of their ancient dominion, was driven there and confined there by other peoples arriving or growing up behind them. This general movement of

[1] Loth, **CCLXX**, i, pp. 210 ff., " Le Songe de Maxen Wledig." Macsen is simply the usurper Maximus, who commanded in Britain under Gratian, was proclaimed Augustus in A.D. 383, and was defeated and slain by Theodosius in August, 388.

expansion and contraction taking the Celts to the west and confining them there may be called the law of Celticism. It must be studied as a capital fact of European history.

IV

WHAT REMAINS OF THE CELTS AND THEIR PART IN HISTORY

The greatness of the Celts has gone, but what has it left behind ?   A remnant of Celtic tongues, of which only one, Irish, is endeavouring to-day to become once more the speech of a nation ; a fringe, of varying depth, in which Celtic died out only recently and its long survival is attested by place-names and folk-lore ; and, lastly, in regions where the Celts were subdued, assimilated, or wiped out in ancient times, recognizable descendants, traces of their social structure, the spirit of their civilization, or, at least, the dead records of history and archæology.   The Celts, who have almost disappeared from Western Europe, are one of the chief elements of which it is composed.   In one place this element reveals itself in individual characteristics ; in another in collective characteristics.   This is particularly the case in France, where the Celtic inheritance seems to be greatest and least diffused.

The Celts were preceded in Gaul by Iberians and Ligurians, who left indelible traces of their occupation in the names of rivers and mountains [1] and perhaps of a few towns.[2] They have bequeathed to the French much of their blood, but apparently nothing of their social structure.   They were clearly not mere hordes, but organized societies.   Records of that pre-Celtic past, such as the megalithic monuments, bear witness to common effort and a social life.   But all that has survived of that is preserved only within the structure of Gaulish society and under Gaulish names.   While the physical geography of France is dotted with Ibero-Ligurian names, the oldest features of her political geography are Gaulish, and these are the fundamental features.

---

[1] For the Ligurians, see d'Arbois, **CCCI**, ii, pp. 87 ff. ; Dottin, **CCCXXI**, pp. 180 ff. ; for the Iberians, Philipon, **CCCLXIX**, pp. 161 ff.
[2] For the Ligurians, see Philipon, op. cit., pp. 129 ff. ; **DXVI**, p. 180.

The large towns of modern France, save for some exceptions which are easily explained, were the capitals of Gallic peoples or of sub-groups which formed those peoples. Their boundaries are almost exactly followed by modern administrative divisions. Arras was the town of the Atrebates ; Amiens, of the Ambiani ; Rheims, of the Remi ; Soissons, of the Suessiones ; Senlis, of the Silvanectes ; Paris, of the Parisii (the Silvanectes and Parisii were sub-groups of the Suessiones) ; Troyes, of the Tricasses ; Langres, of the Lingones ; Chartres, of the Carnutes. At the time of the Roman Conquest the peoples were in process of becoming cities. Their meeting-places or strongholds were developing into towns. That is why most French towns are called after the names of peoples. The old names of Rheims (Diviocortorum), Paris (Lutetia), and Soissons (Noviodunum, now Pommiers, near that city) have vanished. The territories of the Gallic peoples became those of the Roman *civitates* and *pagi*, the centres of Roman Gaul, and these became bishoprics and bailliwicks (the latter word being perhaps Celtic).[1]

Of these Gallic peoples some may have previously been Iberian or Ligurian. But even in the south, in Aquitaine, where the foreign character of the communities was manifest to outsiders like Cæsar and his men, the political stamp of the Gauls was deeply impressed.[2] But it must not be thought that Gaul was mainly an Iberian or Ligurian society, politically assimilated by its conquerors and supplied by them with names with Celtic inflexions. It was not. In the greater part of Gaul the Celts chose their places of residence for themselves. Where they established themselves on the site of earlier settlements, these latter seem as a rule to have already disappeared when the Celts took possession. There were in Gaul cities or fortified villages of the Neolithic and Bronze Ages. The Celts did not settle in them at once, or if they did they abandoned them and did not return till long afterwards. In short, they did not take over from the first inhabitants. They built their own houses and cities ; they arranged the country to suit themselves, and as they arranged it so it still remains, for wherever the Celts

---

[1] Irish, *baile*, district, estate of a great family.
[2] See the following volume in this Series.

established themselves permanently, without exception the French have remained. They were the founders of the towns and villages of modern France. Doubtless, the Celts had neither the same needs nor the same methods of making use of the soil as their forerunners. That is why they settled in other places. They have bequeathed to France habits which have outlived the reasons for them. For example, they have left their system of land-measurement. The Gaul which Cæsar conquered was so well surveyed that the officials of the Roman *fiscus* had only to enrol the Gallic surveyors, from whom they took over some technical terms, and in any case their measures; the *arpent* and the *lieue* are Celtic.[1] The face of France is still very much what the Celts made it.

In short, from the coming of the Celts to France, and from then only, the groups of men established there adopted a structure which is still to be seen in French society. The origins of the French nation go back to the Celts. Behind them there is a formless past, without a history or even a name.

Our societies—nations, as they now are—are complex things, composed of elements of different kinds, some physical and some moral. They are not formed by the mere adding on of features. Their growth may be compared to that of a crystal. In French society the first element to cause the mixture to crystallize was the Celtic element, and the process of crystallization has been so well defined that the crystal has preserved its bold edges and its clear facets.

It is more correct to say that Gaul first began to look like France when the main body of the Celtic peoples was settled west of the Rhine. At that time there were still Celts in Spain, in Italy, and in Asia Minor, but after that, as one section after another was conquered by alien races, they disappeared or lost their identity. These were not driven into Gaul. Those on the right bank of the Rhine were driven to the river after long wars. In Gaul they formed a more concentrated mass, and were able to assimilate everyone else. A fairly loose political organization was formed; a national consciousness, cloudy but capable of occasional flashes, came into being. The nation was in process of formation when the Romans conquered it. It did not sink

[1] *Arpent = arepennis,* Irish *airchenn;* *lieue* (league) = *leuca.*

in the wreck of the Roman Empire.[1] Like Poland, it survived conquest.

Thus I am inclined to think, without being quite sure, that the conflicts which ended with the Celtic peoples finding themselves west of the Rhine contributed to the making of the nation. I say that I am not sure because, among the information which has come down to us from the ancient writers, there is no sign that the Belgæ, who were the last to have to maintain these conflicts, were conscious of any opposition, racial or national, between themselves and the Germans. On the other hand, it is my belief that the invasion of the Cimbri had quite certain effects. We see from reading Cæsar that that of Ariovistus threatened to be followed by others.

But if a nation already existed it was because that which makes the deep-seated unity of a nation existed—a common ideal, the same ways of thinking and feeling, in short, everything that nations express by symbols and all the most intimate part of their civilization. For the Celts, like the Greeks, were more united, more consciously united, by their common ways of thinking and feeling than by their sense of nationality. In speaking of them one may, without paradox, use the word " civilization " in its widest sense. The Greeks and Romans regarded them as barbarians, but as barbarians of a superior kind. They held that the Druids preserved the Pythagorean tradition. Cicero makes the Druid Diviciacus (an Æduan who really existed, a combination of churchman and warrior) a speaker in one of his dialogues.[2]

The ancients credited the Druids with metaphysical speculations of which all trace has vanished. I should say, rather, that the Druids—judges, physicians, directors of consciences, and poets as they were—were moral observers and psychologists. It is true that they studied the metaphysics of death, but that borders on psychology. The Celts thought much about death ; it was a familiar companion whose alarming character they liked to disguise. All that has come down to us from the Druids themselves is one of the tripartite maxims of which the Celts are known to have been fond. This is the form in which Diogenes Laertios gives it in the

---

[1] Jullian, **CCCXLVI,** pp. 154 ff.   [2] *De Div.*

preface to his *Lives of the Philosophers*: Σέβειν θεοὺς καὶ μηδὲν κακὸν δρᾶν καὶ ἀνδρείαν ἀσκεῖν—" To worship the gods, to do nothing base, and to practise manhood." [1] It is a moral maxim of a fairly noble and manly kind.

But we catch a glimpse of the spirit of their doctrine and the soul of Celticism in the literatures of Ireland and Wales. These literatures, especially the Irish, are to a great extent sententious, or gnomic. Even in the narrative parts the gnomic spirit appears frequently. But these narratives are surprisingly successful in the creation of characters, especially for a literature which has left no trace of drama. In the epic of Ulster the hero Cuchulainn, King Conchobar, the Druid Cathbad, and Queen Medb are types whose individuality is all the more remarkable since the works in which they appear are not altogether works of art. The Celts of Gaul deliberately jettisoned the whole of their epic tradition for the sake of the more sophisticated culture which the Romans brought. But they must have kept its spirit; it is to that that I should attribute the dramatic character which the history of France spontaneously assumes in the writings of its chroniclers. For in what other history are social standpoints so happily expressed in the typical figures of heroes ?

The archæology of Roman Gaul is deceptive as to the kinship of the French people. The Gallo-Romans mostly continued to be disguised Celts. So much was this the case that after the Germanic invasions we find modes and tastes which had been those of the Celts reappearing in Gaul. They survived the impress of Rome. Romanesque art often recalls Gallic art, or that of the Gallic stone-masons working in the Roman manner, so that one is sometimes misled. [2] But that is only one sign. Language is another. The Romans slowly imposed their speech on Gaul. But French is Latin pronounced by Celts and applied to the needs of Celtic minds. The analytical character of the verb, the use of demonstratives and demonstrative particles, the turn of the spoken sentence, are common to French and the Celtic languages. [3]

In short, the civilization of the Celts lies at the bottom of

---

[1] 6.

[2] e.g. the monument at Virecourt, sometimes regarded as Romanesque, sometimes as Gallic.

[3] Dottin, **CXCVI**, pp. 77–9.

French civilization, just as the nation into which the Celts of Gaul were beginning to form is at the bottom of the French nation. It is a commonplace to tell the French how Gallic they are. Much of the Celts, then, remains where the Celtic name is lost.

But so far as Celtic social organization is concerned, all the upper parts have gone. The state in France is not Celtic ; it is Germanic or Roman. No Celtic state has survived ; Scotland is the ghost of one, and Ireland is a new creation. Celticism has left only possibilities of nations. It survives only in the foundations of our Western Europe and has made hardly any contribution to its superstructures. It failed through defects of organization which we shall have to examine.

The part played by the Celts in history was not political, for their political formations were unsound. But it was the part of civilizers. One especially characteristic thing happened when they absorbed Roman civilization—the wonderful development of Roman schools, which succeeded the Celtic schools of the Druids.[1] Gaul got her classical culture from Gallic teachers, trained by the Druids, and, what is more, some of them were fit to teach in Rome. Naturally they could interpret Mediterranean civilization— science, art, philosophy, and moral culture—to the Gauls better than foreigners could have done. But it is an interesting fact that they did so act as interpreters. Later, in the Middle Ages, Irish monks brought Europe back to the cultivation of letters and Greek and Latin philosophy. Earlier the Celts had been the middlemen who brought Greek civilization to Central Europe, where they had not failed to propagate their own culture.

The Celts were torch-bearers in the ancient world, and the French have succeeded them. With their love of beauty and general ideas the French have acted in Europe as the middlemen through whom it has received the lofty, mellow civilizations of antiquity which they have helped to make into the civilization of the world. The Celts contributed certain forms of sensibility and humanity which are still the possession of Western Europeans and of the French.

---

[1] e.g. the school of Autun (Tac., *Ann.*, iii, 43).

V

CELTS OF THE CONTINENT AND CELTS OF THE ISLES

When ancient historians speak of the Celts, they usually confine themselves to those of the Continent ; in other words, to the Celts of Gaul, the Gauls, whose progress can be followed with the aid of those writers and whose antecedents have been indicated above. The Celts of the British Isles are left to the Celtic student, and we have to turn to the philologist and other specialists. In this work we shall deal both with the Celts of the Continent and with those of the islands, and we shall most certainly find that we cannot possibly understand the history of the former if we ignore the latter.

The Celts of the islands have a literature which, except for a few Gallic inscriptions, constitutes the whole written tradition of the race. It is true that that literature all belongs to a time later than our period, and that the oldest of the manuscripts in which it is preserved is not earlier than the twelfth century.[1] The languages in which it is presented are already a long way from the stage at which Gaulish stopped. At first sight, it seems rash to connect data which appear so far removed from each other and so unrelated in time or place.

Nevertheless, the very difference between the dialects, Irish on the one hand and Welsh or British on the other, brings us face to face with a really fundamental fact in the history of the Celts—with a kind of prehistoric cleavage of the Celtic body, parallel to a similar cleavage of the Italic peoples, to which I call attention at this early stage of my work, because archæologists who study the Celts [2] do not take it into account, or not sufficiently.

As for their literature, it is already generally accepted that it represents a tradition much older than the earliest date at which the surviving works were set down in writing. In the descriptions of objects of which the ancient literature of Ireland is so full, attempts have been made to identify weapons and jewels of the Hallstatt period,[3] but this is,

---

[1] Dottin, *Les Littératures celtiques*, pp. 17 ff.
[2] Déchelette, ii, 2, pp. 572 ff.
[3] MacNeill, CCCCXLI, chap. ii.

in my opinion, a mistake. In any case, it contains traces of things belonging to a time three or four hundred years before Christ, of which we shall have to take note in our survey. I believe that its origins are still older and that it contains large remnants of a Pan-Celtic tradition, going back beyond the time when the Celts reached the British Isles. By analysis and comparison one may distinguish the different strata of this literary tradition. Even if its antiquity were less likely it would be unscientific to ignore it and deny its existence.

For the history of Celtic civilization, be it that of technical processes, trades, and domestic life, or that of social organization, clans, tribes, kingdoms, confederations, and the way in which they changed the face of the land, or, again, that of art and religion, the actual materials will be supplied chiefly by the literature and the law of the island Celts. But whether we consider institutions or characters—for it is very tempting to look to the Celtic epics and tales for psychological illustrations to a rather dry history—we must never forget that the Gauls whom Cæsar conquered had already advanced far beyond the type of civilization represented by the laws and epics of Ireland.

Lastly the island Celts are of interest to us in their development of the Celtic tradition, which, on the Continent, was diverted from its original course by the Roman conquest.

There are, moreover, several ways of utilizing literary or linguistic data to reconstruct the history of the Celts. Some very dubious methods have been employed—with some good result, to tell the truth, for it was the wild imaginings of the Celtic Academy that opened the way to prehistory. I shall try to adopt the sternest and most austere method.

VI

PLAN OF THIS WORK

First of all, we must try to define what we mean by " Celts ". There is no real obscurity about the matter, but obscurities have arisen from the differences of the various groups of students which have dealt with the Celts, each from its own point of view. The elements from which we have to make up our picture do not agree exactly. We must interpret, select, and give each element its true and proportionate value. That which is least subject to controversy is the linguistic element. Celtic speech is the chief sign of Celticness, if one may use the word. Anyone who spoke Celtic was a Celt, wherever he came from. Those who ceased to speak it disappeared among the peoples who absorbed them, and ceased to be Celts. But the smallest trace of Celtic speech, in names of men or places, in inscriptions or in later languages, proves beyond doubt the presence of the Celts at a certain place and at a certain date. We may accept it that the boundaries of the Celtic tongues correspond roughly to those of the Celtic communities and civilizations.

Secondly, we have to determine their changing boundaries, and for that purpose to discover the facts which make up the internal and external history of their communities, which have no history properly so called, so that we may see how they grew, how their tribes were grouped and how subdivided, and follow their wanderings, their colonizations, the concentric waves of their successive advances, their new settlements, the states which were created, and the nations which accumulated at the end of their journey to their Chosen Land.

Our evidence will be names—place-names, personal names, names of peoples attached to places. On the way, we shall come upon archæological facts. These will take their place among the other evidence, and we shall see how fruitful that assemblage of different kinds of evidence can be.

In the course of this inquiry it will be necessary to venture outside our limits and to attempt a systematic account of Celtic civilization. We shall have to anticipate, and to define the civilization of La Tène, that is to describe the series of characteristic objects which the term covers, because those characteristic objects are just what we have to use as indications of race. For the same reason we shall have to note their chronological classification and the different forms which objects have in different periods.

The last part of this work will be a study of Celtic civilization. Here some of the archæological facts will come in again to bear witness to the industrial capacity of the Celts, their wealth, their trade, their way of life, and their dress. But we shall above all consider the structure of Celtic communities, the units of various sizes—family, tribe, nation—and the social activities—religion, art, etc.—which developed in those communities.

PART ONE

WHAT THE CELTS WERE

CHAPTER I

THE NAME AND THE RACE

WHAT, then, were the Celts ? We must first have some idea of what they were if we are to find out where they were. Every group of men living together forms a physical, social, and moral unit. Its members know one another and are known to others by their physical type, and, still more, by their manner of life, their language, certain sides of their civilization, their name, if they have a common name implying that they belong to the group, or some other symbol. Let us see how these various indications will help us in our study of the Celts.

I

THE NAME OF THE CELTS

The ancient Greek writers who have left information about the Celts used the name Κελτοί, Latin *Celtæ*, as a general racial designation applying to large peoples living a long way off. At the beginning of the third century before Christ, a new name, that of Galatians, Γαλάται, appears for the first time in the historian Hieronymos of Cardia,[1] who wrote of their invasion of Macedonia and Greece and their settlement in Asia Minor. It appeared in the epitaph of young Cydias, who was killed at Delphi in 279.[2] It is probable that the name of *Galli* came into use among the Italians, as a rival to the old name of Celts, about the same time or a little before. The words Galatians and Galli were likewise used as general terms, and were not the names of small groups which became generalized.

[1] *F.H.G.*, ii, 450–461.   [2] Paus., x, 21, 5.

These various designations were used concurrently. The ancients tried to give them special application,[1] and modern historians have attempted to assign them to different groups of Celtic tribes.[2] The tribes did, indeed, form groups of different kinds, but we must give up any attempt to divide them into Celts and Galatians.[3]

These names came from the Celts themselves. The proper name Celtillos, the name of the Celtici (a Celtic people), and the personal names found in Spain—Celtigum, Celtus, Celticus [4]—lead one to think that the root-word was, indeed, Celtic. As for the word *Galli* its equivalent is found in the Irish texts. There were in Ireland tribes of Gaileoin or Galians. In the *Táin Bó Chuailgné* (the Cattle-lifting of Cooley), in which a contingent of them forms part of the army of Connacht, they are distinguished from the other Irish by their military habits and strict discipline ; they have the air of foreigners—almost of foreign mercenaries.[5] They were Gauls settled in Ireland. At the beginning of a poem describing the marriage of Cuchulainn, the *Tochmarc Emire* (the wooing of Emer), the hero, Forgall Monach, Emer's father, comes to the court of Conchobar, King of Ulster, disguised as an ambassador of the King of the Gauls, with gifts, which are objects of gold and wine of Gaul (*fin Gall*).[6] In these two cases we have, not tribal names, but general names, although they do not apply to born Irishmen or to the whole of the Celtic countries.

We need not, therefore, make too much of Cæsar's definition at the beginning of the Commentaries : *Qui ipsorum lingua Celtœ, nostra Galli appellantur*—" Who are called Celts in their own language, and Gauls in ours." [7] At the very most, the passage might mean that Cæsar considered that there were two different pronunciations of the same word.

[1] Diod., v, 32 ; Strabo, iv, 77. On the use of the two names in Polybios, see Bertrand, CCCIII, p. 433.
[2] Bertrand, ibid., pp. 249 ff. ; Bertrand and Reinach, DXLII, pp. 28, 36 ; Jullian, CCCXLVII, i, p. 316 ; Read, CCCLXXXIV, p. 47.
[3] Rhys, CCXXX ; Ripley, CCCLXXVIII, p. 127.
[4] Schulten, DXIX, i, pp. 26, 107.
[5] Windisch, CCXCVI.
[6] *Tochmarc Emire*, in CXL, xi, p. 442. The later copyist did not understand *Gall* to mean Gaul ; for him, *Gall* meant Norwegian, and he combined the two words.
[7] *Bell. Gall.*, i, 1.

The number and the doubtfulness of the etymologies suggested leads us in the same direction.[1] It is not surprising that these names are hard to explain and that their etymological meaning has gone. All that matters from this point of view is that they are not too alien to the Celtic languages in appearance. Probably we are dealing with three forms of one same name, heard at different times and in different places by different ears, and written down by people with different ways of spelling. The initial guttural was transcribed by a surd in the Western Mediterranean area, and (perhaps under the influence of the Tartessians, who sailed to the Celtic countries before the Greeks) by a sonant in Greece. It is equally probable that the same word had two forms, one with a dental at the end and one without.

The fact that there was something that could be called by a name, whether the name was Celts or Gauls, was forced upon the ancients, no doubt by the bearers of the name themselves. But did these general names apply to the Celtic peoples as a whole, or only to some of them ?

Did they apply to the Celts of Ireland ?   When the ancient

---

[1] The following are the usual conjectures : *Celta* is supposed to come from a root *quel*, implying the notion of raising. It is the root of *celsus*, and of Lithuanian *kélias* "elevated ". It has been compared to an Old Irish word, a dictionary word, *cléthe* (Stokes, **CCXXXVI**, pp. 70–1, gloss of O'Davoren) "great, noble, elevated ". In composition, the root is found in Old Irish *ar-celim*, Middle Irish *ar-chell-ain*, " I carry off," and the substantive *tochell* " victory, gain ". D'Arbois supposes that the Germanic -*childis* (Brunichildis), O. Nor. *hildr*, O. Sax. *hild*, is derived from it through a word *Celtis* (the word *Held*, O. Sax. *helid*, A.-S. *hœlep*, O. Nor. *holdr* and *halr*, O.H.G. *helid*, is derived from the Celtic : Irish *calath*, Breton *calet* " hard ").

There was another root *quel* which meant " strike ". It occurs in the Latin -*cello* (*percello*), *calamitas*, *incolumis*, *cladus*, and *clava*, and in the Lithuanian *kalti* " strike ".

The word *Celta* may also be connected with the root of Sanskrit *cárati* " it goes round ", in Greek τέλομαι " I go round, I flow ", and in Latin *cultura*, *cola*, *incola*, *inquilinus*, *exquiliœ*. In Old Irish, the verb *imm-e-chella*, 3rd person, means " goes all round, starting from the sun and moon " ; *timchell* " the act of going round " ; *tóichell*, " journey ". If *Celta* was connected with this root, it would mean something like " the inhabitants ".

When we think of the association of the name of the Belgæ with their dress, we may be inclined to refer to the Scottish kilt. Cf. Joyce, ii, p. 203 ; Cormac, s.v. " Celt vesta ". Welsh *celu* ; Indo-Eur. *quel*.

Galli has been connected with the Old Irish and British word *gal*, which means " worth ", " war ", " power ", " heat ", etc.—i.e. something strong and unpleasant. In Middle Irish there is a word *gall*, meaning " foreigner ", which was used by the English of the Scandinavians. Possibly it comes from *Gallus* (Zimmer), and is a memory of the inroads of the Gauls into Ireland. It has also been ascribed to the root which gives Latin *hostis* (*ghas*, *ghaslo*) (Stokes). The root of the Latin *garrulus* has also been suggested. But what has not ?

writers, in describing the races of the West, started to speak
of the Celts instead of the Ligurians, they imagined, in the
place of the great Ligurian region (*Ligystike*), a great Celtic
region (*Keltike*), which covered the whole West, including
the islands. The islands disappeared into the region as a whole.
The Celts were the great people of the West. Did the islanders
really call themselves Celts ? That is another question,
and one that was probably not asked. It is extremely
doubtful whether the inhabitants of Ireland ever gave
themselves a name of the kind.[1] Moreover, the Irish seem to
have exhausted the resources of their ethnographical sense
when they described themselves in reference to themselves
and distinguished the elements of which they were composed.
The Celts of Britain behaved differently ; indeed, it is just
possible that the Galians of Ireland were recruited among
them.[2]

The names of Celt and Gaul are properly the names of the
Celtic peoples of the Continent.

It is, too, on the eastern limit of the Celts that the evidence
found regarding the use of these racial names and the resulting
distinctions are of value and usefully supplement linguistic
and other indications. In the East there were isolated peoples,
thrown out in advance of the main body, which were called
Celtic—the Cotini and Osi in Silesia, the Scordisci, the
Iapodes. On the other hand, a certain number of Belgic
peoples styled themselves Germanic ; yet the Belgæ were
called Gauls and Galatians, just like the Gauls of Lugdunensis
and Cisalpine Gaul.

We can, to a great extent, trust the ancient authors in
their use of the name of Celts, although it is not always
ultimately based on native evidence. Such terms as Celto-
Ligurian, Celtiberian, Gallo-Greek, Celto-Scythian, reveal
an appreciation of shades of difference, a fairly conscientious
interest in the racial distinctions expressed by names. They
are not, indeed, all of equal value ; Celto-Scythian,[3] for

---

[1] On the names of the Goidels and Brythons, see below, pp. 197 ff.
On the ethnology of Ireland, see below, pp. 207 ff.

[2] The name of Wales, given to that country by the Saxon conquerors,
does not come into the question here. It is the name of a particular Celtic
people, the Volcæ, which was first extended by the Germans to all their
Celto-Romanic neighbours (*welsch*) and then appropriated, as often happened.

[3] Strabo, xi, 6, 2 ; cf. i, 2, 27 ; Plut., *Mar.*, 11 ; Heracl. Pont., in Plut.,
Cam., 22, 2. D'Arbois, CCCI, i, pp. 233-4.

example, merely designates an unknown man who was neither a Celt nor a Scythian. But the use of a racial designation covering more than the group which obviously forms one community is always vitiated by the same causes of error, whether the term be used by a geographer or by an explorer or by a native. Artificial, preconceived classifications are among the most dangerous.

As to the area covered by the name of the Celts, the evidence of the ancients is based on their notion of the racial arrangement of the world, according to which there were great barbarian peoples spread equally all round the circumference.

Unfortunately the Greek writers somehow came to combine their idea of the Celts with that of the Hyperboreians. Many use the two words as synonyms.[1] From this confusion the Greek geographers got the idea that there was a Celtic belt covering all Northern Europe as far as Scythia, and thus were led into mistakes about the relations of the Celts and the Germans,[2] and the true extent of the Celtic region.

Another confusion, that of the Cimmerians and the Cimbri, which was started by Poseidonios,[3] has raged like a pestilence among modern historians,[4] and has recently been given a new lease of life by the latest work dealing with the Celts and Celtic archæology.[5] This theory enlarges their domain considerably towards Eastern Europe, with very little trouble. It is accepted that the Welsh call themselves Cymry. By connecting this name with that of the Cimbri it was natural to hang it on to the Belgæ. But " Cymry " has nothing to do with " Cimbri ". At the time of the Cimbrian invasion the word Cymry must have had the form Combroges [6] (people of the same country, brog). The word still had this form when it was taken over by the Irish

[1] Dottin, **CCCXXII**, p. 22. Hecatæos of Abdera said that, opposite the Celtic country, there was a large island inhabited by the Hyperboreians, which was the British Isles (*F.H.G.*, ii, 286, fr. 2).

[2] In the time of Augustus, Dionysios of Halicarnassos (fragments of Bks. xiv and xv, 1) made Germany part of the Celtic region. Cf. Plut., *Mar.*, 11, 6. D'Arbois, **CCCI**, ii, p. 303.

[3] In Strabo, vii, 2, 2. He was speaking of the Cimmerians of the *Odyssey*, whom he confused with those of Scythia and Asia Minor, the Gimicai of the Assyrian inscriptions. His opinion was adopted by Diodoros (v, 32, 4) and Plutarch (*Mar.*, ii, 9). Cf. Dottin, **CCCXXII**, p. 20.

[4] On this confusion cf. Dottin, op. cit., p. 23.

[5] Peake, **CCCCXLVII**, p. 162.

[6] Or *Combrogi*. Loth, in **CXL**, xxx, p. 384.

(*combreic*, dative of the adjective, " Cymric ").[1] Who were
the Cimbri ?   Probably Germans, doubtless very much
Celticized. But if there can still be any doubt about their
race there is none at all about that of the Cimmerians. They
were Thracians, or a kindred people.[2]

The efforts of the myth-writers to bring the Celts into
mythological tradition, by giving them a place in the two
cycles which are divided into compartments—that of Heracles
and that of Troy [3]—has led to trouble of another kind. They
encouraged the Celtic peoples to forge Mediterranean pedigrees
for themselves at the expense of their Celtic inheritance.
In Gaul, the Ædui and the Arverni connected themselves
with the Trojan stock, by lines unknown to us, and thereby
justified themselves in maintaining or adopting a pro-Roman
policy.

> *Arvernique ausi Latio se fingere fratres,*
> *Sanguine ab Iliaco populi—*

" And the Arvernian peoples, who dared imagine themselves
brothers of the Latin, from their Trojan blood." [4]   The
Irish did likewise, and this was the beginning of their history
writing.[5]   They took bits from the Bible and the Latin
historians and geographers. They placed themselves among
the great peoples of the world. The only connection they
did not boast was the Celtic. They claimed kinship with
the Iberians because they called themselves *Hiberni*, and with
the Scythians because they called themselves *Scotti*.   They

[1] D'Arbois, **CCCI**, i, pp. 257–8 ; Müllenhoff, ii, pp. 116–121.
[2] D'Arbois, op. cit., p. 251 ; Dottin, **CCCXXII**, pp. 169–172. But quite
lately they have been turned into Tokharians (Charpentier, **CLXVI**, 1917,
p. 347). According to this theory, the Cimmerians of the shores of the Black
Sea were divided by the Scythians into two sections, one of which moved
south towards the Danube and so into Asia Minor, where it came into conflict
with the army of Gyges, while the other was driven eastwards and settled
in Turkestan. Some of them remained in the delta of the Danube and formed
the nucleus of the Celtic settlements which we shall find in that region later.
The whole construction is highly fanciful.
[3] They gave the Galatians an eponymous hero—Galates, whom some
made a son of Heracles and a Celtic woman (Diod., v, 24) and others a son
of Polyphemos and Galateia (Γαλατία, in Timæos). Jullian, **CCCXLVII**,
ii, p. 417.   On the possible identification of the Celts with the Læstrygons,
see Dottin, **CCCXXII**, p. 26.
[4] Lucan, *Pharsalia*, i, 427–8, and scholia.   Amm. Marc., xv, 9, 5 ;
Propertius, ii, 13, 48 ; Tac., *Germ.*, 3 ; Hirschfeld, **CXLVIII**, 1897, pp. 1105 ff. ;
T. Dirt, in **CXLIV**, 1896, pp. 506 ff. ; Weerth, **XXXVII**, lxix, 1880, p. 69 ;
Castra Trajana, (near Xanten) = *Trojana* ; Sieburg, **CLX**, 1904, p. 312.
[5] E. MacNeill, **CCCCXLI**, pp. 11 ff., 93 ff.

credited their forbears with the wildest of wanderings, but they did not make them come from the lands which really were the Celtic cradle. So the Celts assumed an illustrious classical pedigree, which they could share with the great civilized peoples, but disowned themselves and their own forefathers. A whole movement of ideas, partly scientific and partly political, the effects of which are still in operation, had to take place before the intellectuals of the Celtic countries, the scholars of Ireland, Scotland, Wales, and Brittany, recovered the consciousness of their racial kinship.

There was a time when the Celts were sufficiently aware of that kinship to impress foreigners with the notion of their unity and to give themselves a name which, if not common to all, was at least very general. But their racial consciousness was too incomplete, and was too often destroyed. They have left us evidence that distant or different groups considered themselves as being of one race, and we shall consider that evidence carefully. The existence of an institution like that of the Druids must have helped to keep the feeling alive. Nevertheless, it weakened, becoming limited to such groups or political relationships as could keep it up, and declining even there. So the Celts are not good witnesses to the use of the name of Celt. When the ancients used it, they generally had very good reasons. Moreover, we are not compelled to accept their evidence without being able to criticize it.

II

THE ANTHROPOLOGICAL EVIDENCE

A wind of confusion has blown among the anthropologists whenever they have come to deal with the Celts, and they have dealt with them far too much. For a long time their great aspiration was to attach racial proper names to pure races. It was with the Celts as with the Aryans. Attempts were made to give their name to one or another of the physical types prevailing in Europe. Not all students, luckily, have fallen into this quagmire, and in the works of Messrs. Boule, Deniker, Ripley, and Fleure [1] the most reasonable discussions

---

[1] Boule, *Les Hommes fossiles*, p. 320 ; Deniker, **CCCXX** ; Ripley, **CCCLXXVIII**, pp. 124–5 ; Fleure, **CCCXXVIII**, *passim*.

will be found. But errors of simplification, which are the most natural of all, continue to create trouble in the language of science long after they have been exploded. An anthropologist who speaks of the Celts must always make a moral effort in order to restrain himself from applying the name as a label to a series of similar skulls. It would be better never to use it at all.

The Greek and Latin writers who speak of the Celts regarded them as a tall people, with lymphatic bodies, white skins, and fair hair.[1] They alarmed the Italians by their resemblance to large, though magnificent, beasts.

Aurea cæsaries ollis atque aurea vestis :
virgatis lucent sagulis : tum lactea colla
auro innectantur [2]—

" Golden is their hair, and golden their garb. They are resplendent in their striped cloaks, and their milk-white necks are circled with gold." Since the ancients return over and over again to their fair hair and their milk-white skin, modern writers have supposed that the bands which invaded Italy and Greece were recruited among the tall, fair longheads of Northern Europe.

Others of the ancients knew that there were Celts who were less fair than the rest, particularly the Britons [3]; that the Celts were not so fair as the Germans ; and that to produce a parade of tall, fair Celts it was necessary to pick out suitable specimens and dye their hair. Suetonius, for instance, tells us that Caligula, wishing, after an alleged campaign against the Germans, to increase the number of prisoners who were to follow his chariot in his triumph, picked out the tallest Gauls that could be found and made them let their hair grow and dye it red.[4] The Greek and Roman writers knew plenty of Celts, if it was only as slaves, Gallic and British, for these must have been very numerous ; but, being used to the dark-skinned, black-haired people of the South, they especially noticed foreigners who had fair or red hair. There were doubtless many dark Gauls.

---

[1] Diod., v, 28 ; Amm. Marc., xv, 12, 1 ; both passages come from Timagenes. Livy, v, 48 ; xx, 55 ; xxviii, 17, 21 ; Silius Ital., iv, 201–3 ; Martial, xi, 53 ; Pliny Eld., iv, 31. Claud., *Stil.*, ii, 651. Cf. Boule, op. cit., pp. 348–350.

[2] Virg., *Æn.*, viii, 658–660.   [3] Tac., *Agr.*, xi.   [4] *Cal.*, 62.

Since Broca wrote, the name of Celts has been attached to the type of dark round-heads of Western Europe and the Alpine regions.[1] This, too, is done in virtue of an ancient authority, namely the first words of Cæsar's *Commentaries : Gallia est omnis divisa in partes tres, quarum unam incolunt Belgæ, aliam Aquitani, tertiam qui ipsorum lingua Celtæ, nostra Galli appellantur*—" Gaul is divided into three parts, one of which is inhabited by the Belgæ, another by the Aquitani, and the third by men who are called Celts in their own language and Galli in ours." [2] The dark type, which is widespread in Central France, has been attributed to the Celts. Broca assigned the fair type to the Belgæ.

Still keeping the Celts round-headed, other anthropologists have identified them with the tall brachycephals or mesaticephals of the north and north-west of Europe, often designated as the Borreby type,[3] who are distinguished from the other European round-heads by the height of the face, the accentuation of the supraciliary ridge, the pentagonal shape of the skull as seen from above, and the stature. The very strange term of " Celto-Slavs " which has been applied to all brachycephals as a whole is due to the diffusion of this special type all over Northern Europe, from east to west.[4] The descendants of this type who are found from England to Russia lead one to think that we have to do with fair brachycephals, perhaps the result of crossing between Nordic long-heads and Alpine round-heads. Herr Schliz, of Heilbronn, an anthropologist whose work deserves to be followed very closely, since he makes an interesting attempt to establish a concordance between forms of civilization and physical types in the centre and north-west of Europe in prehistoric times, has selected this very type to assign to the Celts.[5] For, he says, this is the type found in the graves of the La Tène period in Bavaria, and it is beyond dispute

---

[1] P. Broca, **LXXXVIII**, 1860, pp. 1–56 ; **XLI**, 1860, pp. 457–464, 557–562, 569, 573 ; 1873, pp. 247–252, 317–320 ; 1874, pp. 658–663. Beddoe, **XCVIII**, 1864, pp. 348–357 ; **XLI**, 1877, p. 483. Virchow, **LXXXII**, 1895, pp. 130–3 ; Ranke, **CCCLXX**, ii, pp. 261–8 ; F. W. Rudler, **CXXVII**, 1880, pp. 609–619 ; Ripley, **CCCLXXVIII**, pp. 125 ff.

[2] *Bell. Gall.*, i, 1.

[3] Ebert, **CCCXXIV**, ii, p. 121 ; Ripley, **CCCLXXVIII**, p. 212 ; F. G. Parsons, **LXXVI**, 1913, p. 550.

[4] Ripley, op. cit., pp. 355 ff. (following Topinard) ; Sergi, **DXL**, chap. vi.

[5] Schliz, **XXIII**, 1909, pp. 239 ff. ; 1910, pp. 202 ff., 355 ff. ; id., **LXXXV**, 1911, p. 313.

that the country was at that time occupied by Gauls. If Herr Schliz is in error, he is only partly so, for there certainly were Celts of this type. It is the type represented by the great figures of Galatians which are supposed to have adorned some Pergamene trophy, such as the Dying Gaul of the Capitol and the Ludovisi Gaul. These round heads, the high faces, the straight foreheads with strongly marked brow-ridges, the noses set back at the base, and the stiff hair with rebellious locks, are evidently copied from nature, and the copy is true, for the type is familiar to the modern Frenchman ; he finds it all round him. But it is also the typical Gaul as described by the ancients, tall, fair-haired, and white-skinned, and he is not a dolichocephal.

It is certain that the three types described above existed among the Celts, both on the Continent and in the islands. Here the Irish texts bear their witness. In the *Táin* there are fair heroes (*find-buide*) and also a few dark ones (*dond-temin*).[1] One is called Fiacha Cinn Fionnann, or Fairhead.[2] But no one has any objection to admitting the fact. For even the extremist can save the situation by talking of non-Aryan peoples which have been Aryanized and non-Celtic peoples which have been Celticized. It has, moreover, been almost universally admitted since the time of Roget de Belloguet[3] that the Celts were never more than an aristocracy in the lands which they occupied.

But the difficulty comes just when one passes from determining the anthropological composition of the groups which are known to have been designated as Celtic to giving a name to something formed by those groups. It is in this respect that the attribution of names to one type rather than to another is apt to produce contradictions between the ethnographical conclusions of the anthropologists and those of the archæologists, philologists, or historians. Are the Celts Nordic heroes, who conquer and rule majorities of brunets, Alpine or Mediterranean ? Or are they the brunets of Western or Central Europe, absorbing minorities of Nordic heroes[4] ? The whole meaning of history alters according

---

[1] CCXCVI, ll. 5173, 5186, 5245.
[2] Cf. Kuno Meyer, CCLXXIII, i, for fair hair.
[3] CCCLXXIX, iii, pp. 370 ff. ; Ripley, CCCCXXVII, p. 127.
[4] Peake, CCCCXLVII, pp. 81 ff.

to the answer, and the question cannot be settled by anthropological prejudices.

Herr Schliz, who is very dogmatic, gives the following account of the succession of human types in Southern Germany, which is the field of his studies, during the Hallstatt and La Tène periods.[1] At the beginning of the Hallstatt age there were in that region short, dolichocephalic men, of Mediterranean appearance, who had apparently come from the South-west. At the height of the same period their place was taken by tall men, also dolichocephalic, who, he says, came from the Balkans. The tall brachycephals appear only in the La Tène period. Herr Schliz makes them come from the West or North-west, and he makes them Celts, so presenting yet another view of the history of that people. This substitution of one unmixed anthropological type for another in succession, which Herr Schliz holds to have taken place in Germany, whenever civilization took a new turn, needs to be considered. Herr Schliz restores to favour the idea of peoples of pure race which has lost ground considerably.[2] To compel acceptance of it is another affair.

One must not resort to that inexhaustible source of errors and contradictions, save with great moderation and in a very critical spirit ; it must not be forgotten that peoples and races, being different things, do not necessarily coincide, and, in fact, never coincide exactly. We do not know of any human group in Europe, from the Quaternary Period and the age of chipped stone downwards, which is not composed of different anthropological elements. The physical characteristics of these groups vary, and they can do so without their variations having the least connection with their history. They may change automatically, as it were, without any new element coming in, through variation of the proportion of the elements of which they are already composed ; or they may change with the introduction of new

[1] Schliz, pp. 237 ff.
[2] If we examine Herr Schliz's writings carefully, we notice that he is working on very few facts. He is one of those men who never have the luck to find exceptions on their path ; but they may lie at one side. So far as the Iron Age in Germany is concerned, archæology furnishes nothing to correspond to the racial revolutions which he supposes. Where he sees discontinuity, I see continuity, and continuity in the Celts. Moreover, the tall, long-headed type existed in Germany before the La Tène period ; it has been reported, in particular, in the zoned-vase graves of the beginning of the Bronze Age.

elements, such as slaves or resident aliens, which do not shift the political axis of their composition. Races and peoples have their variations. These do not necessarily take place in the same direction ; they may possibly run counter to each other.

In any case, it is very rash to identify the Celts with one of the elements found in one of their groups. We shall see that the composition of the groups is different from the very beginning.[1] It is particularly rash to identify the Celts with the dominant elements in their Western groups which were not autochthonous and were altered from their original type by the large proportion of alien elements which they must have absorbed. It is unscientific to label a group of men, ancient or modern, by physical characteristics defined in that way. It is equally unscientific to go on from that to searching in the anthropology of Europe for Proto-Celts.[2]

It is, however, true that the Celts formed a racial unit, or several kindred racial units, in which common life produced a kind of unification of physical types in a sort of *habitus* common to all. So an ideal type was created, to which all strove to approach. The Gauls dyed or bleached their hair, and with that object had invented the prototype of soap, *sapo*.[3] They painted their bodies.[4] Just as, in our time, the individuals of any nation have the family likeness by which they are recognized as French, English, Italian, or German, so the ancients could recognize a Celt.

In short, while anthropology has nothing to tell us about the Celts, and, in spite of many efforts, has never told us anything, the anthropological materials which it collects and studies should be taken into account with our other evidence when we try to describe their groupings and look for their ethical relationships.

[1] CCCCLXXXIV, p. 82 ; Ripley, CCCLXXVIII, p. 298 ; F. Dumas, CXLIII, 1908, p. 338 ; cf. Hamy, XV, 1906, p. 1.
[2] Kossinna, LXXXV, 1909, pp. 26 ff. ; 225 ff. ; 1910, pp. 59 ff.
[3] Pliny Eld., xxviii, 191 ; cf. Dottin, CCCXXII, p. 283.
[4] In XXIII (1913), Hoefler published an excellent article entitled " Somatologie der Gallo-Kelten " (pp. 54 ff.), in which he examines the little that we know of this artificial aspect of the Celts. From our point of view, this manner of studying the anthropology of a human society is the safest. Unfortunately, it does not help us to find out and bring together the relics of the Celts.

CHAPTER II

LANGUAGE

I

LANGUAGE AS THE MARK OF A SOCIETY

THE Celts were not a race, but a group of peoples, or, to speak more accurately, a group of societies. Language is one of the clearest and truest characteristics of societies. Among the cultural facts which are bounded by the boundaries of a community, it is one of the most typical or the most apparent. There are exceptions to this rule. France is, perhaps, the best example of the rule and of the exceptions. In that country there are spoken, in addition to French, dialects of the *Langue d'oc*, Basque, Breton, Flemish, German, and Italian. Except the *Langue d'oc* dialects, which are fairly widespread, these tongues are spoken by comparatively small groups on the fringes of the nation. For all these groups, French is the language of civilization. The French-speaking countries beyond her frontiers have the closest social and moral relations with France. Such is France and such are the French-speaking countries. National states which speak two or three languages, like Belgium and Switzerland, are really societies divided by language, whose moral and political unity is maintained by veritable social contracts. The great states (which, in any case, were short-lived), such as those of Asia, in which many languages were spoken, were never anything but empires, and never had any unity but that of the sovereign. On the whole, to speak roughly, the language coincides with the society.

We may, therefore, say that the Celts are the group of the peoples which spoke or still speak dialects of a certain family, which are called the Celtic languages. Wherever the Celts have lived they have left place-names, inscriptions with personal names, and in history the memory of other names, which can be recognized as different from all others and, in general, are the same everywhere. The faintest traces of Celtic speech are certain evidence of the presence of the Celts

33

at a certain place at a certain time. They enable us to stake out the domain of the Celts and its changing boundaries with a maximum of confidence.

But for the history of ancient peoples, especially when it is transmitted only by scanty and uncertain evidence, the consideration of their language, or of what remains of it, is equally useful from another point of view. Languages, in their constitution, show how different societies have been related to one another by blood or neighbourhood. The Celtic languages are not something quite apart among the European tongues. It is, therefore, possible, by comparing them and the other families of languages to obtain information as to where they stand in the genealogical tree of the Indo-European languages, which are, for the greater part, the languages of Europe, what neighbours the Celts had at different moments in their past, and, consequently, where they lived. Nothing else could take the place of this kind of information. That is why we must spend some time in examining the Celtic languages and their affinities.

II

THE CELTIC LANGUAGES [1]

We know of almost as many Celtic languages as separate groups of Celts.

The modern languages are, on the one hand, Irish,[2] comprising three groups of dialects,[3] the Gaelic of Scotland,[4] and the Manx of the Isle of Man [5]; and, on the other hand, Welsh,[6] including two groups of dialects,[7] Cornish, which

---

[1] Vendryès, in Meillet and Cohen, **CCXVIII**; Pedersen, **CCXXVII**; L. Weisgerber, " Die Sprache der Festlandkelten," in **XXIX**, xx, 1930, pp. 147–226.

[2] O'Donovan, **CCXXV**; Molloy, **CCXIX**; O'Nolan, **CCXXVI**.

[3] The southern dialect of Munster (Henebry, **CCV**; J. Loth, **CXXXIII**, iii, p. 317); the western dialect of Connacht (Finck, **CXCIX**; G. Dottin, **CXL**, xiv, p. 97; xvi, p. 421; xx, p. 306); and the northern dialect of Donegal (Quiggin, **CCXXVIII**; Sommerfelt, **CCXXXIX**).

[4] Gillies, **CCIII**, 1902; Reid, **CCXXIX**.

[5] H. Jenner, " The Manx Language," in **CLIV**, 1875.

[6] Rhys, **CCCCLIII**, ch. xii; Morris Jones, **CCVIII**, with the additions and corrections of J. Loth, **CXL**, xxxvi (1915), pp. 108 ff., 391 ff.; xxxvii (1917–19), pp. 26 ff.

[7] The dialects of the north (Anglesey, Carnarvon, and Merioneth) and south (Cardigan, Carmarthen, and Glamorgan) (Fynes Clinton, **CXCII**; Morris, **CCXX**).

died out in Cornwall at the end of the eighteenth century,[1] and Breton, with its four dialects, Trégorois, Léonard, Cornouaillais, and Vannetais.[2] The former are called Goidelic, from the name Goidel, that is Irish; the latter are called Brythonic, from the name of the Brythons, the ancient inhabitants of Britain.[3] There are great differences between the two groups.

The many ancient Celtic languages are represented by what is called Gaulish or Gallic,[4] which covers the remnants of several dialects, if not of several languages,[5] spoken on the Continent and in Britain. These remnants include about sixty inscriptions,[6] some of which, written in Etruscan or Greek characters, range from the descent of the Gauls into Italy to the conquest of Gaul, while others are in Latin characters, epigraphic or cursive,[7] the latest belonging to a time shortly after the Roman conquest. The remainder consists of proper names, some inscribed on coins and others preserved by Græco-Roman tradition, and a few common nouns.[8]

Old Irish is known from inscriptions written in what is known as the ogham alphabet, the oldest of which date from the fifth century,[9] from a few inscriptions in Latin characters, and from copious glosses of the eighth and ninth centuries.[10] Ancient British is known from much briefer glosses of the same period [11] and from proper names preserved in Christian inscriptions of Britain and in Breton tradition.[12]

Between these somewhat incomplete records of the ancient state of those languages which still survive and the Gallic inscriptions or other contemporary documents, we may place

[1] J. Loth, **CXL**, xvii–xxiv, xxxii–xxxvii; H. Jenner, *Handbook of the Cornish Language*, London, 1904.
[2] Loth, **CXL**, xxiv, p. 295, and **CCXIII**; Vallée, **CCXLI**; Ernault, **CXCVIII**.
[3] Macbain, **CLXXXIX**.
[4] G. Dottin, **CXCVI**.
[5] e.g. the Coligny Calendar has been regarded by Sir John Rhys as representing a language similar to Irish (Rhys, **VIII**; cf. Nicholson, **CCXXIV**; Macbain, **CLXXXIX**, iii; cf. below, pp. 233 ff.
[6] Dottin, **CXCVI**, pp. 136–212.
[7] Abbé Hermet, **CCVI**; J. Loth, **CXL**, xli, 1.
[8] Dottin, op. cit., pp. 223–302 (glossary); 133 (history of the Gaulish glossary); Roget de Belloguet, **CCCLXXIX**, i.
[9] Macalister, **CCXV**.
[10] Stokes and Strachan, **CCXXXV**.
[11] J. Loth, **CCXIV**.
[12] Loth, **CCXIII**.

a certain number of Latin glosses,[1] and also the Gaulish formulæ [2] given in the *De Medicamentis* of Marcellus of Bordeaux, who wrote about A.D. 400,[3] and a small Gaulish vocabulary which is preserved in a manuscript of the eighth century in Vienna,[4] but must date from the fifth century.[5] It is called Endlicher's Glossary, after the philologist who discovered it.

This, then, is our chain of evidence on the Celtic languages. It looks fairly loose and exiguous. The Celtic dialects of the islands seem to be à long way from ancient Gaulish, which itself is but little known. It is not surprising that it took a long time to discover their kinship, once the tradition was broken, and that, down to the nineteenth century, historians and antiquaries looked for equivalents of Gaulish words anywhere but in the living Celtic dialects.

With the *Grammatica Celtica* of Zeuss, published in 1853, the scientific comparative study of the Celtic languages began. It is an old book, which has been superseded but not forgotten. In the very first edition Zeuss instituted a methodical comparison between Goidelic, Brythonic, and the remains of ancient Gaulish, and since then the fact of their relationship has been accepted. Zeuss belongs to the same generation as Bopp ; and one of the great scientific achievements of that generation was to disentangle the science of language and to put it together again.

III

AGREEMENTS BETWEEN THE CELTIC LANGUAGES

The kinship of the Celtic languages appears, first, in the agreement of their vocabularies, two or three of which will express the same idea by the same word. Sometimes these words are lacking in other languages, such as **magos*, plain (Gaulish Noviomagus, Noyon, New Plain ; Irish *magh* ;

---

[1] For old Celtic in general, the most complete collection is Alfred Holder's *Altceltischer Sprachschatz*, 3 vols.

[2] Pliny, xxvii, 101 : *limeum = cervarium* ; cf. Jullian, **CXXXIV**, 1911, p. 844.

[3] Dottin, **CXCVI**, p. 214.

[4] Ibid., p. 212. We have six other manuscripts of this text, less complete and later than that mentioned.

[5] H. Zimmer, **CLXXIV**. xxxii, pp. 230–240.

Welsh *ma*; Breton *maes*),[1] or they may be found in other forms, for example, the Gaulish adjective *nŏvios* (as in Noviodunum), formed by adding the suffix *-io-* [2] to the root, as contrasted with the Germanic **nĕvios*, of which we have evidence in the Gothic *niujis*, modern German *neu*, etc., and with the Latin *nŏvus*, a simple stem in *o*, and the Greek *νέος = nĕvos*. One has only to glance through the comparative lexicons to see how general this is.[3] Out of the thousand Gaulish words or parts of words contained in M. Dottin's glossary [4] there are very few for which there is no corresponding word in Welsh or Irish, or both. For these last two languages, philologists have endeavoured, by using the comparative method, to draw up an ancestral vocabulary,[5] representing a common Celtic, from which the Gaulish dialects themselves were derived in ancient times.

Moreover, the Celtic vocabularies resemble one another not only in their simple words, but in their compounds. Many are of the same type,[6] and some are actually alike, in Irish, Welsh, and Gaulish. For the Gallic Vernomagus we have the Irish Fernmag, Alder Field; for the Welsh Trineint, Three Valleys, we have the Gaulish Trinanto. A name like Senomagus (Senan, in Loiret) at once strikes us; it is the Irish Sen Mag, the Old Plain, not just any plain, but a mythical plain, the earthly equivalent of which lay in the centre of Ireland, just as the country of the Carnutes, of which Loiret was part, lay in the centre of Gaul.

The few words which we know of the Celtic dialects of the Continent outside Gaul have equivalents in the Gaulish of Gaul and the languages of the islands. Celtiberian *viriæ* corresponds to Gaulish *viriolæ*,[7] from which French *virole* ("ferrule") comes, and to Irish *ferenn* "belt". For Spanish *gurdus* "heavy" [8] there is the Gallo-Roman derivative *gurdunicus*,[9] *gwrdd* in Welsh, and *gourd* ("numb") in French.

---

[1] D'Arbois, **CCCI**, ii, p. 268. The root may be the Indo-European **magh-*, from which words meaning " great " are derived—Skt. *mahas*, Lat. *magnus*.
[2] Ibid., p. 256. O. Irish *nue*, *nuide*; Mod. Irish, *nuadh*; Welsh *newydd* (the regular termination of stems in *-io*); Breton *nevez*.
[3] Stokes, **CCXXXVII**.
[4] Dottin, **CXCVI**, pp. 217–302.
[5] Ibid., p. 80.
[6] Ibid., pp. 85–6, 105 ff.
[7] Pliny, xxxiii, 40.
[8] Quintilian, i, 5, 57.
[9] Sulp. Sev., *Dial.*, i, 27, 2.

Spanish *acnuna*[1] is explained by the Gaulish *acina*, a land-measure. Many Spanish proper names are like Gaulish or British proper names (Boudica, cf. Boudicca, the correct form of Boadicea), or are explained by common nouns belonging to the other Celtic tongues (Broccus : Irish *broc*, Welsh *broch*, a brock or badger), or are formed like Gallic names (Medugenus).[2] The same is true of the Cisalpine and Galatian dialects. For Cisalpine Gaulish μανιάκης, a collar, we have Irish *muince* and Old Welsh *minci*. *Rumpus*,[3] a vine which grows attached to trees, and *rumpotinus*, the tree which supports it, recall, less directly, Old Welsh *rump* (?), an auger. *Sasiam* (acc.),[4] the name for rye among the Taurini, a Ligurian people which had taken much of its civilization from its Celtic neighbours, is the same as the Brythonic word for barley (Welsh *haidd*, Breton *heiz*). In Galatian μάρκαν (acc.) is exactly like Irish *marc* and Welsh *march*[5]; ἄλκη is like Gallic *alce* " dash "; ἀδάρκης,[6] a medicinal plant, is like Irish *adarc* " horn ". Here, too, the evidence of the common nouns is confirmed by that of the proper names which are our only witnesses for the language of the Celts of the Upper and Lower Danube.

This agreement extends to peculiarities in the declension of nouns[7] and conjugation of verbs.[8] One example taken from conjugation will be sufficient to show it. There are traces in Irish and Welsh of an ancient conjugation in which the first person singular of the indicative ended in *u* (Old Celtic -*ō*) : Irish *biu, tau* " I am ", *tiagu* " I go ", *tongu* " I swear ". In Welsh the *u* became *i* : *carais* = *cărăsĭ* " I have loved ". There is an example of this conjugation in the bilingual Latin and Gaulish inscription found at Todi in 1839,[9] which

---

[1] **I**, ii, 430.
[2] Dottin, **CXCVI**, p. 22.
[3] Varro, *De Re Rust.*, i, 8, 4.
[4] Pliny, xviii, 141. It is not surprising that in these two instances the resemblance is only approximate. In each case the civilization is borrowed, and the Celtic words are modified.
[5] Paus., x, 19, 11 ; Dottin, **CXCVI**, p. 24. It is probable that the words recorded by Pausanias belong to the dialect of the Celts who invaded Greece and Thrace, i.e. the Galatians.
[6] Dioscorides, v, 136 ; *adarca*, Pliny, xx, 241.
[7] Dottin, **CXCVI**, pp. 81, 112 ff., esp. pp. 117–19, on stems in *o* with genitive in *i*, stems in *a* with genitive in *as*, stems in *i* or a consonant with genitive in *os*.
[8] Ibid., pp. 122 ff.
[9] Ibid., p. 153. The inscription has two faces, which partly complement

contains the word *karnitu*. The two texts differ slightly, for the Latin sentence is in the third person, as is usual in inscriptions (*locavit* and *statuit*), whereas the Gaulish sentence must be in the first person (the use of the first person in dedicatory inscriptions is attested by Latin inscriptions found in Gaul). In *karnitu*, which corresponds to *locavit* and *statuit*, we find the root of the Gaelic *cairn* ; it means " I heaped up ".[1]

So the grammar of Gaulish coincides to a remarkable extent with that of the living Celtic languages. Unfortunately we have not much information about it, and all the resources of the comparative grammar of the Celtic tongues which have been applied to the subject have not succeeded in making it easy for us to read the Gallic inscriptions. The reason may be that the surviving remnants of Gaulish contain elements which cannot be fitted together by the methods of reconstruction employed by Celticists, or, more probably, that they are so fragmentary that they are doomed to remain an insoluble mystery.

M. Dottin suggests that it was probably very different from the Celtic spoken in the islands, Goidelic or even Brythonic. The two following facts, however, studied by M. Loth [2] show that phonetic development took place along the same lines in the islands and on the Continent ; this means that the languages were fairly alike, and that the people who spoke them had the same tricks of pronunciation, which they had inherited from their ancestors who all spoke the same speech and which they kept up by their intercourse.

First, the group of letters *ct* became *cht* in Irish and *ith* in Old Welsh ; that is, in both families of languages the guttural tended to become a sort of spirant. It was the same in Gaulish. There is evidence of this in the oldest Gaulish

one another. Face B, restored, runs : *Ategnato Drutei urnum Coisis Drutei f. frater eius minimus locavit et statuit. Ateknati Trutikni karnitu artuass Koisi Trutiknos.* The termination *-knos* is the patronymic suffix. In *artuas* we see the Irish *art*. The monument in question is of stone, and that, doubtless, is the meaning of the unknown Italic word *urnum*. The inscription means : " To Ategnatos, son of Druteos, I, Coisis, son of Druteos, his youngest brother, raised this monument." It should be noted that this bilingual inscription was found in Italy, on the border of the Celtic and Italic domains.

[1] See also d'Arbois, **CLXXXVIII**, pp. 122–4. Pedersen holds that there is a third person singular deponent (**CCXXVII**, i, p. 245 ; ii, p. 406) ; Dottin, op. cit., p. 122.

[2] J. Loth, **CXXXIX**, xiii (1922), pp. 108–119.

inscriptions in which the uniformity of the Latin alphabet has not yet prevailed. We find the name of the man whom Cæsar calls Lucterius written as Λυχτεριος, with a χ. In Irish it is *luchtaire*, glossed as *lanista*, master of gladiators (Old Irish *lucht* " portion ", " troop " ; Welsh *llwyth*). Gaulish wavered between the two sounds.

The second fact is the variety of ways in which the sounds usually written *ss* and *s* are written. The spelling hesitates between *s, ss, ds, d, sd, st, θ, đ*, and *đđ*. For example, the name of the goddess Sirona is written as Dirona and Đirona.[1] On coins we find Veliocassi and Veliocaθi. One name is variously spelt Assedomarus and Addedomarus, the first element of which is found in the form Adeda in Carinthia.[2] So, too, the Fair Iseult appears in Welsh as Etthilt, Ethylt, and Essylt. The sound in question was probably a cerebral, that is a dental pronounced with the tongue pressed very high above the alveoli.

The starting-point is the same, there is the same initial impulse or the same environment—that is the reason of these resemblances. These languages were the same or similar at the beginning, and they were still so to a great extent at the time of the facts which we are discussing, because the reasons for their identity or similarity still existed. Of British and Gaulish Tacitus says in his *Agricola* that they are very little different, and we have no reason to doubt his evidence. As for Goidelic, I have been struck by the fact that in all the stories of Irishmen travelling to Britain and Welshmen travelling to Ireland there is never a word of interpreters. Indeed, there were British colonies in Ireland and Irish colonies in Britain. There is no suggestion that their languages were different. I am inclined to believe that, in the time of the Roman Empire, even the most different of the Celtic languages were not so different that their speakers did not understand one another. In the absence of other evidence, the great number of Irish words which can be shown to have been borrowed from Welsh and vice versa before the literary period of the history of those languages may serve as a proof. The learned Danish scholar, Holger Pedersen,[3] has made

---

[1] Loth, **CXL**, 1911, p. 416. Two etymologies are possible : (i) Welsh *seren*, Breton *sterenn*, " star " (Dottin, **CXCVI**, p. 287) ; (ii) Irish *sir*, Welsh *hir* " long ", i.e. the Longlived One.

[2] Dottin, **CXCVI**, p. 52.   [3] **CCXXVII**, p. 23.

out a long list of these reciprocal borrowings, which prove that the speakers of the two languages understood one another and that the two languages were spoken together.

St. Jerome, a great traveller, says in his commentary on the *Epistle to the Galatians*,[1] that the Galatians of Asia Minor spoke a Celtic dialect which was much the same as that of the people of Treves, among whom he had stayed. The Galatians were Belgæ, and the language of the Belgæ was a Brythonic dialect. St. Jerome lived at the end of the fourth century after Christ, and the Celts had settled in Galatia in the third century B.C. After seven hundred years, cut off from their main stock and living in a country where the common tongue was Greek, the Galatians had kept their language such that it could be recognized and understood by their linguistic kinsfolk. Doubts have been cast on St. Jerome's authority, quite undeservedly ; it has been supposed that he copied an earlier author. This criticism is absurd, for two or three centuries more or less do not affect the value of the fact in the least.

The Goidels and the Brythons had been separated, in my opinion, for a much longer time, yet not so long that they had become incapable of recognizing and understanding each other. The Celtic languages which bear their names have very marked and significant characteristics which I shall discuss in their place. But at the time of the ogham inscriptions the laws by which they became differentiated had left in each tongue many words which were similar to words in the other or could be understood by speakers of the other.[2] It is certainly true, on the other hand, that what remains of Gaulish is very different from the living Celtic languages, and that it lacks some of the characteristics of the modern Celtic group.[3] But it would be a marvel if Gaulish, like those languages, had accomplished a phonetic evolution which is parallel to that which has produced the Romance tongues ; syntax and conjugation are just that side of Gaulish of which we know least, and it is at any rate very remarkable that one of the inscriptions of Alise contains an example of relative conjugation similar to that of Irish.[4]

[1] In Migne, *Patrologie latine*, xxvi, 382.
[2] Cf. Gaulish *enigeno-*, ogham *inigena*, Irish *ingen* "girl" ; Gaulish *magalo-maglo*, ogham *maglus*, Irish *mál* "prince". Dottin, **CXCVI**, glossary, s.v.
[3] Ibid., p. 125.　　　　　[4] **CXCVI**, p. 160 ; cf. p. 122, *dugiiontiio*.

So the unity of the Celtic languages is plain. There were very close similarities between them, such as did not exist between any of them and any other language. They were homogeneous, they had attained a certain degree of stability, and they were still fairly far, at the time when we shall have to bid the Celts farewell, from the differentiation which they present to-day.

IV

THE CELTIC LANGUAGES AND THE INDO-EUROPEAN LANGUAGES

Some years before the publication of Zeuss's *Grammar* Bopp caused the Celtic languages to be finally received into the family of Indo-European tongues by a treatise which for a long time was regarded as authoritative.[1] It is, then, generally admitted that the Celtic languages are Indo-European languages, and have a certain place in the whole body of those languages. That is how they are defined. A definition is a classification. Classification results from comparison ; it is based on the recording of resemblances and differences. We must, therefore, survey the work which has been done in this matter by philologists ; we must try to see on what branch of the family tree of the Indo-European languages the Celtic languages grew, whether any other elements went to their make-up, and what these were.

The data for this study are, on the one hand, grammar and phonetics, and on the other vocabulary. Philologists have established a whole system of equations between the consonants and vowels of the various Indo-European tongues.[2] They have done the same for the grammatical forms of conjugation and declension, for the elements which are added to a word to make noun-stems and verb-stems of it, or to give it different meanings, and, lastly, for the roots themselves.

One of the objects of this study is the reconstruction of theoretical prototypes for each series of words and elements. When all the supposed prototypes for all the Indo-European

---

[1] **IX**, 1838, pp. 187–292.   [2] Meillet, **CCXVII.**

languages are collected together we have the hypothetical
" Indo-European ".   Another object is the establishment
of the genealogical order of the languages.   This gives us
groups of languages which are especially closely related,
and an order of derivation between groups and individual
languages.   Modern philologists no longer believe that
" Indo-European " is even the shadow of a spoken language.
But whether it was spoken or not does not much affect our
power to draw conclusions of all kinds from its composition
and its relationship with languages which really have been
spoken.   It is a system of linguistic facts.

From the composition of the vocabulary, conclusions
have been reached regarding the date when the Indo-
Europeans split.   They already knew of copper at the time.
Conclusions have likewise been reached regarding their first
habitat, which is supposed to have been bounded by the
southern limit of the beech, their manner of life, their social
organization, their crafts, and their ideas about this world
and the next.   The same has been done for the various groups
of Indo-Europeans as for the Indo-Europeans in their
undivided state, but with less strictness and regard for detail.

These conclusions have been corrected.   It has been
pointed out that the historical interpretation of the data of
the Indo-European problem was open to serious criticism.
Nevertheless, the same method has in quite recent years
produced some admirable and instructive works,[1] even if,
like those which preceded them, they sometimes exaggerate
the importance of the similarities and differences of languages.

The kinship of the Celtic and the Indo-European languages
is attested by their grammars and confirmed by a comparison
of these with the grammars of languages which are not Indo-
European.   Take, for example, Semitic grammar ; it is
impossible to mistake a Semitic verb, with its many voices,
for an Indo-European verb, which is richer in tenses.   But the
comparison of the vocabularies furnishes plainer arguments.

The word for " mother ", for example (Old Irish *máthir*,
gen. *máthar* ; Gaulish *matres*, *matrebo*), is the same in all
the families of Indo-European languages (Old Icelandic
mader ; modern German *Mutter* ; Latin *mater* ; Doric
Greek μάτηρ ; Sanskrit *mātár* ; Armenian *mayr* ; Tokharian

---

[1] Hirt, **CCCXXXVIII** ; Schrader, **CCCLXXXI** ; Feist, **CCCLXXVI.**

A *mācar* ; Tokharian B *mādhar*). The word has hardly changed at all.

Old Irish *fert*, modern Irish *feart*, meaning "tomb, tumulus", but also "ditch, enclosure",[1] has an exact equivalent in Indo-Iranian : Sanskrit *vrtih* "hedge, enclosure" ; Zend *varetiš*.[2] The root of these words has supplied words to the whole Indo-European family—Greek ἔρυσθαι (Ϝερυσθαι) "protect", "repel" ; Gothic *warjan* "protect" ; modern German *wehren* "defend". From the sense of enclosure, one passes easily to that of territory, boundary of territory. Irish has *ferann* (*fearann*). The word corresponds, letter for letter, with the Sanskrit *varanáh* "entrenchment", "dike", and the Zend *uarənā* "envelope", "cover". The same extension of the meaning occurred with other words, for example Greek ὄρος (that is Ϝορϝο) ; Corcyraean ὄρβος, hορϝος ; Ionic οὖρος ; Cretan ὦρος ; Old Latin *uruus*. The word is translated in a gloss by *circuitus civitatis*. *Amburuare* means to surround with a furrow as a boundary ; *ueruactum* "fallow land". In Umbrian *uruvú* is frontier .[3]

The Celtic languages are distinguished from all the other Indo-European languages by very clearly marked and quite constant features. These are of a phonetic nature.[4]

(i) The most striking of these phonetic changes is the dropping of the Indo-European *p* at the beginning or in the middle of a word.[5] In the name Aremorici *are* comes from an old **pare*, equivalent to Greek παρά, Latin *prae*, and modern German *vor*. They were the people who lived by the sea, *mor*.[6] In " Vercingetorix " we have *ver*, which is *for* in

---

[1] Cf. *Grab* and *graben*, *fert-i-cladh*.

[2] Walde, **CCXLIII**. Cf. Skt. *api-vṛṇoti* "he closes" ; *apa-vṛṇoti* "he uncovers". Sanskrit employs the same prefixes, *api* = ἐπί = *ob* and *apa* = ἀπό = *ab*. This concordance shows that the root keeps throughout its length the meaning of an action the direction of which is undetermined. Cf. Lithuanian *ùžveriu* "I close" ; *àtveriu* "I open".

[3] Ibid. From the same root, which I have chosen in order to give an example of the luxuriant growths which sprang from Indo-European roots, several Indo-European languages have derived the word for " door "—Oscan *ueru* "door" ; Umbrian *uerofe* "to the door", and *uerisco* "door, little door" ; Latin *uesti-bulum* ; Lithuanian *vaŕtai* (plur.). With the Greek θυραῖος, "public, outside the door", we may compare the Czech adjective *veřejný* and the Oscan substantive *uerehia* "the public as a whole ".

[4] D'Arbois, **CCCI**, p. 270.

[5] Ibid., p. 275 ; **CCXCIX**, p. 17.

[6] D'Arbois, **CCCI**, ii, pp. 175-7.

Irish and *guor* in Old Welsh, corresponding to Greek ὑπέρ. The name means " Chief King of those who march against the foe ". For Latin *pater* and Sanskrit *pitár* we have Old Irish *athir*, and for Latin *plenus*, Sanskrit *prânas*, we have Old Irish *ldn*, Welsh *llawn*, and Breton *leun*.[1]

The *p* is perhaps preserved in the group *pt*, as in Neptacus, Mœnicaptus.[2] It is certainly preserved in the group *ps* and in the group *sp* between vowels, but only to become a guttural afterwards—Ucsello, Latinized as Uxello ; cf. Welsh *uchel*, Old Irish *uasal*, from *upsello* (cf. Greek ὑψηλός) ; Crixos, Welsh *crych* ; cf. Latin *crispus* " curly ".[3]

(ii) Indo-European had vowel-consonants, which are called sonants—m̥, n̥, r̥, l̥. The r̥ is regularly represented by *ri* before a consonant in Celtic.[4]

(iii) The Indo-European diphthong *ei*, which was at first partially preserved,[5] became *ē* in Celtic.[6] *Dēvos*[7] was the Gaulish pronunciation of a word, the Indo-European root-word of which contained the diphthong *ei*.[8] In Irish *dēvos* is represented by *dia* ; when the inflexion was dropped *dé* was left, and this *ē* in a syllable not followed by an *i* split up into *i-a* in Irish.

[1] Ibid., p. 277.

[2] The form Neptacus is not certain, the *P* being possibly an incomplete *R* (Holder, **CCVII**, s.v.). Nor is Moenicaptus. Irish *cacht* " servant " (Welsh *cacth*, Breton *caez*), may be derived from the Latin. On Old Irish *secht*, Welsh *seith*, see Dottin, **CXCVI**, p. 286 ; Philipon, **CCCLXIX**, p. 198. For the passing from labial *p* to gutturals and vice versa, see below, p. 52.

[3] Philipon, **CCCLXIX**, pp. 198 ff. Cf. Old Breton *guohi*, Cornish *guhienn* " wasp ", from *uops*, Latin *vespa* ; also Welsh *ucher* " evening ", Latin *vesper*, Old Irish *fescor*.

[4] Ibid., p. 196. In a certain number of cases, r̥ is rendered by *ar*, even before a consonant : *artos*, from r̥kto, Greek ἄρκτος ; *carros*, Old Irish and Welsh *carr*, from kr̥sos, Latin *cursus*.

There was a Gaulish word *rĭtu-*, meaning " ford ", which appears in place-names—Novioritum (Niort), Ritumagos (Radepont). The word is *rhŷd* in Welsh, *rit* in Old Breton, *rid* in Cornish, *rith* in Irish. It is formed by the addition of a noun-suffix to the root *per*, pr̥ : pr̥-tu. Latin gives *portus*, and Germanic *furt*, both with the sense of " passage ". Zend has *pertu*.

The l̥ has the same vocalization. Old Welsh *litan* and Breton *ledan* reproduce an adjective *litanos*, which is attested by place-names : Litanobriga, the forest Litana (in Cisalpine Gaul). It comes from a word *pl̥tanos*, to which the Greek πλάτανος, from πλατύς " broad ", corresponds. Before a vowel, r̥ and l̥ were vocalized as *ar* and *al* : Gaulish *carnu-* " corn ", Welsh *carn* ; Gaulish *talo-s* " brow ", Breton *tal*.

[5] **CCCLXIX**, p. 194. Deiviciacos, on a coin from Soissons ; Deivaru, in a Latin inscription from Brescia (**CXLIX**, v, 4164).

[6] D'Arbois, **CCCI**, ii, p. 270.

[7] I, xii, 140. Cf. Deva and Devana, the names of British rivers. In France, Devona was Latinized as Divona.

[8] Old Prussian *deiws*, Lithuanian *deive* " ghost ", Oscan *deivai*.

(iv) The Indo-European $\bar{e}$ became $\bar{\imath}$ in Celtic.[1] Typical examples are supplied by the contrast between Latin $r\bar{e}x$ and Celtic rix, and by that between Latin $u\bar{e}rus$ and Irish $f\bar{\imath}r$, or Old Breton $guir$. In the fifth century the Celts gave i a sound intermediate between i and e, and in the Romanic language they confused Latin i and e.[2]

These four facts clearly mark off Celtic from the other Indo-European languages. If we compare the grammars and fragments of grammars of the Celtic tongues [3] we shall find other indications of a less general and a less certain nature—the change of Indo-European $\bar{o}$ to $\bar{a}$,[4] wavering between the diphthongs eu and ou, ou and au,[5] the assimilation of ns into ss and rs into rr,[6] the dropping of v in initial groups of a dental $+ v$,[7] uncertainty in the pronunciation of occlusives between vowels.[8]

Some of the characteristics of modern Celtic languages [9] had not yet appeared in Gaulish, or we have no evidence for them ; in particular the extreme variability of their initial phonemes and the extreme irregularity of their verb-inflexions. But Gaulish changed,[10] and changed quickly, and it was developing in the same direction as the languages of the islands. We have indications of this, and, in particular, of the weakness which was already appearing in the two sounds s and v,[11] the dropping or aspiration of which is

---

[1] D'Arbois, **CCCI**, ii, p. 273.

[2] Consentius, in Keil's *Grammatici Latini*, v, p. 394 ; Dottin, **CXCVI**, p. 96.

[3] Philipon, **CCCLXIX**, pp. 193 ff.

[4] Ibid., p. 194 : Virido-mârus, cf. Greek ἐγχεσί-μωρος ; Gaulish *gnatos*, Greek γνωτός, Latin *notus*.

[5] Ibid., p. 195 : Teutates and Toutos, Toutiorix ; p. 196, Caunus and Counus.

[6] Dottin, **CXCVI**, p. 100 : *essedum*, from *en* and *sed*, "to sit" ; *carrus*, from *carsus*. Cf. Pedersen, i, p. 25.

[7] J. Vendryès, "À propos des groupes initiaux dentale $+ v$," in *Miscellany presented to Kuno Meyer*, Halle a. S., 1912, pp. 286 ff.

[8] Dottin, op. cit., p. 101 : Cevenna and Cebenna, *vertraha* and *vertragus*, *arcanto* and *arganto*, *verco* and *vergo*, Carpento.

[9] Ibid., p. 123.

[10] Pedersen, **CCXXVII**, i, pp. 532–3.

[11] Ptolemy, 2, 9, 1. The evolution of s into an aspirate, which is characteristic of Welsh (Irish *sét* "road" ; Welsh *hynt*), was not completed before the Saxon conquest of Britain, but it is possible that the group *sr* had already become *fr* both in British and in Gaulish. With Φρούδις, the R. Bresle (Ptol., 2, 9, 1), cf. Welsh *ffrwd* "torrent", and Irish *sruth* "river". The dropping of intervocalic v, attested by the Vienna Glossary (*brio* for *brivo*), doubtless appears in the Gallic *druida* (*druvida*). Dottin, op. cit., p. 237.

characteristic of Irish and Gaulish. So, too, the development of u into *gw* (*f* in Irish), which is characteristic of Brythonic (Gaulish *vindo-*, Welsh *gwynn*, Irish *find*), went on in Gaulish in spite of the spelling, since it appears suddenly in French words like Gande, the name of a stream, from Vinda (the White), which was Vuinda or Vuanda in the tenth century, or the River Gartempe, from Vertimpa, Vuartimpa (A.D. 825).[1]

In their vocabulary the Celtic languages present a very great number of peculiarities, which cannot, unfortunately, be made into a system. They are negative facts. Certain Indo-European words and roots are lacking in Celtic, and their place has been taken by others. Before we compare the Celtic languages with the other Indo-European groups, can we at this stage obtain any light on the history of the Celts from these peculiarities ?

One postulate of the earliest comparative studies of the Indo-European languages was that there were unmixed peoples, just as it was postulated that there were unmixed races ; such changes as had taken place in these peoples were supposed to have occurred in each independently, as a consequence of its growth. On this assumption every fact revealed by comparison of their languages was used in a kind of genealogical classification, many parts of which are still useful. But the postulate has been abandoned. There are no unmixed peoples, and doubtless there never were any. But in that case a comparative study of languages may reveal their heterogeneous elements, and consequently those of the peoples which spoke them. We may, therefore, hope to find in the Celtic languages traces of the languages previously spoken by peoples, Indo-European or other, which had dealings with the Celts or were absorbed by them. One would expect them to have passed on to the Celts some part of their vocabulary and some of their ways of speaking. So the innovations which appear in Celtic would come from its associations with foreign tongues.[2]

So far as vocabulary is concerned, the hypothesis leads nowhere, for the Western associates of the Celts spoke languages which have been almost entirely wiped out or

---

[1] Philipon, **CCCLXIX**, pp. 199 ff.   [2] Zimmer, **CLXXXI**, ix, pp. 87 ff.

cannot be compared to any known stock, except Basque (which has yielded nothing) and Indo-European. There were probably other Indo-Europeans in the West before the Celts. The contribution which they left in the Celtic vocabulary cannot be identified.

Another thing postulated in the earliest comparative studies of vocabulary was that the Indo-European roots had very definite meanings, and therefore strictly determined uses. Consequently, great attention was paid to the absence or the replacement of a word. Ultimately it was admitted that the meanings of the roots were vague, and continued to be so save for a few words. We ourselves are constantly describing concrete objects by abstract words (e.g. " rule "), giving special meanings to words whose meaning is general (" chalk "), and, more frequently, generalizing words of special meaning or giving them a new sense, by analogy (" rubber sponge "). It is not surprising that a vocabulary consisting of such indefinite words should not have been used consistently. That one approximate term should have given place to another approximate term is of no importance. The moral is that we must not exaggerate the importance of negative facts when comparing vocabularies. In the case of the Celtic tongues such comparison reveals nothing but accidents of speech, which are quite common and are chiefly due to chance. Let us see some examples.

There was an Indo-European word for a house, which Celtic has lost. It was a word with a definite meaning. It is found in Sanskrit véçaḥ, in Greek [Ϝοῖκος], and in Latin uīcus.[1] This word, as is shown by the Sanskrit and Latin forms, meant the great house, the house of a great family, in which there might be several establishments. It is not found in Celtic. This is not because the Celts did not have great houses ; we shall see that the case was quite the contrary. It is not because the great family had broken up among them ; on the contrary, the Celtic family was a great family of people descended from a common forefather, in which several generations, several branches, and swarms of individuals lived a common life. It was a typical Indo-European family. In Irish the property on which the family lives is called baile. Is this an Indo-European word ? We

---

[1] Meillet, CCXVII, p. 357.

are not sure. It is even supposed to come from the root *bhu-*,
" to be ". *Baile* implies a word **balios*, which implies a pre-
Celtic *bhu-alio-*, " the place where one is ". In any case,
the word must be an old word kept in Irish alone, or
a suppletory term of general meaning.

Here is another accident. Indo-European had a root *sē*,
which meant to sow, but in a very indefinite sense. Welsh
has kept it in the verb *hau* " to sow "; Irish has lost it as
the root of a verb, but has kept it in the substantive *síl*
" posterity ", and expresses sowing by the verb *cuirim*,
meaning " I throw ". The process is comparable to what
happened at the passing from *ponere* to *pondre*, from *trahere*
to *traire*, and from *tirare* to *tirer*. In the same way Irish lost
the Indo-European word meaning to glean, while Welsh
kept it (*medi*). Instead Irish uses *bongim* " I cut "; *buain*,
a verbal noun, means " harvest ", and is a thoroughly Indo-
European word (Sanskrit *bhanajmi* " I break "; Greek
$\phi\alpha\gamma\epsilon\hat{\iota}\nu$).

In the third example the case is different. There was an
Italo-Germano-Celtic word meaning furrow : Welsh *rhych*,
Old Breton *rec* (modern Breton *reguenn*). From it Low Latin
got *riga*, French *raie*, and Provençal *riga*. In Latin the word
existed in the form *porca*[1] " a furrow " (*porculetum*; Umbrian
porculeta). Germanic produced modern German *Furche*
(O.H.G. *furh*, *furuh*), English *furrow*, and Old Icelandic *for*.
All these words come from one word, **prko/a*, the formation of
which is clear. It contains an element *-ko*, which is added to
prepositions or adverbs to form adjectives and nouns, as
in $\dot{\epsilon}\pi\iota\sigma\sigma\acute{o}\varsigma = \epsilon\pi\iota\text{-}k\text{-}yo$ ($\ddot{\epsilon}\pi\iota\sigma\sigma\alpha\iota$, " younger daughters "),
and $\pi\epsilon\rho\iota\sigma\sigma\acute{o}\varsigma = \pi\epsilon\rho\iota\cdot k\cdot yo$. The first element is *per*,
the preposition meaning across. The idea is of a line
drawn across a field. This word does not exist in Irish, and
perhaps it never did. The corresponding word is *etrech*,
which in modern Irish is *eitre* or *eitriach*, with plural *eitreacha*.
An ancient form *etarche* is given in the *Sanas Cormaic*.
But it has been formed in the same way as the other. It is
composed of *etar* + *k* + *yo*. *Etar* is the Irish equivalent of
inter. These two formations are absolutely parallel.

This example is most instructive. The Indo-European

---

[1] This seems to be proved by the Germanic in the concordance of Welsh
rhych, Latin *porca*, and Mod. German *Furche*.

dialects, before they were finally differentiated, were, like all primitive unwritten languages, very fluid.   Out of a fairly few elements they made a great variety of fairly mobile combinations. Their needs of expression were amply supplied by comparatively humble instruments, and they doubtless used more than one equivalent for the same requirement. When dialects were improved it was not only by increase, but also by selection.   Sometimes one equivalent remained in use, sometimes another.

There are other accidents of language, which are yet more obviously arbitrary, for they are intentional and deliberate. These are the disappearances of words on account of religious scruples. They have been studied by philologists for some time past. Certain names were avoided and replaced by approximations—those of the pig, the bear, the bee, certain degrees of kinship, and others.

When we study the vocabulary of the Celtic languages we find a fairly large residue of words which do not appear elsewhere. Most of them are produced by derivation from other words. A very large number are quite modern ; the ancient forms are too uncertain for it to be possible to say anything about them. Some may be vestiges of the most distant Indo-European past.[1] Still there are some left over. Are they an Iberian or Ligurian inheritance ? This remnant does not, so far, seem to me of great importance.

The facts of grammar and phonetics can be interpreted in the same way. According to one linguistic theory, that of *Lautverschiebung*, or permutation of consonants, which created some stir and will be examined in the volume of this series dealing with the Germans, the modifications to which Germanic subjected the grammatical and phonetic structure of Indo-European, are due to the fact that Germanic was an Indo-European language learned by a non-Indo-European people.

We can see examples of languages changing for ourselves. In France French is spoken by a whole part of the nation, which had another language of its own, but has adopted French as its language, namely the people of the Midi, of the *Langue d'oc*. They speak French with a pronunciation of

[1] Meillet, **CCXVI**, p. 2.

their own, different from that of other Frenchmen. If
a strictly phonetic spelling were adopted for French there
would be a danger of it breaking up into more than one
language, with a common vocabulary but different phonetics.

French itself is a result of the changes which the phonetic
habits of the Gauls brought into Latin. For example, they
introduced *u*. Here is another example. The name Mézières
comes from the Latin *maceria*. When the Latins came to
Gaul Gaulish was in process of changing its surd gutturals,
such as *k*, to *chuintantes* [1] and sibilants. I have chosen this
instance because the word has also been adopted by the
Brythonic of Britain. But in Britain Latin never became
a popular language. Such borrowings as were effected were
of a learned kind. *Maceria* produced *magwyr* in Welsh and
moger in Breton, both meaning " wall ". These learned
borrowings always show an uncertainty in pronunciation :
magwyr comes from *măcēria*, having *a* for *ă* and *wy* for *ē* ;
moger comes from *mācēria*, with *o* for *ā* and *e* for *ē*.

The Celts of the British Isles altered Germanic as the
Gauls did Latin. For instance, the Britons imposed their
cerebrals on English.

When a people adopts another language it brings some of
its old habits of speech into it, or else it distorts it in its efforts
to form new sounds and new associations of sounds. Thus
the non-Indo-European Germans introduced curious changes,
similar to those to which their descendants still subject the
words which they borrow.

But if the Germans were not Indo-Europeans, we may ask
whether the Celts were. They, too, altered the aspect of
Indo-European phonetics, and we shall see that in more than
one point the Celtic innovations coincide with the Germanic.

These new considerations of linguistic ethnography very
much obscure the old picture which students tried to make
of the descent and relationship of the Indo-European
languages. They tend to give a much larger part to the
aborigines, the associates, the vanquished, in the final result
of the analysis. On the other hand, our belief in the dialectal
unity of the parent languages from which the kindred
languages are descended is strengthened, for we must now

---

[1] Sounds represented in French by *ch* and *j*, sometimes called " blade-
point consonants " or " spirant palatals " in English. Trs.

presume that we are dealing with single languages which fell apart as their speakers came into contact with different peoples.

But to return to Celtic, we should note that its phonetic innovations are not to be compared to the chief innovation of Germanic, which started the arguments mentioned above. This consisted in the change from easily pronounced consonants—*b*, *d*, *g* (sonants), to consonants whose pronunciation requires more effort, the surds—*p*, *t*, *k*, *q*—and from these to aspirates and then to spirants—*f*, *þ*, *χ*. All the consonants of a borrowed language are pronounced with an effort. To pronounce a language with greater difficulty than it is naturally pronounced may be the case of a foreigner who is making an effort to speak it, or already speaks a language whose sounds are less easy.[1] But the modifications peculiar to Celtic were not such as made the previous pronunciation more difficult. Far from it. Celtic was on the road of phonetic laziness, the normal cause of change in a language. We have evidence in the dropping of *p*, a perfectly articulated surd consonant being replaced by a mere breath. The intermediate stage was probably marked by the consonant being pronounced as a spirant ; *p* must have become *f*. Therefore, while Germanic, in view of the aspect of its phonetics, may be regarded as a borrowed language, it is not so with Celtic. From this point of view, the Celts show themselves Indo-Europeans by origin, not by adoption.

They evidently met on their way with peoples whose speech was not Indo-European. Some they may have assimilated. Their language incorporated non-Indo-European elements. But these elements do not appear in its phonetics, and they are hard to discover in its vocabulary. In the composition of Celtic the old Indo-European predominates enormously. This is an established fact of great importance.

We now have to consider the parent dialect which produced Celtic as it extended its domain, and, with that object, to compare Celtic with the languages of the neighbouring peoples. This inquiry cannot fail to give us valuable indications about the history of the Celts.

[1] Meillet, **CCXVI**, p. 6.

CHAPTER III

LANGUAGE (*continued*)

I

THE *CENTUM* GROUP AND THE *SATEM* GROUP

PHILOLOGISTS have made a first classification of the Indo-European dialects into two groups according to the way in which the initial consonant of the word meaning hundred developed. The word began with a palatal, which among some peoples became a sibilant, while with others it remained an occlusive. There are *satem* peoples and *centum* peoples. The Hindus say *çatám*, the Iranians said *satem*, and the Lithuanians *szimtas*, whereas the Latins said *centum*. The Goths said *hund*, the Greeks ἑκατόν. The Irish said *cét*, now *céad*, and the Welsh say *cant*. Celtic, therefore, is one of the *centum* languages.[1] The value of the distinction appears problematical and the attachment of Celtic to the *centum* group of little significance, if we remember that French, which is one of the heirs of Celtic, has transformed the Latin occlusive into a sibilant. But one should mention the matter.

But let us consider Fig. 1 for a moment. This diagram, devised by M. Meillet,[2] shows the Indo-European languages grouped according to their affinities. At the same time it shows their topographical distribution. The vertical diameter divides the *satem* peoples from the *centum* peoples. Each group is continuous. The dialects of each have been spoken by peoples which are or were neighbours. We shall see other evidences of their kinship. The symbol chosen is not perhaps the most expressive possible, but the thing symbolized is certain.

One group is missing from the diagram, namely the Tokharians of Turkestan. They, surrounded by peoples which spoke languages of the *satem* type, Indian or Iranian, spoke languages of the *centum* type. But we have more than

---

[1] S. Feist, **CCCXXVI**, p. 50.   [2] **CCXVI**, p. 134.

one reason for believing that these Tokharian dialects have affinities with the Western group of Indo-European languages.

The slanting diameter which runs right across the diagram sets apart, in the same half of the ellipse, the Balto-Slavonic, Germanic, Celtic, and Italic tongues. This grouping expresses a different kind of relationship from that which associates Greek with the three last-named dialects to the left of the vertical diameter. The peoples of North-Western Europe had a certain number of roots in common, which the others lacked. They had bonds of civilization, a common life.

It may be said, without much danger of error, that the Indo-European languages have the same relationship to one another as the geographical areas which they cover. It is

Fig. 1.   The Indo-European Languages, arranged according to their affinities. (Meillet, *Dialectes européens*, p. 134.)

highly probable that the affinities of various kinds existing between these dialects fairly represent racial affinities of the peoples.

II

THE WESTERN GROUP : ITALIC, CELTIC, AND GERMANIC

As we follow up this comparison between the Celtic and the other Indo-European languages, two groups of languages seem by the nature of things to call for attention at the outset, namely the Germanic and Italic tongues.

The former covered an area which was continually in contact with that of the Celtic languages, and it is also probable that Celtic and Italic were spoken in neighbouring regions before the Italici settled in their peninsula,[1] and that the Gallic invasion of Italy merely revived contacts which had existed in prehistoric times. In view of the relationships which appear between these two groups and Celtic, one might possibly regard them as one family, the Western family of the Indo-European languages,[2] which, moreover, would show considerable associations with two other neighbouring groups, the Baltic and the Slavonic [3] (which belong to the *satem* group). Confining oneself to Celtic, Italic, and Germanic, one might suppose that these three groups formed a single unit comparable, to some extent, to that formed by the Celtic languages among themselves, but more comprehensive and differentiated earlier and more completely. But the matter is not so simple as that.

Of the phonetic and morphological facts in which the relationship of these three linguistic groups is shown, some may, perhaps, date from the remotest past of Indo-European and be features of one of its dialects.[4] But there are others which appear as absolute innovations, the most important of which is the modification of the linguistic rhythm. Now, the rhythm is a very stable element of a language, and still more so of a way of speaking and pronouncing. In Indo-European the accent of a word seems to have been very weak. It was musical; it fell anywhere, according to the sense. In Celtic and Italic, as in Germanic, the qualitative rhythm of Indo-European deteriorated. The accent gradually became an accent of stress, fixed to a definite place, usually the first syllable, which finally assumed a preponderant position in the word. A fact of this kind may be attributed to the influence of foreign elements, probably in part the same elements, entering in different proportions into the formation of the three groups of peoples concerned. Italic, which changed its abode, resisted these tendencies at first, but finally succumbed to them. " Germanic and Celtic, on the other hand, which remained in neighbouring regions,

---

[1] Meillet, **CCXVI**, p. 12. [2] Ibid.
[3] Ibid., 2nd ed., Avant-propos, pp. 3, 5, etc.
[4] Ibid., Avant-propos, p. 2.

developed partly along parallel lines." [1]   The parallelism is most complete between Gælic and Germanic.[2]

M. Meillet, in the work from which I have taken these remarks, points to other facts which seem to tell the same story [3]—in phonetics the weakness of the final, in consequence of the strengthening of the initial, the alteration of intervocalic consonants, the sensitiveness of vowels to the influence of neighbouring phonemes [4] ; in morphology the accentuation in the verb of the notion of tense, which is shown by the creation of special forms to express the preterite and the distinction of a past subjunctive.   These last observations are equally true of the Baltic languages.

Moreover, the Western Indo-European languages have drawn on a common vocabulary. They alone possess certain roots, certain forms of the same roots, or certain senses which these roots may take.

Latin *hasta* represents a Western root which appears in Irish *gas* " stalk ", Gothic *gazds* " goad ", and Old High German *gert* " rod ".[5]

Latin *ueru* " spit " represents another, which produced Irish *bir* " point ", Welsh *ber* " spear ", and Gothic *qairu*.[6]

Irish *fáith*, genitive *fátha* " bard ", " soothsayer ", corresponds to Latin *vates* and modern German *Wuth, wüthen*, and probably *wuotan*.

Here, now, is the name of an animal : Latin has *merula* " blackbird ", probably for **misula*. Welsh has *mwyalch*, which comes from a primitive **meisalko-*, and Old High German has *meisa*. Modern German *Amsel* " blackbird " has a kindred root.

A root *vē*, which means " to blow " (Sanskrit *vāti* " he blows " ; *vāyuḥ* " wind " ; Lithuanian *vajas* " wind "), assumes the form of a participle in the Western tongues, " the blowing one " ; Latin *ventus*, Gothic *winds*, modern German *Wind*, Welsh *gwynt*. Irish *feth* " breath " is probably derived from the same root, but it is abnormal.

A root *bhu*, which means " to be " and has given φύσις

[1] Ibid., Avant-propos, p. 5 ; Paul the Deacon, i, 325 ; iii, 788 ; Dottin, **CXCVI**, p. 103.
[2] Meillet, p. 6.   [3] Ibid., Avant-propos, p. 132.
[4] Ibid., Avant-propos, p. 5 : *uolo, uolens* ; *uelim, uelle*.
[5] Feist, **CCCXXVI**, p. 217.
[6] Avestic *grāva* " staff ", and Greek ὀβελός " spit ", which have been ascribed to this root, are a long way off it.

("nature") to Greek, has been used for the Western languages in the formation of the verb of being: Latin *fui* "I was"; Irish *buith* (**bhuti*) "to be"; modern German *bin* "am"; English *be*. There is complete concordance between Irish *biu*, Latin *fio*, and Old Saxon *biu*.

Now let us look at a case where it is various forms of one same root that show its continuity. Latin *liquidus* has a root **vleiq*, which has assumed different forms, *vl̥* and *volq*, from which come Irish *flechod* "rain" (subst.), *fliuch* "wet", *folc* "a wave", Welsh *gwlych* "wetness", *gwlyb* "wet". Modern German *Wolke* "cloud" (Old High German *wolcha*) represents a variety of this same root, **vl̥g-*.

These similarities of vocabulary form a very large mass of facts [1] which is comparable to the similarities of Iranian and Sanskrit, and it is still larger if we add to it the words which also appear in the Baltic and Slavonic languages, whose connections with the Western languages deserve to be considered all together and more closely. So, then, Celtic seems to have been taken from a linguistic mass which might be the remains of an Indo-European dialect, split into several fragments.

But in the vocabulary, as in the grammar, the philologists try to discover the influence of foreign elements, in the shape of words whose structure is not clearly Indo-European. They point to the word for "apple", which is *abal* in Irish, *aval* in Welsh, and *Apfel* in modern German; the name of the town of Abella and the epithet of *malifera* ("apple-bearing") which Virgil gives it [2] suggests that Italic once had the word and then lost it. This is one of the words which also belong to Baltic and Slavonic. There is a village named Aboul on the island of Œsel, Slavonic has *jablŭko*, Lithuanian has *óbŭlas*, and Old Prussian had *woble*.

III

CELTIC LANGUAGES AND ITALIC LANGUAGES

Apart from these features shared by Celtic, Italic, and Germanic all together, Celtic has some peculiarities in common

---

[1] Cf. Vendryès, **XCIII**, xxi, pp. 41 ff.: Lat. *nux*, Ir. *cnu*, Mod. German *Nuss*; Lat. *salebra*, Ir. *sal*, O.H.G. *salo*.

[2] *Æn.*, vii, 740.

with one or the other of these languages. In come cases
one language of the group has had losses or a development of
its own ; in others there have been special relations between
two languages or the peoples which spoke them.

The Italic and the Celtic tongues present similarities of
structure which compel us to think that there were once
a great many more, which only disappeared after a separation
which does not seem to have occurred very early.[1]   The
resemblance is of the same order as that subsisting between
the languages of India and the Iranian languages ; that is, the
two language-groups to which the name of Aryan is best
confined. Now we have very strong evidence of a common
Aryan stock about 1400 B.C.   In the inscriptions of Boghaz-
Keui, Indian and Iranian gods, who afterwards became
enemies, are mentioned together in the same invocation.[2]
There was one religion, one people, a common language.
No doubt it was the same with the Celts and the Italici.
It is usual to speak of the Italo-Celtic language and of an
Italo-Celtic stock. I have only to show that the separation
took place a little earlier.

The only Italic language of which we possess a complete
vocabulary, Latin, has absorbed a whole Mediterranean
lingua franca as a result of being transplanted into
Mediterranean life.   Hence comes its kinship with Greek,
obscuring its Celtic kinship. Nevertheless, many fragments
of an Italo-Celtic vocabulary remain in the Italic languages.
There remain, for example, those important words,
prepositions, and prefixes to verbs.[3] Latin *de* corresponds to
Irish and Brythonic *di*[4] ; Latin *cum* to Irish and Brythonic
com or *co-* (*Combroges).

It is a strange coincidence that both groups have two
forms of the same adjective to say " other ", one from a stem
ali- and the other from a stem *alio*. The Italic group has *alis*
and *alid* (whence *alter*) from the former and *alius* and *aliud*
from the latter. Celtic also has two words, Welsh *eil* and Irish
aile, which correspond to their Latin equivalents letter for
letter. *Eil* means " the second ", like *alter*. The very illogical-
ness of this duplication is what invites credence.[5]

---

[1] D'Arbois, **CCC**, p. 10.   [2] Moret, **CCCLX**, English, pp. 303 ff.
[3] Meillet, **CCXVI**, p. 37.   [4] Sommerfelt, **CCXXXIII**.
[5] Walde, **CCXLIII**, s.v. " alius."

There are semantic resemblances, morphological resemblances, common roots, common forms of a same root, common meanings. From a special root $\sqrt{gn\bar{e}}$, meaning " do ", Latin has kept *gnāvus* (from **gnōvo-*), Irish has *gníu* " I do ", *gnim* " deed ", *fogniu* " I serve ", and *fognom* " service " and Welsh has *gweini* " to serve ".[1] The root $\sqrt{g^{w}ei}$, which means " life ", has given *vita* to Latin and *bwyd* " food " to Brythonic.[2] The root $\sqrt{ner}$, which appears in Sanskrit and Greek in words meaning " man ",[3] appears in Irish as *nert* " strength " (Gaulish **Nerton*, as in Nertomarus), in Sabine as *Nerio*, with the same meaning, whence the name Nerio, the wife of Mars, and in Umbrian as *nerf* (accusative plural), the dead, that is the Strong Ones.[4] *Terra* corresponds to Irish *tir*[5]; *tellus* to Irish *talam*.[6] With *sæculum*,[7] from a stem **saitlo*, are connected Welsh *hœdl*, Old Breton *hœtl*, and the name of the Gallic goddess Setlocenia. And there are other instances.[8]

The phonetic and grammatical similarities are of even more weight.

We shall consider the chief resemblance in phonetics— the change from $p \ldots k^{w}$ to $k^{w} \ldots k^{w}$, which gave words of the *quinque* type to Latin and words of the *coic* type to Irish, and the transformation of k^{w} into p in Brythonic and Osco-Umbrian[9]—when the time comes to extract its full significance.[10]

The grammatical similarities are morphological resemblances in declension and conjugation.

The genitive of stems in *o* was formed in *i*: Segomaros, Segomari = *dominu-s, domini*. In Old Irish, *maqi* was the genitive of *maqos*, and in Middle Irish *fir* was the genitive

---

[1] Ibid., s.v. " nāvus."   [2] Ibid., s.v. " vĭta."
[3] 'Ανήρ, *nar* = Skt. *nāra*.   [4] Ibid., s.v. " neriosus."
[5] Ibid., s.v. " terra "; Vendryès, **XCIII**, xiii, p. 385.
[6] Walde, s.v. " tellus."   [7] Ibid., s.v. " saeculum."
[8] Vendryès, " Un Rapprochement celto-ombrien," in **CXL**, 1914, p. 212; Loth, " Notes étymologiques," ibid., 1917–19, p. 314.
[9] Meillet, **CCXVI**, p. 33. Other resemblances are : The treatment of $\mathfrak{r}$, $\mathfrak{l}$, and $\mathfrak{n}$ before a vowel as *ar*, *al*, and *an* (ibid., pp. 33 ff.) ; the change from *bh*, *dh*, *gh* to *b*, *d*, *g* (Dottin, **CXCVI**, p. 98) ; the passing from *gw* to *b* (Philipon, **CCCLXIX**, p. 204). Cf. Windisch, **CCXLV**, pp. 390, 393.
[10] Windisch, **CCXLV**, pp. 390–4 ; cf. **XXX**, 1918, p. 71 ; Meillet, op. cit., 2nd ed., p. 9 ; Moulton, **CCXXI**, p. 6 ; Taylor, **CCCLXXXVI**, p. 192 ; Giles, **CCII**, p. 26 ; Meillet and Cohen, **CCXVIII**, p. 53. The similarities of Celtic and Italic institutions and rites will be discussed in the following volume in this series.

of *fer* (* *uiro-s*), the *i* of the root-word being due to the *i* of the lost termination, of whose existence it provides evidence.[1]

In both groups the superlative was formed by adding -*samo*-, whence come Latin -(*s*)*im*- and Celtic -(*s*)*am*- or -(*s*)*em*-, to the positive. " Nearest " is *proximæ* in Latin, *nessimas* in Oscan, *nesimei* in Umbrian, *nessam* in Old Irish, and *nesaf* in Welsh. Modern German, on the other hand, says *nächste*, and the other Indo-European languages have a formation in *st* : Sanskrit *svadiṣṭhah*, Greek ἤδιστος, Old High German *zuozisto*, whence *süsseste*.[2]

The verb systems of the two groups, which are fairly different from Indo-European and are in part refashioned from new sources, present the same innovations. Both have the future in -*bo* and two forms of the subjunctive. *Amabo* and Faliscan *carefo* are like the Irish futures in -*f* and -*b* : *legfa, ni legub*, from *legaim* " I read ".[3] *Feram* is equivalent to Irish *bera*,[4] *faxim* to Irish *tiasu, teis*.[5]

The forms of the middle voice with a reflexive meaning (cf. Greek λύομαι " I wash myself ", λύει, λύεται) disappeared in Latin [6] and in Celtic, whereas they survived to some extent in Germanic.[7] To take its place, Latin and Celtic created what is called in Latin grammar the deponent, the inflexion of which in certain forms is marked by final *r* and is the same in both languages down to the smallest detail : *loquor = labrur* ; *loquitur = labrithir* ; *loquimur = labrimmir*.[8]

---

[1] D'Arbois, **CCC**, p. 10 ; Meillet, op. cit., p. 35 ; id., "La Forme du génitif pluriel en ombrien," in **XCIII**, 1922, p. 258 (gen. plur. in *o* : Umbrian *fratrom* ; Irish *fer*, from *uiron*, whence oghamic -*a*) ; Pedersen, **CCXXVII**, i, p. 248 ; ii, p. 84 ; Windish, **CCXLV**, p. 395.

[2] Meillet, op. cit., p. 37. Suffix -*tei* broadened by a nasal suffix : *natio*(*nis*) ; Irish *toitiu* (gen. *toimten*) "thought" (cf. *natine*, an Umbrian ablative). Windisch, op. cit., p. 395. Suffix -*tāt* : *unitās* (*tātis*), Irish *oentu* (gen. *oentath*).

[3] Meillet, op. cit., p. 37 ; Vendryès, **CLXXXI**, p. 557, and **CXL**, xlii, p. 887.   [4] Meillet, op. cit., p. 36.   [5] Ibid.

[6] Ibid., p. 35 : Except in the first person singular of the perfect.

[7] Gothic *bairada*, from *bairan*.

[8] Vendryès, **CXL**, xxxiv, pp. 129 ff. Gaulish had the same conjugation (Loth, **LVIII**, 1916, p. 175 ; Dottin, **CXCVI**, p. 123). The deponent, like the Greek middle, is used as an active for a certain number of words which express psychical operations, and so imply some reflexion of the subject about his own action, such as *reor, arbitror*. The semantic distinction between the deponent or middle and the active is a delicate thing, which tends to fade out. It disappears in Celtic. Moreover, as the semantic distinction goes, the corresponding forms disappear likewise. While they are more or less preserved in Old Irish, only a few scant traces of them remain in Brythonic (*gwyr* "he knows").

In Latin the conjugation of the deponent is indistinguishable from that of the passive. Moreover, there are traces in Latin of an impersonal passive: *itur* " people go "; *quom caletur* " when it (the weather) is hot " (Plautus, *Captivi*, 80). Umbrian had *ferar* " let someone carry "; so, too, Oscan had *sakrafir* " let sacrifice be made ". This is the only passive that Celtic has. The Irishman, for example, says *berir* " it is carried ", " someone carries ". To express the first or second person passive the personal pronoun is added, either before or after the verb, in the accusative, as a complement: Irish *no-m-berar* " it (is) me is carried "; *glantar mé, thú, é,* " it (is) me, thee, him is purified." It is the same in Brythonic: Middle Welsh *ym, yth gelwir* for " I am, thou art, called "; in Modern Welsh one can still say *fe'm dysgir, fe'th dysgir,* as well as *dysgir fi, di* for " I am, thou art, taught ".[1]

The impersonal passive indicates that the action of the verb is being done or has been done. In this respect it resembles another form, whose termination also contains an *r*, namely the third person plural of the preterite (*fecere* " they made "). Celtic has the equivalent of this form. It has two preterites—a sigmatic preterite, with a sigmatic *s* added to the stem (*legsit* " they read ", from *legaim*), and a radical preterite, formed directly on the root-word, which is either reduplicated or lengthened. This latter preterite makes the third person plural by adding *r* to the termination *nt*; for example, *lingim* " I leap ", *roleblangatar* " they leaped " (*nt* + vowel + *r*). But here we find ourselves on wider ground, for there is a similar plural in Sanskrit: *asthiran* " they held themselves ", the aorist plural of *sthā* " to hold oneself ". This usage, and its extension, constitute a fairly large system, but one which is on the decline; and the fact that it survives in more complete form in Italo-Celtic than elsewhere is one of our best evidences of Italo-Celtic unity.[2] There is, however, one other language which presents the same features, with a few differences, namely Tokharian.[3]

---

[1] Rowlands, **CCXXXI**, p. 86.
[2] Dottin, **CXCVI**, pp. 122–3; Meillet, " Sur les désinences en -*r*," in **XLVII**, 1924, pp. 189 ff., shows that there is evidence for these terminations in Phrygian, Pseudo-Hittite (3rd pers. plur. of the preterite), and Armenian.
[3] Vendryès, **CXL**, xxxiv, pp. 129 ff.

Again, Italic and Celtic are at one in the formation of the passive preterite. It is composed of the same noun-form, the adjective in -*to*- : Latin *cantatus est* (cf. Oscan *teremnatust* = *terminata est*). So, too, Irish said *rocét*, from *canim*, " it was sung ".[1]

These are facts of great significance, these common innovations in the mechanism of the verb (that chief element in the sentence) and common loyalties to obsolete forms. The kinship and life together attested thereby must be regarded as an established fact before we start to look for the first home of the Celtic peoples and to study how they divided. We shall come across it more than once in the course of this work.

IV

CELTIC LANGUAGES AND GERMANIC LANGUAGES

The special affinities of Celtic and Germanic are quite different. Here agreements in vocabulary are far more interesting than phonetic or grammatical similarities. Indeed, examination of the grammar reveals a considerable gulf between the two groups of languages.

There are capital differences in the declension of the substantive and adjective.

(i) In Indo-European, nouns whose stem was formed by the addition of *o* or *a* to the root had their plural in *s*, while the *o* or *a* became long ; for example, *equŏs, equōs* (Sanskrit *açvah, açvāḥ*). For this termination Greek, Slavonic, Latin, and Celtic substituted the old termination of pronouns : *poploi* (*populī*) ; Gaulish *Tanotali-knoi*. Germanic, alone of European languages, remains faithful to the ancient form : Gothic *fiskōs* " fishes " ; Anglo-Saxon *fiscas*. Hence come the plurals in *ar* (= *as*) of Old Scandinavian and those in *er* of Danish (*kjökkenmöddinger*).[2]

(ii) Germanic and the Slavonic languages have different inflexions for the adjective according as the adjective is, as it is called, determinate or indeterminate.

---

[1] Meillet, **CCXVI**, p. 35.

[2] D'Arbois, **CCCI**, ii, p. 330. Note, too, that Germanic has not the genitive in *i* of Italo-Celtic.

(iii) Old Slavonic, Lithuanian, and Germanic agree in marking the dative plural of the declension by a termination of which *m* was the characteristic feature : Gothic *vulfam* " to wolves " ; Lithuanian *vilkum* ; Old Slavonic *vlŭkomŭ*.[1]

(iv) The superlative in the Germanic languages was formed in accordance with the Indo-European type, as we have seen above. Old High German had *suozisto* (modern German *süsseste*),[2] like the Sanskrit *svádiṣṭhaḥ*, whereas Italic and Celtic had adopted a form in -*(s)amo*.

Germanic, therefore, is distinguished from the Celtic languages by peculiarities, some of which it shares with no other European language, while others connect it with the Balto-Slavonic languages of the North.

It has also peculiarities which mark it off from all the Indo-European languages. There is its famous permutation of consonants (*Lautverschiebung*),[3] and there is the quite special poverty of its verb forms. Germanic, while expressing the notion of time very vigorously, like the other Western tongues, has cut down the Indo-European verb to two tense-forms, one for the present and one for the past, sufficient to supply words for the singular and plural and for the indicative and subjunctive (*nehme*, *nahm*, *nähme*). It is a cut-down language, a language which has been learnt. The same hypothesis satisfactorily explains the two facts.

But if we must accept this hypothesis of the adoption of an Indo-European language by the ancestors of the Germans, it is not possible, as those who adopted it thought at first, that the language borrowed was Celtic,[4] or even Italo-Celtic. Really the Germans borrowed from more than one Indo-European language, Italo-Celtic among them.

Yet, different as they are in grammatical structure, the two families of languages show the most significant likenesses in their vocabulary. These have been frequently pointed out and interpreted.[5]

[1] Ibid., p. 333.
[2] Kluge, CCX, pp. 481–4.
[3] On *Lautverschiebung*, see above, p. 50.
[4] Feist, CCCXXVI, pp. 482 ff. Van Ginneken, in CCIV, pp. 475 ff., maintains that the change of surd explosives and aspirated sonants in Germanic into fricatives began inside words after vowels, liquids, and nasals, under the influence of the ancient Celtic, from 700 to 600 B.C. Cf. Loth, " La Première Apparition des Celtes dans l'île de Bretagne et en Gaule," in CXL, 1920–1, p. 261.
[5] D'Arbois, " Les Témoignages linguistiques de la civilisation commune

The name of the sun is common to both. In modern German it is *Sonne* (Old High German *sunno*), in Welsh *huan*, which, like *Sonne*, is feminine.[1] The Coligny Calendar gives a word *Sonnocingos*, which clearly contains the same word.[2] Celtic and certain Germanic dialects also had the root of *sol* in common with Latin.

An important group of common topographical terms meaning the ground, accidents of the ground, the adaptation of the ground to human life, is of some interest, because it may tell of a life lived in common in the same region[3]: English *floor*, modern German *Flur*, is the same word as the Irish *lár* and Welsh *llawr*. It is from an ancient *plāros*. Gothic *waggs*, used to translate παράδεισος, and Old Icelandic *vongr* " field " seem related to Irish *fagh*, meaning " territory ". Gothic *sinþs* " road " (whence *Gesinde* " servants ", " the people who accompany you on your way "), is the same as Irish *sét* and Welsh *hynt*. Modern German *Rain* " ridge " (Old High German *rein*, meaning " rampart of earth ", " boundary between field and wood "), is the same as Irish *roen* " road ", and Gaelic *raon* " field ". It gives us a vision of rather swampy country, where roads could only be on raised embankments. English *wood* (Old High German *witu*, which is found in the name Widukind) is the same word as Gaulish *vidu-*, which appears in Viducasses, *vidubion*, Irish *fid*, and Welsh *gwydd*. These words mean " trees ", " timber ", " a forest ".

There are many technical terms, the names of materials, such as metals and instruments.[4] Modern German *Eisen*, Gothic *eisarn*, is the same as Gaulish **isarno-* (in *isarnodori*, glossed by *ferrei ostii*), Irish *iarn*, and Welsh *haiarn*. Old High German *lôth*, English *lead* (the metal), is the same as Irish *luaidhe*. Modern German has another word, *Blei*, of uncertain origin.

So one can make up a long list of words which are both

---

aux Celtes et aux Germains pendant les Vᵉ et IVᵉ siècles av. J.-C." in **CXLI**, 3rd ser., xvii, p. 187 ; id., " Unité primitive des Italo-Celtes," in **LVIII**, 1885, pp. 316 ff. ; id., **CCCI**, ii, p. 330 ff. ; Kluge, **CCXI**, i, pp. 234 ff. ; Bremer, " Ethnogr. der germ. Stämme," in Paul, **CCCLXVII**, ii, pp. 787 ff. ; Pedersen, **CCXXVIII**, i, pp. 21 ff. ; Dottin, **CXCVI**, pp. 128 ff. ; Meillet, *Lang. germ.*, pp. 208 ff. ; Munsch, s.v. " Kelten ", in Hoops, ii, p. 26 ; Meillet and Cohen, **CCXVIII**, pp. 65 ff.

[1] Kluge, **CCX**, s.v. " Sonne ".   [2] Dottin, op. cit., pp. 175, 191.
[3] D'Arbois, **CCCI**, ii, pp. 359 ff.   [4] Ibid., p. 362.

peculiar and common to Celtic and to Germanic, or, more correctly, to the whole extent of the Germanic world. These words are substantives.

Do they come from a common parent-tongue ? Were they borrowed by one language from the other ? [1] There are words which Celtic borrowed from Germanic, but that happened quite late, and we need not linger over them. They are, in particular, the words which Irish took from the Scandinavian tongues in the time of the Vikings. There are authenticated cases of borrowing by Germanic from Celtic.

First of all there is a series of words which have not undergone the Germanic permutation of consonants, and were probably borrowed after that practice had ceased, or, at least, after it had ceased to affect spelling.[2] Gaulish *carruca*, whence comes French *charrue* (" plough "), gave to Old High German *charruh*, modern German *Karch*. Gaulish *keliknon* " tower ", " upper storey ", was taken over unchanged by Gothic. Modern German *Pferd*, Old High German *pferfrit*, comes from Gaulish *paraveredus*. We should note that a great number of words dealing with horses and vehicles are common to Germanic and Celtic, and there is every chance in the world that the former got them from the latter.

English *breeches* (Old Icelandic *brok*) comes from Gaulish *braca*.[3]

Other words were borrowed by Germanic after Celtic had lost *p*.

German *Land* comes from a Celtic *landâ*, which produced Irish *lann* and Welsh *llan*. In the Middle Ages it meant both waste land and the ground surrounding a church. It comes from the root of *plānus*.

German *Leder* " leather " comes from a Celtic word represented by Irish *lethar* and Welsh *lledr*. The root contained the *p* of Latin *pellis* and English *fell*.

In the presence of these facts some scholars, like d'Arbois de Jubainville, have been led to suppose that many

---

[1] The question is discussed systematically in Kluge, **CCXII**, p. 325.
[2] Ibid., ii, p. 324 ; Feist, **CCCXXVI**, p. 482.
[3] Here the derivation may have happened the other way round. Vendryès, **CXL**, 1912, p. 377.

words were borrowed before the Germanic permutation of consonants took place or the Celtic languages lost *p*.[1]

Among the terms common to both groups of languages, there is a whole series of political, legal, and military words. Some of them were certainly borrowed from Celtic, and it is hard to deny that all were.[2] The Gaulish *ambactus*, meaning " servant " (ἀμφιπόλος), but in a sense which tended towards that of " minister ", gave O.H.G. *ambaht*, with the same meaning, and German *Amt*. Gothic *reiks* " prince " and *reiki* "kingdom" come from Gaulish *rīx* and -*rigion* (Irish *ríge*), not from Indo-European *rēx* and the associated words. The Indo-European *ē* would have become *â* in German. The resemblance of the following words is explained in the same way :—

Irish *oeth*, German *Eid*, English *oath*.

Irish *luge* " oath ", Gothic *liuga* " marriage ". Here the borrowed word has been given a more special meaning.

Irish *fine* " family ", Old High German *wini* " husband ". Old Scandinavian *vinr* means " friend " (the same specialization).

Welsh *rhydd* " free ", modern German *frei*.[3]

Irish *giall* " hostage " (**geislos*), modern German *Geisel*.

Irish *orbe* " inheritance ", modern German *Erbe*.

Irish *air-licim* " I lend ", represents a Celtic word corresponding to Gothic *leihvan* and modern German *leihen* " to lend ".

Old Breton *guerth* " value ", " price ", represents the prototype of Gothic *wairþs* and modern German *Werth* " value ".

Modern German *Bann* " order ", comes from a Celtic word represented by Irish *forbanda* " legal order ".

Now for terms of warfare :—

Modern German *Beute* comes from a Celtic word *bōdi*, which is found in the name of Boudicca (Boadicea), Irish *buaid* " victory ", and Welsh *budd* " prey ", " booty ".

Modern German *Brünne* " breastplate" comes from a Celtic word represented by Irish *bruinne* and Welsh *bronn* " chest ".

---

[1] Feist, op. cit., pp. 170, 482 ; Kluge, CCXI, p. 787.
[2] D'Arbois, CCCI, ii, pp. 335 ff. ; id., CCXCIX, p. 170.
[3] From an Indo-European form *prijo-s* ; cf. Skt. *priyaḥ* " loved ". D'Arbois, CCCI, ii, p. 337.

The war song of the Germans, the *barditus*, bears a name, the origin of which can be perceived through Welsh *barddawd*, the science of the bards. It was a song sung by the Germanic bards. In all ages, as we know, the best equipped and best ordered troops have supplied others with their military vocabulary.[1]

The similarities of the Celtic and Germanic vocabularies bear witness to a long period during which they lived together. If we suppose that the Celts and Germans ever spoke the same language their intercourse went on long after their dialects were separated. But it is hard to believe that they were ever brothers in speech, in view of the different structures of their languages.[2] Probably they were only brothers by adoption. The most characteristic instances quoted may be explained as borrowing by Germanic from Celtic. They are the borrowings of a people which goes to another for things and ideas of civilization, for things and ideas designated by substantives. The Celts seem to have been for long ages the schoolmasters of the Germanic peoples. Perhaps one may go further still; I am very much inclined to believe that one cannot dismiss the hypothesis which has already been put forward, particularly by d'Arbois de Jubainville, that some political relations existed between the Germans and Celts, whatever may have been their nature—alliance, domination, or the formation of a common *Reich*—and whatever their extent.[3]

So the relations of Celtic and Germanic are of a very different kind from those of Celtic and Italic. In the latter case we have two languages born of a parent tongue which lies not very far behind, and in the other the formation of a common stock of words due to the contact of two peoples, one of which was much influenced by the other, at different times, in any case from an early period, and without their ever ceasing to be neighbours.

In this influence of Celtic on Germanic it is not possible to determine the proportionate share of each of the Celtic

---

[1] We may add some religious terms : e.g. Old Saxon *nimid* (*de sacris silvarum quae nimidas vocant;* cf. d'Arbois, op. cit., p. 377 ; Feist, op. cit. p. 354) = Gaulish *nemeton* ; and the name of Velleda among the Bructeri = Irish *ban-file* " prophet-woman " (see the following volume in this series).

[2] Kluge, **CCXI**, p. 324 ; Mansion, **CXXXI**, lvi, pp. 191–209 ; **CXL**, 1914, p. 387.

[3] D'Arbois, **CCCI**, ii, p. 323 ; Bremer, in **CCCLXVIII**, iii, p. 787.

dialects. The ancestors of the Irish may well have been in contact with the Germans, no less than the Britons and the Gauls. Secondly, the borrowed words are found in the Eastern and Northern dialects of Germanic, such as Scandinavian and Gothic, as well as in the Southern and Western.[1] All the Celtic world influenced all the Germanic world. Its influence extended even beyond and through the Germans to the Balto-Slavs and the Finns.

V

CELTIC LANGUAGES AND BALTO-SLAVONIC LANGUAGES
THE VOCABULARY OF THE NORTH-WEST

It has already been observed above that the signs of kinship with the Western languages extend in part to the Slavonic and Baltic tongues. But philologists have been especially struck by the fact that these languages have in common a great number of words which are lacking in Indo-Iranian, Armenian, and Greek. They therefore infer that all North-Western Europe had a vocabulary of its own, as opposed to the Mediterranean vocabulary.[2] These represent two areas of civilization, two areas of intercourse. It is needless to demonstrate that one of them was the Mediterranean basin. The belt in which the North-Western vocabularies are supposed to have been used was the scene of cultural events of a general nature which are revealed by prehistoric archæology—the spread of the rite of incineration in the Bronze Age, the diffusion at the same time of pottery of the Lausitz type,[3] and the amber-trade.[4] All these mean

---

[1] Fischer, **CC**, 1909, No. 85. Cf. **CXL**, 1912, p. 377. As we see, Celtic cannot be shown to have supplied Germanic with all its Indo-European words. Germanic has words in common with Latin which are lacking in Celtic ; perhaps it got them from Italo-Celtic. But it also has words which are part of the common stock of the Indo-Europeans and are lacking in Italic and Celtic. It has even some which it shares with the Indo-Iranian languages alone ; e.g. such a religious word as the Old Icelandic *draugr* " ghost ", which is the same as the Vedic Sanskrit *druh* and the Avestic *druj* (Feist, op. cit., pp. 189, 191, 195, 214, 223 ff., 263).

[2] Meillet, **CCXVI**, i, p. 17, on the vocabulary of the North-West.

[3] Déchelette, **CCCXVIII**, ii, i, p. 385 ; Hubert, " La Poterie de l'âge du bronze et de l'époque de Hallstatt dans la collection de Baye," in **CXLIII**, 1910, pp. 5 ff.

[4] Déchelette, op. cit., ii, i, pp. 623–7.

intercourse within a given belt, the climate of which, moreover, is much the same throughout, suits the same crops, and bears the same flora. Communications of this kind are calculated to encourage interchange among languages ; some words correspond to the features of civilization which are found in the two different parts of the belt, while others are picked up by men going about in it. We may suppose that there was a lingua franca for North-Western Europe as there was for the Mediterranean.

The Italic languages extended their domain southwards, and the Celtic languages south-westwards, of the great plain of Northern Europe, to which the North-Western vocabulary belonged, but they had their share in it. In its Mediterranean evolution Italic drew close to Greek, but many similarities prove that it is connected with the languages of the North. So, too, Celtic contains many words which have equivalents in the Slavonic languages on the one hand, and in the Baltic tongues—Lithuanian, Lettic, and Old Prussian—on the other. It is an interesting fact that both Italic and Celtic preserve, as records of their origin, their share of the Northern vocabulary.

Long lists have been drawn up, from which we shall draw with due caution. Of the words contained therein, some are shared only by Celtic and the languages mentioned (the question of borrowing has even been raised, as in the case of Germanic), and the rest appear also in Germanic and in Latin.

All these languages had one same word for the sea. They pronounced it differently—Celtic with an *o*, *mori* (Morini, Aremorici), Irish *muir*, Breton *mor* ; Latin with an *a*, *mare* ; Germanic and Balto-Slavonic with an *ŏ* or an *ă*, Old Icelandic *marr*, modern German *Meer*, Slavonic *morje*, Lithuanian *maris*.[1]

Some of the words in which these languages agree refer to social life, such as the word for " people ", which appears in the following forms : Irish *tuath*, Oscan *touto*, Gothic *þiuda*, Lithuanian *tauta*. A root *val-vla*, meaning " power ". " greatness," " territorial dominion," " territory," comes into Latin *valere*, modern German *walten*, and Slavonic *vladi*, and is represented in Celtic by Irish *flaith* " dominion ",

---

[1] Meillet, op. cit., p. 22. For the following words, see ibid., pp. 18 ff. ; Berneker, **CXCI**, s.vv.

"territory", and Welsh *gwlad*, whence comes *gwledic* "prince".

Most of the common words deal with agriculture, plants, and animals. Old Slavonic *zrŭno* "seed" and Lithuanian *zirnis* "pea" correspond to Latin *grānum*, Irish *grán*, Gothic *kaurn*, and English *corn*. Russian *bórošno* "rye-meal" corresponds to the Gothic adjective *barizeins* "of barley", Latin *farina*, and Welsh *barra* "bread". The word for apple has been discussed above.[1] The pig, Latin *porcus*, was called *orc* in Irish, *farah* in Old High German, *pârszas* in Lithuanian, and *prase* in Old Slavonic. Latin *faba* "bean" corresponds to Old Prussian *babo*.

Naturally Celtic and Germanic present more similarities to the Baltic dialects, shared with them alone, than Italic does. The resemblances in Latin are survivals. Those in Germanic have been kept up by the relations of the two peoples as neighbours, and this is also to a great extent true of Celtic. The Baltic and the North Sea united the peoples which dwelt on their shores just as the Mediterranean did. It is possible, too, that in the centre of Europe the Celts had once been neighbours of the earliest Slavs as of the Germans.

The following words are found only among the Celts, Germans, and Slavs. There is a plant-name, variously used for the yew and the willow: Welsh *yw* "yew", Old High German *iwa*, *Eibe* "yew", Old Slavonic *jiva* "willow". The word for the metal lead, *luaidhe* in Irish and *lôth* in Old High German, is found in Russian in the form *luda*, meaning tin.

The Balto-Slavonic languages have more likenesses to Celtic than to Germanic. This may be due to the loss of words by Germanic. But the resemblances may also be special and typical. Some of them consist of terms of abstract or general meaning relative to qualities, to manners of being, and bear witness to a common past, perhaps a remote one. Thus, Irish *cotlud* (gen. *cotulta*) "sleep", "to sleep", is a compound of a verb which Lithuanian possesses in its simple form *tuleti* "to be quiet". Irish *gal* "worth", "power", is found in Lithuanian *galeti* "to be able" and Old Slavonic *golemŭ* "great". Others are names of concrete

[1] P. 57.

things or social notions. For example, Irish *mraich, braich*,
Welsh *brag*, Gaulish *brace* " malt ", correspond to Russian
braga, with the same meaning. Irish *sluag* " troop ", corresponds to Slavonic *sluga* " servant " and Lithuanian *slauginti*.
Mr. Shakhmatov [1] has drawn up a long list of words of the
common Slavonic tongue, which he holds to have been taken
from Celtic, but it is open to criticism. We must, however,
suppose that some of the similarities between Celtic and
Balto-Slavonic are due to the latter language borrowing
words through Germanic or over the head of Germanic.

Even the Finnish languages borrowed some words from
Celtic. But here there is no question of a common past. We
only note these borrowings because they give an idea of
the distance to which Celtic civilization shed its influence.

Some of the political and legal terms which Germanic
took from Celtic were passed on to Slavonic and Finnish.[2]
Such are : the word for debt, Old Irish *dliged*, to which
Slavonic *dlŭgŭ* [3] corresponds, through Gothic *dulgs* ; the
word for inheritance, *arbe* in Finnish ; the word for
worth, *verta* in Finnish ; the word for kingdom, *rikki*
in Finnish (these last two words were borrowed fairly
late) ; the word for office, *ammatti* in Finnish.

In the above words it was probably the intermediate
Germanic form that was borrowed. Celtic influence was
only transmitted ; the connection might be quite close, but
it might be very distant. As an instance of direct borrowing,
on the other hand, we have Finnish *tarvas* and Celtic *tarb*
" bull ". Here there is no intermediate Germanic word.

These facts show how Celtic civilization circulated and
expanded in the cultural area of the north-west.

[1] In **XXIV**, xxxiii, pp. 51–99 ; **CXL**, 1912, pp. 391 ff. The author connects
Russian *bojarinu* " leader " with Irish *bo-aire* " cattle-owner, landowner " ;
Slavonic *otici* " father ", with Irish *aithech* " master of the house ". Many
of the words in his list are common, not only to Celtic and Slavonic, but also
to Germanic and Latin. Cf. Meillet, in *Revue des Études slaves*, i (1921), p. 190,
n. 1 ; Lubor Niederlé, **CCCLXIV**, i, pp. 24 ff.

[2] D'Arbois, **CCCL**, ii, p. 348.

[3] Old Slavonic *dlugu* and Russian *dolgu*, from the root *dhlegh*, which gave
dliged " duty, law ", to Irish, *indulgere, indultum* " authorization ", to Latin,
and *dulgs*, " debt ", to Gothic, are derivatives from Germanic. See Vendryès,
" La Racine occidentale *dhlegh*," in **CXL**, 1923, p. 429.

CHAPTER IV

LANGUAGE (*concluded*)

I

CELTIC LANGUAGES AND INDO-EUROPEAN LANGUAGES OF THE EAST AND SOUTH-EAST. CONCLUSION

CELTIC came into contact with other languages than Germanic, Slavonic, and Italic. When the Latins and Umbrians went down into Italy they left the Celts uncovered on the east. In that quarter, various Indo-European languages were spoken, which it would be interesting to know, in order to have a complete notion of the affinities of Celtic. These were Illyrian, Thracian, Dacian, and Getic. The Illyrians had historical relations with the Greeks, and so did the Dacians, but how far did they go back ? There were certainly religious resemblances between the Thracians and the Greeks which may have come down from very ancient cultural relations. These various languages did not vanish without leaving a trace. Something of their vocabularies remains in those of the Slavonic tongues, Rumanian, Albanian, and Greek.

This last language is highly complex. It inherited something from the languages which were spoken on Greek soil before the Hellenes, properly so called, arrived there, and among these there were Indo-European tongues which we cannot classify. It also picked up many words from neighbouring dialects. The scholars of Greece were interested in these foreign elements in their speech, and faithfully collected them in their dictionaries.

Greek has a certain number of words in common with Celtic—either with Celtic alone or with it and other of the languages which we have been considering. Usually they are rare words,[1] or, to be more accurate, the most striking cases are rare words, that is, foreign words. Thus Greek, which is

---

[1] Βρένθιξ, Hesych., Βρένθος. Cf. Welsh *bryn* "hill"; Gaulish, *ex monte Brenno*. Holder, **CCVII**, i, p. 525.

only distantly related to Celtic, has preserved words which bear witness to languages which were much closer to it. For example, the name 'Ακράγας contains a word κράγος, which does not mean " cry ", but " rock ", like Welsh craig.[1] The word may be Sicel or Ligurian ; now Celtic, like Sicilian Greek, absorbed some of the Ligurian vocabulary. There are, too, reciprocal borrowings, for which Greek travellers and colonists were responsible. Greek πρῖνος " ilex " is Gaulish prenne (Irish crann).[2] Old Irish meccon " root " and Gælic meacan " carrot " recall Greek μήκων " poppy ", as do Old Slavonic makŭ and modern German Mohn.[3]

Greek has also preserved some relics of the ancient tongues of Asia Minor, some of which, such as Phrygian, which is a form of Thracian, belong to the group of European languages enumerated above, while the others are at least in part Indo-European, such as Hittite. Here we can glean a few similarities to Celtic.[4] Another descendant of these tongues is Armenian, which is difficult to place exactly in the body of Indo-European languages. It seems to be even more distant from the Celtic group than Greek. The further apart dialects lie on the map the fewer similarities do we seem to find.[5]

Nevertheless, the two groups of Indo-European languages whose areas are furthest removed from Celtic and which lie at the opposite pole of the Indo-European expansion have very singular affinities with it, the systematic nature of which calls for attention.

[1] Pedersen, LXX, xxiv, p. 270.
[2] Boisacq, Dic. étym. lang. gr., s.v. πρῖνος ; Pedersen, CCXXVIII, i, pp. 44, 159.
[3] Macbain, CLXXXIX, s.v. " meacan." Other resemblances which exist between Greek and Celtic alone are so singular that they must be merely apparent ; e.g. the similarity of Welsh cerd " art " to Greek κέρδος, and that of Irish cian " long " to Greek κεῖνος (i.e. " distant "). Cf. Boisacq, s.v. κέρδος ; Macbain, s.v. " cian."
[4] e.g. Δίνδυμος ; cf. Irish dind ; Old Icelandic tindr ; modern German Zinne.
[5] The Celts of the British Isles have preserved several types of boats made of hides over branches, which are called by the generic name of currach or coracle—Irish curach, Welsh cwrwg, Low Latin curucus. These coracles are exactly like the gufas of the Tigris and Euphrates, and many Assyrian monuments portray these ancestors of the modern coracle. The various forms of this vessel were used in Armenia, as appears from the accounts of the Armenian campaigns of Assyrian kings. In Armenian, kur means boat. This very striking coincidence does not seem to be mere chance. It is tempting to connect the word with an Indo-European root, that of corium " leather " (Macbain, CLXXXIX, s.v. " curach." See below, p. 195, n. 2).

The kinship of Celtic and Indo-Iranian is shown by a common vocabulary, but this only contains a very few words which really count—a few craft-terms, if any, the feminine forms of the nouns of number " three " and " four ", and a considerable group of religious or politico-religious words. In this domain, Italic has much in common with Celtic, and both with Indo-Iranian ; institutions have even been preserved which correspond to this vocabulary or explain its preservation.[1]

Celtic has two words to designate religious belief, Irish *crabud* (Welsh *crefydd*) and Irish *iress*. There is nothing corresponding to them except in Indo-Iranian, namely Sanskrit *viçrabdhah*, meaning believer, and Pahlavi *parast* " worshipper ". Sanskrit *çraddha* " confidence in the virtues of the offering " has equivalents in Latin *crēdō* and Irish *cretim*.[2] Latin *jus*, preserved in Irish *huisse* (*justiios*), corresponds to Zend *yaoš* (Sanskrit *yoḥ*). The word for king is the same in both groups : Sanskrit *rāj* (stem *rāj*) and *rājan*-, Latin *rex*, Celtic *rix*. The root meaning " drink " has kept the same form : *pibāmi*, *bibo*, Irish *ibim*. To drink the sacred liquor is an essential part of worship. Lighting the fire is another, and here, too, the roots reappear and can be recognized by their nasals : Irish *-andaid* " to light ", Sanskrit *inddhé* " he lights ". Greek says αἴθω. For milk, a religious drink, Irish has two words, both of Indo-Iranian kinship : *gert* " cream ", which recalls Sanskrit *ghṛtam* " rancid butter ", and *suth*,[3] Sanskrit *suláḥ* " pressed ", that is the *sómaḥ*. The root *bhewd* has given *bhāvayati* " he causes to prosper " to Sanskrit, the name of the god Faunus to Latin, and that of the goddess Buanann to Irish.

The Latin name Neptunus, which recalls the Irish Nechtan, one of the secondary names of the sea-god Nuada Necht, has often been connected with Sanskrit *napta*-, and the Irish *triath* or *trethan* " sea " with the Sanskrit name of the god Tritaḥ (Tritaḥ Āptyaḥ, Trita of the Waters), Zend *Þraētaonō*.[4] M. Vendryès adds to these names of water-gods,

[1] Vendryès, " Les Correspondances de vocabulaire entre l'indo-iranien et l'italo-celtique," in **XCIII**, xx (1918), pp. 265–285.
[2] Id., **CXL**, xliv, 90.
[3] On *suth*, see **XCIII**, p. 277. The word is preserved in a gloss of Cormac (*Sanas Cormaic*, ed. K. Meyer, p. 111, No. 1283).
[4] Pedersen, i, pp. 132, 179 ; cf. Greek Τρίτων.

the only divine names corresponding in the two groups, those of the rivers Sionann (Shannon) and Sindhuḥ, and that of the Danuvius and Zend *danuš* " river ".[1]

The affinities of the dialects now called Tokharian [2] with Celtic are grammatical, like those of Celtic and Italic. It has a medio-passive or deponent with verb-forms in *-r-*.[3] It also has, like Latin and Celtic, a subjunctive in *-a-*, taken from a stem different from that of the indicative.[4] I have already said that it belongs to the *centum* group of languages, and other analogies of structure have been pointed out.[5] These analogies, which are very unlike those of Celtic with Indo-Iranian, suggest a relationship something like that between Celtic and Italic, only blurred by time. The Tokharians lived in the Indian orbit, and were fed on Indian thought and literature, and their vocabulary shows the effect. It is the structure of their language which tempts one to seek kindred for them in the West. But are we to suppose that they travelled from Europe to Asia ? Prehistoric archæology has noted many traces of migrations from Europe to Asia, at dates which do not agree with that which can be assigned to the breaking up of any Western group to which the Tokharians could have belonged. I am convinced that there were other migrations, from Asia to Europe, at that very date.[6] I also believe that the discovery of Tokharian, like that of the Hittite inscriptions, compels us to move the cradle of the Indo-European tongues eastwards, and that they were to some extent differentiated before they expanded towards the West.

Some little contact with the Greeks or the peoples whose languages are unknown save through Greek forms ; frequent intercourse with the Balto-Slavs, either by immediate contact

[1] I shall return to the parallel between Celtic and Indo-Iranian institutions in the following volume.

[2] Meillet, **CLXII**, i, pp. 1–19 ; Lévi and Meillet, **XCIII**, xviii (1914), pp. 1 ff. ; Meillet, **CXXXVII**, Aug., 1912, pp. 136 ff. ; Pedersen, **CCXXVIII**, ii, pp. 396, 673 ; Feist, **CCCXXVI**, pp. 428 ff.

[3] Vendryès, " Les Formes verbales en *-r* du tokharien et de l'italo-celtique," in **CXL**, 1913, pp. 129 ff. : *aikemar* " I know " ; *dhatmasdhar* " thou art born " ; *ayitr* " he attributes to himself ". We may contrast the Latin line, *tunicaque inducitur artus* (Virg., *Æn.*, viii, 457), with the Tokharian sentence, *wastsi* (cf. *vestis*) *yamassitr*. Cf. Meillet, **LXXV**, 1911, i, p. 454.

[4] **LXXV**, p. 142 : *wärpnātr* " he admits " ; subjunctive *wärpatar*.

[5] Meillet, **XCIII**, xviii, p. 24.

[6] Feist, **CCCXXVI**, pp. 423 ff.

in the centre of Europe or through the Germans; contact on a very wide front on the Germanic side; more or less complete unity with the Italici at a fairly recent date, broken, however, as we shall see, before the Celts finally moved away to the West—these are the facts which first emerge from a comparative examination of the Celtic languages and the Indo-European tongues of Europe. The region in which these complex relations can have existed almost completely and simultaneously during the time when the Italo-Celtic community was breaking up is near the centre of Europe, probably round about Bohemia. The comparisons which have been made between Celtic and the Eastern branches of Indo-European—Indo-Iranian and Tokharian—open vistas into a more distant past; they forbid us to place the separation of the groups which are geographically furthest from each other too far back, and suggest that the point of junction of the neighbouring groups should be shifted eastwards, where I shall not try to locate it exactly.

In defining the Celtic peoples by their speech, I based my definition on a factor which holds good for peoples which are completely constituted, however they may have been formed and whatever elements they may have absorbed, and it is so that I prefer to consider them. The brief comparative study which we have just made has given us much information about the element which supplied the language, or the bulk of the language, and the very definite affinities which it presents with the most distant groups of Indo-European leave no doubt that that element was of the same stock as the speakers of those tongues. But it has shown from the very first, unfortunately not in at all a clear manner, that the composition of the Celtic peoples was complex, and that in the differentiation of their languages a share must be ascribed to the alien tribes which they absorbed.

II

IBERIAN, LIGURIAN, AND RÆTIAN

The ancient Greek and Latin writers from whom we obtain some of our information about the Celts mention them in the West of Europe in opposition to two peoples which inhabited large areas, the boundaries of which changed from time to time and are very problematical—the Iberians and the Rætians—and these peoples themselves evidently stand for many others.

The ancients speak of the Iberians as being in the British Isles. Is this because of the likeness of name between the Iberians and the people after which Ireland was called, the Hibernians ? Or is it on account of the great number of dark-skinned folk in the West of England, which struck Tacitus ? [1] In the time of Cæsar the Iberians were spreading very much into Gaul in Aquitania.[2] In another direction they are said to have occupied the whole of Italy and also Sicily, the earliest historical inhabitants of which, the Sicani, are supposed to have been Iberians.[3] In the Iberian Peninsula, which they had long shared with the Ligurians,[4] the Iberians appear to have been so long established that we can hardly take them for anything but aborigines.

But the problem is quite clearly presented, and admits of several solutions. One consists in identifying the Iberians and the Basques, who are supposed to be the inheritors of their language in modern Europe. Although this view has its adherents, it is hardly tenable from the point of view of language,[5] and indefensible from that of archæology.[6] The Basques are the remnants of prehistoric populations confined in the Pyrenees. We have already seen that the comparison of Basque with the Celtic tongues leads to nothing. If Iberian were represented by Basque we should evidently learn nothing about the part played by the Iberians in the constitution of the Celtic societies from philology.

Next, the Iberians have been connected with the Berbers of North Africa, whose languages had already been compared to Basque.[7] Herr Schulten and his Spanish pupils and colleagues, Sr. Bosch Gimpera among them, have given a scientific form to this solution of the problem [8] in a series

[1] Philipon, **CCCLXIX**, p. 296 ; Tac., *Agr.*, 11.
[2] Caes., *Bell. Gall.*, i, 1 ; Strabo, iv, 1, 1 ; 2, 1 ; Philipon, **DXVI**, p. 302 ; cf. d'Arbois, **CCXCIX**, p. 91.
[3] Philipon, **CCCLXIX**, pp. 304, 160, 305.
[4] Schulten, **DXVIII**, i, p. 54 ; Bosch Gimpera, **DIII**, p. 49 and passim; Avien., *Ora Maritima*, 195 ff.
[5] Philipon, **DXVI**, pp. 1 ff. ; **CCCLXIX**, pp. 158 ff.
[6] Bosch Gimpera, op. cit.
[7] Philipon, **DXVI**, pp. 1 ff. ; Boudard, **DVI**, p. 92.
[8] Schulten, **DXVIII**, i, pp. 50–1 ; Bosch Gimpera, **DIV**.

of important works, in which they have supplemented these linguistic data by archæological arguments of great value.[1] In this way they have reconstructed a very convincing picture of the expansion of the Iberians in Spain.

M. Philipon, a pupil of d'Arbois de Jubainville, has on two occasions put forward another theory,[2] based on absolute distinction between the Tartessians and Iberians [3] and the elimination of the Ligurians from the Peninsula.[4] According to his view, the Tartessians occupied a large part of Gaul,[5] and the Iberians almost the whole country, at different but fairly recent dates. Both peoples were Indo-Europeans [6] who came from Asia, the former by way of the sea and Africa, the latter by land and the North.[7] M. Philipon has drawn up for the Iberians a vocabulary which is distinct from the Tartessian. It is based on geographical names and proper nouns in which he finds words which are plainly Celtic, like *gurdus*,[8] and others which have usually been assigned to Ligurian, such as Rhodanus (the Rhone), Sequana (the Seine), Isara (the Isère), Alba, and Albion,[9] and even Albis (the Elbe), which is certainly Germanic.[10] His vocabulary, therefore, is very like Celtic and not very different from Ligurian. The consequence would be [11] that Iberian left place-names all over France,[12] even the names of towns,[13] and also in Western Germany to the Elbe,[14] in Britain,[15] and throughout Italy, to say nothing of the traces of their journey from east to west.

Unfortunately, M. Philipon supports his ethnological conclusions with no archæological fact and very little chronology. To my mind, accepting as I do, with reservations,

[1] See below, pp. 282 ff.
[2] Philipon, CCCLXIX, pp. 151 ff.
[3] Ibid., p. 51.
[4] Ibid., p. 133.
[5] Philipon, DXVI, p. 53 ; CCCLXIX, p. 154.
[6] DXVI, pp. 50, 57 ff. ; CCCLXIX, pp. 155, 163, 165, etc.
[7] This would explain the red-haired Iberians of Silius Italicus (16, 472).
[8] Philipon, CCCLXIX, p. 159. See above, p. 37. The question of *briga* will be discussed below, pp. 293-4.
[9] Ibid., p. 299.
[10] Ibid., p. 300.
[11] M. Philipon also attributes words in -*asc*-, -*osc*-, to Iberian (see below).
[12] Ataravus, the Arroux ; Vesera, the Vézère. Philipon, op. cit., p. 300.
[13] Agedincum, Avaricum. Ibid., p. 303.
[14] Ambra, the Ammer ; Visera, the Weser ; Leisura, the Lieser. Ibid., pp. 295, 300.
[15] Tamaros, Isca. Ibid., p. 296.

many of M. Philipon's views, and regarding the ethnological testimony of the ancient authors as most important, the only set of archæological remains which could correspond to the area which may be defined with the aid of these selected data, is the series of tombs containing bell-shaped vases adorned with incised bands,[1] bored flat objects known as bracers or bowman's wrist-guards, conical buttons, and daggers of flint or copper, which are found from Sicily to the north of Italy, in Sardinia, in the Peninsula from Catalonia to Baetica and the neighbourhood of Lisbon, in France from the Pyrenees and Provence to Brittany, in the British Isles, in Holland, in the valleys of the Rhine and Danube, in Bohemia, and on the middle Elbe. It is just to these tombs containing bell-vases that the Sican period in Sicily may correspond.[2] Their area of expansion coincides in part with that of the megalithic monuments, but it is wider. The Iberian name is the last left to us to attach to that civilization of Western Europe, chiefly on the coasts, of which the megalithic monuments are the most distinguished representatives. If this is the case, the Iberian element must have formed a considerable ingredient in the composition of the Celtic peoples. It is therefore possible that in what survives of Celtic there is some Iberian, but it is difficult to place one's finger on it.

[1] Déchelette, i, pp. 549–552; A. del Castillo Yurrita, **CCCIX**.
[2] **CCCIX**, pp. 126 ff.

CHAPTER V

The Archæological Evidence

I

ARCHÆOLOGICAL TRACES OF THE CIVILIZATION OF THE CELTS.
THE CIVILIZATION OF LA TÈNE. THE GALATIANS AND THE
GAULS OF ITALY

ARCHÆOLOGY has often been mentioned in the preceding chapters, for it is next to impossible to separate archæological and ethnological data completely in the history and prehistory of ancient peoples. Each set of facts helps to explain the other, and each fills gaps left by the other. Archæology brings together the scattered data of the ethnography of peoples whose civilization is known chiefly by remnants which it has left in the ground. These are legitimate indications of vanished peoples, like their place-names, to the full extent to which the postulate of ethnography, which represents and distinguishes peoples by their civilizations, is justified. Unfortunately they are incomplete indications, since from the period in which they help us to find traces of the Celts nothing has come down to us but somewhat scattered objects and ruins.

We must now take a general survey, as we did with the language, and run over all that it is strictly necessary to accept as known, in order to visualize the Celts on the archæological map of Europe, at least at the height of their greatness and expansion, before we can follow the whole of Celtic archæology in the order of its obscure periods. It is, it is true, begging the question to describe archæological finds as Celtic before we have tried to lay down the limits of the area covered by the Celts at the date of the objects discovered. But we can do so, starting from a certain point.

In drawing up the scheme of periods and ages by which time is measured with reference to prehistoric archæology, archæologists have distinguished a second Iron Age, which is

80

also known as the Marne or the La Tène period,[1] after the stations or groups of stations taken as typical, and corresponds to a civilization which by common agreement is attributed to the Celts. We shall see presently that the attribution is justified. During the time when that civilization flourished, that is from the fifth to the first century before Christ, we know roughly the area over which the Celts extended. The area of the La Tène civilization coincides with it, or goes beyond it only to testify to the influence exercised over their neighbours by the Celts, who at the time were the ruling power of barbarian Europe.[2] That that civilization should be attributed to the Celts is as self-evident as that the language of the region should, and requires no proof.

But if proof is wanted, the data collected on the southern and south-eastern borders of the Celtic world, where the Celts came late and did not maintain themselves as a people, where they were in contact with peoples which have a history and whose civilization is known, are certainly decisive. Galatia would furnish the best, if it supplied many. We must wait on the excavations, which will one day show results.[3] In the meantime, the Galatians have given us the orthodox portrait of the Gaul. All the ancient monuments depicting Gauls are derived, more or less directly, from those which commemorated the great Gallic inroad of 279 B.C., the victories of the Kings of Pergamon over the Galatians settled in their neighbourhood, and various episodes in the wars of the East.[4] They represent Gauls of the La Tène epoch, with typical ornaments and arms—the characteristic torque and the horned helmet which tradition ascribes to them. The Dying Gaul of the Capitol has sunk down on

[1] General bibliography : Déchelette, **CCCXVIII**, ii, 3 ; Dottin, **CCCXXII** ; Lindenschmit, **CCCXCIX** and **CCCCVI** ; Vouga, **CCCCXCIV** ; Allen, **CCXCVIII** ; Hoernes-Menghin, **CCCXXXIX** ; Smith, **CCCLXXXIV** ; Reinach, **CCCLXXIII** ; Morel, **CCCCLXXXIV** ; Montelius, **CCCLVII** ; Holmes, **CCCCXXXIII** ; Schumacher, **CCCCIX**, i.
[2] Siret, **DXXIII** ; Bosch Gimpera, **D** ; Pič and Déchelette, *Le Hradischt de Stradonič en Bohème* ; Parvan, **DXLVIII**.
[3] Reinecke, **CCCCVI**, v, p. 293, n. 2 ; R. Zahn (in **CLXIII**, 1907, pp. 638 ff. ; **XX**, 1907, p. 225) is endeavouring to find Galatians in the pottery of Gordion, Boghaz-Keui, and Priene.
[4] In this connection it is most important, for the study of Gallic weapons, to take into account the trophies and other monuments on which they are represented in Asia and Gaul. They add to what we already know, and they supply dates. Cf. Couissin, in **CXXXVIII**, 1927–8.

a shield with metal-work like that of the shields from the
Marne cemeteries, especially those of that date ; his horn
might have come from Gaul or Ireland ; his sword,
unfortunately, is merely fanciful (see Plate I).

The excavations which have been systematically conducted in Italy for some years in the neighbourhood of Ancona
have given results which are of great importance for the
identification of the Gallic civilization. The first discoveries
were made at Montefortino, two miles from Arcevia and
twenty-five miles from Sinigaglia (Sena Gallica). This was
in the territory of the Senones, who settled there after
390 B.C., but departed (or at least their chiefs did) after
285 B.C. Here there was found a cemetery of rectangular
graves, lying east and west, in which the dead were buried
stretched on their backs, surrounded by a whole paraphernalia
comprising weapons, ornaments, and funerary vessels.
A large number of the objects found in these tombs are of
Etruscan make. But the tombs themselves are different
from those of the country ; they are like those of Champagne,
and contain exactly the same weapons as they.[1] It is a Gaulish
cemetery, a Senonian cemetery, and, what is more, a dated
cemetery.

Moreover, it is not an isolated case, for there is a whole
series of cemeteries, from the Alps to the Apennines, which
resemble those north of the Alps, period for period, in the
funeral rites which have been observed in them or in part
or all of the grave-goods.[2] Some lie in country which was
actually occupied by the Gauls, others in Ligurian country
which was subject to Gallic influence,[3] or in Venetian country
which they encroached on or visited frequently.[4] The
information furnished by the graves corroborates the picture
which the ancients drew of the Gauls.[5]

[1] For Montefortino, see Déchelette, **CCCXVIII**, p. 1088 ; Brizio, in **CVI**,
ix, 3 (1901), pp. 616 ff. ; cf. Déchelette, in **CXXXVIII**, 1902, i, p. 245. Later
excavations have yielded gold objects adorned with figures just like those
of the Gundestrup cauldron.

[2] Cf. Déchelette, pp. 1086 ff.

[3] Giubiasco, Ornavasso.

[4] Alfonsi, " Tomba pre-romana di Este del IV periodo," in **LIII**, 1911,
p. 125.

[5]

Aurea cæsaries ollis atque aurea vestis ;
virgatis lucent sagulis ; tum lactea colla
auro innectuntur ; duo quisque Alpina coruscant
gaesa manu, scutis protecti corpora longis.

Virg., Æn., viii, 659–662 ; cf. Sil. Ital., iv, 154–6.

In short, we know the civilization of the Gauls of Italy, and that gives us a certain foundation for ascribing to the Gauls a similar civilization which we find elsewhere—namely, the civilization of La Tène. There are compelling reasons for ascribing it to the Gauls of the fourth and following centuries, and strong grounds for supposing that it was peculiar to them. The remains of that civilization, from its beginning onwards, will be described in this chapter as archæological indications of the Celts.

With regard to the La Tène civilization, certain archæologists and historians have made a mistake which must be corrected. The Celts have been the subject of a false argument in archæology similar to those committed with regard to them in anthropology. Such indications as we possess have been given a too general significance, and they have been taken to mean that La Tène civilization and the Celts were one and the same thing. One school [1] has in this way abbreviated the history of the Celts in Ireland in the most misleading way, making it begin with the earliest La Tène objects found in the island. It is necessary here, at the outset, to state, as a matter of principle (we shall have to prove it later), that the civilization of La Tène really corresponds to only one of the groups of the Celts, who had split up long before the fifth century before Christ. It is the culture of the Continental Brythons,[2] who afterwards became leaders of the other groups. It is not that of the Goidels of Ireland. The civilization of the Celts became uniform later, in consequence of the overflow of the Brythons over the whole Celtic world.

Moreover, the Celts left relics of civilization in the ground before the La Tène period. But these cannot be defined *a priori* as Celtic ; they do not bear the recognizable stamp of a Celtic civilization, and before we can attribute one or another series of objects to the Celts it will be necessary to examine systematically all the historical and linguistic evidence which leads one to look for the presence of that people at the places where the objects have been found. It does not seem to have been until the fifth century B.C.

[1] MacNeill, CCCXLI ; Macalister, CCCCXXXIX.
[2] Déchelette, p. 575.

that Celtic society attained the degree of development and self-consciousness implied by the production of a distinct and complete style for every kind of tool, weapon, and decoration. The finds of the La Tène period present just the homogeneity and originality that one would expect in such a civilization and such a stage in the life of a people. When, therefore, we inquire whether some set of earlier remains is to be put down to the Celts, we have to arrange in chronological series all that preceded the La Tène civilization in certain regions and led up to it. Thus, the exposition which follows in this chapter will serve as a basis for our inquiry into the archæological materials for the history of the Celts.

In the course of it we shall make an analysis, as we did with the language. The material which makes a civilization for the archæologist is made up of elements ; it is a compound, like the civilization itself. The La Tène culture, homogeneous and original as it is, has clearly been influenced from outside and has its foreign ingredients. Thus it reveals some of the relations which the Celts had with their predecessors and their neighbours.

Lastly, this civilization displays variations which are certainly not due to mere chance. We may try to attach them to one or another group of the Celtic peoples, or to one or another Celtic nation. In this respect archæological research is one of the methods by which we may resolve the problems which history will put to us. We shall take due note of these variations when the time comes to do so.

II

THE LA TÈNE CULTURE AND ITS SUBDIVISIONS. THE STATION
OF LA TÈNE

The civilization with which we are dealing is now most usually known by the name of one of its chief centres.[1]

The station of La Tène has been known for a long time,[2]

---

[1] Id., pp. 911–941 ; E. Desor, " Les Constructions lacustres du lac de Neuchâtel," in CIX, 1864, p. 63 ; Vouga, CCCXCIV.

[2] It was brought to light in 1857 by the level of the lake falling. The first excavations took place in 1874.

but quite recent excavations [1] have made our knowledge of
it very complete. It stands at the outflow point of the Lake
of Neuchâtel, by the side of an ancient bed of the Thielle.
At first, since it was covered by the waters of the lake, it
was taken for a lake-village. Really it was a post on the edge
of the water, with bridges and store-houses on piles, guarding
the lake and the river, a military post, and one where there
had been fighting. There were found many fragments of
harness and vehicles, weapons of all kinds, the tools needed
in the station, and skeletons which told of tragic episodes in
its history. It was probably a toll-station.[2] The Gauls made

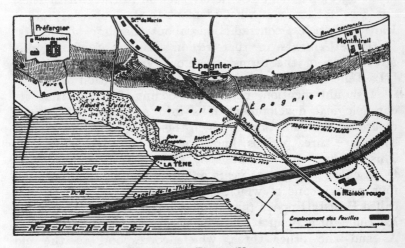

MAP 2. La Tène. (Vouga.)

profit from the trade-routes,[3] and La Tène commanded that
which led from the Rhone to the Rhine and another
connecting the valleys of the Rhone and the Doubs. Tolls
may have been paid in kind, and the proceeds piled up in

---

[1] V. Wavre and P. Vouga, " La Tène. Fouilles de 1907," in **CIX**, 1908,
pp. 59–69 ; " Fouilles de 1908," ibid., 1909, pp. 229–237 ; Vouga, " Troisième
Rapport. Fouilles de 1909," " Quatrième Rapport. Fouilles de 1910–11,"
and " Cinquième Rapport, 1912–13," ibid., 1910, pp. 183–9, 1912, pp. 7 ff.,
and 1914, pp. 49–68 ; " Note sur les fouilles de 1917," ibid., 1917, pp. 94 ff. ;
id., **CXVIII**, 1912, p. 218 ; **XVII**, 1915, pp. 196–222 ; Heierli, **XLVIII**, iv,
p. 105.

[2] Déchelette, p. 939.

[3] Thus, Dumnorix levied tolls for the Æduan country (Cæs., *Gall. War*,
i, 18).

the store-houses, unless the post contained an entrepôt for other purposes.

The choice of the name of La Tène for the civilization in question is not altogether happy, for the site only represents one period of that civilization. Nor is it any better to call it, as some do, after the hundred and ninety-one cemeteries of the Marne.[1] These have yielded earlier types, but not the whole series. No one site covers the whole range of those few centuries. As for the expression " Late Celtic ",[2] used by British archæologists, which suggests the idea of the latest developments of Celtic civilization in the British Isles, one does not know at what moment to start using it, and it leads to hopeless contradictions about the date of the first Celtic settlements in that region. In spite of the disadvantages of the terms, therefore, I shall speak of the " La Tène period " and the " La Tène civilization ".

I should mention, before proceeding further, that its chronological development falls into a system of periods regarding the definition of which there is general agreement. There are three periods, known as La Tène I, II, and III. This system was instituted by the German archæologist, O. Tischler.[3] For some years another system, distinguishing four periods, one of which is intermediate between the so-called Hallstatt epoch (first Iron Age) and that of La Tène, has come into favour.[4] This first period is called by the letter A, and the other three, which correspond to the old classification, are likewise marked by letters. The arrangement is based on the observation of data in Germany. At the end of the development of the Hallstatt civilization, the appearance of the objects changes, and they assume forms which announce the coming of the later culture. This latter, which we shall continue to call La Tène, appears earlier in Germany than elsewhere. This observation takes us a step nearer one of the conclusions to which we are moving.

---

[1] Déchelette, p. 929.
[2] CCCLXXXIV, p. 83. Similar ambiguities arise from the use, in German, of such terms as *Früh-La-Tène, Spät-La-Tène*, as in Forrer's " Früh-La-Tène-Gräber bei Blosheim," in LIV, 1919, p. 983, which deals with La Tène II.
[3] Tischler, in LXI, 1885, p. 157 ; Reinach, in LIX, Monaco, 1900, p. 427.
[4] Reinecke, CCCCVI, pp. 1, 7, 11, 13 ; CCCXCIX, v, pp. 50, 57, 8, 15, 51.

The forms assumed in succession by the objects of each
of the classes which we are about to examine can be classified
chronologically according to these periods.

III

WEAPONS OF OFFENCE

The objects to which the civilization of La Tène has
given a style are weapons, jewels, and other articles of wear,
and vases of earthenware and metal. We shall examine them
in turn, starting with the weapons.

Of offensive weapons the most characteristic is the sword.
Moreover, the sword seems to have been the chief weapon
of the men of this civilization.[1] It is fairly frequent in the
tombs, although economy may have been exercised with
regard to it.[2] Moreover, these swords seem to be good,
well-forged weapons,[3] in spite of the contrary remarks of
Polybios in his account of the campaign of the Consul C.
Flaminius against the Insubres in 223.[4] The swords of the
Gauls, he says, bent at the first stroke, and had to be
straightened with the foot. The Gallic sword of La Tène I
was so good that it was probably adopted by the Romans.
Those of the third century had defects, but these were
tactical, not technical.[5]

The tactics of the Gauls, like those of the Romans, consisted in the close combat with the sword, the attack being
prepared by volleys of javelins. It was *infantry* fighting, at
least at the beginning. In any case, the infantry were always
more numerous than the cavalry. In Cæsar's time there
were in Gaul large forces of mounted nobility, but these

[1] Jullian, **CCCXLVII**, ii, p. 195. On the divine nature of the sword, see
d'Arbois, **CCXLVIII**, i, p. 73.

[2] To tell the truth, many tombs of armed men contain no sword. That
means that it was so precious that the survivors did not always sacrifice
it for the sake of an uncertain future life. Chiefs may have been regularly
buried in battle-gear or state costume. Common men were probably content
with scanty funeral furniture. Here, as elsewhere, I attach more importance
to positive evidence than to negative.

[3] Déchelette, ii, 3, p. 1129.

[4] ii, 53; Plut., *Cam.*, 41. Cf. S. Reinach, "L'Epée de Brennus," in
XV, 1901, p. 344.

[5] Livy, xxii, 46 : At the battle of Cannæ the Iberians and the Gauls
had the same weapons, but the Gauls cut, while the Iberians thrust.

were not the mass of the army.[1] The use of chariots, which preceded that of cavalry and still existed in Britain when Cæsar came, did not affect tactics. Troops engaged with

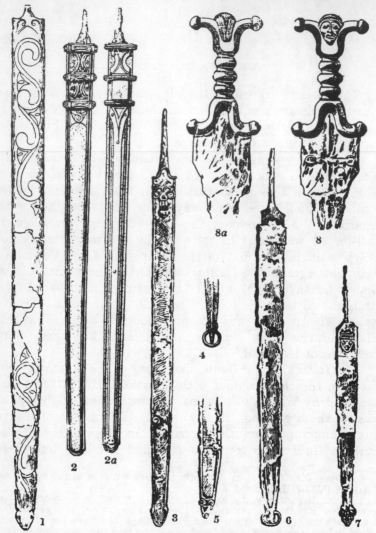

FIG. 2. Swords and Scabbards. (Déchelette, ii, 3.) 1, La Tène, Switzerland (fig. 463). 2, R. Witham, Lincs (fig. 645). 3, La Tène (fig. 459.) 4, The Rhine at Mainz. 5, Castione, Ticino. 6–7, Marson, Marne (fig. 457). 8, Chaumont, Hte.-Marne (fig. 474).

[1] The army of Vercingetorix contained only fifteen thousand horse in the last rising of Gaul. Cæs., *Gall. War*, vii, 64 ; cf. Cic., *Pro Font.*, fr. 12.

the sword, and the chariots were mingled with the infantry.[1]
It was the same with all the Celts, for the old Irish poems
describe the same tactics.[2]

This form of fighting, common to the Celts and Latins,
was very different from that of the Greeks. The Greek
phalanx was a body armed with long, heavy spears. For the
Greek hoplite, the sword was an auxiliary weapon, not the
chief one. Like the medieval knight, he only resorted to it
when his spear was broken.

The swords of La Tène are of quite a peculiar kind.[3]
They are derived from the latest type of Hallstatt sword.
This was a dagger, from 16 to 24 inches long, the hilt of which
branched out into antennæ of various shapes. The edges
were sharp and straight, and to a certain point parallel.
The scabbard ended in a chape, which took two forms :
sometimes it terminated in a ball, and sometimes in a crescent
or fish-tail. In the history of weapons one sees alternately
the dagger lengthening into a sword and the sword contracting into a dagger. Some La Tène swords still have the
remains of the antennæ of the Hallstatt dagger. But the
kinship of the two types is chiefly shown by the chape of
the scabbard. The earliest La Tène swords have an open-
work chape (Fig. 2, Nos. 4, 6). The ends of the crescent of
the Hallstatt chape have grown longer and come round to
meet the edges of the scabbard. The Gauls were in the habit
of giving life, as it were, to structural forms, and the horn
of the crescent, curving like a swan's neck, was given a swan's
head, often with a piece of coral for the eye. The early swords
are still fairly short ; the average length is from 24 to
26 inches. The scabbards were of metal—first bronze, and
then iron. The mouth curved upwards in the shape of an
arch, and fitted into the guard, the shape of which we do
not know.

The sword grew longer steadily. Those of the second
period of La Tène are about 96 inches long. The handle

---

[1] Tacitus gives a description of a typical battle of this kind (without,
however, properly understanding it) in *Agr.*, xxxvi. The cavalry was at first
employed in the same way, mixed with the infantry.
[2] d'Arbois, **CCXLVIII**, vi, pp. 332–3, 340.
[3] Déchelette, ii, 3, pp. 1107 ff. ; **CCCLXXXIV**, p. 58, fig. 56 ; p. 59,
fig. 58 ; Nicaise, **CCCCXXXV**, pl. iv ; Vouga, **CCCCXCVI**, coll. 31–45 and
pl. i–viii.

remains as before. The scabbard still has an arch-shaped mouth. It is usually of iron. Whether it is of iron or of bronze, it is often adorned with fine engravings (Fig. 2, No. 1). The chape has altered ; the horns of the crescent have been flattened right down on to the scabbard, and the open-work has gone (Fig. 2, Nos. 1, 3).

The latest swords are still longer. The scabbard has a straight mouth, and is often made of wood. There is no trace of the original form of the chape. The scabbard has no ornament, and is bound with a network of wire which is a development of a transverse bar which existed on earlier types. The point of the sword has been rounded off (Fig. 2, No. 2). It is a wholly different weapon from that of La Tène I.

When the weapon intended for close combat can only be used for cutting, the warrior needs a second weapon with which he can thrust. This is almost a general rule. So we find the dagger with antennæ reappearing, this time with an " anthropoid " handle (Fig. 2, Nos. 8, 8a). This weapon is derived from the earlier swords, in which the end was still pointed, and the mouth of the scabbard and the chape recall the swords of La Tène II.[1]

The sword was slung on the right, not the left, and from a waist-belt, not a baldric.[2] The strap which held it ran through two rings and a metal loop at the upper end of the scabbard. The belt did not consist of a metal chain, as Diodoros says ; it was only partly of metal, being a leather strap ending in bronze or iron chains which formed the two sides of a clasp. These belt-ends are often found in Gallic tombs.

The late La Tène swords found in Britain, which were made locally after the conquest of Gaul by the Romans, have the suspension-loop about the middle of the scabbard. They must, therefore, have balanced differently. There are other peculiarities about them. The hilt sometimes ends in a globular pommel, like those of the Hallstatt swords. The chape spreads out into a winged form, and is derived from

---

[1] Déchelette, ii, 3, pp. 1137 ff. ; S. Reinach, in **XV**, 1895, pp. 18 ff. It is hardly probable, as M. Reinach supposed, that these daggers, which are found far apart but are not numerous, are of Helvetian origin.

[2] Diod., v, 30 : ἀντὶ δὲ τοῦ ξίφους σπάδας ἔχουσι μακρὰς σιδηραῖς ἢ χαλκαῖς ἀλύσεσιν ἐξηρτημένας παρὰ τὴν δεξιὰν λαγόνα παρατεταμένας.

those of La Tène II.[1] They were, too, pointless swords, used only for cutting.[2]

These swords are quite different, not only from the straight sword and κοπίς of the Greeks,[3] the iron sword used in Italy before the country was united,[4] and the curved sword which the Iberians are commonly supposed to have used [5] at the time when the Roman army might have adopted it, as it is alleged to have done, but also from the Germanic imitations and adaptations with two cutting edges or one single one.[6]

Heads of spears and javelins [7] are much more frequent in the stations and tombs than daggers and swords. It is difficult to tell spear-heads from javelin-heads, and it is not always possible to distinguish them from those used in other periods and by other civilizations. The oldest resemble the Hallstatt types,[8] being long and shaped like a willow-leaf, sometimes with a not very pronounced midrib. Some are very long, measuring from 16 to 20 inches. In La Tène II spear-heads become broader [9] and assume fanciful shapes. Some are flame-shaped, with sinuous edges, others have crimped edges, and others have pieces cut out of the edge or middle. Some are very finely decorated. The heads of spears and javelins are either socketed or tanged.

One often hears of a javelin which was peculiar to certain Celtic nations, namely the *gaesum* ; its shape is not known.[10]

A recent find of arrow-heads in a Marne burial has settled the much disputed question as to whether the bow was used in Gaul.[11]

---

[1] Déchelette, ii, 3, p. 1123 (cf. figs. 466, 464).
[2] Tac., *Agr.*, xxvi. It should be noted that the late La Tène sword of the British type is shorter than its predecessors, probably in imitation of the Roman *gladius*.
[3] Daremberg and Saglio, **CCCXV**, s.v. " Copis " ; Déchelette, ii, 3, p. 1125.
[4] Déchelette, p. 1137, n. 1.   [5] Ibid., p. 1134.
[6] Ibid., pp. 1126, 1132.   [7] Ibid., pp. 1143 ff.
[8] Ibid., ii, 2, p. 744.
[9] Diod., v, 30, says that the Gauls had spears with heads a cubit long and nearly two spans broad.
[10] A. J. Reinach, " L'Origine du pilum," in **CXXXIX**, 1907, i, p. 424. The Gaulish cemeteries of the Pyrenees and Spain have yielded javelins with long shafts of iron, the σαύνια ὁλοσίδηρα, *soliferrea*, which, according to the ancient writers, the Iberians used (Déchelette, ii, 3, p. 1151). A more frequent type of javelin has a long prolongation of the socket (ibid., p. 1147 ; cf. A. Blanchet, " Note sur le *gæsum*," in **CXL**, 1904, p. 229, on a Roman *denarius* bearing the figure of a Gallic warrior casting a broad-headed javelin).
[11] A. J. Reinach, " La Flèche en Gaule," in **XV**, 1909, p. 14 ; Vouga, **CCCCXCIV**, pl. xiv.

IV

DEFENSIVE ARMOUR

The commonest arm of defence was the shield, which is represented by a great number of bosses and a few plates found at La Tène.[1] For a long time the Celts, like almost all the peoples of Northern and Central Europe, used round targets of wicker or metal.[2] The shield of the Celts of history, Gauls and Irish,[3] was a large, long buckler, oval or oblong in shape, and sometimes fairly narrow. They were recognized by this shield.[4] Except the square shield with double bosses found in the Hallstatt tumulus at Huglfing, near the Würm-See in Bavaria,[5] our oldest evidence for it consists of artistic representations—a sword-sheath of La Tène I, found at Hallstatt (Fig. 19), on which warriors carrying shields are engraved,[6] Italic vases adorned with figures, like the Certosa *situla*,[7] and a stele at Bologna,[8] all dating from just before the great Gallic invasion of Italy. But no trace of a shield has been found in the tombs of La Tène I.[9]

The shields of La Tène II had the " trigger-guard " boss, consisting of a strip of metal rising into an ellipsoidal half-cylinder, the flat wing on each side being riveted to the surface of the shield. Another type had in addition a brace running in a ridge down the axis ; this is the shield of the Dying Gaul (Plate I), and it appears in the monuments commemorating the Galatian wars and in works derived from them. A more useful representation from this point of view is a statue found at Mondragon, in Vaucluse, now

[1] Vouga, op. cit., pls. xv–xviii. Shields similar to those of La Tène have recently been found in Denmark, in a boat of that period (" Oldtidsbaaden fra Als ", in **CCCCI**, pp. 21–3, figs. 11–12). These are Celtic shields adopted by the Germans.

[2] On these shields, see Déchelette, ii, 3, pp. 1167 ff.

[3] Joyce, **CCCCXXXIV**, p. 124. This is the shield to which the Irish word *sciath* and Welsh *ysgwyd* are applied.

[4] In the reliefs of Osuna, in which warriors appear, some bearing round targets and others large oblong shields, the latter represent Gauls (P. Paris and A. Engel, " Une Forteresse ibérique à Osuna," in **CXIII**, xiii). The auxiliary at Borgo San Dalmazzo is shown to be a Ligurian by his target.

[5] Déchelette, ii, 2, p. 719 ; Naue, **CCCCII**, pp. 46, 100, pl. xv ; id., in **CXXXIX**, 1895, 2, p. 55.

[6] Déchelette, ii, 2, p. 770, fig. 297.

[7] Hoernes, **CCCXXXIX**, p. xxxii.

[8] **CVI**, ix (1901), p. 56 ; cf. Grenier, **DXXIX**, pp. 455 ff.

[9] Déchelette, ii, 3, p. 1167.

WARRIOR FROM MONDRAGON
Avignon Museum

[face p. 92

at Avignon (Plate II).[1] This shows that the shield of
La Tène II must have been still in use at the time of the
Roman conquest. Most of the bosses found in the trenches
at Alesia are of this form.[2]

But a new type had been introduced, with a conical boss,
attached to the surface by a circle of metal, rivetted on.
This is represented on the arch at Orange,[3] on an altar found
at Nîmes,[4] and in the statue of a Gallic chieftain found at
Vachères (Basses-Alpes) (Plate III).[5] It has lately been
put forward that these bosses should be regarded as
Germanic, because the Germans adopted and developed
them.[6] Cæsar's German cavalry are supposed to have left
some at Alesia. It is more likely that the Gauls copied them
from the armament of the Romans, which they readily
imitated, than from the Germans, who were still subject to
Gallic influence.

The British shields of the first centuries before and after
Christ still recall that of La Tène II by their pointed oval
boss.[7] The round boss also appeared in this country, but with
the wealth of decoration peculiar to British art.[8]

These Gallic shields were richly ornamented and bore
emblems [9] ; for example, those represented on the arch at
Orange and that found in the River Witham with the emblem
of a boar. The Gauls were organized in clans, and clans have
always had their own colours and emblems. The Scottish
clans still have colours ; those of the other Celts must have
had them once.

The rank and file wore no breast-plate. It is part of the
gossip of ancient history that the Gauls fought stark naked.[10]
The Gauls of the East, however, adopted the Greek breast-

---

[1] Espérandieu, **CCCXXV**, No. 271 ; cf. the frieze at Nîmes, ibid.
[2] Déchelette, ii, 3, p. 1172 ; S. Reinach, **CCCLXXIII**, ii, p. 121. For
contemporary finds in Germany, see **CLX**, 1897, p. 348 ; 1899, p. 400 (grave
at Weisenau, peat-bog at Mainz).
[3] S. Reinach, op. cit., i, p. 45, fig. 36 ; cf. id., in **CXXXIX**, 1889, i, p. 201.
[4] Espérandieu, op. cit., i, No. 431.
[5] Ibid., No. 35.
[6] M. Jahn, in **LXXXV**, 1913, p. 75.
[7] Déchelette, ii, 3, p. 1175 ; **CCCLXXXIV**, pp. 104–6, figs. 114–115 ;
Kemble, **CCCL**, pl. xiv, 1 (shield from the R. Witham).
[8] Déchelette, p. 1176 ; **CCCLXXXIV**, frontispiece ; Kemble, **CCCL**,
pl. xv, 1.
[9] Diod., v, 30 ; Livy, vii, 10, etc. ; Dottin, **CCCXXII**, p. 213 ; Déchelette,
p. 1174 ; Joyce, **CCCCXXXIV**, i, pp. 127 ff.
[10] Diod., loc. cit.

plate.[1] The leaders wore it.[2] What is more, ancient Celtic had a word for it—Irish *bruinne*, French *broigne*. It can be seen on trophies and some other monuments. The ancients mention coats of mail.[3] Varro says that these were invented by the Gauls,[4] and their skill in metal-work makes this likely, but only late fragments of them are known.[5] The Vachères statue (Plate III) shows that these coats of mail had broad shoulder-pieces of the Greek type. Breast-pieces of scales are represented on the arch at Orange, and fragments of them have been found at La Tène.[6]

One usually thinks of the Gauls in helmets with plumes and horns. The arch at Orange shows these,[7] but only one actual specimen exists, and it is not like them. It is a bronze helm found in the Thames at Waterloo Bridge (Fig. 4, No. 4),[8] and consists of a plain metal cap with two conical horns. The helmets represented on the Gundestrup cauldron have analogies with this specimen.[9]

Most of the Gaulish helmets of the La Tène period are Italo-Greek helmets, either imported into Celtic countries or copied with the addition of elaborate Celtic decoration. The finest was found at Amfreville-sous-les-Monts (Eure).[10] It is covered with bands of ornament, some in embossed gold and the others inlaid with enamel. The decoration includes palmettes, more or less modified, at the level of the chin-strap, and a band of triskeles, standing for a vine-tendril motive (Fig. 4, No. 2). These helmets consisted of a head-piece of varying height, with a very short neck-guard and cheek-pieces which are often missing, but must always have been of the triangular type.[11] Sometimes the

[1] Lucian, *Antioch.*, 8. The Galatians who fought against Antiochos Soter wore breast-plates of bronze.
[2] Plut., *Marcel.*, 7, 8 ; *Cæs.*, 27.
[3] Diod., loc. cit.
[4] *De Lingua Lat.*, v, 24, 116.
[5] De Bonstetten, **CCCCLXVIII**, p. 3, n. 2.
[6] Vouga, **CCCCXCIV**, col. 57.
[7] Déchelette, pp. 1156 ff. ; monument of the Julii at St.-Rémy (Espérandieu, **CCCXXV**, i, p. 93) ; relief from La Brague (ibid., i, p. 31) ; trophy in the Vatican (Déchelette, p. 1157) ; bronze in the Berlin Museum (Schumacher, **CCCCX**, fig. 5).
[8] **CCCLXXXIV**, p. 107, fig. 116.
[9] C. Jullian, in **CXXXIV**, 1908, pls. 1–10.
[10] Déchelette, p. 1164 ; *Gaz. archéol.*, 1883, pl. 53 ; Coutil, *Le Casque d'Amfreville*, pp. 2 ff.
[11] Déchelette, p. 1161.

FIG. 3.   Iron Gallic Helmets of La Tène III.   (Déchelette, ii, 3, fig. 491.)
1, *Oppidum* of l'Hermitage near Agen.   2, Alise-Ste.-Reine, Côte d'Or.

FIG. 4.   Celtic Helmets of La Tène.   (Déchelette, ii, 3.)   1, Berru, Marne.
2, Amfreville-sous-les-Monts, Eure.   3, La Gorge-Meillet, Marne (fig. 490).
4, Bed of the Thames (fig. 487).

head-piece was of a plain spherical shape, and sometimes it rose to a cone, with a knob on the top. These helmets with a terminal knob grew longer and were developed into a particular type of which the cemeteries of the Marne furnish some examples. The finest specimens, those of La Gorge-Meillet and Berru (Fig. 4, Nos. 1, 3), were adorned with studs of coral.[1]

The Gauls had a helmet of another kind, having a spherical head-piece round which ran a line in relief, with a concave band below it, from which the rim spread out, and asymmetrical cheek-pieces like those of the Roman helmet (Fig. 3). This helmet and its cheek-pieces have been found in the circum-vallations of Alesia. It is the helmet of La Tène III,[2] and it is also an Italic helmet ; indeed, it is derived from bronze Italic models which are earlier than those from which the preceding Celtic types were copied, namely the great Hallstatt helmet with a double crest or its variant with a plain ridge.[3]

In fact, in the La Tène period as before, the helmets of Central Europe were always importations or copies. It must have been very difficult in the Gallic Wars to tell the helmet of a legionary from that of a Gaul. Moreover, helmets were rare. Most warriors fought bare-headed or in leather caps.[4]

V

ORNAMENTS AND ACCESSORIES OF DRESS

Brooches.—The Gauls were fond of ornament.[5] The finds of the La Tène period show this, although almost all the gold is gone and little but the copper remains of their jewellery. They made delightful things out of the hooks of their belts and the pins with which they fastened their

[1] Ibid., p. 1163. A helmet of the Berru type is shown on the Pergamon trophy (S. Reinach, s.v. " Galea " in Daremberg and Saglio).
[2] Déchelette, pp. 1165–6.
[3] The statuette of a warrior found in the necropolis of Idria in Istria wears a helmet of this type (Szombathy, in CIV, 1901, p. 6, fig. 9). Others have been found in that of Giubiasco. Gallic warriors were not all equally up-to-date in their armour, and one may occasionally have seen, as in the romances of chivalry, dinted old armour and, doubtless, ancient swords of forefathers.
[4] But all the warriors on the Gundestrup cauldron seem to have helmets.
[5] Diod., v, 27.

WARRIOR FROM VACHÈRES
Avignon Museum

[*face p.* 96

cloaks (*sagum*).[1] Their *fibulæ* or brooches are of an originality and variety which make them especially instructive for deciding questions of date and race.

The La Tène brooch is derived from the Hallstatt brooch which immediately preceded it. This latter had a very arched bow, which tended to become slenderer than in the old types. The foot had grown much longer, and had a knob which kept the catch pinched together. The spring, formed of only a few coils, was on one side of the bow only.[2] At the very end of the Hallstatt period the spring had grown longer ; it had been made to coil on both sides of the bow, and, at once leaping to the extreme of the fashion, was made so long that the brooch looked like a cross-bow.[3] At the same time the foot had been curved back, first slightly and then at a right angle. Such is the type named after the Certosa (Charterhouse), near Bologna (Fig. 5, Nos. 1–2), and it seems to be the point from which the La Tène brooches started. The Certosa brooch seems to have been native to Italy.[4] That of La Tène originated in a country which was in frequent communication with Northern Italy and was influenced by the fashions prevailing there.

The oldest La Tène brooches often have a highly arched bow. The foot is sometimes slightly turned up, and sometimes tends to curl back to the bow. There is a great variety of shapes. The makers experimented, and displayed ingenuity.[5]

Among the brooches with a slightly raised foot some have a fairly thick bow, moulded in quaint reliefs, the chief element in which is a human head. The knob is in the shape of a head (Fig. 5, No. 5). In some cases the decoration is carried beyond the head of the bow over the spring, on a broad tongue (Fig. 5, No. 7). Other brooches, of the same early period, have a curling-up piece on the head of the bow, and

---

[1] Sometimes brooches are found in pairs, joined together by a chain. In this case they fastened a cloak which hung over the shoulders and left the chest bare.

[2] Déchelette, ii, 2, p. 847.

[3] Ibid., p. 849.

[4] Ibid., p. 848.

[5] Ibid., ii, 3, pp. 1247 ff. ; Viollier, CCCCXC, pls. iv, v, xi. All these brooches belong to La Tène A. Recently M. Viollier has selected them, with others of a simpler form, as characteristic of a first subdivision of La Tène I. P. Reinecke, " Fibeln der La Tène Zeit aus der süd- und norddeutschen Zone," in CCCXCIX, v, pl. xx ; Beltz, in CLXIX, 1911, p. 665.

this portion and the turned-up foot become absolutely symmetrical. Sometimes these ends are shaped like the heads of birds (Fig. 5, No. 6).

Among the brooches whose foot turns back to the bow there is a whole series in which it has the form of a hollow

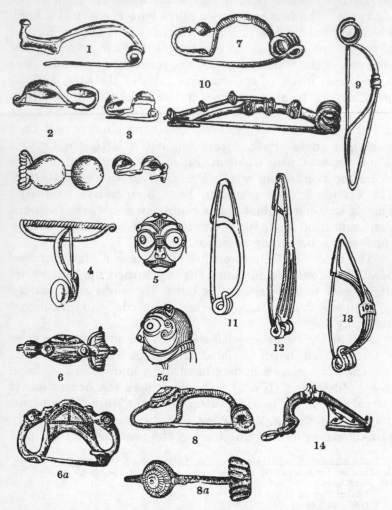

FIG. 5. Brooches. (1–13 from Déchelette, ii.) 1–3, Certosa, Italy (figs. 348, 350). 4, Heiltz-l'Évêque, Marne (fig. 350). 5, 5a, Parsberg, Upper Palatinate. 6, Nierstein, Rheinhessen. 7, Ciry-Salsogne, Aisne. 8–9, Vevey, Switzerland (fig. 533). 10, Dühren, Baden (fig. 535). 11–12, Stradonitz (fig. 537). 13, Puech de Buzeins, Aveyron (fig. 538). 14, Backworth (B.M. *Guide* to the Iron Age, fig. 102).

kettle-drum. The main part of the bow is broadened so as to form the same shape.

After these there comes a type with a spring formed of only a few spirals and a thick depressed bow, adorned with motives in relief. The foot ends in a broad disc set with coral (Fig. 5, No. 8).

The brooches which come next are simpler. The foot ends in a complicated knob, which recalls the birds' heads mentioned above, and the spring generally has one more coil.

So much for the brooches of the first La Tène period. In the second period the foot comes closer to the bow, until at last it is attached to it by a ring. This ring is at first near the centre of the bow, and then it shifts towards the head. The knob is at first recognizable, and then ceases to be. Both bow and foot have more than one knob. At the same time, the spring tends to become longer. At this date brooches of iron and also of silver are made (Fig. 5, Nos. 9, 10).

As time goes on the brooch of La Tène II comes to receive its shape in the casting. The bow and the turned-back foot are made in one open-work piece (Fig. 5, Nos. 11, 12). This type continued to be in use after the Roman conquest of Gaul, at which time it presented a great number of varieties. The La Tène II brooch was also developed in a form which is fairly easy to recognize, in which the connecting ring comes close to the head of the bow and the latter is surrounded by the wire of the spring (Fig. 5, No. 13).[1]

The succession of types was the same in Britain. There it continued in various kinds of brooch, differing from the Roman brooches in the style of their decoration (Fig. 5, No. 14).

In the family tree of the brooches we find occasional " sports "—disc-shaped brooches,[2] the earliest of which are the kettle-drum brooches, in which the whole mechanism is covered by the drum-shaped bow, and the ring-brooches of the Pyrenean and Iberian stations, which are mounted on a ring passing through the head and the foot.[3]

Torques.—After the brooch the torque, or collar, is the

---

[1] Almgren, " Fibules d'Alésia et de Bibracte, deux dates fixes dans l'histoire de la fibule," in **CLXXXV**, p. 241.

[2] Déchelette, ii, 3, p. 1251 ; Kropp, **CCCXCVIII**, p. 16 (a brooch found at Ranis).

[3] Déchelette, p. 1269.

most characteristic article of Gallic adornment and that
which presents the greatest number of classified and dated
varieties. *Torques* is the name which the Latins gave to it,
because it was often made of a twisted strip of metal, with
very sharp edges. The Greeks have preserved the Celtic
name for it in the form μανιάκης.[1] Irish *muince*, Old Welsh
minci (modern *mynci*) " collar ", may come from the same
root. The torque is not peculiar to the civilization of La Tène.
At the end of the Bronze Age magnificent gold torques with
hooked ends were made in England.[2] But in Western Europe
the torque was still rare in the Hallstatt period, and came
into general use immediately afterwards.

Perhaps it was not merely an adornment. We have
figures of Gaulish gods, holding a torque in the hand and
apparently elevating it ritually (Fig. 7, No. 1). Another
figure of one of these gods, in Paris, bears a torque on his
horns.[3] It was an ornament with which, it seems, representations of the gods had to be provided. It was even added
to the figures of Roman gods.[4] It was an offering. Quintilian
tells us that the Gauls offered to Augustus, who was a god,
a gold torque weighing a hundred pounds.[5] On an altar
dedicated to Tiberius, found in Paris, we see armed Gauls
bearing a huge circle or hoop before a seated personage.[6]
Perhaps this was a torque of the kind.

Except in three instances,[7] torques have been found only
in the graves of women.[8] On the other hand, the monuments
regularly show them on the necks of men, and the whole of
written tradition, Irish included,[9] confirms their evidence.
The Gauls who invaded Italy may have worn it already, if
we are to believe the story of Manlius Torquatus,[10] and their
successors always wore it.[11] There may be differences of
race ; there are certainly differences of date. The torques

---

[1] Polyb., ii, 31 ; cf. Dottin, **CXCVI**, p. 269.
[2] E. Toulmin Nicolle, in **XLVI**, 1912. Cf. Déchelette, ii, 1, p. 316.
[3] Espérandieu, **CCCXXV**, No. 3653.
[4] The Hypnos in the Besançon Museum (S. Reinach, **CCCLXXII**, fig. 102).
[5] vi, 3, 79.
[6] The monument of the Nautæ (Espérandieu, op. cit., No. 3132).
[7] Déchelette, ii, 3, p. 1209 ; Brizio, in **CVI**, i, ix (1901), pp. 724 ff.
[8] Déchelette, loc. cit.
[9] *Táin Bó Chuailgné*, xxii ; **CXL**, 1910, p. 10 ; Joyce, **CCCCXXXIV**, i,
p. 99.
[10] D'Arbois, **CCXLVIII**, xii, p. 126 ; cf. Déchelette, p. 1210.
[11] Déchelette, p. 1208 ; Armstrong, *Celts*, 24.

found in female burials date from La Tène I ; the monuments are of La Tène II. The fashion had changed. Women ceased to wear the collar of rigid metal ; men, and perhaps only the chieftains, wore it.[1]

The earliest torques are very simple, some being formed of a hollow tube of bronze bent into a hoop, and others of a solid rod, plain or twisted, and ending in hooks for the

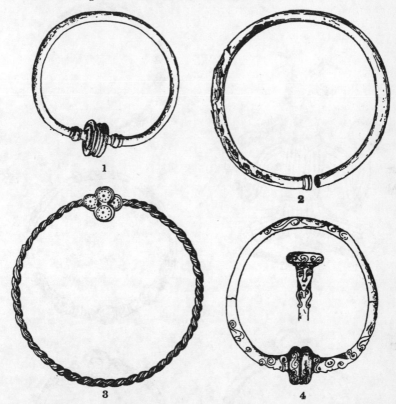

Fig. 6. Torques. (Déchelette, ii, 3, fig. 515.) 1, Bussy-le-Château, Marne. 2, Schirrhein, Alsace. 3, Étrechy, Marne. 4, Courtisols.

clasp or in buffers (Fig. 6, Nos. 1, 2). These are attributed to the beginning of the first period. Gradually the ornamentation grew richer. There were buffer-torques,

[1] This is the explanation of Déchelette, with which I fully agree. He adds (p. 1210) that the Celts of the Danube took the practice of wearing the torque as a national emblem from the Scythian chiefs. He suggests that they even imported Scythian torques, or at least models ; see below.

the hoop of which was thick with relief decoration (Fig. 6, No. 1), sometimes including human faces (Fig. 6, No. 4). Then there was a whole series of torques, completely closed or having a movable segment, the ornament on which was similar, but was distributed symmetrically in three groups (Fig. 7, Nos. 2, 4) or asymmetrically on one part of the hoop

FIG. 7. Torques. (2–5 from Déchelette, fig. 516.) 1, Horned God on the Gundestrup Cauldron, elevating the Torque (*Mémoires de la Soc. des Antiquaires de France*, 1913, p. 259). 2, Aube. 3, Schlettstadt, Alsace. 4, Pleurs, Marne. 5, Marne.

only. This decoration consisted of discs set with coral
alternating with bosses adorned with spirals. In some cases
it might be open-work and consist of separate pieces fixed
on to the collar (Fig. 7, Nos. 3, 5).[1]

From La Tène II we have a few torques, such as the
plain wire type with the ends bent into an S. The torques
which warriors were beginning to wear as badges were of
precious material, gold,[2] and have therefore usually disappeared. There is, however, a group of torques of this date,
most of them in the Toulouse Museum and found in that
neighbourhood,[3] with a voluminous decoration of bosses
bearing scroll-work distributed all round the hoop or beside
the terminal buffers. The buffers were fastened together by
T-shaped tenons. A torque of this family has been found in
Hungary, at Herczeg-Marok (near Baranya),[4] and two others,
with less violent decoration, come from Clonmacnoise and
Broighter in Ireland.[5]

From La Tene III we have thick torques with
a quadrangular section, ending in large knobs.[6]

Bracelets.—It is not always easy to distinguish La Tène
bracelets from those of the preceding period.[7] But there are
quite special types, and these can be classified chronologically.
Their classification follows that of the torques, and they have
the same characteristics.[8]

Like the torques of the tombs of the Marne, bracelets
were almost exclusively worn by women. But, like the
torques, they were sometimes worn by men, especially
chieftains. In that case they were valuable objects, like the
gold bracelet found on the arm of the warrior buried in the
grave at La Gorge-Meillet.

Corresponding to the simple early torques, there is a series

[1] Déchelette, ii, 4, pp. 1211 ff.
[2] Id., ii, 3, p. 1208 ; Roget de Belloguet, **CCCLXXIX**, iii, p. 89 ; Dottin,
CCCXXII, p. 133 ; S. Reinach, s.v. " Torques ", in **CCCXV**.
[3] At Cordes, Montans, and Lasgraïsses in Tarn, Fenouillet in Hte.-Garonne
(Déchelette, ii, 3, pp. 1339 ff.), and Serviès-en-Val in Aude (P. J. Cros, in
XCI, iv, p. 143).
[4] Costa de Beauregard, in **LX**, Autun, 1907, p. 826 ; Coffey, **CCCCXXVIII**,
p. 80, pl. ix ; Sir A. Evans, in **XVII**, 1897, p. 400.
[5] Déchelette, pp. 1208, n. 1, 1217.
[6] **CLXIX**, 1904, pp. 54 ff. ; analogies between the bracelets and rings of
La Tène and the earlier forms of the Caucasus and Hungary.
[7] Déchelette, pp. 1218–1230 ; Viollier, in **CLXXX** ; Brizio, in **CVI**, 1901,
p. 30.
[8] Heierli, in **XLVIII**, iv, pp. 126, 131, 137.

of bracelets found in the same tombs—tubular bracelets, open or closed, bracelets formed of a sharp-edged rod ending in knobs, ribbed bracelets, and others with slight bosses (Fig. 8, Nos. 1, 2).[1]

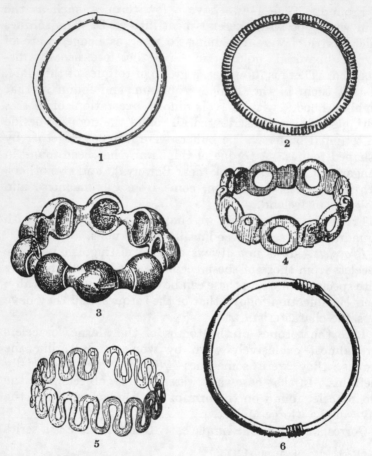

FIG. 8.   Bracelets. (Déchelette, ii, 3.) 1, Marson, Marne. 2, Caranda, Aisne. 3, Bydžov Novy, Bohemia (fig. 517). 4, St. Rémy-sur-Bussy, Marne. 5, Marne (fig. 519). 6, Stradonitz (fig. 520).

Another series corresponds to the second series of torques and presents many of the same characteristics. The bosses become larger, they are arranged in groups, and they have additional S-shaped ornamentation.

[1] Allen, CCXCVIII, p. 113 ; Anderson, CCCCXIV, p. 141.

When the torque disappears the bracelet continues to develop. It is now that the bracelets formed of hollow semi-ovoid bosses with *appliqué* or relief ornamentation appear. Some of these are fairly heavy, having the clasp made in a separate piece. There are also types containing open-work and others formed of an undulating wire (Fig. 8, Nos. 3–5).

All this series belongs to the second period of La Tène.

In the third period a type appears which lasted long afterwards. This consists of a plain wire with the ends twisted round each other and some way along the hoop. At the same time bronze comes to be used less frequently in the making of bracelets. Glass bracelets become more numerous, especially in Switzerland. Some are of white or transparent glass; others of blue glass, sometimes relieved with yellow or white enamel. They are of native make, or, at least, come from Cisalpine Gaul (Fig. 9, Nos. 1–3). The Gauls also made use of Kimmeridge shale, or lignite, but the lignite bracelets of the La Tène period are narrower than the Hallstatt lignite bracelets of barrel form.

At the end of the development of La Tène civilization heavy bronze bracelets are found in Scotland, which are adorned with reliefs or enamels and look as if they were made of three bracelets stuck together.[1]

Belts.[2]—The belts with iron chains of which I have spoken date from La Tène II. Before that time the Gauls wore belts of leather or cloth with clasps.

These clasps are derived from Hallstatt types, and keep their general form. They consist of a metal tongue, usually not decorated, sewn on to the material, and one or two cross-bars, forming tags, attached to it. The hook springs from a plate of bronze, or iron, or even gold, attached to the last bar. It is triangular, like that of the Hallstatt clasp, but it often has rich open-work ornamentation, derived from the Greek palmette or composed of confronted animals (Fig. 9, Nos. 6, 7).

The later we come down the more massive these hooks become, just like the torques and the bracelets. There are balls and bosses and reliefs (Fig. 9, No. 4); and finally, at the end of the La Tène period, they are simplified into thick rings. In this last type the hook is at the end of a triangular

---

[1] Déchelette, ii, 3, pp. 1230 ff.   [2] Ibid., pp. 1263–1270.

piece, mounted on a ring which is supported by two crescents (Fig. 9, No. 6), or it is concealed under a palmette, the base of which is an oblong slot (Fig. 9, No. 5). Belt-hooks are found in the graves of both men and women.

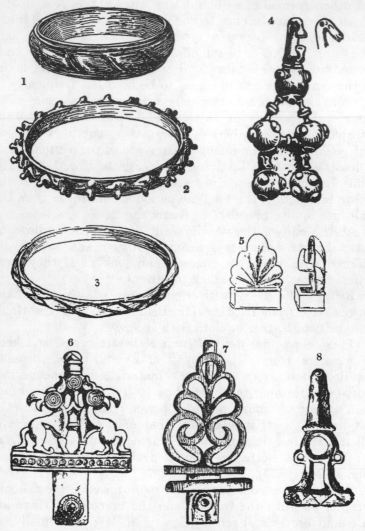

FIG. 9. Bracelets and Belt-clasps. (Déchelette, ii, 3.) 1, Val d'Aosta. 2-3, Münsingen, Switzerland (fig. 580). 4, Gröbern, Saxony (fig. 526). 5, Stradonitz (fig. 528). 6, Somme-Bionne, Marne. 7, La Motte-St.-Valentin, Hte.-Marne (fig. 524). 8, Stradonitz (fig. 527).

Hooks of this kind are found on very beautiful chain-belts of bronze which women wore at the end of La Tène II. These are made of circular rings or of rings alternating with ornamented oblong bars, and have pendants hanging from them.

Various Objects.—To obtain a complete picture of Gaulish adornment in the La Tène period we must note, in addition

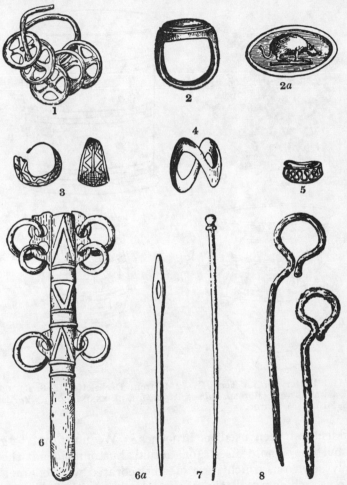

Fig. 10. Various Objects. (1–7 from Déchelette, ii, 3.) 1, Naix, Meuse (fig. 560). 2, Stradonitz (fig. 546). 3, Étrechy, Marne (fig. 542). 4, Steinhausen, Switzerland (fig. 544). 5, Münsingen (fig. 545). 6, 6a, La Tène (fig. 559). 7, La Motte-St.-Valentin, Hte.-Marne (fig. 541). 8, Bonchester Hill (*Proc. Soc. Antiq. Scotland*, xliv, p. 235).

to the brooches, torques, bracelets, and belts, the earrings of bronze and of gold, shaped like boats,[1] and the rings, most of which are small bracelets (Fig. 10, Nos. 3, 5).[2] In La Tène III seal-rings appear (Fig. 10, No. 2). These were borrowed from Italy and Greece. Some rings have a bent form (Fig. 10, No. 4). But we also have silver rings with this saddle-shaped bend, which must have gone on the

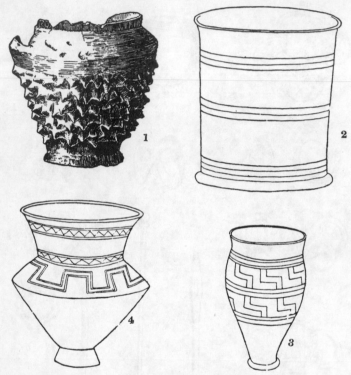

FIG. 11. Pottery of La Tène I. (2–4 from Déchelette, ii, 3, fig. 659.) 1, Caranda vase (Moreau, *Album Caranda*, i, pl. xxxix, fig. 1). 2, Aisne. 3, Aisne. 4, Marne.

shoulder and been used as brooches.[3] We must not forget the buttons, those used for actual buttoning and those merely sewn on, which were often decorated with enamel [4]; the pins, which recall the Hallstatt pins, with button and swan's neck heads (Fig. 10, Nos. 8, 9), the buckles, the

[1] Ibid., p. 1264.   [2] Ibid., p. 1244.   [3] Ibid.   [4] Ibid., p. 1289.

needle-cases (Fig. 10, No. 6),[1] the mirrors,[2] the combs,[3] and the amulets of all kinds, especially those consisting of wheels (Fig. 10, No. 1).

VI

POTTERY [4]

The pottery of La Tène, although unequally distributed,[5] is very abundant and varied, and includes many forms which certainly show their origin, but also show how freely the people of that time made use of the heritage of the past.

The first types which strike one in a collection of vases from the cemeteries of the Marne are those with straight sides and angular shoulders. These " carinated " vases, as they are called, have necks either high or low. They belong to the first period (La Tène I), as do the beaker-shaped vases, sometimes small and sometimes very large, and others which are cylindrical (Fig. 11, Nos. 1–4).

These vases are of a fairly fine paste, covered with a brown or blackish burnished slip. They are engraved with patterns of straight lines, filled with red or white paint.

Some of the short-necked vases have the belly covered with a decoration like the heads of nails.[6] These curious vessels look as if they were made of metal, and, indeed, they are copied from metal originals.

The carinated vases are derived from the Italic pails (*situlæ*) of riveted bronze, which are frequent in Hallstatt tombs (Fig. 12, No. 1).[7] The cylindrical vases are modelled on the cordoned buckets known as *ciste a cordoni*, and their incised decoration recalls the cordons of the buckets.[8] Nor

---

[1] Ibid., pp. 1286–9. [2] Ibid., pp. 1284–6. [3] Ibid., pp. 1292 ff.

[4] Ibid., pp. 1258 ff.; Morel, **CCCCLXXXIV**; Moreau, **CCCCLXXXIII**.

[5] It is completely absent in Central and Southern Gaul (Déchelette, op. cit., ii, 3, p. 1459) and at La Tène (Vouga, **CCCCXCIV**, 26–8). It is very abundant in the Marne cemeteries, especially for the first period. In the Cisalpine cemeteries Italic pottery to a great extent took the place of the native ware.

[6] Déchelette, ii, 3, p. 1467. Similar vases are found in the Cisalpine cemeteries. Cf. Schumacher, in **CCCXCIX**, v, pl. lxx, 1320.

[7] There are many examples of similar imitations in the earlier Italian pottery.

[8] The handles even of late buckets were reproduced in earthenware. Cf. vases from the tumuli of the plateau of Ger (Pothier, p. 57, fig. 11).

are these the only La Tène vases derived from metal prototypes. A vase found at St. Pol de Léon bears, no doubt in an exaggerated form, the palmette which adorns the junction-point of the handle in the corresponding Italic

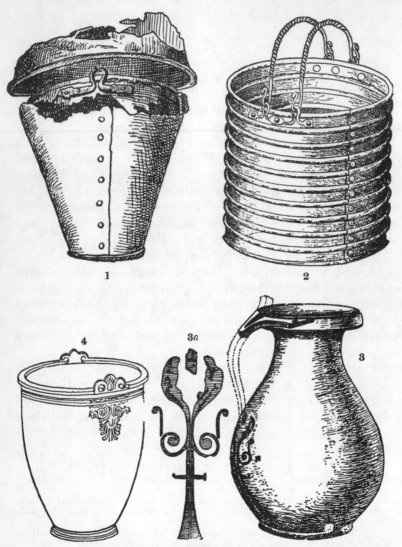

FIG. 12. Metal Prototypes of La Tène Pottery. (Déchelette, ii, 3.) 1, Pail from Plougoumelen, Morbihan (fig. 292). 2, Cordoned bucket from Reuilly, Loiret (fig. 299). 3, 3a, Aylesford, Kent (fig. 652). 4, Montefortino (fig. 646).

buckets (Fig. 13) ; compare, too, the ornament on the metal jug from Aylesford (Fig. 12, Nos. 3, 3a). Another, from Lann-Tinikeii, in the commune of Plœmeur, in Finistère,

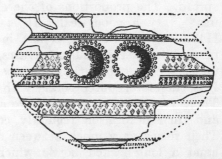

FIG. 13.   Vase from Saint-Pol-de-Léon. (Déchelette, ii, 3, fig. 663.)

FIG. 14.   Vase from Lann-Tinikeii, Morbihan. (Déchelette, ii, 3, fig. 665.)

is an imitation of a vessel made of riveted metal bands (Fig. 14). Others, by their incised decoration of *pointillé* arches and large dots, recall the Veneto-Illyrian bronzes.[2]   There are

FIG. 15.   Vase from Mané-Roullarde, Morbihan.   (Déchelette, ii, 3, fig. 666.)

not many vases copied from prototypes in riveted metal-work in Gallic countries, but some have been found, for example, in Brittany (Fig. 15).   There the cordoned bucket

[1] Déchelette, **CCCCLXXXVIII**, ii, 3, p. 1468 ; Du Chatellier, **CCCCLXXI**, pl. xiv, 1, 2 ; pl. xvi, 1.
[2] Reinecke, **CCCXCIX**, p. 24.

produced local imitations richly decorated (Figs. 15, 16, No. 4). While the prototype of the carinated vases has not yet been discovered among Celtic remains, buckets of cast metal are fairly frequent.

The tombs of the Marne have yielded many examples of a baluster-shaped type of vase which is much more widespread. The proportions of the elements in this " pedestal urn " vary a good deal. It is derived from the typical Hallstatt vase in two portions ; indeed, the most remarkable peculiarity of the Hallstatt vases, the sagging of the belly under the weight of the upper part, can still be seen in it. It is, therefore, contemporary with the beginnings of La Tène. These vases almost always have a moulding round the foot and their decoration regularly contains cordons in relief.[1] Their forms vary much between two extremes—on the one hand a long-necked bottle which is characteristic of the earliest La Tène sites in South Germany (Fig. 16, No. 1), and, on the other, a kind of jar with a wide mouth surrounded by the same cordon-moulding and a foot which tends to be very simple (Fig. 16, No. 3). In Germany these vases sometimes have an incised decoration which recalls the Hallstatt metal vases (Fig. 16, No. 1a). In France they are often covered with a very broad curvilinear pattern, painted in brown on red or incised.[2]

The pottery of the second La Tène period seems to be especially rich in vases of this family,[3] and they continue into the third period.[4] Either they are monochrome, and plainly decorated with their relief cordons or lustrous lines put on with the burnishing point, or they are painted with red or brown motives on a smooth white ground (Fig. 17, Nos. 4, 5, 8).

This ware is more varied than the preceding one, because it is not only a funerary ware. It comprises all the usual crockery, great jars for provisions, plates, vases with handles, etc. Many are adorned with hatchings or dots, put on with the punch or the comb (Fig. 17, Nos. 1–3). Most of the pottery

[1] These cordons are sometimes distributed down the whole body of the vase, dividing it into regular bands as in the pottery of the Venetian area.
[2] Cf. vases of the Glastonbury type (Déchelette, ii, 3, p. 1473 ; CCCLXXXIV, p. 137).
[3] Déchelette, pp. 1460 ff., 1480 ff.
[4] Ibid., pp. 1481 ff. ; Laville, " Sépultures marniennes de Valenton (Seine-et-Oise)," in XLI, 1910, p. 571.

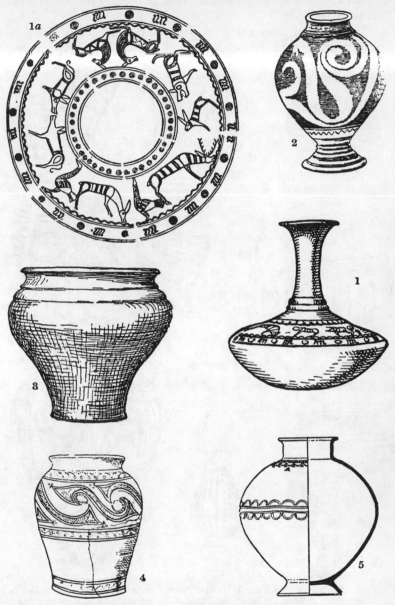

Fig. 16. Pottery of the Marne, Brittany, and Central Europe. (Déchelette, ii, 3.) 1, 1a, Matzhausen, Upper Palatinate (figs. 671–2). 2, Beine, Marne (fig. 660). 3, Manching, Upper Bavaria (fig. 675). 4, Plouhinec, Finistère (fig. 663). 5, Praunheim, Hessen-Nassau (fig. 673).

at Mont Beuvray is like this, but painted pottery is also plentiful there.[1]

The painted decoration of pottery develops especially in the area of the southern expansion of the La Tène civilization,

FIG. 17. Pottery of La Tène III. (1–7 from Déchelette, ii, 3.) 1–3, Mont-Beuvray (fig. 677). 4, Montans, Tarn. 5, Lezoux, Puy-de-Dôme (fig. 683). 6, Shoebury, Essex (fig. 681). 7, Stradonitz (fig. 677). 8, Celles (Pagès-Allary, in *l'Anthropologie*, 1903, p. 402).

[1] Déchelette, pp. 1485 ff.

in the south of Gaul and in Spain.   In the south of Gaul
very curious vases were manufactured, with a flower or fruit
ornament on a slip.[1]   But painted ware spread all over
Gaul, and was manufactured at more than one place.[2]
Sometimes its decoration includes relief friezes which were
kept up in the pottery of the Empire.[3]

Arms, ornaments, and vases—that is what constitutes the
main part of the furniture of the graves of La Tène.   It is
also what constitutes most of the finds made in the dwelling-
places.   It does not, of course, represent the whole material
side of the civilization of the period.

Many remains of vehicles have been found.   The Gauls
had a reputation as cartwrights.   There are also many
portions of harness and horse-trappings, the interest of which
for this chapter lies not in their form but in their decoration.
Fire-dogs have been discovered, and keys, and a fair number
of iron tools.

This is not the place to present a systematic picture of
the whole civilization of the Celts and all the things which
they produced or used in the La Tène period, but to point
out those objects and characteristics of objects which allow
us to attribute one or another series of finds to the Celts
or their influence and to date them.   To this end some facts
still remain to be noticed.

VII

DECORATIVE ART

Many of the objects of which we have been speaking are
decorated, and some very richly.   The taste, the style, the
fashion to which they bear witness are expressed, not only

[1] Ibid., pp. 1488 ff. ;   cf. R. Zahn, in **CLXVIII**, 1907, pp. 338 ff. ;   **XX**,
1907, p. 226.   For Galatian sherds with painting on a slip, see Déchelette,
CCCCLXXIII, i, p. 130 ;   Mazaurie, " La Céramique polychrome des Celtes ",
in **CXXXIV**, 1901, p. 82.

[2] Carlier, " Vases peints du Musée archéologique de Genève," in **CXXXIV**,
1908, p. 257 ;   Marteaux and Leroux, **CCCCLXXXIII**, p. 417.   For painted
vases from the Æduan district, see Déchelette, ii, 3, p. 1491 ; Abbé Philippe,
CCCCLXXXVIII, p. 23 ;   Lindenschmit, **CCCXCIX**, i, vi, pl. 6.

[3] Painted La Tène vase with frieze of birds in relief, at Lochenstein,
near Balingen (G. Bersu, in **LXV**, 1924).

in their form, but in characteristic ornament. In particular there is no mistaking the decoration of metal objects of La Tène for that of any other period. Moreover, it is certainly Celtic, for the tradition of it continued in Celtic countries after the conquest of the Continental Celts and was perpetuated in the Christian art of Ireland.[1]

It is purely an ornament of line, in which the zoomorphic

FIG. 18.   Bracelet from Rodenbach, Rhenish Bavaria. (Déchelette, ii, 3, fig. 583.)

elements, human heads, etc., mentioned above, take a predominant place, and indeed these are distorted so as to fit into the linear decorative scheme (Fig. 18).[2] The type of stylization which was the result was quite new in ancient art.

Needless to say, the La Tène decorators often got their effects with less trouble. They had preserved, at least in

[1] Allen, **CCXCVIII,** p. 125 ; Déchelette, ii, 3, pp. 1525–7.
[2] Lindenschmit, op. cit., iii, i, and suppl.

pottery, the rectilinear patterns of Greek frets, chevrons, zigzags, and crosses practised in the preceding period. Metal objects are often adorned with plain ribs and grooves,

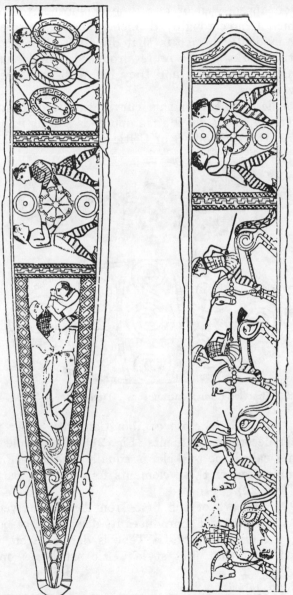

Fig. 19. Sword-scabbard from Hallstatt. (Déchelette, ii, 2, fig. 297.)

and some of them are not always easy to tell at first sight from things made earlier, later, or elsewhere.[1]

But in every series of manufactured objects the decoration approached at one time or another to the ideal type which I have roughly defined. The decorative art of La Tène evidently turned in that direction. The people for whom the works of art were produced found that type satisfying to their taste, and they had a distinct preference for curved lines.

The chief element in this curvilinear decoration is the double volute with a thick stem and ends curling in opposite directions, the symbolic S of Celtic ornament.[2] It is found

FIG. 20.   Bracelet from Montsaugeon.   (Déchelette, ii, 3, fig. 697.)

isolated, and also in close combination with other volutes and other decorative elements (Fig. 21). The triple volute, sometimes called the triskele, is equally frequent (Fig. 20).[3] The combination of these elements forms a rich pattern of curves (Fig. 22).

Just as the art of the first Iron Age is derived from Græco-Asiatic art, and reproduces its decoration of bands of animals, the ornament of La Tène is derived from a later Greek art. Of that first style Celtic art keeps only the

[1] Déchelette, pp. 1505 ff.
[2] Ibid., pp. 1514 ff.
[3] Ibid., p. 1518 ; **CCCLXXXIV**, pp. 17 ff. ; Hœrnes, **CCCXXXIX**, p. 662, figs. 197–8.

confronted animals.[1] The palmette, which is its favourite
motive, is the source of the Celtic volutes.[2] It is certainly the

FIG. 21. Bracelet
from Bologna.
(Déchelette, ii,
3, fig. 519.)

FIG. 22. Triskele-pattern on Gold Plaque
from the Tumulus at Schwarzenbach. (Déchelette, ii, 3, fig. 698.)

Greek palmette, with its long, wide-spreading leaves, first
stiff and then drooping (Fig. 23, No. 1), and not the more
softly curving Egyptian or Oriental palmette which is one

1   2   3   4

FIG. 23. Palmettes. 1, Drooping palmette on a pail from Waldalgesheim
(B.M. *Guide* to the Iron Age, 1925, p. 19, fig. 10). 2, Detail on a torque
from Waldalgesheim (ibid., p. 20, fig. 12). 3, Classical palmette (ibid.,
fig. 13). 4, Stiff palmette on the handle of an oenochoë from Somme-
Bionne (Déchelette, ii, 3, fig. 641).

of the most ancient motives in decorative art.[3] The Celtic
artist broke up the palmette and simplified it (Fig. 23,
Nos. 2, 4). Moreover, he took his inspiration from the two

[1] CCCLXXXIV, p. 17.   [2] Déchelette, pp. 1513 ff.
[3] Montelius, CCCLVII, i, pp. 77 ff.

FIG. 24. Ornament of the Bronze Vase from Saulces-Champenoises, Ardennes.
(Déchelette, ii, 3, fig. 655.)

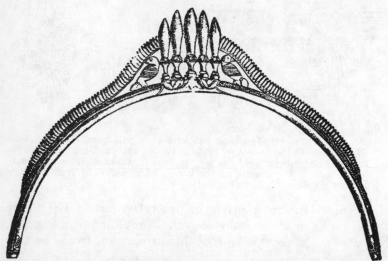

FIG. 25. Torque from Besseringen, Rhineland. (Déchelette, ii, 3, fig. 584.)

types of Greek palmette, that of the sixth century and the classical type (Fig. 23, No. 3).

The Greek palmette is a somewhat complex ornament. It is composed of petals, spreading from a stylized calix represented by volutes. From these volutes spring accessory ornaments—the palmette in bud, the palmette seen sideways on. The palmettes and buds may be enclosed by the network formed by the volutes.

Celtic art took the volutes chiefly and made them into its S decoration and, by combination, its triskeles. It reduced the number of petals of the palmette, which was from nine to eleven, to three. It adopted the profile palmette (Fig. 24), the bud (Fig. 25),[1] and the encircling of the palmette by volutes (Fig. 26). Having

FIG. 26. Disk from Auvers, Seine-et-Oise.
(Déchelette, ii, 3, fig. 694.)

FIG. 27. Sword from Lisnacroghera.
(Déchelette, ii, 3, fig. 469.)

[1] The grouped balusters on the Besseringen torque (CCCXCIX, ii, ii, pl. i) are, in my opinion, palmette-buds, and so are those on the Rodenbach bracelet.

broken up the elements of its models, it spread them out along its sword-scabbards (Fig. 27).

Celtic ornament is incised, or embossed in relief, or cast in relief, or cast and then treated with the engraver. It favours bosses. It also favours very sharp ridges, producing definite shadows. It also favours open-work, and has left

FIG. 28.　Horse-trappings from Somme-Bionne.　(Déchelette, ii, 3, fig. 506.)

very strong and graceful examples of this method in metal (Fig. 28). One at once compares this art to French Gothic art, but there is no transition between them. The execution of this decoration varied much in the course of the period, in the manner indicated in the preceding paragraphs. The ornament of La Tène I is more varied, more mingled with

FIG. 29.　Coral Boss from the Marne.　(S. Reinach, *Catalogue du Musée de Saint-Germain*, ii, p. 245, fig. 133.)

zoomorphic motives, and generally slenderer than that of La Tène II. The art of this period tends to approach to the classical models, imitating, for example, the bands of vine-tendrils, which had hitherto not been attempted.[1] No really local style was produced except in the British Isles.[2]

[1] On the Gundestrup cauldron, for example.
[2] Déchelette, ii, 3, pp. 1526–7; **CCCLXXXIV**, p. 29.

One peculiarity of La Tène art is the use of other materials in the decoration of metal. Two are of especial interest—coral and enamel.[1] The people of this age had at first a marked liking for the red of coral. The coral was set in sunk beds on the surface of an object (Fig. 29), or affixed by small nails or rivets to a support of iron or bronze, as in the brooches adorned with coral knobs. Sometimes the coral was carved.

The objects adorned with coral belong to the first La Tène period. Either taste changed, or supplies were cut off; at a certain date they vanish from Celtic jewellery.[2] Pliny states [3] that the coral-producing countries one day started to send such large quantities of it to India that it became rare in the centres of production. M. Salomon Reinach explains

FIG. 30.   Cross with enamel inlay from La Gorge-Meillet.   (Déchelette, ii, 3, fig. 508.)

that this must have happened after the expedition of Alexander, that is, at the end of the fourth century. It is just at this time that coral disappears from Celtic lands.

Its place was at once taken by enamel. This was a red enamel, the colour of blood, which is described by Philostratos.[4] It seems to have been a Celtic invention. Enamel was at first used as a substitute for coral, and in the same way, being either riveted [5] or fixed in a setting in small solid pieces, while cold (Fig. 30). The fusibility of enamel allowed of greater liberty of treatment. The *champlevé*

---

[1] Déchelette, pp. 1547 ff. ;   Allen, **CCXCVIII**, p. 94.
[2] Déchelette, pp. 1330 ff.
[3] *N.H.*, xxxii, 2 ; S. Reinach, " Le Corail dans l'industrie celtique," in **CXL**, 1899, pp. 24 ff.   [4] *Icones*, i, 28.
[5] This process continued in vogue in Britain after the Roman conquest, as in the Battersea shield (fig. 31, below ; **CCCLXXXIV**, pp. 101 ff.).

process was invented. The enamel was poured hot into sunk beds, which were made larger as time went on. Finally the whole surface to be decorated was covered with enamel and the sunk parts were separated from one another only by a slender net-work of metal. Enamelled decoration of this kind appears on the Amfreville helmet. These different methods were practised during the second La Tène period.[1] Later the Gauls came to use enamel yet more freely. They made objects entirely covered with enamel, held on a grooved ground.[2] They used it in particular for buttons, especially at Mont Beuvray, at Bibracte, where enamellers' workshops have been excavated.

It is not certain whether enamel-work continued without interruption in Gaul after the Roman conquest.[3] In Britain it certainly developed, particularly in adding blues, yellows, and reds to its range of colours.[4] The use of enamel to cover large surfaces is one of the characteristics of the art which developed in Britain while Roman art was taking the place of Celtic in Gaul.

The popularity of enamel did not preclude a liking for glass and a certain skill in making it. I have already spoken of glass bracelets, and many glass necklace-beads have been found.[5] The Celts at first went to Italy for their glass-work, but they soon made their own. Later the Gallo-Romans were remarkably skilful and inventive in this craft.

We have chiefly to do with a purely ornamental art decorating useful articles. The richness of the ornament and the freedom with which it was used makes some of these useful articles real works of art (Fig. 31).[6] But plastic art properly so called is very poor.[7] Nevertheless, it shows a taste and a style of its own. The most remarkable specimen of it that we have, the silver vessel found at Gundestrup in Jutland, outside the Celtic countries,[8] is adorned with divine figures and symbolical scenes which make it an ethnographical document of inestimable value for the history of the Celts (Plate IV).

[1] Déchelette, ii, 3, p. 1549. [2] Ibid., pp. 1551–5. [3] Ibid., p. 1547.
[4] CCCLXXXIV, pl. viii. [5] Déchelette, pp. 1314 ff.
[6] e.g. a plaque from Auvers (Seine-et-Oise), a bracelet from Rodenbach, and the Battersea shield.
[7] Déchelette, ii, 3, pp. 1531–9 ; De Gérin-Ricard, CCCCLXXVI,
[8] Drexel, "Über den Silberkessel von Gundestrup," in LXXIII, 1915, pp. 1–96.

[face p. 124

THE GUNDESTRUP CAULDRON

Denmark (Sophus Muller, *Det store sølvkar fra Gundestrup i Jylland*, frontispiece)

Fig. 31. The Battersea Shield. (B.M. *Guide to the Iron Age*, frontispiece.)

VIII

CHRONOLOGICAL SUMMARY AND CONCLUSIONS

The characteristics of the La Tène periods, including the intermediate period which Herr Reinecke's arguments compel us to take into account, may be summarized as follows :—

La Tène A : Tumulus-tombs, with cremation and with inhumation ; swords like the Hallstatt sword with antennæ ; very varied brooches, closely derived from the Certosa types, and, in particular, kettle-drum brooches.[1]

La Tène I (B) : Inhumations under tumuli and in flat-graves ; swords with curved scabbard-mouth and open-work chape ; brooches with turned-up foot ; torques, except at the end ; pottery like the Hallstatt types or carinated ; coral ornament.[2]

La Tène II (C) : Flat-graves ; cremation is practised again ; tumuli rare ; long swords, without open-work in the chape ; long brooches, with the foot attached to the bow by a ring ; pedestal vases ; enamel decoration.[3]

La Tène III (D) : Cremation ; long swords with blunt point ; scabbards with a straight mouth ; cast brooches ; pedestal vases ; lavish use of enamel.[4]

Each period is represented by typical sites—La Tène A, by the rich tumuli of Bavaria and the Middle Rhine ; La Tène I, by the cemeteries of the Marne ; La Tène II, by the station of La Tène itself ; La Tène III, by Mont Beuvray and the Hradischt of Stradonitz.

This series of periods is conventionally taken to end with the conquest of Gaul. But La Tène civilization lasted longer in Britain and Ireland. We can distinguish a La Tène IV, the Late Celtic of British archæologists, the characteristic of which is the extreme development of the decoration,

---

[1] Reinecke, CCCCVI, pp. 2–6, pl. vi ; id., CCCXCIX, v, p. 50.
[2] Id., CCCCVI, p. 7 ; CCCXLIX, v, pp. 8, 57.
[3] Id., CCCCVI, p. 11 ; CCCXLIX, v, pp. 15, 57 ; Déchelette, ii, 3, p. 931 ; CCCLXXXIV, p. 71.
[4] Reinecke, CCCCVI, p. 13 ; CCCXCIX, v, p. 51 ; Déchelette, ii, 3, pp. 931–2 ; CCCLXXIV, pp. 74, 76 ; XV, 1903, pp. 385 ff. (tumulus at Celles) ; XXXVIII, 1897, pp. 553 ff. (tomb at Cernon-sur-Coole) ; CCCCLXXXIII (Presles, St.-Audebert).

the main features of which we have been considering.[1]
The last heir of that art, which was crossed about the sixth
century with Germanic art, is the art of Ireland of the time
of Charlemagne, with its illuminated manuscripts covered
with twining decoration and its gorgeous gold-work.[2]

The positive dates of the first four of these types of culture
are established, like all positive dates in prehistory, by
reference to the historical civilizations of the Mediterranean,
in virtue of the various contacts which took place between
them and of dated objects which were imported into the
regions which have no written history. The Celts were visited
by traders of Marseilles,[3] and later by others from Italy.[4]
Meanwhile the Gauls had descended at historically known
dates into the peninsulas of the Mediterranean, and the areas
which they occupied varied in a manner which is of great
interest from a chronological point of view.[5]

The extreme terms are supplied by the excavations at the
camp of Château-sur-Salins and those at Mont Beuvray.
At Château, the presence of red and black Attic pottery
similar to that found on the Acropolis among the rubbish
resulting from the burning of 480, gives a date to a fairly
complete series of cross-bow and kettle-drum brooches.
La Tène I brooches, of the earliest type, were found above
this layer.[6] So La Tène A corresponds to the fifth century,
and to the whole length of it. Later Greek vases, such as the
ovoid pail with movable handles, are found with objects of
La Tène I.[7]

The finds from Mont Beuvray give another term,
for the site was abandoned for that of Autun in the year
5 B.C. The series of coins stops at this date, which may be
taken as the final date of La Tène III.[8]

[1] Déchelette, ii, 3, pp. 934, 1525–7.
[2] Allen, CCXCVIII, pp. 163 ff.
[3] List of Greek vases found in La Tène burials, in Déchelette, pp. 933–4 ;
list of objects of Greek, Italo-Greek, or Etruscan manufacture found north
of the Alps, ibid., pp. 1599–1607.
[4] Vases of the potter Aco, ibid., p. 1579.
[5] See above, pp. 1 ff.
[6] M. Piroutet and Déchelette, "Découverte de vases grecs dans un
oppidum hallstattien du Jura," in CXXXIX, 1909, i, pp. 183, 201 ; Piroutet,
"Essai de classification du hallstattien franc-comtois," ibid., 1928, ii,
pp. 266–7 ; Déchelette, ii, 3, p. 697 ; Reinecke, CCCCVI, pp. 2 ff.
[7] Reinecke, op. cit., p. 7 ; tumulus at Waldalgesheim, near Bingen.
[8] The finds at the Hradischt (oppidum) of Stradonitz, in Bohemia, give
another term. But the site was first abandoned by the Boii in 58, and then

Intermediate terms are supplied by Italy. M. Viollier has observed that his first subdivision of La Tène I (La Tène I*a*) is not represented in that country. That period, therefore, came before the great Gallic invasion of 390. The excavations at Montefortino have yielded objects belonging to the last phase of La Tène I (La Tène I*c*), but none of La Tène II. Now the country was recovered from the Gauls in 283.[1]

But from this point onwards coins come to our aid— coins of Marseilles, Greek coins from Europe and Asia, Roman coins.[2] The cemetery of Ornavasso, near Novara, has yielded a series from La Tène II and La Tène III, some of which are dated quite closely by Roman consular coins.[3]

From all this evidence we obtain the following scheme :—

La Tène A	. .	500–400
La Tène I*a*	. .	400–375
La Tène I*b*	. .	375–325
La Tène I*c*	. .	325–285
La Tène II	. .	285–100
La Tène III	. .	100–1

The civilization of La Tène begins with the Golden Age of Greek civilization. The innovations which mark the former were stimulated by those of the latter.[4] From then onwards the surfaces of contact steadily increased, and, in spite of some appearances to the contrary, the influence of the Mediterranean peoples and the amount of things imported increased likewise, until the civilization of La Tène was absorbed by that of Rome.

Italic influence, which seems to have been that to which the Hallstatt culture was chiefly subject, continued to affect the succeeding civilization ; the zone of intercourse and

conquered by the Marcomanni in 12–10 B.C. There is, therefore, an uncertainty of nearly fifty years. It is true that some hold that it was the Marcomanni that brought the series of La Tène civilizations to an end at the Hradischt, but this is quite wrong. The civilization of the Hradischt is too like that of Mont Beuvray to be that of another people. Cf. Déchelette, **CCCCLXXII.**

[1] Viollier, " Giubiasco," in **CLXXX,** pp. 229 ff.
[2] Reinecke, op. cit., p. 11 ; **CCCXCIX,** v, p. 15 (burials at Dühren in Baden, La Tène II) ; Blanchet, **CCCVI,** ii, p. 531.
[3] Déchelette, pp. 1093–4.
[4] Furtwängler, in **XX,** 1889, pp. 43 ff. ; Reinecke, **CCCCVI,** pp. 3 ff. ; Déchelette, p. 1508 ; E. Maassen, " Die Griechen in Südgallien," in *Œsterr. Jahrhft.*, ix (1906), p. 181. See below.

exchange seems to have extended between Venetia and Bavaria.[1] Later, the presence of Celtic settlements in Italy must, until Cisalpine Gaul was conquered by the Romans, have contributed to the influence of Italic civilization over that of La Tène.

Lastly, the wanderings of the Celts and their extension eastwards brought them into touch with the Scythians and the Hellenized Asiatics of Asia Minor. Here they got the torques with heads of serpents, the animal-headed torque of Vieil-Toulouse, the similarity of the torques of Lasgraïsses to that of Herczeg-Marok, and, what is still more significant, certain figures on the Gundestrup cauldron.

But what the men of La Tène borrowed they usually adapted and transformed in a fashion quite their own. Never before, among all the arts borrowed by the civilizations of Central Europe from the more advanced cultures of the South, had such originality been displayed. The development of such a strongly marked style implies a society which is populous, united, prosperous, and full of life—and perhaps more than a society, a nation.

Besides, the art of La Tène is not all borrowed from foreign peoples. It is derived directly from what it inherited from the Hallstatt civilization, as it was in the fifth century before our era in Western Germany, Upper Austria, Switzerland, Lorraine, the Franche-Comté, and Burgundy. The civilization of these regions, which I shall show to have been the heart of the Celtic world, had for long ages been steadily growing more united and homogeneous.

The constancy, the homogeneity, of the La Tène civilization all over the area which it covered is one of its most striking features. That is why one should pay the greatest attention to any local variations which it shows at one same date, and need not make too much of the many lacunæ in our archæological maps.[2] In archæological ethnography most negative facts are inadmissible.

---

[1] Reinecke, **CCCXCIX**, v, p. 284.
[2] Déchelette, ii, 3, pp. 1120–1 (the distribution of La Tène swords in France) and map iv.

PART TWO

MOVEMENTS OF THE CELTIC PEOPLES

CHAPTER I

The Origins of the Celts

I

THE SEPARATION OF THE GOIDELS AND THE BRYTHONS

WE now have to try to find out whence they came, where they went, how they expanded, and where they stopped—in short, to trace their history—and that will be the second part of our inquiry.

The fact which dominates the whole history of the Celts, and apparently starts it, following as it did closely upon the breaking-up of the Italo-Celtic community (if that abstract concept ever corresponded to the existence of a definite social group), is their separation into two groups of peoples, whose languages became different as has been explained above—that is, the Goidelic, or Irish, group, and the Brythonic group, which includes the Gauls.

The separation of the Celtic dialects is a fact of far greater importance than the supposed distinction between the Celts and the Gauls.[1] It implies a fairly deep division between the peoples which spoke these two groups of dialects, and also a fairly long separation,[2] a fairly long interval between the migrations of the two Celtic bodies, a rhythm in those migrations not unlike that assumed by those historians who speculate on the distinction between Celts and Gauls, but much ampler. In other words, it leads one to believe that the occupation of the British Isles by the Celts and of Ireland by the Goidels took place long before—centuries before— the historical movements of the Brythonic peoples. These latter expanded about the sixth century before Christ. We must go back to the Bronze Age for the earlier invasion.

---

[1] Dottin., **CCCXXII**, pp. 12 ff.

[2] Sir John Rhys once tried to explain the phenomenon of labialization by the absorption of the Continental Celts by non-Aryan peoples (**CCXX**). Cf. S. Reinach, *Origine des Aryens*, pp. 108–112. D'Arbois has refuted this theory (**CXL**, 1891, p. 477).

Many historians and archæologists ignore this cleavage, or do not attach enough importance to it.[1] But Celticists and philologists are as divided over its importance as over its date. Mr. Eoinn MacNeill,[2] after making the mistake of identifying the Celts with the La Tène civilization, and making the movements of the Celts, all the Celts, date from the beginning of that culture, is obliged to conclude that the Goidels and Brythons arrived in Great Britain and Ireland together, and in the fourth century B.C. at the earliest. Had they become different before that ? Did they become so after their settlement in the British Isles ? The question does not seem to have occurred to him. In any case he does not think that the facts on which the distinction of the Celtic dialects is founded are important. Phonetic changes of this kind, he says, are not necessarily bounded by racial frontiers. They propagate themselves in some mysterious way, and stop equally without apparent reason.[3]

It is true that many of the things which make the difference between the two groups of Celtic dialects are of fairly late date. But that is not the case with the most characteristic of all, the labialization of velar consonants,[4] our chief indication of the softening of the consonants in Brythonic, which has given Welsh its present form.

Labialization had already become general at the time when the Goidels and Brythons accomplished together, according to Mr. MacNeill, the Celtic colonization of the British Isles. The name of the islands, Πρετтανικαὶ νῆσοι, which dates from the voyage of Pytheas, would be valuable evidence of this, were it not that it is derived from the name

---

[1] Continental archæologists seem quite unaware of this distinction between the two groups of Celts, although they admit in a general way that Britain was occupied by Celts long before the historical migrations (Déchelette, ii, 2, p. 573). The historians pay no more attention to it than the archæologists. M. Jullian (**CCCXLVII**) does not trouble about it. Niese (in Pauly and Wissowa, **CCCLXVIII**, vii, p. 611) holds that the distinction between Goidels and Brythons appears only at the end of ancient times.

[2] **CCCCXLI.**

[3] J. Loth, in **CXL**, 1922, pp. 4 ff. Mr. MacNeill is an admirable Celticist, and his learning gives great authority to his opinion. His theory was, however, greeted with some surprise. It is, of course, true that phonetic facts, like archæological, have no absolute racial significance. Their significant value follows from their circumstances, their context, the chronological indications attached to them, their recurrence in similar conditions, or some other adventitious element in their definition. It is from these that conclusions must be drawn.

[4] See above, pp. 39–42.

of the Picts (*Pretanni, Prydain*), the Celtic origin of which is doubted. It is hard to believe that two peoples which spoke very similar tongues, which may be supposed to have lived fairly close to each other in the country from which they started, should have engaged in similar adventures, perhaps together, at any rate with the same object, in the same direction, and at the same time—adventures such as would bring them closer together, and, indeed, mingle them inextricably—and yet have had no influence on the phonetic development of each other's speech. Yet, when we do find such influence at work in Ireland it is only in the case of particular words, which Irish quite definitely and consciously takes over. The *p* of Brythonic,[1] and even that of Latin,[2] is carefully changed to *k* in Irish, although the Latin *p* is sometimes kept.[3]

While always remaining the same language, Irish did, no doubt, in the long run take something from the neighbouring tongue. It only resisted it as well as it did because its own characteristics were already quite definitely established, and it had had time to fix them; this always implies a fairly long separation. In fact, while all the Celtic dialects which make up Gaulish for us, without exception, as we shall see, underwent labialization, Irish alone escaped because it was cut off from the rest for a long time.

But how far must we go back to find the date of labialization, considered as the chief indication of the distinction of the dialects, and the date, doubtless far earlier, of the separation of the peoples [4]? The close kinship of Celtic and Italic will serve us as a guide, and will give us

[1] Welsh words transcribed with *k*.

[2] From *purpura* they made *corcur*; from *pascha, case*; from *presbyter, cruinther*; from Patricius, Cothraige. We see that this last transcription dates from before the dropping of *qu*; Cothraige comes from Quatricius. But the process was not quite universal, for to some Latin words they applied the dropping of *p*, as in *saltir* (*saltir na ram*), from *psalterium*.

[3] A great road in Middle Irish is called *prim roen*; a sin, *peccad*; a parish, *parche*; etc. The same thing had already happened in Old Irish, but, except where it was used for *b*, it was not used to transcribe Latin words.

[4] M. J. Loth, who, in a reply to Mr. MacNeill's book, has assembled most of the reasons for believing that the Goidels settled in the British Isles at a very early date, nevertheless declares that the differentiation of the two groups of languages does not date from more than a few centuries before our era (in CXL, 1920-1, pp. 282 ff.). In the preface to his vocabulary of Old Breton, emphasizing the close kinship of Gaelic and Brythonic, he explains that their differentiation must date only from the first centuries of our era, that is, from the conquest of Brythonic lands by the Romans.

means to interpret the data of the problem. We shall also find archæological data coming to confirm those of language.

For the Italic dialects present exactly the same cleavage with the same chief indication,[1] but in circumstances which entitle us to interpret it boldly as I have proposed above for that of the Celtic dialects. From this point of view the parallel between the two groups of dialects is quite remarkable. It has not failed to impress philologists strongly.[2] The most cautious and critical try to keep their conclusions within modest bounds.[3] But the similarity of the facts is too marked and the languages are too closely allied for their agreement in this particular case to be fortuitous. Celts and Italici doubtless lived near enough to each other for the same linguistic fashions to spread from one group to the other. On each side a body broke off which remained faithful to an ancient condition of its language. The groups of men among whom the velar was labialized had certainly remained very close to each other, unless they were brought together by some chance. A good scientific method makes as little use of chance as possible.

It should be noted that the same thing happened in the Greek dialects and in the Illyrian dialects. Greek ἵππος ousted an older ἵκκος, which corresponds to Latin *equus*. The word is known from the *Etymologium Magnum*.[4] The Homeric language, the literary Ionic, keeps the guttural in cases where the common Greek has lost it : κοῖος, κῶς, instead of ποῖος, πῶς. The Athenians · gave the name of Πυανόψια to a feast which the Samians called Κυανώψια, the Beanfeast. Among the Illyrian dialects, Venetian kept the velars (Liquentia, Aquileia, Mogiancus, ᾿Αρουκία),

---

[1] See above, p. 57.

[2] Cf. Meillet, in **XLVII**, 1918, xxi, 1.

[3] Meillet, loc. cit. ; id., **CCXVI**, p. 53 ; J. Loth, in **CXL**, 1920–1, p. 278, n. 1 ; Philipon, **CCCLXIX**, p. 204 ; J. Vendryès, in **CXL**, 1923, p. 174. These do not allow that the similarities between Italic and Celtic mean very much ; they hesitate to compare the breaking-off of the Goidels and the Latins from their respective groups, and they hold that labialization occurred independently in Brythonic and Osco-Umbrian. MM. Meillet and Vendryès allow, however, that there are more connections between Celtic and Osco-Umbrian than between Celtic and Latin (Meillet, in **XCIII**, xv, p. 161 ; Vendryès, **CXL**, xxxv, p. 212).

[4] Ridgeway, **DLIII**, p. 672. Boeotian had πέτταρες and Æolic πίσυρες for " four ", like Umbrian *petora*, whereas the form τέτταρες prevailed in Greek.

whereas the dialects of the Balkans labialized them (Pempte, Λυππείος, 'Αρελάπη, Arupi).[1]

It is not likely that the fact is to be explained in exactly the same way in Greek and Illyrian as in Italic and Celtic. It is equally unlikely that it did not occur, where it is observed, in comparable conditions. In any case, if we can take it as proved that the Greeks came from the North, that is from Central Europe, we may suppose without unlikelihood that they were once neighbours, not only of the Illyrians, but of the Italo-Celts, and even of the Celts, and that contact was not completely broken at the time when the labialization of the velars took place, that early indication of the cleavage of the Celtic dialects. Now it is certain that the Greeks did not leave their original home all in one body,[2] and yet labialization took place in the mainland dialects of Greek— Doric, Attic, the common Greek. Ionic merely gutturalized the velar, like Goidelic, but much earlier. The Dorians were evidently the latest of the Greeks to come south. The Ionians, who were the first to settle on the eastern fringe of the Greek world, came before them. In fact, everything seems to have happened as if labialization was the work of the last wave of Greeks, the last who remained in contact with their Indo-European neighbours of Western Europe, among whom labialization also took place.

Roughly the Dorian invasion coincides with the disappearance of the Mycenæan civilization, with the Middle Ages of ancient Greece, and with the beginning of the Iron Age. Its true date is probably not far off the traditional date.[3] Ionic was probably the dialect of the Greeks who settled in Greece in the Mycenæan period, or even before it, whose remote history is beginning to be revealed by the Hittite records.[4]

Things went on in exactly the same way among the Italici and at about the same time. The position of one part of them, the Umbrians, can be determined very exactly in relation to the Etruscans[5] from the moment when they descended

[1] Philipon, CCCLIX, p. 99. Cf. the variation between dentals and gutturals pointed out by Kretschmer, 259 : 'Ιάποδες = 'Ιάπυγες.

[2] Jardé, CCCXLV, English, pp. 71 ff.

[3] Ibid., English, pp. 75–7 ; Fougères, Contenau, Grousset, Jouguet, and Lesquier, CCCXXXI, i, pp. 292 ff.

[4] Meyer, CCCLIV, i, 2, pp. 800 ff. ; H. R. Hall, in CLXXXVI, pp. 297 ff.

[5] Grenier, DXXIX, pp. 460 ff., 500 ff. ; Homo, CCCXLI, English, pp. 50 ff., 54 ff. ; H. Hubert, in CXL, 1914, pp. 20 ff.

into Italy. Between the Umbrians and Etruscans there were relations, not only of immediate proximity, but of intimate penetration. The Etruscans were strangers to Italy, and won their land from the Umbrians. Historical tradition, at least, says that they took from them the northern part, the region of Bologna. In brief, the Umbrians and the Etruscans were two elements, and the two chief elements, of the population north of Central Italy and south of the plain of the Po. Now we know quite well the archæological remains which represent the Etruscans.[1] There are tombs in Etruria which resemble those of Asia Minor, whence the Etruscans came. In these, pottery and other objects of Eastern origin are found. At Bologna [2] a part of the cemetery which extends from the town to the Certosa contains tombs similar to those of Etruria and equipped with Etruscan furniture. Nearer to the town there are tombs of another type, small pits with ossuaries of a characteristic shape, and older objects of various kinds. All this is also found in Etruria, side by side with the remains of the Etruscans. These objects mark the civilization called after Villanova, where a similar cemetery was found. It is the civilization of the Umbrians.

This culture has very many affinities with that which prevailed on the other side of the Alps, in the valley of the Danube. Its most significant feature is the ossuary, which is like that of the tumuli and tombs of Hallstatt.[3] This latter has its ancestors in the common pottery of the end of the Bronze Age, north of the Danube Valley.[4] From the route followed by these technical developments we may infer that of the advance of the peoples which had that civilization in Italy, if they really were newcomers in that country. Now in Italy, in Northern Italy, there had formerly been a fairly dense population, which had built, on both sides of the Po, rectangular villages reared on piles, the remains of which are known as *terremare*.[5] The *terremare* had disappeared. Were the Villanova men descended from their inhabitants? Certainly not.[6] The people of Villanova took the place of

---

[1] Grenier, op. cit., passim ; Homo, op. cit., English, pp. 55 ff.
[2] Grenier, op. cit., pp. 160 ff., 127 ff.
[3] Ibid., pp. 133–5.
[4] H. Hubert, in **CXLIII**, 1910, pp. 5 ff.
[5] Homo, op. cit., English, pp. 30 ff. ; Montelius, **DXXXV**, pp. 55–89, pls. v–x ; Modestov, **DXXXVI**, pp. 156–215.
[6] Déchelette, ii, 1, p. 23, n. 1 ; ii, 2, p. 537, n. 2.

those of the *terremare*; they were not descended from them.

There is, therefore, reason for believing that the Umbrians arrived in Italy about the beginning of the Iron Age.[1] They came from north of the Alps, and it was in that region that they had been in contact with the Celts.[2]

Where, then, do the Latins come in?[3] Latin and Irish being in the same position in relation to Italic and Celtic respectively, the Latins and Goidels must have been in like positions with regard to the larger groups of which they formed part. The Goidels had advanced furthest west of the Celts (ἔσχατοι ἀνδρῶν), and the Brythons seem to have followed in their footsteps (but this has still to be proved). The Latins, then, should be those of the Italici who first moved away from the common cradle of the race and first settled in Italy.

At the date of the foundation of the first villages which were to unite to form Rome, Latium was evidently the centre of the Latins. Their archæological domain is distinguished fairly clearly, save on the Etruscan side, from that of the Umbrians. Its characteristics are the hut-urn and the funerary *dolium*.[4] Other urns are found, covered with helmets or with caps, crowned by the *apex* of the Roman priests.

The Sabellians, whose language has the same differential characteristics, were their neighbours on the south-east.[5] But where had they been before? Must we not give a place to the Iberians and Ligurians in the prehistoric civilizations of Italy in the Bronze Age and before it?[6]

Several important features of Roman civilization, such as the form of the city (*Roma quadrata*) and of the camp, with its quadrangular plan and its two main streets crossing each other and aligned on the cardinal points, and the College

[1] Cato, quoted by Pliny, *N.H.*, iii, 114, says that the Umbrians founded Ameria 963 or 964 years before the war of Perseus, i.e. about 1134 B.C.

[2] Hence the theory of some ancient grammarians that the Umbrians were a branch of the Gauls; Solinus, ii, 11 (according to Bocchus, a historian of the first century); Isidore of Seville, *Orig.*, ix, 2, 87 (Dottin, **CCCXXII**, pp. 25–6). This error is the foundation of Bertrand's hypothesis (**CCCIII**, pp. 27–32) on the first Celtic invasion of Italy. Cf. Thierry, **CCCLXXXVIII**, i, xlii.

[3] Homo, op. cit., English, pp. 41 ff.

[4] Ibid., English, pp. 75–80; Modestov, **DXXXVI**, pp. 248 ff.

[5] Walde, **CCXLIV**.

[6] Déchelette, ii, 1, p. 23, n. 1; Homo, op. cit.; Philipon, **CCCLXIX**.

of Pontifices, recall the *terremare*, with their ritual regularity of plan, their moats and bridges.[1] Did the Latins, then, once live in the *terremare* of the plain of the Po ? It is probable that they did, and that they there mingled with the Ligurians, with whom historical tradition represents them as associated down to the foundation of Rome.[2] When we look among the remains of the *terremare* for signs of the arrival of the Latins we are faced with an *embarras de richesses*—handles with crescent-shaped projections,[3] vases with wart-ornament,[4] tanged swords,[5] pins with ring-heads, coin-necklaces.[6]

So the Latins descended into Italy some time before the Umbrians. Since they were separated from the rest of the Italic peoples, their language did not share in the evolution of their dialects. That was how Latin became different from the other Italic languages. All this gives us at least a presumption to explain what happened to Celtic.

But we must go further. The Villanovan civilization was introduced into Italy almost at the same time as the successors of the Mycenæans entered Greece. About the beginning of the first Iron Age, at the end of the second millennium before Christ, a certain stirring took place in Europe, which is revealed in prehistoric archæology by many novelties,[7] and the result of it was that new Aryan bodies descended into the Mediterranean world. A similar agitation had occurred earlier, at the end of the first period of the Bronze Age, and had had the same effects.[8]

The movements of the Celts were, in my opinion, likewise in two waves, and must have been governed by the same demographic laws, by the same general facts in the history of civilization. In other words, the breaking-off of the Goidelic group, and probably the first Celtic colonization of the British Isles, must have occurred at the same time as the descent of the Latins into Italy, and that of the first Greek invaders into Greece. The differentiation of the

---

[1] Peet, **CCCCXLVII** ; Homo, op. cit., English, p. 50.
[2] Homo, op. cit., English, pp. 45 ff.
[3] Ibid., English, p. 50. See also Pigorini, in **LII**, 1900, pp. 21 ff. ; Modestov, op. cit., pp. 156–225, 288 ff. ; Peet, in **CLXI**, 1910, 2, pp. 386–7 ; Grenier, in **CXXXIX**, 1914, i, p. 328.
[4] H. Hubert, loc. cit.
[5] Modestov, op. cit., pl. xix, and pp. 187 ff.
[6] H. Hubert, in **CLIII**, 1925, p. 25, n. 3.
[7] Déchelette, ii, 3, p. 1289.
[8] Id., ii, pp. 2, 6 ff.

Brythonic, Umbrian, and Doric dialects took place afterwards at some time unknown, among the groups which had remained behind and in contact with one another. The migratory movement of the peoples speaking these dialects occurred about the same time, but after their dialects had become differentiated, and the result of it was that they became definitely different languages.

In short, the dividing of the Celtic peoples into two groups is an ancient event, of very great importance, connected with the great facts of European prehistory. It is the consequence of the breaking-up of the Italo-Celtic community.

This demonstration is based mainly on three hypotheses, which it may be as well to state here. The first is that linguistic affinities indicate at least the proximity of the races concerned. The second is that certain concordances must have originated not only in one neighbourhood, but about the same time. The third is that each separate set of archæological facts is a set of ethnographical facts, which may correspond to one or other of the ethnographical facts implied by the various dialects concerned.

There is nothing extravagant in these hypotheses.

II

THE CRADLE OF THE CELTS. VARIOUS THEORIES

Before we inquire what sets of archæological facts correspond to the breaking-off of the Goidels and the separate existence of the Goidels and the Brythons, we must determine, if it can be done, the place from which both bodies set forth. The cradle of the Celts was, no doubt, quite close to the cradle of the Italici. Now these latter came to Italy from the north and north-east, not from the west or north-west, of the Alps. It is, therefore, north of the Alps, whether close to them or far away, that we must look for the Celts.

There are two contradictory traditions regarding the origin of the Celts. One places them where the ancients knew them ; the other, further east, along the North Sea. In the time of Tarquin the Proud, we read in Livy,[1] the Gauls were strongly established in the centre of what is now France.

---

[1] v, 34.

They centred round the Bituriges and their king, who at that time was called Ambicatus. Besides the Bituriges, the confederation comprised the Arverni, Senones, Ædui, Ambarri, Carnutes, and Aulerci, that is, the peoples which in Livy's time occupied the very centre of the Celtic world. " Gaul," he says, " was so fertile and populous that the immense multitude threatened to be hard to rule. So the King, being old and wishing to relieve his kingdom of its excess population, declared that he would send his sister's sons, Bellovesus and Sigovesus, who were energetic youths, to whatever country the gods should indicate by omens, and they could take as many men as they wished, so that no people should be able to resist their advance. The omens assigned the Hercynian Forests to Sigovesus, and to the much more fortunate Bellovesus the road to Italy."

The ancient historians were fairly clear as to the limits reached by the Gauls. They were so well established in Gaul in the first century before Christ that it required an unusually critical spirit to doubt that Gaul was the cradle of the race. The invasions by which they extended their frontiers were supposed to have started from Gaul.

But the tradition recorded by Livy is by no means to be despised. The names are good Gallic—Ambicatus " He-who-gives-battle-all-round ", Bellovesus " He-who-can-kill ", Sigovesus " He-who-can-conquer ". They may be fancy names, but the fancy is native. Therefore the tradition must be a Gallic one, which Livy doubtless got from Cornelius Nepos, that is, from the Gallic historian Trogus Pompeius.

Cæsar says as much [1] : " There was a time when the Gauls surpassed the Germans in valour, carried war into their country, and sent colonies across the Rhine to relieve their own territory of its excess population. It was in this way that the Volcæ Tectosages came to take possession of the most fertile districts of Germany, near the Hercynian Forest, which seems to have been known to Eratosthenes and some other Greeks under the name of Orcynian. There that tribe has maintained itself to this day, and enjoys a great reputation for justice and courage. Even now they live in the same poverty and with the same frugality as the Germans ; they have adopted their manner of life and their dress " (Cæsar

[1] *Gall. War*, vi, 24.

is seriously misleading as to the poverty of the Volcæ).
Tacitus, in his *Germania*,[1] repeats Cæsar's opinion, and
mentions other peoples east of the Volcæ—the Boii in
Bohemia and the Cotini in Silesia.

But there were other traditions which are echoed in the
ancient historians. Ammianus Marcellinus, in a long passage
about the Gauls, writes as follows : " *Drasidæ memorant
revera fuisse populi partem indigenam* (the Druids relate
that part of the population was really indigenous), *sed alios
quoque ab insulis extimis confluxisse et tractibus Transrhenanis*
(but that others had come in from the outermost isles and the
regions beyond the Rhine)." [2]   The aborigines are the
Ligurians or other races, and the newcomers are the Celts.
Ammianus Marcellinus or his source, Timagenes, says a word
on the reasons for their migration.   " They were," he says,
" driven from their homes by the frequency of wars and
violent rising of the sea—*Crebritate bellorum et adluvione
fervidi maris sedibus suis expulsos.*"   So the Celts had come
from beyond the Rhine, but more especially from the low
countries washed by the North Sea.

Further evidence for the marine upheavals of which the
Celts are reported to have been victims was furnished by
the historian Ephoros [3] ; it is quoted by Strabo, who is, however, sceptical.   Ephoros described the Celts as obstinately
remaining in their threatened lands, and losing more lives
in the floods than in war.[4] The legend of the Celts advancing
against the waves with their weapons probably goes back to
this tradition,[5] to which there is an allusion, of still more
respectable antiquity, in the *Ora Maritima* of Avienus.[6]
The passage must be quoted, for it resumes some centuries
of Celtic history in ten lines.[7]

The voyager who has left Britain on his left and sails
northwards comes to the land of the Ligurians, *cæspitem*

---

[1] xxviii.
[2] xv, 9, 2. Ammianus's source is Timagenes of Alexandria, a valuable
historian who gave most of the classical traditions about the Gauls their
accepted shape. O. Hirschfeld, in **XXXVII**, 1894, p. 36.
[3] In *F.H.G.*, i, 243–4 ; Dottin, **CCCXXII**, p. 300.
[4] Strabo, vii, 2, 1.
[5] Arist., *Eth.*, ii, 7.
[6] See above, p. 3.
[7] 140–5. In Pytheas's time there had long been no Celtic peoples on
the coast, but the Germans of Jutland and the Danish islands, where the
amber-trade was conducted, were very much Celticized.

Ligurum subit, which is empty of inhabitants, emptied as a result of the attacks of the Celts. They, too, were a fleeing people, *fugax gens hæc quidem*.

> *Diu inter arta cautium duxit diem*
> *secreta ab undis. Nam sali metuens erat*
> *priscum ob periclum ; post quies et otium,*
> *securitate roborante audaciam*
> *persuasit altis devehi cubilibus*
> *atque in marinos jam locos descendere.*

Avienus's source, better informed than Ephoros and Timagenes, made the Celts move backwards and forwards between the sea and the mountains.

Pytheas found the Celtic country on the coast, some days' sailing from Cantion, that is Kent, but his valuable evidence needs to be interpreted.

We are treating the ancient writers with a respect which they do not quite deserve if we rely on the documents which we have just been considering to place the Celtic cradle either in Gaul or on the very shores of the North Sea. Nevertheless, modern theories of the origin of the Celts, whether based on the observation of archæological facts or on the interpretation of historico-linguistic facts, are falling into line with the ancient beliefs.

Three of these theories must be discussed separately and set aside. The most learned of Rhenish archæologists, Herr Schumacher, maintains that the movements of the Celts went from west to east. The Celts who peopled the Rhineland, he says, came from Gaul.[1] A general shifting from west to east set up among the Celtic peoples during a period which, in his view, begins in the middle of the Hallstatt age. The Sequani, starting from the Seine, reached the Franche-Comté ; the Mediomatrici left the Marne to settle on the Meuse ; the Helvetii were Helvii from the banks of the Allier ; the Volcæ, the Bituriges Cubi, and the Turones were spread out from the Danube to Thuringia. The Treveri

[1] Schumacher, "Die Erforschung d. röm. u. vorröm. Strassennetzes in Westdeutschland," in **XXIX**, 1906, p. 25 ; id., in **LXXXIV**, ii, pp. 16, 18 ; id., in **CXVIII**, 1916, p. 133 ; id., in *Nassauische Annalen*, 1917, p. 175 ; id., in **LXV**, N.S., i, 1917–1922 ; id., **CCCCIX**, i, pp. 214 ff. ; H. Hubert, in **CXL**, 1925, pp. 254–7.

were of the same origin.[1] Their arrival in the valley of the Rhine is attested by a type of Hallstatt urn common in the region centring on the mouth of the Main, which resembles more southern types save in the poverty of its decoration. Herr Schumacher calls this the Mehren type.[2] The Celts, he says, reached the Rhine through the Palatinate and the Hunsrück. Crossing the river they came to the Taunus, the Westerwald, and the Vogelsberg. He follows them in the valley of the Tauber and the Odenwald. They stopped on the line of Hagenau, Rastatt, and Stuttgart. Later contingents, coming up, reinforced the first settlements, and introduced and established the civilization of La Tène. The name of the Roman Province of Rætia points to the resistance of the old Hallstatt population. This latter was Ræto-Ligurian, and had been reinforced by Illyrian elements.[3] Herr Schumacher, who has spent his life following the traces of prehistoric man on the map, has very justly remarked that the oldest roads climbed the hillsides and followed the watersheds. It was by these upland roads that the Celts advanced. He likens their movements to the treks of the Boers. They were pastoral folk, extending their grazing-grounds.

But when one starts pricking out routes on a map one is too easily led into imagining movements and directions. The discovery of groups of similar objects on a line which may have been a route does not show in which direction the route was followed. In reality the proofs are but slender. No doubt the pottery of Haulzy may resemble that of the Hunsrück. Herr Schumacher errs as to the direction in which Celtic civilization spread, because he has not seen the poverty and the wealth of the French Hallstatt period for himself. To him the immense mass of tumuli in the Franche-Comté perhaps represents the Celts in their original home. But if we look closely we can only regard that district as a jumping-off point.[4] Herr Schumacher's hypothesis, based on such a complete knowledge of the archæological evidence and such a sure judgment in matters of detail, only shows what

[1] Schumacher, in **LXXXIV**. 1916, pp. 133 ff.
[2] Id., in **LXVII**, 1918, pp. 98 ff. ; **CCCCIX**, p. 89.
[3] A. Schliz, in **CLXV**, 1908, pp. 426 ff. ; id., in *Heilbronn. Festschr.*, 1911, pp. 41 ff. ; Schumacher, **CCCCIX**, p. 109.
[4] Cf. certain pages of Schumacher, following on Helmke's work on the excavation of tumuli in **CLIX**, i, ii, 1918–19.

a delicate matter the racial interpretation of prehistoric archæology is.

M. Camille Jullian, after having followed the tradition of Ephoros and Timagenes,[1] propounds an entirely new theory of the origin of the Celts which, if it were accepted, would change the ground of part of the problems which we have still to settle.[2] He would obliterate all frontiers between Celtic and Ligurian.[3] In his view Ligurian is the pre-Celtic language, or, rather, a common language spoken alike by Celts and Italici, in fact, Italo-Celtic. The undivided Italo-Celtic body, instead of having been confined to Central Europe north of the Alps, as I have suggested, covered the whole of Western Europe. One fine day it resolved into its divergent elements ; M. Jullian does not tell us how. It is, indeed, difficult to imagine this dissolution if one adopts M. Jullian's theory, for, pursuing his theory as far as it will go, he makes the Italo-Celtic world a sort of united empire, the unity of which alone made possible the cultural developments which took place in it. He is thinking particularly of the trade in bronze. It is a plausible theory, for there were Italo-Ligurians in Italy, just as much as there were Celto-Ligurians in Gaul, but, although it is advancing in favour, it is only a surmise.

It must be dismissed as non-proven in the present state of our knowledge, for several reasons. First, there is not one single word attributed to Ligurian with good reason which has any one of the characteristics peculiar to Italic and Latin. We can suppose, from its wretched remnants, that it was something like Italic and Celtic, but we are not in a position to regard it as their original source. Secondly, the area covered by place-names in *asco*, *osco*, and *usco* does not correspond on its eastern border with that which I shall show reason for assigning to the earliest Celts. Thirdly, the ancient writers, who seem to be perfectly well acquainted with the Ligurians and use the name of Ligurian, not for an enormously spread-out nation, but as the generic name of an immense number of tribes—Salyes, Taurini, Sicels, Ambrones—always distinguish them from the Celts and the

---

[1] Jullian, **CCCXLVII**, i, pp. 227 ff.
[2] Id., in **CXXXIV**, 1917, p. 124 ; 1918, p. 43.
[3] Sir John Rhys made a similar attempt, but made Ligurian a Goidelic language of Gaul.

Italici. There were Ligurians in Rome, but they were driven out of Reate by the Sabines,[1] that is to say, by Latins. The Celto-Ligurians of Gaul are evidence of the almost generic difference between the two elements of which they were composed. Lastly, the fact remains that Ligurians were left over who did not become either Celts or Italici. Therefore the whole area covered by the Ligurians cannot be regarded as the domain of the Italo-Celts before they split ; that must be defined on its own account.

This new theory has not provided a solution, but a new and unnecessary name for the old problems. It has introduced into archæology a most vexatious tendency, which has been too readily accepted [2] ; namely, that notion of a prehistoric empire which has the air of a sociological or historical interpretation of facts. Now nothing in the prehistoric archæology of the Celtic world or the Ligurian world gives the least suggestion of an empire, even in the nature of the Aztec Empire.

A third theory has lately been put forward by Mr. Peake.[3] This is based on the interpretation of a piece of archæological evidence and of one only, namely the so-called flat-tanged sword. The hilt of this sword consists of a metal tang springing from the base of the blade and shaped to fit the hand, with pieces of other material rivetted on to its two faces.[4] Swords of this type were first used as a sign of race by Herr Kossinna,[5] who regarded them as evidence of the expansion of the Germans. He drew up a chronological classification of them which still holds good.

The early swords have only one or two rivets at the guard and none on the hilt. Most were found in Schleswig-Holstein (about thirty in all), and the rest not far off. They date from the middle of the second period of the Bronze Age.[6] The next type, belonging to the end of that period, has rivets on the hilt and, without exception, more than two pairs of rivets on the guard. The swords of the third period of the Bronze Age are distinguished from their predecessors by the fact that the edges of the hilt and guard form one continuous

[1] Dion. Hal., ii, 49.   [2] Homo, **CCCXLI**, English pp. 46–7.
[3] **CCCCXLVII**, pp. 81–103.   [4] Déchelette, ii, 1, pp. 208–9.
[5] Kossinna, in **LXXXV**, 1912, pp. 275 ff.
[6] H. Hubert, in **XV**, 1920, pp. 575–6.

concave curve. Most of the examples of this type also come from Schleswig-Holstein. Here Herr Kossinna stops, but the history of these swords went on much longer, well into the Hallstatt period. Hallstatt swords of this class have at the base of the blade notches to which a guard was probably attached.[1]

Mr. Peake has no difficulty in showing that Herr Kossinna's statistics are incomplete. He adds a long series of swords from Hungary and the north of Italy.[2] He concludes that the Celts originally came from the middle valley of the Danube. Thus he is opposed to both the other theories which I have discussed. But it is evident that he confounds the area of extension of the Celts with that of the Indo-Europeans of Europe.[3] In trying to settle the question of race by examining one single indication, he has taken a cultural fact of far too general a kind as the indication of a particular race.

The problem of the origin of the Celts can only be solved by following the data given in the preceding chapters. They were allied to the Italic peoples in language, and their routes crossed. They rubbed shoulders with the Germans, lived in the same climate as the Slavs, and perhaps encountered the Illyrians and Greeks near their cradle. Furthermore, the main body of the Celts and the leading nations among them were certainly settled in the region where the civilization of La Tène was formed, that is, where it could receive the decisive influences of Greece and Italy direct, where industry displayed the greatest inventiveness and the relics of human life bear witness to wealth in the most settled condition.

[1] I have called attention (ibid.) to the fact that the area in which these swords were found stretched far further, but westwards (Western Germany, France, Spain, the British Isles), than Herr Kossinna made it do ; so much so, that I regard it as one indication of the extension of the Celts. In proof, I only cited the collection in the Saint-Germain Museum, which is large and very representative (Déchelette, ii, 1, pp. 208–9). I am of opinion that this type of hilt is not of Northern origin, but was used in Ægean and Hungarian daggers. If so, the flat-hilted swords of Mycenæan type are not imports from the North. For the significance of these swords with regard to the ethnology of the Celts, see below, p. 177.

[2] CCCCXLVII, pls. x, xiii.

[3] Same work.

III

THE AREA OF CELTIC NAMES IN GERMANY

Western Germany fulfils these conditions exactly. It is full of place-names of Celtic origin, quite especially in the south-west. A very large number have survived in recognizable form.

First there are the *names of towns*.[1] In Bavaria, Carrodunum (Karnberg), Cambodunum (Kempten),[2] and Locoritum (Lohr); in Wurtemberg, Virodunum (Wirtenberg); in Baden, Tarodunum (Zarten), near Freiburg-in-Breisgau, Bragodunum or Bragodurum (Brännlingen), and Lopodunum (Ladenburg) on the Neckar, near Mannheim; in Hessen and the Rhine Province, Tredentus (Trans) near Mainz,[3] Bondobriga (Boppard), Vincum (Bingen), Valandra (Vallendar), Vosavia (Wesel), and, right in the north, Mediolanum (Meteln-an-der-Vichte).[4]

All these names have been changed and Germanized in different degrees. Others have been completely altered, or cannot be identified exactly with the names of towns now existing. Near the Main, Segodunum is doubtless Würzburg; Bamberg was Devona; Rottenburg on the Neckar was Sumelocenna. In Bavaria, Boiodurum has become Innstadt, a suburb of Passau, which was Batava Castra, and Ratisbona has become Regensburg (Ratisbon). Stranting was Sorviodurum. In the south-east of Bavaria there was a town of Artobriga, which may be Burgerwald, between Teissendorf and Traunstein, and in the Taunus, near Frankfort, there was an Aretaunum.

It is needless to demonstrate the Celtic character of all these names. It is apparent at first sight. It is due to obviously Celtic elements—*dunum, durum, bona, ritum, briga, cenna, lanum, are*.[5] Moreover, many of these names are found also in Gaul.[6]

---

[1] D'Arbois, **CCXCIX**, pp. 9 ff., 127–131; Müllenhoff, **CCCLXII**, ii, p. 227; Grupp, **CCCXCIV**, p. 69; Cramer, **CXCV**.

[2] P. Reinecke, in **LXI**, 1912, p. 4.   [3] D'Arbois, **CCCI**, ii, p. 324.

[4] Schumacher, in **CX**, 1917.

[5] I have not mentioned the names in -*acus* (Abudiacus, Eppach; Cassiliacus, Kisslegg; Lauriacum, Lorch), which may be Gallo-Roman place-names of the time of the Empire.

[6] Tredentus or Tridens (Trans) = Tredentus or Tridens, in the diocese of Le Mans = Tridentum (Trent) in N. Italy (D'Arbois, loc. cit.).

The Celtic place-names of Western Germany include, too, a series of names of mountains and a still larger number of names of rivers.

Names of Mountains.[1]—Ercynia Silva, the Erzgebirge ; Gabreta Silva, the Goat Mountain, the Böhmer-Wald, also in Bohemia. In Gaulish, the word for goat was **gabros* (Irish *gathar*, Welsh *gafr*, Breton *gabr*). The Finne, a range in the basin of the Saale north of Saxe-Weimar, south of the Harz, has a name of Celtic origin, *pennos*, head (Welsh and Breton *pen*, a Brythonic word, the Irish form being *ceann*).[2] The name of the Taunus is not Germanic, and may be Celtic. I do not venture to suggest a derivation. Some have connected it with *dunum*.[3]

Names of Rivers.[4]—First of all the Rhine (Rēnos) and Danube (Danuvius) have Celtic names. In Irish *rian* corresponds to Rēnos exactly, the Irish diphthong standing for an *e* in ancient Celtic ; the word means the sea. The name Danuvius is applied to the upper course of the Danube, which flowed through a Celtic country ; in Irish *dana* means swift. Ister is the Illyrian, eastern name of the river.

The Danube has tributaries and sub-tributaries with Celtic names. The Laber (Labara), which flows into the Danube on the left bank, near Ratisbon, is the Talking River (Irish *labrur*, Welsh *llafar*, Breton *lauar*). The Lauterach, a sub-sub-tributary, flowing through the Vils and the Naab into the Danube near Ratisbon, has a name in which the Celtic **lautron* can be recognized.[5] Near Salzburg, in the valley of the Inn, there is a Glan. Glan is Glana, the Pure (Old Irish *glan*). There is another in Rhenish Bavaria. A tributary of the Upper Danube, the Brege, gets its name from a Celtic Bragos.[6] We should note that river-names, which were masculine in Celtic, were made feminine by the Germans. It is supposed that the name Licus, the Lech, is likewise Celtic.[7]

---

[1] W. Krause, **CCCXCVII**, p. 39.

[2] Doubts have been cast on the Celtic origin of the name Finne. Vendryès, in **CXL**, xlii, p. 194.

[3] Holder, **CCVII**, s.v. " Taunos ".

[4] D'Arbois, **CCXCIX**, p. 6 ; Grupp, **CCCXCIV**, p. 69.

[5] Endlicher's Glossary : *lautro* = *balneo*. Dottin, **CXCVI**, p. 265 : Ir. *loathar* " basin " ; Breton *louazr* " trough ".

[6] Bragodunum, in the Rhine valley, stood on another Bragos.

[7] Licorix, 'Αμβιλικοι, in Pannonia.

In the basin of the Rhine, Celtic names of rivers are still more numerous. That of the Neckar, Nicer, may be Celtic. That of the Main, Mœnus, probably is ; in any case, the diphthong is not Germanic.[1] That of its tributary, the Nida, is certainly Celtic ; it is shared by the Scottish Nith and the Nied, an affluent of the Saar, in Lorraine. The Tauber, a tributary of the Main on the left bank, was called Dubra, the nominative plural of *dubron*, a Celtic word meaning water.[2] Near the Tauber there was a Vernodubrum ; that is, an Erlenbach ; now there is an Erlenbach just there, and there are some others in the same district, whose names may perhaps have the same origin.

The name of the Lahn, Logna,[3] is not Germanic, and may be Celtic. In any case, Nassau, through which it flows, has a name which recalls Nasonia (Nassogne in the Belgian Luxemburg) and Nasium (Naix-sur-Ornain, in the department of the Meuse). The Ruhr, Raura, has the same name as the Hérault, Arauris.[4] The Embscher, which is called Embiscara in tenth-century documents, was once Ambiscara, in which one can see two Celtic elements, *ambi* and *isca*, a word for water which has furnished river-names in Britain, to which a suffix *ara* or *ala* has been attached. So, too, we have Iscara, Iscala, from which come the Ischar in Alsace and the Ischl in Austria, near Salzburg. The Lippe (Lupia or Lupias) has a name of uncertain origin, but it flowed by Aliso, the name of which is very like Alesia.[5] There is the same proportion of Celtic names on the left bank of the Rhine.

So much for the valley of the Rhine. The origin of Amisicus, the name of the Ems, is uncertain.[6] In the valley of the Weser, the Wümme had the name, perhaps Celtic, of Uimina, which was also borne by the Visme, an affluent of the Bresle. But some have regarded it as Ligurian.[7]

[1] It recalls the Irish *muin* "neck" (Welsh *mynci* "collar" ; see above, p. 38).
[2] Ir. *dobor*, Welsh *dubr*, *dwfyr*, Bret. *dubr*, *daour*.
[3] Laugona, Loucona.
[4] The Sieg (Sigina) bears the name of the Seine (Sequana) Germanized. But it is not certain that the latter is Celtic ; it may be Ligurian (Jullian, CCCXLVII, i, p. 115) or Iberian (Philipon, DXVI, p. 128).
[5] Alesia may be explained by Old Irish *all*, gen. *aille* (from *als-* ; cf. Germanic *fels* "rock") ; Alesia would mean Rocky Hill.
[6] H. M. Chadwick, in CLXXXII, p. 318, n. 2.
[7] Müllenhoff, CCCLXII, ii, p. 232.

The Leine, further south, seems to have the same name as the Lahn.[1] The Weser itself has an indubitably Germanic name, Visurgis, which may, however, conceal a Celtic name.[2] The name of the Elbe either is Germanic and the same as the Swedish word *elf*, meaning river, or belongs to the family of the Aubes, Albes, Albion, which is pan-European. The names of its tributaries are probably Germanic, except, perhaps, that of the Saale ; and this, like the other names of rivers in Western Germany, may equally well be Celtic or Germanic.[3] In Thuringia three Wippers have a name, the Celtic origin of which has lately been revealed, as in the case of the Wupper in the Rhine basin.[4]

The list of Celtic river-names in Germany has been extended by the incorporation of a long series of names (mostly of streams) ending in -*ef*, -*pe*, -*p*, and -*ft* (Olef, in the Eifel ; Wörpe, an affluent of the Wümme ; Erft, near Neuss), the Latin name of which end in -*eva*, -*efa*, -*apa*, -*afa*, -*affa*.[5] For these names have equivalents in Britain,[6] such as Ἄβος (the Humber) (Ptolemy), Abona (the Avon) (Tacitus), Αὔσοβα, Τοίσυβις, Τονέροβις. This makes it probable, if not certain, that they are Celtic.[7] They are very frequent in Flanders, Brabant, Holland, and the German provinces west of the Rhine, and extend north-eastwards to a line which runs up the Weser valley, goes through Hanover, and stops at the ridge of the Harz, embracing the greater part of Westphalia. They become very rare and finally disappear south of the Harz. So, if we add this series of names, they extend the area of Celtic place-names towards the north-east and give us its limits in that direction more accurately.[8] But on the whole, Celtic names, which are

[1] Ibid. Its Latin form, *Laina*, may be a Germanization of a Loina, Logna (cf. Mœnus).

[2] Cf. La Vesdre, a tributary of the Ourthe, which then became Liez, and the Wear in Durham.

[3] Müllenhoff, op. cit., ii, p. 213. Cf. Salzach, which flows into the Plattensee, Seille (Salia), and Selse, near Alzey (Salusia).

[4] Ibid., ii, p. 214.

[5] Ibid., ii, pp. 207 ff. ; C. Tauber, in **LXIX**, 1910, 2, p. 333 ; Chadwick, same article, p. 315 (cf. **CXL,** xxxviii, p. 283). Many of the names in this series now have a termination in -*er* ; e.g. Hesper (Hesapa), on the Ruhr.

[6] Abusina (Abens) near Ratisbon ; Apala (Appel) near Kreuznach (Müllenhoff, op. cit., ii, pp. 227–230).

[7] Ibid., ii, p. 231, comparing Olef, Olpe, Oleve, with Ὀλίνας (the Orne), Olario, Oléron.

[8] Ibid., ii, p. 232.

very frequent in the valleys of the Rhine and Danube, grow scarce before we reach the Elbe, and are almost wholly absent in Frisia and the northern part of Hanover. If the Celts ever were in those parts they were driven out at a very early date.

What do these Celtic place-names mean ? That the Celts set out from Germany, or that they conquered it ? There is

MAP 3. Northern Germany.

strong reason for believing that the names are aboriginal, or, at least, very ancient, since there are so many names of rivers and mountains among them. We know that such names are almost rare in Gaul.[1] Many names of French rivers and mountains come from the Ligurians, if not from still further back.[2] Now the names given to the land and its natural features are the most enduring of place-names. The

[1] Dottin, **CXCVI**, p. 74.   [2] Jullian, **CCCXLVII**, i, p. 114.

first occupants of a country always pass them on to their successors. These latter sometimes add a name of their own. The Gauls did this in Gaul. To the Araris, a tributary of the Rhone, they gave the name of Souconna, Saône. But the new name has not always won the day. In Germany, likewise, we find some Ligurian or Iberian names, perhaps even east of the Rhine [1]; but among the non-Germanic names a very large number, and those very ancient, are Celtic.

There is one which bears in itself evidence of its great antiquity, and that is the name of the Hercynian Forest. It is a relic of a very ancient state of the Celtic world. It had probably remained attached to the place which it designated ever since it took its earliest form. At that time the Celts were neighbours of the Italici in that region. The name appears in different forms—Hercynia, Ἀρκύνια, Ἑρκύνια, Ὀρκύνια, Ἑρκύνιον ὄρος.[2] The initial h is uncertain. In any case, the etymology seems clear.[3] The word is derived from a name of the oak, common [4] to Celtic, Italic, and Germanic, perqʷ, which is preserved unaltered in the name of the Lithuanian god Perkunas. Old High German forhe attests it equally, although it has changed its meaning. Latin made perqʷos into quercus, following the rule which I have explained before. Celtic, following the same rule, should have produced first *Querqunia and then *Perpunia in Brythonic. But, before the rule took effect, the velar in the second syllable was probably changed, as in a certain number of words, to k. The p, having then escaped assimilation, maintained itself (Gothic Fairguni [5] may, perhaps, be evidence of this stage in the history of the word), and was later dropped, as p usually was in Celtic. In short, the name of the Hercynian Forest dates from an age before the Celtic dropping of p and the Italo-Celtic assimilation of p to the velar in two-syllable words of the form $p \ldots q^w$. Now, it is a fossil,

---

[1] Even if Sieg is Ligurian or Iberian, in any case, the Beybach, near Neumagen on the west bank of the Rhine, was called Rodanus (Venantius Fortunatus, 3, 12, 7 ; cf. M. Müller, in **CLVII**, 1906, pp. 51–9) ; not to mention a tributary of the Upper Danube on the right bank.

[2] Holder, **CCVII**, s.v. " Ercunion ".

[3] The Welsh verb er-chynu " to rise " has been mentioned in this connection ; but the prefix was are in Gaulish (Müllenhoff, op. cit., ii, p. 243).

[4] D'Arbois, in **CXL**, 1890, p. 216 ; Kluge, in Pauly and Wissowa, i, col. 325.

[5] Wiedenann, in **CCXXXVIII**, xxviii, 1904, i.

for the Celtic languages took the common name of the oak from other roots ; and the fossil is *in situ*.

D'Arbois de Jubainville has extracted from the names of German rivers indications regarding the direction in which the Celtic peoples moved.[1] He has observed that many of these peoples were called after places, and particularly after rivers, which seem to have been in their neighbourhood.[2] In Italy there were the Ambisontes, who were Gauls settled astride of the Isonzo ; in Illyria, the Ambidravi on both banks of the Drave ; in Gaul, the Ambarri on both banks of the Arasis, or Saône.[3] The Taurisci were the Gauls of the Tauros, that is, the Tauern ; the Scordisci, those of the Shar-Dagh ; the Sequani, those of the Sequana. This kind of name was especially suitable for groups which had broken off from larger groups and had not yet got a name of their own, or chance groups whose unity, while they were still settling, was chiefly geographical. Now, we always find them in process of forming or of breaking off.

Some of these names taken from places show that their bearers had changed their abode. The Sequani, for example, who lived in the Franche-Comté were nowhere near the river to which they owed their name, the Sequana, or Seine. We shall see how they came to leave it.

Now, we know Gallic peoples whose names recall those of rivers in Germany which have kept their Celtic name.[4] Near Basle there dwelt the Raurici ; the Raura is the Ruhr, and there is no other river of the name. Avranches is the town of the Abrincatui ; the Abrinca is the Vinxtbach, which flows into the Rhine on the left bank, south-east of Cologne. D'Arbois de Jubainville [5] adds to these the Salassi or Salluvii of the Alps, who perhaps came from the banks of a Sala in Saxony or Lorraine. But it is not certain that they were Celts. At the very most they were Celto-Ligurians.

The same reasoning would lead one to suppose that the Volcæ, Cenomani,[6] Turones, Santones,[7] and Lemovii or

---

[1] D'Arbois, **CCXCIX**, p. 129.

[2] Philipon (**CCCLXIX**, p. 153, n. 7) declares that the Iberians can be recognized by these names of peoples taken from names of rivers ; e.g. Iber and Iberes, Astura and Astures.   [3] Pauly and Wissowa, i, col. 1795.

[4] D'Arbois, op. cit., p. 130.   [5] Ibid., p. 154.

[6] A subdivision of the Volcæ ; cf. Cenomanni (ibid., p. 153).

[7] On the Main, in the Odenwald (Zangemeister, in **I**, xiii, 2, i, p. 283, No. 6607 ; Norden, **CCCCIV**, p. 257).

Lemovices,[1] who appear distributed between Germany and Gaul in Cæsar's time, originally came from Germany, not from Gaul.[2] This was what the Helvetii did, who left behind them, on the right bank of the Rhine, the desert of the Helvetii. One part of them, the Tigurini, has left place-names

MAP 4. Germany between the Rhine and Elbe.

in Bavaria to tell of their former presence in that country. Another, the Raurici, were once, perhaps, on the Ruhr, and their last migration was the cause of Cæsar's intervention in

[1] Tac., Germ., 43 ; **CLXVIII**, 1930, p. 153.
[2] Cf. Jullian, **CCCXLVII**, i, p. 251, n. 8. According to him, the Volcæ lived in the valleys of the Doubs, Saône, and Marne, and joined in the migration to the Danube.

Gaul, as was that of the Boii, who followed the same route at the same time. The Helvetii and Boii were the last of the Celtic peoples to move, and their movement, related in some detail by an eminent contemporary, can be regarded as the last wave of the general movement in which the Celtic peoples were involved.

With regard to the Volcæ, one of the oldest groups and one of the first to leave their old homes, bodies of whom went to the ends of the Celtic world and were in the position of an advanced guard in Gaul, a recent conjecture corroborates our hypothesis regarding their original habitat. That very ingenious philologist, M. Cuny, has compared the name of the Volcæ to that of the Volsci of Latium,[1] and suggests that the two peoples had the same name, having the termination -co in one case and -sco in the other. Both terminations were used alternatively in what was apparently the old name of the Oscans, Opisci, or, as the Greeks said, ’Οπικοί. If M. Cuny is right we have to do with a name which was common to the vocabularies of the Italic and Celtic groups. Since racial names do not seem to turn up in two neighbouring racial spheres by mere chance, the Volcæ or Volsci may be a people divided between the two groups, belonging to one and having sent out emigrants to the other. Their presence in Bavaria and their obstinacy in remaining there are most significant facts. The Volcæ did not go to Bavaria ; they were there, and quite close to the probable point of contact between the Italici and the Celts.

To sum up, the names of places and peoples which have been enumerated cover the south-western corner of Germany. The area in which they are found is a vast irregular triangle with one point on the Rhine near Cologne and another beyond Bohemia.[2]

Between Bohemia and the Rhine we have definite trace of a frontier. It lies in Thuringia. Along the ridge of the Thüringer Wald a very regular grassy track runs through the trees. It is called the Rennstieg, and marks the present

[1] In **CXXXIV**, 1911, p. 178.
[2] The Boii held an advanced position on this side down to the first century. Their domain is marked on the east by the towns of Mediolanum (Wolkersdorf, north of Vienna), Eburodunum (Brünn in Moravia), Meliodunum on the border of Moravia and Bohemia, Budorigum (Brieg in Silesia), and Lugidunum (Liegnitz). To the north-east there are still some names, but they are very infrequent and doubtful (Müllenhoff, op. cit., ii, map 1).

frontier of Gotha. It has always been a frontier, and its name has been supposed to come from the mounted wardens who guarded it, as if it was derived from *rennen* and *steigen*; not a very satisfactory explanation. Now, it is the name of a road.[1] Further west, running roughly north and south, is a small range, once the frontier between Franconia and Thuringia, called the Rhön, a name for which Germanic furnishes no plausible explanation.[2] Celtic, on the other hand, gives us two words, which may be one and the same. First, there is Middle Breton *reun*, Irish *roen* " a hill ". *Run* implies a Gaulish **roino*. In Irish *roen* means a road, that is, a raised road, and in Gaelic *raon* means a stretch of land (cf. *céte* " hill " and " road "). Secondly, Gaelic *roin* or *rann*, corresponding to Welsh *rhan*, Cornish *ran*, and Breton *rann*, means a division. Now both the Rennstieg and the Rhön are at once heights and boundaries [3]; and, what is more, these parallel ranges, running in two successive lines across the horizon from the Elbe to the Rhine, are crowned with prehistoric forts, for here Celts and Germans were for a long time in conflict.

We can, then, have some idea how far the Celtic domain extended northwards and eastwards at a time which is not so remote that all memory of their occupation is gone and over a period which was long enough for it to leave permanent traces.[4]

Did that domain not extend further ?

Beyond the Boii, in the time of Tacitus, it seems—at least, Tacitus is our informant—there was a Celtic people, the Cotini,[5] speaking its own language, between the Quadi, who were Germans, and the Sarmatians, who were Slavs or Indo-Iranians. They must have been somewhere near Galicia. They paid tribute, and, what should be noted, were the people who worked the iron mines. Whether they were

---

[1] Bædeker, *Mittel- und Norddeutschland*, p. 419 (Leipzig, 1885).

[2] Krause, **CCCXCVII**, pp. 8 ff.

[3] Müllenhoff, op. cit., ii, pp. 207 ff. ; Goetze, in **LXXXV**, Erganzgsb., ii, 1910–11, p. 91.

[4] Reinecke, **CCCCVI**, p. 9, draws the line, at the beginning of the La Tène period, along the Thüringer Wald, Frankenwald, and Erzgebirge, taking in Silesia. Bremer, in Paul, **CCCLXVII**, iii, p. 774.

[5] *Germ.*, 43 : *Cotinos Gallica . . . lingua coarguit non esse Germanos et quod tributa patiuntur. Partem tributorum Sarmatœ, partem Quadi ut alienigenis imponunt.*

a remnant left by the Celts in a region which they had abandoned, or the lost outpost of a Celtic expedition into north-eastern Europe, we should have no means of deciding (even if we have to accept blindly the statements of the ancient interpreters on which Tacitus's information is based), did ethnographical archæology not here furnish its decisive testimony.

Another piece of linguistic information, apparently less valuable, also supplied by Tacitus, has in recent years given rise to a number of rather adventurous theories. In the south-east corner of the Baltic lived the Æstii, or Esthonians.[1] Through the amber trade they had dealings with the Teutons of the Cimbric Peninsula, or Jutland, and the coasting traders of the West. Tacitus says that they were akin to the Celts in language—*lingua Britanniæ propior*. This is possible, but they were not Celts. The Celtic etymology ascribed to the Polish, Lithuanian, Lettish, and Esthonian names of rivers and other place-names is purely fanciful, where they are not derived from pan-European roots.[2] The similarity of Ptolemy's name for the Oder, Οὐιαδούα, to that of the Irish river Οὐίδονα,[3] is deceptive. The likenesses between Celtic, Balto-Slavonic, and even Finnish do not compel one to conclude that the Celts dwelt for hundreds of years on the Vistula.

The most serious argument is the resemblance in name between the Wends, the Veneti of Morbihan, and the Veneti of Venetia.[4] But here again, as in the case of the Volcæ and the Volsci, we may have an old name which survived in differentiated branches of the Indo-Europeans, or even the name of an old people which split up among differentiated linguistic groups. Neither history nor archæology allows us to suppose that Europe was divided racially into clearly defined, watertight compartments. Movements, larger and smaller, were always taking place, raids of varying amplitude, which broke down frontiers, obliterated distances, and threw up unexpected colonies in the remotest quarters. These incidents upset the composite picture of the Europeans which we laboriously try to put together by assembling the remains of their cultures and their

[1] *Germ.*, 45. [2] Niederlé, **CCCLXIV**, i, p. 24.
[3] Bremer, in Paul, op. cit., ii, p. 774. [4] **LXXXV**, 1922, p. 59.

languages. We must accept that disorderliness, and regard the past, like the present, in all its complexity.

The question whether the Cimbri and Teutons were Celtic is of quite a different kind. Their chiefs have Celtic names, and in their country the most important specimen of Celtic plastic art was found—the Gundestrup cauldron. They held in their hands the amber trade, that favourable soil for racial cross-breeding. The ancient geographers dispose of the problem by describing the Teutons and the peoples who traded in amber between Esthonia and the mouth of the Elbe as Celto-Scythians.[1] We have not advanced much further than they. Are these folk Germanized Celts? Are they Celticized Germans? And from when does the mixture date? The question will arise again, when we have to study the fluctuations of the Celto-Germanic frontier.[2] As for the question whether the Celts at some time occupied the seaboard extending from the root of Jutland to the mouth of the Rhine, it must remain open until further arguments have been examined.

On the west and south, the original domain of the Celts, or of those Celts of whose domain we can at this stage have any idea, comes to an end where names of the Ligurian or Ræto-Ligurian type begin.

These are the ancient place-names of Liguria properly so called, names which have the same terminations ; names, particularly of rivers, which are found (on the Italian side, for instance) outside the limits ever reached by the Celts, names also of physical features which are unintelligible in Celtic (though this method of determination is not trustworthy), and names found in Celtic lands which present phonetic peculiarities which are foreign to Celtic.

Names ending in -*usco*, -*asco*, -*osco* are the most typical. They appear in numbers in the oldest documents regarding the geography of the Ligurian country (Neviasca, Tulelasca, Veraglasca, Vinelasca, streams in the neighbourhood of Genoa) and wherever the ancient historians mention the presence of Ligurians.[3] Peutinger's Map gives a station of Caranusca (cf. Carrara and Caria, now Chieri) on the road

[1] Strabo, xi, 6, 2 ; cf. i, 2, 27 ; Plut., *Mar.*, ii.
[2] See the following volume in this series.
[3] D'Arbois, **CCCI**, ii, pp. 68 ff.

from Metz to Treves.   In the Eifel there were a Pagus
Carouuascus,[1] a Carascus (now Karsch) near Treves, and an
Yvasco ; near Malmédy, a Via Masuerisca, mentioned in
a Merovingian document ; in Luxemburg, a Villa Marisca.
In Bavaria, south of Munich, probably near Tolz, there was in
the ninth century a Radinasc.[2] These names mark the extreme
north-east frontier of names in -asco, -osco, and -usco.   That
frontier is important.

But it is not the extreme limit of all Ligurian names.[3]
Names of rivers have been found beyond.[4] Certainly more
have been found than ever existed.[5] We must, too,
distinguish Ligurian names from the Iberian names which
also came so far. For example, the various rivers called Dore,
Dorre, etc., have their counterparts in the Rhine Valley,
such as the Thur, a tributary of the Ill, which was once
Dura.[6] Fortunatus mentions a Rodanus, an affluent of the
Moselle.[7] The name of the Drôme, Druna, reappears in
Bavaria in the Traun, a sub-tributary of the Inn.[8]

The Isar (Isara) has been regarded as having a Ligurian
name no less than the Isère, and so have the Isen (Isana),
Ammer (Ambra), and Lieser (Lesura).[9] The valley of the
Moselle, down to the neighbourhood of Treves, and a great
part of the left bank of the Rhine were Ligurian country ;
the right bank of the Danube, all that constituted Vindelicia,
had been Ræto-Ligurian and doubtless remained so in part.
If we are tempted to recognize Ligurian names beyond, we
must examine them very critically.

It is probable that the Celts took a great part of their
domain in Germany from the lands of the Ligurians and
Iberians, but that was doubtless at a very early date.   It
is also probable that their advance for a long time halted on

[1] Ibid., p. 70.
[2] Cf. Livy, xlii, 7 : In Liguribus . . . ad oppidum Carystum (or Caruscum).
[3] Cramer, CXCV.
[4] The Celtic name of Worms, Borbitomagus, contains a non-Celtic
element. This is found again in the name of a god, who is sometimes called
Bormo and sometimes Borvo. He was the god of hot springs. The variation
between m and v is not Celtic.   It only appears in the name of the Cevennes.
Cf. above, p. 50.
[5] e.g. the name of the Vimina and that of the Albis   (Philipon, CCCLXIX,
p. 300), which is certainly pan-European.
[6] Holder, CCVII, i, p. 1378.
[7] M. Müller, in CLVII, 1906, pp. 451–550.
[8] Holder, op. cit., i, p. 1331.
[9] Philipon, op. cit., pp. 295, 300.

a line running through Treves, the Vosges, and Upper Bavaria.[1] That, roughly, is the south-western limit of the oldest Celtic domain that can be determined by the method which we have so far followed. It would, moreover, be rash to try to make the line too straight and simple.

IV

THE DOMAIN OF THE CELTS IN GERMANY.
ARCHÆOLOGICAL DATA [2]

On the north-east the frontier of the Celtic civilization of La Tène coincides roughly with that which we have obtained from the linguistic evidence. We shall now see that on that line, from the end of Neolithic times, there was established a fairly stable archæological frontier, which can only be the frontier of the Celts and the Germans.

It ran at the beginning of the La Tène period a little to the east of the ridge of the Thüringer Wald, between the upper valleys of the Saale and the Weisser-Elster.

Excavations conducted in this region near Ranis, east of Saalfeld,[3] have revealed a certain number of contemporary cemeteries belonging to that time. Some are composed of inhumation-tombs and others, known as urn-fields, were confined to cremations. Their distribution is somewhat confused. The inhumation-cemeteries belong to the Gauls, although that race continued to practise cremation at the beginning of the period ; the urn-fields are, at least chiefly, the work of the Germans, who adhered to the old rites.

At the level of Weimar the urn-fields are found west of the Saale. Below the mouth of the Saale the cemeteries contemporary with La Tène I are urn-fields (Map 5).

---

[1] It should be observed that the name of the Argonne may be connected with that of the Hercynian Forest (Wiedemann, in Bezzenberger, xxviii, 1904).

[2] See recent publications of Herr G. Kraff, *Die Kultur der Bronzezeit in Süddeutschland* (Augsburg, 1926) ; "Beiträge zur Kenntniss der Urnenfelderkultur in Süddeutschland," in **XXXVII**, cxxxi, 1927, pp. 154 ff. ; "Urnenfelder in Westeuropa," ibid., 1929, pp. 47 ff.

[3] Déchelette, ii, 3, pp. 1074 ff. ; Reinecke, **CLVIII**, p. 480 ; Kropp, **CCCXCVIII** (cf. H. Hubert, in **CXL**, 1912, p. 364) ; K. Jakob, " Die La-Tène-Funde der Leipsiger Gegend," in **LXXIV**, ii, 1907 ; H. Busse, *La-Tène-Gräberfeld bei Schmetzdorf* ; W. Hindenburg, " Neue Funde der La-Tène-Zeit aus dem Kreise Tetlow," in **LXXXV**, ii, pp. 194 ff. ; K. Wasse, " Möritzer Funde," ibid., i, pp. 273 ff. ; E. Wahle, " Ein Grabfund der Spät-Latènezeit von Zahna," ibid., 1912, pp. 306 ff.

Objects of a Celtic type of manufacture are found in the Germanic cemeteries, but are less and less frequent the further away one goes. Also cultural differences in craftsmanship appear on the racial frontier. For instance, the copies of pottery-types are less well executed, and hand-made vases are more frequent. The shape of objects, too, is altered; for example, that of swords and scabbards. Scabbards of the Germanic type have been found in the upper valley of the

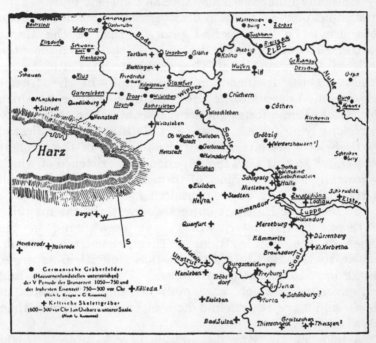

MAP 5. The Frontier between Celts and Germans in La Tène. Legend: ● Germanic urn-fields of the fifth period of the Bronze Age, 1050–750, and earliest Iron Age, 750–500. ✛ Celtic inhumations, 600–500, in the Eastern Harz and on the lower Saale (Kossinna, *Ursprung und Verbreitung der Germanen in vor- und frühgeschichtlicher Zeit*, Mannus-Bibliothek, No. 6, Leipzig, Curt Kabitzsch, p. 32, fig. 45).

Saale, at Grossromstedt in the Kreis of Apolda.[1] This is as far as they reach towards the south and west.

On the Lower Rhine the boundary was at the level of Cologne.[2] Below that the La Tène civilization is confined

[1] See Kossinna, CCCXCVI ; for brooches, see R. Beltz, in CLXIX, 1911 pp. 664 ff. ; 1912, pp. 660 ff. ; Motefind, ibid., 1913, pp. 101 ff.
[2] Rademacher, in LXXXV, i, pp. 83 ff.

to the left bank. Upstream it is not really well represented on the right bank until one comes to the Neuwieder Becken, near Coblenz.[1]

Between the Rhine and the Elbe, it is absent in Westphalia and Hanover, where the previous civilization persists, very little influenced by the new fashions.[2]

In the south-western corner of Germany the La Tène culture was particularly rich and brilliant. It is represented by especially numerous and especially ancient finds.[3] It is on account of these German discoveries that we have had to recognize a La Tène period prior to that of the Marne burials.[4] The map (Map 6) drawn by Déchelette to show the finds of Greek and Italo-Greek objects in Celtic tombs brings out the frequency of these tombs in the district between the Lower Moselle and the Upper Danube, of which the Middle Rhine forms the axis, in contrast to their rarity in regions lying further west. The Hallstatt finds indicated by Déchelette are late Hallstatt,[5] and some of them might be ascribed to this La Tène A period, the existence of which is generally accepted. Most of them were made in the south of the region which we are considering.

To these late Hallstatt objects we must add the majority of those, scarcely later, which have been found in the region of the Middle Rhine. They come from tumuli, similar to the Hallstatt tumuli—those of Klein-Aspergle, Dürkheim, Rodenbach, Armsheim, Waldalgesheim, and Schwarzenbach—which were most certainly the tombs of chiefs, and have been found here in greater numbers than anywhere else.

A map showing the distribution of gold objects would look very much the same,[6] but with one addition, namely, an important group of finds in the country of the Volcæ Tectosages in France, at Cordes, Montans, and Lasgraïsses in the department of the Tarn, and at Fenouillet in the Haute-Garonne.[7] Here there was, without any doubt, a very wealthy

[1] Gunther, ibid., iii, pp. 1 ff.; Schumacher, **CCCCIX**, pl. viii.
[2] W. Schulz, in **LXXXV**, x, pp. 108 ff., 226.
[3] Déchelette, iii, 3, pp. 1063 ff.
[4] See above, p. 126.
[5] Kappel-am-Rhein, Vilsingen, Pisek (Déchelette, ii, 3, pp. 1597, 1596, 1599). The finds marked in the east (the Vettersfelde treasure and the Vogelsang bracelet) are Scythian.
[6] Ibid. pp. 1332 ff.   [7] Ibid., pp. 1339 ff.

colony, the colony of a wealthy people. But the bulk of the gold objects were in Germany, and it was between the Moselle and the Danube that the axis of the Celtic world still lay in La Tène I. It was in this region that the wealthiest aristocracy remained established. The Volcæ and still more

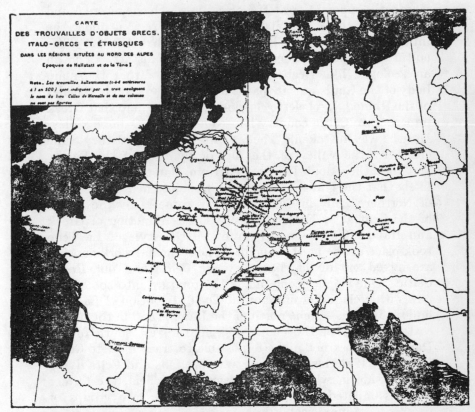

MAP 6. Finds of Greek, Italo-Greek, and Etruscan Objects north of the Alps in Hallstatt and La Tène I. Legend : Hallstatt finds (i.e. earlier than 500 B.C.) have the name of the place underlined. Those of Marseilles and its colonies are not given. (Déchelette, iii, map v.)

the Helvetii, who for a long time occupied the south-western corner of this region, left behind them a reputation for riches, riches in gold, which they doubtless obtained by washing the sand of the Rhine.[1]

[1] For the collection of gold in rivers among the Celts, see Athenæos, vi, 233, following Poseidonios ; for the wealth of the Volcæ in gold, see Strabo, vi, 1, 13.

The great tumuli of which I have spoken contained either skeletons or ashes. But inhumation, which came to prevail in La Tène I, even in this part of Germany, had not yet become general, and still less had burial in flat-graves. Therefore the great majority of the Greek objects found were early importations. The places in which they were found lead one to think that it was just in this region, under the influence of Greek or Italo-Greek art, that the La Tène culture became different from that of Hallstatt. For an archæologist like Déchelette they are proof that the main body of the Gauls was at that time in Germany, on both sides of the Rhine.[1] Déchelette concluded from his map that Greek imports into Celtic country had come by the Danube valley. Here he was mistaken.[2] The map itself shows that they came either by the valley of the Aar or by that of the Saône, and that they doubtless started from Marseilles. But it is likely that the Italian objects which maintained the fashions of Northern Italy in Celtic countries came in by the passes of the Central or Eastern Alps.[3] The conjunction of Greek and Italic influences which produced the style of La Tène took place at the meeting-point. The style and workmanship are mixed, no doubt, but they are Celtic and not Ræto-Celtic. One single people made the mixture into something new with a character of its own. The distribution of La Tène finds in Bavaria—some north of the Danube and in the north-eastern corner of the country [4] and the rest south of the Danube [5]—does not make it possible to trace a Ræto-Celtic frontier. If at this time there were Rætians and Celts living side by side in what was afterwards Vindelicia, the former were assimilated or the settlements of the two groups of peoples were inextricably interspersed.[6]

So in La Tène I the archæological map still coincides, on the whole, with the linguistic map. The movements of the Gauls westwards and southwards had not yet shifted the former balance of their settlements. Their old homes were in Germany. There they remained for a long time yet. Afterwards, when the Celtic body had extended indefinitely,

---

[1] Déchelette, ii, 3, p. 913.
[2] Piroutet, in **XV**, xxix, pp. 213 ff. ; xxx, pp. 31 ff. ; cf. Hubert, in **CXL**, 1925, pp. 252 ff.
[3] See above, pp. 128–9.
[5] Ibid.
[4] Reinecke, **CCCCVI**, p. 5.
[6] Mehlis, **DXLV**.

examination of their funeral rites, failing other information, shows that one of its chief centres was there. For it was there that they introduced the new and there that they maintained the old. There they continued to build tumuli until La Tène II; there they began making them again in La Tène III; and it was probably there that the practice of cremation, which had long been preserved there, was revived.[1]

In Bohemia the Celts did not yet occupy more than the south-western corner of the country at the beginning of

FIG. 82. Hallstatt Pottery from Germany. (Schumacher, *Siedelungs- u. Kulturgesch.*, figs. 28, 31, 33.) 1–3, Gündling type. 4, Salem type. 5, Koberstadt type.

the La Tène period.[2] Their La Tène burials are there found in tumuli; at Pisek, an early Greek *œnochoë* and a basin, also Greek, have been discovered. Then, in the course of the first La Tène period, they expanded towards the line which I have indicated. The cemeteries which they have left there are like those of the Marne.

---

[1] Schumacher, **CCCCIX**, pp. 144 ff. For tumuli of La Tène II, see P. Horter, in **LXXXV**, x, p. 231; H. Hornung, in **LXVII**, v, pp. 19, 102. For tumuli of La Tène III, see Reinecke, in **LXXXI**, 1919, p. 12.
[2] Déchelette, p. 1078.

In the Hallstatt period the same state of things already obtained all over this region. From Bohemia and Bavaria to the neighbourhood of Cologne we find the same tumuli, with some local differences in construction which are hard to reduce to a system.[1] In these tumuli there are the same urns, shaped like tops, which are unlike the Hallstatt urns of the Middle Danube and are, on the whole, decorated in the south and plainer in the north (Fig. 32), their differences perhaps corresponding to tribal divisions, but to divisions inside one same group of peoples.[2] The urns are accompanied by grave-gear which varies greatly between the beginning of the Hallstatt period and the end, being richer in pottery at the beginning and in ornaments and arms at the end,[3] but includes brooches related to the Italic types [4] and unlike the two-piece brooches common to the centre and coastal districts of Germany, and iron swords.

The north-east frontier is the same. The urn-fields of Westphalia and Hanover lie outside it.[5] Hut-urns extend as far as it, and there stop.[6] The deposit discovered at Wahren, near Leipzig, in 1915,[7] is a typical find. It includes an engraved iron collar with buttons set at right angles on the ends. This is a type of collar which is found in Eastern Germany as far as the Baltic, but doubtless comes from the Illyrian countries. The deposit also contained an ingot of iron in the shape of a double pyramid. This is the easternmost find of an ingot of the type, which is very frequent in the southern angle of the Rhine. It is probable that the Celtic countries supplied the Germanic lands with iron at the time, and this would agree with the fact that the Germans took the word for " iron " from Celtic.

On the western side there are the same outlying sites as in La Tène I,[8] but again the great majority of tumuli are in Western Germany.

In relation to the culture of Western Germany the superiority belongs to that of the Middle Danube, which had

[1] Ibid., ii, 2, pp. 606 ff.
[2] Schumacher, op. cit., p. 86 ; Hubert, in **CXL**, 1925, p. 125.
[3] F. Kaufmann, **CCCXLVII**, i, p. 196.
[4] D. Viollier, in **CCCCXC**, pp. 26 ff. ; Beltz, in **CLXIX**, 1912, pp. 660, 26 ff.
[5] Schulz, in **LXXXV**, x, pp. 108 ff.
[6] Schumacher, **CCCCVIII**, p. 38.
[7] M. Næbe, in **LXXXV**, 1915, p. 83 ; G. Kossinna, ibid., p. 84.
[8] See the following volume in this series.

a different history. This alone would suffice to explain how Illyrian elements entered into the population of Southern Germany with the Illyrian civilization.[1] It seems, too, to be as difficult to trace a Ræto-Celtic frontier in Bavaria in this period as in La Tène I.[2] In Bohemia the area of the tumuli, which I have regarded as coinciding with that of the Celts, was the same.

If it were possible to use the argument of permanence of habitat there would be no doubt that the same men lived all over this region in the Hallstatt and La Tène periods. But habits of life changed much in the course of the Iron Age, and the population shifted accordingly.[3] Only in a few places can one definitely say that it stayed where it was— about Hagenau, at Grossgartach, on the Heiligenberg near Heidelberg, on the Hennenberg near Riedlingen.[4] But it moved within only a small area. The archæological maps of the Hallstatt and La Tène periods coincide in great part.[5] Herr Schumacher has made the continuity of population all over the Rhineland quite plain.[6]

If we go back yet further in time we find the archæological map of the third and fourth Bronze Age periods [7] much like that of Hallstatt, but with narrower extensions westwards. Again there are tumuli and special types of pottery from Bohemia to Cologne and from Cologne to Switzerland, with changes in fashion [8]; the same weapons and the same bronze objects appear in tombs and deposits.[9] The same line forms a rough frontier, not between an area of tumuli and one of urn-fields, for funeral practices were generally much the same on both sides, but between two kinds of metal-working, with distinctly different characteristics. The thick-hilted Germanic swords, the Baltic axes, the gorgets, the

[1] See above, pp. 128–9.
[2] J. Naue, in CXXXIX, 1895, 2, p. 40 ; XV, 1897, p. 641 ; M. von Geyer and P. v. Goessler, in X, 1917, p. 29.
[3] T. Voges, in LXXXV, i, p. 288.
[4] For Hagenau, see Schumacher, CCCCIX, i, p. 66, n. 33 (see also Schæffer, CCCCVII) ; for Grossgartach and the Heiligenberg, ibid., p. 135 ; for the Hennenberg, G. Bersu, in LXV, 1917, p. 22. Herr Schumacher does not raise the question, and that is perhaps why he does not answer it ; my own personal notes are also unsatisfactory.
[5] Maps : For the Forest of Hagenau see Schumacher, op. cit., i, p. 67, fig. 21 ; for Grossgartach, ibid., p. 44, fig. 14 and pls. iv–x.
[6] Ibid., map, pl. x.
[7] Cf. Lissauer's maps, in CLXIX, 1904–7.
[8] Schumacher, op. cit., i, p. 61.   [9] CCCXCIX, v, p. 38.

large cast brooches, hardly extend beyond Thuringia, on the one side; the axes, swords, pins, and general knick-knackery of Western Germany hardly pass it, on the other.[1] On the one side industry is connected with that of Switzerland, Eastern France, and Italy; on the other, with that of the Danube valley and Hungary.

An archæological map of the second period of the Bronze Age would present an utterly confused picture. Moreover, it is difficult in the archæology of the beginning of the Bronze Age to say how much is due to native settlements, to trade, to itinerant craftsmen, and to the influences of other civilizations.

Meanwhile, something happened which adds much confusion to the picture of the archæology of the West, namely, the spread of the civilization which is chiefly represented by the curious pottery known as Lausitz or Lusatian ware.[2] This culture stretched in a belt, narrowing west of the Rhine, from Galicia to France, where traces of it are found in Normandy and Dordogne,[3] leaving pottery with relief decoration in countries where pottery was incised and urn-fields in countries of tumuli and inhumations. The phenomenon may be the result of one of those abnormal movements of peoples, as we may call them, which are known to have occurred several times in the history of the world, which, without altering the racial maps permanently, have upset them considerably. This movement had a great effect on the civilization of Western Europe, and it must have brought very large bodies of settlers to the west of Germany, for at the end of the Bronze Age their funeral practice prevailed everywhere, and it persisted into the Hallstatt period.[4]

In the region which has thus been defined archæology reveals nothing corresponding to the separation of two groups of peoples, related yet having linguistic differences which imply a real separation. On the contrary, everything points to unity, concentration, and increasing concentration. In that region there was only one group of Celts, that of the Brythonic Gauls. Also, as we have seen, the place-names show that p was used, as in Lopodunum (Ladenburg), Lupias (the Lippe), and the Finne, from pennos.

---

[1] See map in Kossinna, **CCCXCVI**, fig. 17.
[2] H. Hubert, in **CXLIII**, 1910, pp. 5 ff.   [3] See below, p. 251.
[4] H. Horter, in **LXXXV**, 1913, p. 307.

V

THE GOIDELIC CRADLE

But whence did the Goidels come, and when did they come ? Where must we look for their earliest home on the Continent and their starting-point ? Probably they came from north of the Brythonic domain, and it is to them that tradition refers when it tells that the Celts used to live on the low coasts of the North Sea. They must have left those shores very early, for hardly a trace of them remains there.

Such was not the opinion of the great Celticist, Zimmer.[1] He maintained that the Goidels came from France, and probably by the Atlantic coast, starting from south of the mouth of the Loire. He has set himself to study the relations of the British Isles with the Continent. He had collected a great number of facts about the trade which went on at the beginning of the Middle Ages between Ireland and the French coast, especially the wine-trade, and he held that men had gone to Ireland by the same route as goods. But there is not only one route by which goods or men could have gone from the Continent to Ireland. There are at least two others, one by which the Angles and Saxons went from the mouth of the Elbe to the east coast of England and over England to Ireland, and one which the Vikings of Denmark and Norway took round the north of Scotland and past the Isles to the north of Ireland and the gates of the Irish Sea.

But at what date did the Goidels cross over ?

An orthodox but unfortunate answer is supplied by the use of the word κασσίτερος in Homer to mean " tin ".[2] The tin which was worked up in Greece came from the Cassiterides Islands, which may have been Scilly and were, in any case, a Celtic country[3] ; it was Celtic tin, τὸν κασσίτερον τὸν Κελτικόν, according to the author of the

---

[1] In **IX**, pp. 1–59.
[2] D'Arbois, **CCXCIX**, p. 19 ; S. Reinach, in **XV**, 1892, p. 275.
[3] L. Siret (in **XV**, 1908, p. 129) places the Cassiterides in Brittany ; G. Bonsor (in **XXXIV**, 1921, p. 60), in Bætica (Mons Casius, in *Avienus*, 259–261). Cf. J. Loth (in **CXL**, xxxviii, p. 260), on ancient tin-working in the Scilly Isles. Carty (in **LXXXVIII**, 1924, pp. 166–7), commenting on a very troublesome passage in Pliny (vii, 119), supposes that the sea-route to the tin countries was discovered in the sixth century by a Phocæan navigator named Midacritus.

Marvels attributed to Aristotle.[1] If tin is Celtic its name may be. D'Arbois de Jubainville saw in it a Celtic stem, *cassi-*, meaning " pleasant ". The Irish noun *caise*, containing this stem *cassi*, means " esteem ", " love ", while the adjective *cais* means " elegant ".[2] M. Salomon Reinach has suggested that *kassiteros* got its name from the Cassiterides ; d'Arbois was of opinion that it was a Celtic comparative.[3] So the Celts and, at least, the Goidels, must have held the Western tin-mines about 800 B.C., and doubtless had done so for a long time.[4] The reasoning is satisfactory, but the premiss is doubtful. Its chief weakness is that there is no equivalent for the word at all in Celtic. Tin is called *stan* in Irish and *ystaen* in Welsh.[5] These may have been borrowed from the Latin ; but it is not likely that a word describing an important product which was almost peculiar to the Celts would have disappeared, particularly since it was supported by Greek usage.

A preferable etymology [6] makes κασσίτερος a Greek comparative, and connects it with κασίγνητος, a close relation. It is a term of kinship which belongs to the dialects of Asia Minor, attested by the lexicographers in the forms κάσις, κασσᾶς, κάσας, κασύας, and κασσύας, and meaning very close relationship. So κασσίτερος refers to the kinship of tin and lead, which are always brought together and always compared to each other. Tin was called *plumbum album*.[7]

We must turn to archæology in order to go back so far, and even further, in the history of the movements of the Celts. The Hallstatt period is out of the question. Except at the end it is hardly represented in the British Isles, and

---

[1] Ps.-Arist., *De Mir. Ausc.*, 1, 834a, 6.

[2] **CCXCIX**, p. 19. The stem is very well represented in Celtic. The Gauls had gods called Casses, there was a British people of the Cassi, and it appears in many compound names—Cassivellaunos, Cassignatus, etc.

[3] A comparative of equality. The comparative of superiority is in -*yos-*, like the Latin comparative, and the Greek comparative in ιων.

[4] Mr. MacNeill (**CCCCXLI**, p. 47) believes that the word is Celtic, but that it does not prove that the Celts were in possession of the country where tin was extracted.

[5] Middle Irish also said *cred* (O'Curry, **CCLXXVIII**, p. ccccix).

[6] S. Reinach, in **XV**, 1892, pp. 275 ff.

[7] Pokorny (in **CLXXI**, 1913, pp. 164 ff.) derives the word from the Elamite *Cassi*, which appears in the name of the Kassites, *Kassi-ti-ra*, whence Sanskrit *Kastira*. Cf. Hüsing, in **CXIV**, 1907, p. 25 ; Bork, in **CLXIII**, 1917, p. 541 (*Kassitú*, the name of an Elamite god).

what we know of its last phase is not enough for us to imagine a Celtic colonization of any magnitude distinct from that which took place in the La Tène period. But the archæology of the Bronze Age presents two series of facts which must be considered. Apart from those scholars who do not think that there were any Celts in the British Isles before the La Tène period, opinions are divided between two hypotheses which place the arrival of the first wave at the beginning and at the end of the Bronze Age respectively.[1]

In the first period of the Bronze Age there arrived in the British Isles, coming from the Continent, people with very marked characteristics.[2] The old Neolithic inhabitants (among whom I include those of all the beginning of the

FIG. 33. Bronze Age Pottery from England. Zoned Beakers from the Round Barrows. 1, Lambourn Down, Berks. 2–3, Goodmanham, Yorks (Ebert, *Reallexicon*, 2, pl. 248 ; B.M. *Guide* to the Bronze Age).

Bronze Age) were long-heads of Mediterranean type, who built for their dead, or, at least, for the more distinguished of them, tumuli with a funeral chamber known as " long barrows ", in which one sometimes finds those curious bell-shaped beakers adorned at regular intervals with bands of incised or stamped decoration, of a very simple and austere type. The newcomers were of quite a different type, and had other funeral practices.[3]

They buried their dead under round tumuli, known as

[1] D'Arbois (**CCC**, p. 16) says that the Goidels imported metal-working into the British Isles, but did not arrive there until between 1300 and 800, i.e. at the very end of the Bronze Age or well within the Hallstatt period. Cf. Allen, **CCXCVIII**, p. 21.
[2] A. Keith, in **LXXVI**, 1915, p. 12 ; J. Loth, in **CXL**, xxxviii, p. 271 ; Holmes, **CCCCXXXIII**, p. 119.
[3] Keane, **CCCXLIX**, p. 527.

" round barrows ", in graves in which the body was placed
in a crouching position on one side and enclosed in stone
flags or woodwork.[1] Later they burned them. In their graves
there were zoned beakers (Fig. 33), but of a late type in which
the neck is distinguished from the belly, or vases derived
from these beakers.[2] The funeral urns descended from them.
The grave-goods comprised buttons with a V-shaped boring,
flint [3] and copper daggers, arrow-heads, and flat perforated
pieces of schist which are " bracers ", or bowman's wrist-
guards.[4] The skeletons were of a new type : tall, with round
head of a fairly constant shape, the brow receding, the
supraciliary ridge prominent, the cheek-bones highly
developed, and the jaws massive and projecting so as to
present a dip at the base of the nose. I have already described
them as one of the types represented in Celtic burials.[5]

The association of the physical type of this people with
the beaker has led British anthropologists to call it the
Beaker Folk. Some of the invaders landed in Britain on the
east, in the region of York and about the Firth of Forth ;
others landed in the south and established themselves on
the Downs, where they were very densely grouped about
Salisbury.[6] In Scotland they were accompanied by other
brachycephals, with a higher index and of Alpine type.[7]
In general they advanced from south to north and from east
to west, and their progress lasted long enough for there to
be a very marked difference in furniture between their oldest
and latest tombs. As they advanced they scattered, and they
are comparatively few in the north of Scotland and in Wales.[8]

[1] Holmes, op. cit., p. 179. For variety in the construction of tumuli,
ibid., p. 175.
[2] Abercromby, in **LXXVI**, 1902, p. 373.
[3] For the chronology of the flint daggers, see Smith, in **CXXXIII**, 32.
It must not be forgotten that all these things are later than the introduction
of metal, and that the flint daggers are contemporaneous with the bronze
ones.
[4] Evans, **CCCCXXIV**, pp. 420 ff. ; del Castillo, **CCCIX**, pls. cxcv ff.,
p. 185.
[5] See above, pp. 29 ff. ; Loth, loc. cit., p. 272 ; Keith, loc. cit.
Index, between 68 and 88 ; average height, 5 ft. 7½ in.
[6] O. G. S. Crawford, in **LXVI**, xl, 1912, p. 184. Loth (loc. cit., p. 275)
notes about 2,000 tumuli in Wiltshire alone. A. Dote, in **CXXIV**, 1911–12,
p. 15.
[7] Loth, loc. cit., p. 273 : Index, between 82 and 92 ; height, 5 ft. 5 in. ;
Keith, loc. cit. ; Fleure, **CCCXXVIII**, p. 51.
[8] List of beakers found in Wales in *Bull. Bd. Celt. Soc.*, i, p. 182 ; ii–iv,
p. 389 ; E. M. Wheeler, in **XVI**, 1923, p. 21.

Their progress was a conquest. It is evident that they subdued and assimilated the previous occupants of the country. It is true that they did not come in sufficient numbers [1] to alter the average type of the population, whose descendants still formed a considerable minority,[2] but they were strong enough to impose certain important and predominant features of their civilization down to the end of the Bronze Age and later still.

But whence came these invaders ? The beakers and their very ancient forms are found in Sicily, Sardinia, and Italy, but above all in Spain,[3] and it has become the practice to regard them as having originated in that country.[4] In any case, they are one of the relics of the civilization which produced the megalithic monuments. The diffusion of the bell-beaker in Western Europe is a sign of the unity of that civilization. It is the typical vase of the megalith-builders, and in the greater part of France all their pottery recalls it more or less. With the beakers, one finds in this part of the area covered by them the bowman's bracers, the daggers of flint and copper, and the buttons with the V-shaped boring, which are found in the round barrows of Britain. But they do not accompany the same type of skeleton. The beakers themselves are more like those of the British long barrows than those of the round barrows. Between these last no transitional form has yet been reported, and the difference between them, in spite of their indisputable kinship, is what has first struck all observers.

The bell-beaker spread in the seaboard region of Northern Europe, in the area of the megalithic monuments, and, though no perfectly normal specimens are found in Denmark, variants of it are found in many Danish burials.[5] But others are found elsewhere, outside the region of the megaliths. The German archæologists call them zone-beakers,

[1] Abercromby (**CCCCXII**, p. 69) places the number of invaders very low, basing his calculation on the number of tombs found, and gets a figure of about 600. Keith rightly objects to this method of reckoning.

[2] Keith, loc. cit. : 20 per cent of a West End club, representing civil servants, squires, and professional men, were found to be of the round-headed type of the invaders.

[3] Del Castillo, **CCCIX**.

[4] H. Schmidt, in **CLXIX**, 1913, p. 235 ; Åberg, **CCCCXCV** ; Bosch Gimpera, **DII** ; del Catillo, op. cit., pp. 29 ff.

[5] Del Castillo, op. cit., pls. ccv, ccvi, 1, 3, p. 191.

Zonenbecher,[1] to distinguish them from the bell-shaped vases. They have a flat bottom, sometimes a foot, and are taller. Sometimes they have been manufactured in the country. The zones are treated differently, tending to fall into groups on the neck of the vase and on the belly, the curve of which is broken, sometimes near the top and sometimes near the bottom.

These zoned vases seem to have come into the Rhine valley from the west. The agricultural peoples of the Rhine, who were very peaceful folk, found themselves at the beginning of the Bronze Age face to face with bowmen, probably coming from the Vosges or the Ardennes, whose armament and dress must have been the same in every detail as those of the Beaker Folk of Britain. They had, too, almost exactly the same funeral practices. They were also round-heads of a particular type, very ancient in Western Europe, which has been compared to the type of Grenelle and that of Ofnet, but certainly resembles the British type of the round barrows.[2]

The map of the distribution of the zoned vases [3] and other objects which go with them is most interesting to study. They are crowded in the Dutch provinces of Guelderland and Drenthe, and along the Rhine from Coblenz to Cologne and, especially, from Mainz to Spire. They have been found in the Taunus, in Hessen, in Hessen-Darmstadt, along the Main, in the valley of the Neckar, and in Bavaria. They appear in Bohemia, crossing it from north-west to south-east. They are, indeed, so numerous there, and the pottery which accompanies them is so varied, that one may ask whether they did not originate there, or come there direct through Italy and across the Danube. Both suggestions seem doubtful. The first, indeed, seems hardly possible, for the zoned vases found in Bohemia appear in a belt, marking the line of a movement which cuts across the settlements of the aborigines.[4] North of Bohemia and the Thuringian mountains, they are numerous in the valley of the Saale and north of it, between Magdeburg

---

[1] Bosch Gimpera, s.v. "Glockenbecherkultur," in Ebert, **CCCXXIV**, del Castillo, op. cit., pp. 141 ff.

[2] A. Schliz, in **XXIII**, 1909, p. 263 ; A. Stocky, in **CXV**, 1919–1920.

[3] Del Castillo, op. cit., map i.

[4] Cervinka, in Ebert, op. cit., s.v. "Böhmen-Mähren" ; del Castillo, op. cit., p. 149.

and the Harz. Further east, in the basin of the Oder, they have been found in Silesia along the Sudeten and about Breslau, and northwards they appear in Westphalia, the province of Osnabrück, Mecklenburg, and the island of Rügen. They are concentrated along the Rhine, in Bohemia, and in Saxony, and scattered in all the rest of Germany west of the Elbe. They are still more thinly spread between the Elbe and the Oder. We must imagine warlike bodies moving fairly fast, for their cemeteries are generally small, ravaging the country but holding it, for the cultures which they found in possession have vanished while theirs has lasted.

This tremendous journey of the bell-beakers and the zone-beakers is still full of mysteries. It was clearly not the same men who used them in Spain and in Bohemia, and one mystery which we should be glad to solve is the origin of the Continental branch which covered Germany and flourished there. We do not find it commencing in France, and the type of man which accompanies it is absent from the normal French series of Neolithic skulls.[1]

It is at least certain that the Beaker Folk went from Germany to Britain, and not from Britain to Germany. The typical round-heads of the round barrows are a Nordic type, which may have grown up on the plains of Northern Europe. No doubt the state of things revealed by British remains of the beginning of the Bronze Age is complex, and one must not draw too close a comparison between the round barrows and the German and Bohemian tombs containing beakers. Other things are found in the round barrows besides beakers and brachycephals. But, apart from these two features, three things have to be considered, which point in the same direction; first, the comparatively large number of cremations; secondly, the similarity of the British barrows to the tumuli of North Germany at the beginning of the Bronze Age and the constant practice of burying the dead, when inhumation is practised, in a contracted position, as in Central Germany; and, lastly, the similarity of many of the urns of the round barrows, which are late developments of the zoned beaker, and of other vases found there, to the so-called Neolithic pottery of North Germany in the region

[1] Cf. Poisson, in **CXXXVIII,** 1929.

of the megaliths.[1] They are a development or a degradation of the same species.

At this point it is legitimate to ask what became of all the people who set up the megalithic monuments in the north-west of Germany, and what became of the tribes of bowmen who were mingled with them, for it is a dogma of German *Siedelungsgeschichte* that all the north-west seaboard, Westphalia, and Hanover were emptied of their inhabitants before the second period of the Bronze Age.[2]

Many scholars, British, German, and French, have accordingly thought that the mixed population of this part of Germany, which one day set off and emigrated, was the original stock of the Goidels.[3]   Others have denied this [4] because very few beakers have so far been discovered in Ireland.[5] Their contention is plainly absurd, for there are two chances out of three that the Goidels crossed Britain in order to reach Ireland, and if the beakers themselves are rare in the country their derivatives are plentiful.[6] But the positive statement requires further proof.

It is not likely that North-Western Germany was depopulated and part of its inhabitants went over into Britain all at once. It is certain that the movement of trade connecting the British Isles with the Continent across the North Sea was not at once affected. At that same time objects manufactured in Ireland—which was rich in metal, especially gold, and much visited by sailors—were travelling as far as the Danish archipelago : axes with very slightly flanged edges and incised and hammered decoration, and gold lunettes.[7] In the period when metal-working was spreading the British Isles had been a half-way house on the route to the north, and now things went on as before.

From the second period of the Bronze Age onwards this current seems to have flowed in the opposite direction.

[1] Del Castillo, op. cit., pp. 161 ff.   For the *Trichterbecher*, cf. **LXXXV**, 1921, pp. 13 ff., 143 ff., 239 ff.
[2] Kossinna, **CCCXCV**, iii.
[3] J. Loth, loc. cit.
[4] Holmes, **CCCCXXXIII**, p. 195.
[5] **CXXXIV**, 1904, pp. 316–17 ; Armstrong, **CCCCXV** ; **CXVIII**, 1911, p. 184 ; A. del Castillo, in **LXXXV**, 1915, p. 34 (Knockmaa, co. Galway) ; W. J. Dargan, ibid., 1916, p. 77 (co. Wicklow).
[6] Holmes, op. cit., p. 187 ; **CCCLXXXIV**, p. 44 ; J. Loth, op. cit., p. 273.
[7] Montelius, **CCCC**, p. 79 ; Déchelette, **CCCXVIII**, ii, 1, pp. 354 ff.

Objects have been found in Ireland and Great Britain which are or may be derived from prototypes in Northern Germany and the Danish archipelago. Does this stream of imports point to a movement of men ? Messrs. Crawford [1] and Peake [2] believe that it does, and that those men were the Goidels.

Their attention is chiefly directed to the flat-tanged swords of which I have spoken above, which are represented in the British Isles by some specimens of their early types. [3] But swords were not the only imports. The great symmetrical brooches of cast bronze passed from Germany into Ireland, where they were made in gold, without pins, and became a kind of clip, used as a fastening. [4] The great torques with turned-back ends of the fifth period of the Germanic Bronze Age followed the same road, [5] as did the breast-ornaments of the same time, formed of several torques set edge to edge, which were imitated in gold wrought in one piece. [6] The curved, broad-headed pins of Eastern Germany are found in Ireland and Scotland, with their characteristic annulations and curved ends. [7]

The Western German pins with the bulge in the middle are found in England. [8] While many of the bronze tools of the British Isles are like those of Western Europe, Spain, and even the Mediterranean countries, some of the latter are noticeably lacking, such as the sickle with a lateral button, and as time goes on a fair number of Northern types and objects come in.

Is all this the consequence of the exodus of the populations once established in Frisia, Hanover, and Westphalia ? It cannot be denied that the facts brought forward are, after all, very meagre, [9] and might be explained without supposing great shiftings of peoples. The practice of cremation, which was general in the British Isles, prevents

[1] O. G. S. Crawford, " A Prehistoric Invasion of England," in XVI, ii, p. 27.

[2] See above, pp. 145 ff.   [3] Peake, CCCCXLVII, pl. xiv.

[4] Coffey, CCCCXXVIII, pl. v.   [5] Ibid., pl. viii.

[6] Ibid., pl. ii.   [7] Childe, *The Bronze Age*, 1930, fig. 14.

[8] Ibid.

[9] Messrs. Crawford and Peake also argue from the appearance in England, at the end of the Bronze Age, of large vases surrounded by lines of finger-prints, which were very common on the Continent at the time. But these are too common objects and too vague characteristics to be used as indications of race.

us from identifying the new invaders, if there were any. Moreover, the British barrows and pottery of the end of the Bronze Age appear to be developments of the barrows and pottery of the beginning.

VI

A VIEW OF THE ORIGINS OF THE CELTS AND ITALO-CELTIC RELATIONS. TRACES OF THE GOIDELS AT THEIR STARTING-POINT

In working up to the origins of the Continental, Brythonic branch of the Celts, we had to stop at the second period of the Bronze Age. At this time, according as one adopts one or the other of the hypotheses set forth above, either the migration of the Goidels was beginning, and their establishment in the country from which they started was much earlier, or else it was over, and we must go back in our search for an undivided Celtic race, to what many still call the Neolithic Age, that is, the long succession of centuries during which metal was slowly coming into use in Western and Northern Europe.

The picture presented, at this approximate date, by the prehistoric archæology of the region which we are considering, is very involved. An attempt has been made to bring some order into the facts revealed by the excavations by distinguishing different civilizations by their pottery. For the pottery (Fig. 34) is very plentiful and varies greatly, whereas this cannot be said of other objects. For types of pottery students have sought corresponding types of man, not without contradictions ; behind civilizations they have tried to detect peoples.[1]

The pottery has been classified in types—that of the megaliths of Northern Germany, that of the lake-dwellings, that which is adorned with incised bands, the beakers on which a pattern has been impressed with cords, the zoned vases, and a number of wares adorned with deeply impressed dots, called after Schönfeld, Rössen, Nierstein, Grossgartach, and other sites.

The pottery of the lake-dwellings and the hill-stations

---

[1] A. Schliz, in **XXIII**, 1909, p. 263 ; **CXVIII**, 1912, pp. 36 ff., 220 ff. Wilcke, ibid., 1909, 3, p. 336 ; Kossinna, in **LXXXV**, 1911, pp. 313 ff.

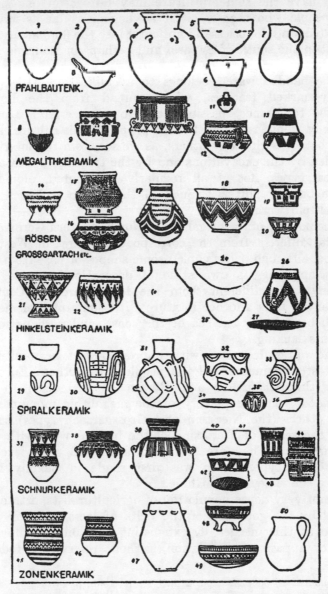

FIG. 34. Neolithic Pottery of Germany. (Schumacher, *Siedelings- u. Kulturgesch.*, p. 58, fig. 18.) The types, reading down, are : Pile-dwelling ; megalith ; Rössen, Grossgartach, etc. ; Hinkelstein ; spiral ; cord-impression ; zoned.

which have the same furniture may be set on one side.[1]
The people who used it, after advancing as far as Mainz,
retreated, and doubtless did not enter into the final amalgams
except in the south of Bavaria and perhaps in Bohemia and
Austria.

The banded ware [2] belongs to a civilization with very
clearly-marked features, which spread from the Lower
Danube to France, passing north of Switzerland, almost
certainly from east to west. The people of this culture came
into contact with many others, as we see from the mixtures
revealed by the excavations and by the frequent appearance
of local types, not at all regularly distributed, alongside
of the banded pottery. Such in the Rhine valley is the
Hinkelstein ware.[3]

The pottery of the megaliths of North-Western Germany [4]
is quite different from the corresponding wares of Western
Europe, although it has copied some shapes of vase from the
latter, applying its own style of decoration.[5] It is not
fundamentally different from the local wares of Central
Germany. It is another mixture with some new elements
added, brought by the sea or the coast, and perhaps some
elements lacking.

The wares decorated with impressed dots bear witness
to a taste common to all the peoples of Northern Europe.
Some (the Schönfeld [6] and Rössen [7] types) seem to be
descended from the pottery of the megalithic monuments,
while others (the Nierstein and Grossgartach types) seem
to be the result of a crossing of the banded ware with the
Rössen type. They are found in a limited area, except
the Rössen type, which was first made in Saxony and
reached the valley of the Rhine.[8]

A not very dense population of agriculturalists, attracted
chiefly by the good soil of the belts of loess, clearing the
ground as they needed it, exhausting the soil and moving
on ; or a pastoral population, without reserves of fodder

---

[1] Schumacher, **CCCCIX**, i, pp. 21 ff.   [2] Ibid., p. 31.
[3] Ibid., p. 34.   [4] Ibid., p. 30.
[5] Kossinna, **CCCXCVI**, pp. 155 ff.
[6] On Neolithic pottery, see Reinecke, in **CLX**, 1900, p. 232 ; Kossinna,
in **LXXXV**, i, 26, 255 ; ii, 59.
[7] Kossinna, **CCCXCVI**, p. 164.
[8] Schumacher, op. cit., i, pp. 39 ff.

and therefore scattered—such was the bulk of the people. Among them tribes of hunters, fishermen, or brigands went about—warlike, conquering tribes, drawn by the woods and the high ground, or by the rivers. These were the men who

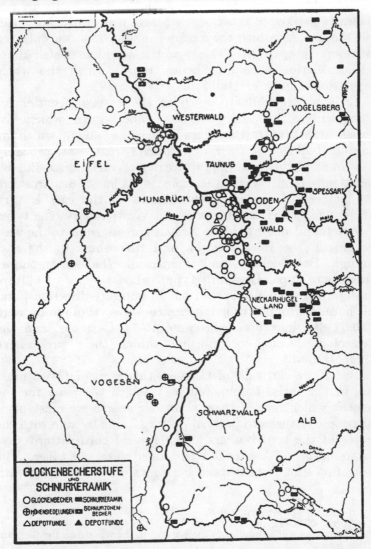

MAP 7. Distribution of Zoned Beakers and Cord-impression Vases in the Rhine Valley. Legend : ◯ Bell-beakers. ⊕ Hill-settlements. ▬ Cord-impression ware. ◙ Schnurzonenbecher. △▲ Deposits. (Schumacher, *Siedelungs- und Kulturgesch.*, pl. iv.)

produced the zoned pottery,[1] or the cord-pattern pottery which is very like it.[2] (Map 7.)

This state of things prevailed roughly in all the districts between the North Sea and Switzerland, and between the Meuse and the Oder. The western and eastern limits are not so clearly marked as those which I have previously described, and the peoples which they bounded were less concentrated and more interwoven. This was the world in which those Celtic societies came into being, round which the whole population finally crystallized.

It is worth while to consider the eastern frontier for a moment. The valley of the Elbe, down which the agriculturalists of the Danubian Plain came [3] and up which the megalith-builders or their descendants went, was, probably as a result of their meeting, a district of variations. But we should note that it was at the same time a line of demarcation. The pottery of the megalithic tombs of the east is very different from that of Hanover and Westphalia.[4] The types of ware found side by side in Anhalt spread, some to the west (Schönfeld, the Rössen type), and the others to the east through Brandenburg and Pomerania (balloon-amphoræ, Molkenberg type, Bernburg type). Local types of culture sprang up there which spread out in opposite directions, and the human groups turned opposite ways, those who were to be Celts and those who were to be Germans, and the archæological map of Europe shows their progressive differentiation.[5]

But if we can talk of Celts at this early date we must look in the racial hotchpotch of Western Germany for the element which formed them.[6] In our search we must place the people of the cord-pattern pottery [7] side by side with the people of the zone-beakers. The typical cord-pattern vase is a round-bellied beaker like the zoned vase, but taller. The decoration usually consists of horizontal lines impressed with

[1] Ibid., p. 49.
[2] Ibid., p. 47.
[3] Kossinna, op. cit., pp. 165 ff.
[4] Åberg, CCXCVII, pp. 151 ff.
[5] These facts will be studied in more detail in the volume on the Germans in this series.
[6] G. Wilcke (in LXXXV, 1918, pp. 1–54) regards the Rössen-Nierstein ware as an indication of the Celts.
[7] Schumacher, op. cit., i, pp. 46 ff. ; Åberg, op. cit., pp. 97, 178, 182, 190, and maps iv, xi ; Schuchardt, CCCLXXXIII, pp. 108 ff.

cords on the fresh paste and (only in late or degenerate specimens) of bands of engraved herring-bone pattern, sometimes vertical. It is an almost general rule that this ware is chiefly of a funerary nature. It is found in tumuli erected in a few cases over cremations and usually over graves in which the body was laid out at full length. These tumuli are generally in high, wooded places.

This cord-pattern ware is most frequent in the valley of the Saale. It is very common all over Saxony, from the Elbe to the Thuringian mountains. (Further north, between Magdeburg and the Harz, a few specimens have been found, and also on the right bank of the Elbe and even in Jutland [1]; but this was the domain of another people.) There is hardly anything between the Elbe and the Oder, and nothing between the Oder and the Vistula. East of the Oder two objects only, one in Silesia and the other in Volhynia, have been assigned to it. It is very frequent in the north of Bohemia. Westwards it appears beyond the mountains of Thuringia, and extends through Hessen and along the Taunus to the Rhine and Neckar. Specimens are found as far as Switzerland in the lake-villages. In South-Western Germany the men who made this pottery seem to have lived alongside of other groups without either colliding with them or mixing with them. Perhaps they lived a different manner of life. They were warriors or hunters. But if they lived side by side with the agriculturalists of the plain their relations must, on the whole, have been peaceful.[2] What were their relations? We are free to imagine them as we like. Certainly they were very considerable.

The makers of the zoned vases and those of the cord-pattern beakers lived in the same districts in Saxony, in Bohemia, and in Western Germany. If maps showing their distribution were placed one over the other they would fit, and each would complement the other. We now have to inquire whether they came into contact and, if they did so, whether either side influenced the other. We have only one proof of their meeting. In a burial at Hebenkies,[3] near Wiesbaden, a zoned vase has been found together with

[1] Åberg, op. cit., p. 182.
[2] Schumacher, op. cit., i, pp. 44–5 ; A. Schliz, in *Heilbronner Festschr.* pp. 10 ff. ; Kossinna, op. cit., pp. 173, 180, 183.
[3] Åberg, op. cit.

cord-pattern vases, and the decoration of this zoned vase is produced by the impression of cords. A certain number of these *Schnurzonenbecher* have been found along the Rhine.[1] They may be hybrids, and Herr Schumacher believes that it was under the influence of the people of the cord-pattern beakers that the tumulus was adopted by the tribes of the zoned vases.[2] In any case, the two ceramic types crown the development of the so-called Neolithic pottery of Western Germany.

Thus, as early as this time, in this region two groups of warlike tribes insinuated themselves concurrently among the old inhabitants, and formed a kind of network round and between them. It has been suggested that one of the two groups was Celtic, because it sent out to the British Isles the only large colonies which they received before the La Tène period.[3] The relative position of these two groups in Germany, which reveals, even before that colonization, the principle of a differentiation comparable to that of the Goidels and Brythons, affords a very strong argument in favour of that hypothesis.

But two points remain to be considered.

A certain number of Scandinavian and German archæologists have held that the people of the beakers with stamped decoration had also crossed over the Lower Elbe into Jutland, and there formed a very large colony, which exerted a considerable influence all round and is certainly one of the chief elements in the formation of the Germans.[4]

The racial mark by which this Jutland folk is known is the round tumulus covering a pit, in which the dead man was laid in a contracted position, which is called the single-burial tomb in contrast to the megalithic funeral chambers. In it we find beakers, sometimes similar to those of Saxony, some amphoras of the same type as those which almost always accompany the cord-pattern beakers, and asymmetrical perforated axes, the most perfect of which is the boat-shaped axe, well known to prehistorians. If the hypothesis mentioned above were true, either the people

---

[1] Schumacher, op. cit., i, pl. iv and p. 49.

[2] Ibid.

[3] Kossinna, in **LXXXV**, 1913, pp. 31 ff. ; Schumacher, in **XXXI**, x ; Wilcke, in **LXXXV**, 1918, p. 50.

[4] See the volume in this series on the Germans.

of the cord-pattern beakers was itself an element of the Germanic race, its western extensions being submerged in the mass of the Celts, or else it split and produced a nucleus of Celts and a nucleus of Germans.

Our previous examination of linguistic relations does not fit well with this hypothesis. But there are positive reasons for rejecting it. The national weapon of the people of the cord-pattern beakers was an asymmetrical perforated axe like the battle-axes of Jutland, but shaped in longitudinal facets. It went with its bearers when they expanded towards the Rhine. It is entirely absent north of the Elbe. It is unlikely that the Jutland battle-axes are derived from the faceted axe. It is equally unlikely that a people, whose remains are remarkable for their uniformity, and thereby bear witness that it expanded rapidly, as conquerors, should, where it is found to have been, have kept only part of its characteristic gear, and that not its weapons, in one particular region into which it advanced. The culture of the single-burial tomb and the culture of the cord-pattern vase are mixed formations of the same kind, the former being probably older than the latter, and are composed of the same elements, which were supplied, some by the megalith-builders of the seaboard (axe, type of beaker, tumulus), some by the aborigines of the Baltic plains, and some (funeral rites and part of the pottery) by the peoples which came from Central Europe.

The second point concerns the kinship of the Celts and the Italici.

The cultures of the cord-pattern beakers and the zoned beakers were succeeded in Bohemia by what is called the civilization of Aunjetitz, or Unetice,[1] which corresponds to a more advanced stage of the Bronze culture, extending considerably beyond its first period. This civilization extended its frontiers greatly in all directions. Later the migration of the folk who had made it left the actual centre of their habitat empty. The main movement was to the south. The culture is found, complete and unaltered, south of the Danube. The civilization of Northern Italy presents such close similarities to it that one is justified in looking here for the ancestors of the Italici and, more particularly, of the

[1] L. Niederle, in **LV**, i, 1907 ; cf. Déchelette, **CCCXVIII**, ii, 1, pp. 89-90.

Latins. But this culture also spread between the Saale and the Oder, in the Saxon area of the cord-pattern beakers, and then westwards along the upper valley of the Danube and to the Rhine, where its collars and pins with rolled heads and racket heads are found, together it is true, with a pottery derived from zone-beakers (Adlerberg type).[1]

Was it descended from the two cultures whose place it took ? In that case these would represent the undivided stock of the Celts and Italici. Does it itself represent that undivided stock ? Neither supposition is probable. The people of Aunjetitz was itself a mixed people, containing a smaller proportion of Nordic types than the people of the cord-pattern beakers, and other types than the people of the zoned vases ; it had taken some features from the cultures between the Elbe and Oder and it kept the funeral customs of the Danube valley. It is, then, as it were, parallel to the two others, and not derived from them.

Furthermore, since there is nothing recalling it in the archæology of the British Isles, it is probable that the Italici and Celts had parted before it appeared. The Italici had begun to develop on their own lines in the south-east of Bohemia, in Moravia, and perhaps in Silesia [2] ; the Celts did likewise between the Upper Danube, the Saale, and the North Sea, where they already formed a community divided into two sections. But they were not so much separated as to have no intercourse and never to borrow from one another. Above all they were not so firmly settled down that parties could not cross from either side of the vague frontier to the other. We must not imagine these prehistoric peoples as keeping strictly within neat frontiers.

Dim and hypothetical as this reconstruction of Italo-Celtic origins still remains, it can be traced with some probability to the beginning of the Bronze Age. We can see that the formation of distinct groups, the concentration of the Celts on the border of Thuringia, the departure of a first Celtic migration to the British Isles, and that of a first Italic migration to Northern Italy, happened roughly at the same time, as has been indicated at the beginning of this chapter.

---

[1] Schumacher, op. cit., i, pp. 63–5 ; **CCCCVIII**, p. 89.
[2] Meillet, **CCXVII**, p. 376 ; Peet, **DXXXIX**, pp. 509–510 ; Homo, **CCCXLI**, English, p. 48.

Another result of our archæological inquiry is to show, as our linguistic inquiry might already have made us foresee, that the elements of which these societies were composed were very fluid and themselves composite.

The most obscure point in the hypothesis adopted is the original position of the future Goidels, for if the zone-beaker folk was the nucleus which organized them it is very hard to determine where it was itself formed. Moreover, it spread over almost the whole of the Celtic domain and left

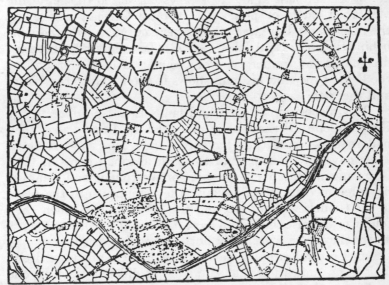

FIG. 35. Distribution of Cultivated Land and Dwellings in Ireland. (Meitzen, *Siedelung und Agrarwesen*, fig. 19.)

descendants there. In any case it occupied all the seaboard districts between the Rhine and Elbe which remained outside the frontiers previously mentioned. These were the districts which were emptied by the migration of the Goidels to Britain. It is possible that the consequences of this migration affected peoples dwelling east of the Elbe. But it is certain that it did not cause any movement on the part of the interesting culture which developed in the Bronze Age in the Cimbric Peninsula, the Danish islands, and Pomerania.

Was it a total or only a partial emigration? It was probably partial, for there remained what is usually left behind by peoples which have been a long time in a country where they have been engaged in adapting the ground to human life, namely the distribution of dwellings and the shape of villages and fields. In the western part of North-Western Germany, in Western Hanover, and Westphalia, cultivated land and dwellings are arranged in a manner which is foreign to Germany, or has become so. It is the arrangement found in Ireland (Fig. 35), part of England, and France. The houses stand alone in the midst of their fields, and the villages are of the simplest kind. It is a system suited to the raising of horned cattle or pigs. The typical German village, on the other hand, is a large village, very irregular, with gardens behind the houses and fields, very regular, all round. Meitzen [1] designated the former type of occupation of the ground as the Celtic type, and his map shows it extending to the Weser and the Sieg.

This disposition of men and lands is not peculiar to the Goidels alone. Perhaps they inherited it. In any case, they had it, and where they have remained they have kept it. They have left it in part of their old German domain. The Germanic inhabitants of this part of Westphalia and Hanover have retained it, either because they stepped into the place of the Goidels without altering the arrangement which they found, or because they left a large number of the old occupants where they were ; probably both things happened.

Agricultural peoples never change their abode entirely. This is an indication that the Goidels did not leave in one body, and that they did not all leave.

What was the reason of their emigration ? It was certainly not weakness or poverty. Perhaps there was some encroachment of the sea on a coast which has altered much. Perhaps some invention in the matter of navigation was discovered. The megalith-builders whom the Goidels surrounded were certainly sailors who were not afraid of crossing the North Sea.

---

[1] CCCLIII, i, pp. 174–232 and fig. 19. Beyond the zone of the Germanic villages he places the villages and cultivated lands of a type very familiar to us, which, indeed, is like the Germanic type ; it is that of the Brythonic Celts, where the villages are large, but there are also big isolated farms and houses.

CHAPTER II

THE EXPANSION OF THE CELTS IN THE BRITISH ISLES

I

THE BRITISH ISLES BEFORE THE COMING OF THE CELTS

IN the following chapters we shall consider how the various elements of the Celtic population emigrated in succession and made new Celtic countries. In this respect the British Isles, where we saw the Goidels landing in the last chapter, give a condensed picture of the Celtic world and the clearest picture of it. They must, therefore, be studied separately and before the other Celtic countries. It is, moreover, here, and here alone, except in Brittany, that the Celts survive otherwise than in a diffused condition, for they here form communities, one of which is to-day a nation. Here the two first Celtic groups can be distinguished, not by mere conjecture but by their still living languages. Here the chain of facts is complete. But we shall find in the ethnology of the British Isles other races which I have not yet mentioned, and the Belgæ in particular. All the groups of Celtic peoples which we shall find playing their part on the Continent reappear in the British Isles, and in circumstances which are favourable to study.

Furthermore, we can see here, thanks to data which are lacking for the study of the Continental Celts, the natives whom the Celtic peoples absorbed. Once these were assimilated, they certainly went for much in the making of the Celtic peoples and their civilization. The two strains had for some time remained distinct. They appeared so to foreigners, and the natives were conscious of their different origin.

In relating his first expedition to Britain Cæsar wished to say a few words about its population, and he gives us a first brief account of the races of the country. " The interior of Britain," he writes, " is inhabited by people who, according to their own tradition, are aborigines. The coast is occupied by others, who came from Belgium on looting or warlike expeditions, and have almost all kept as tribal names those of the tribes from which they are descended. Brought in by war, they settled down and proceeded to cultivate the land." [1] So Cæsar knew that the population of Britain comprised at least two different elements, and that the later comers were distinguished by their relationship to the Celtic peoples of the Continent, and particularly by their names, which bore certain testimony to their origin.

Unfortunately he is not as clear as he is concise and positive. He knew the peoples of Belgium well, and he must have seen for himself that their names recurred in Britain. It is a pity that he has not told us those which attracted his notice. Ptolemy [2] mentions a *civitas Belgarum*, which covered eastern Somerset, Wiltshire, and the north of Hampshire. One of their towns was called Venta Belgarum, now Winchester. North of the Belgæ, in what is now Berkshire, was the *civitas* of the *Atrebates*. From the Thames northwards to the Wash, in what are now the counties of Hertford, Bedford, Cambridge, Huntingdon, and Northampton, were the Catuvellauni, in whose name we can, without much strain on our goodwill, see that of the Catalauni, of which it was probably the older, uncontracted form. Further north the Parisii occupied part of Yorkshire between York and the sea. But the Parisii were doubtless not Belgæ.[3] This does not amount to much in all, and the Belgæ no longer existed in distinct communities on the coast where Cæsar could have come across them. It is probable that the people of the British Belgæ was formed by the union of scattered elements which had kept their tribal names for a time and, when they combined, contented themselves with their race-name.

Cæsar has given us another piece of information about the adventures of the Belgæ in Britain. Before describing his campaign of 57, he gives a brief history which he had obtained from the Remi about their neighbours [4] : " Their

---

[1] *Gall. War*, v, 12, 1–2 ; MacNeill, **CCCCXLI**, p. 54 ; A. Mahr, "Das frühe Inselkeltentum im Lichte neuerer Ausgrabungen," in Archäol. Inst. d. Deutschen Reiches, *Bericht über die Hundertjahrfeier*, pp. 310–12 (Berlin, 1930).

[2] 3, 13 ; Holmes, **CCCCXXXIII**, pp. 232–3.

[3] See below, p. 214.

[4] *Gall. War*, ii, 4, 6–7.

neighbours were the Suessiones, who owned a very extensive and extremely fertile territory. At a time within recollection they had a king named Diviciacus, who was the most powerful man in Gaul, and established his supremacy over a great part of the land on this coast and over Britain." The Belgæ of England may have been remnants of the forces of Diviciacus. Their number had increased even in Cæsar's time.[1]

But what were the aborigines ? Were they the first Celtic colonists or the predecessors of the Celts ? Were they Brythons ?   Or Goidels ?   Or Picts ?   Or still earlier inhabitants ?   Scholars are divided. Cæsar's expression is probably very comprehensive, but it leaves us wondering.

II

THE MYTH OF IRISH ORIGINS

Ireland has always liked to make out that her origins are mixed, and her latest national historians are quite enthusiastic in proving that she is not thoroughly Celtic,[2] and only became so very late in the day.

The Irish have imagined their island as peopled by a series of invasions. The *fili*, the official bards, corresponding to the *vates* of Gaul, developed this tradition into a theory. The catalogues of the poems which the *fili* had ready for the entertainment of their hearers give the titles of the principal works into which these various parts had been crystallized. The poems are lost, but they are found again in a compilation of the eleventh century, entitled the *Leabhar Gabhála*, or *Book of Invasions*.[3] It is a composition of theorists and mythographers. But it was accepted. Local tradition (the

---

[1] Holmes, op. cit., p. 232, n. 3.

[2] In the Middle Ages a legend of British origins was developed, of which it would be unnecessary to speak, if it had not been cited by an anthropologist of the learning of Mr. H. J. Fleure (**CCCXXVIII**, pp. 65–71), who gives it an appearance of truth. This legend connects the history of Britain with that of Rome and the Trojan cycle. The myth of Irish origins is of the same class, but of better quality. It has the merit of having been made by Irishmen for Irishmen, and of expressing a part of the national beliefs. The legend of British origins was in part made by foreigners for foreigners.

[3] On the mythical invasions of Ireland, see Czarnowski, **CCCCXXIII**, pp. 97 ff.

Dinnshenchas) and heroic epic show that the mythical invaders of prehistoric Ireland were familiar characters in Irish mythology, or at least some of them.

The *Leabhar Gabhála* tells the story of five invasions.

The first was that of Partholon. Partholon left Spain after killing Bel, the king of the country, and arrived in Ireland on the very day of Beltane, the Feast of Bel, on the 1st May. Ireland was at that time occupied by a race of spirits or demons from the sea, the Fomorians (Fomóraig),[1] and Partholon fought them. His race was, however, carried off by a pestilence, which broke out on the day of Beltane and lasted a week. The scene of the death of the sons of Partholon was a plain called Sen Mag, the Old Plain, where the whole tribe had gathered to bury its dead. Sen Mag is a mythical plain ; but another version of the story places the event in the plain of Breg near the east coast, that is, in the religious centre of pagan Ireland, where the most famous graves are.

The second invader, Nemed, also came from Spain, and also landed on Beltane day. It was the great spring festival. Nemed and some of his people were slain by a pestilence ; the rest were subdued by the Fomorians, who made them pay a tribute of two-thirds of their children, harvests, and milk. The sons of Nemed rose and besieged the Fomorians in a tower of glass in Tory Island (Tor Inis, the Isle of the Tower). The revolt failed, and the remainder of the sons of Nemed were wiped out.

Then came the Fir Bolg, with the Fir Domnann and the Galians (Gaileoin), who are included under the name of Fir Bolg. We shall meet them again. These people sided with the Fomorians, and we are given a most unpleasant picture of them.

The following wave brought the Tuatha Dé Danann, that is, the Tribes of the Goddess Danu. They were amiable gods, doing good and bringing civilization, and among them were Nuada, the sea-god, Manannán mac Lir, another sea-god, and Lugh, the sun-god. There were other gods in Ireland who are classed among the Fomorians and are associated more or less closely with the Tuatha Dé Danann. The Tuatha Dé

---

[1] *Fomóraig* means " deep, submarine "; *fo* = ὑπο ; *mor* = *mare*.

Danann, arriving at Beltane, engaged in battle with the Fomorians, whom they defeated at Moytura in Connacht on the day of the feast of Samhain, the 1st November, six months, or two seasons, later.

Fifth came the Goidels, or, more accurately, the sons of Mile, son of Bile, from Spain, like Partholon and Nemed. But Spain had been only a previous stage on their journey, and they came from much further away. Arriving in Ireland, they fought and did business alternately with the Tuatha Dé Danann. In the end they had the better of them and the Tuatha Dé Danann retired into the *sidhe*, the great megalithic tombs, such as New Grange and Brugh-na-Boyne.

But this was not all, for in the second generation of the Milesians (as the sons of Mile came to be called), the Cruithnig, or Picts, appeared. The Milesians had encountered them already on their way, and we shall come back to them later.

We might regard this whole story as a curious attempt to fit the mythical prehistory of Ireland into the history of the world as it was conceived by the last Latin writers and the Christian Church.[1] Possibly it was so. But the learned author or authors of the work of which the *Leabhar Gabhála* is the latest edition found the materials of their compilation all there, waiting for them. They did not invent the Fomorians or the Fir Bolg or the Tuatha Dé Danann. Most of the episodes revolve round the great seasonal feasts of the Irish year. They are myths, subjected to various degrees of euhemerization. But among these myths there are traditions of a historical kind, and names which belong to history. Two facts, at least, should be kept in sight. One is that the Goidels did not regard themselves as the builders of the great megalithic funerary chambers, which became the dwellings of the gods. The second is that with strange insistence, the authors of these stories make the first settlers in Ireland come from Spain, and that probability is on their side. It is a pity that they have not told us equally clearly whence the last arrivals really came.

These Irish traditions have their chronology, given in annals the authenticity of which can be checked by reference to the technical inventions ascribed to the kings who appear

[1] Bede, *Eccl. Hist.*, i, 1.

there with their dates.[1] One date which interests us is that of the discovery of gold, both gold mines and the manufacture of gold objects. Ireland was a sort of Eldorado. It is possible that its wealth in gold attracted visitors and settlers. The most ancient gold objects are the crescent-shaped things called lunettes. Leinster tradition ascribed the invention of gold-working to King Tighearnmhas. The discovery is supposed to have taken place in the auriferous region traversed by the Liffey. Tighearnmhas was a Fomorian king who lived during the reign of Nuada, and also saw the coming of the Milesians. Other traditions place him among the Milesian kings. In any case, the chronicles place him between 1620 and 1036 B.C. Even the earlier date is, in my opinion, too late for the beginnings of gold-working in Ireland, but not very much so, and it is about the probable date of the landing of the future Goidels in the island. So part of the traditions survives checking.

We shall now try to see what really lay behind these tales. At the same time we shall see how much truth is condensed in the picture drawn by Cæsar.

III

THE NON-CELTIC ELEMENT IN THE POPULATION OF IRELAND, ACCORDING TO MR. MACNEILL. THE GOIDELS AND THE SUBJECT PEOPLES. THE ERAINN

Anthropologists have observed in the present population of the British Isles certain aberrant types, which they hold to represent the aboriginal inhabitants. These, according to Mr. Fleure, are found, at least in Wales, in the remoter and wilder districts.[2] We hear of long-headed Mongoloids, akin to the Eskimos, and these are said to appear also in Ireland, and to be descended from its first occupants.[3] But to them we must add the far greater number of descendants of the megalith-builders and the navigators, long-headed or short-headed, who first spread the knowledge of metal in Western

---

[1] Miss M. Dobbs, in **LXXX**, 1914, p. 24 ; Macalister, **CCCCXXXIX**, p. 120. The memory of Tighearnmhas is associated with the institution of the worship of Cromm Crúaich ; that is one reason for believing that something like his real date has been preserved.

[2] In **LXXVI**, 1916, p. 35.

[3] Pokorny, in **CV**, xlix, 1919 (repr.) ; **CLXXI**, 1915, pp. 231, 308-357.

Europe.[1] Attempts have been made, with varying success, to credit these forerunners of the Celts with such institutions as that of the Druids, with technical processes, and with certain weapons.[2] Certain words, too, must be ascribed to them—the names of rivers and peoples and individuals, which have survived. But one may try to see them in intact social formations. That is what Mr. MacNeill has done for Ireland, by extracting new pieces of information from the written tradition of the country, and it is worth while to examine his findings closely.[3]

He supposes that when the original inhabitants were amalgamated by the Goidels into their political organization they kept their old constitution in part and were incorporated as ready-made social units into the Goidelic system. As a sign of their incorporation and their dependence, special burdens of a political kind were laid on them, as a tribute. For there were in Ireland a great number of vassal clans—Celticized clans, speaking Celtic and ruled by Celtic lines, but keeping their old names and compelling their masters to assume them, just as, later, the Angles and Saxons imposed their names on the Norman barons. These clans were called *Aithech-thuatha*, the lower-class clans.[4]

These clans seem to have been comprised under the general name of Féni (singular Féne) in Old Irish.[5] This name may have become Middle Irish Fianna (singular Fian). The Fianna were a permanent fighting force, which might be created by a levy of subjects, for the Goidels were not liable to military service beyond certain limited contributions. Finn mac Coul, the hero of the Fianna, belonged to a subject clan of Leinster, one of Galians.[6]

---

[1] Fleure, in **LXXVI**, 1918, p. 155.
[2] For the name of the coracle, which Pokorny ascribes to the aborigines of Ireland, see J. Loewenthal, in **CLXIV**, vii, p. 177. The root must belong to the North-western vocabulary (O. Nord. *hgrunde* " skin " ; O. Slav. *kora* " bark " ; Lith. *karna* " lime-bark "). See above, p. 73.
[3] MacNeill, **CCCCXLI**.
[4] *Duanaire Finn*, introd., xxxi ; MacNeill, op. cit., p. 148. *Aitheach* " giant, soldier, peasant ", etc.
[5] MacNeill, op. cit., p. 150 ; J. Loth, in **CXL**, xli, p. 350 ; *feni* means " kinsfolk, men of the same race " (*uenioi* ; cf. Gwynedd = **ueiniia*) ; the name of the people must at an early date have become that of a social class, the clan of free tenants ; *fiann* " troop " from *ueinā*. Ptol., ii, 2, 3 : Οὐέννικνιοι perhaps comes from the same root, and may be the tribal name of a group of Féni.
[6] MacNeill, op. cit., p. 149.

The rent-paying clans have all been put down in a list like so many things in Ireland. We have several manuscripts of a treatise giving the names and positions of these old non-Gaelic communities.[1] They are so numerous and so widely spread that one grows anxious for the Goidels. One regards the latter with surprise and admiration when one thinks that they imposed their language on that great mass of subjects so easily and so completely that nothing is left but dead words to show that another tongue was ever spoken in Ireland. When an invading people has imposed its speech on the inhabitants of a conquered country it has always had some superiority over them in numbers, in civilization, or in political organization, which we do not seem to see in this case. But it appears elsewhere, in the names of divisions of the country and towns and villages, which are Celtic, whereas the names of rivers are not,[2] and also in a tradition which relates that the Goidels cleared all Ireland of forest, but that the plain of Breg, Magh n-Ealta, called the Old Plain, where the great tumuli of the lower Boyne lie, was already cleared when they arrived.[3] Moreover, non-Gaelic does not necessarily mean non-Celtic. Subject clan does not necessarily mean non-Gaelic clan. Lastly, even if the subject clans and the ruling clans are racially of different origin, the fact that some were subject does not at all imply, as Mr. MacNeill supposes, that they came to Ireland before their rulers.

Ireland, as we know her, is a kind of feudal organization, in which clans have their order of rank like individuals. But their ranks were never fixed once for all. We know, for example, that in the first half of the second century after Christ there was a general rising of the rent-payers under Cairbre Cat-head.[4] In the course of the history of Ireland many clans rose or fell in rank through force of circumstance or arms. Their very unstable order of eminence only existed *de facto*. Those which forced their way up justified their action by history and legend, inventing titles to the possession of their rank.

---

[1] Ibid., p. 73. One MS. of this treatise has been published in **CXL**. The treatise goes back to the eighth century.
[2] Macalister, **CCCCXXXIX**, p. 252. [3] MacNeill, op. cit., p. 72.
[4] Ibid., p. 119 ; Macalister, op. cit., p. 290 ; E. MacNeill, *Duanaire Finn*, i, p. lvi.

This is, in particular, true of the reigning lines which gave Ireland a kind of unity at the time when St. Patrick began, or was about to begin, his preaching of Christianity. These were the lines, this was the aristocracy, gathered round the High Kings of Tara, who called themselves the Milesians, the sons of Mile. They caused a Milesian literature to come into being.[1]

The list of the subject peoples brings all the elements which, apart from the Goidels, made up the population of the British Isles before us in review. We must, however, set aside a certain number of clans which, if their names have any qualifying sense, can only be industrial castes formed into territorial clans. The list mentioned above [2] includes in the territory of the Desi in Munster, where there are copper mines, a Tuath Semon. This was the clan of the Rivet, *seim*. In the mining district of Béarra in Western Munster were the Ceardraighe, the Smiths. A Tuath Cathbarr, or Helmet Clan, was distributed over the counties of Tipperary, Limerick, Cork, and Kerry. Whether they were Gaelic or non-Gaelic we have no idea, and perhaps there is no occasion to ask. They were not racial formations, but social. We shall also set aside a clan named Fir Iboth or Ibdaig,[3] which is placed in the lower valley of the Shannon, in Counties Galway, Tipperary, and Limerick. It has the same name as the Ebudæ, or Hebrides. According to Solinus,[4] the people of those islands lived on fish and the milk of their cattle. Were there Hebrideans in Ireland ? Was it the common name of a caste of fishermen ? We have no reason for inclining to either view.

Among the subject or rent-paying peoples one of the largest seems to have been that of the Erainn, who apparently gave their name to Ireland,[5] which the Goidels continued to call by it. Ireland is called Eire, Old Irish Eriu. The Greek and Latin forms, Ἴερα (νῆσος), whence Avienus gets his Sacra Insula, Strabo's Ἰέρνη, Ptolemy's Ἰουερνία, the Iverna of Pomponius Mela and Juvenal, and the Hibernia of Cæsar, render the old root-word as exactly as possible. The Irish Erenn, the genitive of Eriu, and the

---

[1] *Duanaire Finn*, i, p. xxxviii.   [2] MacNeill, op. cit., p. 75.
[3] Ibid., p. 74.   [4] *Collectanea Rerum Memorabilium*, 22, 42.
[5] The accusative plural Erna has provided the stem of a more modern form of the word.

Welsh form Iwerddon,[1] take us back to a term containing an *n* : *Iuerion, genitive Iuerionos.

The Erainn were the Iverni. Ptolemy places the people of the 'Ιουέρνοι in the south-west of Ireland.[2] Now this was just where the Erainn had their principal centre in the time of the oldest epics. The list of rent-paying peoples places the Erainn, or rather the Sen-Erainn, the old and authentic Iuerni, in the district of Luachair, covering the north of Kerry and the adjacent parts of Limerick and Cork ; here stood Teamhair Erann,[3] that is Tara of the Erainn, which had been the chief burying-ground and meeting-place of the Erainn before it became one of the religious centres of Munster. At the beginning of our era the Erainn of Munster were subject to the dynasty of the Eoganachta of Cashel, a thoroughly Celtic line.[4] But there were also Erainn in Connacht and Ulster,[5] where they appear as the scattered remnants of an ancient population, driven by invaders into corners where they make a stand.

But what were the Erainn ? It is possible that they were not Celts. It is tempting, on the other hand, to compare the names of the Iverni and the Iberians.[6] The likeness of these names naturally leads one to infer relationship between the peoples. That likeness is even more complete than it first seems. For the *n* of the stem both of Erainn and of Ierne is an addition. The Erainn, like all the peoples of Ireland, got their name from an eponymous ancestor. Theirs was called Iar (in two syllables). This name is directly descended from an Old Celtic word *Iueros*. It is easy to conclude that there were two race-names corresponding to the name of Ireland—Iueri and Iuerni. Now " Iueri " and " Iberi " are almost identical. Spain and Ireland lie near enough and have always had enough intercourse for this similarity to be at least taken into consideration.

---

[1] The *dd* represents a *y*. The *h* in the form Hibernia, Hiberio, is adventitious. Rhys (**CCLXXXI**, p. 130) wrongly connects the form *ywerit* with the name of Ireland (cf. Skene, **CCLXXXVII**, i, p. 295 : Bran mab Ywerit) ; Ywerit is the same as Welsh *gwerydd* and O. Irish *fairge*, "the Ocean," and Ywerit is the wife of Llyr, the sea-god. Cf. Ptol., ii, 2, 5 ; 3, 2 ; vii, 3, 2, Ούεργιουος, Ούεργιουιος. In Mela, ii, 78, the name of Ireland appears in the form Bergyon (Hercules fights with Albiona and Bergyon), which = Iberygon or Ivorygon. MacNeill, **CCCCXLI**, p. 67.
[2] Ptol., ii, 2, 6.   [3] T. J. Westropp, in **LXXX**,1918, pp. 111 ff.
[4] MacNeill, op. cit., p. 65.   [5] Ibid., p. 66 ; e.g. in Antrim.
[6] Ibid.

The authors of the *Leabhar Gabhála* have found worthy successors in the scholars of our time who have endeavoured, with much learning, labour, and ingenuity, to detect the Iberian element in the racial antiquities of the British Isles.[1]

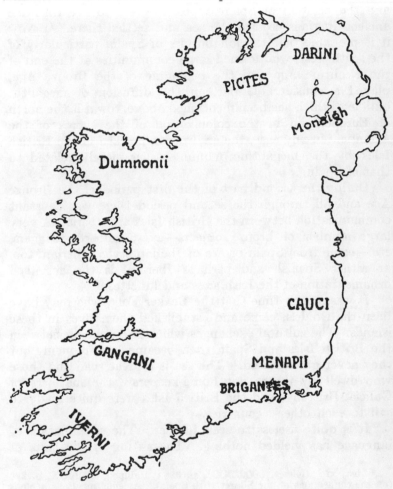

MAP 8. Ireland about A.D. 90. Pictes = Picts (French map).

Their pains have been ill-rewarded, for, while it is almost certain that there was this Iberian strain, and that it was considerable, anything definite to be said on the subject can be summed up in a very few words.

[1] Sir J. Rhys, in **CXLVII**, 1890.

Tacitus remarked that there were dark-skinned men in Britain who were very numerous in Wales among the Silures, who occupied the south-west of that region : " The dark faces of the Silures, their usually curly hair, and the position of Spain opposite, are evidence that the ancient Iberians crossed the sea and settled there." [1] Now it is probable that the inhabitants of Spain, particularly of the south-west, who formed large communities at the end of the Neolithic Age and the beginning of the Bronze Age, played a considerable part in the diffusion of megalith-building, which has been mentioned above, towards the north of Europe, and in the colonization of the shores of the Atlantic. In any case, the civilization marked in the British Isles by the megalithic monuments is closely related to that of Spain. [2]

During the second part of the first period of the Bronze Age and all through the second period there was constant communication between the British Isles and Iberia. A very large number of bronze objects—axes, halberts, daggers, etc.—come from Spain or are of Iberian style. Iberian, too, or rather Spanish and perhaps Iberian, is the engraved ornamentation of the Irish axes and lunettes.

It was at this time that the Beaker Folk, who may have been the Goidels, came and established themselves in these islands. The cultural exchanges which had gone on between the British Isles and Spain then became less frequent, but they never quite ceased. [3] The sea is a great road and those who dwell by it are not home-keepers ; the mariners of Galicia, Brittany, and the British Isles were quite ready to sail to each other's countries.

It is quite useless to seek further. The examination of language has yielded nothing. The sifting of the cults of

---

[1] *Agr.*, xi ; Holmes, **CCCCXXXII**, p. 398 ; Philipon, **CCCLXIX**, p. 296 (on the connections of the Silures with Spain). Avienus mentions a Mons Silurus (433), and the proper name Silur has been found in Spain (**I**, ii, 5923). MacNeill (op. cit., p. 61) maintains, over-critically, that the Iberian theory of the population of the British Isles has no other foundation than the passage in Tacitus. Cf. Dion. Perieg., *Orbis Descriptio*, 563–4, on the Hesperides, the land of tin, islands inhabited by the wealthy children of the noble Iberians.

[2] J. Loth, in **XCII**, 1925, p. 137 ; 1926, p. 1 ; Bosch Gimpera, in **CXXXIX**, 1925, 2, p. 191 ; Breuil, ibid., 1925, 1, p. 79 ; Breuil and Macalister, in **CXXII**, p. 921.

[3] Examples of ear-rings of Portuguese type, **LXXX**, 1917, p. 30 ; R. Severo, in **CXVII**, ii, pp. 405–412 ; Anderson, **CCCCXIV**, pp. 144, 149, 208, 210.

Ireland and the folk-lore of Britain has been equally fruitless,[1]
for what do we know about the Iberians, their language or
their religion ? A few rare place-names [2] add their testimony
to archæological probabilities to assure us that there were
Iberians in the British Isles. The Iverni may perhaps have
been among them. It cannot be shown that Ireland was ever
called Iberia. Indeed, there is a set of names, similar to
Eire and Erainn, which are the names of rivers in Britain—
the Scottish Earn and Findhorn [3] and the Iwerne in Dorset
(cf. 'Ιουερνία).[4] If the name of Ireland is to be explained
in the same way as those of the rivers, it does not come from
a racial name, but from an adjective of quality. Iverjon
would come from *Piverjo-, which is comparable to Sanskrit
pivari, Greek πιαρός, " fat ", and would be parallel to
Pieria, the home of the Muses.[5] It would have nothing in
common with the name of Iberia, and would even be a Celtic
word, by the loss of the radical *p*.

The name of Britain, Albion,[6] in company with which
that of Ireland appears from the earliest times,[7] tells us as
clearly as possible that it is not Celtic. The Irish kept it in the
forms Alba, Alban, Alpe, to designate the whole of the sister-
island, but more particularly Scotland. It belongs to a family
of names : Alba, Albona, Albis, Alpes, Albani, Albioeci, etc.,
the names of towns, rivers, mountains, and peoples, which is
perhaps the most numerous family of European place-names
and is certainly the most widespread. It is highly probable
that these names are Indo-European and are connected with
the same root as Latin *albus*. But Celtic has lost just this very
root. In Western Europe these geographical names seem to
belong to the Ligurian vocabulary, which is Indo-European,
or to the Iberian vocabulary,[8] if it is Indo-European, or to
the Italic vocabulary. For they appear both in Spain and in
Sicily ; in Gaul, as the names of peoples, they are confined to
Narbonensis ; lastly they are represented by several instances
in Liguria properly so called.

In my opinion the names of the two islands date from
before the coming of the Celts and are an inheritance from

[1] Rhys, **CCCCLI**, vii.
[2] Philipon, op. cit., p. 296, Tamaros and Isca, in Cornwall.
[3] MacNeill, op. cit., p. 67.   [4] See above, p. 197.
[5] Thurneysen, **CCXL**.   [6] Holder, s.v.
[7] Avien., *Ora Mar.*, 112.   [8] Philipon, **DXVI**, passim.

their predecessors in Western Europe, Iberian or Ligurian. While the Iverni had kinsmen of the same name in Spain, there were also Albiones in Spain, on the north coast, in Asturias. They are mentioned by Pliny.[1] These were doubtless old Ligurians. But I do not insist on this point, for I do not want to have to demonstrate against learned Spanish scholars that the islands of Ierne and Albion were off the coast of Spain, like the still vex'd Cassiterides.

IV

THE PICTS

So the Neolithic population had left remnants in the two islands, and, also in the two islands, there had been Iberian settlers. But the racial map of Britain shows nothing corresponding to the Erainn. On the other hand, there is another group of tribes which is common to both islands ; it, too, was very considerable, and in the north of Ireland it formed a mass comparable to that formed by the Erainn in the south. These were the Cruithnig. The Cruithnig are the Picts, who were a distinct people in the larger island, occupying all or part (but the chief part) of Caledonia before the Scots— that is the Irish, the Gaels—came into the country and hewed a domain for themselves out of their land.[2] In Ireland the Picts held a large part of Ulster, where they were so numerous that they became the preponderant power.[3] In Connacht there were communities of Picts near Cruachain, the capital, and there were others in Munster, Meath, and Leinster. The Cruithnig of Ireland are called *Picti* in the Irish annals.[4] The Caledonian Picts are called *Cruithnii* or *Cruthini populi* in Adamnan's *Life of St. Columba*,[5] and the Irish list of the Pictish kings begins with an eponymous founder, Cruidne.[6] It is, therefore, certain that the two terms are equivalent.

[1] *N.H.*, iv, 111 : *a flumine Navia Albiones*, etc.
[2] Pedersen, **CCCXXVII**, i, p. 12 ; Windisch, **CCXLV**, p. 28 ; Nicholson, **CCXXIII**, pp. 20–97, 100–3 ; S. Ferguson, in **LVI**, 1912, pp. 170–189.
[3] D'Arbois, **CCXCIX**, p. 26 ; MacNeill, op. cit., p. 63.
[4] Holmes, **CCCCXXXIII**, pp. 411–12.
[5] Ibid., p. 422.
[6] D'Arbois, **CCC**, pp. 35–6, n. 6.

The Pictish people took up enough space to give its name to the whole of the British Isles. If we suppose that the *c* of Cruithnig represents a *qu*, which was destined to become *p* in Brythonic, we can go back through the forms of the sister language to a form Qurteni (Qartani) or Qretani. The corresponding name for the country was pronounced Pretani in Brythonic, from which comes Welsh Prydain. Ynys Prydain is the name of the island of Britain. Pytheas heard this name about 300 B.C., and very correctly called the two islands Πρεττανικαί νῆσοι. But it is uncertain whether he heard them called by this name in Gaul or in Britain itself.[1]

The name is intelligible in Celtic. It is generally traced back to Irish *cruth*, Welsh *pryd*, meaning " form ".[2] The Picts had a name among the Romans for tattooing themselves with animal and other forms.[3]

The word Pict has no such ancient ancestry. It is first met in a panegyric of 296 in honour of Constantius, who commanded in Britain.[4] It has been thought that it might be merely a Latin name given by the Romans, a kind of nickname afterwards consecrated by the chronicles. Cæsar, in his account of the Britons of the interior, says that they painted themselves for war with woad.[5] *Picti Britanni*, Martial repeats.[6] So the Picts would be Britons who still remained savage outside the Roman frontier. A Celtic explanation of the word has, however, been put forward. It is supposed to come from a root meaning " to tattoo ", beginning with *qu*, which became *p* in Brythonic. From the same root came Irish *cicht*, meaning " engraver ".[7] The Gaulish proper names Pictillus, Pictilus, Pistillus are diminutives of a term which may have been identical with the name of the Picts and has not been preserved.

These two doublets explain one another. All the same, the very existence of the duplication is perplexing, and the fact that that one of the two terms which seems to have

---

[1] Holmes, op. cit., p. 413.
[2] Ibid., p. 418, n. 5.
[3] Herodian, iii, 14, 17 ; Claudian, *Goth. War*, 416–18.
[4] Incerti Panegyricus Constantio Augusto, c. 7 : *Caledonum aliorumque Pictorum silvas*.
[5] *Gall. War*, v, 14.
[6] xiv, 99, 1.
[7] Holmes, op. cit., p. 414 ; Rhys, op. cit., pp. 215–16.

prevailed in Britain does not appear in the Irish traditions in the vulgar tongue, but only in Latin annals, would need explaining.

The Pictish question is one of those most hotly debated in the ancient history of Britain, but it does not seem to have received much illumination in the course of these unending battles. Many historians and philologists have maintained that this little-known, mysterious people, with its reputation for wildness, relegated to the north of Britain or scattered about in Ireland, was the remnant of the pre-historic inhabitants. Sir John Rhys regarded them as the chief representatives of the prehistoric population of these islands,[1] the Erainn being only a branch of them. But really the Erainn and Picts are very clearly distinguished from one another; in Antrim, for example, the north, Dal Riada, was Hibernian, and the rest was Pictish.

At the time when the Venerable Bede wrote his *Ecclesiastical History* the Picts, according to his statement, spoke a language which was different both from that of the Scots, who were Goidels, and from that of the Britons.[2] Moreover, Adamnan, in his *Life of Columba*, tells us that when the Saint evangelized the Picts he spoke to them through an interpreter.[3] But this separate Pictish language may have been Celtic. The six inscriptions which are said to be Pictish, found in the east and north of Scotland, afford no evidence on one side or the other, being indecipherable.[4]

The principal argument to which recourse is had is one based on the prehistoric customs of the Picts, and in particular on their law of succession. In Bede's time, that is in the sixth century, the succession in the Pictish royal families went in the female rather than in the male line.[5] Thus, a king of the Picts of the beginning of the seventh century, Talorcan, was the son of a Saxon refugee named Eanfred

---

[1] Op. cit., p. 272.
[2] i, 1; iii, 6; MacNeill, op. cit., p. 63.
[3] i, 33; ii, 33; Rhys, loc. cit.; Holmes, op. cit., p. 421.
[4] They are in oghams or in minuscule characters; only one is in disfigured Roman capitals; Rhys, in CCXIV, xxvi, p. 263; CCCCL, ii, p. 681, 2; Macalister, CCCCXXXIX, p. 253.
[5] Bede, i, 1; H. Zimmer, in CLXVII, xv, 1894, pp. 209 ff.; Skene, CCCCLVII, i, p. 232; Rhys, op. cit., ii, p. 682 (compare the succession of the sister's son in the royal families of the Berbers); Macalister, op. cit., p. 242. The last author observes (p. 244) that the same rule of succession obtained under the Irish kings.

and a Pictish princess.[1] Intermarriages between Picts and Scots, with similar consequences, are mentioned in all the chronicles. The Irish related that the Picts invaded Ireland shortly after the settlement of the sons of Mile. Herimon, the chief of the Milesians, drove them out and settled them in Alban (Scotland). But he gave them for wives, since they had none, the widows of the warriors of the race of Mile, who had perished at sea before the conquest of Ireland, on the condition that in the future inheritance should go through the woman, not through the man. The mythological explanation confirms the fact.

This mode of succession created particularly close relationships between men and their mothers' brothers. Tacitus had noticed this among the Germans,[2] and a votive inscription found at Colchester shows that it was the same among the Picts, probably even outside the royal lines. Here it is :—

DONVM. LOSSIO. VEDA. DE SVO
POSVIT. NEPOS. VEPOGENI. CALEDO.

" Presented at his own cost by Lossio Veda, nephew of Vepogen, a Caledonian." [3] It is a unique thing in Latin epigraphy for a man to indicate his family by the name of his uncle and not his father. In the history of the family the right of cognates, kinsman on the distaff side, has always been opposed to that of the agnates, kinsman on the male side. The evolution of the Indo-European *gens* evidently reached a form in Greece, Rome, Ireland, and Wales in which the right of the agnate prevailed over that of the cognate, and in consequence the facts noted among the Picts have been regarded as alien to Indo-European law.

But the law to which these facts bear witness also obtained among the Goidels of Ireland, and even among the ancestors of the Welsh. Considerable traces of it are to be found in their legal texts, their history, and their epics. The Irish gods and heroes are called after their mothers ; Lugh is the son of Ethniu, Cuchulainn is the son of Dechtire.[4] The Welsh god Gwydion is the son of Don.[5] The Celtic family is a fairly complicated institution, not quite like the Latin

---

[1] This is exactly what Bede relates. Cf. d'Arbois, CCI, i, p. 265.
[2] *Germ.*, 20.　　　　　[3] Holmes, op. cit., p. 415.
[4] Rhys, CCCCLII, p. 15.　　　　[5] Ibid., pp. 14, 37, 46, 56, 68.

family, and it has varied since the time at which we first know anything of it.

So there is nothing to prove that the Picts were not Celts. On the other hand, we have some reason for believing that they were a Celtic people, doubtless including a large proportion of foreigners and aborigines, but not more or less, no doubt, than the other Celtic peoples.

The names of the Pictish tribes—Cornavii, Smertæ, Cæræni, Carnonacæ, Creones, Lugi, Decantæ, Epidii, Tæzali, Vacomagi, Dicaledonæ, Verturiones [1]—contain Celtic sounds. So do the names of individuals—Argentocoxos, Togenanus.[2] Examination of the ancient and modern place-names of the Pict country leads to the same result [3]; Albhais (Alves in Morayshire) is to be compared to Alventium (Avin in Belgium) and Alvinca. Aberlour in Banffshire gets its name from Labhair, which is the same as Labara (*labrur* "I speak"). Dea'in, the Aberdeenshire Don, which is derived from $\Delta\eta o\acute{v}a\nu a$, the name of the town of the Tæzali, now Aberdeen, belongs to the same family as Devona in Gaul. Fuirgin (Foregin, a farm in Inverness-shire) corresponds to Vorgium, a town in the country of the Osismi in Gaul.

It is true that among the place-names of the Pictish country there are some in *ar*, of the type of Isara, Araris,[4] which might be Ligurian or Iberian, and stems which are usually regarded as Ligurian.[5] These are the contribution of the aborigines or of the previous inhabitants, whatever their position was, who survived among the Celtic tribes of the Picts.[6]

If the Picts were Celts so were the Silures. The names of their towns—Venta Silurum, Isca Silurum [7]—are Celtic. Another town, Abergavenny, was called Gobannium; it was the town of the smiths, for *gof* in Welsh means " smith ".[8] But perhaps they were only very much Celticized.

---

[1] D'Arbois, **CCXCIX**, p. 21.
[2] Ibid., p. 29.
[3] Diack, in **CXL**, xxxviii, p. 109 ; H. Marwick, in **CXXIV**, 1922–3, p. 251.
[4] Ptolemy's $O\dot{v}\acute{a}\rho a\rho\iota\varsigma$ $\epsilon\acute{\iota}o\chi\nu o\iota\varsigma$ is the same word as Farair, the R. Farrar (Inverness-shire) ; Diack, loc. cit.
[5] Diack, in **CXL**, 1924, p. 125 ; Bodotria (Tac.), $Bo\delta\epsilon\rho\iota a$ (Ptol.), cf. Bodincus, the Po ; Turcid, cf. Nematuri (in Liguria), Furobriga, Furia (in Spain) ; ibid., 1920–1, p. 109.
[6] Windisch, **CCXLV**, p. 25.
[7] Holder, s.v.
[8] D'Arbois, op. cit., p. 30 ; cf. Zimmer, in **IX**, 1912, p. 16.

In the lists of Irish subject tribes there are other Celtic tribes—the Fir Domnann, the Galians, and even the Fir Bolg. But before we come to them we must place the Picts in relation to the Goidels and the Britons. In doing so we shall obtain information about the three groups, which we shall suppose to be distinct.

V

GOIDELS, PICTS, AND BRITONS

The Picts and Goidels seem to have followed the same route and, in general, to have gone about the extension of their settlements in the same way. Landing on the south and east coasts of Britain, they would cross the country and, coming to the opposite shore, each in turn reach Ireland, while keeping one foot on the larger island. The archæological evidence seems to confirm this view. The builders of the round barrows slowly came to Ireland, and all the successive strata of British archæology are found in their order in that country.[1]

The traditional history of Ireland shows something of the same sort. King Ugaine the Great reigned over both Ireland and Britain to the English Channel. Some annals make him a contemporary of Alexander.[2] At that time there were Britons in Britain, for Pytheas encountered them there; but they had not been very long established. It seems doubtful that if the Britons on their arrival found a great Celtic kingdom, or something like it, spread over both sides of the Irish Sea, it was a Goidelic kingdom. But the question deserves discussion, and we have to find out whether the Picts or the Goidels established themselves in the British Isles first. M. J. Loth has recently maintained that the Picts were first, and that they were the builders of the round barrows.[3]

Why should the Britons have called their new country the island of the Picts if they found one or more Goidelic states established there? If they heard it called Quretenion

---

[1] See above, pp. 171-2.
[2] According to the *Annals* of Tighearnach, he became king in the eighteenth year of Ptolemy, son of Lagos, i.e. in 306.
[3] In CXL, xxxviii, pp. 259 ff.

it was because the Picts were the predominant or the most numerous part of the population. And if this was so it was probably because the Picts had superseded the Goidels, and in that case had come later than they.

It may be argued that the Britons got the name of the island from the Goidels. But the Irish probably never used the name Cruitheantuaith for the whole island of Britain. By it they meant the land of the Picts, Scotland.[1] It is not likely they ever meant a wider region, for which they had another term, Alba.[2]

But why suppose that the Picts came before the Goidels ? For once the mythical tradition of Ireland, which makes the Goidels come after most of the foreign peoples which they conquered or absorbed, represents them as followed by another Celtic people [3]; what need is there to reject it in this one case ?

In my view, then, the Picts were not the first, but the second body of Celts to enter the British Isles, and it is they who may be represented in the archæological remains by the series of bronze objects mentioned above.[4] But we must not draw too hard a line between the second and third wave of invaders.

To tell the truth, the archæological evidence of a second invasion of the British Isles in the Bronze Age is so elusive that at first we must try to use it sparingly. It is hardly likely that the Picts were a division of the Goidels, and arrived at about the same time as they. But it is not at all certain that they were fundamentally different from the Britons.[5]

First of all the language of the Picts, however much it may have differed from Brythonic in the eighth century of our era, had by then undergone the change characteristic of Brythonic, the Brythonic change of qu to p, which is attested in Pictish, apart from the name of the people itself, by that of the Epidii,[6] a Pictish tribe dwelling north of the Wall of Antoninus.[7] According to Bede, they called the end

---

[1] Marstrander, in **CXL**, xxxvi, 1915, p. 362. Loth (op. cit., p. 280) distinguishes between Prydyn, Scotland, and Prydain, Britain.
[2] **CXL**, xxxvi, 1915, p. 380.
[3] D'Arbois, **CCXCIX**, p. 25.
[4] See p. 177.
[5] D'Arbois, **CCC**, p. 33; Frazer, **CCI**, p. 9.
[6] Ptol., ii, 3.
[7] Skene, **CCCCLVI**, 4.

of that vallum Pean Fahel, while the Angles called it Penneltun.[1] So the place-names of Britain seem to have been homogeneous and free of Goidelism before the arrival of the Scots.[2]

Secondly, the Pictish kings, of whom we have a list, had Welsh names, such as Mælchon[3] and Drust.[4] Some of their names can actually be contrasted with Irish forms. One king is called Wurgust, which is Uorgost, Uurgost, Gurgost in Old Breton, and Gwrgwst in Welsh, while the Irish equivalent is Fergus. It means " superior choice ". The first part of the word is $u[p]per$. The initial vowel, becoming a consonant in both families of languages, tended towards f in Goidelic and to g in Brythonic.

Lastly, one tribe of the Picts, which lived in Caithness in the north of Scotland, was called the Cornavii,[5] and seems to have been the double of a much larger British tribe of Cornavii in Cheshire, on the north-eastern border of Wales.

So we have the same language and the same tribes. Are the Picts really different from the Britons ? Was Cæsar not thinking of the Picts when, in contrasting the tribes of the interior with those of the coast, whose manners seemed to him to resemble those of the Gauls, and whom, as we have seen, he described as Belgæ, he ascribed strange matrimonial customs to the former ?[6] " The women are held as wives in common by groups of ten or a dozen men, who are generally brothers, fathers, and sons. Any children born are regarded as belonging to the men who have taken the mothers into their houses as virgins." Cæsar does not express himself well, and he is translated worse. According to this account the Picts were polyandrous. Polyandry is not matriarchy. But both terms are used equally inaccurately by ethnologists, anthropologists, and archæologists to describe the facts which result from a very well-known condition of social constitution. Surely the truth is that there were exogamous clans which went in pairs, all the men and all the women of one clan being supposed to be the husbands and wives

---

[1] Bede, i, 12.
[2] *Parisii, Petuaria, Pennocrucium.*
[3] Welsh Mailcon (*Annales Cambriae*, passim).
[4] Welsh Drystan (*Mabinogion*).
[5] Rhys, CCCCLIII, pp. 111–13.
[6] *Gall. War*, v, 14 ; cf. MacNeill, CCCCXLI, p. 59.

respectively of the other clan, without that legal relationship being necessarily exercised or preventing the formation of small families consisting of married couples.[1] In this state of society the children usually belong to the clan of the mother, and this gives rise to conditions which are labelled matriarchy. Cæsar was fairly well informed, and the manners which he describes have no doubt more connection with those of the Picts than that of mere oddity. It does seem, too, that in the centre of Britain the royal families were organized like those of the Picts. The Queen, through whom the royal blood and rank came, must have enjoyed an esteem which, when she knew how to use it, gave her considerable authority ; witness Boudicca, the Queen of the Iceni of Norfolk and Suffolk, who led the rising against Suetonius Paulinus in A.D. 61.[2]

So if we follow and interpret Cæsar there were only two bodies of organized peoples in Britain at the time of his landing—Belgæ and Picto-Britons or Picts—and in that case the arrival of the latter can be placed much nearer that of the former, that is about the time when the use of iron was introduced into the country, at the beginning of the La Tène period.

The question would be finally decided against the distinction of Picts and Britons if it could be proved that they really bore the same name.[3] But in the history of the Britons and of their name, one fact of peculiar importance stands out. At the time of the Anglo-Saxon invasions, between the sixth and eighth centuries, with the rebirth of a kind of national sentiment, the Britons felt the need to give themselves a name. They called themselves the Combroges, the Fellow-countrymen, the Kymry (Cymry).[4] That is the national name of the Britons. It has not much meaning, and it does not suggest that it took the place of another more or less obsolete name. Britanni was not a national name, but a geographical designation given to the inhabitants of South Britain, first by the Gauls and then by the Romans. The Britons themselves probably adopted it (whence would come personal names like Britto and Brittus), but not so completely as to be content with it.

---

[1] Holmes, op. cit., p. 415. [2] Ibid., pp. 269, 297.
[3] Ibid., pp. 460 ff. [4] Ibid., pp. 449 ff.

If this was so we have to suppose that between the settlement of the Picts, who called themselves the Qretini or Pretini in virtue of their nationality, and the first incursions of Belgæ, a mass, even a considerable mass, of Celtic invaders arrived, for whom, though we cannot give them any particular name, we shall reserve that of Britons. Cæsar, who only knew them from the other side of the line of battle, may have thought that they were the same as the Picts. But they were conscious of their difference, and they made others see it. We shall see that the Goidels did not confuse the Picts with the various groups of Britons with whom they came into contact.

As for the Picts—of whose manners and institutions Cæsar ascribed what he had heard tell to all the inhabitants of the interior as a whole—they had certainly come to Britain so long before the Belgic invasions that they had acquired the right to be regarded as aborigines.

But were they, if not *the* Britons, at any rate Brythonic, in the general sense in which I have used the word ? That is to say, had their language, when they arrived in Britain, changed *qu* to *p* ?

The Goidelic form of their name, Cruithnig, cannot be adduced as proof of the negative, since the Goidels were aware that the *p*'s of Brythonic corresponded to the *qu*'s of their own tongue. In the Irish texts which have come down to us we find them transcribing the *p*'s of Brythonic and even of Latin as *qu*, that is as *c*. Thus, *purpura* became *corcur*, and Patricius (St. Patrick) became Cothraige.

We have nothing certain in support of the affirmative. If the Picts arrived at the end of the Bronze Age, it seems to me scarcely probable that their language had not yet undergone the mutation of the velars.[1] It is certain that it offered it no resistance, either because it was already tending that way or because the Picts adopted the language of the people who came after them. The British emigrants arrived with the prestige of a superior craftsmanship and a better-armed civilization. They could impose their language. I should, moreover, be very ready to believe that there was fairly thorough interpenetration between the Pictish and British tribes. Were the Cornavii of Cheshire and those of Caithness,

---

[1] See above, pp. 132 ff.

living so far apart, Picts ? Were they Britons ? In any case, one fraction of them was surrounded by alien groups. The Epidii of Argyll were, perhaps, a British tribe which had pushed northwards, like the Novantæ who were opposite them across the Firth of Clyde. But, on the whole, when we come to the Celtic peoples of the Continent, we shall find reason for thinking that the Picts were probably closer to the Britons than to the Goidels.[1]

VI

PICTS, BRITONS, AND BELGÆ IN BRITAIN

So, after the settlement of the Goidels, there were three Celtic colonizations of Britain, by the Picts, by the Britons, and by the Belgæ, following each other at fairly long intervals.

The first to come were the Picts, who followed the Goidels about the middle of the Bronze Age. Their movement had come to an end when the civilization of Hallstatt, or rather its second period, that of the large iron swords, was beginning on the Continent. The civilization of this period is hardly represented in the British Isles.[2]

When Cæsar says that the peoples of the interior of Britain, as opposed to the agriculturists of the coast, were pastoral folk, living on meat and milk and clothing themselves in the skins of their cattle,[3] he is probably speaking of the Picts. The economic life of the Continent in the Bronze Age, and still in the Hallstatt period, was pastoral rather than agricultural.[4]

They did not make a complete clearance of the builders of the round barrows of the beginning of the Bronze Age, whom I have identified with the Goidels, for down to the La Tène period and during it the inhabitants of Britain continued to erect round barrows, under which contracted skeletons have been found in graves.[5] This is a fact which

---

[1] See below, pp. 230 ff.
[2] CCCLXXXIV, pp. 82–3 ; Déchelette, ii, 2, p. 729 ; E. C. R. Armstrong, in XVI, 1922, p. 204, points to only one large iron Hallstatts word, and there is not one short Hallstatt III sword (against this, see Déchelette, loc. cit., p. 737).
[3] Gall. War, v, 14 ; Holmes, op. cit., p. 267.
[4] See below.
[5] Holmes, op. cit., p. 287.

we must take into account, in order to understand what sort of connections there were between the various elements composing the Celtic population of Britain.[1]

A new body of colonists arrived at the beginning of the first period of La Tène. These were the Britons,[2] and their settlement must have been completed about 300 B.C., when Pytheas made his voyage.[3] The new civilization brought a new economic life. The British settlers were agriculturists. Pytheas observed this besides practices which were new to him, such as that of threshing in barns and not out of doors.[4] In Cæsar's time things in general must have been very much as in Gaul. But agriculture did not change the face of the land so completely as in certain parts of Gaul. The Britons were not settling in a depopulated country. Agriculture took its place in a countryside which had already been adapted to pasture, and the English countryside remains the same to-day.

The first Britons seem to have arrived at the very beginning of the La Tène period, perhaps even a little earlier, between 550 and 500. In the excavations conducted in 1911 and 1912 at Hengistbury Head,[5] in a fortified settlement on the spit separating Christchurch Harbour from the sea, pottery was found very similar to that of the tumuli of the south of Gaul [6] and that recently discovered near Penmarch,[7] a squat ware, still reminiscent of those of the Bronze Age and Hallstatt. For some time past many objects of this period have been found in the south of England.[8]

---

[1] Cf. Nicholson, in **CXL**, 1904, p. 350. Some have connected the Picts with the Pictones of Poitou. I see no great reason for either agreeing or doubting. But I am inclined to think that a generalized designation like that of " Picts " is ancient, and everything seems to show that early racial names, like those of the Picts and the Pictones, do not recur independently.

[2] Holmes, op. cit., pp. 232–3.

[3] Ibid., p. 229.

[4] Ibid., p. 224, and, for the economic condition of Britain, pp. 357 ff.

[5] J. P. Busche-Fox, in **CXXVIII**, iii, 1915 ; cf. Hubert, in **CXL**, 1927, pp. 398–9.

[6] Déchelette, ii, 2, pp. 663 ff.

[7] Favret and Bénard, in **CXXXIX**, 1924, i, pp. 179 ff. In France, these wares are of the end of the Hallstatt period or the very beginning of La Tène. They come from Gallic settlements.

[8] See C. Hawkes and G. C. Dunning, " The Belgæ of Gaul and Britain," in *Archæol. Journ.*, 1930, pp. 150 ff. ; Hawkes, " Hill-forts," in *Antiquity*, v, 1931, pp. 60 ff. ; Hawkes, Myres, and Stevens, *St. Catherine's Hill, Winchester*, 1930 ; Bushe-Fox, **CCCVIII**, for Scarborough ; E. Cunnington, in **XVI**, 1922, pp. 14 ff., for All Cannings Cross, and ibid., 1921, p. 284, for various finds.

The oldest and largest group of barrows of this epoch is that at Arras in Yorkshire.[1] These tombs contain furniture which is very like that of the Marne burials. In particular it includes remains of two-wheeled chariots like those of Champagne.[2] But the bodies are mostly contracted, instead of being laid out at full length as in France.[3] The new culture, therefore, did not prevail in Britain in its pure form. That of the previous inhabitants did not completely disappear. It is, however, to be supposed that the newcomers were sufficiently numerous at the beginning to spread their technical methods and their tastes all over the country fairly soon.

We can judge of the numbers of the Britons from the number of their tribes. Under the Roman Empire there were about twenty *civitates*,[4] that is, British tribes, each of them a composite formation. Most of these are found in Britain alone. It follows that either they were formed in the country with a Celtic organization and native material, or they were already complete, organized social bodies when they arrived. In either case, we must suppose a fairly large number of Britons. Only three British tribes, the Brigantes, Parisii,[5] and Cassi,[6] one of which occupied the greater part of Yorkshire and Nottinghamshire, and another Holderness in Yorkshire, left a portion behind them on the Continent. There were Parisii in the neighbourhood of modern Paris. The Brigantes came from Switzerland and Upper Bavaria ; Bregenz was originally Brigantum, and Cambodunum (Kempten) was a town of the Brigantes. They founded another Cambodunum on the road from York to Chester.[7] Although the Brigantes come before us as a fraction of a people, they were one of the most numerous tribes in Britain, if we are to judge from the map, in which the names of their towns are sown thick. The Cassi must have belonged to the

[1] CCCLXXXIV, pp. 115, 119 ; Déchelette, ii, 3, p. 1102.
[2] Chariot-burial at Hunmanby near Hull ; R. A. Smith, in CXVIII, 1909–1910, pp. 403 ff.
[3] The previous types persist in these burials. Also, the British ingredient was composed of the same strains as the Goidelic and Pictish : round-heads and long-heads of the North, with a few Alpines. For the ethnology of Britain at this time see Holmes, op. cit., p. 234.
[4] Ibid., p. 234.
[5] D'Arbois, CCC, p. 26.
[6] Cæs., *Gall. War*, v, 21.
[7] Camboritum, in *Itin. Anton.*, 474, 7 ; cf. Chambourcy, Chambord.

same group as the Veliocasses, Viducasses, Baiocasses, and Tricasses ; this group perhaps gave its name to Hessen.

MAP 9.   Britain at the time of the Roman Conquest.   (C. Hawkes and G. C. Dunning, *The Belgæ of Gaul and Britain*, fig. 33.)

The presence of the Parisii, Brigantes, and Cassi among the Britons shows that they were related to the Celtic peoples of the Continent, and also points to the part of the Celtic world in which we should look for the origins of which they preserved the tradition.[1] Intercourse and exchanges of all kinds kept alive that likeness between Britons and Gauls which is a sign of their kinship.[2]

At a much later date new Celtic invaders landed in the British Isles. These were the Belgæ.[3]

Did the Belgæ form a body within the whole Celtic mass in any way comparable to the Goidelic and British groups ? [4]

From the linguistic point of view, no. The Belgæ spoke the same tongue as the Gauls, whose language belonged to the Brythonic group.[5] The names of places and persons, which are all we have to represent the Belgæ, are similar to or identical with Brythonic names.[6] No linguistic fact has been discovered to distinguish the language spoken by the Belgæ from Brythonic. Celtic developed in the same way among them as among the Britons. The two peoples lived close to each other and mixed with each other.

But this is only a partial answer, for in other respects the Belgæ could be regarded as a solid, distinct group of peoples, conscious of their unity and finding the principle of their destinies in themselves. We can only judge of the matter when we have formed some judgment of the size of the Belgic peoples and of the history of their migrations.

In any case, they felt the need of expressing their unity and independence by having a racial name of their own.

The passages in Cæsar regarding the ethnology of Britain,[7] properly interpreted, place their first inroads in the first half of the second century B.C. The archæological evidence confirms this. The appearance of the culture of La Tène II, followed by that of La Tène III, can be explained by the

[1] Many place-names are common to Britain and Gaul, and suggest the same inferences as Cambodunum. Cf. Sorviodunum (Old Sarum) and Sorviodurum near Straubing in Bavaria, also Uxellodunum, Noviomagus, Mediolanum, Condate, Segodunum.

[2] Tac., *Agr.*, 11 ; cf. Pliny, *N.H.*, xvii, 4 ; xxxii, 6 ; Mela, iii, 3 ; d'Arbois, **CCXCIX**, p. 32.

[3] See below, p. 221.

[4] See below, p. 229.

[5] Yet Cæsar declares, on the first page of his *Commentaries*, that the Belgæ differed in dialect from the other Gauls. Strabo (iv, p. 176) more accurately speaks of slight differences of dialect.

[6] D'Arbois, op. cit., pp. 25 ff.

[7] See above, pp. 210–11.

arrival of a new stratum of immigrants.[1] Cremation-tombs of La Tène II and III have been found in the south of Britain. The largest group of such tombs is that of Aylesford, in Kent.[2] They are small pits, 2 or 3 feet deep, containing funeral urns, sometimes arranged in circles.

Not all tombs in Britain contain cremations from La Tène II onwards.[3] Even in the south cremation was not the universal custom. The new rite, therefore, seems to be an indication of the new race ; cremations mean Belgic tombs.[4]

There are, perhaps, other traces of the passage of the Belgæ besides those which I have mentioned. The *Antonine Itinerary* gives a Blatobulgium in Scotland, which was doubtless Blebo (representing an earlier form Blathbolg), near St. Andrews. We shall see that it was possible for the first vowel to waver between *e* and *o*. Bolge, or Bolgios, has been found among Pictish masculine names. In Aberdeenshire the name of Strathbolgin (Strathbogie) contains the same element, which may be evidence of the Belgæ.[5]

It is probable that the Belgæ, like the Britons, advanced as far as they could. But they did not arrive in masses to be compared to those of the Britons. Cæsar says that they came on warlike expeditions, which were probably little more than pillaging forays—either organized attempts at conquest from a centre which remained on the Continent, like that of Diviciacus, or else a succession of raids on a small scale on the part of adventurers and seekers of loot. There was no movement of a whole nation. The invaders were bands, some organized in " cities " and some composed of detachments from various " cities ", which were usually too small to form complete social units when they settled in the country. The actual peoples remained in Gaul. In the racial make-up of Britain, then, the Belgæ were not nearly so large an ingredient as the Britons.

[1] Bushe-Fox, in **CXXVIII**, 1925, p. 31 ; shield of La Tène II with elongated boss, found at Hod Hill, in **XVI**, 1922, p. 98.

[2] Déchelette, ii, 3, p. 1102 ; **CCCLXXXIV**, pp. 124 ff. ; for tomb at Welwyn, Herts, see R. A. Smith, in **CXVIII**, 1912, p. 170.

[3] Holmes, op. cit., p. 287.

[4] I shall have occasion to point out that the rite of cremation never ceased to be practised by one branch of the Belgæ from the Hallstatt period onwards, and that it spread in Gaul at the time of the Belgic ascendancy.

[5] Rhys, **CCCCL,** ii, p. 206.

Nevertheless, the Belgæ, like the Britons, added their contribution to the civilization of the country.[1] When they first landed Greek coinage was beginning to be disseminated in Britain.[2] The Belgæ doubtless helped to spread its use. At all events the culture which was theirs and that of their age spread like the previous civilization and equally widely.[3]

But the Belgæ were not the only Celts who arrived in Britain in La Tène II and III. One of the most remarkable

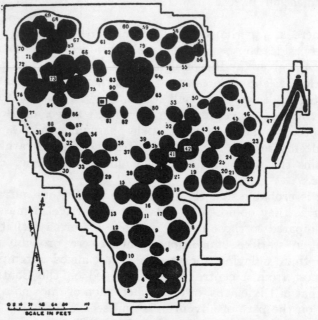

FIG. 36. Plan of the British Village at Glastonbury, Somerset. (Déchelette, ii, 3, fig. 405.)

Celtic settlements in Britain is the pile-village at Glastonbury (Fig. 36), in Somerset.[4] It contains the same incised pottery (Fig. 37) as is found in the Celtic cemeteries and *oppida* of Finistère (the cemetery of Kerviltré, the *oppidum* of Castel-Meur).[5] It was probably imported from Brittany; at least,

[1] For their importation of Greek and Italian objects, see Holmes, op. cit., p. 246.
[2] Ibid., p. 248.
[3] In particular, the swords of La Tène II and III. The Caledonians of Galgacus had them (Tac., *Agr.*, 36).
[4] Bulleid and Gray, CCCCXVII.
[5] Ibid., ii, p. 494. Cf. Déchelette, ii, 3, p. 1473. For the Brittany origin of the Marlborough bucket, see A. J. Evans, in XVIII, ix, 1890, p. 373.

it is evidence of relations, perhaps of a commercial kind, especially affecting the south-west of England. This pottery is found at Hengistbury Head, with coins of the Curiosolites and Andecavi.

The Glastonbury village is the largest and richest crannog known, and is the best excavated.[1] Is it to the Belgæ or to the Britons that we must ascribe the building of these curious structures,[2] standing on piers of timbers, clay, and stones

Fig. 37. British Vases with Incised Decoration from Glastonbury. (Déchelette, ii, 3, fig. 668.)

held in place by piles, which resemble the lake-villages of Central Europe but are quite unconnected with them? Crannogs are found all over Great Britain and Ireland. They date from the La Tène period, but they outlived it, and they reveal, with the forts, how insecure life was in the troubled times in which the Celtic settlement of the British Isles was nearing completion.

[1] Coffey, **CCCCXXVIII**, p. 103 ; Macalister, **CCCCXXXIX**, p. 50.
[2] I should ascribe them to the Belgæ, for piles have been found in the rivers of Northern Gaul, and the swampy districts from which the Belgæ of Britain came were better suited to this kind of dwelling than those occupied by the Britons.

There was, perhaps, a fourth strain in the population of Britain when the Romans conquered it, namely the Germans. Tacitus [1] ascribes Germanic origin to the Caledonians on account of their red hair and great height. It is not a very good reason, but it is quite likely that a few Germans came to Britain in the wake of the Belgæ, considering how long the Germans had lived close to the Belgæ and that, as we shall see, they started moving after the Belgæ and in just the same manner.[2] But Tacitus might well have connected what he tells us of the maternal family of the Germans in their own country with what he could have been told of the customs of the Picts.[3] If the Picts set forth after the Goidels from the German coasts of the North Sea, it is probable that they drew some Germans along with them.

If the archæology of Britain reflects, as it is reasonable to suppose, its racial vicissitudes—if, that is, the arrival of each of the elements in its Celtic population is to be connected, as has been done above, with a phase of its civilization, as revealed by the remains left in its soil, the Belgæ having contributed the culture of La Tène II and III, the Britons that of La Tène I, and the Picts that of the end of the Bronze Age—then we have nothing to ascribe to the Goidels but the culture of the beginning of the Bronze Age, and they must be identified with the Continental invasion which took place in Britain at that time.

In the preceding pages it has been sufficiently established that that first influx of Celtic population was not driven out by the succeeding waves. Indeed, traces of it are found down to the Anglo-Saxon conquest. The remnant, incorporated in the political organization of the later comers, kept its funeral customs, that is, a part of its morals. It made such a lasting impression that the face of the countryside to this day is as its ancestors had made it. If the south of England, which is so very like the French coast opposite, presents such a different appearance, that is certainly partly due to the persistence of a strong Goidelic strain in people and civilization. But these first invaders likewise allowed their predecessors to survive. There was room for these latter to live within the network of the Goidelic occupation. The

[1] *Agr.*, 11. For the Caledonians, see **CXL**, xxxix, p. 75.
[2] See above, p. 214.   [3] See above, p. 205.

Goidels borrowed some things from them,[1] and certain imported objects in Goidelic tombs show that they took over the Western and Mediterranean connections of the aborigines.[2]

But we have something still better, namely an evidence of the mixed civilization which grew out of the contact of invaders and invaded and implies some association between them.   That is Stonehenge, the largest of the megalithic monuments.[3] The Goidels must have provided the religious idea, their predecessors the method of construction.[4] The grouping of a large number of round barrows about the monument,[5] its successive transformations, revealed by the latest excavations,[6] its constant use until after the Roman conquest,[7] and, lastly, the ancient tradition of a circular temple of the Sun among the Celts of the Ocean,[8] all compel one to ascribe its construction to the first Celtic occupants of Britain.[9] It implies the highest degree of power and organization of which prehistoric times have left a trace. It has, too, been thought that the great number of barrows surrounding Stonehenge proves that men came from far away to be buried near the holy place.[10] These funeral pilgrimages would demand roads, such as the well-known Pilgrims' Way,[11] a prestige as a sanctuary, and a social unit of vast extent and influence, something like the great Goidelic Kingdom of Britain, the memory of which has been preserved, but post-dated, by tradition.

VII

THE BRITONS AND BELGÆ IN IRELAND.   FIR BOLG, FIR DOMNANN, GALIANS

The Britons and Belgæ, like the Picts, went beyond Britain and crossed the Irish Sea on their westward way.

[1] Abercromby, CCCCXII.   [2] Cylinders and various beads ; ibid.
[3] Hawley, in XVI, 1921, pp. 19 ff.
[4] Astronomical considerations tend to fix the date of the building of Stonehenge about the second millennium (Holmes, op. cit., pp. 475 ff.).
[5] Hawley, loc. cit., 47.
[6] Ibid. Romano-British pottery and coins of Claudius II Gothicus found during excavation.
[7] For stone rings in Scotland, see CXXIV, xlv, 1910, p. 46 ; lvii, 1922–3, pp. 20, etc.
[8] Hecat. Abd., in F.H.G., ii, p. 387 ; cf. Diod., ii, 47, 2 ; Pindar, Pyth., x, 29–30 ; Olymp., iii, 16.   [9] Holmes, op. cit., pp. 475 ff.
[10] Ibid., pp. 113–14.   [11] Ibid., p. 247.

Ptolemy shows us in the south of Ireland a settlement of Brigantes,[1] in what is now Waterford, and, by the side of them, in Wexford, one of Menapii, with a capital called Menapia [2]; the former are Britons, and the latter Belgæ from the Finnish coast. He also mentions an 'Επίδιον ἄκρον, or " Horse Promontory ", a name familiar among Celtic place-names, the π of which—certain evidence that it is Brythonic—was disguised as *ch* in the Irish name Aird Echdi.[3] On the other side of the Menapii, further north, in Wicklow, were the Cauci. These are Chauci, that is Germans from the Hanoverian coast,[4] who had followed the Belgæ over the sea.

The Menapii seem to have pushed their way forwards in Ireland, for we find later a scattered people of Monaigh or Manaigh.[5] One branch of them was established in the east of Ulster, near Belfast, and another in the west, where their name is preserved in that of Fermanagh. The Irish genealogies make them both come from Leinster, where the Menapii were settled. South-east of Fermanagh lies County Monaghan, the name of which perhaps has the same origin.

With the coming of these Britons and Belgæ, the civilization of La Tène was introduced into Ireland. The arms, pottery, and art of La Tène were imposed on Ireland as they had been on Britain. Mr. Coffey has maintained, arguing from Zimmer's hypothesis regarding the Goidels, that this civilization came direct from Gaul.[6] It probably came from both sides, Britain and Gaul. Besides, it came in two instalments, one of La Tène I [7] and one of La Tène II [8]; the former was probably Brythonic, coming from Britain, and the latter Belgic, coming from Gaul. In Ireland, as in

[1] ii, 3, 10. Cf. Westropp, in **CXXII**, 1918, p. 131 ; J. Loth, in **CXL**, 1914, p. 111 ; Rhys, **CCCLI**, p. 285.
[2] ii, 2 ; d'Arbois, in **CXL**, 1898, p. 249.
[3] ii, 3, 1. Aird Echdi, Height of the Echdi. Cf. Feist, **CCCXCVI**, p. 58 ; K. Meyer, " Zur keltischen Wortkunde," iii, No. 41, in **CXLVIII**, 1913, p. 445.
[4] Ptol., ii, 2, 8. Pokorny (in **CLXXI**, xi, pp. 169–188) sees further traces of the Germans in the ethnology of Ireland. He Germanizes the Galians; according to him the Coriondi, Cuirenzige, would in Germanic be *Hariandiz, and the Cauci are Chauci, Chauchi, transformed into Ui Cuaich.
[5] MacNeill, **CCCCXLI**, p. 58.
[6] In **CXXII**, xxviii, c, p. 96, where he gives a summary of La Tène objects found in Ireland. Those which best support his view are the carinated vases of Marne type found near Dublin.
[7] Coffey, loc. cit.
[8] Ibid. The Menapians of Labraid Loingsech (see below, p. 225) arrive with spears with long, broad heads.

Britain, the Britons or Belgæ built crannogs,[1] the distribution of which corresponds to the extension of their settlements.

The Fir Bolg, Fir Domnann, and Galians are simply colonies of Belgæ, Britons, and Gauls. In the list of subject tribes they appear as foreigners allowed to remain on sufferance as metics. If they are placed before the sons of Mile in the order of invasions, it is by an artifice of what is known as Milesian literature.

The Fir Bolg, Fir Domnann, and Galians go together in the *Leabhar Gabhála* and in history.[2] Therefore, what can be proved of one group is true of the others, and even of people who are constantly associated with them, such as the Luaighni.[3] In any case, Milesian literature is equally censorious about them all. This is how they are described in the *Book of Genealogies* of Duald mac Firbis[4] : " Black-haired, talkative, treacherous, tale-bearing, a clamorous, contemptible folk ; miserly, vagrant, instable, harsh, and inhospitable ; slaves, thieves, boors ; foes of music and noble pleasures, troublers of feasts, fomenters of strife— such are the descendants of the Fir Bolg, the Galians, the Luaighni, and the Fir Domnann in Ireland." These Belgæ and Britons (for they, I believe, were the peoples in question) no doubt brought material civilization and plastic art to Ireland, but it is possible that their manners and customs did not appeal to the previous inhabitants of the country. We may suppose, too, that the portrait is not a true one, especially in the matter of the colour of their hair.[5]

The Fir Domnann,[6] to take their name literally, were the men of Domnu, just as the Tuatha Dé Danann were the tribes of the Goddess Danu.[7] They were called after a hypothetical eponymous goddess. But, while Danu is a dim

---

[1] Ibid., p. 103.

[2] M. E. Dobbs, in **LXXX**, 1916.

[3] The Luaighni were established in the east, from the Shannon to the Irish Sea. The barony of Lune in County Meath is called after them. They formed one of the chief forces of the army of Leinster. That is why they are placed with the Galians, who were so numerous in Leinster, among the Gallic or British invaders of the Iron Age. Cairbre Cat-head, who led the rising of the subject peoples, was chief of the Luaighni (MacNeill, op. cit., p. 80).

[4] *Duanaire Finn*, i, p. xxxi.

[5] The Belgæ were fair.

[6] Dobbs, op. cit., p. 168. They came after the Fir Bolg, according to the *Leabhar Gabhála*.

[7] Squire, **CCCCLIX**, p. 48 : Domnu, the mother of the Fomorian gods. Rhys, **CCCCL**, ii, p. 208.

enough figure, Domnu is only a name in the genealogies. It can only be a racial name, presented in the Irish fashion. The people were also called Domnanid and Domnannaig.[1]

Now one of the principal British tribes was that of the Dumnonii,[2] who lived in Cornwall. There was another of the same name in the south of Scotland, between Galloway and the Clyde, which Ptolemy calls Δαμνόνιοι. *Dumnonii* should become *Domnain* in Old Irish. Such proper names as Inber Domnann, River-mouth of Domnu (Malahide Bay, north of Dublin), and Erris Domnann, Land-bridge or Promontory of Domnu (in the north-west of County Mayo, in Connacht), suggest incursions of Dumnonii on the Irish coast.[3]

The similarity of the names affords valuable evidence. These people are Celts, it is true, but Celts belonging to another group than the Goidels—that is Britons. A gloss informs us that one thing remembered about the Fir Domnann was that they dug wells.[4] If they had come from the region about Devon and Dorset, to which the domain of the Dumnonii was still confined at the time of the Roman occupation, they must in many places have found it necessary to dig wells in the chalky soil in order to get water. Ireland is not so dry.

Another British tribe, the Setantii,[5] who lived along the coast of the Irish Sea, south-west of the Brigantes and north of the Cheshire Cornavii, must have made a name for themselves in Ireland. The greatest hero of the Irish epics, Cuchulainn, was really named Setanta.[6] It is a foreign name, and the foreign form of the stem is preserved ; in Irish it would have become *Setéta. It is curiously like the name of the Setantii. Moreover, according to a tradition related by Duald mac Firbis,[7] Cuchulainn belonged to a subject tribe, the Tuath Tabhaira.

So there are three Brythonic tribes in Britain, all living on the Irish Sea, of which we find settlements, or at least

[1] **CXL**, xxxi, p. 15.
[2] Rhys, **CCCCLI**, p. 298 : The Dumnonii were a political formation. Windisch, **CCXCVI**, p. 25.
[3] Rhys, **CCCCL**, ii, p. 208 ; MacNeill, op. cit., p. 79.
[4] *Coir Anmann*, **CCXCV**, iii, p. 381.
[5] Ptol., ii, 3, 3.
[6] Holder, s.v.
[7] MacNeill, op. cit., p. 79 : Ferdiad is a Fir Domnann.

traces, in Ireland. They probably invaded Ireland soon after they had settled in Britain.

The Galians were closely connected with the Fir Domnann. They had the same ancestor, and they had chiefs from among the Fir Domnann.[1] I have already shown that their name came from that of Gaul and the Gauls.

A further proof of this with a date is given by the pair of stories entitled *Longes Labrada*, the *Sailing* or *Exile of Labraid Loingsech*,[2] and *Orgain Dinn Rig*, the *Destruction of Dind Rig*. Labraid Loingsech was the grandson of King Lægaire Lorc, Ugaine Mor's son, who was murdered with his son Ailill by his brother Cobthach. Labraid Loingsech fled. " He set out eastwards and came to the isle of the Britons, and then he went among the young men with speckled hair who dwell in the country of Armenia and entered the service of the King of Armenia." Where this Armenia was is disputed. D'Arbois de Jubainville proposed the reading Fir Menia, the men of Menia, that is of the country of the Menapians. But what follows is the important part. " The Galians fed him during his exile in the land of Gall." So he went to Gaul after a stay in Britain. He came back with a band of Galians, and with their help he destroyed Dind Rig and avenged his father and grandfather.

For this series of kings the annals give dates varying between the fifth and third centuries.[3] But the story itself provides an archæological date. It tells that Cobthach, in order to take his brother by surprise, decided to sham dead, and so had himself laid out on his wagon with his weapons in his hand, and when Lægaire leant over him to embrace him he killed him.[4] The murderer was imitating one of the chariot-burials which are found in the tombs of the Marne, and are not later than the first period of La Tène, that is 300 B.C. So the usages of the La Tène civilization had entered Ireland before that date, and Britons or Gauls were certainly established there.

This story might even be a history of the arrival of the Menapii, that is of the first Belgæ, in County Wexford and Leinster. For everything happens there. Lægaire is murdered at Carman, in County Wexford. Dind Rig is the chief

[1] Dobbs, loc. cit.   [2] d'Arbois, in **CXL,** 1909, p. 212.
[3] Dobbs, op. cit., p. 72.   [4] *Coir Anmann.*

residence of the Kings of Leinster. Leinster, too, seems to have been mainly peopled by foreigners. It was there that the Galians were massed as the Erainn were in Munster, and they were the chief strength of the troops of Leinster. In the great poem of the Ulster cycle, the *Táin Bó Chuailgné*, much is made of their military organization, which may originally have been due to the superiority of the iron weapons which they had brought from Gaul. I am not sure that the people in the story of Labraid are Menapii ; we are dealing with Gauls coming to reinforce their British brethren, and they come from Gaul like the Belgæ, who, in any case, cannot have arrived long after them.

The examination of certain proper names borne by Galians or found in the district occupied by the Britons leads to the same conclusion. Finn mac Coul (mac Cumhail) belonged to a Galian clan, the Ui Tarsigh. The name of his father, Cumhal, corresponds to that of the Gallic and British god Camulos, who was worshipped by the Remi. Several ogham inscriptions from County Waterford mention a person named Neta Segamonas. This name may mean Champion of Segomo. Now Segomo is not a god of Ireland, nor even of Britain ; he is a Gallic god. These inscriptions belong to a group (all found in the same county), the proper names in which appear in the dynasty of the Eoganachta of Cashel, who ruled over Munster in the time of St. Patrick. There Neta Segamonas appears in the form Nia Segamain. It is to be supposed, and Mr. MacNeill is of this opinion,[1] that the Eoganachta were a family of Gallic origin, which had risen to importance.

But the best reason for thinking that the Galians were not Belgæ is that they distinguish themselves from their successors, the Fir Bolg. For them, too, the mythologists invented a goddess, Bolga, an even more elusive being than Domnu. But the etymologists could dispense with her, for the meaning of the name is perfectly clear. The Fir Bolg are the Men with the Bags. *Bolg* means a bag ; *di bolg*,[2] the two bags, means the bellows. Mr. MacNeill makes the Fir Bolg one of his industrial classes, the Bag-makers. There was a legend that, having emigrated to Greece and become serfs, they were employed in carrying earth in leather

[1] Op. cit., p. 127.   [2] G. H. Orpen, in **LXXX**, 1911, p. 180.

bags and spreading it over rocky ground. According to another they did trade with the Eastern world, and sent to it leather bags filled with the soil of Ireland, which was scattered around the cities to kill the snakes.

An opinion which is supported by the authority of Sir John Rhys [1] and d'Arbois de Jubainville identifies the Fir Bolg with the Belgæ. The first syllable of the name of the Belgæ contained a vowel which might be an *o* ; witness the name of the Galatian chief Bolgios, who, as we shall see, was a Belgian. This explanation does not exclude the other. It does not compel us to abandon the etymology proposed above. The word *bolg* is not peculiar to Irish. *Bulgas Galli sacculos scorteos appellant*, Festus says.[2] " The Gauls call leather bags *bulgæ*." In Welsh *boly* (*bola, bol*) means " bags ". It is probable that this word existed in Belgic, too, and possible that it came into the racial name of the group. Its employment in the formation of a racial name is explained in a poem attributed to Columba.[3] The author speaks of *fir i mbolggaib* " men in bags ". Here the bags are garments— trousers. So trousers are called " bags " in English. The name Gallia Braccata, applied to a people from its national garb, makes it quite credible that a name of this kind should have been adopted to describe the Belgæ. The large wide trousers in which we usually imagine the Gauls are the trousers of the Belgæ. The Gauls properly so called, those of Gallia Lugdunensis, wore another kind of trousers, which appears on the Gallo-Roman monuments, a short, close-fitting garment which was adopted by the Roman army. This is the *bracca*, short drawers not reaching below the thighs.

As for the Goidels, they wore no trousers at all. Thus the costume of the Highlander is a faithful witness to the Goidelic origin of the Scots.

The name of the Belgæ, then, is a racial nickname, and the name of the Men with the Bags of Ireland is the name of the Belgæ.

It is under their common name that the Belgæ are designated. It may, perhaps, be worth while to examine the names of the Belgic clans in detail. One clan of Fir Bolg

[1] Rhys, CCCCL, ii, p. 205.
[2] G. H. Orpen, op. cit., p. 145.
[3] Frag. 8 *b* 3. *Fir bolgg*, ibid., 131 *a* 1.

was named Clan Morna.[1] The Clan Morna were the enemies of Cumhal, and are mentioned as such in the oldest poem of the Finn cycle. Perhaps they are the Morini of the Pas-de-Calais, who are themselves Belgæ and, what is more, neighbours of the Menapii on the north.

On the whole the list of the non-Gælic tribes of Ireland is not mainly a list of non-Celtic tribes. It does not provide material for a picture of the population of the island before the advent of the Goidels, but it records the successive waves of Celtic colonization, of which that of the Goidels was the first.

But from the position of the later colonies, Gallic, British, and Belgic, in relation to the Goidels we can draw conclusions. The arrival of the new settlers did not affect, as in Britain, the racial and social balance of the country. They took their place in a system which they did not transform. If they came to conquer they failed, and were content to be received as serfs, as in the legend of the Fir Bolg in Greece.[2] They certainly did not come in sufficient force to obtain the ascendancy.

There were no migrations of whole peoples. The biggest perhaps were those of the Brigantes, the Menapii, and the Cauci, whose combined settlements covered a large area. The Dumnonii ranged the coasts of Ireland in scattered bands of pirates or traders. The Belgic and Gallic bodies probably comprised men of various races, for the names of the clans seem to be mostly new. It is possible that they sometimes arrived in armies ; it is more likely that they came in bands ; and one would naturally suppose that these bands consisted of men only.

Having entered Ireland these bodies of Britons, Gauls, and Belgæ went all over the country ; their inroads reached far. Irish tradition is full of their exploits, and they provided its chief heroes, such as Cuchulainn and Finn, and doubtless some of its episodes. But, contrary to what happened in Britain, they became merged in the mass of the Irish ; they founded no great independent settlements ; they were assimilated by the first Celtic occupants of the island.

[1] *Duanaire Finn*, intr., xxx.
[2] MacNeill, op. cit., p. 76.

VIII

THE RACIAL COMPOSITION OF IRELAND

But there they were, and they had their own place. The bodies of Celts represented in Britain appear in Ireland. We shall see as we go on that there were no others. It would seem that each wave of invading Celts, exactly following its predecessors and tending to spread on the top of them, went as far as it could until it was forced to stop.

Let us look at our map of Ireland (Map 8) for a moment and consider the motley spectacle which it presents in the time of Ptolemy.[1] In the south-western corner are the Iverni, who are not Celts. In the north-eastern corner the Darini may likewise be a remnant from the pre-Celtic past. They lived on in the history of Ireland, but they changed their ground. They are the Deirgthene of Munster, who seem to have been a tribe of Iberians. In the south-east are the territories of the Britons and Belgæ, to which we should probably join that of the Gangani in Munster.[2] In this last name we recognize the names of Gann and Genann, who were Fir Bolg who landed in County Clare, at the mouth of the Shannon. Ptolemy's map tells us nothing about the Picts of Ulster and elsewhere, nor about the scattered groups of Fir Bolg, Dumnonii, and Galians which were to be found almost everywhere, but we must bear them in mind. The true domain of the Goidels probably covered barely half the country.

As a matter of fact, the various groups were all becoming assimilated. An expression like Erna Dé Bolgæ, the Erna or Erainn of the Goddess Bolga, which combines the name of the Iverni with that of the eponymous goddess of the Belgæ, is significant of what was happening. No less so is the way in which the ruling aristocracy took over the traditions of the subject tribes. We have seen that the chief Irish heroes, Cuchulainn and Finn, were not Goidels. The heterogeneous mass was gradually becoming a nation, which afterwards absorbed yet other elements.

Ireland gives an exceptionally complete picture of what

[1] LXXX, 1918, pp. 131 ff.   [2] Ibid., 1920, p. 140.

was likely to happen wherever the Celts established themselves—the survival and incorporation of the aborigines, the superimposition of Celts, and the amalgamation of all these various elements into new social and political bodies, which were the final form of Celtic societies. In addition, in Ireland, the organization was provided by the first invaders.

CHAPTER III

CELTIC EXPANSION ON THE CONTINENT IN THE BRONZE AGE. GOIDELS AND BRYTHONS

I

DID THE GOIDELS TAKE PART IN THE CELTIC MIGRATIONS ON THE CONTINENT ?   TRACES OF THE GOIDELS IN SPAIN

IN the following chapters we shall consider how the Celtic domain on the Continent was constituted by the extension of the original Celtic domain to the west and south. The Celts met on their south-westward march the same foreign peoples, Iberians and Ligurians, as in the British Isles. But the first question which arises is whether the migrating bodies contained the same Celtic elements and were composed in the same fashion ; we already know that the great mass consisted of Gallo-Britons and Belgæ. Did they also include Goidels and Picts ?   It is an old question which has been revived, but with particular reference to the Goidels.

Zimmer's hypothesis as to the ports from which they sailed [1] implies that they had advanced at least as far as the Loire before they crossed to the British Isles. If we reject it, as I have done, as insufficiently proved, we do not necessarily deny that they went still further without crossing the sea.

But whereas in Ireland the Goidels were preserved by their isolation, and first their power and sovereignty and then their racial character were to a great extent protected by the sea against the encroachment or influence of the other Celts, it could not possibly be so on the Continent, and if any settlement or group which was originally Goidelic survived into historical times we have no means of recognizing it as such. Our task, therefore, is not to look for vanished settlements, but to gather up such scattered memories as they may have left behind them and, above all, such facts as show that Goidelic was spoken on the Continent outside the places of its origin.

---

[1] In **IX**, 1912, pp. 1–59 ; cf. J. Vendryès, in **CXL**, 1912, pp. 384 ff.

The town of Acci, in Spain, now Gaadix in the province of Granada, had a war-god who was called either Netos (genitive Neti) or Neto (genitive Netonis). His worship is attested by Macrobius [1] and also by two inscriptions in Estremadura and Portugal. He has been regarded as Celtic for various reasons.[2] Now the Goidels had a war-god named Nét.[3] *Nét* implies an earlier Netos, genitive Neti. Are these two the same god [4] ? The answer is doubtful, for if the Irish Nét's name is Celtic,[5] it seems to come from a root *nant*, which appears in the name of the Gallic goddess Nantosuelta,[6] and there is no reason to suppose that the disappearance of *n* before *t* or *k* [7] had already taken place at the time when some of the Goidels reached Ireland and others of them, from some other direction, could be supposed to have invaded Spain. Nor is there any ground for imagining that the dropping of the *n* occurred among two branches of the Goidels which were not in contact with each other, whereas having become the rule among the Irish Goidels it neither spread to their near neighbours the Britons nor developed independently among them. Lastly, it is not certain that the people of Acci or the other worshippers of the Spanish Netos were Celts.

In the case of France facts can be produced which are still the subject of controversy. If they were as important as they are made out to be they would go beyond the object of our present inquiry and prove that Goidelic was not quite a dead language in Gaul when the country became Roman. Does not Cæsar state, at the beginning of his *Commentaries*, that the various parts of Gaul spoke different languages [8] ? Some scholars, such as Sir John Rhys, have thought it possible to determine those of the peoples of Gaul which were Goidels [9] ; for instance, the Arverni and Sequani, and

---

[1] *Saturn.*, i, 19, 5 : *Accitani etiam, Hispana gens, simulacrum Martis, radiis ornatum, maxima religione celebrant, Neton vocantes.*

[2] **I**, ii, 3386 (Acci) ; 5278 (Turgalium, Trujillo) ; 365 (Conimbriga, Condeixa-a-Velha, near Coimbra) ; Roscher, *Lexikon*, s.v. ; Holder, **CCVII**, s.v. ; Leite de Vasconcellos, **DXIII**, ii, 309 ; Toutain, **CCCLXXXVIII**, iii, 136. Schulten (**DXVIII**, p. 83) regards him as Iberian. Cf. Philipon, **DXVI**, p. 209.

[3] **CXL**, 42, 215.

[4] Hubert, in **CLXXX**.

[5] Nét is a Fomorian god.

[6] D'Arbois, in Reinach, **CCCCLXXIV**, i, 224.

[7] Pedersen, **CCXXVII**, i, 51.

[8] *Gall. War*, i, 1, 2 : *Hi omnes lingua, institutis, legibus inter se differunt* ; Strabo, iv.

[9] **CCXXX**, passim, esp. p. 59 ; Nicholson, **CCXXIII**, 6, p. 116 ; Holmes, *Cæsar's Conquest of Gaul*, p. 319.

behind them all the peoples of their faction and all those of Aquitania. These were the *Celtæ*, the rest being the *Galli*. By this side-road Sir John has brought back the old distinction between the two names. The proofs adduced are a very few words, mostly proper names, which appear to contain the old *qu* of Celtic. Some are furnished by inscriptions, the others are place-names.

The principal document is the Coligny Calendar, in which three words of Goidelic appearance are found [1]—the name of the month Equos, the Horse month, which should be *epos* in Brythonic Gaulish; the name of the month Qutios or Cutios,[2] which Sir John explains by the Welsh word *pyd* " dangerous ", and compares to Latin *quatio*; and the word *quimon*, which he suggests is an abbreviation of a word pronounced *quinquimon* (*coic*, *pump* or *pimp*), comparing it to the Latin distributives *bimus*, *trimus*, *quadrimus*.[3] The Calendar also presents words for which Goidelic alone is said to have equivalents—Ciallos, which is like Irish *ciall* " collection ", " total ", and *lat*, followed by a number, which might be the Irish *láthe* " day ", for which there is no Brythonic equivalent.[4]

If these arguments hold good we have a document, and a most important one, establishing the use of Goidelic words in Gaul at the time of its Romanization. Were there considerable survivals of Goidelic in the religious vocabulary, or did the language continue to be spoken? The district is the middle valley of the Rhone. It is likewise in the south-east and south-west of France that almost all the evidence in question has been collected. The observations made on the Coligny Calendar called attention to other documents, particularly a lead plaque, bearing on its two faces a cursive Latin inscription, found at Rom, in Deux-Sèvres,[5] and a few scattered formulæ in Marcellus of Bordeaux.[6] Little by little one-half of the Gaulish inscriptions has been grouped round

[1] J. Loth, in **CXL**, 1904, pp. 113 ff.; S. de Ricci, ibid., pp. 10–27; Rhys, in **CXXI**, 1910.
[2] Rhys, **CCXXX**, p. 28; Dottin, **CXCVI**, p. 280. S. de Ricci compares the word to the name of the month Κούτιος in the Locrian calendar of Chalæon, in **CXL**, 1898, p. 218.
[3] Rhys, op. cit., p. 5.
[4] Ibid., pp. 6, 7.
[5] C. Jullian, in **CXL**, 1898, p. 168; Nicholson, op. cit., p. 127; Rhys, in **CXXVII**, 1900, p. 895.
[6] Nicholson, op. cit., pp. 6, 7; Holmes, loc. cit.

these documents. What are these facts worth ? We need not pay attention to the Rom tablet or the formulæ of Marcellus of Bordeaux,[1] for the text of both is disfigured. But we must discuss the evidence of the Coligny Calendar.

Coligny lies in the ancient domain of the Ambarri, or perhaps in that of the Sequani, already discussed. Another inscription was found near Coligny, at Géligneux, in Ain,[2] which proves clearly that the same language was spoken in that part as in the rest of Gaul, namely Brythonic. It is a Latin funerary inscription, containing Gaulish words. One M. Rufius Catullus, Curator of the Nautæ of the Rhone, has built himself a funerary chapel and made provision for the maintenance of worship there by a foundation which provides, among other things, for a funeral feast to be held periodically. *Et ad cenam omnibus tricontis ponendam (denariorum binorum) in perpet(uum), sic ut petrudecameto consumatur.* This means that the banquet is to take place on the 14th day of every thirty-day month. *Tricontis* is the dative of a word meaning 30, a cardinal number ; in Breton *tregont* ; in Old Irish *tricha*, genitive *trichat* (= *tricos*, *tricontos*). *Petrudecameto* is an ordinal number, 14th.[3] But it is a Brythonic ordinal number. In a Goidelic-speaking country it would have been *quadrudecameto*. Therefore the Goidelic words in the Coligny Calendar could only be, at the most, survivals in a special vocabulary. The Calendar itself contains Brythonic words which can be recognized as such from the use of *p—prinni*,[4] *petiux*.[5] But its Goidelisms are

---

[1] D'Arbois, in **CXL**, 1904, pp. 351–3 ; 1906, p. 107.

[2] **I**, xiii, 2494 ; Allmer, in **III**, 753 *b* ; J. Loth, in **VIII**, 1909, p. 21 ff. Loth has corrected Hirschfeld's interpretation very happily : Géligneux belongs to the bishopric of Belley, i.e. to the old *pagus Bellicensis* ; just as the bishopric of Belley comes directly under the archbishopric of Besançon, so the *pagus Bellicensis* depended, under the Empire, on the province which bore the name of Maxima Sequanorum ; it formed part of the *civitas Equestrium*. In the Coligny Calendar, the months of thirty days are described as *matu* " good, fortunate " (Irish *maith*, Gaelic *math*, Welsh *mad*). The only exception is the month of Equos. It is true that it is not certain whether Equos had twenty-nine or thirty days. The only day which has the indication that it is a *dies fas*, namely, *mat*, written out in full in the Coligny Calendar, is the 14th of the month of Riuros. In the matter of funeral rites, in India, the fourteenth day is set apart for banquets in memory of those who have died young or by force of arms.

[3] O. Irish *dechmad*, Welsh *degfed* " tenth ".

[4] With *prinni*, cf. *prenne* (translated *arborem grandem* in the Vienna Glossary) ; Welsh *pren* " wood " ; Irish *crann* " tree ". Loth, in **CXL**, 1911, p. 208 ; Dottin, **CXCVI**, p. 279.

[5] With *petiux*, cf. Welsh *peth* " a certain amount " ; O. Irish *cuit* " part ". Rhys, **CCXXX**, p. 36 ; **VIII**, p. 53.

doubtful. Common sense forbids us to suppose that a language which was hardly ever written should have preserved, in the spelling of certain words, sounds which it no longer pronounced. It is, on the other hand, probable that the *q* taken by Gaulish from the Latin alphabet stands for other sounds in these inscriptions than the old Celtic velar.

M. Loth supposes that the words in question are compound words, in which *qu* does not stand for a single letter, and should be expressed by the double sound *co-w*.[1] There are instances of such fusions of sounds.[2] If we break up *equos* we get an element *ek*. Now the month Equos is February; in the Irish calendar February begins with a great feast, called *oimelc*. This word is explained in the *Glossary* of Cormac. It is the month in which the milk comes to the ewes.[3] This indication gives the key to the element *ek*. *Eko* could be the Celtic equivalent of *(p)ecu*, *pecus*, with the initial *p* dropped. There was an equivalent for *pecus* in Celtic, doubtless confined to religious parlance; it is represented by the name Eochaid,[4] which corresponds, letter for letter, to Sanskrit *paçu-pátiḥ*. So Equos must have been, not the month of the Horse, but a month which affected the sheep. M. Loth has compared *quimon* with *Quigon*, the cognomen of a citizen of Treves,[5] which breaks up into **co-uigon* " fellow-traveller ", Welsh *cy-waith* " fellow-worker ".[6] As for Qutios, the spelling is not certain and it is more often written Cutius. Of all the hypotheses put forward to explain the obscure passages in the Coligny Calendar, those which try to find Goidelic words in it are among the least probable.

In the same fashion M. Loth has explained the name of the Sequani, over which Celtic scholars have been justifiably concerned and which they have made out to be Ligurian,[7]

---

[1] In **LVIII**, 1909, p. 20.
[2] The name of Bituitus, the chief of the Arverni, is an excellent example. A coin found at Narbonne gives the spelling : Bito-uniotouos (Amardel, in **XXXIII**, 1906, 412, p. 426).
[3] Irish *melg* " milk "; *oi*, *ui* " ewe ".
[4] *Eochaid* = *(p)e(ç)u-(p)ati*.
[5] Bulliot, in **XII**, 1863, p. 142 ; **CXXXIX**, 1863, p. 275.
[6] The country of the Treviri furnishes another example of a false velar in the name of Dinquatis (a Gallic god), which is given to Silvanus as an epithet on two inscriptions found at Géromont in Belgium (**CXLIX**, xiii, 3968).
[7] D'Arbois, **CCCI**, ii, pp. 130–3.

Iberian,[1] and Goidelic [2] in turn. He regards the name of Sequana, their eponymous goddess, as a complex stem which can be analysed into *Seko-uana* or *Seko-ou-ana*.[3] If this is so the Goidelic air of the name of the Sequani is deceptive, and it could not be otherwise, since they spoke Brythonic at least from the time when they founded their city of Epamanduodurum,[4] and they did not alter their name.

Other words found in the south of Gaul give rise to other reflections. One is the proper name Κοναδροννία, which appears in an inscription found at Ventabren, in the Bouches-du-Rhône.[5] It is a prænomen of numerical type (like Sextus), equivalent to the Umbrian Petronia. Its Gaulish form would be Petronia. But is it certain that this name is Celtic? And are the names Quiamelius (Antibes) [6] and Quariates (Queyras) [7] any more so?

These names cannot be dismissed like those discussed before. But we should note that they come from the south of Gaul, where the Gauls did not arrive till fairly late, and there always remained a substratum of the native Ligurian population. That the Goidels should at a very early date have advanced further in that direction than the Brythons is highly improbable. So the words which have detained us are not at all likely to be Goidelic words. They may be Ligurian. Mixed groups of Celto-Ligurians, such as the Salyes round about Marseilles, were formed in this region. It is to be believed that the two strains in their composition appeared in their speech, and that this contained at least some proper names of Ligurian origin, correctly pronounced. The same may be said of the name Aquitania. A curious passage in Pliny seems to mean that the district was once called Aremorica.[8] *Aremorica* is Celtic, and means the country

---

[1] Philipon, **CCCLXIX**, p. 299.   [2] Nicholson, op. cit.
[3] Root *seig*; cf. Mod. German *seihen* " to filter " ; O. Slav. *seknati* " to cut " ; Sanskr. *secanam* " pouring " ; root *sek* " to cut ", from which come Lat. *seco* and Irish *sgathaim* " I cut ".
[4] The City of Men who deal with Horses ; -*mandu*-, -√*mendh* " to deal with ". Cf. Viromandui, Manducus.
[5] Dottin, **CXCVI**, p. 149 ; d'Arbois, **CCXCIX**, p. 87 ; cf. Κου or *Koui* in the Cavaillon inscription (Dottin, op. cit., p. 152) ; Loth, in **CXXXIV**, 1918, pp. 38 ff.   [6] **I**, xii, 226.   [7] **I**, xii, 80.
[8] Pliny, *N.H.*, iv, 105 : *Gallia omnis Comata uno nomine appellata in tria populorum genera dividitur, amnibus maxime distincta. A Scalde ad Sequanam Belgica ; ab eo ad Garunnam Celtica eademque Lugdunensis ; inde ad Pyrenaei montis excursum Aquitanica, Aremorica antea dicta.* Rhys, **CCXXX**, p. 57.

by the sea (*are, mor*). *Aquitania* may have meant the same thing in a language in which the word for water, or the sea, was of the same form as Latin *aqua*. That language may have been Ligurian.[1] It was natural for the part of Gaul in which the natives remained distinct down to the Roman conquest to have its name from a non-Celtic language. But the supporters of the Continental Goidels do not see things so. We shall not follow them.

All the unintelligible inscriptions of the Rhone valley and all the words presenting anomalies from the Celtic point of view have been assembled round the facts furnished by the Coligny Calendar and brought forward by Sir John Rhys as witnesses to a language which he calls " Celtican ", which is at once Ligurian and Goidelic.[2] He identifies the Goidels with the Ligurians, and so gives the Goidels of Gaul a substantial reality. Thus his Ligurians spoke a Celtic language, namely Goidelic, and they were the first body of Celts to break away towards Western and Southern Europe. If so, we should have to increase the domain of the Celts by the whole domain of the Ligurians. But we should also have to be able to explain as Celtic every peculiarity of language revealed by Ligurian names and names of Ligurian type, and for that we should have to invent a pre-Celtic language, extending wider than the pre-Goidelic tongue. If we extend the limits of Celticism as much as this we shall obliterate them altogether.

One of Sir John Rhys's arguments is furnished by the name of the god Segomo. The inscriptions show that his worship extended from Nice to the Côte d'Or. He was a Mars. Now we have already met him ; in the ogham inscriptions of County Waterford the proper name Nia Segamain Segomo's Champion, appears three times. Moreover, Segomo's name recalls that of the Segobrigii, an Alpine people described as Ligurian.[3] Therefore Ireland and the south-east of Gaul had a common god, whose name had an element in common with that of a tribe situated in that part

[1] Cf. Aquincum (Budapest). Celtic also had the equivalent for *aquae*— Irish *uisge*, Welsh *aw*.

[2] Rhys, op. cit., p. 78 ; S. de Ricci, in **CXL**, 1898, pp. 213 ff. ; 1900, p. 27.

[3] Rhys, op. cit.

of Gaul where the Ligurians are placed. So far so good ; but County Waterford happened to be peopled by Gallic colonies. The Celtican hypothesis, which identifies Goidels and Ligurians, is as vain as that which regards the Ligurians as the Italo-Celts in their undivided state.

There are, then, no certain linguistic traces of Goidelic in Gaul, nor are there any in the Continental extensions of the Celtic domain. If any Goidels stayed there they have left no sign of their presence. It does not follow that the ancestors or the first cousins of the Goidels did not spread into those parts.[1] Above all it does not follow that the ancient Celtic tongue was not spoken there before its velar was transformed. There are two questions mixed together, and they should be kept distinct. They can only be answered consistently and separately by the use of other arguments which are of an ethnographic nature.

II

FRANCE AND SPAIN AT THE BEGINNING OF THE BRONZE AGE. IS THE CIVILIZATION OF EL ARGAR CELTIC ?

We may say boldly that there is nothing in the archæology of France and the Iberian Peninsula corresponding to the invasion of England by the builders of the round barrows. Bell-shaped beakers are found there, and in great numbers, but they are of an early type.[2] They are the beakers of the megalithic monuments. There are still, perhaps, scholars who are prepared to believe that this mode of construction spread from the Scandinavian or German north to the Mediterranean.[3] But for years nobody has thought of regarding them as the work of the Celts. We have, therefore, no archæological indication of the migrations of the Celts along the western coasts of Europe before a relatively late period of the Bronze Age ; and if the Goidelic invasion of Britain is represented by the civilization of the round barrows, and particularly by its characteristic tombs and pottery, it was confined to the British Isles. But our archæological evidence is incomplete.

[1] D'Arbois, CCC, p. 12 ; Rhys, CCCCLI, p. 4.
[2] Del Castillo Yurrita, CCCIX, pp. 105 ff.
[3] S. Reinach, in XV, 1893, p. 731.

M. Louis Siret,[1] who was one of the founders of prehistoric archæology in Spain, has maintained that the Celts arrived in that country about the same time (in the Bronze Age), and by sea. He holds that it was the Celts who introduced bronze into Spain, and that they brought it from Bohemia, but that they came by sea, after a halt in the British Isles (for we have no trace of their transit overland), and that they founded in Spain, as in Britain, a colony of metal-workers.

He ascribes to them a series of stations in the province of Almeria, and among them the famous station of El Argar.[2] But similar sites are found from Catalonia to Portugal. They are fortified hill-stations, not having cemeteries separated from the town. The burials are in among the houses, and even in the houses. Herein they differ greatly from the earlier towns with their separate cemeteries of megalithic monuments such as Los Millares and Fuente Vermeja.

The houses and tombs have yielded a very complete series of objects. Objects of copper and bronze are very numerous.[3] In the making of tools, metal had taken the place of flint. The most characteristic object is the halbert. Since halberts are abundant in Ireland and a few have been found in Northern Germany, M. Siret makes the colonizers of Spain arrive by that route.[4]

He compares the tombs of El Argar with the Bohemian tombs of the beginning of the Bronze Age, those of what is called the Aunjetitz or Unetice civilization.[5] They are cists, some of them made of very well dressed slabs, in which the body was laid in a contracted position.[6] There are also large urns, sometimes placed in pairs, mouth to mouth.[7] The tombs are similar, and M. Siret has drawn up a list of the furniture in which the objects correspond piece by piece.[8] Not only the metal objects, but the vases are similar. M. Siret lays particular stress on the likeness of the carinated forms, with an angular profile, and of the vases with feet.[9]

[1] **DXXII**, i, pp. 103 ff., 195 ff.
[2] Siret, " Orientaux et Occidentaux," in **CXXXVI**, 1927, pp. 231–7 ; Déchelette, in **CXXXIX**, 1908, 2, pp. 244 ff. ; Schulten, **DXVII**, pp. 166 ff. ; Bosch Gimpera, **DV**, pp. 157 ff. ; J. Cabré Aguilo, in **XCVII**, i, pp. 23 ff.
[3] Siret, **DXXII**, pl. viii.
[4] Ibid., p. 194.
[5] See above, p. 185.
[6] Siret, op. cit., pl. xiii.
[7] Déchelette, op. cit., pp. 256, 260.
[8] Op. cit., p. 154.
[9] Ibid., pl. ix.

Moreover, this pottery is generally blackish, like the wares of Central Europe.

M. Siret considers that Bohemia, being supplied with tin by the deposits of the Erzgebirge and the neighbouring deposits of Lausitz, was one of the first centres of the Bronze civilization; that it was in a position to act as distributor to countries which were less favoured in this respect, as he imagines to have been the case with Spain,[1] believing that its tin-mines were not discovered until later; and that the peoples which had this mineral wealth in their territory (which at that time, he thinks, were the Celts) were likely to be eager for conquests and adventures.

The Aunjetitz period is contemporaneous with the time when the supposedly Goidelic invaders of Britain were beginning to cross to Ireland. But it is very doubtful, as we have seen,[2] that the Aunjetitz civilization was a Celtic culture. It is still more doubtful that that of El Argar was, and M. Siret's hypothesis has been keenly combated.[3] Even the resemblances of the two civilizations have not the significance which he attaches to them. Déchelette says that the relationship is that of cousins, not, as M. Siret holds, of mother and daughter.[4] El Argar and Aunjetitz stand on two routes from the Eastern Mediterranean, where the prototypes of their funeral customs and technical processes were to be found. The distribution of the halberts, on which M. Siret bases the route taken by his alleged Celts, is not quite what he believes it to be. The halbert was used in Italy. It is represented in carvings on the rocks of the Lac des Merveilles.[5] It was used in Hungary,[6] whence it may have come into Italy. It seems to be absent in Bohemia. Moreover, the German halberts are very different from those of Ireland and Spain. They have the handle attached by a metal socket to which the blade is riveted,[7] whereas in Ireland and the Peninsula the blade is fixed directly on to the wood, and these are probably the earlier types.[8] The resemblances in

---

[1] Ibid., p. 138; Schulten, op. cit., p. 74.
[2] See above, p. 186.
[3] In particular, by Déchelette, op. cit., pp. 261 ff.
[4] Ibid., pp. 251 ff.
[5] Montelius, **DXXXV**, ii, pl. cxxvii, figs. 1–3.
[6] Ibid., p. 93.   [7] Ibid., p. 36.
[8] G. Coffey, in **CXXIII**, xxvii, p. 94; H. and L. Siret, **DXXI**, pl. xxxii; L. Siret, **DXXII**, p. 168.

culture between the British Isles and Spain can easily be explained by trade with the people of Tartessus.[1] Their differences, on the other hand, which are patent, are hard to explain if it is assumed that they were colonized about the same time by the same people.

But besides all this it is very difficult to imagine that the Celts were able at that time to send colonies to the British Isles and to Spain at once. It is enough to remember how extremely hard it is to determine their traces in the archæology of their original home at the end of Neolithic times or at the beginning of the Bronze Age, and to interpret them. They are indeed fleeting, shadowy traces ! That means that the Celts had not yet attained to unity in their first habitat. They were the most vigorous folk there, but they may not have been the most numerous. In any case they were not sufficiently homogeneous peoples, peoples sufficiently aware of themselves, to build up a single civilization of their own. Young, strong peoples have made very distant raids. Several times in prehistory we find identical remains in quite small settlements separated by great distances, and may infer that such a raid had taken place. The adventures of the Normans in the eleventh century were a repetition of many earlier adventures. But to populate a country on a large scale something more was wanted, namely numbers, mass.

At the beginning of the Bronze Age the Goidels had already grown sufficiently to found a lasting settlement in the British Isles. They were not capable of founding another in Spain.[2] Nor did they found one in France.

[1] Avien., *Ora Marit.*, 113 : *Tartessiis qui in terminos Œstrymnidum negotiandi mos est.*

[2] Nevertheless, I do not think that Déchelette has disposed of the problem raised by M. Siret. There is too much difference between the civilization of Los Millares and that of El Argar to be explained by mere development. I myself regard it as a difference of race. What can the new element be ? It is not quite true to say that there are no tombs between Spain and Bohemia like those of El Argar. There are the cists of Chamblandes in the canton of Vaud. There are those of the Valais, which contain just those objects which I have mentioned above as being identical with the Bohemian objects of Aunjetitz. Also, I am very much struck by the fact that, in stations of the El Argar type, the tombs are in the town, under the houses. It is the same in the Neolithic fortified dry-land stations of the Michelsberg type, in the pile-villages, and at Fort-Harrouard. Now, I have already admitted that the people of the Swiss pile-villages must have been Ligurians.

I wonder, therefore, whether the appearance of the El Argar civilization in the Peninsula does not correspond to the arrival of the Ligurians, whom all the ancient authorities unite in placing in that country. There were apparently Ligurians all the way to Cadiz. The resemblance of culture

III

THE FLAT-TANGED BRONZE SWORD IN SPAIN AND FRANCE. PICTS AND PICTONES

But could the Goidels not have come later ?   Let us see the facts which we have to interpret.

The Bronze Age in Spain after the coming of the El Argar culture is very little known.[1] Axes have been found, some of Mediterranean types and others related to types in France and the British Isles. But the series of bronze tools is still very incomplete.

At the very end of the Bronze Age a series of swords appears. These are the flat-tanged swords, in which the base of the blade is carried on in a tongue, to which the two pieces of which the handle is composed is riveted.[2] The number of such swords found was greatly increased in 1923 by the dragging of the harbour of Huelva.[3] From within a small space the drag brought up over 150 bronze weapons and other objects, with a good number of swords among them. They may have been a cargo which went to the bottom. But had the ship taken them on at Huelva, or had she come there to unload them ?   The question is of importance for interpretation of this type of sword as an indication of race. Huelva is in the copper country, and near the Rio Tinto.[4] Can it have been the distributing centre for the flat-tanged swords, which have hitherto been regarded as Northern ? Nothing of the kind. The Spanish examples, including those from Huelva, are late types, with concave hilt, an oblong slit in the place of rivet-holes, and notches at the base of the blade. If they were manufactured at Huelva they were

between El Argar and Aunjetitz which has raised the whole question would be explained at the same time. For the supposed Ligurians of the pile-villages formed one element of the population of Bohemia in Neolithic times. The pottery of Aunjetitz, which is generally compared to that of northern Germany, has as many likenesses to the pottery of the pile-villages. In bronze objects, the same relationship can be pointed out, and, on the whole, apart from one object, a diadem (which may be native), the metal objects of the El Argar tombs are not different from those of the same date found in the Swiss palafittes.

[1] Déchelette, **CCCXVIII**, ii, 2, p. 47 ; Bosch Gimpera, **CCCCXCVIII**, pp. 175 ff. ; Leite de Vasconcellos, in **XXII**, 1906, p. 179 (tombs of Bronze Age II).

[2] Déchelette, op. cit., ii, 1, p. 208 ; Cartailhac, **DVII**, pp. 221 ff.

[3] J. Albelda, in **CXXXIX**, 1923, 2, pp. 222 ff.

[4] C. Jullian, in **LVIII** 1923, pp. 203 ff.

imitations. Besides, the find as a whole was a mixed one, including Italian brooches as well as these Northern swords. If it was a cargo it can only have been the cargo of a coasting trader, putting in along the coasts of the Western Mediterranean and Atlantic. But there is in the appearance of this series of swords a suddenness, an unexpectedness, which tempts one to interpret it as the sign of the appearance of a new racial element. Unfortunately it is a very inadequate sign.

These Spanish swords come from France, where older forms of them are found and in larger numbers.[1] But there they are associated with other objects.

In the founder's deposit at Petit-Villatte (Cher)[2] we have a sword-hilt of cast bronze of a type which is found from Danzig to Silesia.[3] The same deposit includes a fragment of a blade, which must have been fitted to a hilt of this kind. It also contained two fragments of the curious bronze boxes which were made in the second half of the Bronze Age in the neighbourhood of the Scandinavian Straits. Those of Petit-Villatte are not of the latest type, but of one contemporary with the fourth period of the French Bronze Age. A similar box was found in the pile-village of Corcelettes on the Lake of Neuchâtel, which yielded two brooches consisting of symmetrical discs and an independent pin,[4] likewise from Scandinavia.

From the same region come the gold objects—vases and bracelets—of the treasure of Rongères (Allier).[5] This treasure includes a type of bracelet, with the ends splitting into two horns rolled in spirals, which was made in bronze in Bohemia in the second period of the Bronze Age and was afterwards manufactured as far away as Sweden.[6] The vases are adorned with concentric circles, which form the decoration of the latest of the bronze boxes mentioned above.[7] Their origin is revealed by their distribution.[8] The largest treasures, and far the largest, are those of Messingwerk near Eberswalde

[1] Déchelette, ii, 2, p. 208.
[2] Kossinna, in **LXXXV**, 1918–19, pp. 173, 185.
[3] Déchelette, ii, 1, p. 396, and fig. 157, 2.
[4] Montelius, **CCCLVII**, 57.
[5] Déchelette, in **CVII**, xix, 185, pl. xv.
[6] Ibid., pp. 187, 195–6 ; **CCCXVIII**, ii, 1, p. 315.
[7] Montelius, op. cit., p. 67.
[8] Kossinna, in **LXXXV**, 1914, p. 308.

in the Kreis of Oberbarnim in Brandenburg and Boeslunde in Seeland. A very great number of finds have been made within a line embracing Westphalia, Lower Saxony, part of Brandenburg, and Mecklenburg, with especial density in Jutland and the islands.

Another vase of the same origin, found at Villeneuve-Saint-Vistre (Marne), resembles almost in every detail one discovered at Werder on the Havel in Brandenburg.[1]

But apart from the swords the objects enumerated are rare, and, if we leave the swords out of account, they have the air among the other objects of the regions in which they are found of being exotics. But objects are not all of equal importance to ethnology, for the reason that they are used for purposes which do not all affect the consciousness of the human group to the same degree. A community will change its fashions in the matter of pottery or armament sooner than in the matter of religion or the treatment of the dead. It is more liable to go after strange drinking-vessels than after strange gods.

Among the gold objects discovered in France which are of the style of the Rongères vases there is an idol, or a fragment of one, known as the Quiver of Avanton (Vienne) (Fig. 38 b).[2] A similar object, but more complete, the Golden Hat of Schifferstadt (Fig. 38 a), was found in the Palatinate, on the left bank of the Rhine.[3] On the " brim " of this two bronze axes with the stop-ridge had been laid. A similar thing, likewise flanked by two axes, is engraved on a slab of the monument at Kivik in Skåne,[4] the other slabs of which are also covered with religious subjects or emblems. They are clearly bætyls, and they recall those which have been found in the region of the megalithic monuments in Spain at Los Millares.[5] But we cannot suppose that at that date they came from the south-west to Poitou and the Rhine. We must suppose that, in the form of the Schifferstadt Hat and the Avanton Quiver, the bætyl travelled from north-east to south-west. It is not likely that these idols were brought in by merchants. They represent a cult and a group of men who

[1] Ibid., p. 295.
[2] Déchelette, ii, 1, pp. 362 ff.
[3] Lindenschmit, **CCCXCIX**, i, x, pl. iv.
[4] Norden, **CCCCV**, p. 33 ; Montelius, **CCCC**, p. 68, n. 3.
[5] Siret, **DXXIII,**, p. 41.

practised that cult, and that group came from Poitou, from the Rhine, and from beyond.

So, then, in France and in Western Europe a certain number of objects dating from the end of the Bronze Age

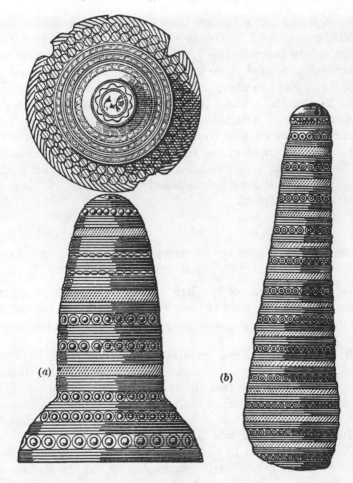

(a)   (b)

FIG. 38. The Golden Hat of Schifferstadt (a) and the Quiver of Avanton (b).
(Déchelette, ii, 1, fig. 144.)

have been found, and among them one of first importance, the Avanton Quiver, and a series of very considerable importance, the swords, which develop from originals which are found at the point where the Celtic and Germanic countries meet.

These facts can be interpreted like the similar facts presented by the British Isles. There we are compelled to look to archæological facts, which might have another significance, for evidence of additions to the population which did actually take place and have left no other visible trace. Do they, first in France and then in Spain, represent a late Goidelic invasion [1]? Not being tempted to interpret the corresponding facts in the British Isles in this manner, we are obliged to regard them as an indication of the coming of the Picts. I have made no objection to the association of the names of the Picts and the Pictones.[2] Without disguising the meagreness of the facts which I have brought together in order to lead to this conclusion, I have no objection to regarding this people of the Pictones as one of those earliest established on the soil of Gaul, and permanently settled in its domain, whence it may be supposed to have sent out bodies of settlers into Spain.

IV

THE BRYTHONIC CELTS OF SOUTHERN GERMANY IN THE EAST OF GAUL. TUMULI OF THE BRONZE AGE

But in the course of the Bronze Age things happened in the eastern part of what is now France, the racial character of which is quite clear, and they went on in the Hallstatt period.

From the first period of the Bronze Age burial under tumuli was practised in the east of France, in the Jura.[3] These were no longer tumuli over funerary chambers but tumuli over a cist, a sort of coffin of flags, a *loculus* of stones put together more or less roughly, or merely the remains of the dead man, who at this date was laid on his back.

The objects found in these tombs are of the same family as those found, in different circumstances, in the tombs of the Valais [4] and in the Cevennes district, where, for example,

---

[1] Peake, **CCCCXLVII**, p. 164. Mr. Peake imagines the Goidels established in the region of the Swiss palafittes and attacked by the Brythons, after which they went to Gaul with the flat-tanged sword, the Sequani forming their rear-guard.

[2] See above, pp. 202 ff.

[3] Déchelette and Piroutet, in **CXXXIX**, 1909, i, pp. 216 ff.; Piroutet, in **XV**, 1918–19, pp. 213–249, 423–447; 1920, pp. 51–81.

[4] Déchelette, ii, 1, p. 137; Viollier, in **XVIII**, pp. 125 ff.; id., **CCCCXCII**, pp. 23 ff.; Behrens, in Ebert, **CCCXXIV**, s.v. " Schweiz ".

the dolmen of the Liquisse (Aveyron) [1] has yielded the same trefoil-headed pins as the tumuli of Clucy (Jura).[2] But these same pins also appear in Southern Germany.[3] The fact is that the distribution of bronze objects has not really any ethnological meaning. In general they spread along trade routes, not in areas of occupation.

Funeral rites have a very different significance. That just described is new in France. On the other hand, it had been practised in Central Germany during the vague period which is variously assigned to the Neolithic, Copper, and Bronze Ages. The beakers with cord impressions are usually found in tumuli, and under those tumuli the dead were laid on their backs when they were not burned.[4] It is therefore in the direction of Germany that we must seek the origin of the new methods of burial and the starting-point of the men who introduced them. In Switzerland,[5] where tumuli going back to the beginning of the Bronze Age, if not to the Neolithic, have been reported and excavated in certain places in the north-east, between the Aar and the Rhine, they likewise represent an encroachment by the peoples of Germany on the domain of the palafitte-builders.

On what scale was this westward movement ? It is not easy to say. The tumuli which can be referred to the first period of the Bronze Age on the strength of datable objects are not many. The systematic exploration of the neighbourhood of Salins adds one or two to their number every year.[6] But all round these dated tumuli there are thousands which contain nothing but a few bits of flint or polished axes and shapeless potsherds. They might equally well be attributed to Neolithic times or to quite late periods. The discovery of a bronze pin in one tumulus in a group must suffice to date the group ; the proximity of a settlement of known date gives the indication needed for others.

If this is the case with the neighbourhood of Salins we are clearly justified in looking for tumuli of this date among

---

[1] Déchelette, ii, 1, pp. 137 ff.
[2] Ibid., p. 137.
[3] e.g. at Haberskirsch, near Friedberg (Upper Bavaria). G. Behrens, CCCXCI, p. 3.
[4] See above, pp. 183 ff.
[5] Viollier, CCCCXCIII, p. 31.
[6] See p. 246, n. 3. M. Piroutet's reports on the exploration of the country round Salins are in the *Archives de la Direction générale des Beaux-Arts*.

the countless *marchets* of the Province of Namur,[1] which have for choice been attached to the Hallstatt series, or further south among the tumuli without furniture of the Haulzy,[2] Penborn, and Grossblittersdorf[3] group, and among those of the group of the Naquée, near Clayeures (Meurthe-et-Moselle).[4] These are sufficient to represent many others and bear witness that the tumulus-builders who, from Thuringia, reached the Rhine, spread widely in the first period of the Bronze Age beyond the left bank of the river in Switzerland, Franche-Comté, and Belgium, without leaving any trace in their tombs (which, besides, were ill-suited to the preservation of their contents) of the characteristic furniture which distinguishes them in Germany.

Is it to a better method of building the tumulus, or to the chances of the wanderings of a small, better-provided group, that we owe the preservation in Brittany of a very few vases with one or two handles, which, from their horizontal ornament, can only be compared to the Adlerberg type of pottery[5]? Only the distance makes one hesitate to recognize the kinship. Two of these vases were the urns of a cremation-burial,[6] two others stood in their tumulus beside skeletons laid on their backs,[7] one skeleton being enclosed in a wooden coffin. These tumuli are quite different from the round barrows of England, both in the funeral rites to which they bear witness and in the pottery which they contain. They are also different from the German tumuli which yielded the zoned vases, for in them the dead were laid on one side and contracted. In their funeral rites they only resemble the tumuli of Saxony, Thuringia,[8] and the Rhenish area, in which vases with cord-impressions were

[1] De Loe, *Congrès de Dinan*, i, p. 269 ; Bosch Gimpera, in Ebert, **CCCXXIV**, s.v. " Belgien ", i, p. 401.

[2] Goury, **CCCCLXXVII**, p. 95 ; Rademacher, s.v. " Haulzy ", in Ebert, op. cit.

[3] Beaupré, **CCCCLXII**, pp. 29, 34–5.

[4] Ibid., p. 36. Id., repr., from **LXXIII**, 1909, for three funerary sites of the Bronze Age, at Benney, Azelot, and Bezange-le-Grand, the last two groups being of Bronze Age I.

[5] Du Chatellier, **CCCCLXXI**, pl. xiii.

[6] Tumuli of Kerougant in Plounévez-Lochrist (id., **CCCCLXX**, p. 88) and Run Mellou Poaz in Spézet (ibid., p. 168).

[7] Tumuli of Kervern in Plozévet (ibid., p. 282 : coffin) and Ruguellou in La Feuillée (ibid., p. 217). Cf. J. Loth, in **CXL**, 1920–1, p. 287, for tumulus of La Garenne at Keruzun (vase with four handles).

[8] Schumacher, in **XXIX**, x, p. 13.

found [1]; for in these tombs also cremation was found side by side with inhumation.[2] The culture which they represent contributed to the making of that of the Adlerberg. Now, we have regarded the people of this culture as the core round which the Brythonic Celts formed.[3] Must we not conclude that these were the folk who suddenly shot out a tongue as far as Brittany after advancing slowly but on a wide front stretching from Belgium to Switzerland [4]?

Some tumuli in the Jura have been attributed to the second period of the Bronze Age, and doubtless others which have no furniture are of the same date.[5] At any rate, opposite the little camp of Mesnay which overlooks Arbois (this camp probably belongs to that time), the ground is dotted with small tumuli without furniture, which may be the tombs of the people of this and the neighbouring stations. What is more, the second period of the Bronze Age seems to have been a time of great disturbance. Our best evidence of this is the discovery of almost inaccessible refuge-caves, like that hollowed in the face of the cliff overhanging the source of the Liron north of Salins. It can only be reached by rope-ladders, and it contains hearths dating from that period. The people who then lived in these parts, whoever they were, had enemies from whom they had to protect themselves in impregnable retreats.

The third period of the Bronze Age is what Rhenish archæologists call the Tumulus Period in Western Germany.[6] This was the age of unification. The tumuli become more frequent in France, too, and their area of extension becomes wider. But they are still collected, at least at the beginning, chiefly in the eastern departments of France, those of Lorraine, Burgundy, and Franche-Comté, which have been better explored or are richer. The tombs, like the famous one at Courtavant in the Aube,[7] are exactly like those on the other side of the Rhine. The various modes of erecting tumuli are

[1] Åberg, CCXCVII.
[2] Schumacher, CCCCIX, pp. 63 ff.
[3] See above, p. 185.
[4] Did their area of extension run out to another point in the south? Tumuli, Neolithic or of the Bronze Age, are found in the Alpes-Maritimes and Provence. M. Piroutet (in XV, 1915, p. 78) is inclined to think that they are local derivatives of the dolmen-tumulus.
[5] Piroutet, in XV, 1903, pp. 458 ff.
[6] Behrens, CCCXCI, p. 93; Schumacher, in XXIX, x, pp. 39 ff.
[7] Déchelette, ii, 1, p. 148.

common to both regions, whether they cover an oblong grave with stone walling, like that at Courtavant, or a small vault of unshaped stones built over the body.[1] But the weapons and ornaments of the dead are also the same, and some of them, such as the bracelet with coiled ends depicted in Fig. 39, come from beyond Germany and must have had their origin in the wealthy industry of the Hungarian region.[2]

At the end of this period, or in the fourth period of the Bronze Age, the tumuli are found a little further west than before, except for the extension into Brittany which I have mentioned. Southward they reach to the Lozère,[3] and northward to the Haute-Marne.

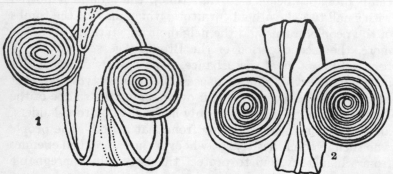

FIG. 39.   Bracelets with Coiled Ends.   (Déchelette, ii, 1, figs. 47, 46.)
1, Swabian Jura.   2, La Combe-Bernard, Côte d'Or.

The funeral customs are now slightly changed. The dead placed in the tumuli were burned, not in all cases, but in some. But cremation seems to have come from the same country as the tumulus, for it was established in the Celtic territory in Germany before it reached France.

Not everything, however, that came to France from over the Rhine was Celtic. We know of cremation-cemeteries of this time which have no tumuli—those of Pougues-les-Eaux, Arthel in the Nièvre, and Dompierre in the Allier.[4] These cemeteries are rich in pottery, and their pottery is of a type which comes from a distance. It consists of carefully made

[1] Schumacher, op. cit., p. 73.
[2] Richly, **DLII.**
[3] Tumulus of La Roche-Rousse in the commune of Esclanèdes (Lozère) (Déchelette, ii, 1, pp. 154 ff.) ; other funerary types (ibid., p. 153).
[4] Ibid., p. 155.

vases, turned on the wheel, of fine clay, decorated with horizontal, perpendicular, or slanting grooves, cupules, and bosses surrounded by circular grooves. Similar cemeteries with the same pottery are found in greater numbers east of the Rhine,[1] but also a long way further east, even in Poland.[2] The pottery in them is the so-called Lausitz ware. It is fairly widespread in France,[3] and we shall find that it is still more so when we examine it more closely. It was imported or manufactured as far west as Dordogne and the depths of Brittany.

The Celtic settlements in Germany and Eastern France were not yet so dense but that there were gaps into which other peoples might insinuate themselves. The pottery of the Lausitz type was imported by other foreigners moving westwards, who came from further than the Celts. Perhaps this hypothesis gives the key to the problem raised by the appearance of the name of the Veneti by the Baltic, on the Po, and in Brittany.[4] In any case, we have to do with one of the groups of migrants, prehistoric or historic, of which there were many, nomadic or semi-nomadic. They contributed to the formation of the communities into which they were absorbed, and there seems to be only one left at this day, because it alone refuses to be absorbed—the Gypsies. We know so little about what goes on in our own world that we cannot ask for much more about prehistoric times.

At the end of the Bronze Age the tanged sword extended over an area which covered that of the tumuli and reached somewhat further to the west and south. This sword has been found near Paris, and in the departments of the Cher,

---

[1] Behrens, op. cit., pp. 160 ff. ; Schumacher, in **XXIX**, x, p. 45. Herr Rademacher, in Ebert, **CCCXXIV**, vi, p. 282, s.v. " Kelten ", suggests that the men of the *Urnenfelder*, being of Alpine stock, formed the Celtic race by uniting in Western Germany with the men of the tumuli. He also regards their invasion as being of a violent nature. The facts are not so clear, and one may differ entirely from his view.

[2] See above, p. 168.

[3] Hubert, in **CXLIII**, 1910, pp. 108 ff. ; Bleicher and Beaupré, **CCCCLXVI**, p. 33 (cave of la Baume, Doubs) ; Philippe, **CCCCLXXXVIII**, pp. 50 ff. (Fort-Harrouard).

[4] **LXXXV**, 1922, p. 59. The pottery with deeply in-cut decoration found in the tumuli of the Charente, the Gard, and the forest of Hagenau is to be contrasted with that of Lausitz. According to Herr Rademacher (in **LXXXV**, 1926, pp. 14 ff.), vases with this decoration are further evidence of the expansion of the Celts in the Bronze Age. If so, we must slightly increase the area occupied by them in France at that time.

Vézère, Vaucluse, Drôme, and Var. Until we have more information we can admit that both swords and tumuli represent the area covered by the Celts in France in the Bronze Age, but that the latter alone represent the slow, age-long advance of the Celts of Southern Germany, the Brythonic Celts.

CHAPTER IV

CELTIC EXPANSION ON THE CONTINENT IN THE HALLSTATT PERIOD

I

THE CELTS IN THE EAST OF FRANCE

IN Germany it is to the third period of the Bronze Age, in France to the Hallstatt Period, that archæologists have given the name of the Tumulus Period.[1] For the practice of burying under tumuli became general in the eastern departments of France and made its way to the western departments. These tumuli,[2] which vary very much in size, and are often enlarged by secondary burials, are in the main composed of a stone erection, which unfortunately has always fallen in, formed of large rubble pieces arranged in vaulting, covered by a pile of smaller material and sometimes by a chape of beaten earth. The remains of the man for whom the tumulus was originally built were laid on a floor or in a pit. The monument was completed by circles of stones, which sometimes constituted the whole monument, unless the rest has been removed in later times.[3] The dead were interred or burned according to the place, time, tribe, and social conditions.[4] The French tombs resemble those of Germany [5] in characteristic details of construction as in contents. The invasion which had gone on through the Bronze Age seems to have continued, but without the participation of the people of the urn-fields, who still kept themselves distinct from the rest on the other side of the Rhine.

The tanged bronze swords and the thick-hilted bronze swords of the Mörigen type,[6] which we have considered above

---

[1] Déchelette, ii, 2, p. 630.
[2] Ibid., pp. 631 ff.; Viollier, **CCCCXCI**, pp. 35 ff.
[3] Déchelette, p. 649 (Pommard), 641 ff.
[4] Inhumation seems to be prevalent in eastern France and at the beginning of the Hallstatt Period (ibid., p. 632). Cremation is general in the south-west and in Brittany at the end of that period (ibid., pp. 681–2).
[5] Schumacher, in **XXIX**, x, p. 51; Behrens, in **CLXXVII**, 1927, pp. 125 ff.
[6] The first phase of the Hallstatt Period (Hallstatt A), according to Reinecke, **CCCXCIX**, v, pp. 231–247.

as indications of that invasion, are already in great part
Hallstatt swords (Map 10). The large, blunt-ended bronze
swords with nicks at the sides of the base are even fairly
far advanced in the series of products of the Hallstatt culture.
Some have been found in tumuli.[1]

MAP 10. Swords and Daggers in the Hallstatt Period. + = bronze swords ;
o = large iron swords ; ● = iron daggers with antennæ. (Déchelette,
ii, 2, map ii.)

Tumuli which from their large iron swords must be
assigned to the middle of the Hallstatt Period have been
explored in Belgium [2] and in the French departments of the
Meurthe-et-Moselle, Vosges, Haute-Marne, Côte d'Or, Jura,

[1] Those of the Combe d'Ain (E. Clerc and J. Le Mire, in LXXXIV, 1877,
p. 471), the Barrières at Miers (Lot) (Prunières, in XXVI, 1887, Toulouse,
ii, p. 698), the Roche-Rousse at Esclanèdes (Lozère) (ibid.), and St.-Aoustrille
(Cher). Cf. the statistics in Déchelette, ii, 2, p. 725.
[2] Court-St.-Etienne (Comhaire, in XLIII, 1894–5, pl. vi, pp. 53–4 ;
Déchelette, p. 615).

Ain, Nièvre, Cher, Vienne, Cantal, Lozère, Aveyron, Lot, and Drôme.[1] In the Cher particularly several groups of large, rich tumuli show that there was already a considerable settlement, and not mere isolated colonies. Déchelette's map of the distribution of the large iron sword in France gives a fair notion of the extension of the tribes from across the Rhine in that country. It only differs from the map which one might make for this period in that it represents larger and more homogeneous settlements than yet existed.

But it is in the Côte d'Or and Francho-Comté, particularly about Salins, that is in the country which had long been occupied by the tumulus-builders, that we can best judge of their increase.

The Moidons forest,[2] between Salins and Arbois, is an immense cemetery of tumuli. The number has been reckoned at about forty thousand. The group of tombs at Alaise, north of Salins, is also very large. Far the most of the datable tumuli are of the Hallstatt Period. Another considerable group extended north of Dijon between the upper Seine and the upper Aube, and there were others to the south.

These huge cemeteries represent a large population. They were a people attached to the country, who had adapted it to their own practices. There were strong towns, refuge-camps, such as the camp of Château-sur-Salins, which covers about fifty acres. Here four fortified towns overlooked the ground where the small town of Salins now stands, on the hill of the camp of Château, on Mont St.-André, on Mont Poupet, and on the hill of Fort Belin. In Burgundy [3] a line of fortified enclosures ran along the heights overlooking the valley of the Saône. These Hallstatt Celts seem to have settled for choice on high ground, and as a rule in places where there are now forests or brush, for it is always there, all over France (and the same might be said of Germany), that their tumuli and their fortified towns (when these have not survived as modern towns) are found.

They evidently did not live too far away from their tombs and their strongholds. There they had their fields, sometimes overlooked by tombs, as in Bavaria in the Bronze Age, and

---

[1] Déchelette, p. 728.
[2] Piroutet, in **XV**, 1900, pp. 369 ff. ; 1908, pp. 437, 700 ; 1904, pp. 297 ff. ; **CXXXIX**, 1904, 2, pp. 52 ff. ; 1928, 2, pp. 220 ff. ; Déchelette, p. 750.
[3] Déchelette, pp. 641 ff., 693 ff.

their clearing of the fields of stones still shows the regular lay-out of the fields ; there they had their peace-time and summer dwellings. If we were to add to this picture the immense labour of clearing the forests we should have to imagine the districts in which they were in force as being at least as densely populated as they are to-day. But the Hallstatt people were pastoral, and had herds of goats which helped to keep down the forest, which only developed after their time. The country was traversed by roads or tracks of a fairly fixed kind,[1] the line of which was determined by the configuration of the land, and these have been grooved with deep ruts by the small four-wheeled chariots of which remains are found in many tombs. We can form a fairly true picture of the warriors, with shaven faces (they look their razors with them into their graves), long, broad iron swords with heavy conical pommels and wooden sheaths, seldom wearing helmets, and wearing Italic helmets when they did, seldom having breastplates, and carrying round shields of which only a very few metal specimens survive.

The disposition of their tumuli gives a somewhat vague idea of their social formations. A group like that of Magny-Lambert, with the heaps of stones which accompany the monuments and may be either houses or other buildings, the form of which we cannot restore, recalls the tribal centres, the meeting-places which were also burying-grounds, the most typical examples of which are to be found in the Irish epics. Others represent centres of only relative density.

Now just at the end of this Hallstatt Period we are able to give their true name to the inhabitants of the Franche-Comté.

Marseilles was founded about 600 B.C. About 500 the Massaliots were importing into the districts of Dijon and Salins and further north amphoras, probably full of wine, craters for the preparation of drinks, œnochoës, and painted cups from Attica.   These were fragile goods which would not have stood a long journey overland, and were probably carried by boat up the Saône and, for Salins, up the Loue, which is navigable as far as Port-Lesney. The Greeks, therefore, knew something about the ethnology of the region. The

---

[1] E. Euvrard, in **XLV**, 1924, p. 103 (Gallic road from Besançon to Beures, Aveney, and Chenecey).

ancient geographers make the border-line of the Celts and the Ligurians run somewhere about the Lake of Geneva and the middle course of the Rhone. If they had been precise folk they would doubtless have told us that the Celts were already on the left bank of the Rhone in Haute-Savoie, and even further west, for tumuli have been found in the Hautes-Alpes (at Chabestan), Vaucluse (at l'Agnel in the commune of Pertuis), Bouches-du-Rhône, and Gard. But these are the remains of small isolated groups, not to be compared to those of the north and north-west. In any case, in the fifth century, if the Ligurian peoples mentioned by Apollonios and Avienus were still to be found on the shores of the Lake of Geneva they were surrounded by Celts ; and it may be that they existed only as a memory.

If the people on the right bank of the Rhone at that time were Celts, we can hardly doubt that their Bronze Age predecessors were Celts, too, at least in great part. If the persistence of the funeral rites did not prove it, the presence of Bronze Age and Hallstatt tombs side by side in groups of tumuli which appear to have been tribal cemeteries should convince us. It is, however, certain that the signs of the expansion of the Hallstatt culture are not explained by the normal growth of population. New tribes came from east of the Rhine, with the large bronze sword and with the iron sword. This latter was made on the spot in Burgundy and Berry, where iron was plentiful and easy to work. But the models came from Central Europe and with them all the Italic bronze vessels, the *ciste a cordoni*, the riveted pails, etc., which are characteristic features of the richest sepultures of the earlier Hallstatt Periods.

It was, moreover, not until the second half of the Hallstatt Period that the Celtic population of Lorraine, Franche-Comté and even Burgundy reached its maximum, if, indeed, we can yet argue from the chronological results of the latest excavations. The statistics of the discoveries made in the region of Salins show very clearly that far more tombs have been found dating from the second half of the Hallstatt Period than from the first. The population may have increased naturally in peace and prosperity. It may also have received augmentations from outside. This hypothesis fits the facts better. It seems still more reasonable, if we take into account a series of other facts which we are now going to examine. It has sometimes been thought that the hypothetical movements of peoples gave rise to violent conflicts, and that the first occupants resisted the newcomers by force of arms. They certainly had many fortresses with walls built in the Gallic fashion of a combination of beams and stones, against which the backs of their houses were set. These have been exalted by some students into scientific systems defending tribal territories. The insecurity of a disunited society is perhaps sufficient to explain the great number of these works.

II

THE CELTS IN THE DOMAIN OF THE PILE-DWELLERS

What was happening on the outskirts of the Celtic world, enlarged in the manner described above, and, first of all, what was happening on the other side of the Jura in Switzerland ? Switzerland is one of the countries of Europe whose prehistory is not only best known but clearest. Of it, as of the British Isles, one might say that the general currents of prehistory end there, but they only filter in.

During a considerable part of Neolithic times and all the Bronze Age, Switzerland was the chief home of the builders of palafittes or lake-villages. On the shores of the Swiss lakes they had found the conditions of life which they wanted. They lived crammed between the forests, which probably came further down than to-day, and the lakes ; and their dwellings, tilled fields, and pasturages doubtless took up every scrap of habitable, cultivable, and pasturable ground in that inconvenient and unattractive country. We know that they had other settlements in France, Southern Germany, the Danube basin, and Northern Italy, which progressively broke away, shrank, and became absorbed in those of their neighbours.[1] We are almost justified in giving them a name.[2]

It would seem that in the height of the Bronze Age the people of the lake-villages enjoyed the maximum of comfort in their habitats. The level of the lakes fell, the sign of a drier and hotter climate, and it is noted that the buildings of this

[1] Munro and Rodet, **CCCLXIII** ; Ischer, **CCCCLXXXIX** ; Ebert, **CCCXXIV**, s.v. " Pfahlbau ".

[2] They were probably Ligurians. Déchelette, ii, 1, p. 15.

time stand at some distance from the ancient shore-line.[1] The forests probably became clearer through the same causes, and the grazing-grounds wider. This change of climate was not peculiar to the region of the lake-dwellings. The Swedish geologist Sernander has studied it in the peat-bogs of the north,[2] which present everywhere, at the same level, a stratum of dry ground corresponding to the same epoch. Just as in the milder climate of the Bronze Age the civilization of the Baltic straits rose to a dazzling prosperity, so that of the pile-villages blossomed out, and its influence spread to Celtic Germany and to Eastern Gaul, which was in process of becoming Celtic.

One point in the civilization of the lake-dwellers remains a mystery. How did they dispose of their dead [3] ? There are not many sepultures contemporaneous with the lake-villages, and they may be the work either of the descendants of tribes which had previously held the country or of small groups of newcomers which were absorbed to a greater or less extent. Perhaps the practice was not definitely established, and varied. But it is probable that the people of the pile-villages kept their dead near them, as they did in their terrestrial stations,[4] or in the late palafitte of Donja-Dolina.[5] They could keep them on the palafitte itself, or put them in coffins between the piles, or throw them into the water. Now, at the beginning of the Bronze Age, there were tumulus-builders in the north of Switzerland,[6] in the obtuse angle formed by the Aar and the Rhine, in contact with Germany ; their funerary ritual clearly distinguishes them from the lake-dwellers.

At the end of the Bronze Age or, more exactly, after the first Hallstatt Period, that of the short bronze sword,[7] the lake-villages were abandoned, and it would seem rather suddenly. The excavations reveal traces of burning ; but accidental fires cannot have been infrequent. Skeletons

[1] Ischer, pp. 140 ff. ; Déchelette, ii, 1, pp. 112 ff.
[2] Ebert, op. cit., vii, 6 ff., s.v. " Klimatverschlechterung " ; Gerland, *Beiträge zur Geophysik*, 1912, pp. 115 ff.
[3] Viollier, CCCCXCII, pp. 10 ff.
[4] Stations of the Michelsberg type (Schumacher, CCCCIX, i, pp. 26 ff. ; W. Brehmer, in Ebert, CCCXXIV, s.v. " Michelsberg-Typus ").
[5] Truhelka, DLVI, 1902, pp. 1 ff. (Donja-Dolina).
[6] See above, pp. 247–8.
[7] This sword is found in the palafittes and is there classified as the Mörigen sword (Ischer, op. cit., pl. xiii).

and remains of skeletons have been found, and I have given the reason. There is no patent incontestable fact to show that there was a catastrophe or a battle or violence of any kind.[1] The climate became wet and cold again, and the villages were submerged.

What became of the inhabitants ? They lived on in the mountains, where they clung to their old economic habits, tilling minute fields and raising large flocks and herds. They kept their old methods of building. The barns reared on posts which are dotted about the valley-sides faithfully repeat the construction of the lake-dwellings, of which the chalets are a more distant reproduction. When iron came into use the people of the pile-dwellings, who had had to cut quantities of wood painfully with axes of stone or bronze, found themselves in possession of an excellent stock of woodman's tools, which enabled them to move up to less damp areas in the bottoms of high-lying valleys at a level of about 3,000 feet. It is true that no trace of them is to be seen there.[2] But perhaps this objection is not fatal. For one thing, the lake-dwellers can never have been very numerous ; and when they were dispersed over an area wider than their previous habitat they must have been few and far between. For another the Swiss archæologists who have devoted themselves to the study of the palafittes and of the Gallic tumuli and cemeteries have not yet found any trace of the people, and perhaps have not sought it much. It is revealed by its work, which is the clearing of the forests on the first plateaus. Besides, history implies its existence.[3]

The second change of climate was general, like the first. The Scandinavian peat-bogs present above the dry stratum later formations of peat, which in some cases can be dated. In the north of inhabited Europe the climatic change resulted in depopulation and southward movements which determined the distribution of the Germanic peoples in the centre and east of Germany for a long time. In the west we can imagine flooded coasts, overflowing swamps, the Germans of the North Sea making for warmer climes and coming into contact with the Celts, and the latter beginning to leave the

[1] Schæffer, in **CXXXVIII**, 1926, p. 228.
[2] Schumacher, s.v. " Schweiz ", in Ebert, **CCCXXIV**, ii, pp. 403 ff.
[3] See the following volume in this series, *ad init.*

wet forests of Westphalia, Hessen, and the Bavarian Alps and establishing themselves in numbers on the other side of the Rhine. It has been supposed that the drying of the forests in the Bronze Age opened up those of Alsace to the Celts [1] and encouraged their expansion. The return of the cold and of abundant rainfall may have had much the same result.

At the time when the palafitte-builders were retreating new tumulus-builders arrived in Switzerland, apparently by two routes.[2] Some crossed the Rhine about Schaffhausen and advanced as far as the Reuss. The others crossed about Basle, reached the Aar, and ascended its valley and those of its higher tributaries. So they came to the neighbourhood of Lausanne. They did not, properly speaking, supplant the people of the pile-dwellings, and they seem to have stopped at the lakes of Thun, Zug, and Zurich.

Their tumuli are in quite small groups. From this it is easy to infer that the builders never stayed very long in one place. As in France, too, they stand on the medium heights overlooking the great Swiss valleys. They are the relics of tribes of stock-raisers and hunters. But those tribes never formed large, permanent settlements like those of France.

Moreover, the Hallstatt tribes of Switzerland did not comprise very large numbers. Their tumuli can be reckoned not in thousands, but in hundreds, and there are but few hundreds.

This somewhat sparse population was increasing in the second half of the Hallstatt Period.[3] Far the most of the tumuli belong to this time. In this respect the situation is the same in Switzerland as in the French Jura.

We may ask whether at least some of the Hallstatt tribes of Switzerland did not come from France. The objects found in the tumuli on both sides of the frontier are the same.[4] Fashions changed in both countries in the same way. But most of the Swiss tumuli contained cremations.[5] Among the

---

[1] Schæffer, in **CXXXVIII**, 1926, pp. 222–9 ; cf. Hubert, in **XVI**, 1929, pp. 132–5.

[2] Déchelette, ii, 2, pp. 612–615 ; Viollier, **CCCCXC**, p. 4 ; id., **CCXCII**, pp. 81 ff. For their tumuli, see the Swiss journals, esp. **XVII** : J. Wiedmer, 1908, p. 89 (near Subingen) ; von Sucy and Schultheiss, 1909, p. 1 (Gaisberg near Kreuzlingen) ; H. Breuil, 1910, p. 169 (the Murat wood near Matran) ; Viollier and Blanc, 1907, p. 93 (Niederwenigen) ; etc.

[3] Viollier, **CCCCXCII**, p. 51.

[4] Wiedmer, in **XVII**, 1909, i (tumuli, Nos. v–viii, xi).

[5] Viollier, loc. cit., and map 4.

inhumations, moreover, there is a large proportion of La Tène tombs dug in the tumuli. Again, the Swiss tombs are as rich in pottery as the French are poor. The tumulus-builders seem, therefore, to have come straight from Bavaria, where the two rites were practised, cremation being preferred.

There is no doubt that they were Celts. Although they did not come from Franche-Comté, the demonstration made in the case of the people of Franche-Comté holds equally for them. They were Celts, come direct from the cradle of the Celtic peoples.

Small as the Hallstatt population of Switzerland was, it none the less represents a migration of people from the south of Germany which, if only as an indication, is of importance. This shifting of population probably took place in more than one wave, at least in two, at the beginning of the Hallstatt period and towards the middle, like the migration into France ; but ,what is still only a hypothesis in the case of France can be taken as a certainty in that of Switzerland.

To perceive the full significance of these facts we must set them in their place in the whole of archæology and ancient history. At the beginning of the Hallstatt period there were movements of peoples from the centre of Europe to the south, the scale of which we can estimate. This was when the Umbrians descended into Italy. There they took the place of the people of the *terremare*, as the Celts of Switzerland had taken the place left empty by the lake-dwellers. A date for this event is provided by Cato the Elder, quoted by Pliny.[1] It took place at the time of the foundation of the Umbrian town of Ameria, which occurred, we are told, 963 years before the war of the Romans with Perseus, that is in 1134. About the same time the Dorians invaded Greece, forming the last wave of the Hellenes.[2]

Whence did the Dorians come ? From the North and from Illyria. Whence did the Umbrians come ? They certainly descended gradually from somewhere about Bohemia, in the neighbourhood of the Celts. It is impossible that movements of tribes on such a scale should have had no effect on their neighbours, setting them free to move or

---

[1] *N.H.*, 111, 114 ; Grenier, **DXXIX**, pp. 505 ff. ; Homo, **CCCXLI**, English, pp. 50–1.

[2] Jardé, **CCCXLV**, English, pp. 75–6.

encouraging them to follow, to say nothing of the change in climate, creating new vacancies and new attractions, and the migrations which it provoked. The emigration of the Celts must have been connected with the great movements of peoples which were happening at the same time, and it probably did not fall short of them in size. Moreover, about the beginning of the Hallstatt period, the Celtic peoples of Western Germany had quite emerged from the stage of incohesion corresponding to the first half of the Bronze Age. Their numbers were great. The use of iron had increased their powers tenfold. They could cut roads through the forests.[1] They had wagons, of which they have left specimens.[2] Above all, they had new and better weapons. That is why the beginning of the first Iron Age witnessed a tremendous commotion among the Celtic peoples. It did not subside altogether. The movement began again some centuries later. We shall now see how far it went.

III

THE FIRST DESCENTS OF THE CELTS INTO ITALY

By the end of the Hallstatt Period the Celts had already advanced considerably beyond the limits of the area which we have been surveying. They had crossed them on the south-eastern side and joined their Osco-Umbrian cousins in Italy. These latter had probably come in by the eastern passes of the Alps, whereas the Celts entered by the western passes, having come either through the Valais, where they had not halted,[3] or through Savoy, where they have left some traces of their stay.[4]

This was the date which Livy [5] gives to the Gallic invasion of Italy, which, he says, occurred in the time of Tarquin the Elder, between 614 and 576. Also, according to Plutarch,[6] a Greek poet named Simylos ascribed the tragic death of Tarpeia to the Celts, and not to the Sabines. Historians

---

[1] J. Fleure, in **LXXVI**, 1916, p. 143.
[2] Déchelette, ii, 2, pp. 747 ff.
[3] Viollier, in **XVII**, 1912, map.
[4] See above, p. 257.
[5] v, 33 : *Prisco Tarquinio Romæ regnante.*
[6] *Rom.*, 17.

are divided as to the amount of faith to be placed in these statements.[1]

If we adhere to the historical texts rigidly we cannot say that there were Gauls in Italy before the fourth century ; at the earliest, they can only have come a few years before the battle of the Allia.[2] Livy's story does not conflict, save in the date, with the others, but he indicates in a sentence, to which too little attention has been paid, that the invasion of Bellovesus had been preceded by another. " They crossed the Alps," he says, " by the country of the Taurini and the valley of the Dora Baltea, defeated the Etruscans near the Ticino, and hearing that the place in which they had halted was called the Plain of the Insubres (*agrum Insubrium*), that is by the very same name as a sub-tribe of the Ædui (*cognomine Insubribus, pago Hœduorum*), regarded this as an omen, which they followed, and founded a city there (*ibi omen sequentes loci condidere urbem*)." This was Milan. So Bellovesus had been preceded by a body of Insubres who had at least left, near Milan, their name, which was still known at the time of the great invasion. The passage should be borne in mind, for it gives the most ancient name of a Celtic people which we can put down on our historical maps.

The question now takes on a very different shape.

In 1827 at Zignano, in the valley of the Vara, the chief tributary of the Magra, which flows into the Mediterranean south of the Gulf of Spezia, a cippus was found surmounted by a very crudely sculptured head and bearing an inscription in Etruscan characters, running downwards, which reads *Mezunemusus*. A series of similar cippi have been found in the same region, but in these the head rises from a body, still incorporated in the block, but having arms, legs, and attributes which, as we shall see, have an ethnological meaning. A first group of four stones comes from the communes of Villafranca (the wood of Filetto and the castle of Malgrate) and Mulazzo (the parish of Lusuolo). One bears

---

[1] They have been accepted by many, including Alexandre Bertrand, who placed the descent of the first Celts into Italy still earlier, about 1000 B.C. It is true that he did not disguise the fact that these first Celts were Umbrians. The Umbrians were Celts, properly speaking. Those who came later were the Gauls. See Bertrand and Reinach, **DXLII**, pp. 43 ff.

[2] Meyer, **CCCLIV**, v, p. 153 ; Mommsen, **CCCLIX**, English, vol. i, pp. 337–8 ; Müllenhoff, **CCCLXII**, ii, p. 247 ; Jullian, **CCCXLVII**, i, p. 289 ; Niese, in **CLXVIII**, 1898, pp. 113 ff. ; id., in **CCCLXVIII**, vii, pp. 613–17.

an inscription, which is unluckily indecipherable. Three represent armed warriors ; the fourth a woman.[1] Another group of more archaic character was afterwards discovered in the commune of Fivizzano, in the parish of Cecina.[2] These stones stood in their original place and position, set in a regular row in a black soil revealing traces of animal matter. A third group also has been published.[3]

By the peculiarities of their armament the warriors of the first group have been identified as Gauls. They are naked, with the sword attached not to a baldric but to a waist-belt, and on the right, not the left. In their right hand they hold an axe which may be the *cateia*, and in their left javelins, which may be *gœsa*.[4]

If the figures are Gauls the inscription should be Gallic. Attempts were at first made to read it as Etruscan, but with no success whatever. But the Celtic appearance of the word will at once emerge if we take the various values of the Etruscan z into account. On the one hand it is equivalent to *ti, di*.[5] In that case *Mezunemusus* can be read as *Mediunemusus*, and can be compared with the place-names Νεμωσσός (Nemours, Clermont-Ferrand),[6] Medionemeton (Kirkintilloch, near Glasgow), and Mediolanum. Mediolanum probably means the Middle Sanctuary ; the cippus is a boundary-mark, not a tombstone. Secondly, the z may represent the dental sibilant of Celtic, which is expressed in writing by δ, ð, *d*, or *s*, either single or duplicated.[7] So *Mezu* would be *Meddu*, which appears in the names Messulus, Meddilu, Methillus, etc. The meaning of the word is indicated by Irish *midiur* " I judge ", " I measure ". *Mezunemusus*, then, would mean " he who takes care of the holy places " or " who measures them ", and would be the proper name of a man. The main thing is that the word is Celtic and that the presence of the Celts on the coast of Liguria, in the valleys of

[1] U. Mazzini, *Monumenti celtici in Val di Magra*, repr. from **LXVIII**, 1908, p. 29 ; Hubert, in **CXXXIX**, 1909, ii, pp. 52–4 ; id., in **CXL**, 1913, pp. 418 ff. ; M. Giuliani, *Di nuovi studi sui Celtici in Italia secundo monumenti recentemente scoperti in Italia*, repr. from **LXVIII**, 1923.

[2] U. Mazzini, in **LIII**, 1909, pp. 65 ff.

[3] Id., ibid., 1923, p. 73.

[4] They had no shield. Cf. Varro, *De Vita Pop. Rom.*, iii, 14 : *qui gladiis cincti sine scuto cum binis gaesis essent.*

[5] Vendryès, in **CXL**, 1913, p. 423.

[6] Strabo, iv, 2, 3.

[7] Rhys, in **VII**, 37.

the Vara and Magra, is attested by a group of monuments
which are certainly akin and probably contemporaneous.

Their date is indicated by that of the sword represented
on the stones of the first group. It is the Hallstatt dagger
with antennæ, a number of specimens of which have been
unearthed by excavation in Celtic lands.

Of these daggers with antennæ, the first origin of which
was perhaps Italian, forms are known which are peculiar
to Italy ; but it is not with them that we now have to deal.[1]
Those on the cippi are imported weapons, and earlier than
the great historical invasion of the fourth century. They
had gone out of use when this took place ; the dagger with
antennæ had lengthened and become the La Tène sword
which is described by the ancient writers and discovered by
archæologists.[2] Any Gauls who can at that time have come
as far as Liguria had certainly not preserved an obsolete
armament. It is almost universally agreed that the daggers
with antennæ represented on our cippi were used within the
extreme dates of 700 and 500 B.C. They are among the features
usually taken as characteristic of the last phase of the
Hallstatt culture. These dates suit the Italic buckets and
bronze plaques on which much the same weapons are represented as on the cippi.[3] They also suit the whole set of objects
(including the bucket) found in the famous tomb of Sesto
Calende on the Ticino, south of Lake Maggiore, among which
there is a short sword with antennæ.[4] Lastly they suit the
late part of the cemeteries of Golasecca, Castelletto Ticino,
etc., which form a large and peculiar necropolis on the
plateau of Somma Ticinese, south of Lake Maggiore.[5] They
must suit our cippi. From these chronological considerations
one must conclude that the Gauls descended into Italy earlier
than is usually supposed.

The cippi of Cecina are still older. Two of them represent
men, with a dagger engraved, horizontally, below the hands.
It is not the dagger with antennæ depicted at Villafranca,
but one of more ancient appearance, which might be of

[1] Déchelette, ii, 2, pp. 740 ff.
[2] Hubert, loc. cit.
[3] On the bucket from the Certosa of Bologna, the man doing sacrifice
holds a sword with antennæ.
[4] Montelius, **DXXXIV**, pl. lxii ; Hoernes, in **XXIII**, 1905, 294 ; Déchelette,
ii, 2, p. 721.
[5] Montelius, op. cit., p. 233.

bronze, but which might also be a sword, a sword with a heavy round pommel like those of Hallstatt, conventionally reduced to the size of a dagger. These cippi are too crude to be used as an argument. They complete the series, that is all. If the others are Celtic these must be, and this conclusion will hold good so long as Liguria as a whole does not yield others which demand another hypothesis.

The valleys of the Magra and its tributary the Vara make passages in the Ligurian Apennines, descending from passes to which the valley of the Taro on the other slope gives access. This is a gateway into the country; indeed, it is the most convenient entrance. One can easily understand an advanced body of Gauls establishing themselves there, in Ligurian territory. Our cippi, confined as they are to a small area, certainly look as if they had belonged to an outpost, a colony in a strange land.[1]

But an outpost implies an army. Behind the advanced guards, camping in the passes which led to the coast over the Apennines from the plain of the Po, there must have been other bodies at intervals. If there were no trace of these it would be hard to imagine a small Gallic colony established in the sixth century beside a mountain route hundreds of miles from any Gallic country. But the necropoles of the Ticino are probably traces of their main settlement.[2]

The western cemeteries of the Po valley are sufficiently unlike those of the east at this time to forbid us to ascribe them to the same peoples.[3] In each case there was a new civilization, without any very perceptible connection with that of the previous occupants of the country, who lived in

[1] Issel, **DXXX**, p. 673; cf. ibid., p. 594. Sig. Issel observes that the country had many attractions, including mineral wealth—the mines of Serravezza (in the Apuan Alps), il Mesco, Sestri Levante. For Celtic penetration in Liguria, see ibid., p. 670; on its date, Sig. Issel is as vague as can be.

[2] Montelius describes the tomb at Sesto Calende as Gallic, but we may suspect that he makes it too late. Ridgeway, Pigorini, A. Bertrand, and S. Reinach regard it and those of Golasecca as Celtic. But their definition of the Celts is rather loose, and has included, at once or alternatively, the Ligurians, Umbrians, Illyrians, and Rætians. It is not likely that when the Italici entered Italy they were already differentiated, not only from the Celts, but from one another. Montelius, op. cit., p. 64, 6; Ridgeway, **DLIII**, pp. 48 ff.; Pigorini, *I Primitivi Abitatori della valle del Po*, repr. from **CXXV**, 1892, fasc. 3; Bertrand and Reinach, **DXLII**, pp. 57-8, 63, etc. Cf. Hubert, loc. cit.

[3] Montelius, op. cit., pp. 232 ff.; Déchelette, ii, 2, p. 536; Sergi, **DXL**, passim.

the pile-villages and *terremare*. The latter had ceased to build their quadrangular towns in the north of Italy at the dawn of the Iron Age, or before it. The civilization of the eastern side, which is called after Villanova, was that of the Umbrians, the last Italici to arrive, since it flourished at Bologna before the Etruscans took possession of it.[1] The western culture, to which archæologists attach the name of Golasecca, may be that of the first Celtic invaders.

It is very clearly distinguished from the other by its pottery and the construction of its tombs. We do not find in Lombardy the characteristic biconical urn of Villanova. Nor do we find the pit-grave of the Umbrian country. The pottery consists chiefly of spherical urns and vases with a hollow foot. The oldest urns are adorned with parallel bands of incised triangles. In the latest vases these bands are separated by cordons in relief, and are either smooth or filled with criss-cross lines made with the burnishing-tool. This ware was evidently influenced by that made at the same time in the east of the Po valley, around Este, among a third people, the Veneti.[2]

The tombs either are tumuli of rubble, like that at Sesto Calende, or consist of a stone cist buried not very deep but surrounded by a stone circle, the circles being connected by parallel lines of rubble. These stone circles suggest tumuli of earth washed away by rains. Lastly, tombs of the Golasecca type have been explored at Castello Valtravaglia, in the province of Como, on which there were stelæ—absolutely formless, it is true.[3]

But it is not altogether evident that the civilization of Golasecca was not connected by some obscure links with the autochthonous culture of the Ligurians who had previously occupied the lake stations, at that time deserted, at the foot of the Alps.[4] The excavations at the Isola Virginia by the shore of Lake Varese have yielded some fragments of a pottery resembling that of Golasecca.[5] It is, therefore, quite possible that the lake-village which formed the Isola Virginia was still occupied at the time when the cemetery of Golasecca

[1] Modestov, **DXXXV**, pp. 287 ff. ; Grenier, **DXXIX**, pp. 460 ff. and passim.
[2] See below, p. 275.
[3] Magni, **DXXXI** ; Montelius, op. cit., pp. 252 ff. (Castello Valtravaglia).
[4] Pigorini, in **XXVII**, 1884 ; Déchelette, ii, 2, p. 536.
[5] Castelfranco, **DXXVI**, pls. xii ff. ; Munro, **CCCLXIII**, p. 195.

was opened. But it certainly did not last so long. Moreover, except for these few potsherds, the objects found at the two sites have nothing in common. On the contrary, these abandoned villages and these tombs of a new form, grouped in new districts, mean that great changes had taken place in the country, changes of race. In Switzerland the same signs led us to infer a settlement of the Celts. In Italy (if it is admitted, for similar reasons, that the Umbrians occupied about the same time the Veronese and Emilia) we are justified in thinking, with all the reservations entailed by our ignorance, that the same Celts then descended into Lombardy and Piedmont.

What is more, the tombs and the pottery have equivalents in Celtic lands. The lines of stone connecting the tumuli

FIG. 40.   Tall-footed Vase from the Tumulus of Liviers, Dordogne.
(Déchelette, ii, 2, fig. 330.)

are found in Bavaria as early as the Bronze Age, and in Burgundy and the forest of the Moidons. The stone circles are found with the tumuli in Burgundy and in the districts last conquered by the Hallstatt culture in the south-west of France.[1] The vases characteristic of the cemetery of Golasecca have their prototypes in the Bavarian tumuli of the end of the Bronze Age. It is in the West, in the pottery of the Lake of le Bourget, in the tumuli of Aquitaine (Fig. 40), and even in the Hallstatt stations of the English coast, that we see their closest kindred.[2]

This culture of the western plain of the Po had penetrated

[1] Naue, CCCCII, pls. xli, 1 ; xlii, 2 ; xliii, 2 ; xliv, 1 ; xlv, 2 ; Bertrand and Reinach, op. cit., 82.
[2] Naue, ibid. ; Morin-Jean, in LX, Chambéry, 1908, p. 600 ; Déchelette, ii, 2, pp. 815; 817 ; CCCLXXXIV, pp. 24–8.

into Liguria. There the same tombs have been found, consisting of chambers of badly hewn slabs containing ossuaries and other vases, without decoration save in a few rare cases, but showing distant resemblances to those of Golasecca. These tombs are not very numerous. But what is remarkable is that most of them are found in the valleys of the Lunigiana.[1]

In short, if there were any Celts in Northern Italy before the invasion of the fourth century, they lived on the plateau of Somma, and the cemetery of Golasecca holds the remains of one contingent of them. Now, if we interpret the cippi of Villafranca and the inscription of Zignano aright, there were. Behind the advanced point to which these belong the main body occupied the banks of the Ticino. If these folk were not the forces of Bellovesus, they were perhaps the first Insubres.

They probably arrived as early as the first half of the Hallstatt Period, and were armed with large swords. But it was not until the second half that they settled in any force. This first colonization of Italy took place in two waves, like that of France and Switzerland, with a greater interval between them.

At the time when the cippus of Villafranca was carved, that is not long after the opening of the cemetery of Golasecca, the Etruscans, advancing northwards, crossed the Apennines and civilized and subjugated Umbrian Emilia. Certain Etruscan stelæ found at Bologna represent foot-soldiers, naked or armed, fighting Etruscan horsemen. These are probably all Gauls. The naked ones with long shields certainly are.[2] Their appearance would not have been familiar to the people of Bologna if there had been large, unbroken masses of Veneti on one side and Iberians or Ligurians on the other between them and Etruria before their sudden irruption. Polybios was therefore right in saying that the Gauls had been in immediate contact with the Etruscans[3] long before the collision of the fourth century.

This prolonged contact, first with the Umbrians and then with the Etruscans, had a civilizing influence, the results of which are apparent. Whether the stones of the Lunigiana

---

[1] Issel, op. cit., pp. 593 ff. ; Montelius, op. cit., pls. clxiv–clxv ; Issel, in **LIII**, 1912, pp. 39 ff.

[2] Grenier, **DXXIX**, pp. 453–5.

[3] ii, 17.

were idols or tombstones, they are something quite unique among Celtic finds. They are the oldest stone monuments which the Celts have left, their oldest attempts at sculpture with their oldest inscriptions. These efforts, ancient and crude as they are, might be worse. At first they were called menhir-statues.[1] But the cippi of Liguria have nothing in common with the French menhir-statues of the Aveyron— neither the shape nor the technique, nor the things represented, nor, above all, the date. They are like the Villanovan stelæ with a human outline of San Giovanni in Persiceto or Bologna.[2] So the Celtic colony in Liguria must have taken both its writing and its art from its neighbours. That means that it had other dealings with them than fighting and pillage.[3]

Let us try to imagine this first settlement of the Celts in Italy. First of all, the invaders came from a long way off. The occupants of the plateau of Somma Ticinese were in the habit of leaving much pottery in their tombs. It was not so in the Celtic countries nearest to Italy, Franche-Comté or Switzerland, but it was so in Lorraine and Bavaria. Therefore the bands which entered Italy passed beyond the tribes which were settled down on the fringe of the Alps and in the Jura. Their advance was in no way delayed by the barrier of the mountains, over which trade had long had its tracks.

Although the cemeteries of the Somma plateau are comparatively large, these first settlers did not come in solid masses. We must think of bands of Celts squeezing into the country among the Ligurians, now as guests and now as conquerors, but so few in numbers that they were bound to be absorbed and lost.

In his description of Cisalpine Gaul, Polybios describes a pastoral people living in a very primitive fashion [4] : " They live scattered in unwalled villages. The thousand things

---

[1] Cf. Hubert, in **CXL**, 1914, p. 41, n. 3. The only objects in France to which they can be compared are some small stelæ found at Orgon (Bouches-du-Rhône), on which the same semi-cubical owl-head appears. These might belong to the same family of monuments ; apart from that, they are equally unique.

[2] Ducati, in **LIII**, 1923, 83 (Saleta, N. of Bologna) ; Hoernes, **CCCXXXIX**, pp. 218 ff., 642 ; Grenier, op. cit., p. 416.

[3] Pettazzoni, in **CIII**, xxiv, p. 317.

[4] ii, 17.

which make life pleasant are unknown to them. Their only bed is hay or straw, their only food is meat, and, in short, they lead the simplest life. Strangers to anything outside war and stock-raising, they are ignorant of all science. Their wealth consists entirely in gold and in beasts, which are the only things that they can take away with them in all circumstances and move about at will." These features contrast with the account which he has given a few lines above of the fertile Cisalpine country and its agricultural wealth and with what we know of the Gallic settlements of the fourth century. They fit the Hallstatt Celts, who were generally pastoral.

In Italy they were barbarians, but inquisitive and well-meaning barbarians. Whether they allowed themselves to become absorbed or suffered severe set-backs, their settlements must have been steadily dwindling, if not absolutely deserted, when a second wave of Celts came down.

IV

THE CELTS ON THE NORTH-EAST OF ITALY

Another inscription, which has only just been translated satisfactorily by the Norwegian Celticist Marstrander,[1] shows that the Celts had about the same time reached the eastern end of the Alps, and were flowing over into Italy on that side. At Negau in Lower Styria, a short distance north-east of Marburg on the Drave, a deposit was found in 1912 containing about twenty bronze helmets of the Etrusco-Illyrian type represented on the Italic buckets which I have mentioned above.[2] On two of them there are *graffiti*, written in an alphabet of Etruscan type, like the Zignano inscription, in which the letters common to both are the same. The wording runs from right to left. Mr. Marstrander reads on one helmet :—

Siraku gurpi sarni eisvi tubni banuabi

that is, Sittanku Chorbi ; Isarni Tisuvii ; Dubni Banuabii. All these words are proper names, and they are all Celtic. In each case a man's name is followed by that of his father ;

---

[1] *Les Inscriptions des casques de Negau*, repr. from **CLII**, 1925, p. 37.
[2] Giovannelli, *Antichità scoperte presso Martraj*, p. 47, pl. ii ; Mommsen, in **CI**, vii, p. 208 ; S. Reinach, in **CXXXIX**, 1883, ii, p. 272.

the first is the signature of the maker, and the two others are the names of successive owners.

The second inscription yields a more unexpected reading :

harigasti teiva . . . i . . .

This is a Germanic proper name followed by a patronymic formed from the name of the god Tiwaz.

The date of these inscriptions is clearly that of the type of the helmets. Now these spherical bronze helmets (Fig. 41) continued in use for several centuries.[1] An example appears in the tomb of Sesto Calende,[2] and is probably the earliest. A bronze statuette found in the Illyrian cemetery of Idria near Bača [3] represents a warrior wearing a helmet of the same type, and it cannot be nearly so old. Others have been

Fig. 41. Spherical Helmets. (Ebert, *Reallexicon*, v, pl. lxxxix. Natur-historisches Museum, Vienna.) 1, Magdalenenberg, near Laibach. 2, Etruscan type. 3, Watsch.

discovered in the Ticinese cemetery of Giubiasco with swords of La Tène III, and are of the first century before or after Christ.[4] It is true that the type developed. The spherical helmet was at first forged and made of plates riveted together ; later it was cast, the crown of the earlier type serving as a model. A concave band appeared between the brim and the spherical crown. The latter was provided with one or two crests, or was pinched together at the top. The Negau helmet is intermediate between the archaic types of the seventh or sixth century and the later examples from Giubiasco. It is like the ogee-shaped helmet of the cemetery of Watsch in Carniola,[5] and is probably contemporaneous with it. One

---

[1] S. Reinach, in Daremberg, **CCCXV**, s.v. " Galea " ; E. Sprockhoff, in Ebert, **CCCXXIV**, s.v. " Helm ".

[2] See above, p. 266.

[3] Szombathy, in **C**, 1901, p. 6.

[4] Viollier, in **XXVI**, 1906, p. 97 ; **CLXXX**, p. 229.

[5] Much, **CCCLXI**, lii, 1. The incised decoration of this Watsch helmet is like that of Negau helmet No. 2.

can well believe that an ancient type of armour should have been preserved in isolated examples at the bottom of a remote valley, but twenty specimens all together, and of such a rare piece of armour, can only date from the time in which it was normally made. Whatever the nature of the deposit may be—armoury, armourer's shop, trophy—the conclusion must be the same. Besides, one of the Giubiasco helmets, too, bears an inscription, produced in the casting; it is in Latin, and in fairly late characters.[1] The Negau *graffiti*, on the other hand, are archaic, and are certainly earlier than the inscriptions of Branio and Todi,[2] which are of the time of the great invasion.[3]

Therefore Celts came into Styria at the end of the Hallstatt period, and their presence there is attested a little later than in Lombardy.[4] Like their compatriots to the west, they were assimilated to the peoples whose guests or conquerors they had been. These folk, who fought bare-headed,[5] have left nothing behind them but helmets, and helmets which they had made themselves. This fact at least suggests that they did not pass through the country like a whirlwind, but were settled there. Their remains are merged in those of the native peoples. We do not know how far they may have advanced on this side, nor how many they were. But we do know that great changes took place in all this region comprising the Austrian slope of the Alps at the end of the first Iron Age. Cemeteries and dwelling-places were moved. The site of Hallstatt itself seems to have been abandoned. One way of explaining these facts is to suppose that foreign contingents came in, large enough to upset the old settlements and to create new ones.

[1] Rhys, in **VII,** p. 19.
[2] Dottin, **CXCVI,** p. 154.
[3] Marstrander, on the other hand, does not think that the inscription is earlier than the settlement of the Celts in the Danube valley in the second century. He even says first century. For he observes that in the word *banuabi*, w is written as *u*, as in Latin, and concludes that the inscription is later than the conquest of the Cisalpine country. The same sound is written as *f* in another word in the same inscription. I do not think that this difference in writing need be taken into account.
[4] This is what Bertrand and Reinach maintain (**DXLII,** pp. 122–144). But their argument is based on the confusion mentioned above (p. 267). They confuse Celts and Illyrians, as they confused Celts and Umbrians.
[5] On the belt-plaque from Watsch there is a scene of a helmeted horseman fighting with a bare-headed horseman; the latter may be a Celt (Bertrand and Reinach, op. cit., p. 107).

Did the Celts descend on this eastern side as far as Italy ? We do not know. But, like the Illyrian peoples among whom they settled, they were affected by the influence of the civilizations of Italy, that of the Veneti of Este or that of the Etruscans of Bologna. One can imagine that these Celtic colonies, established in Italy or on the outskirts of it, borrowed with profit not only to themselves but to the Celtic country behind them. Their presence must have stimulated trade between the plain of the Po and Western Germany or France. It is possible that they had a great influence on the turn which Celtic civilization was to take. If we admit their existence we can easily understand how the Certosa brooch was the prototype of the Celtic brooches of La Tène.[1] Even the dagger with antennæ which has enabled us to date the Ligurian cippi, may have been borrowed from Italy, where it appears to have come directly after the bronze sword with antennæ.[2]

The second Negau inscription informs us that there were Germans among the Celts who came at the end of the first Iron Age to fight on the Italian border.[3] This is a most valuable piece of information regarding the fact, already pointed out, of Celto-Germanic collaboration, for it gives us one date for it. We must suppose that at this time, in the north-east of their domain, the Celts were the leading people of their neighbourhood. This is not clear from the archæological data, which show that the Germans were at that time subject to the influence of the Illyrian culture. But the inscription is convincing.

V

CELTIC EXPANSION IN THE SOUTH-WEST OF FRANCE AT THE
END OF THE HALLSTATT PERIOD

In the south-west the tumuli of the earlier Hallstatt periods stop about Cahors, and do not reach the Garonne. They go beyond the crest of the Central Plateau, but not far.

---

[1] The Certosa brooch must have reached the Celtic world, chiefly by the east. See Reinecke, CCCCVI.

[2] Déchelette, ii, 2, pp. 730 ff.

[3] Marstrander suggests the Bastarnæ. But there cannot have been any Bastarnæ in this region yet, at the date which I have adopted.

There was a sudden expansion at the end of the Hallstatt
Period ; and there had certainly been no previous incursions

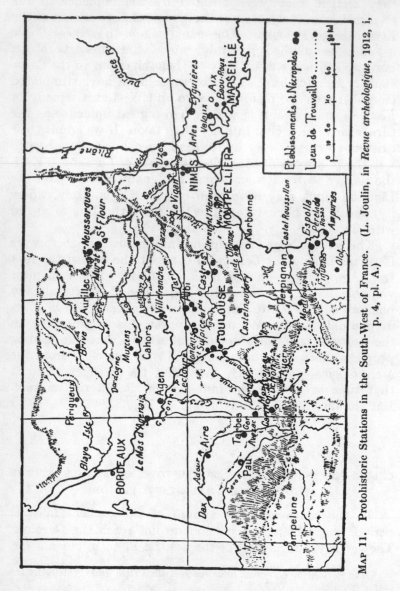

MAP 11. Protohistoric Stations in the South-West of France. (L. Joulin, in *Revue archéologique*, 1912, i, p. 4, pl. A.)

to prepare for this. We have evidence for it in the cemeteries
(Map 11) which are distributed in fairly large numbers

between the crest of the Plateau and the Pyrenees.[1] It even went a long way beyond the mountains. Most of these cemeteries are composed of tumuli containing cremations ; the mounds themselves may have been worn down by water flowing down the sides, but either stone circles [2] or recognizable traces remain. In other cemeteries the graves are flush with the ground and arranged in regular lines.[3]

They are in three main groups, in two of which they are concentrated in fairly large numbers. The chief group is spread along the line of the Pyrenees from the watershed between the Mediterranean and Atlantic, through the departments of the Ariège, Haute-Garonne, Hautes-Pyrénées, and Basses-Pyrénées, into the Landes and Gironde. The largest collection is on the plateau of Ger,[4] overlooking the Adour, in the Hautes and Basses-Pyrénées. Further south there are the tumuli of Bastrès (canton of Lourdes) and Ossun [5] (arrondissement of Tarbes), and further north, on the plateau of Lannemezan, is the cemetery of Avezac-Prat.[6] Behind, east of the basin of Arcachon, the cemetery of Mios [7] speaks for the same civilization, but the tombs in it are flat-graves.

A second group extends from Albi to Toulouse, and includes the cemeteries of Saint-Sulpice, of Sainte-Foy, a mile from Castres, of the Lacam and Mons plateaus, near Roquecourbe, of Montsalvi in the commune of Puygouzon, of Lavène, near Montsalvi, of Saint-Roch, near Toulouse, etc.[8]

The third is a more scattered group, with Agen as its centre.[9]

Other tumuli have been excavated farther north, at

[1] Déchelette, pp. 663 ff., 671 ff. ; Joulin, in **CXXXIX**, 1908, ii, 1, p. 193 ; 1912, i, 1, p. 235 ; 1914, i, p. 59 ; 1915, i, pp. 47, 259 ; 1918, ii, p. 74 ; 1922, i, 1 ; Bosch, Gimpera, **CCCCXCIX**, 13.

[2] Déchelette, pp. 666, 669 : Stone circles at Garin (Hte.-Garonne). It is possible that the tumulus degenerated into a circle of stones, as in Burgundy (Auvenay road) or at Golasecca.

[3] J. Sacaze, in **XXVI**, 1880, ii, p. 877 (plain of Rivière) ; Joulin, in **CXXXIX**, 1912, i, pp. 33 (necropolis of Sainte-Foy, Tarn) and 4 (Saint-Roch, near Toulouse) ; 1915, ii, p. 82 (Mios).

[4] Pothier, **CCCCLXXXVIII** ; Déchelette, pp. 663 ff.

[5] E. Piette, in **LXXXVI**, 1881, p. 522 (tumuli at Bastrès and Ossun).

[6] Piette and Saccaze, ibid., 1879, p. 499 (Avezac-Prat).

[7] See n. 6. Cau-Durban, in **XXVI**, 1887, ii, p. 737 (cemetery of Ayer, Bordes-sur-Lez, Ariège).

[8] Déchelette, p. 671 ; Joulin, in **CXXXIX**, 1912, i, p. 60.

[9] Déchelette, p. 676.

Liviers near Jumillac-le-Grand in Dordogne [1] and, at the other end of that vast domain, in the environs of Nîmes.[2]

All these tombs are dated by the swords and brooches found in them. The swords are invariably of the type with antennæ.[3] But they are not the old dagger with antennæ of the necropolis of Hallstatt. They are small swords, the handle being usually of iron, and the shape of the pommel is quite unlike the model furnished by the earlier bronze sword with antennæ. The two antennæ have a right-angled bend in them, and end in fairly large knobs, which soon afterwards are all that is left of them.

The brooches are of iron, with a highly arched bow and a large cross-bow spring. They are like the Certosa type. The perpendicular continuation of the foot ends in a flat circular button. Others are of the kettledrum type, which is contemporaneous in Central Europe with the Certosa brooches, but are mounted on a ring which runs through the coils of the spring and the end of the foot ; these are a new type which is peculiar to the region and developed in it.

If we are to place these Aquitanian cemeteries in the third Hallstatt period it will be more accurate to place them at the end of it. It is even probable a priori that the Hallstatt culture lasted longer in this region than elsewhere.

The civilization represented by these tombs does not carry on that of the first Hallstatt settlements in Gaul. It is in the east of the Hallstatt area that we must seek the equivalents of certain metal objects found in the French tumuli, and, still more, of their pottery. Among the weapons there is a javelin made entirely of iron, which we shall find again in Spain. This all-iron javelin has already been reported among the arms of the necropolis of Hallstatt itself.[4] In pottery these tumuli are distinguished from those of the rest of Gaul, firstly by its abundance. There is not much in the Hallstatt tumuli of Eastern and Central France. There is more in those of Champagne and Lorraine, but it is different from the Aquitanian ware. On the whole, this latter has a curiously archaic look. With its ornament of grooves and bosses, like the Lausitz type of pottery, it might belong to

[1] Ibid.
[2] Ibid. ; Bosch Gimpera, op. cit., p. 47, n. 1.
[3] Joulin, op. cit. (Sainte-Foy).
[4] Déchelette, pp. 746, 668, fig. 254 ; Sacken, *Hallstatt*, pl. vii, 2, 3.

the Bronze Age. But there can be no mistake about it, for it includes earthenware copies of the great cylindrical bronze pails with vertical handles which must be placed between the cordoned buckets of the Hallstatt period and the British cist-type buckets of the La Tène period.[1] It also includes vases with a hollow foot shaped like a truncated cone, which cannot be placed very far back among the wares of the Continent. It is in the pottery of the Bavarian [2] and Bohemian tumuli that we find the equivalents of the Aquitanian pottery, and everything seems to suggest that large bodies of Celts from Bavaria and Bohemia had come, without halting on the way, right through France to establish themselves between the Central Plateau and the Pyrenees.

There are obviously exceptions, which do not invalidate this general conclusion. For example, the cemeteries of Roquecourbe have yielded a cup painted with red triangles on a black ground, which recalls the Hallstatt pottery of the Franche-Comté and Southern Germany.[3] Moreover, the various groups differ to some extent from one another in this or that part of their grave-gear.

One thing to note is the similarity of a certain number of vases to the early vases of Golasecca. They have the same round belly and wide neck, the same parallel bands of chevrons and zigzags, and the same high hollow foot. The construction of the tombs presents similarities of the same order. I have compared the stone circles of Golasecca to washed-away tumuli. The tumuli of the plateau of Ger and the Haute-Garonne have stone circles, sometimes several, which in some cases are all that survives, the earth of the mound having been carried away by water. Indeed, we must be in the presence of an event which is not only comparable but parallel to that of which the cemetery of Golasecca is the chief record.

In each case the domain of the Celts was extended, on the whole, suddenly. In each case I imagine that the new settlement was the work of the Celts in the rear, and not of those who had just before established themselves on the front line. History will afterwards show them established in south-western France, Volcæ and Boii—Volcæ Tectosages

---

[1] Déchelette, pp. 815 ff.
[2] Naue, CCCCIII, pll. xliv ff.   [3] Déchelette, p. 673.

round Toulouse, Volcæ Aricomii behind them in the Gard, and Boii or Boiates round the lake of Arcachon.[1] Both Volcæ and Boii had come from Bavaria and Bohemia. If they had not all arrived at that time, that at least shows that the Celts were capable of sending out colonies to great distances, and as a fact they were. The colonization which took place in the third Hallstatt period can be followed on its way through France by the distribution of certain types of sword.[2] It seems to have halted a moment at the foot of the Pyrenean passes, just as, in Livy's story, on the other side of Gaul, the army of Bellovesus halted at the foot of the Alps.[3] The result of this halt was the chain of settlements along the mountains. They lasted, too, perhaps because of the salt-deposits of Salies-de-Béarn and the district. But they did not last as long as the settlements beyond the crest of the Pyrenees, from which they got some of their implements and part of their civilization, as we shall see.

VI

CELTIC EXPANSION IN THE EXTREME WEST OF EUROPE

The earliest pottery of the Iron Age found in the south of England, first at Hengistbury Head near Southampton and then at All Cannings Cross Farm in Wiltshire,[4] is very like that of the Pyrenean tumuli. Did the Britons whose arrival it represents come direct from the same regions ? Did they pass through Aquitaine ? And did they take ship from the Loire, as Zimmer supposes the Goidels to have done, or from the Garonne ? They probably came from Brittany, where an exactly similar pottery has been found in the cemetery of Roz-an-Tremen near Penmarch.[5] We should note here that the pottery immediately above this stratum at Hengistbury Head consists of vases decorated with cordons in relief,[6] which are of the same type as those of the second

---

[1] Peynau, **CCCCLXXXVI**, i.
[2] Henry, "Les Tumulus du Département de la Côte d'Or," École du Louvre thesis, in "Rapport sur l'administration et la conservation des Musées nationaux" (*Journal officiel*, 24th August, 1928).
[3] Livy, v, 34.
[4] See above, p. 213.
[5] Favret and Bénard, in **CXXXIX**, 1924, i, pp. 178 ff. ; Bénard, *Les Deux Nécropoles de Saint-Urnel et de Roz-an-Tremen*, repr. from **XLIII**, 1922.
[6] J. P. Bushe-Fox, **CCCVIII**, pp. 34 ff.

period of Golasecca, and seem to have been made fairly soon after them. These different facts lead one to think that bands of emigrants moved at this time from the east of the Celtic world, some towards the extreme west of Europe and some towards the south-west, and that the flow, at least on the western side, was for some time continuous.

CHAPTER V

CELTIC EXPANSION ON THE CONTINENT IN THE HALLSTATT PERIOD (*continued*). THE CELTS IN SPAIN

I

CELTIC CEMETERIES AND TUMULI

THE drive to the south-west was not exhausted when it reached the Pyrenees. Many bodies crossed them.

We must observe first of all that they never lost contact with the settlements in Aquitaine. In the tombs of that region, more particularly near the Pyrenees, objects are found which are really Spanish, invented south of the Pyrenees, where they were copied from Greek or Italic models. Such, for instance, are the belt-clasps (Fig. 42).[1] The presence of these Spanish objects helps to give the Hallstatt civilization of Aquitaine its characteristic appearance, which is so different from that of all other parts of the Celtic world. It also shows that the settlements to the north of the Pyrenees and those to the south constituted one single group, a single racial unit, the connecting links of which we may usefully consider (Map 12).

There have been found south of the Pyrenees a series of tumuli with cremations, and also cemeteries—very large ones—with cremations, dating from the end of the third Hallstatt period. The tumulus without any interior chamber and the practice of cremation were alike novelties in Spain at this time. These tumuli and cemeteries are dated by brooches of the various types already mentioned, swords with antennæ, and pottery like the Pyrenean wares of France.

---

[1] These belt-clasps are related to the Hallstatt clasps with a single hook of Central Europe ; they differ from them in having more than one hook and in having oblong holes in the base of the hooks. Clasps of this kind have been found at Olympia and in the ruins of the Greek colony of Ampurias. From this Déchelette concludes that they were Greek (" Agrafes de ceinturon ibériques d'origine grecque," in **CLXXXV**). Bosch Gimpera thinks that they may have come to these places as trophies, or that they belonged to auxiliaries (**CCCCXCIX**, p. 30). For the archæology of the Celts in the Peninsula, see Bosch Gimpera, *L'Arqueologia y l'arte ibericas*, vol. i. *Etnologia de la Peninsula iberica*, pp. 452 ff., Barcelona, 1931.

The earliest, therefore, date from the middle of the sixth century.[1]

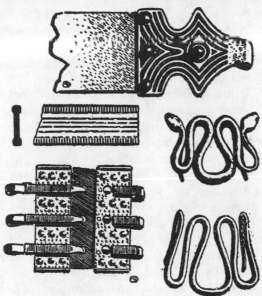

FIG. 42. Iberian Belt-clasps.
(G. Bonsor, *Colonies agricoles*, figs. 9–13.)

The tumuli are in groups on the little hills, the Alcores, which fill the great bend made by the Guadalquivir before

[1] Sr. Bosch Gimpera and some other Catalan archæologists think that the Hallstatt culture had entered Spain by the Mediterranean coast two or three centuries before. Cremation-cemeteries, without tumuli, have been explored in Catalonia (Espolla, Tarrasa, Sabadell, La Punta del Pi), where vases have been found which resemble those of the earliest Hallstatt sites of the south of France, and must date from about the eighth century (Bosch Gimpera, J. Colominas Roca, " La Necropoli de Can Misert," Tarrasa, in **XV**, vi, 1920 ; Bosch Gimpera, **DV**, pp. 175 ff. ; **DII**, p. 45 ; **CCCCXCIX**, p. 14 ; **DXVII**, p. 179 ; Péricot, **DXV**, p. 47). Sr. Bosch Gimpera at first thought that these might represent the advance of early bodies of Celts by the east coast of Spain, two or three centuries before the date assigned to the first Celtic settlements in the country. The natives maintained themselves in the more mountainous parts of Catalonia, where their archaic civilization is represented by a certain number of stations, while the influence of the Hallstatt culture, spread by the Celts, made itself felt farther south as early as this time in the province of Almeria, where, with the Hallstatt period, cremations in graves and stone tumuli appear (Siret, **DXXIII**, vii, fig. 69 ; Déchelette, ii, 2, p. 686 ; Péricot, loc. cit. ; Bosch Gimpera, **DII**, p. 53). Afterwards Sr. Bosch Gimpera talks of nothing but Ligurians. But the cemeteries in question are quite remarkably poor. There are no weapons in them which might date them beyond dispute, and the pottery is hardly older in type than that of the Pyrenean tumuli. Provisionally, I regard them as of the same date as these latter, and I do not take them into account in reconstructing the history of the Celts in Spain.

it reaches the sea, and are there contiguous to inhumation-cemeteries without tumuli. They were found to contain the pottery which we already know and brooches of the serpentine and Certosa types, all mixed with so many Phœnician objects that the excavator did not hesitate to ascribe the tombs to Carthaginian colonists. But the Carthaginians and their Libyan subjects did not burn their dead.[1]

To the Marquis of Cerralbo we are indebted for our knowledge of the great cemeteries of the two central provinces of Soria and Guadalajara, which lie side by side, one in the south-east of Old Castile and the other in the north of New Castile.[2] There, too, there was salt, which might keep the population in the place. In these two regions a dozen cremation-cemeteries are known. The largest is that of Aguilar de Anguita in the province of Guadalajara, near the sources of the Salon, the ancient Salo, the valley of which was a channel of intercourse between the Ebro and the Tagus.

In this cemetery and others the urns were arranged in several parallel rows, a yard or five feet apart. In other cemeteries, which are just the same in respect of the objects found in them, this arrangement can no longer be seen, if it ever existed. There were no tumuli. Above the urn a tombstone was set, which, with one exception, was quite plain.[3]

The characteristic objects of the grave-gear are the same as north of the Pyrenees. The sword is of the type with antennæ. There are several forms, from those with bronze antennæ and semicircular iron antennæ to that with atrophied antennæ.

The brooches (Fig. 43) are the iron brooch with a perpendicular foot and a button, the ring-brooch, and

[1] Bonsor, **CCCCXCVI**. He ascribes the tombs with zoned vases to the Celts. Déchelette (in **CXXXIX**, 1908, 2, pp. 391 ff.) does not hesitate to regard these tombs as Celtic. Cf. Reinecke, in **CLXIX**, 1900 ; **CLVIII**, p. 162. Recently, MM. Bonsor and Thouvenot have explored a necropolis in the province of Seville, the furniture of which presents analogies with that of the tombs in the valley of the Bætis (**CCCCXCVII**). These tombs are really native (those containing bell-beakers) or Iberian (containing painted pottery), but they show signs of Celtic influences.

[2] Cerralbo, in **LIX**, Monaco, 1912, i, pp. 593 ff. ; Déchelette, ii, 2, p. 687 ; id., in **LVIII**, 1912, pp. 433 ff. ; Bosch Gimpera, **DXVIII**, p. 189 (bibliography) ; Schulten, **DXVIII**, p. 199 ; Bosch Gimpera, **CCCCXCIX**, pp. 13 ff. ; **DII**, p. 55 ; Péricot, **DXV**, p. 47 ; **CXVIII**, 1911, p. 384.

[3] Déchelette, ii, 2, p. 688, i.

another Hallstatt brooch which is absent, as far as I know, in the series from the French side of the Pyrenees, that in the shape of a horse or of a horse with rider. This last appears at Hallstatt itself. It is of Italian origin, and it was probably from Italy that it came to Spain. It is possible that the belt-clasps, which are of quite a peculiar kind, were likewise imported direct, and developed independently in Spain.

The pottery, which consists chiefly of funeral urns, is in part related to that of the north of the Pyrenees. This

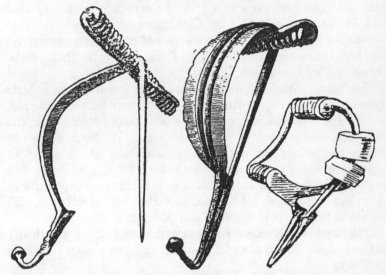

Fig. 43. Hallstatt Brooches from Spain. (Bonsor, *Colonies agricoles*, figs. 6, 96–7.)

part of the pottery of the cremation-cemeteries persists in the latest necropoles.

For not only did these cemeteries last a long time, but the communities which left their dead in them adhered, like those of Aquitaine, to ancient forms. We may merely note this in passing ; we shall have to return to it later. It cannot have taken less than two or three hundred years for the Hallstatt types to develop as they did in Spain [1] and the Pyrenees. After that the civilization to which they belong outlived itself. Dates are furnished by the discovery of Greek

[1] Bosch Gimpera, **CCCCXCIX**, pp. 20 ff.

vases of the fifth and fourth centuries in a similar necropolis at Alcacer-do-Sal[1] in the south of Portugal and by that of painted Iberian vases of the third century in several others.[2]

Let us now go over the area. Brooches of the series described above and isolated daggers with antennæ, or contemporary cremations, have been discovered in certain *citanias*, ancient towns of masonry construction, in Portugal,[3] in Cantabria and Galicia in the north, and in the south at Almedinella in Andalusia,[4] and at Villaricos in Almeria, on the Mediterranean coast.[5] In the north-east the dagger with antennæ has been found in the cemeteries of Gibrella[6] and Perelada (Gerona). In Catalonia, in the provinces of Gerona and Barcelona, a whole series of cremation-cemeteries has been explored, the pottery of which recalls that of the cemeteries of the Tarn.

In fact, almost all over the Peninsula the objects characteristic of this culture, which, it must be remembered, was far from remaining pure, have been found isolated on the outskirts and crowded in the centre. Without apparent connection with the previous civilizations, the nearest of which are almost completely unknown to us (we have not one late Bronze Age station in Spain), this culture came in at a time which may be placed, in virtue of the daggers with bronze antennæ, between 600 and 500 B.C.

North of the Pyrenees we have attributed it hypothetically to the Celts. South of the Pyrenees we have positive reasons for doing so.

II

THE ANCIENT HISTORIANS

North of Italy and the Adriatic, where the Celts had advanced in the sixth century, the Greeks did not come into direct contact with them. The result is that their advance

---

[1] Estacio da Veiga, **DXXIV**, iv, xxxiii, 268 ; V. Correia, *Uma Conferencia sobre a necropole de Alcacer do Sal*, repr. from **XXXIII**, 1925.

[2] Bosch Gimpera, **DXVIII**, p. 189.

[3] Cartailhac, **DVII**, p. 246, figs. 358–60 ; Déchelette, ii, 2, p. 686 (Cividade Velha de Santa Luzia) ; Bosch Gimpera, **CCCCXCIX**, pp. 40 ff. ; Mendez Correa, **DXIII**, passim.

[4] Cordova Museum. Bosch Gimpera, op. cit., p. 51.

[5] Siret, **DXXIII** ; H. Sandars, " The Weapons of the Iberians," in **XVIII**, 1913, pp. 205 ff.

[6] Bosch Gimpera, op. cit., p. 14 ; **XV**, 1920, vi, p. 590.

went unrecorded in classical literature (except in Livy, who may have had other sources), ánd therefore we have not been able to argue anything from this absence of evidence in the ancient authors.

In Spain Greek mariners were doing trade before the sixth century,[1] and we have an uninterrupted series of testimonies about the Peninsula and its people, some furnished by sure witnesses, namely writers who had travelled and seen what they described with their own eyes. Now among the inhabitants of the country they mention the Celts fairly early, and after them the Celtiberians.

The first [2] to speak of the Celts in Spain is Herodotos.[3] " The Danube," he says, " starts from the country of the Celts and the city of Pyrene. It flows through Europe, which it divides down the middle. The Celts are outside the Pillars of Heracles and march with the Cynesii, who are the western-most people of Europe." Herodotos's geography, so far as the interior of Europe is concerned, is vague ; but it is definite in respect of the coasts. He belonged to a people of sailors, which would naturally have nautical information, and his geographical sources must have been of the *periplus* class, which is very well represented in Greek literature. The Cynesii were a Ligurian people, whom Polybios calls Κόνιοι. Their cities were Conistorgis, the site of which is not known, and Conimbriga, which was well to the north ; both were in the south-western end of the Peninsula, between the Guadiana and Cape St. Vincent.[4] Aristotle, in his *Meteorologica*, faithfully records the information supplied by Herodotos [5] ; he speaks, if not of the city, of the mountain of Pyrene, *in the Celtic country*, from which, he says, both the Danube and the Tartessus rise.

About this Tartessus, that is the Guadalquivir, and its valley, which was a sort of Eldorado to the ancient mariner,

---

[1] The voyage of Colæos of Samos, about 660 : Hdt., iv, 152 ; d'Arbois, **CCCI**, ii, p. 306 ; Schulten, **DXX**, p. 25. Tradition of the voyages of Heracles : Pherecydes of Samos (ca. 480 B.C.), p. 33 ; Sil. Ital., iii, 357 ; Philipon, **DXV**, p. 83.

[2] Unless we are to see a distortion of the name of the Celts in that of the Γλῆτες, mentioned with the Cynetes and Tartessians by Herodoros of Heracleia (ca. 500 B.C.), frag. 30 ; A. Blasquez, in **XXXIV**, 1915, lxvi, p. 164. Strabo, iii, 4, 19, gives Ἰγλῆτες ; Philipon **DXV**, p. 132.

[3] ii, 33.

[4] Schulten, **DXIX**, p. 91.

[5] i, 13, 19.

Herodotos gives a detail which has not received the attention which it deserves. It is the name of the King of Tartessus, Arganthonios,[1] who was on the throne when the Phocæans were making their first attempts at colonization, round about the time of the foundation of Marseilles. Herodotos says that Arganthonios gave them money to build the wall behind which Phocæa for some time defied the Persians of Cyrus. Tartessus was famed for its silver mines ; Arganthonios is the Silver King. If his name were Iberian, like the name of Tartessus itself, there would be a very great argument, though perhaps an only one, for classifying the Iberians as Indo-Europeans. But it is based on the Celtic form of the word for silver—*arganto*.[2] Either there were Celts at Tartessus, or the Phocæan legend of the Silver King contains an admixture of Celtic elements. The Celts of the Alcores were not far away, and there is no reason why a Celtic chief should not have become king of the Iberian state of Tartessus, perhaps by marriage, or even that he should not have made a name for himself in the world.

Arganthonios was dead when the Phocæans founded Alalia in Corsica in 564. He was a semi-legendary person, and had been given a reputation for proverbial longevity. Herodotus says that he reigned eighty years and lived a hundred and twenty ; later they gave him a hundred and fifty or three hundred. In any case, we must suppose that he reigned roughly about 600 B.C., and place the arrival of the Celts in Bætica as far back as that. The tombs of the Alcores are older than the cemeteries of Castile, and contain objects earlier than the Certosa brooches.

About 350 Ephoros, in his history of the world, described the extent of the Celtic domain, which reached as far as

---

[1] Hubert, in **CXL**, 1927, pp. 78 ff. ; Hdt., i, 163.
[2] According to Schulten (op. cit., p. 61), the name is Ligurian. But the Ligurians probably had another name for silver, from the same root as the English word. The name of Piz Silvretta, near Klosters, in Grisons, a region of Ligurian place-names, bears witness to it. Also, the Ligurian place-names of the south of Spain, among which are a Mons Argentarius (Avien., *Ora Marit.*, 291) and an 'Αργυροῦν ὄρος (Strabo, iii, 148), include a Mons Silurus (Avien., 433), which seems to form a pendant to them, to say nothing of the people of the Silures. The Celtic etymology of Arganthonios presents two difficulties : (1) the writing of the dental in the stem ; but the Negau inscription shows that in the sixth century the Brythonic *t* was pronounced in such a way that it could be expressed by a letter bordering on θ ; (2) there was, in Bithynia, an Arganthonion, first mentioned by Apollonios of Rhodes (i, 1176). Cf. Philipon, **DXVI**, 55, 65.

Cadiz.[1] At the end of the century Aristotle gave the name of
" Celtic " to the whole mountain mass of the Peninsula.[2]
Some years later Pytheas made his voyage, the account of
which was largely used by Timæos and Eratosthenes.
Timæos speaks of the rivers which flow into the Atlantic as
going through the mountains of the Celtic country.[3]
Eratosthenes was censured by Strabo because he said that
the western coasts of the peninsula belonged to the Celts.[4]
But with Timæos and Eratosthenes, the Celtiberians seem
to have made their first appearance in literature. Celtic
expansion in Spain had reached its maximum. Henceforward
we shall only see it recede.

About the time of Herodotos, the author of the *periplus*
which Avienus used in his *Ora Maritima* gave the names of
the Celtic peoples which had settled close to the Portuguese
coast. " North of the Cynetes," he says [5] :—

> *Cempsi atque Saefes arduos colles habent*
> *Ophiussae in agro, propter hos pernix Ligus*
> *Draganumque proles sub nivoso maxime*
> *Septentrione conlocaverant larem.*

The country was called Ophiussa. These people who had
squeezed themselves in between the Ligurians and the
Cynetes, pushing back the former to the north into the
Pyrenees and beyond, are probably the Celts of Herodotos.[6]
The Cempsi must have bordered not only on the country of
the Cynetes, but inland on the northern frontier of the
kingdom of Tartessus. The Saefes must have been a continuation of them northwards.

In the east the same author tells us for the first time of
another Celtic people. He has just spoken of the River
Tyrius, now the Turia, and adds : " But as the country lies
further from the sea it stretches out in ridges covered with

---

[1] In Strabo, ii, 19 ; Schulten, op. cit., p. 93.
[2] *De Animalium Generibus*, 38.
[3] Schulten, op. cit., p. 96.
[4] Strabo, ii, 4, 4.
[5] 195 ff. ; Schulten, **DXVII**, p. 80 ; id., **DXIX**, p. 89.
[6] Bosch Gimpera, **CCCCXCIX**, p. 5. For a contrary view, see Philipon,
op. cit., p. 71. The name of the Cempsi, which is also mentioned by Dionysios
Periegetes (338), may be connected with the Celto-Ligurian root of the name
of the Cevennes, *cemm*. The Cempsi had come down further south and
occupied the island of Cartare, not far from Cadiz (Avien., 255).

undergrowth. There the Berybraces, a rude and savage people, used to wander among their great herds of cattle. Living on a hard fare of milk and fatty cheese, they showed a spirit like that of wild beasts." [1] The Berybraces, elsewhere called Bebryces, are much better known than the two other peoples. They are definitely described as Celts by the *perigetes* Scymnos of Chios, who summarized the geography of Ephoros.[2] We have no difficulty in associating their name with a family of Celtic words—Bebrinium, Bebriacum, Bebronne, Bibrax, Bibrori (in Brittany)—which contain the name of the beaver, *bebros*.[3] Writers whose evidence, it is true, is not of much value for these distant times, Dion Cassius,[4] Silius Italicus,[5] and Tzetzes,[6] place the Bebryces at various points along the coast.

Whereas the Marseilles geographer used by Avienus shows the interior of the Peninsula as being in the possession of three great Celtic tribes, he mentions no one in the Pyrenean isthmus except the Dragani, who were Ligurians. Here he apparently contradicts the archæological data. We must presume from what he says either that the Celts only occupied limited districts between the central plateau and the Pyrenees, or that their settlements there did not last as long as those in the south and on the coast. There is nothing against this in the archæological finds.

Avienus's three tribes vanished from history after the time of Ephoros. Later writers mention only a very few names of Celtic peoples outside the Celtiberian group. The Berones,[7] in the upper valley of the Ebro, are described as Celts. Their neighbours, the Autrigones,[8] may be Celts, too.

---

[1] 483 ff. :—

> *At qua recedit ab salo tellus procul,*
> *dumosa late terga regio porrigit ;*
> *Berybraces illic, gens agrestis et ferox,*
> *pecorum frequentis intererrabat greges.*
> *Hi lacte semet atque pingui caseo*
> *praedure alentes, proferebant spiritum*
> *vicem ad ferarum.*

[2] In *F.H.G.*, 199 ; Avien., 483–9 ; Schulten, **DXIX**, p. 35.
[3] Jullian, **CCCXLVII**, i, p. 259. Philipon (op. cit., xiii) makes them an Iberian people.
[4] Frag. 53.
[5] 3, 442.
[6] In Lycophron, 1305 ; Schulten, op. cit., pp. 91 ff.
[7] Strabo, 3, 4, 5. Cf. Scholia on Lucan (Usener's ed.), iv, 10 ; Isid., *Orig.*, ix, 2, 114. " Gallohispani," St. Jerome, *Comm. on Isaiah*, xviii, 66, 9.
[8] The towns of Uxama Barca and Deobriga are in their country.

So may the Turmogidi,[1] on the other side of the watershed between the basins of the Ebro and Douro. I should say the same of the Nemetati,[2] whom Ptolemy mentions on the right

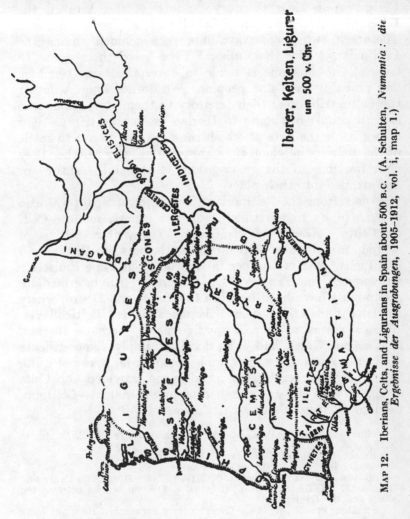

MAP 12. Iberians, Celts, and Ligurians in Spain about 500 B.C. (A. Schulten, *Numantia : die Ergebnisse der Ausgrabungen, 1905–1912*, vol. i, map 1.)

bank of the Douro in the north of Lusitania ; we see in their name a Celtic word, *nemeton*. Further north were the Artabri, whose name, formed on the model of that of the Cantabri,

---

[1] With the town of Deobrigula.
[2] Ptol., ii, 6, 40.

also appears as Arotrebæ, which may be Celtic [1]; they had three towns with Celtic names—Ardobriga, Acobriga, and Brigantium, not to mention the Promontorium Celticum (Cape Finisterre) in their territory. South of the Artabri, the Bracari,[2] with their town of Caladunum, appear to be Celts. These last two peoples are, however, included among the Lusitanians,[3] like the Callæci [4] (who gave their name to Galicia), whose name is made to cover the same territory and probably the same peoples. We do not know whether the Celtic tribes had their territory to themselves, or shared it with people belonging to Iberian or Basque tribes. Nor do we know the date at which these peoples began to settle in the districts in which they are reported, nor whether they were fractions of the great groups of the sixth century or had stepped into their place.

Apart from the Celtiberians, the Celts of Spain are also designated by names which look like generic names—Celti or Celtici, Κελτοί or Κελτικοί. The writers tell us of a group of Celtici or Celti in the south, between Bætica and the Tagus,[5] and of another in Galicia about Cape Finisterre and astride the Tamara (the Tambre).[6] An intermediate group must have lived between the Tagus and Douro, where we later find a city near Salamanca named Celticoflavia. Κελτικοί seems to be a derivative name, perhaps Iberian, if it is not Greek and if it does not imply some delicate distinction, meaning, for example, people who were not quite Celts.[7] In any case, this racial name provided the Celts of Spain with a large number of proper names—Celtigun, Celtillus, Celtius, Celtus, Celtitanus.[8]

[1] Pliny, iv, 3, 119; Mela, iii, 13. Cf. Irish *Artaige* (M. E. Dobbs, in **LXXX**, 1916, p. 168).

[2] *Braca.* Cf. Holder, **CCVII**, s.v.

[3] Strabo, iii, 147, 151, 154 (Celtiberians).

[4] Sil. Ital., iii, 344 ff.; Norden, **CCCXIV**, p. 145; Hübner, in Pauly and Wissowa, **CCCLXVIII**, s.v.; Isid., *Orig.*, ii, 2, 110 (similarities between the Callæci and the Gauls).

[5] Schulten, op. cit., p. 109. Their territory approached the right bank of the Bætis. Pliny, iii, 11, *oppida Hispalensis conventus*: *Celti, Axati*, etc.; iii, 13; *Ant. Itin.*, 414, 5; Ravennas, 44, 315, 2.

[6] Celtici Nerii, Præstamarici, Superstamarici; Mela, ii, 2; Pliny, iv, 3; Jullian, op. cit., i, p. 307.

[7] Pliny, iii, 13: *Celticos a Celtiberis ex Lusitania advenisse manifestum est sacris, lingua, oppidorum vocabulis, quae cognominibus in Bætica distinguuntur.*

[8] Schulten, op. cit., p. 107; Fidel Fita, in **XXXIV**, 1916, lxix, p. 114 (inscriptions of Peñaflor).

Does this mean that the Celts of Spain and, by extension, those of the first migrations were Celts as opposed to the Gauls ? No doubt there were slight differences of vocabulary and pronunciation between the Celts of Spain and the Gauls of Gaul. We have a great number of Celtic names from Spain. There are none ending in -*marus* among them. I know of only one instance of a name in -*rix* (Thiureigs). On the other hand, the names Boutius, Cloutius, and Mælo are found there. Ambactus appears in the form Ambatus, and Camulus in the form Camalus.[1] But these differences are not to be compared to those separating Goidelic from Brythonic.

III

THE TERRITORY OCCUPIED BY THE CELTS

The Celtic place-names of the Peninsula enable us to determine fairly accurately, if not the whole extent of the territory occupied by the Celts, at least that of the country in which they were established long enough to leave place-names. The most interesting are the names of towns. Among these there is a series which seems to go back to the first Celtic immigration, namely those in -*briga*, such as Segobriga (Segorbe) and Laccobriga (Lagos).[2] This ending appears so often in Spain that it has been regarded as Iberian.[3] This is quite wrong. Names in -*briga* are found in regions in which the Iberians certainly never lived—Admagetobriga in the Franche-Comté, Artobriga in Bavaria, etc.[4] It is the Gaulish equivalent of German *burg*.[5] The name of the goddess Brigid comes from the same stem, with the vowel *i*. There is no doubt, therefore, that the word is Celtic.[6] It is true that it is found attached to names, the first part of which is not or does

[1] Schulten, op. cit., p. 31, n. 5.
[2] D'Arbois, **CCXCIX**, 98 ; Schulten, op. cit., pp. 23, 110 ; Schumacher, **CCCCIX**, 122 ; according to whom it applies to river-crossings.
[3] Philipon, **DXVI**, p. 158 ; id., **CCCLXIX**, p. 217 : Names ending in -*briga* were formed by the Latins from race-names in -*q*, based on town-names in -*bri* (e.g. Segobriges ; Hübner, *Monumenta Linguæ Ibericæ*, Berlin. 1883, pt. i, Nummi, No. 89).
[4] D'Arbois, op. cit., p. 98.
[5] In Irish, *bre*, gen. *breg*, means "hill". In Welsh, *bre*, plur. *breon* ; Penbre. *Brig* meant "end".
[6] Jullian (in **CXXXIV**, 1906, p. 47) has tried, on not much ground, to make it a Ligurian word.

not seem to be Celtic—Uollobriga, Langobriga, Talabriga, Conimbriga, Cottaiobriga, etc.[1] Some, too, are Latin names in a Gaulish dress—Augustobriga, Cæsarobriga, Juliobriga, Flaviobriga.[2] But there are enough wholly Celtic names to make it unnecessary to look for the origin of the first part in another language. There are, for instance, Eburobriga,[3] Nertobriga,[4] Medubriga,[5] Nemetobriga,[6] Deobriga, etc.[7] All the same, only six names in *-briga* are known in Gaul and Germany, whereas there are thirty-five of them in the Peninsula.[8] On the whole they are more numerous in the west and centre than in the south and east.[9] They are lacking in Catalonia, in the provinces of Valencia, Alicante, and Murcia, and in the governments of Granada and Seville. There are thirteen in the province of Corunna, four in the Douro, and three in Portuguese Estremadura.

There are other Celtic names, distributed in the same manner, which corroborate the Celtic nature of those ending in *-briga*—Brigantium, Trigundum, Novium, Deva, Uxuma, Ugultiniacum, Ebora, Eburobritium,[10] Ocelodurum.

The limit of the Celtic settlements [11] can be traced by Deobriga among the Autrigones, in the valley of the Ebro, and Nertobriga, in the valley of the Jalón ; on the east, going through Contrebia on the Jiloca, by Segobriga, the town with a Celtic name which on this side is nearest the coast ; and on the Andalusian side by Mirobriga and Nertobriga in the Sierra Morena.

North of the Ebro, in Aragon, the River Gallicus and the

---

[1] D'Arbois, op. cit., p. 99.
[2] Ibid., p. 108.
[3] Irish *ibar* " yew ". Dottin, **CXCVI**, p. 255.
[4] Irish *neart*, Welsh *nerth* " strength ". Ibid., p. 275.
[5] Irish *mid* " mead " ; Welsh *medd*. Ibid., p. 271.
[6] Irish *nemed* " sanctuary ". Ibid., p. 224.
[7] *Devo-* : Irish *dia*, gen. *dié* " god ". We might add Segobriga, which Philipon makes an Iberian name and Schulten a Ligurian one (**DXIX**, p. 68). It is true that *sego* comes into many Ligurian place-names (Segusio, (?) Susa ; Segobrigii, above, p. 237), but it perhaps comes into more Celtic names (Segodunum, Rodez and Würzburg ; Segedunum in Britain ; Segura, Bressuire). Irish *seg* " strength ".
[8] D'Arbois (op. cit., p. 98) adds fourteen names in *-obre*, which he derives from ancient names in *-briga*—Canzobre, Cillobre (p. 103). The derivation is doubtful. Names in *-briga* produced names in *-brega*, and those in *-obre* may have come from town-names in *-bris*. Philipon, *Peuples*, p. 216.
[9] Schulten, op. cit., p. 110.
[10] *Eburo-* is likewise Ligurian. D'Arbois, **CCCI**, ii, 199.
[11] Schulten, op. cit., p. 106.

towns of Forum Gallorum and Gallica Flavia seem to belong to a later stratum of Celtic names.[1] Further west the region covered by Celtic names reaches the coast in two rivers called Deva, one among the Carietes and the other among the Cantabri. The Celts, who did not drive out the previous occupants of the Pyrenees, certainly mixed with them.[2] In the east, between the Celts and the coast, there was a tract of Iberian settlements into which they certainly penetrated, but without apparently making a serious breach in them. In the south were the Tartessians. The west coast, on the other hand, is dotted with Celtic names along its whole length, and the Celtic towns are on the shore.

If we were to make up a map from these names it would not quite correspond to the archæological map. It would leave outside the Celtic area the cremation-cemeteries of the provinces of Gerona and Barcelona on the one hand [3] and, on the other, the Alcores district with its cremation-tumuli. From this I conclude that in both cases the archæological finds represent settlements which did not last long. Catalonia and Bætica were the chief territories of the Iberians and Tartessians. That small bands of Celts should have passed through the one and insinuated themselves into the other, or even established themselves there, is of little consequence ; either they were absorbed or they have slipped through the meshes of the net of history.

This map based on names seems to indicate the route of the Celtic invasion.[4] The main route, in any case, seems to have been by the western passes of the Pyrenees, the famous road of Roncesvalles. From there it must have run to the valley of the Ebro by Suessatium [5] among the Varduli, a town with a Celtic name recalling that of the Suessiones, and Deobriga, to ascend the plateau by the Pancorbo gorge. Beyond, it followed the valleys of the Pisuerga and Douro. From the plateau they must have spread over the rest of the Peninsula. I am quite prepared to believe that smaller bands entered by the eastern passes of the Pyrenees ; but I am

[1] See the following volume in this series.
[2] Schulten, op. cit., p. 23, n. 5 : Celtic personal names.
[3] Bosch Gimpera, " La Necrópolis de Perelada," in **XV**, vi, 1915–1920, pp. 590 ff.
[4] Schulten, op. cit., p. 106.
[5] D'Arbois, **CCXLVIII** (Droit), p. 41.

not at all inclined to think, as some have suggested, that the Celts came by sea and worked up the great rivers of the west.[1]

Like the Celts of Aquitaine, they must have come from a great distance. It is not certain that the name of Suessatium, with its resemblance to that of the Suessiones, dates from the earliest Celtic settlements.[2] But that of Brigantium,[3] the Celtic town which stood on the site of Corunna, among the Cantabri, probably belongs to the oldest stratum of Celtic names in Spain. Now this is significant. It is the name of Bregenz on the Lake of Constance, and it is the name of the Brigantes who must have come to England from the same region.

The place-names also give an important piece of information about the character of the Celtic settlements. Whereas in Gaul there are plenty of names in -*magus* and -*ialum*,[4] common nouns meaning " plain " and " field " which designate settlements in the plains, probably agricultural, the abundance of names in -*briga*, indicating settlements on hills and fortified hills, is very significant. These names tell of insecurity, a state of war or danger of war, and we can imagine the Celts of Spain who had conquered only the least attractive parts of the country, scattered in the midst of Ligurian tribes, driven off, broken up, but still formidable and keeping watch on the Iberian or Tartessian states whose military power is always represented as considerable in the ancient writers. That power held the fertile valleys of the south and east, which the Celts were powerless to seize from it. The rapid advance of the Celts in such a huge country was able to set up a chain of posts all over it, but could hardly establish a continuous mass of population.

The historians [5] represent the Celts of the Spanish plateau as leading a hard and penurious life as very savage herdsmen. The mountaineers, the herdsmen and peasants of the *meseta*,

---

[1] Philipon, **DXVI**, p. 140 ; id., **CCCLXIX**, p. 190 ; Hirt, **CCCXXXVIII**, i, p. 168.
[2] See the following volume in this series.
[3] D'Arbois, **CCXCIX**, 121.
[4] Ibid., 90 : -*magos*, Irish *mag*, Welsh *ma* " plain " ; -*ialon*, Welsh *ial* " open space ". Cf. Dottin, op. cit., s.v.
[5] See the passage of Avienus about the Berybraces above, p. 290 ; Schulten, op. cit., p. 106.

still live fairly roughly. But by their side live a middle class of townsfolk and an aristocracy.

Now the Celts had dealings with Tartessus. It was through Tartessus that the gold, copper, and tin of the Celtic country were exported in the time of Ephoros.[1] They were, therefore, linked up with the general economic life of the world, and they profited by it. The Celts were never, in any country, people to resist civilizing influences from outside. As a fact, the Celts of Spain have left evidence of the great extent to which they borrowed from others. Those who buried their dead in the tumuli of the Alcores were well supplied with Carthaginian articles of bronze and ivory.[2] Those of Aguilar de Anguita and other places in Castile and Portugal bought Iberian and Greek pottery.[3] They adopted part of the armament of the Iberians—their round shields, the iron portions of which are found in their tombs, their body-armour,[4] composed of two round plates held on by braces, which the Iberians had copied from the Italians, the bits of their horses, and even the horse-shoe,[5] which appears here for the first time in the Celtic world.

But the things taken from foreign cultures become scarcer as one approaches the Garonne, and the sepultures of Aquitaine, taken as a whole, if compared with contemporary tombs of the Rhine valley and Southern Germany, give an impression of being poor, particularly in articles of luxury of Greek manufacture.

Altogether, then, there are very extensive but not at all populous settlements of pastoral and warlike peoples, which very rapidly spread across the plateaus and made their way to the sea down the great rivers of the Atlantic side—the Douro, Tagus, and Guadiana. They easily conquered the first Ligurian occupants of the country. But they stopped at the edge of the fertile valleys and coasts already occupied by the Tartessians and Iberians. These last give the impression of being the powerful peoples of the Peninsula, and the story of the Celts will be chiefly subordinate to theirs.

[1] Ibid., p. 92.
[2] Bonsor, in **CXXXIX**, 1899, 2, pp. 251, 280, 288.
[3] Déchelette, ii, 2, p. 692 ; Bosch Gimpera, **CCCCXCIX**, pp. 38 ff.
[4] Déchelette, p. 688 ; cf. p. 692, n. 1.
[5] Ibid., p. 690.

IV

THE SURROUNDING OF THE CELTIC SETTLEMENTS.   THE
IBERIAN INVASION OF LANGUEDOC AND AQUITAINE

Some decades after the Celtic invasion the Iberians of the Ebro valley gained ground to the north at the expense of the Ligurians.[1]   They probably organized military expeditions against the Ligurians and waged a war of destruction on them.   But they followed up these ravages by extending their settlements.   It is possible that the whole series of Iberian states was involved in this movement, or that it was produced by pressure, of which we know little at present, from the south.[2]

At the time of Hecatæos of Miletos the region of Narbonne, Béziers, and Montpellier was held by the Ligurians.[3]   There one Ligurian people, the Elisyces, formed a state which was known far and wide, almost as well as Tartessus.   In the days of the Homeric poems it stood for the wonderful West, the happy, distant land to which the dead retired.[4]   When the Carthaginians fell on Gelon of Syracuse in 480, when he was about to go to the help of the Greeks against the Persian invaders, and were defeated at Himera, there were Elisyces serving in their fleet as mercenaries, with Ligurians, Sardinians, and Corsicans.[5]

At the time when the Marseilles *periplus* used by Avienus was written, the glory of the Elisyces was only a memory. " The nation of the Elisyces," Avienus writes,[6] " first occupied these parts, and Narbo was the chief head of its haughty realm."   He bears witness to the destruction wrought by the Iberians on their way.   " Ancient tradition tells that Bezera (Béziers) stood there,[7] but now the Heledus (the Lys) and the Orobus (the Orb) flow through empty fields and piles of ruins which speak of the prosperity which is gone." [8] At that time, according to the same author, the Iberian

---

[1] Schulten, op. cit., pp. 81 ff. ; Jullian, **CCCXLVII**, i, p. 265.
[2] R. Lantier, in **LI**, xxvi, p. 18.
[3] Hecat., frag. 19.
[4] Müllenhoff, **CCCLXII**, i, pp. 63 ff.
[5] Hdt., vii, 165.
[6] *Ora Marit.*, 586.
[7] Philipon, **CCCLXIX**, p. 155.   The Tartessian name of Béziers seems to indicate an earlier advance of the peoples established in the south of Spain (ibid., p. 303).
[8] 591–4.

frontier reached the Hérault (Oranus) and the lake of Thau (Taurus palus).[1] Later it extended as far as the Rhone.[2]

It is possible that the Iberians went up the Rhone valley. A great part of ancient ethnology has come down to us in the form of fables and myths through the epic and lyric poets and the polygraphers. The author of a Περὶ Ποταμῶν ascribed to Plutarch speaks of one Κελτίβηρος, brother of Arar, who seems to be a river which flows into the Saône.[3] Here we perhaps have a recollection of those ancient campaigns of the Iberian bands. One may, too, wonder whether the advance of the Iberians in the fifth century was not preceded by extensive movement in both directions on the Ibero-Ligurian borders.

On the other side the Iberians established themselves in force between the Pyrenees and the Garonne. Eliberre (Auch), Hungunverro,[4] between Toulouse and Auch, and Calagurris,[5] between Toulouse and Saint-Bertrand, were Iberian towns, as were Elusa (Eauze), Iluro (Oloron), Tolosa (Toulouse), and Carcaso (Carcassonne).[6] To these we must add Burdigala [7] (Bordeaux) and perhaps Corbilo [8] (Nantes). The foundation of these cities shows that the Iberians left other things than ruins in their track. They left remains of their civilization, and in particular their pottery,[9] which is

---

[1] 612–614, 628–630. The Ceretes of Cerdagne and the *litus Cyneticum* extend beyond the Pyrenees (ibid., 550–2, 566).

[2] Scylax, 2. Cf. Strabo, iii, 4, 19 (166) ; Pliny, xxxvii, 32 ; Scymnos of Chios, 206–8.

[3] Pseudo-Plut., 6 ; Schulten, op. cit., p. 22.

[4] *Jerusalem Itinerary*, 550, 10.

[5] *Antonine Itinerary*, p. 457.

[6] D'Arbois, op. cit., p. 91 ; Strabo, iv, 1, 1.

[7] Jullian, op. cit., i, p. 264, n. 4.

[8] Schulten, op. cit., pp. 82–3.

[9] Déchelette, in **CXXXIX**, 1908, 2, pp. 400 ff. ; id., *Man.*, ii, 3, pp. 1492 ff. ; Joulin, in **CXXXIX**, 1920, 2, pp. 296 ff. ; P. Thiers, *Recherches sur les Ibères du Roussillon*, repr. from **XL** ; H. Rouzaud, *Notes et observations sur le pays narbonnais*, repr. from **XL**, vii ; id., " L'Oppidum pré-romain d'Ensérune " in **XL**, 1923 ; E. Pottier, " Les Fouilles de Montlaurès," in **LVIII**, 1909, pp. 981 ff. ; P. Thiers, " Fouilles de Castel-Roussillon," in **XXXVIII**, 1910, p. 149 ; E. Pottier, *Les Fouilles d'Ensérune* ; A. Mouret, " Note archéologique sur la céramique d'Ensérune," in **CCCXIII** ; G. Vasseur, " Découverte de poteries peintes à décoration polychrome dans les environs de Marseille," in **LVIII**, 1905, pp. 383 ff. ; id., " La Poterie ibérique pseudo-mycénienne aux environs d'Arles," in **XLIV**, 1907, p. 54. Although there are geometric vases of the fourth century among this pottery, it does not all date from the Iberian occupation ; imported vessels may have been added to it. Besides, it lasted longer than the Iberian occupation, and seems to be the prototype of the painted ware of Montans (La Tène III).

well known from the exploration of Montlaurès, Ensérune, Castel-Roussillon, and le Baou-Roux. It has been found at Marseilles and in the environs of Arles. Sculptured monuments, such as the Grézan statue [1] with the Iberian belt and the bust from Substantion (Sextantio),[2] which wears the same hood as the Grézan statue, tell the same story even more definitely.

The establishment of the Iberians in Aquitaine in the fifth century had one consequence of great importance to the Celts of that region and those of Spain. They were cut off for a long period from the main Celtic body. They no longer received anything from it, and lived on the old stock of Celtic culture which they had brought with them. This is the reason of their local peculiarities. For two or three hundred years there can have been very little direct communication between the Celts of Spain and those of Gaul and Britain, except by sea. There was some, but it has left no visible trace save in the west, besides some indirect traces on the southern edge of the Peninsula, where a few gold or bronze torques and a few brooches of La Tène I have been found, which are absent everywhere else.[3]

The Iberians seem to have held their ground in the Pyrenean country west of the Garonne. But in Languedoc they retreated after less than a hundred years. The *Periplus* of Scylax, attributed to an admiral of Darius but really written about 350 B.C., gives a very different picture of the region from that of Avienus. It places the limit of the Iberians near Emporion, south of the Pyrenees. Between Emporion and the Rhone the Iberians and Ligurians are mixed together—Λίγυες καὶ Ἴβηρες μίγαδες.[4] So the Ligurians had returned as the conquerors had retreated, and the latter had come to terms with them or were holding themselves on the defensive.

---

[1] Espérandieu, **CCCXXV**, i, 427.

[2] Bonnet, in **XC**, 1924, p. 14. We should also add the two busts found at St.-Chaptes, which have the same hood (Espérandieu, op. cit., No. 7614).

[3] Bosch Gimpera, **CCCCXCIX**, p. 41 ; F. Macineira, in **XCVII**, 1923, p. 80 (Gallic gold torque) ; Mariano Sanjuan Moreno, in **XXXIV**, 1916, lxvii, p. 181 (brooches of La Tène I at Castellar de Santisteban, Jaen). Cf. Lantier, **DXI**, pp. 109 ff.

[4] Scylax, 3, D, 17. Cf. Pseudo-Scymnos, 199 ff. He places the Ligurians after the Bebryces, in the neighbourhood of Emporion (Ephoros, 357) ; Schulten, op. cit., 93.

This fact is important for us, for behind the Ligurians as they flowed back came another wave of Gauls, and the return of the Iberians into Spain had consequences on the Celtic settlements in the country which we must examine.

V

THE CELTS ON THE COAST OF PROVENCE

Two hundred years afterwards Timæos, writing about 260, included the Provençal coast of the Mediterranean in the Celtic world. In the *Marvels* attributed to Aristotle there is a passage, which probably comes from Timæos, describing the Heraclean road, that is the Corniche road which runs along the coast of Italy in the Celtic country and passes through the Celto-Ligurians to Iberia. "They say that from Italy into the Celtic country, among the Celto-Ligurians and the Iberians, there is a road which is called the Heraclean Road." [1] This is the oldest historical document which definitely mentions the Celtic country as coming down to the Mediterranean. It is to be supposed that the facts to which that was due, which are not mentioned before this date, happened at least a hundred years before, and are connected with the retreat of the Iberians, for which Scylax is the earliest evidence.

It is true that the Celts had come almost to the coast of Provence long before.[2] But evidence of a less conjectural kind than that with which we have been dealing hitherto is now furnished of their presence.

We read in Justin that about two hundred years after the foundation of Marseilles, that is about 400 B.C., the city was attacked by a coalition of peoples of the neighbourhood, which had taken for its leader a petty king named Catumandus.[3] You could hardly find a more thoroughly Gaulish name than that. Catumandus is He-who-directs-the-battle.[4] The coalition laid siege to the city, but its plans were

---

[1] Pseudo-Arist., 85. Hence the name of Gallicus Sinus given to the Gulf of Lions. Livy, xxvi, 19 ; Strabo, iv, 137 ; Ptol., ii, 10, 2 ; viii, 5, 2 ; d'Arbois, in **CXL**, 1983, p. 85.
[2] See above, pp. 251–2.
[3] Just., 44, 5 ; Schulten, op. cit., p. 93 ; Niese, in Pauly and Wissowa, **CCCLXVIII**, vii, p. 615.
[4] *Catu* : Irish *cath*, Welsh *cad* " battle " (Dottin, **CXCVI**, s.v.).

upset by some religious sign, so it abandoned the attack. The Marseilles people sent gifts of thanksgiving to the Temple of Delphi. On the return their messengers brought news of the capture of Rome by the Gauls. Therefore the incident occurred about 390.

The Celts had lived along the coast, associated or mingled with the Ligurians, since the end of the fifth century. I have said that the Carthaginians recruited mercenaries among the Elisyces on the coast of Provence in 480. Henceforward they would come there for Celtic or Gaulish mercenaries. In 263, when the Romans sent two legions into Sicily after concluding an agreement with Hieron of Syracuse, the Carthaginians sent there an army of Iberian, Ligurian, and Celtic mercenaries.[1] The last-named were not Celts of Spain, for at this time, as we shall see, these would have been not Celts but Celtiberians. They were Celts of Gaul. This recruiting must have started a long time before, for these are probably the men to whom reference is made in a curious speech which Thucydides makes Alcibiades address to the Spartans. It is during the Sicilian war, in 415. Alcibiades has been banished and turns traitor ; he proposes to go and enlist an army of Iberians and other very special barbarians who have appeared in that quarter : καὶ ἄλλους τῶν ἐκεῖ ὁμολογουμένως νῦν βαρβάρων μαχιμωτάτους (" and others who are recognized to be the most warlike of the barbarians now there ").[2]

Having arrived on the Provençal coast in the last years of the fifth century, the Celts, who in this district never succeeded in completely absorbing the Ligurians, continued their advance in the direction of Languedoc.[3] The Iberians did not resist, and Polybios, an accurate and well-informed historian, wrote about 150 : " One meets nothing but Celts from Narbo and its neighbourhood to the Pyrenees." At all events, when Hannibal, sixty years before, in 218, passed through Roussillon and Languedoc on his way to the Alps, with an army largely composed of Celts, it seems that he met nothing but Gauls.

[1] Pol., i, 17, 4.
[2] Thuc., vi, 90, 3.
[3] Joulin, in **CXXXIX**, 1923, 2, p. 197. La Tène tombs with red-figured Attic pottery at Toulouse, Ensérune, Mataro, and San Feliú de Guixols.

INDEX

Note.—References are given to figures and notes, but only where there is no reference for the subject to the text of the same page.

BOOK
II

(The publishers wish to point out that the original page numbering has been retained for this volume, *The Greatness and Decline of the Celts*.)

THE
GREATNESS
AND
DECLINE
OF THE
Celts

HENRI HUBERT

CONTENTS

v

CONTENTS

PART TWO

THE END OF THE CELTIC WORLD

PART THREE

THE CIVILIZATION OF THE CELTS

CONTENTS

MAPS

FOREWORD

THE CELTIC GENIUS

I HAVE already explained and justified the division of Hubert's work on the Celts into two volumes.

With the present volume we find ourselves in the La Tène period. It begins by describing a new expansion, then a retreat, the florescence and decline of the Celtic world.

It is about 500 B.C. that the La Tène civilization appears with an increase of the population, which descends from the heights into the plains, an advance in technical processes, and a growth of prosperity which give rise to the great historical expeditions. The movements which now take place are different from those described in the previous volume, about which we have little direct information. From definite evidence it can be seen that operations now assume a " co-ordinated, concerted, and, one might say, political character " (p. 18), and that is a great novelty among the Celts. All round the circumference of the Celtic world this activity manifests itself—first in Italy, the Danube Valley, and Britain, and then in Eastern Europe and Asia Minor, the south-west of France, and even in Spain. They found settlements, or rather the previous inhabitants mingle with them, and they contribute and receive in varying proportions. But what the advanced bodies receive— for example, the idea of a political life in Italy, and intellectual and moral culture in Greece—will benefit the whole Celtic world, doubtless in different degrees. The Celts " enter the history of the world " (p. 32). " Unsettled and unruly elements," bands of barbarians, " great companies," will still break in ; the energy, courage, and " roving spirit " of the Celts will make some of them mercenaries in great demand, free-lances scattered among many peoples. " Mercenary service was a regular Celtic industry, and a well paid one " (pp. 64, 66, 90). But the mass of the race is settled, and the Celts are involved in the politics and economics of the whole world. Being both inventive and receptive, they are agents for the unification and progress of mankind. There are, it is true, Gallic Celts and British Celts, Celts of the Danube and

ix

Germany and Italy ; but a Celtic civilization has grown up which is comparatively homogeneous and comparatively native in its character.

From the end of the third century onwards the Celts are in conflict with Rome on every side. Their civilization stands face to face with a different, and in some respects higher, civilization, while from behind they are pressed by a people of lower culture, the Germans, with whom, as we know, they have a real " intimacy " (p. 93). The more active the civilizing and political influence of the Celts is in Germany, the harder they will be pressed by their neighbours, to be finally driven back. There was a twofold process— " a process of assimilation of the German world on the one hand, but on the other, as a result of that very assimilation, a process of penetration by the Germans into the Celtic world " (p. 103). The Cimbri, Teutones, Suevi were Celticized Germans, mixed with Celts to a various extent.

Gradually the Celts are driven back on themselves. The Rhine becomes the frontier of the western Celts. In the course of their disturbed history main peoples and subordinate groups have parted, reunited, mixed, and passed one another. Now they are in what are almost their final positions. The Celtic world has assumed what Hubert strikingly describes as " the face under which it was last known to antiquity, and it was a face of death ". At this moment " its features appear in broad daylight and that thanks to its conqueror " (p. 119). The Romans, and Cæsar above all, help us greatly to picture them.

Hubert, in the part of his work describing the civilization of the Celts, begins by studying their social structure. As a sociologist, he compares one Celtic society with another, he compares them with other Indo-European societies and points out their common characteristics, and he looks in them for survivals of primitive organizations, earlier than the Indo-European societies, traces of clan life (pp. 190, 198, 201). For this task he gets valuable information from Irish and Welsh sources, his use of which he justifies. In short, he is concerned with the evolution of society as such, and, if he draws upon his general sociological knowledge for the study of the Celts, he makes repayment in bringing interesting data and confirmations to sociology.

In doing this Hubert followed his natural inclination ; he was applying and reinforcing the knowledge born of his wide interest. But he was also adhering to the programme of this series. One feature of this synthesis, l'Évolution de l'Humanité, *is that it presents sociology and history in intimate association. Not only do we, in the case of each human group, pay due attention to the study of institutions, but we endeavour to determine the role of society as society, to make plain the relations of the social and the individual. Our readers know this ; and they also know that, on account either of the subject or of the bent of the author, some volumes more than others enable us to set the social in its place in history and to reflect on problems of a theoretical nature.*

Hubert's work, in its contribution to the study of the Celtic societies and of society in general, raises some most interesting problems.

Although he speaks here and there of Celtic " nations " and seems in one passage to credit the Celts with a national consciousness,[1] he points out clearly in several places the distinction between society and nation. There was no more a Celtic nation than a Greek.[2] The Celts are no more a nation than they are a race [3] ; they are " a group of peoples, or, to speak more accurately, a group of societies " (Rise of the Celts, *p. 33). As the greater Celtic world missed the opportunity to become a kind of great confederation, so the smaller Celtic world of Gaul " missed, in Vercingetorix, the opportunity of becoming, side by side with the Roman Republic, the prototype of the modern great nation " (pp. 147–8). Now—and this is the important point—that was because Gaul " had not at that time acquired the rudiments of a state structure without which a nation cannot be made " (ibid.).[4] A society may have every kind of aptitude for forming a nation but fail to be a nation if it is not strongly rooted in a soil and definitely organized as a state. And, however wide a society, or a collection of societies having the same civilization, may be, one cannot speak of empire (as I have said) [5] when no central power has asserted itself, when there is no unifying state.*

[1] *" But if a nation already existed, it was because that which makes the deep-seated unity of a nation existed—a common ideal, the same ways of thinking and feeling, in short, everything that nations express by symbols and all the most intimate part of their civilization "* (Rise of the Celts, p. 13).

[2] *See* Jardé, Formation of the Greek People, *in this series, pt. iv. Cf. Jullian,* Histoire de la Gaule, *i, ch. ix.*

[3] *See* Rise of the Celts, Foreword, *p. xiii.*

[4] *In a Celtic society, the state usually remains rudimentary and almost undifferentiated. . . . The Celtic societies are at the tribal stage, and have only a private law "* (p. 196).

[5] Rise of the Celts, Foreword, *p. xx.*

Of Celtic civilization, on the other hand, we can speak, for the various branches of the Celts had a real sense of oneness, a family likeness, a common language, and we know that language is among the most typical phenomena of a culture (p. 187 ; Rise of the Celts, p. 33). But among all these phenomena a distinction must be made, and this is important. And, although the study of civilization and that of society seem to coincide, all that constitutes a civilization (and goes on in a society) is not properly and essentially social.

With the conception of sociology now in vogue (which is ethnographic) and the present conception of history (which is in a certain sense synthetic), the word " civilization " is used more and more in a broad and sometimes rather vague way. No doubt there is no reason why one should not, in describing racial groups and in order to define them, make use of political and economic institutions, arts, crafts, and religion, all together and as of equal relevance. There is no reason why one should not, under the word " civilization ", include the most diverse manifestations of human activity. From any point of view other than that of scientific causality, of synthesis of the second degree, there is no need for a closer discussion of the valuable information which Hubert presents in the third part of this volume, entitled " Civilization " under the headings " Structure of Society ", " Setting of Social Life ", and " Social Activities ". But for a fundamental explanation it is possible and legitimate to consider matters in more detail.

Hubert himself would not deny it ; and we found in his work, here and there, statements which enable us to press our explanation deeper. When, for instance, he says : " Every group of men living together forms a physical, social, and moral unit " (Rise, p. 21), he makes an interesting distinction. And when he says elsewhere that the love of the Celts for general ideas helped to make the lofty, mellow civilizations of antiquity into the civilization of the world (Rise, p. 15), he quite clearly shows the part played by the logical factor, as distinct from the social.

What strikes one in the Celts is just the fact that the part which they played in history was logical, and civilizing in the limited sense of that term, rather than social in the proper and strict sense of the word.[1] If they do not seem to have excelled as citizens, if they failed politically, " through having no sense of the state or an insufficient sense of discipline," they take their revenge and are

[1] See Rise of the Celts, p. 15.

important in history by the value of the individual and the develop-
ment of personality (pp. 9–10, 271, 276). The tribal system lasted a
long time among them ; gradually, through contact with the land, it
became aristocratic, feudal ; then, in town life, an urban class
grew up. As always happens where the social organization is not
heavy, oppressive, centralizing, and levelling, the conscience was
able to waken and the mind to exert activity.[1] The Celts were at
once inventors (p. 260) and ready assimilators.

"Eager for everything that was not Celtic" (p. 140),
"with their curiosity about civilization" (p. 10), they fell
surprisingly quickly into the ways of the more civilized peoples
with which they mingled or had dealings of any kind (p. 55).[2]
"The stranger from the Mediterranean always had a special
charm for them" (p. 140). So, with their physical mobility
and mental elasticity, they acted as middlemen of civilization ;
they were "torch-bearers" in Europe (p. 62 ; Rise, p. 15).

But, receptive though they were, they had their own native
character, a common ideal, a "soul of the people", one might
say, of course, without giving the words a metaphysical meaning.
Camille Jullian has said that Celtic unity was "in the domain
of poets rather than of statesmen"[3] ; it was, indeed, a work of
the mind, the work of the poets—and of the Druids. Druidism
was the chief uniting factor, the "cement" of Celtic society
(p. 227). There was nothing of the priest-king in the Druids ;
their part was more specifically spiritual. They were men of
God, depositories of wisdom and science, directors of consciences,
and teachers of the young and of their whole people.[4] Their
doctrine turned towards nature, in agrarian festivals, but still
more towards man, in its concern for morals. With a high,
manly ideal of life, they at once despised death and aspired to
the immortality of the soul. "To worship the gods, to do nothing
base, and to practise manhood"—this Druidical axiom, which
Hubert takes from Diogenes Laërtios, is admirable.[5] Certain
elements of Druidism come from the Indo-European foundation
and are related to the teaching of the Brahmins, of the Magi,
of the Orphicists[6] ; but the accent of their religion is

[1] *Cf.* Formation of the Greek People, *Foreword, p. xii ;* Israel, *Foreword ;*
both in this series.
[2] *Cf.* Primitive Italy *and* Ancient Persia, *both in this series, Forewords.*
[3] *Jullian,* Hist. de la Gaule, *i, p. 381.*
[4] *Cf. Albert Bayet,* La Morale des Gaulois, *pp. 163–4.*
[5] Rise of the Celts, *p. 14 ; cf. below, p. 271.*
[6] *See the volumes in this series on Greek religion, ancient Persia, and India.*

thoroughly Celtic, deeply human, as it is in its haunting sense of death and its worship of heroes.

Hubert follows Celticism, after its collapse, in its various survivals. He shows it holding out with its language in the extreme west of Europe, cherishing and writing down its legends, and long afterwards, in the twentieth century, making an independent nation in Ireland.

But the essential survival of Celticism he finds and shows us in Romanized Gaul, in the France of all ages. We cannot conceal the fact that this historian, with all his devotion to objective science, seems to have a sort of tenderness for the Celtic genius. I do not think that it leads him astray, but it infuses emotion into many pages of his work, particularly those which tell of the effects of Celticism on the history of the French nation.

The Celts made the France of to-day. They are responsible for the appropriation of the soil, the judicious choice of dwelling-places and roads. Above all, into this setting they introduced their " soul of the people ". For Gaul to acquire a true national consciousness, only a strongly organized state was needed. We have, too, seen a wonderful agent of unification, social discipline, and energetic but elastic government come into being and grow up in Rome.[1] With a dim sense of what they lacked the Celts welcomed Roman rule with astonishing readiness. For, in the penetrating words of Renouvier, " what they liked was not so much independence as to be dependent only on what they liked." [2] In their evident superiors the Celts were willing to see friends and guides.[3] They yielded, and at the same time they resisted. They accepted the authority and culture of Rome, but they kept their Celtic soul, or the essential part of it. " The Gallo-Romans mostly continued to be disguised Celts (Rise, p. 14).

[1] Primitive Italy and Roman Political Institutions ; cf. below, pp. 69, 154.
[2] Introduction à la philosophie analytique de l'Histoire, p. 390 ; " Their devotion to Julius Cæsar, who defeated them for ten years, followed on their devotion to Vercingetorix, who defended their liberty. . . . From the Druids they accepted a kind of Papacy. . . . Of Rome, lastly, that is, of the Empire, they at once appreciated the scientific administrative methods and the admirably formulated law, so much so, that they set themselves up as the successors and, when necessary, the substitutes of the last Romans. That, in fact, is what they became, and among modern peoples the principle of the strong state for a long time had them for its champions."
[1] For the relations of the Celts and Rome, see pp. 86, 97, 148. See also Bayet, op. cit., p. xi.

Like Chapot in his account of Roman Gaul in The Roman World, *Hubert here in his account of the Gallic Celts finds the intellectual and moral foundations of France. It is true that the Romans, for all their tolerance, seem to have persecuted the Druids, but Romanization, which was accepted partly willingly and partly perforce, allowed certain mental qualities of Celticism to survive, and, indeed, developed them in Gallo-Roman civilization, and those qualities are an essential part of the spirit of France—observation, justice, measure, elasticity.*

Plastic art rose to no great heights in Gaul, but decorative art adorned everything with that delicate sense of the beautiful which is called taste.

The Latin language, adopted by the Gauls, not only retained certain Celtic ingredients, but was intimately transformed, becoming analytical. We see the men who gave it a new character as " great talkers " ; they had talents for eloquence and poetry, for an eloquence which aimed at action and for a poetry which readily turned to the dramatic or gnomic.

Of the literature of the Celts, which for a long time was popular, oral, a somewhat untrue idea was at first formed, as a result of Renan's famous article on the poetry of the Celtic races.[1] It was supposed to be elegiac and very feminine in character. This conception was only justified by the state of Celtic studies at the time. Since then, the labours of such men as Gaidoz, d'Arbois de Jubainville, Loth, Ernault, Le Braz, and Dottin have revealed a poetry "bursting with heroic sap", the expression of " vehement, passionate, almost brutal natures, eager for action and intoxicated with movement and noise".[2] No doubt the Celts gave a very large place to woman, both in life and in lyric poetry. But the romantic and marvellous, the workings of love and fate, those themes which surround the adventures of the British heroes—Arthur, Tristram, Parsifal—must not blind us to a whole side of masculine poetry, nor to one of humorous observation.

When the Celts of Gaul had thrown over their epic tradition, " attracted by the more refined civilization which the Romans brought," they kept its spirit, and it is this spirit, according to

---

[1] *In Rev. des Deux Mondes, 1st February, 1854.*

[2] *Anatole Le Braz, " Le Drame dans l'épopée celtique," in Rev. des Deux Mondes, 1st July, 1904 : " A people at once violent and sensitive, imaginative, and pugnacious, greedy for ideals and for action." Dottin, " La littérature gaëlique de l'Irlande," in Rev. de Synth. hist., iii, p. 63.*

Hubert, that animates the work of the French chroniclers and gives them a dramatic character. From Gregory of Tours and the monks of Saint-Denis they made the history of France " the finest historical narrative in the world ". And the actual story of France, like its written history, " the history of that undestroyable people of peasants, warriors, and artists, with its glories and tumults, its hopes and enthusiasms, its discords and rebirths, is surely the story of a nation whose blood and bones are mainly composed of Celtic elements " (Rise, pp. 14–15 ; below, pp. 269, 276).

One cannot lay too great emphasis on the range of the work done by Hubert in this study of the Celts, which will be completed by that of the Germans. It helps one to understand France. It is rich in teaching, without ever revealing a desire to generalize. It makes one see how men, beyond societies, create nations, how they arrive at the feeling and then at the idea of a fatherland. Patria nostra *will soon become* France dulce. *Perhaps the misfortunes of the third century, " by the suffering of the country," contributed to the national education of the people of Gaul. " They gave it those venerable wrinkles which men have always loved to see on the face of their motherland " (p. 155)— an exquisite phrase which is the expression of the whole Hubert, historian, thinker, and writer.*

HENRI BERR.

PART ONE

CELTIC EXPANSION IN THE LA TÈNE PERIOD

CHAPTER I

THE CELTS IN ITALY

I

THE CIVILIZATION OF LA TÈNE. EXTENSION OF GALLIC SETTLE-
MENTS IN GAUL

THE new movements of expansion mentioned in the last
chapters of the previous volume, *The Rise of the Celts*,
are the effects in general history of something that had been
going on inside Gaul and the Celtic regions of Germany
since the time of the first Celtic settlements in Aquitaine
and in Spain and first Celtic inroads into Italy, that is, since
550 B.C. These events are marked in archæology by the change
from the civilization called after Hallstatt to that called
after La Tène.[1] All over the region situated west of the
Alps and the Central Plateau, the change took place in less
than a hundred years. From Provence [2] to Thuringia [3]
the civilization of the first La Tène period is represented.
It begins about 500. The spread of the new styles strikes
one less by its rapidity than by its universality. Everywhere
the Celts fell into line with those who had started the fashion.
This is interesting evidence of the unity and continuity of
the Celtic world. But the fashion did not change merely in
dress, arms, pottery, or art ; funeral rites also changed,
and equally universally. Moreover, the area covered by the
La Tène civilization almost everywhere extends beyond that
of the Hallstatt culture. Inhabited sites are found closer
together ; vacant spaces are filled up. The Celtic population
is at once more numerous and, in general, denser. Certainly

---

[1] See *Rise* (i.e. Hubert, *The Rise of the Celts*, in this series), ch. iv, § i.
[2] Déchelette, **CCCXVIII**, ii, 3, p. 999 ; cf. p. 1055, fig. 435, 6 (Gard).
[3] Schumacher, **CCCCIX**, i, p. 120.

colonization went on inside the Celtic world, and there were shiftings of the population, perhaps conflicts and disorders. But on the whole there was an increase of power which had for consequence the colonizing expeditions into Britain and Italy and, later, into the Danube valley and, lastly, into Spain.

In craftsmanship [1] the civilization of La Tène is the direct continuation of that of the last period of Hallstatt. It develops the legacy of Hallstatt; at least, it implies it as an immediate predecessor. We have seen this already : the La Tène sword is a dagger with antennæ, elongated ; the La Tène brooch is a Certosa brooch, with an upturned foot, the end of which curls back towards the bow ; the bracelets and torques are very much alike ; and the pottery carries on the Hallstatt types with provincial peculiarities. The chief difference comes from the imitation of Greek objects and decoration, due to relations established either on the Marseilles side or by way of the Danube valley. The problem raised by these changes is entirely one of the simple problems connected with the history of the progress of civilizations. It is not so, in my opinion, with the funeral rites. Here the changes come about in quite a peculiar way.

At the end of the Hallstatt period, the practice of cremation was almost universal among the Celts. Moreover, the ashes of the dead were laid in tumuli of the same type as those containing the previous burials. On the other hand, we may say that for a period of over two hundred years, beginning about 500 B.C., the practice of cremation was almost abandoned, and that fairly abruptly, as it would appear. The change was not absolutely instantaneous, nor quite universal. Cremation-tombs of La Tène I have been found in the Haute-Marne and Haute-Saône and, above all, in the valley of the Rhine. But they are exceptional, and we may take it that the exception confirms the rule. It shows that the disappearance of the earlier rite was due to its being dropped by the same people as had formerly practised it, and that, since the new rule did not prevail all at once, it was not adopted as a matter of course.

Furthermore, the use of tumuli was given up in the Celtic world as a whole. The typical tomb of the La Tène period

[1] For changes introduced in material civilization, see *Rise*, ch. v.

is an oblong grave, in which the body is laid with or without a coffin.[1] This change, too, was abrupt in certain parts, but it was not universal.

In the old Hallstatt settlements, the Celts continued to build tumuli in the La Tène period. In Germany [2] all the tombs which can be dated between 500 and 400 B.C. are tumuli, and so are some of those dating from 400 to 300. In Switzerland,[3] this practice continued for about a hundred years, till about 100. In Alsace,[4] Lorraine,[5] Haute-Marne,[6] Burgundy, and Franche-Comté,[7] the vast majority of La Tène tombs were found under tumuli.

But we must make a distinction. For one thing, the Celts of the tumulus countries utilized the old tumuli and dug new tombs in them ; for another, we know a certain number of tumuli which were deliberately erected to cover several burials. So each tumulus might become a little cemetery. But it is none the less true that tumuli were built in the La Tène period in these regions to cover at least one principal tomb. On the whole, tumulus-building lasted in certain parts of the Celtic area until the third period of La Tène, that is, till the first century B.C.

Where Hallstatt tumuli were rare, the La Tène tombs are always flat-graves. This is so in the Department of the Marne, where there are so many La Tène cemeteries.[8]

But here again there is a point to consider. In the cemeteries of the Marne and Aisne, mounds have been noted, which are tumuli, apparently empty. The cemetery of Nanteuil, in the Aisne, consisted in part of a vast tumulus, like the Burgundian tumuli which contain many graves. Lastly, such place-names as Les Buttes, La Motte, La Motelle, La Tomelle, coinciding with Gallic cemeteries, suggest tumuli which have disappeared. What is more, single tombs (like the chariot-burial at Berru) [9] and groups of tombs are

---

[1] Déchelette, ii, 3, pp. 1030 ff.
[2] Ibid., pp. 1063 ff.
[3] Ibid., pp. 1082 ff. ; Gruaz and Viollier in **XVII,** 1914 pp. 257 ff. ; 1915 pp. 1 ff. (Gallic cemetery at St. Sulpice, Vaud).
[4] Déchelette, ii, 3, pp. 1069–1070.
[5] Ibid., p. 1042.
[6] Ibid., pp. 1041–2.
[7] Ibid., pp. 1043 ff.
[8] For maps of cemeteries of the La Tène period in the Dept. of the Marne see ibid., p. 1018, fig. 423.
[9] Ibid., p. 1026, fig. 426.

surrounded by a circular ditch.   Circular enclosure and
tumulus are found simultaneously in yet other regions, in
England for example, and stand for the same culture.   It
should be noted that in two places the tumulus won the day
—in England [1] and in the lower valley of the Rhone,[2] where
there were new Celtic settlements dating from La Tène.
In both cases, we may suppose that the settlement took
place before the time when the flat-grave was beginning to
gain the upper hand.   In England, moreover, the La Tène
tumuli are probably just continuations of the round barrows
of the previous inhabitants.   So there was, at least, a period
of varying practice, which continued longer, or even indefinitely, where there were many tumuli.

We have already seen one group of Celts giving up its
tumuli for cemeteries of flat-graves.   This was the branch
which occupied Aquitaine and Spain.[3] This is a change similar
to that which we have just noted all over the Celtic world,
and it may have come about in the same way.   I am inclined
to think that the flat-graves are tombs reduced to their
simplest expression by communities which were denser than
those of the Hallstatt age, and, therefore, more anxious to
save space and not to spread out their cemeteries.   These
are considerations which matter in the history of funeral
rites.[4]

But we are still left with some novelties—the oblong
grave, the coffin, and, above all, the orientation.   In the
flat-grave cemeteries, the dead are laid east and west, with
the head to the west, and the older the cemetery is the more
regular is this rule.

New practices imply new ideas.   There can be no question
of a cataclysm, with new peoples taking the place of old
peoples wholesale.   The spread of the new ideas may have
been due to propaganda.   More than once, one has to resort

---

[1] Ibid., pp. 1102 ff.
[2] Ibid., p. 1056.
[3] See *Rise*, pp. 283 ff.
[4] Déchelette (ii, 3, p. 1015) ascribes the abolition of the tumulus to a
desire to hide the grave, for protection, from the eyes of the foreigners in the
midst of whom the Celts were advancing.   But it must not be forgotten that
the La Tène flat-graves are grouped in cemeteries.   If they had been completely hidden, these tombs would have been dug one above another or
would have cut one into another.   This does occur, but rarely.   We must
conclude that the graves had outward marks, a monument perhaps or a
small mound, a wooden post, or something of the sort.

to this hypothesis to explain some general phenomenon revealing the moral life of prehistoric peoples. But how did the propaganda take place and who conducted it ? It seems to me that we must imagine imitation on the one side and authority or the preponderance of new elements on the other —in any case, new demographic and social conditions.

For every change in the appearance of the prehistoric civilizations there has been a movement of the population, greater or less. So it was at the beginning of the La Tène period. The arrival of new peoples can be seen clearly at certain points.

One of these is the Department of the Marne.[1] If we go by archæological finds alone, we find it with very few inhabitants in the Bronze Age and almost completely depopulated in the Hallstatt period. In the La Tène period, on the other hand, it was covered with a very dense population. No less than 191 Gallic cemeteries have been found there. Within about twenty years, over a hundred tombs have been explored. In the cemetery of Les Croncs, at Bergères-les-Vertus, over a thousand have been opened. This large number of cemeteries represents a numerous and entirely new population. For one cannot suppose that all Hallstatt tumuli have succeeded in escaping the eye of the antiquary in this department, where tomb-hunting is almost a sport.

Another region, which was, indeed, inhabited in Hallstatt times, but sparsely, received in the La Tène period a fairly large population, quite differently grouped, and that was Switzerland.[2] There the La Tène tombs are distributed in two groups. An eastern group extends from Basle to the lakes of Zurich and the Four Cantons. Near Basle there is a large cemetery, that of Muttenz. The valleys of the Glatt, the Limmatt, and the Reuss contain Celtic cemeteries. A region in which the Aar still receives a few small tributaries divides this group from the western, which extends from the neighbourhood of Berne to the Lake of Geneva. The centre of the first group is Zurich and that of the second is Berne. In the district of Berne alone, in the immediate environs of the city, eighteen cemeteries of the La Tène period are known.

[1] Ibid., p. 1020, and app. v.
[2] Viollier, **CCCCXCII**, pp. 59 ff.

The Hallstatt tumuli were in quite small groups, corre-
sponding to a population which changed its abode easily.
The cemeteries of La Tène are those of a fixed population. In
some of them over two hundred tombs have been opened.
Between these two settlements, the old groupings of the
Hallstatt population do not seem to have been touched.
We shall see later to what extent we must suppose them to
have been penetrated by new elements.

We may picture bodies forcing their way across older
settlements. In Haute-Saône [1] a small Marne cemetery has
been found, which probably represents the settlement of a
small colony of new-comers. Further south, in Dauphiné
and the Alps,[2] cemeteries or single tombs of the Marne type
stand for recent settlements, the density of which we have
no means of estimating. In Provence [3] there are no burials
of the new type, but objects of the first La Tène period found
in the fortified enclosures, particularly brooches, announce the
arrival of Celts in a new domain.

In the west, except in Normandy [4] and certain places in
Brittany [5] and Berry,[6] the chance which guides archæological
discoveries has been very unfavourable to the Gauls. The
archæological map of the cemeteries is almost blank.[7] The
few swords found in the dragging of rivers would not fill it.
And yet we must suppose that at this time there were Celts
settled everywhere between the Seine and the Garonne.
This blank space in the map leaves room for all kinds of
conjecture. In any case, we may suppose that the settlements developed gradually and that those which reached
furthest forward do not belong to the early phase of the
La Tène civilization.

No normal increase of the old Celtic occupants of Lorraine
and Alsace, of Burgundy and Franche-Comté, would have
sufficed for the foundation of the new settlements in

[1] Déchelette, ii 3, p. 1046 (cemetery at Mercey).
[2] E. Chantre, in *Bull. Anthr. et biolog. de Lyon*, 1913–17, pp. 17 ff. (cemetery
at Genas, Isère) ; H. Muller, in **CXLVI**, 1920, pp. 16 ff. (cemetery at Pariset,
near La Tour-sans-Venin, Isère).
[3] Vasseur, in **XI**, xiii, 3, 1903 (Le Baou-Roux) ; cf. Déchelette, ii, 3, p. 1001.
The fortified enclosures of Provence were occupied from 600 B.C. onwards
and abandoned about 125 B.C. Cf. Justin, 43, 4.
[4] Déchelette, ii, 3, p. 1060.
[5] Ibid., pp. 945–6, 1060.
[6] Ibid., pp. 1049–1050.
[7] Ibid., map iii (La Tène tombs and cemeteries in France).

Champagne, Switzerland, Dauphiné, and Provence, to say nothing of the others. We are therefore compelled to imagine something similar to what I have suggested as an explanation of the Hallstatt occupation, a sort of drift of the Celtic tribes from the Rhine valley and beyond, or possibly definite invasions. It is, moreover, hard to believe that the evolution of the Hallstatt types of object from which the types characteristic of the La Tène culture sprang occurred anywhere but in the German domain of the Celts. Indeed, transitional forms abound in Germany whereas they are rare in France. It is in Germany that the civilization of La Tène makes its first appearance and first becomes really rich. I think, therefore, that on the whole it originated in Germany, and that it was from Germany that, between 500 and 400 B.C., the bodies set out which peopled Switzerland on the one side, Champagne on the other, and all the other districts which we can suppose to have been covered by this colonization. From where exactly did they start ? Probably from more than one point in Celtic Germany.[1] The question will arise later.

Lastly, although the funeral rites of the Gauls of this epoch are those of a military people which sends its men into the next world in fighting-gear, or at least in parade-dress, I cannot help noting the peaceful character of the new Celtic settlements.

We must picture the population of Champagne as dispersed in large open villages, which must necessarily have been agricultural villages. Champagne had not attracted the Hallstatt stock-breeders. I am inclined to think that, among the progress made by Celtic civilization in the La Tène period, there was some in agriculture, and that the men who stayed in Champagne knew how to make use of the dry slopes of its hills and, still more, of the richer uplands of the Aisne, with their heavy soil, where we also find them established. It is probable that the plough,[2] a good plough, the Gallic name of which survived in Roman Gaul (*carruca*), with a coulter and probably wheels, was the invention which made it possible to till this ground. I imagine the landscape

[1] Rademacher, in Ebert, **CCCXXIV**, s.v. " Kelten ", vi, pp. 285–6.
[2] Déchelette, ii 3, pp. 1378 ff. ; Dottin **CCCXXII**, pp. 192 ff. ; Reinecke, in **LXVII**, 1919, pp. 17 ff.

which they created in Champagne and the Aisne as something like that part of the country which has not been given over to vineyards, with ploughed fields running down the sides of the hills.[1] Their settlements in Switzerland were of the same character, and presented the same appearance. They still do ; the contrast between the ploughed hillsides and the upland pasture-ground about Berne and the Lake of Thun is very remarkable and strange. It is a spectacle which implies peoples of different economic habits living side by side. But in my opinion it is a prehistoric spectacle.

I have called attention to the great number of Gallic names in *-magus* and in *-ialum* in Gaul properly so called. They designate settlements in the plains, agricultural markets or centres of activity.[2]

But there is something more. Except in Germany and Provence, where special circumstances and the presence of unruly neighbours compelled the Gauls to stand on their guard, there are no fortified places belonging to the earlier periods of La Tène. The Hallstatt forts had been abandoned and the Gallic *oppida* were not yet built. For instance, in Franche-Comté, the occupation of the camp of Château-sur-Salins,[3] which was an admirable site for a fortress, seems to have been interrupted in La Tène I.

It is surprising to come upon a peaceful Gaul just before the invasions of Italy and Greece, but we have to accept it. That all went smoothly always, it would be rash to imagine. That there were no shiftings of population, no fluctuations of frontiers, is very unlikely ; that there were no small wars is impossible ; and we should find evidence of them if we examined these very cemeteries of the Marne. But the Gauls of France did not live in a world of constant violence and strife. Therefore their communities developed and multiplied in peace. Their nations and tribes generally lived on terms of international justice and policy which made it possible for social life to become organized. Indeed, that is why they had the surplus man-power and the inter-tribal concord which allowed them to make the great expeditions to which we now come.

---

[1] H. Muller-Brauel, in **LXXXV**, 1926, pp. 184 ff.
[2] Jullian, **CCCXLVII**, i, pp. 238 ff.
[3] Piroutet, in **CXXXIX**,, 1928, 2, pp. 266 ff.

II

THE GREAT GALLIC INVASION OF ITALY

The civilization of La Tène spread in France between 500 and 400 B.C. It is just about this latter date that we must place the Celtic invasion of Italy which was the first of the great historical expeditions of the Celts.

All the ancient historians agree in describing the descent of the Celts into Italy as a mass invasion on the part of a people which was a huge army, speedily ending in the extermination of the former occupants of the country and the foundation of a very large colony. At the bottom of all their accounts there is doubtless a version written for the occasion which probably comes from Timagenes.[1] But, apart from the fact that Timagenes generally had fairly good information, in the account of the earliest Gallic wars there are probably good traditional elements, for which the Celts themselves were partly responsible. Gallic historians like Cornelius Nepos, who was an Insubrian, and Trogus Pompeius, who was a Vocontian, may have had a part in handing them on. This history, in which both sides have collaborated, is assuredly epic and heroic rather than purely historical.

But after all, the accuracy of the anecdotal details does not matter much. The history of the first Gallic wars appears to have been built up on a fairly sure chronological foundation with materials which are rather fabulous, but nevertheless of very great value, much like all that part of ancient history which has not been written by contemporaries. On the whole, it has survived criticism remarkably well. Archæology adds to it without correcting it.

It is of capital interest to us, in that it gives us the earliest information that we have of at all a detailed kind about the making of a Celtic settlement, and this information seems to be trustworthy. There is an artificial confederation of tribes from different districts, some newly formed, others old, among which foreign bodies may find a place. They go forward. Some settle down at once. Others hesitate and take longer to find their resting-place. They go about the country,

---

[1] Niese, in Pauly and Wissowa, **CCCLXVIII**, vii, col. 613 ; Hirschfeld, in **CLXVIII**, 1894, p. 331 ; d'Arbois, **CCXLVIII**, xii, p. 51 ; Müllenhoff, **CCCLXII**, ii, p. 613 ; Jullian, **CCCXLVII**, i, p. 281.

fighting, treating, employing policy. Others follow them,
summoned by them or tempted by their example. At last
they are so many that they form a huge mass. Corners and
outlines are rubbed away. The Gauls, with their curiosity
about civilization, become assimilated to their new
surroundings. They prosper in peace, but their political
formations disintegrate and finally collapse.

All the historians except Livy [1] run events together,
placing them between 396 and 386 B.C.[2] But Livy's account
is not substantially different from the rest. Of the first
invasion he only gives the date, and on the whole he passes
it over. A certain number of chronological concordances
have been established—the first year of the ninety-eighth
Olympiad and the Archonship of Pyrgion in Athens
(388–387 B.C.),[3] the Archonship of Theodotos, the Peace of
Antalcidas, the siege of Rhegion, and the second year of
the ninety-eighth Olympiad (387–386 B.C.).[4] Cornelius
Nepos [5] places the entrance of the Gauls into Italy at the
same time as the capture of Veii by Camillus, in 396. In
Roman chronology, the uncertainty of the particular date
is due to the way in which dictators may have upset the
reckoning of Consulships.[6] At all events, we may agree
to place the capture of Rome in the year 387–386.

The most interesting thing which Livy adds to the accounts
of his fellow-historians is the idea of a kind of political plan,
which he supposes to have lain behind the expedition. The
Celticum formed a confederation, at the head of which was
the King of the Bituriges, whose name at that time was
Ambicatus.[7] The population exceeded the normal size of
agricultural tribes attached to the land.[8] Ambicatus

---

[1] See *Rise* pp. 263–4.
[2] Homo, **CCCXLI**, English, pp. 165 ff.; Grenier, **DXXIX**, pp. 64 ff.;
Meyer, **CCCLIV**, v, pp. 151 ff.
[3] Dion., i 74; App., *Celtica*, 2, 1.
[4] Polyb., i, 6; Diod., xiv, 113, 1; Just., vi, 6, 5.
[5] Pliny, *N.H.*, iii, 125; Unger, *Römisch-griechische Synchronismen vor
Pyrrhos*, repr. from **XXI**,, 1876, 1.
[6] O. Leuze, **CCCLI**, *passim*.
[7] Livy, v, 34. The Gaul of Ambicatus, with its High King, provided
by one of the confederate nations, is constituted like the Ireland of
St. Patrick's day.
[8] The development of the Celtic family, as we know it in Ireland and
Wales, results in the exclusion of a certain number of individuals from the
original property of the family, and this necessitates periodical divisions of
property between families or emigrations.

resolved to send out two colonies under the command of his nephews on the distaff side,[1] his heirs, Sigovesus and Bellovesus. He made them strong enough to break all resistance.[2] Trogus Pompeius compares the Gallic expedition to a *ver sacrum*,[3] that is to one of the religious emigrations practised by the Italic peoples.

Apart from this difference, the facts are set forth by most historians in much the same fashion.[4] The Insubres, Boii, and Senones destroy a large Etruscan town, Melpum, perhaps Melzo, west of Milan. They found Milan and a certain number of other towns. Following up their successes against the Etruscans, they attack Clusium (Chiusi). The Romans grow disturbed, negotiate, and send a relief army which is defeated on the Allia. Rome is taken, and then saved by the geese of the Capitol and Camillus.

According to some, the Gauls are wiped out. According to others, they retire fairly quietly to their settlements in Romagna, being recalled by an inroad of Veneti.[5] The Gauls are said to have had guides. Some accounts speak of a noble of Clusium named Aruns,[6] seeking vengeance on his wife and his Lucumo ward ; others, more significant, refer to Elico, a Helvetian smith working in Rome.[7]

In every case, it is the riches of Italy, the fruit, the figs, the wine, that draw the barbarians from their less kindly regions. The men who summon them bring them samples of these delights. What all historians have faithfully recorded, is the terror sown among the peoples of Italy by the approach of the Gauls.[8] These queer-looking barbarians, coming from so far, were to the Italy of the fourth century before Christ what the Scourge of God was to the Gaul of the fifth century after Christ, an unavoidable, irresistible, God-sent calamity. The army which came down into Italy is rated at 300,000 men, that which triumphed at the Allia at about 30,000.

[1] Livy, loc. cit. : *sororis filios.*
[2] Ibid. : *ne qua gens arcere advenientes posset.*
[3] Just., XXIV, 4.
[4] Plut., *Cam.*, 15 ; Dion., xiii, 14 ff. ; Polyb., ii, 17 ff. ; Pliny, ii, 125 ; xii, 5 ; Cato, p. 36 ; Aul. Gell., xvii, 13, 4 ; App., *Celtica*, ii, 1 ; *Historia Romana*, iv, 2 ; Diod., xiv, 113, 1 ; Just., xx, 5.
[5] Polyb., ii, 18, 3.
[6] Livy, v, 35 ; Plut., Dion., locc. citt.
[7] Pliny, xii, 5.
[8] Livy, v, 35, 4 ; 36, 2 ; 37, 2 ; 38, 6 ; 39. 1.

These were terrifying hosts for Etruria and Latium, which were only accustomed to wars between one city and another. The battle of the Allia, *Alliensis clades*, was a rout, for which the Romans blushed until the end of the Empire. The war-cry of the Gauls, rising on all sides before the troops made contact, seems to have provoked a wild stampede. As for the evacuation of Rome, of which Livy gives us a remarkably objective picture, it was creditable to a few only. In any case, the Gauls were no gentle foes. They were in the first frenzy of their onrush. They came forward ravaging the country and burning the towns.[1] No doubt, they had a law covering foreign relations and were accustomed to negotiating; indeed, we are told that they did negotiate.[2] But one can easily believe that these parleys gave rise to hopeless misunderstandings. The Gauls, being strong, and not properly understood, were touchy, and they seem to have been lacking in patience.

The deliverance of Rome did not put an end to their attacks. They returned into the valley of the Tiber and to Rome itself in 367,[3] in 361–360,[4] and in 350–349.[5] They descended into Campania in 360 and in 349. In 367 and in 349 they went as far as Apulia.[6] The dates of these expeditions are uncertain, and so is their relative size, but we have one piece of archæological evidence in the shape of a small cemetery at Canossa di Puglia.[7] At the same time they went much further, into Greece, whither Dionysios I of Syracuse sent a body of them which he had taken into his service.[8]

South of the Apennines, these Gallic expeditions were merely raids, which began to turn into expeditions of mercenaries. They had not the rapid successes of the campaigns in the plain of the Po. The fact is, that north of the Apennines the Gauls had had only Etruscans before them,

---

[1] e.g. Mazarbotto (Montelius, **DXXXIV**, p. 410; Grenier, **DXXIX**, p. 99). Herr von Duhn (in Ebert, **CCCXXIV**, s.v. " Kelten ", vi, p. 207) seems to deny that the city was destroyed; but I think he is mistaken. Doubtless it was partially reoccupied by the Gauls.

[2] Livy, v, 35.

[3] Livy, iv, 42, 8; vii, 1, 3; Polyb., ii, 18, 6–7.

[4] Livy, vii, 11, 1; 12, 8.

[5] Ibid., vii, 26, 9; cf. Homo, **CCCXLI**, English, p. 175.

[6] Livy, loc. cit.; Diod., xiv, 117, 7.

[7] *Prähist. Blätt.*, 1898, pp. 49–56.

[8] E. Cavaignac, in **CXL**, 1924, pp. 359 ff. The first relations of Dionysios with the Gauls seem to have been in 379, at the time of the siege of Croton.

who really formed nothing but a fairly recent colony there, and fortified places were rare. South of the Apennines, both in Etruria and in Latium and Umbria, the Gauls found themselves in the midst of a quantity of very ancient little cities, all fortified and perched in good situations. But the strength of their walls was only the instrument of their resistance. The cause of that resistance and its success was that they were political bodies, which refused to yield in a war undertaken *pro aris et focis*, and would not die. The greatest disaster seems to have been that of Rome, and Rome had at once formed again with its army outside its ravaged soil.

Livy, in the chapters of Book V in which he describes the Gallic invasion, makes it plain, with the understanding, lucidity, and descriptive power of a great historian, that the Gauls were not then capable of subduing the determination to live and to conquer embodied in political units which were far superior to their own. Moreover, they did as all conquering armies do in warm and fertile countries. At first they let themselves go, taking what they pleased. Livy shows them to us, gorged with eating and drinking, even rasher and more careless than usual after their too easy victories, and falling into drunken slumber wherever the night happened to overtake them. Then comes the plague, which we may take to have been dysentery. They are encamped among the ruins of Rome, in the dust and ash of the burning city. It is summer, and the weather is hot for these men of the north. Disease spreads among them like cattle-plague, *vulgatis velut in pecua morbis*. Dead bodies accumulate, and have to be burned in heaps (usually they buried their dead). With the plague comes famine. The Gauls are no better organized for conducting large armies than the Italic peoples, but the latter at least know how to conduct small ones. They have no commissariat, and they have laid the country waste. Lastly, they know nothing about field fortification or intelligence, and they allow themselves to be surprised.

None the less, the effects of the terror died hard. Until 349 the Romans remained on the defensive. From that date onwards, it seems, they took courage, and turned upon their enemies. The Gauls were so surprised at the first encounter, Polybios tells us, that they stopped short and scattered.[1]   Indeed, peace seems to have been concluded about 335.[2]

The general outcome was that, while Gallic inroads penetrated as far as the end of Italy, the Gallic conquest stopped at the Apennines. But in what manner did it take place ? Is it true that the Gauls came in like a whirlwind, and where did they make their entry ? That is the first question which we shall discuss. After that, we shall inquire how the Gauls conducted themselves in Italy, what were their general relations with their neighbours, and what became of their civilization in that country.

III

HOW THE GAULS ENTERED ITALY

The Gauls came in, according to Livy,[3] in several bands, crossing the Alps in succession or by different routes.

Bellovesus, who, according to the same author, directed the whole venture, had with him only the Insubres.[4] They arrived first. When their movement had been accomplished, a force of the Cenomani under a leader named Elitovius [5] followed them by the same pass, and Bellovesus assisted them on the way down. Livy then mentions, in vague terms, an advance on the part of the Libui and the Salluvii,[6] but it is doubtful whether they arrived so early. The Boii and Lingones came over together by the Pennine Alps, that is by the Simplon or the St. Gothard, and, passing the first two bodies hustled the Etruscans and Umbrians on the other side of the Po. The Senones arrived last and, passing the leading bodies in the same manner, provided the army of about thirty thousand men which crossed the Apennines and took Rome. Livy does not assert this positively ; he says that he believes it.[7]

To transport over the Alps, without any scientific dis-

---

[1] Polyb., ii, 18, 7.
[2] Ibid., xix, 1 (the Thirty Years' Peace).
[3] Livy, v, 34–5. Cf. Homo, CCCXLI,, English, pp. 165 ff. ; Jullian, CCCXLVII, i, pp. 289 ff.
[4] Livy, v, 34, 9.
[5] Livy, v, 35, 1.
[6] Livy, v, 35, 2.
[7] Livy, v, 35, 2–3.

position of supply-posts, a mass of men large enough to form
a whole nation, with women and children, flocks and herds,
a great number of chariots, and an indefinitely large train
of very primitive little waggons and pack-animals, was an
extremely difficult undertaking. It required at least some
organization if it was, as history relates, a concerted movement. What was done was to divide the host into separate
bodies, and it was most natural to form these according to
tribes. So Livy's account seems quite credible. Recon-
naissances, too, had to be made, guides to be found, extra
provisions to be obtained, and help of all kinds to be secured,
and there must have been negotiations or battles with the
local natives, all combining to delay and slow down the
advance ; and, even if we exclude the suggestion that they
made temporary settlements, it must have been necessary
to clear and till the land which they occupied for the time
being. The passage of the Gallic columns needed a fairly
long time, and we must suppose that there were big intervals
between one body and the next.

But how big were these intervals ? The largest is that
separating the invasion of the fifth and sixth centuries from
that of the fourth.

It is very remarkable that the fourth century Gallic
cemeteries in the Cisalpine country are all south of the Po,
the oldest being round Bologna.[1] Those north of the Po,
which are in two main groups, one west of the Ticino [2] in
the province of Novara, and the other about Como, date from
the last three centuries before Christ.[3] The dead in them
were burned, and their tombs are like contemporary tombs
in the Alpine valleys, but also resemble those of Golasecca.
This looks as if the Gauls of the fourth century had rapidly
advanced on Bologna, leaving Lombardy in the possession
of their predecessors, who had arrived a century or two earlier
and are said to have opened the gates of Italy to them. As
a matter of fact, the earlier settlement no longer existed.
The first Gallic cemeteries north of the Po were broken up
by the construction of towns or by cultivation (*grandiaque*

---

[1] Déchelette, ii, 3, p. 1087.
[2] Ulrich, **DXLI.**
[3] Déchelette, ii, 3, pp. 1093 ff., 1097 ; von Duhn, in Ebert, **CCCXXIV,**
s.v. " Kelten ", vi, p. 286 ; s.v. " Bologna ", ii, p. 112.

effossis mirabitur ossa sepulcris).   A few isolated objects [1]
are sufficient evidence that this district was taken by the
Gauls at the same time as the Cispadane region, or even before
it. The columns of Bellovesus must, therefore, have followed
one on another at intervals of a few years or a few months.
At the very most we may suppose, if we cannot accept this
blank in the archæological map, that the Insubres and
Cenomani arrived after the Boii and Senones with reinforcements which continued to descend from the Celtic interior
for a long time yet.

But this, too, is hard to believe, and the order of march
of the five Gallic nations (apart from the Libui and Salluvii)
is quite as probable. It follows from their position. The
first-comers doubtless stopped as soon as they could. The
way down into the great valleys which spread out towards
the Po is very attractive, and must have been so then. The
country had been brought under cultivation by the people
of the *terremare* and the pile-villages, and here the first
invaders stopped. Those who followed had to go further.
Those who are found at the end of the line are evidently
the last-comers. Thus the Insubres, after their first collision
with the Etruscans, settled south of the Lake of Como,
between the Ticino and the Adda, occupying the provinces
of Como and Milan. The Cenomani, coming next, settle
between the Adda and the Adige, south of the lakes of Iseo
and Garda, around Brescia and as far as Verona. On this
side the Celts were stopped by the Veneti, whom they could
not oust and had to take into consideration. The Boii
occupied the region of Lodi, north of the Po, between the
Ticino and the Adda. There they are said to have founded
the city which is now Lodi (Laus Pompeia). But, finding
themselves cramped, they crossed the Po with the Lingones
and filled the plain under the Apennines between Parma
and Bologna, while the Lingones occupied the whole of
Lower Emilia. The Senones, prolonging the chain of Cisalpine
Gauls, occupied the coast of the Romagna from the Utens
(Montone) to the Alsis (Esino) on the outskirts of Ancona,
according to Livy; but they advanced a little further, to
the valley of the Chienti.[2]

[1] Montelius, **DXXXV**, i, pp. 63–4.
[2] Livy, v, 35, 2–3. Regarding the Senones, Livy is not absolutely

We must suppose that they did not settle down all at once. The *Periplus* of Scylax,[1] written about 350, which enumerates all the peoples of the coasts of the Mediterranean one by one, does indeed speak of the Gauls on the Adriatic seaboard, or, more exactly, of the remnants of the expedition against Rome (ἀπολειφθέντες τῆς στρατείας), but only as covering a small area (ἐπὶ στενῶν). They cannot have occupied more than the mouths of the Po, their territory being bounded on the south by that of the Etruscans, which extended to Spina, an old Greek colony on the southern mouth of the Po, and on the north by that of the Veneti, which extended to Adria, another Greek colony a few miles north of the northern mouth. The mouths of the Po seem to have been in the domain of the Lingones. A too literal interpretation of the text would lead us to look for the Senones here, since it seems to have been they who made the expedition against Rome. But according to the author of the *Periplus* the Adriatic coast between Ancona and Spina still belonged to the Etruscans about 350, not to the Senones. The continuous succession of campaigns between 390 and 350 makes one think that the Senones were not permanently established before 350. One may suppose, too, that they did not occupy the coast but the terraces of the Apennines ; for it is here that Gallic settlements have been found, and not on the coast. In that case the *Periplus* of Scylax, which is really a " Pilot " for the use of navigators, might have ignored them, if we suppose that Ancona and Spina were still in Etruscan hands.

It is about this same date of 350 that the series of Greek vases found in the Etruscan cemetery of Bologna (La Certosa) comes to an end.[2] This means that the Etruscans had maintained themselves in the city, keeping up constant intercourse with the Greek colonies on the mouths of the Po, under the eyes of the Gauls established all round them. In general, the cities in this neighbourhood also seem to have

correct, but he only needs the slightest amendment. The domain of these peoples extended south of Ancona. In recent years, Gallic tombs have been found in the region of Filottrano and Osimo, e.g. that at San Genesto, near Tolentino. See von Duhn, in Ebert, s.v. " Kelten ", vi, p. 292. This observation enables one to judge how much trust one can place in the information supplied by the ancient historians.

[1] Scylax, 18.
[2] Grenier, **DXXIX**, pp. 160 ff., 320 ff. ; id. **CCCLXXVIII**, p. 72.

held out. Como, which has been assigned to the Insubres, and Bergamo, which has been assigned to the Cenomani, did not come under their power until later. Mantua continued to be an Etruscan enclave to the end.

So, from Como to Ancona and from Milan to Verona the five great peoples of which we are speaking made themselves one continuous territory. They had found it there, ready made for them, for the greater part of it coincides with the Etruscan territory on the Po. When the Etruscans were defeated, the political organization of their province had broken down. The five nations which succeeded them sooner or later assumed their position. This fact should be borne in mind, for it explains the cohesion of the group which they formed and the co-ordinated, concerted, and, one might say, political character which the historians ascribe to their first operations.

But there were other Gallic peoples south of the Alps —the Libui and Salluvii, mentioned by Livy.[1] Polybios[2] adds the Libici and Laevi north of the Po and the Ananes, Anares, or Anamari,[3] south of it, west of the Boii. These last two are perhaps not Gauls. But the others certainly are.

The Libui and Libici are probably identical and had Vercellae for their centre ; in their territory was a Rigomagus (Trino). From a somewhat obscure passage in Pliny,[4] the source of which is the *Origines* of Cato, it appears that they were a sub-tribe of the Salluvii. The Salluvii, who are also called the Salassi,[5] must have spoken a Celtic language, for their capital was Eporedia, the name of which is undoubtedly Gallic. They were probably a section of the Salyes of Provence, whom the ancient ethnographers label Celto-Ligurian. Between the Libici and the Insubres were the Vertamocori of Novara, who are described as Ligurians by Cato and as Gauls by Pliny.[6] The latter says that they were a *pagus*, that is a sub-tribe of the Vocontii of Dauphiné. North of the Vertamocori, the Lepontii, established in the

---

[1] Livy, v, 35, 2.
[2] Polyb., ii, 17, 4.
[3] Müllenhoff, **CCCLXII**, ii, p. 267.
[4] Pliny, iii, 134 ; Cato, fr. 27 ; Strabo, iv, 6, 8, on the Rhaetians. Cf. Meyer, **CCCLIV**, iv, p. 150.
[5] Holder, **CCVII**, s.v.
[6] Pliny, iii, 124 ; cf. d'Arbois, in **CXL**, xi, p. 154.

Val d' Ossola and the Val Leventina, were Gauls.[1] At the mouth of each of these two valleys we have a large cemetery, corresponding to their two main settlements, at Ornavasso [2] and Giubiasco.[3] These are La Tène cemeteries. At Ornavasso a certain number of vases have been found bearing *graffiti* which seem to be Celtic so far as they can be read at all.

The Lepontii must probably be attached to the people of the Valais. The Vertamocori and Salluvii are related to the Gauls of Dauphiné and Provence. The two sections were linked up by a series of Gallic peoples occupying the Alpine valleys—the Centrones on the upper Isère, the Medulli in the Maurienne, and the Caturiges on the upper Durance. These last had been settled for a short time in Italy.

The Gallic tribes of Piedmont seem to form a distinct group from the five large nations in Lombardy and Emilia, more recent and less solidly welded together. They are the advanced posts in Italy of the Alpine tribes or of those which had come as far as the foot of the Alps in the Rhone valley and had remained there. Immediately after the fall of Rome, Polybios [4] mentions frequent raids by men from across the Alps as causing agitation among the Cisalpine Gauls, whose successes had tempted them. The arrival of the Piedmontese tribes may correspond to those expeditions.

The Insubres, Cenomani, Boii, Lingones, and Senones came direct from much further away—from the banks of the Rhine, Appian says, and in any case from the interior of the Celtic world.[5]

Livy [6] gives us a list of the peoples among which Bellovesus raised his army, namely the Bituriges, Arverni, Senones, Ædui, Ambarri, Carnutes, and Aulerci, which appear for the first time in history. Over-critical scholars have attacked this list, but unjustly.[7] It is a document of the greatest importance, for it represents a fundamental grouping of the Gallic peoples. It shows what section of them took

[1] Pliny, iii, 134.
[2] Binachetti, in **XXVIII**, vi, 1895 ; v. Duhn, in Ebert, **CCCXXIV**, vi, pp. 292 ff.
[3] Viollier, in **CLXXX**, pp. 229 ff.
[4] Polyb., ii, 18–19.
[5] App., *Celt.*, i, 2, 390 ; cf. Prop., x, 10, 19.
[6] Livy, v, 34.
[7] D'Arbois (**CCXCIX**, pp. 139 ff.) and Bertrand (**CCCIII**, p. 20) regard the Celts of Italy as a colony of the Danubian Celts.

part in the great movement of expansion which was then taking place towards Britain and to the south-east.

The Insubres are Ædui; the Cenomani are Aulerci; the Senones of Italy are doubtless the same as the Senones of Gaul. In the Italian settlement the Bituriges, Arverni, Ambarri, and Carnutes do not appear, but we find the Lingones, who were afterwards neighbours of the Senones and Ædui in Gaul, and the Boii, who were one of the most widely scattered of all the Celtic peoples, but seem to have kept their main body in what I regard as the original home of the Celts, east of the Volcae. So the two lists do not agree absolutely, but there is nothing very disturbing in that.

Later on, we shall inquire where the peoples of the first list can have been at that time. We should note that neither list includes the two nearest neighbours of Italy—the Helvetii and Sequani. They must have had their hands full in their old or new possessions in Switzerland and Franche-Comté. Perhaps they stand in the same relation to the invaders of Italy as the Insubres to the Senones; settling in the country first, they were passed by those who followed them.

By what road had the invaders come? There are two views, both based on the text of Livy, which is in such imperfect condition that both sides quote the same sentence as their authority.[1] The Gauls are said to have come through the country of the Ligurians of Turin (Taurini) and by the Julian Alps (*saltusque Juliae Alpis*). There is no doubt about what Livy thinks, for in the preceding sentence he mentions the Gauls as being in contact with the people of Marseilles. It is hardly credible that they crossed the Julian Alps, for the way was blocked by the Veneti, whom the Gauls did not touch. A happy conjecture has replaced the name of the Julian Alps by that of the River Duria.[2] But the geographical position of the Gauls solves the problem. The Insubres established south of Lake Maggiore and the Lake of Como had not come over by the Mont Cenis and the Val d'Aosta. They had crossed the Alps either by the St. Gothard, coming down on to Lake Maggiore, or by the Maloja, descending on to the Lake of Como. They stopped at the

---

[1] v. Duhn, in Ebert, **CCCXIV**, vi, pp. 285, 292.
[2] Jullian, **CCCXLVII**, i, p. 289, n. 5; p. 291, n. 4.

mouths of the Alpine valleys between the Ticino and the
Oglio. Those who came after gathered round them there,
and went on from there ; those who crossed the Pennine
Alps doubtless came by the Simplon, which brought them
to the same point by the Val d'Ossola. The Celts might come
from Bavaria ; the valley of the Rhine and the Engadine,
leading to the St. Gothard and the Maloja respectively,
were the natural routes up to the crest of the Alps for a people
coming from South Germany. The Boii and Lingones, who
crossed the Pennine Alps, came from the same region, working
round the Bernese Oberland.

It was only later, as I have suggested, that they passed
through the Ligurians who lay between their Lombard
settlements and the French Alps. It does not seem that they
ever went through the peoples that lay to the north-east
of their settlements.

IV

CHARACTER OF THE GALLIC SETTLEMENT IN THE VALLEY OF THE PO

So the Gallic peoples of the Cisalpine country were
portions of certain great Gallic tribes settled in various
other parts of the Celtic world. The invasion had not been
carried out by complete nations or tribes, nor yet by
temporary formations of a purely military kind, having no
political ties. These fractions of tribes had become tribes.
But the various elements in the political organization of
the Celts were perfectly homogeneous and only differed in
size.[1] They had combined to some extent for their venture,
but when their object was attained they at once went back
to their old freedom of action. Thus it is that we find the
Senones operating alone against Etruria and Rome.

How were those bodies made up ? It is an interesting
question, but we cannot answer it completely. Were they
merely composed of the men that each happened to get
together ? Were they sub-tribes or clans ? They were
probably groups which already existed. The Insubres and
the Cenomani, indeed, were either sub-tribes or fractions of

[1] On the divisions of the tribe, see Czarnowski, **CCCCXXIII**, pp. 231 ff.

sub-tribes of the Ædui and Aulerci. The Cenomani were in the same group as the contingents of a people which seems to have formed part of their confederacy, the Andecavi ; this must be the explanation of the presence of the village of Andes [1] on their territory, close to Mantua.

Another question is the size of the bodies. We can form an approximate idea of it. It may be remembered that the ancient historians reckon the victors of the Allia at 30,000 men. It is quite a credible figure. It was required, and it was sufficient, to produce the effect of irresistible mass of which I have tried to give a notion. We must multiply it by at least seven to allow for the women, children, old men, sick, cripples, and slaves. This would bring the number of the Senones up to about 200,000 in all. The Boii must have been about as many. Pliny, still quoting Cato's *Origins*, tells us that they had 112 tribes,[2] no doubt at the time when their country came under Roman sway. By this he must mean 112 clans, 112 groups of a social and territorial nature, each of which must have been of some size. Indeed, the object of the statement is to suggest that the Boii were a very considerable people. Populations of this size were capable of occupying the country effectively, and we must take the historians almost literally when they tell us that they drove out the Etruscans and Umbrians. That a few settlers, a large number of slaves, and perhaps a few subject and associated groups survived[3] is very probable, but it is even more evident that a Celtic occupation took the place of the Etruscan and Umbrian occupation, that it formed a whole new Gallic colony.

Another very remarkable thing is that the Italian colony of the Celts was on the plains. Nothing could show better that something had changed in the civilization of the Celts since the Hallstatt period. The Hallstatt men made for the hills. The Gauls of the La Tène period made for uplands and plains suited for agriculture. The Senones got the worst share,[4]

[1] Moreover, the Cenomani seem to have preserved in both their homes the same habits or rules of place-naming. The name of Tridentum (Trent) is to be compared with that of Tridentus (Trans in Mayenne). D'Arbois, **CCCI**, 2, p. 324.

[2] Dottin, **CCCXXII**, p. 306.

[3] e.g. the Comenses (Como), Ausuciates (Osuccio), Gallianates (Galliano), etc. Cf. Niessen, **DXXXVII**, ii, 1, pp. 185, 188–9.

[4] Diod., xiv, 113, 3. Cf. Jullian, **CCCXLVI**, i, p. 247.

for nothing was left for them but the slopes of the Apennines, though these were far from barren. Perhaps that is what drove them over the crests which barred their way to look for better land. Having failed, they contented themselves with what they had and throve on it. Therefore we cannot picture the Gallic settlers of the Cisalpine country as the nomads and stock-raisers described by Polybios; these characteristics belong to another branch of the Celts. They remained settled on the soil which they had conquered. They really colonized it, and as agriculturists.[1]

It is said that they founded cities—Milan, Brescia (Brixia), Bergamo (Bergomum), Como, Vicenza, Modena (Mutina),[2] and probably Lodi and Sinigaglia (Sena Gallica). Some of these towns no doubt existed before their coming, as was the case with Como, Brescia, Bergamo, and Bologna. To this last they gave a Gallic name, Bononia. Others kept their old names, which came from the Ligurians.[3]

If they did not Celticize the country sufficiently to give Gallic names to the towns, it was still more natural for them to keep the old names of the rivers.[4] The name of the Reno, however, is Celtic. Some have maintained that Benacus, the name of the Lake of Garda, is Celtic, meaning the Lake of the Points (Irish *benn*, " point "),[5] but the derivation is doubtful. Lastly, among the place-names of the country there are to this day many ending in -*asco* and -*usco*, which are Ligurian. Some of these date from before the Gallic occupation; others were doubtless given afterwards, but they were still formed on the same principles.[6]

The Cisalpine Gauls have left behind them funerary inscriptions, *graffiti* on pottery, and manufacturers' marks in surprisingly large numbers for a people which had had no knowledge of writing at the time when it arrived.[7] By a

---

[1] Diod., v, 40, 4–5 ; Dion., xiii, 11.

[2] Just., xx, 5, 8 ; Livy, xxxiv, 9 (Milan) ; Pliny, *N.H.*, iii, 124–5 (Como, Bergamo). Verona is supposed to have been founded by Brescia (Catull., 67, 32) ; its name may be Celtic. Cf. Niessen, i, p. 204. Against this view, see Philipon, **CCCLXIX**, p. 138. For Parma, see Mart., v, 13, 7 (*Gallica Parma*).

[3] Pliny, iii, 17.

[4] Philipon, op. cit., p. 189 ; cf. 139 (Ticinus).

[5] Pokorny, **CCCXIV**, v, in Ebert, p. 297, s.v. " Kelten ".

[6] D'Arbois, **CCCI**, ii, pp. 46, 63.

[7] J. Rhys, **VI**, pp. 59–75 ; Stokes, **CCXXXVIII**, xi, pp. 112–18.

Of the inscriptions published as Celtic, many have nothing Celtic in them but a few proper names. Others are thoroughly Celtic—notably those from

curious chance, far the greatest number have been found north of the Po and on the fringes of the Gallic country. They seem to be later than the best days of Cisalpine Gaul.

The archæological remains, the known amount of which increases constantly, are distributed equally irregularly. Nothing remains of the towns, which were destroyed when Roman towns were built on their sites. The cemeteries represent wealthy but scattered settlements.[1] They confirm history, which fills up the gaps in their evidence.

On the whole, the Gauls formed a compact and lasting settlement in the central part of the Po valley. They took root there firmly enough to change the face of the countryside for ever.

According to historical tradition, the beaten Etruscans retired into the Euganean Hills overlooking Verona, and became the Raetians, so-called after their leader Raetus.[2] The Cenomani had advanced on this side. Justin attributes to them the foundation of Trent, and indeed Tridentum is a Gallic name.[3] North of Trent, in the Val di Non or Nonsberg, the little village of Cavareno has a Gallic name,[4] and the name of the district recalls that of the Anauni, a small people belonging to the group whose centre was Trent; their name certainly seems to be Gallic.[5] Near by, in the valley, a Gallic cemetery has been explored at Mechel-in-Nonsberg.[6] But the slopes of the Alps north of Cisalpine Gaul on this side remained in the hands of the Raeti and Euganeans.[7] Whoever these last may have been, there were undoubted Ligurians among them. There were, for example, the Trumpilini, who have left their name to the Val Trompia. They naturally recall the Trumpilini of the Maritime Alps,

Briona, near Novara, and Brescia. The former contains some Latin names (Legatus, Quintus), and the latter is half-Latin, half-Celtic.

[1] See above, p. 15.

[2] Just., xx, 5, 9.

[3] See above, p. 22, n. 1.

[4] *Cauaros*, hero ; Irish *caur*, giant.

[5] Ptol., ii, 1, 32 ; **I**, v, p. 537. **anavo-*, cf. Welsh *anau*, harmony. D'Arbois, **CCCI,**, ii, p. 159.

[6] Much, **CCCLXI**, lxv, 149 ; further east, is another cemetery in the Val Sugana (v. Duhn, in Ebert, s.v. " Kelten ", i, p. 295). The last Gallic cemetery on the Venetian side is that of Pavigliano Vennese (**CXII**, 1880, pp. 236 ff.).

[7] D'Arbois, **CCXCIX**, p. 143. Cf. Trumpilini, in an inscription from La Turbie (**I**, v, 7817), and Stoeni, in Pliny, iii, 134 ; **I**, i, p. 460 (117 B.C.) ; cf. Holder, **CCVII,** s.v. " Stoeni ".

whose existence and defeat are recorded by the monument
at La Turbie. There were also the Ligures Stoeni, who have
left their name to the village of Stenico, in the upper valley
of the Sarca.

The western edge of the Gallic domain in Italy presents
a similar spectacle. The ethnography of the region must
have been so entangled as to involve the ancient writers
in mistakes without end. Cato seems to have made a serious
effort in his *Origins* to establish the identity of the peoples
in those parts on the strength of the information at his
disposal. The result is that he describes the Vertamocori
and the Salluvii, whom we have good reason to call Celtic,
as Ligurians.[1] The Gallic peoples of the north of Piedmont
were evidently not to be compared to the consolidated peoples
of Lombardy and Emilia. We must imagine them as mixed
up with Ligurians, Gallic villages standing next to Ligurian
villages and inter-marriage going on between the two sides.
The races of the mountain districts must have been equally
intermixed. Switzerland is the proof of it, and, still better,
Upper Piedmont, with its history, its dialect, and its French
villages on the Italian slopes of the Matterhorn separated
from French-speaking Switzerland by a wide belt of German
Swiss.

So we can see how it was that people like the Bagicuni
in the neighbourhood of Cueno, whom all the historians
agree in calling Ligurian, could be regarded as descendants
of the Caturiges,[2] who were Gauls. Associations of all kinds
grew up, for which we can lay down no rules. But on the
whole the Ligurian was on top, or rather he was all round.
Later on the Gallic peoples of the mountains—Centrones,
Medulli, Caturiges—were comprised in the Ligurian kingdom
of Cottius.[3] But, though politically incorporated by the
Ligurians, the Celtic colonies of Piedmont faithfully preserved
their language, as is shown by inscriptions,[4] of which some
at least are not very ancient, and by certain features of
their civilization, long after the Romans had destroyed the
Gallic organization of the Milanese and Emilia. They even
made their neighbours accept them. In short, it does not seem

[1] Pliny, iii, 124.
[2] Pliny, iii, 47, 135 ; Ptol., iii, 1, 31. Cf. d'Arbois, in **CXL**, xi, p. 154.
[3] Müllenhoff, **CCCLXII**, ii, p. 249.
[4] Inscriptions from Briona and Ornavasso (Rhys, **VI**, p. 47).

that there was any conquest or attempt at conquest on the part of the Ligurians. There was certainly association, whatever the causes may have been.

North of the Insubres, in the Como district, similar formations were organized, whose sway extended up to the Ligurians of the Euganean country. In this region, cemeteries and single tombs have been excavated at Introbbio, Civiglio, Soldo, Legnano, Esino, and Pianezzo.[1] These the archæologists generally describe as Gallo-Ligurian, perhaps because most of the tombs contain cremations. Funerary stelæ have also been found here, at Rondineto, Algate, Civiglio, and Cernusco Asinario, and *graffiti* containing Celtic names on the bottoms of vases, for instance at Ornavasso and Giubiasco. But as a whole, those so-called Lepontian inscriptions are probably not Celtic; they belong to a dialect which has a touch of Italic in it, and may be Ligurian, or perhaps stands in the same relation to Italic as Macedonian to Greek.[2]

South of the Po the Ligurians extended to Etruria. There is nothing after the great invasion like the little colony which left the cippi of the Vara behind it. But the boundary may have been vague. Among the Ananes there was a town named Comillomagus, now Broni.[3] This is certainly a Gallic name. But the westernmost of the cemeteries representing Gallic civilization which is yet known was found at Saliceto di San Giuliano, about five miles from Modena.[4]

V

CIVILIZATION OF THE CISALPINE GAULS

In the valley of the Tiber, at Todi, south of Perugia, a funerary inscription has been found, in Latin and Celtic, in honour of one Ategnatos, son of Druteos.[5] It is the

---

[1] Montelius, **DXXXIV**, pls. 63–5; Castelfranco, in **LIII**, 1886, p. 184; A. Magni, in *Rev. archeol. della prov. di Como*, 1907, pp. 3 ff. (Liguro-Gallic cemetery at Pianezzo).

[2] H. Pedersen, in **CXVI**, 1921, pp. 38–54; cf. Vendryès, in **CXL**, 1923, 491; v. Duhn, in Ebert, **CCCXXIII**, s.v. " Kelten ", vi, p. 287. On the other hand, Pokorny declares that these inscriptions are Celtic (ibid., 136–8). Cf. Philipon, **CCCLXIX**, pp. 136–8.

[3] Nissen, **DXXXVII**, ii, 1, p. 271.

[4] **LIII**, 1876, p. 30; 1886, p. 159; 1888, p. 40.

[5] Dottin, **CXCVI**, p. 153, No. 17 *bis*; cf. *Rise*, p. 38, n. 9.

southernmost of the Celtic inscriptions and it stood well inside Umbria, far north of the Latin territory. The Celtic domain certainly did not reach so far as that.[1] It may be a relic of a Celtic expedition like the tombs of Canossa, or it may merely record the fact that a Gallic family came and settled here at an early date, before Rome encroached on the conquests of the Gauls in her work of uniting Italy. But why is the inscription in two languages, and why is one of them Latin? It gives us a glimpse of the kind of society formed by the invaders together with the aborigines. Each side stood its ground and kept its language, but they did not ignore one another, or keep themselves to themselves. This is not the grim picture of the Gallic wars which Livy gives us. Besides, even in that picture we can see some features of policy and social life which correct it.

The same story is told by the tombs of the Senones [2] found at Montefortino, Filottrano, Ripa Bianca, and elsewhere. They are surprisingly wealthy. They are full of gold in two forms—purely Gallic ornaments and Etruscan ornaments. The Gallic ornaments are rings and buffer-torques, recalling those of the Rhine valley. The Etruscan ornaments are crowns of gold foliage, collars with pendants shaped like eggs or amphoræ, of a well-known type, and bracelets ending in snakes' heads. It has been said that, if the Senones took home the thousand pounds of gold which formed the ransom of the Capitol, the wives and daughters of their chieftains must have been richly arrayed. But there are not only articles of adornment to speak of their wealth. There are ivory boxes, bronze vases with richly decorated handles and feet, and painted Attic pottery. The whole points to a taste no less refined than that of the contemporary peoples of Campania and Etruria. Moreover, the Senones copied from the latter the practice of laying in their tombs kitchen utensils, lamps, spits, and lamp-stands, which were unknown to the great majority of Gauls. The men took with them to their graves strigils, which prove that they had adopted the fashion of rubbing themselves with oil. They kept their own swords and spears; but the helmets were Italic, and, it seems, they were beginning, under the influence

[1] Cf. d'Arbois, **CCXCIX**, p. 4.
[2] See above, p. 15; Déchelette, pp. 1088, 1181.

of their neighbours, to give up the war-chariot with which they had descended upon Italy. In short, they had fallen, or were falling, into line with the peoples all round them, they had adopted their manners, because they had dealings with them, and in less than fifty years they had ceased to appear, in their new colony, as wild and terrifying savages. The first generation of Gauls born in Italy was doubtless quite as much Italian as Gallic.

The Gallic cemeteries round about Bologna likewise testify to such extensive borrowing from the civilization of the conquered that one may ask whether the Gauls were there as besiegers or as neighbours and allies.[1]

Besides, they had, in the course of the long succession of wars which we usually have in our minds, long periods of peace. Polybios mentions a period of thirty years between 329 and 299, and one of twelve between 347 and 335.[2] The archæologists of Ancona were led to seek for Gallic tombs by the discovery of open settlements situated on the terraces of the Marche.[3]

We find the same kind of relations with the Veneti of Este. The Gauls were not far from the town; no doubt they came into it, but without hostile intent. They took service as mercenaries, they came as visitors, perhaps they worshipped in the temples; in any case, they were known in the place and attention was paid to them. In the ruins of the temple of the goddess Rehtra, among the votive statuettes, there is one representing a Gallic warrior with a belt and a La Tène sword slung on his right. Another statuette represents a Gaul with a dagger or short sword stuck in his belt on the right. These are votive offerings which may have been dedicated by Gallic visitors. A fragment of a stamped plaque shows a horseman with a La Tène shield. Lastly, in the same area brooches of La Tène Ic have been found.[4]

There were individuals with Celtic names at Este. One of those names is recognizable in its Venetian transcription Verconzarna.[5] If we suppose that the Etruscan z is equivalent

[1] See above, p. 15. Cf. v. Duhn, in Ebert, **CCCXXIV**, s.v. " Kelten ".
[2] Polyb., ii, 19.
[3] Déchelette, ii, 3, p. 1091, n. 2.
[4] Montelius, **DXXXIV**, pls. 61, 4 ; 60, 5.
[5] Rhys, **CCXXX**, 38.

to the Gallic _d_,[1] we get Vercondarna, which falls into the class of Celtic names which includes Vercondaridubnus, Tarcondarius, etc. It is composed of the preposition _ver-_ (= ὑπέρ) and an adjective [2] related to the Welsh substantive _oyndarod_ "rage", and the adjective _cynddeiriawg_ "enraged". Vercondarna is a feminine name, for all its warlike meaning. It probably tells us of mixed marriages between Venetian men and Gallic women, and there must also have been marriages between Venetian women and Gallic men, and that just about the date at which we have halted.[3]

The cultural exchanges to which this intercourse led were chiefly to the advantage of the Gauls, but not entirely so.

In the common vocabulary of the Italic and Celtic languages, there is not only the residue of an old undivided stock; there are words borrowed by one side or the other. Some of those borrowings are ancient, and seem to date from the time when the Italic peoples, and the Latins in particular, found themselves face to face with the Celts. What is more, it was the Latins who borrowed from the Gauls.

It is generally accepted to-day that the Latin word _gladius_ "sword" is of Celtic origin.[4] The Latin grammarians knew that it had once had the form _cladius_, and accordingly they derived it from _clades_.[5] It comes from a word which must in Gaulish have been *_kladios_, which is represented by Welsh _cleddyf_, from which comes Irish _claideb_. The ancient historians tell us that the Romans subsequently adopted the sword of the Celtiberians, which had the advantage of being equally useful for cutting and thrusting. But it is hard to make the adoption of the word _gladius_ as late as the time when the Roman armies were operating in Spain. Besides, the hypothetical word *_kladios_ does not seem very appropriate for a thrusting weapon. It has the same root as κλάδος,

---

[1] See _Rise_, p. 265.

[2] For the suffix _n_, see Dottin, **CXCVI**, iii; cf. Marstrander, in **CLXXI**, 1910, p. 378.

[3] Gallic names survived in Venetia; e.g. (**I**, v, 8740), at Concordia, near Portoginaro, north-east of Venice, ILATEUTA, with which compare Welsh Elltud. Rhys, **CCXXX**, p. 15.

[4] Vendryès, in **CLXXXIII**, p. 309. The _kl_ of the Celtic word became _gl_ in Latin. There are other examples of this mutation, such as the word _gloria_, which comes from a form _klouesia_ and is related to Greek κλέος (κλέϜος). Cf. κυβερνᾶν, _gubernare_. The transformation had taken place in the second century (cf. _Miles Gloriosus_).

[5] Varro.

meaning "stick", Old Slavonic *kladivo*, which means "hammer", and perhaps κόλαφος, meaning "blow". The root *kela* or *kla* seems to have meant striking so as to split, and not so as to pierce. The word well fits the weapon into which the La Tène sword was tending to develop. Derived from the dagger, it was becoming a weapon intended for delivering great cutting blows. In spite of the poor opinion which Livy and Polybios had of the weapons of the Gauls,[1] it is probable that the Roman troops, though better organized and better led than the Gallic, had not really good arms and readily changed them.[2]

The Gauls also had a better shield than the Italic troops, and one which covered them better. It is probable that the Latins adopted it, and with it the word *scutum*.[3] Attempts have been made to explain this word by *obscurus*, or by *cūtis*; it covers and hides, or it is made of skin. Welsh and Irish have the words *ysgwyd* and *sciath* respectively, meaning both "shield" and "shoulder". The semantic derivation of the meaning is quite clear in Celtic, but is absent in Latin. It is to be noted that *scutum* is specially used for a large tall shield. Livy contrasts the Celtic *scutum* of the heavy infantry of the Celtiberians with the Iberian *caitra*, the round target of their light infantry.[4] This contrast is repeated. The Celtic origin of the word *scutum* is therefore probable. The large shield of the Roman infantry is not unlike the La Tène shield. What is more, the innovation is ascribed to Camillus.[5]

Another borrowed word, of a different kind, is *vates*.[6] This word stands alone in Latin. Its close similarity to Irish *faith*,[7] which has exactly the same meaning, Cæsar's use of it to designate the men who in Gaul had exactly the position of the *faith* in Ireland, and Strabo's transcription οὐάτεις with the same meaning, all show that the word was

---

[1] Polyb., ii, 33 ; Livy, xxii, 46 ; S. Reinach, in **XV**, 1906, p. 344.

[2] The word *lancea* was admittedly borrowed, apparently from Spain (Diod., v, 30 ; Aul. Gell., xv, 31, following Varro). Cf. Déchelette, ii, 3, p. 1150. Middle Irish *do-lecim*, I throw, has been compared to Irish *laigen*, Welsh *llain*. Walde, **CCXLIII**, s.v. The word fits the all-iron javelin found in tombs in the Pyrenees and at Hallstatt. Cf. A. J. Reinach, in **CXXXVIII**, 1907, i, pp. 243, 426 ; ii, pp. 125, 225–6.

[3] Walde, **CCXLIII**, s.v.

[4] Livy, viii, 8.

[5] Plut., *Cam.*, 40. Cf. Dion. Hal., xiv, 9 ; Polyb., vii, 7, 2. See Reinecke, **CCCCVI**, p. 10.

[6] Walde, **CCXLIII**, s.v. ; Strabo, iv, 4, 4.

[7] Dottin, **CXCVI**, p. 115.

borrowed and that it kept its special sense. When we read the story of the Gallic wars in Livy or Justin, we find that the barbarians appeared to the Latins, who themselves were pious folk and much given to divination, as superstitious in the extreme. If we suppose that the Cisalpine Gauls had the two castes or colleges of the Druids and the *vates*, and that these latter had the same function, social, political, and religious, as they have in the Irish epics, having a finger in every pie, and being always ready to produce a poem to meet the occasion—satire, war-song, or prophecy—or to interpret in inspired verse all the circumstances which were perturbing their audiences, the presence of the inspired bard in the ranks of their adversaries must certainly have appeared a novelty to the Romans. If the name *vates* really comes from Celtic, it is because there were such bards in Cisalpine Gaul. It is interesting evidence on the history of Druidism, for the word must have been borrowed fairly soon to have passed into common use. It can only have been learned in Italy or Spain, and Italy is the more likely. The Celts have been and still are great versifiers, great lovers of songs and poetry. They certainly were so at that time.

That the Romans benefited by the imagination of the Gallic poets is very possible. The story of the Gallic wars, out of which Livy, a historian of genius gifted with the spirit of divination, has made a very remarkable historical work, is something quite by itself, rather fabulous and very epic. Monsieur Jullian has suggested that the tradition was probably made up of Celtic epics.[1] The well-known story of Valerius Corvus,[2] who was rescued in single combat with a Gallic chief by a crow which pecked the Celt's face and hid the Roman from him with its wings, is an example. The episode is unlike anything else in Roman history and literature. But it is like a famous episode in the great Irish epic of Ulster, the *Táin Bó Chuailgné*,[3] in which the goddess Morrigu attacks Cuchulainn, who has scorned her love, in the form of a crow. The crow is not a mere flight of fancy ;

[1] Jullian, **CCCXLVII**, i, p. 294.

[2] Livy, vii, 26 (the campaign of 345) ; Dio Cass., fr. 34. The interpretation suggested above was put forward in my lecture at the École des Hautes-Études.

[3] A similar episode is represented on one of the decorated faces of an Etruscan alabaster vase in the Florence Museum, among scenes of the Trojan War, although it is foreign to that tradition. Milani, **DXXXIII**, ii.

it is the creature which stands for battle and the gods and goddesses of war. The story of Valerius Corvus came down from the family tradition of the Gens Valeria to Fabius Pictor, from whom Livy got it ; but how did it come in ? Some Valerius must have had dealings with the Gauls, or at any rate a kind of international tradition of those heroic wars must have tended to accumulate.

These separate facts suggest a picture of the little world in which the Gauls of Italy played their part, and give an idea of what they had brought to it and what they had got from it. But the chief novelty which then appeared in the Celtic communities of Italy was of another kind. The small Italian cities of Etruria, Umbria, Samnium, Latium, and Campania were highly developed societies. They had their internal politics, which were party politics, with constitutional problems, of the queerest kind but quite definitely envisaged. The problems were the same as in the Greek cities, but they had been raised and studied, particularly in the Greek colonies of the south of Italy, by Pythagoras and his school. The Italian cities also had a foreign policy with a programme, far-sighted plans, systems of alliance, and even conflicting systems. In all this the Gauls suddenly found themselves involved. When we pass from the story of Ambicatus to the chapter in which Polybios (ii, 19) sums up the events which occurred from 299 onwards, we are in another world. We pass from the world of the tribe to that of the state. In 390 the Gauls attack Etruscans and Latins without distinction. They rush blindly forward and cause their enemies to unite to meet the common danger. A hundred years later most of them have selected their opponent. It is Rome. They enter into alliance with her enemies. They are probably led more then they lead ; but they use diplomatic methods, they have a policy.

In coming into relations with the Italian cities, the Gauls entered the history of the world, and they never fell out of it. We shall see them again once or twice acting in their old character of barbarous hordes rushing to the conquest of fertile lands. But they had learnt to play their game in the manner of the Mediterranean cities, and little by little they all took to it.

The settlement of a large colony of Gauls in Italy had

more effect on the Celtic world as a whole than to attract
new bands of invaders at intervals. In material civilization
there is every evidence that between the beginning of the
La Tène period and its last phase new crafts were acquired,
such as glass-working, the stock of tools was increased,
and habits of life, methods of construction, domestic arrangements, and ideas of comfort were transformed. In all this,
imitation of the Italic peoples and the Greeks was certainly
the chief factor. The civilization of La Tène was affected
by the economic progress of the world in general. But in
the present state of our archæological knowledge we cannot
follow the order of these facts in detail.

VI

THE EARLIEST GALLIC SETTLEMENTS IN THE EASTERN ALPS AND ON THE MIDDLE DANUBE

The Celts expanded in the same period in other directions
as well as into Italy. If the Gauls did not enter that country
by the Danube valley, it does not follow that they made
no advance on that side. They had come there as early as
the beginning of the fifth century. When the Romans found
it necessary to pay attention to what was going on beyond
the Alps, they found Celts in Noricum (Austria) and Pannonia
(Western Hungary).[1] The Carni, who were in the Alps
between the Drave, Istria, the Adriatic, and the Tagliamento,
were Celts.[2] Behind them, a whole new Celtic world reached
as far as the Black Sea. But when did those settlements
begin ?

The tradition used by Livy tells of an expedition, the
counterpart of that of Bellovesus, led by his cousin Sigovesus
into the Hercynian Forest, which had long been occupied
by the Celts but was certainly not the limit of their advance.
Justin's summary is more detailed.[3] According to him, one
part of the Gallic *ver sacrum* made for Illyria *ducibus avibus*,
guided by birds, " for the Gauls are pre-eminent in the augur's
art." The adventurers settled in Pannonia, " had various

[1] See *Rise*, pp. 272 ff.
[2] I, i, p. 460 ; Holder, CCVII, s.v.
[3] Justin, xxiv, 4.

wars with their neighbours which lasted long, and at last reached Greece and Macedonia, overthrowing everything before them." It is an excellent summary of the facts, except that it mentions no interval between the Illyrian wars of the Gauls and their descent on Delphi.

But for a long time yet the Raeti on the one hand and the Veneti on the other remained in the Central Alps and the north-eastern corner of Italy, forming a broad, continuous belt between the Cisalpine Celts and those of the valley of the Danube ; on the Italian side the enclave of the Trentino bit into it but did not pierce it. In 350 there is no question yet of the Carni between the Veneti and Istria. The Veneti march with the Istri, and these latter extend to the Danube.[1]

But about the same time, the Gauls had already come into collision with the Illyrian people of the Ardiaei or Vardaei, which touched the Dalmatian coast opposite the islands of Pharos and Corcyra Nigra (Lesina and Curzola) somewhere near the mouth of the Naron (Narenta). This incident was related by Theopompos, who died in 306.[2]

More serious and more fruitful in results was their encounter with the Antariatae.[3] These seem to have been at that time the predominant people among the Illyrians. At the time of the *Periplus* of Scylax, the Antariatae reached down to the Dalmatian coast at the mouth of the Narenta.[4] They were at constant war with the Vardaei for the possession of the salt-deposits of the upper valley of that river. Inland, they extended to Bulgaria, for they had evicted the Triballi from the valley of the Morava. How far north they went at this date it is hard to say. Their eponymous hero, Antaricos, son of Illyrios, was the father of Pannonios.[5] In any case, they were a very large people and seem to have been then at the height of their military power. They had used it

---

[1] Ps.-Scylax, p. 20.

[2] Theompomp., fr. 41 ; Athen., x, 60 ; d'Arbois, **CCCI**, i, p. 305 ; id., **CCXCIX**, p. 118 ; Schulten, **DXIX**, p. 93.

[3] Or Autariatæ. Antariatae seems to be more correct. The particle *an* is a formative of racial names in Albanian, and there seems to be little doubt that the Albanians are the direct descendants of the ancient Illyrians. The Antariatae are the men of the Tara, a tributary of the Drina, which separates Montenegro from the former Sanjak of Novi-Bazar. Their capital was Tariona (Pliny, iii, 26). Cf. Fischer, in **CLXIX**, 1911, p. 3 ; Baron Nopsca, ibid., p. 913 ; d'Arbois, **CCXCIX**, p. 118 ; Strabo, viii, 5, 11.

[4] Ps.-Scylax, 25.

[5] D'Arbois, **CCCI**, i, p. 303 ; Dottin, p. 152.

against the Macedonians. In 393 the Illyrians, that is to
say the Antariatae, had driven Amyntas II, the father of
Philip, from the throne and had then made him pay them
tribute. In 359, Bardulis, King of the Illyrians, utterly
defeated the army of Perdiccas III, Philip's brother, who
lost his life in the battle. Philip, becoming king, made a
vigorous effort, drove the Illyrian garrisons out of the towns
of Macedonia, and defeated the Antariatae.

It is probable that the Celts came into his political
schemes,[1] but not without payment ; this would explain
the abundance of coins of Philip found among the Celts of
the Danube. The defeated Illyrians became disturbed again
in 335, after the accession of Alexander the Great. We may
suppose that the Celts, whose ambassadors appeared at his
court when he was on his Danubian campaign, kept the
Antariatae occupied while he tackled the Thracians. The
historian of these events, Arrian, who used the " memoirs "
of an eye-witness, Ptolemy, son of Lagos, tells us that these
Celts lived on the Ionic Gulf.[2] Were they the Celts of Italy ?
These have left no Macedonian coins. Did they come on to
the Adriatic north of the Veneti ? Arrian's language is vague,
and doubtless only testifies to the great place that the Celts
of Italy had in the world of that day. Celtic envoys crossed
Asia in 324 to pay their court to Alexander in Babylon.[3] When
the Antariatae caused the Macedonians anxiety, the Celts
kept the former quiet, to their own advantage.

Now, all of a sudden, in 310, the Antariatae were seized
with panic and began to flee in masses.[4] The event appeared
so extraordinary· that historians had recourse to absurd
prodigies to explain it. What had happened was an invasion
of large numbers of Celts, led by a chief named Molistomos.
The flying Antariatae ran into the Macedonians. Cassander
planted some 20,000 on his frontier as military settlers.[5]
Others established themselves among the Veneti and among
the other peoples of the Dalmatian coast.

This fact suggests that the Celtic attack on the Antariatae
at a certain moment assumed the character of a sudden

[1] D'Arbois, CCCI, ii, p. 314.
[2] See Rise, p. 5.
[3] Diod., xvii, 113, 2 ; Arr., Anab., vii, 15, 4.
[4] App. Illyr., 4. Tomascek, in Pauly and Wissowa, s.v. " Autariatai ".
[5] Diod., xx, 19.

cataclysm, and that the original positions of the two peoples
had not been perceptibly altered before then.   The Italian
settlement of the Celts had for a long time lain very much
in front of the Celtic frontiers, being flanked right and left
by Ligurians and Illyrians.   North of the Illyrians, other Celts
had advanced by the Danube, filtering in among the Illyrian
inhabitants.   But they do not appear in large and irresistible
numbers until the end of the fourth century.   That, if one is
to trust the historians, is the position in the south-eastern
part of the Celtic world during the fourth century.

Examination of the archæological finds does not contradict
this view.

It is impossible that the Celts should have arrived in
the middle valley of the Danube in the Hallstatt period.[1]
The Negau helmets are isolated, or rather, apart from the
inscription, they only appear in association with objects
which are not Celtic.[2]   Celtic civilization, and the Celts with
it, gained ground in the first period of La Tène, but more
probably at the end of that phase than at the beginning.[3]

La Tène finds in Upper and Lower Austria are
unfortunately scanty, and do not furnish the answer to our
question.[4]   On the other hand, the cemetery of Hallstatt
itself has yielded an object which, though only one, is of
very great importance.   It is a La Tène sword with a scabbard
of engraved bronze.[5]   The chape is of the type of La Tène I
in appearance but without open-work, and the manner in
which the decorated surface is divided into compartments
recalls the transverse bars with which the scabbards of
La Tène II are strengthened.   On the central part of the
scabbard[6] three foot-soldiers are engraved, carrying a spear
on the shoulder, wearing no helmet, and holding a large
oval shield with a central ridge of the Gallic type.   Behind
the foot-soldiers are four horsemen, advancing with spear
couched, wearing a cap to protect the head and, apparently,
body-armour.   The second seems to have struck with his
spear a foot-soldier, who is lying on his back.   On each side

[1] Cf. Hoernes, in **CXXX**, 1888, p. 333.
[2] See *Rise*, pp. 272 ff.   Cf. Reinecke, **CCCCVI**, pp. 5–6.
[3] Reinecke, op. cit., p. 9.   The La Tène civilization extended into
Transylvania, perhaps from the La Tène period itself (ibid., n. 27).
[4] Déchelette, ii, 3, p. 1081 ; Lindenschmit, **CCCXCIX**, v, p. 284, n. 1.
[5] Ibid., iv, pl. 32 ; Déchelette, ii, 2, p. 770.
[6] See *Rise*, fig. 19.

of these figures is the same scene, of two persons clad in a long-skirted coat and tight striped hose, holding a wheel in their hands. On the chape is a partially serpentine creature struggling with a fallen man. This object is unique, and the art which it represents is very different from the art of La Tène. The costumes are without parallel. On the other hand, the procession of warriors recalls those on the Italic and Venetian buckets. The wheel, doubtless solar, with its two supporters, recalls a motive familiar to the art of Villanova. In fact, this sword from Hallstatt stands not so much for a replacement of Illyrian civilization by Celtic civilization as for the mixed culture which may have been the result of the contact of the two peoples.

There are a certain number of cemeteries in Carinthia and the valley of the Isonzo containing Celtic objects,[1] at Watsch, at Sankt-Michael near Adelsberg, at Nassenfus, at Vital near Prozoz in Croatia, at Idria near Bača in the province of Gorizia. The Celtic objects are isolated, as at Watsch, or late, belonging to La Tène II, as at Sankt-Michael. They are found mixed with Certosa brooches and even with Villanovan brooches which have survived so long.

The cemetery of Idria might have been the successor to the neighbouring cemetery of Santa Lucia.[2] The latter suddenly ceases to be used when the former becomes important. The native town to which the cemetery of Santa Lucia belonged was doubtless destroyed. The population fled. Strangers came and took up their abode elsewhere. But were these Celts? Inscriptions have been found in the cemetery of Idria, and they are not Celtic. We cannot argue from these facts that the Celts began to advance in Friuli at the time when they were making that concentration in the north of Bosnia which caused the Antariatae to leave their homes.

There was the same activity at that time all round the skirts of the Celtic world. The Celtic colonization of Britain was approaching completion. Fresh tribes of Gauls were making their way to the Garonne, where the Iberians held them. Later we shall examine, as a whole, for a longer period, what was going on on the Germanic side.

---

[1] Déchelette, ii, 3, p. 1098.
[2] Szombathy, in CIV, i, p. 318 ; G. Cumin, 1915, p. 219.

CHAPTER II

THE CELTS IN THE EAST

I

THE GAULS IN THE BALKAN PENINSULA

WE have come to the neighbourhood of the year 300 B.C.
At this date, the development of the civilization
of La Tène takes a turn which has long been noted by
archæologists, who have marked it by a new period, La
Tène II. We shall again see, all round the fringes of the
Celtic world, movements similar to those which in the sixth
century took the Celts to the British Isles, Spain, and Italy,
and at the end of the fifth took them to Provence, Italy,
the Danube valley, and again to Britain. We shall see them
spreading and wandering about in the East, establishing
themselves strongly in the valley of the Danube ; new bands
descending on Italy and Spain, and others reaching Britain
and Ireland. A new group of Celtic tribes takes part in those
expeditions or directs them.

When the power of the Antariatae was destroyed, the
conquerors camped in their place, probably in the valley
of the Morava, whence they threatened Thrace, Macedon,
and Greece at once, for they did not settle down at first ;
they remained on the move and no doubt received new
contingents, perhaps summoning them.[1] These great movements of tribes never stop all at once. Besides, if the Gauls
were looking for a settled abode, they could do better than
in the present Serbia.

In 298 a body of them advanced as far as Bulgaria.
They came up against the Macedonians, and were defeated
by Cassander on the slopes of Haemos.[2] A little later a
second body, led by one Cambaules, seems to have reached
Thrace.[3] In 281, the death of Lysimachos and Seleucos and

---

[1] For Brennus's propaganda for the expedition of 279, see Paus., x, 19 ;
Polyaen., *Strat.*, vii, 35 ; Thierry, **CCCLXXXVIII**, i, p. 226.
[2] Jouguet, **DXLIV**, English, p. 176.
[3] Paus., x, 19.

the ensuing prolongation of the dynastic war and the disorganization of the Macedonian kingdom weakened the obstacle which still held the Gauls in check. They saw this, and seized their opportunity.

We are told that they resumed their advance in 280, in three armies.[1] The eastern army, commanded by Cerethrios, attacked the Triballi on the Bulgarian side. The western army, crossing Illyria, must have entered Macedonia somewhere near Monastir; it was preceded by envoys.[2] Ptolemy Ceraunos, who, after betraying and killing Seleucos, was at the time King of Macedon, refused to listen to them. He was utterly defeated and slain. This army was led by a chieftain called Bolgios, whose name we must bear in mind.[3] Historical tradition, which dates from the time of the actual events, records that he crowned his victory by sacrificing prisoners.[4] The Macedonian army was scattered and the state, lacking its head, appeared to be destroyed. The Gauls ranged over the country, looting. Little by little, the Macedonians rallied [5] and by well-conducted warfare on a small scale compelled them to retire behind the mountains.

The central army, commanded by Brennus and Acichorius,[6] had advanced on Paeonia and had to fight throughout the year with the hillmen of Haemos. It did not descend on Macedon until the following year, after it had received large reinforcements, including Illyrian contingents.[7] It was a large host, reckoned by the historians at 150,000 foot and 15,000 or 20,000 horse. Each horseman was accompanied by two mounted servants, the body of three being called a *trimarkisia*. We should note this appearance of cavalry in the Gallic forces. The army seems to have been fairly well organized and skilfully led.[8] In the eighty years

---

[1] Jouguet, **DXLIV**, English, p. 178. Thierry, op. cit., i, pp. 221 ff. ; Stähelin, **DLIV**, p. 2 ; Jullian, **CCCXLVII**, i, p. 300 ; Dottin, **CCCXXII**, p. 316 ; Justin, xxiv, 5–8 ; Paus., i, 4 ; x, 19 ; Diod., xxii, 9. These writers' accounts are derived from common sources, among which we must reckon the history of Hieronymos of Cardia, who lived at the time of the events ; cf. d'Arbois, **CCXLVIII**, xii, pp. 81 ff. ; Jullian, op. cit., i, p. 301, n. 5. Was there a Gallic tradition in this ? See ibid., and F. P. Garofalo, in **CXXXV**, xiii, p. 456.

[2] Just., xxiv, 5, 1.
[3] See below, p. 67.
[4] Diod., xxxi, 13.
[5] Under Sosthenes ; Just., xxiv, 5, 12–13.
[6] Diodoros calls him Cichorios.
[7] Particularly the Antariatae ; App., *Illyr.*, 4.
[8] Especially in the crossing of the Spercheios ; Paus., loc. cit.

or so that the Gauls had been serving as mercenaries by the side of Greek troops,[1] they had learned something and gained experience. Old trained mercenaries may have rallied to the army of Brennus. At all events, it left a name for resourcefulness and alarming ingenuity.[2] Brennus crushed the reorganized Macedonian army, and then descended into Greece by way of Thessaly. At Thermopylae he was met by a force composed mainly of Athenians.[3] While one body, detached on Ætolia, sacked the town of Callion with appalling savagery,[4] the main force managed to turn the position and came by the gorges of Parnassos to Delphi. The Ætolians and Phocians came to the rescue of the god, and the Gauls had to retire to Thessaly.

The Phocians owed something to Apollo, for they had looted Delphi some seventy years before in the course of the second Sacred War, and had come away with considerable sums. They had not, therefore, left much for the Gauls to take, except the statues. Nevertheless, the gold of Delphi has passed into legend.[5] In the great Gallic army there was a body of Tectosages, and the report went about that this treasure had been taken to Toulouse, to other Tectosages, who had migrated there from the same original home. A dark story grew up about this act of pillage and the problematical and accursed gold. The legend-mongers seized upon the sacrilege and gave Brennus a lasting reputation for impiety [6] which placed him on a level with the other Brennus, him of Rome and the Capitol.

Art did its share. This campaign of Brennus was commemorated in monuments. The battle of Thermopylae was depicted on a wall-painting in the council-chamber of Athens.[7] But there were also representations of the sack of Delphi, which were to be seen in various temples of Apollo in Greece and Italy, at Delos, and even in Rome, where, according to Propertius,[8] one of the ivory-plated doors of

---

[1] Jullian, op. cit., i, pp. 324 ff.
[2] Polyaen., *Strat.*, iv, 8 ; vi, 35, 42.
[3] Paus., i, 3, 4 ; x, 19. For the shield of young Cydias, cf. d'Arbois, CCCI, ii, p. 398.
[4] The Oatrians came to the assistance of Callion, and were completely defeated ; Paus., x, 22, 6 ; Cavaignac, CCCX, iii, p. 44.
[5] Just., xxxii, 3.
[6] Diod., xxii, 10.
[7] Paus., i, 3, 4 ; A. J. Reinach, in CVII, 21, p. 192.
[8] Prop., ii, 31, 3.

the temple of the Palatine showed *dejectos Parnassi vertice Gallos*, "the Gauls thrown down from the height of Parnassos," forming a pendant to the story of the Children of Niobe. The whole affair was one of the triumphs of Apollo. One or more of these commemorative monuments furnished motives to the minor arts of Greece or Alexandria. One portrayed a Gaul setting his foot on the cut-off head of the Pythia,[1] another showed Gauls gesticulating against a background of colonnades.[2]

It is certain that the Greeks thought of the Gauls as beautiful. The figure of Brennus in particular has benefited by their æsthetic indulgence. The story ran that Brennus had received three wounds from Apollo's own hand. He gave the order to retreat, and had the strength to lead his men through the gorges of Parnassos to join up with the rearguard of Acichorius, who had remained at Heracleia. He might have recovered, but he felt that he was condemned and determined to die. He got drunk and killed himself. A marvellous little bronze in the Naples museum (a replica) apparently represents the suicide of Brennus.[3]

Although the attack on Delphi did not last long, Central Greece was sufficiently disturbed for the celebration of the Panathenaea to be suspended in 278.[4] The Gallic army retired more or less in good order.[5] We find one section of it in Thrace, in the neighbourhood of Byzantion; it surprised Lysimacheia [6] at the root of the Gallipoli peninsula. Antigonos Gonatas drove the Gauls out of the place in a battle in which he surprised them while pillaging his camp, which he had abandoned to them.[7] This affair took place in 277.

After this victory, Antigonos seems to have taken into his service the force of Ciderios, and perhaps the remnants

---

[1] e.g. on a medallion from Capua; **CXXXVIII**, 1889, i, p. 198.
[2] On the bottom of a *poculum* from the factory of Cales; ibid.
[3] A. J. Reinach, op. cit., pl. xviii (= Bienkowski, **CCCIX**, fig. 117).
[4] Ibid., p. 187.
[5] According to Justin, xxiv, 8, nothing of it remained. But enough must have remained to take the gold of Delphi to Toulouse.
[6] Livy, xxxviii, 16; Just., xxv, 2; Stähelin, **DLIV**, 5. According to Livy, this was the force of Leonnorios and Lutarios; see below, p. 45. According to Justin, they were troops remaining to guard the country. Polyb., iv, 46.
[7] A. J. Reinach, op. cit., p. 37; Just., xxv, 2; Livy, xxviii, 16. For a painted Galatomachia in Athens, see Reinach, op. cit., p. 187.

of the vanquished, who helped him to take possession of
Macedonia. He still had some of them in 274 when he was
defeated by Pyrrhos, who gloried in the fact that he had
triumphed over them.[1] In 265 a body of Gauls, being ill-
paid, mutinied at Megara, and he put them all to the sword.[2]
But Pyrrhos likewise employed Gauls, whom he allowed to
violate the tombs of the ancient kings of Macedon at Ægae [3] ;
he had them in the attack on Sparta ; he had them again at
Argos when he was killed. Down to the very end of these
Macedonian wars of succession, bands of Gauls left their
dead scattered about Greece [4] in the cause of every party.
No tomb of them has survived. We shall return later to the
amazing story of the mercenaries.

A large part of Brennus's army returned to its starting-
point, under the lead of a chief whose name has come down
to us under the distorted form of Bathanattos,[5] and settled
permanently north of Macedonia between the Shar-Dagh
(Mons Scordus) and the Danube.[6] It doubtless consisted of
bodies of mixed origin. They took a name for themselves
from the country, and became the Scordisci. On the banks
of the Danube they founded or took over a capital,
Singidunum, which is now Belgrade.[7]

Among the Illyrian peoples of the coast of Epeiros,
opposite Corcyra, the ancient geographers mention the
Hylli, who are described in the *Etymologicum Magnum*
as a Celtic people.[8] They may, at least, have been Celticized
by their neighbours the Scordisci. The eastern part of the
new domain of the Scordisci was taken from the Triballi
who were driven out, at least to some extent.[9]

Excavation in Bosnia and Herzegovina has revealed
traces, still too rare, of the passage of the Celts and of Celtic
settlements in these new provinces of the Jugo-Slav
kingdom.[10] We know nothing of Serbia itself.

[1] Plut., *In Pyrrhum*, 26 ; Paus., i, 13 ; Just., xxv, 3.
[2] Trog. Pomp., *Prol.*, xxvi.
[3] Plut., loc. cit. ; Diod., xxii, 12.
[4] Just., xxvi, 2.
[5] Ath., vi, 234 *b*.   The name Bathanattos is supposed to have become
a family-name.
[6] Just., xxxii, pp. 3, 7.   It cannot have been that the Tectosages of
Toulouse returned to their own country.
[7] Ptol., iii, pp. 9, 3.
[8] *Etym. Magn.*, 776, 39 ; Scylax, 23 ; Scymnos of Chios, 404.
[9] App., *Illyr.*, 3 ; Niese, CCCLXVIII, p. 618 ; Jullian, op. cit., p. 303.
[10] Patsch, in CV, ix, 1904, p. 241.

Another body, which had likewise belonged to Brennus's army, retired on to the slopes of Haemos under a leader named Comantorios.[1] Little by little it gained the upper hand over the Thracian tribes of the vicinity and founded a Celtic kingdom in Thrace, which lasted until 193 B.C. Its capital was Tyle or Tylis, the site of which is difficult to establish. This people expanded south of Haemos to the basin of Adrianople and north of it, no doubt, to the Danube.

At first the proximity of the Gauls of Haemos perturbed the Byzantines.[2] But they showed themselves such good neighbours that they soon dispelled their alarm. They became Hellenized, and struck coins—very fine ones, with the type of Alexander. Some of these coins bear the name of one of their kings, Cauaros.[3] In short, they lived after the manner of the Hellenistic states of the time, and became so civilized that they finally succumbed to the attacks of the Thracians in 193.[4] Of their Celtic civilization, nothing has survived.

So the invaders of the Balkans who had found no room in the over-populated lands of Greece Proper, covered with cities, had carved themselves kingdoms in the north of the peninsula, among people who were less attached to the soil and did not occupy it so completely, in the wider plains of the Morava, Maritza, and Danube. At intervals along the Danube below the Iron Gates were towns with Gallic names —Bononia (Vidin), Ratiaria (Artcher), Durostorum (Silistria), and Noviodunum (? Isakcha) in the Dobrudja—which were outposts of the state of the Scordisci or of the Celtic kingdom of Thrace.

The forces which had formed the nucleus of these tribes had been very much reduced. We may suppose that they received additions, which cannot have increased the Celtic element in them very much, but there remained all round them Illyrians and Thracians, and even Illyrian and Thracian states,[5] and the states which they formed were composed

---

[1] Polyb., iv, 46 ; Trog. Pomp., *Prol.*, 25 ; d'Arbois, **CCXCIX**, p. 5 ; Jullian, op. cit., p. 303, n. 2 ; Just., xxxii, 3, 6.

[2] A heavy tribute was laid on them by Comantorios, and it continued, in a reduced form, into the time of Cauaros ; Pol., loc. cit.

[3] Blanchet, **CCCVI**, p. 466 ; Forrer, **DXLIII** ; Polyb., iv, 52 (219), for Cauaros.

[4] Ibid., viii, 24.

[5] For a Celtic name among those of the Thracian kings, see Forrer, **DXLIII**, p. 203.

of Celto-Illyrians and Celto-Thracians.[1]   I cannot picture
the Scordisci very clearly. But I imagine the State of Haemos
as something like the first Turkish states which were carved
out of the Arabian Empire round a small band of janizaries.
Those states were as good as their chiefs ; they depended
on the prestige of the chief. The kingdom of Thrace, at least,
seems to have had an admirable head—the King Cauaros
mentioned above.

But there is a region of Celtic names and sites, still more
thinly sown, running northwards along the Black Sea.
North of the Danube, in the angle formed by that river and
the Sereth, Ptolemy [2] mentions the Britolagae, whose name
looks Celtic. So does that of the town of Aliobrix. Further
north, on the Dniester (Tyras), there was a Camodunum
(Zaleszczyki in Galicia). Pausanias [3] speaks of a Gallic people,
the Cabari, remarkable for its great stature, which lived
in the far north on the edge of the frozen desert. If his
information is worth considering, it is hereabouts that we
must place them.

Evidence of the activity of the Celts of this region is
given by an inscription from Olbia on the Bug [4] dating from
the third century, when the city was purely Hellenic,
in honour of a citizen named Protogenes, who had distinguished himself when the place was threatened by the
Galatians. These latter had come and attacked it in mid-
winter, with the assistance of the Sciri, a Germanic people
which lived on the Lower Vistula in the first century of the
Roman Empire.

In addition, Gallic objects of La Tène have been found
in Southern Russia, for example in the cemetery of Jarubinetz
on the Dnieper (Government of Kiev).[5] These are, it is true,
quite recent and they may have been brought in by Germans
who had Gallic objects with them. All these facts are
evidence of the advance either of the Celtic kingdom of
Thrace and the groups which had gone about its territory
in search of settlements, or else of the Boii of Bohemia, of

---

[1] Jullian, op. cit., p. 249, n. 3 ; Strabo, vii, 1, 1. The Ister forms the
northern boundary of the Illyrian and Thracian population, with a certain
number of foreign tribes, some of them Celtic.

[2] Ptol., 3, 10, 7.

[3] i, 35, 5.

[4] Dittemberger, **IV**, 226, 103 ff.

[5] Déchelette, ii, 3, p. 1082.

whose roving spirit we have already seen something. Whichever it was, the Celts went as far as the Sea of Azov (Maeotis). Here the ancient geographers fix the furthest limit of the Celtic world.[1]

II

THE GALATIANS IN ASIA MINOR

In 278 Nicomedes, King of Bithynia, probably through the agency of Antigonos Gonatas, summoned into Asia Minor a body of Celts which may have included some of the men defeated at Lysimacheia.[2] This body was commanded by a chief named Leonnorios. It usually operated with another body, led by one Lutarios. Both seem to have been detached from the army of Brennus before its descent into Greece, to repeat in Thrace the pillaging of Acichorius. Lutarios seized vessels and joined his comrade on the other side of the Hellespont.[3] A treaty was struck,[4] and for some time the Galatians, for thus we must henceforward call them, did good service, duly appreciated, to Nicomedes, or to the Greek cities allied to him, from which they drove off Antiochos the Seleucid who was threatening them from a distance.[5]

The two bodies amounted together to about 20,000 persons, 10,000 of whom were men under arms. They were a difficult host for a petty king of Asia to keep under control. They left Nicomedes and started working on their own account, threatening, ravaging, and negotiating to raise tribute from the terror-stricken cities.[6] We find them at Troy,[7] at Ephesos, at Miletos. In St. Jerome's day people still told of the Milesian Virgins, who had killed themselves to escape outrage and mourned their lot in one of the most beautiful epigrams in the Palatine Anthology.[8] Here again the gods had manifested themselves; the River Marsyas

[1] Plut., *Mar.*, xi.
[2] Stähelin, " Galatia," in **CCCLXVIII** ; Thierry, **CCCLXXXVII**, i, pp. 255 ff., 379 ff. ; Jouguet, **DXLIV**, p. 182 ; Jullian, op. cit., i, p. 303 ; d'Arbois, **CCXCIX**, p. 195.
[3] Livy, xxxviii, 16. Cf. Just., xxv, 2.
[4] Memnon, 20 ff.
[5] Ibid., 11. Cf. Thierry, op. cit., i, p. 260.
[6] See also Ps.-Plut., *Parall. Min.*, 15, 3096 (following the *Galatika* of Cleitophon) ; Strabo, xii, 5, 1 ; xiii, 1, 27 ; Durrbach, **V**, 31.
[7] Callim., *Hymn to Artemis*, v, 257.
[8] *Pal. Anthol.*, vii, 492 ; Paus., x, 22, 4 ; St. Jerome, *Agst. Jovinian*, i, 41.

had defended Celaenae with his waters,[1] and Heracles, Hermes, and Apollo had shown the people of Themisonion a cavern where they could take refuge.[2]

There as elsewhere the Gauls looked for a place in which to settle down. When and how they succeeded it is very hard to say. Livy says that they divided Asia between them.[3] One tribe took the Hellespont; another, Æolis and Ionia; a third, the south of Asia Minor to the Taurus; finally, they had established themselves on the River Halys in the centre of the peninsula, to threaten Syria and exact tribute from it. In writing this part of the history of Asia, Livy and the rest of them lacked objectivity, sense of proportion, and, above all, a good map of Asia Minor. Their judgment was led astray by the terror of those who had lived through the invasions and naturally exaggerated the number and power of the destroyers. However prolific they may have been,[4] the 20,000 Gauls, male and female, of Leonnorios and Lutarios were still, a few years after the invasion, only a very small army, which could not hold a country of that size and was lost when it spread itself.

Antiochos Soter defeated them badly about 270.[5] The Gallic cavalry is said to have been crushed by the elephants of the Syrian army. This battle of the elephants was suitably glorified in after years. The memorial was a painting,[6] which must have been exhibited at Pergamon beside the other " Galatomachies ".

It was probably Antiochos Soter who established the Galatians astride of the Halys and on the Phrygian plateau, for he was the lawful ruler of those regions. This was the most sparsely populated part of Asia Minor, the poorest and least desirable, and it is more likely that the Galatians made the best of what they got than that they chose it for themselves. Their settlement on the plateau of Asia Minor has been compared, with some justice, with their settlement on the plateau of Spain.

[1] Paus., x, 30, 9.
[2] Paus., x, 32, 4–5.
[3] Livy, loc. cit. ; cf. Just., loc. cit.
[4] Just., loc. cit. : *tantæ fecunditatis inventus fuit*.
[5] Celebrated in verse by Simonides of Magnesia (Suidas, s.v.). There is a paraphrase in Lucian, *Zeuxis or Antiochos*, 9–12.
[6] A. J. Reinach, in CVII, xxi, p. 195. Small terra-cotta figures of war elephants are probably derived from this monument.

It was some time before they gave up their wild ways, and the Greek cities had to pay the tax known as *Galatika* (Gaul-Geld) for many years. Moreover, their real military value caused their services to be greatly sought after by one and another of their neighbours. They played a part in the game of Asiatic politics. Their history becomes inter-mingled with that of the Hellenistic states, and ceases to belong to the general history of the Celts. They took sides in the question of the Bithynian succession ; they warred against the Kings of Pontus and the people of Heracleia ; they fought for the pretender Antiochos Hierax against Seleucos II Callinicos. This last war brought them up against the enemy who worsted them, the little kingdom of Pergamon. Having defeated Seleucos at Ancyra, they were beaten in 241 near the sources of the Caïcos by Attalos of Pergamon, who was backing Seleucos. This victory finally established the power of Attalos, who gained the title of King by it. Between 240 and 230, he again defeated one of the Gallic tribes—the westernmost, the Tolistoagii—four times. These defeats were decisive. The Gauls of Asia were confined to their own country, and hardly came out of it again ; even there they were not always independent, but they remained there.

These victories were gloriously commemorated. In any case, the acropolis of the new capital had to be adorned. Attalos and his successor Eumenes set up monuments which must have formed a single scheme.[1] In the excavation of Pergamon bronze statue-bases have been found on which the name of the sculptor Epigonos appears several times. Pliny mentions three other artists—Phyromachos, Stratonicos, and Antigonos. These men did a piece of work, the remnants of which are magnificent. They treated the Gauls admirably, idealizing them just enough. Of these Pergamene statues there are two certain copies in marble—the Dying Gaul of the Capitol and the Ludovisi group of a Gaul stabbing himself with his own sword after having killed his female

---

[1] S. Reinach, **CCCLXXV**, pp. 6 ff. ; A. J. Reinach, loc. cit. ; Pliny, 34, 84. The Thusnelda at Florence has sometimes been regarded as coming from the former monument. Cf. Kossinna, **CCCXLV**, 217, pl. xlv, 1. A statue since discovered in Asia Minor, in the walls of Halicarnassos, seems to be an independent work ; it represents a squatting figure, dressed in thick wool, with tight trousers, a belt, apparently of metal, and a cap (G. Karo, in **CII**, 1920, 160, pl. iv).

companion.   These are Gauls sure enough, recognizable by
some detail of costume, their ornament, their weapons,
and their type, with the prominent eyebrows, deep-set base
of the nose, and stiff, rebellious hair.   But they are also
very noble works of art.   These sculptures did not lack
emotion or sympathy ;   the masterpiece of Epigonos,
according to Pliny, was a dead mother caressed by her
child.   The monuments of the victor certainly contributed
to the glory of the vanquished.

On the Acropolis of Athens, Attalos I dedicated another
monument composed of groups representing four subjects—
a battle of Giants, a battle of Amazons, the battle of
Marathon, and the defeat of the Gauls in Mysia.   Six statues
of half life-size from the battle of Giants are known, dispersed
between the Louvre and the Venice and Naples museums.[1]
There were also paintings in Pergamon,[2] and some of the
small objects representing Gauls are derived from those
famous works of art.

What we know of the Galatian state gives us our first
example of the organization of a Celtic state.

When they started on their migration, there were two
main bodies and seventeen leaders of bands.[3]   Very soon
we find ourselves in the presence of three peoples formed
into twelve groups, four groups to a people—the Tectosages,
the Tolistoagii (or Tolistobogii or Tolistoboii),[4] and the
Trocmi or Trogmi.   The Tectosages are probably Volcae ;
it is very doubtful that the Tolistoagii or Tolistoboii are
Boii ; the Trocmi are not found elsewhere and their name
cannot be explained.   The twelve subdivisions are sub-
tribes, similar to the *pagi* which we shall find in Gaul.   The
names of a few of them are known—the Teutobodiaci among
the Tectosages and the Voturi, Ambituti, and Tosiopes
among the Tolistoboii.[5]   Historians have been misled by
the title of Tetrarch, borne by chiefs of tribes or sub-tribes.
Each of the three peoples, with its four sub-divisions, formed

---

[1] The Vigna Ammendola sarcophagus gives an idea of what this monument
may have been like. S. Reinach, **CCCLXXIII**, i, p. 36 (= Bienkowsky, **CCCV**,
pl. iv).

[2] Cf. **CXXXV**, 1913, p. 392 ; S. Reinach, **CCCLXXVI**, p. 149, n. 4. Attalos
and Nike before a trophy of Gallic arms, on a fresco at Naples.

[3] Memnon, 19 ; Livy, xxxviii, 16.

[4] Stähelin, **DLIV**, p. 42, n. 3.

[5] Pliny, v, 146.

a tetrarchy with proto-tetrarchs.[1] It is an organization, a typical example of which is furnished by Ireland. Each sub-tribe was the quarter of a tetrarchy. At its head was a king (*regulus* or βασιλεύς), assisted by a council of nobles, who were sometimes also called *reguli*. Ireland presents just the same arrangement of royalties of different ranks. For each sub-tribe there was, in addition, a judge (δικαστής) and a military leader (στρατοφύλαξ) with two lieutenants. The Celtic constitutions will give us instances of the same distinction between the judicial, royal, and military functions.

How was the tribe, the *gens*, *populus*, or *civitas* governed? We do not know, but the absence of information seems to indicate that its rulers were only temporary and chosen by common agreement among the sub-divisions. But the three peoples formed a federation, which was exactly translated under the Roman Empire by the expression κοῖνον Γαλατῶν, the Commonwealth of the Galatians. It was governed by a senate composed of the twelve tetrarchs and by an assembly of three hundred representatives, that is twenty-five representatives to a sub-tribe, who met at the common shrine of the Galatians, in a place called Drynemeton.[2] The powers of this assembly seem to have been chiefly judicial. The general policy of the confederate peoples apparently remained independent. We always see them developing separately.

There is something artificial in the regularity of this structure and its numerical symmetry, and indeed it is probable that the Gauls who were collected together from the remnants of military bands, sorely tried by the adventure of Brennus and a succession of wars, bore no resemblance to organized nations when they arrived in Asia Minor. They must then have rearranged themselves, like the Scordisci, on the ideal plan of the Gallic tribe, and we have the good fortune to know how they did it. The plan was not modified for the simple reason that the Galatians remained a closed community. We have proof of this. Another band of Gauls, the Ægosages, were summoned from Thrace in 218 by Attalos of Pergamon, who afterwards tried to get rid of them. They revolted and settled on the Hellespont, where

---

[1] Stähelin, op. cit., p. 43; id., "Galatia," in CCCLXVIII, p. 527.
[2] D'Arbois, CCXCIX, 203; Stähelin, DLIV, p. 43, n. 8.

Prusias I of Bithynia defeated them in 217. They did not attempt to unite with the Galatians of Phrygia.[1]

The three peoples lay one behind the other, from west to east. In the west, the Tolistoboii occupied the upper valley of the Sangarios; Pessinus was their capital and Gordion was probably in their territory. Next came the Tectosages, with Tavium as capital. The Trocmi stood astride of the Halys, reaching westward as far as Ancyra; they had the largest and least populous district.

The Galatians apparently settled down side by side with the Phrygian population without driving it out, by some process of endosmosis which we cannot follow.[2] The association of the new population and the old was probably peaceful. There was nothing to show that it was not, and certain facts suggest that it was,[3] although they do not justify us in supposing that relations were always cordial and that the domination of the Gauls was always endured with patience. They were a foreign minority encamped in the midst of a dense population of Greeks and Phrygians, who kept their own independence.[4] The great centres were not touched, and few new ones were created. Only three or four towns have names which are certainly new and at least partly Gaulish—Tolistothora in the south of the country of the Tolistoboii, Pitobriga in the north of the country of the Tectosages, and Eccobriga among the Trocmi.[5] What were these towns? Were they like the camps of refuge in which, according to the historians, the Gauls shut up their women and children? Where did the Galatians live?[6] Being semi-mobilized and often at war, they remained an army for a very long time. The position of the Galatians in

---

[1] Polyb., v, 111. Cf. Rhigosages, who served in the army of Antiochos III in 220 B.C. against Molon, Satrap of Media (ibid., v, 53, 3).

[2] It has been supposed that they were in cantonments, like Ariovistus among the Sequani (Ramsay, in LVII, xxii, p. 341).

[3] Thierry, CCCLXXXVII, p. 983; Stähelin, DLIV, p. 47.

[4] Pliny, v, 22; 175 settlements in all. For intermarriage, see Livy, xxxviii, 17, 9; O.G.I.S., 545.

[5] We should probably add Trocnades (= Tricomia; cf. I, iii, suppl. 1, 6997), which was probably taken from the Galatians, Peion (cf. Welsh *pau*, " inhabited country "), Blucion (Welsh *blwgh* " box ", γαζφυλάκιον, Strabo, xii, 567), and perhaps also Tavium (Welsh *taw* " rest ").

[6] The mass of the Galatian population lived in villages (Livy, xxxviii, 18), and the chiefs in the φρούρια, some of which were the old cities (Stähelin, DLIV, 46).

Galatia must have been like that of the Franks in Gaul and the Mongols in China.

III

GALLIC MERCENARIES IN EGYPT. THE CIVILIZATION OF THE GALATIANS

Antigonos Gonatas, who had placed Gallic mercenaries at the disposal of Nicomedes of Bithynia, also lent a body of them to Ptolemy II Philadelphos in 277–6.[1] Ptolemy was at war with his brother Magas. He defeated him, but the mutiny of a corps of four thousand Gauls prevented him from following up his victory. Pausanias speaks of a conspiracy to take possession of Egypt.[2] What an adventure as a sequel to the sack of Delphi ! But, however disorganized we may imagine the great kingdoms of the Successors to have been, they were too big for a small band of janizaries, and however mad the Gauls may have been, perhaps they did not go to such lengths as this. More mildly and credibly, the scholiast of Callimachos, who celebrated their defeat,[3] speaks of an attempt to plunder the treasures of Ptolemy. The Egyptians shut up the Gauls on an island in the Sebennytic arm of the Nile. There they all perished, either by starvation or by a kind of ritual suicide of which we shall see other instances. In memory of this affair Ptolemy had a Gallic shield on his coins. The victory was considered of sufficient importance to deserve a monument. A superb fragment of it survives, and possibly three. The first is the head of a Gaul, with an intense expression of anguish, now in the Cairo Museum.[4] The others, which were found at Delos,[5] are a younger head, also expressing pain, and a wonderful headless body of a fallen warrior.[6] The whole monument must have represented the scene of the suicide and must have been a magnificent illustration of the epic of the Gallic mercenaries.[7]

[1] A. J. Reinach, in **CVII**, xviii, p. 37 ; id., in **CXXXIV**, 1910, p. 33.

[2] Paus., i, 7, 2.

[3] Callim., *Hymn to Delos*, 185–8.

[4] A. J. Reinach, ii, pl. vii.

[5] Ibid., pp. 99–101.

[6] S. Reinach, **CCCLXXVII**, ii, p. 199 ; **CXXXIX**, 1909, p. 2, 465. For smaller monuments derived from these great works and small Alexandrian monuments representing Gauls of Egypt, see A. J. Reinach, in **CVII**, xviii, pp. 102 ff.

[7] For collective suicide on the part of the Gauls, see Just., xxvi, 2.

Ptolemy II at the end of his reign, and Ptolemy III after him, enrolled more mercenaries. Under Ptolemy IV, we find some settled in Egypt; those were the κάτοικοι, whose descendants were ἐπίγονοι.[1] Some of their graves, with painted tombstones, have been found in the cemetery of Hadra,[2] south-east of Alexandria. From these men a body of four thousand was raised, which appeared at the battle of Raphia in the Coele-Syrian campaign with ten thousand Gauls from Thrace.

There were likewise Gauls in the army of the Seleucids. Some took part in the campaign against the Maccabees. There was no prince in the East who could do without his corps of Gauls.[3]

Gauls appeared in the army of the Lagids which besieged Abydos in 186–185 in the repression of the revolt in Upper Egypt. Here is an inscription which they left on the walls of the temple of Seti I, in the small chapel of Horus [4]:

Τῶν Γαλατῶν	Of the Galatians,
Θόας Καλλίστρατος	we, Thoas, Callistratos,
Ἀκάννων	Acannon,
Ἀπολλώνιος	Apollonios,
ἤλθομεν	came,
καὶ ἀλώπεκα	and a fox
ἐλάβομεν ὧδε	caught we here.

It is a thrilling monument in its extreme simplicity, scribbled on the walls of the deserted, sanded-up old chapel one evening by men who had wandered there out of idle curiosity and had come on a jackal, which they took for a fox. It brings before one the glorious adventure of those simple-minded men, whose fathers had come from the banks of the Rhine to overthrow the order of sacred things in Greece, and who, since then, had been dragging their heavy hobnailed soles over every battlefield in the East.

But this inscription suggests yet other reflections. Those Galatians could write, and that by itself is interesting enough.

[1] Polyb., v, 65.
[2] A. J. Reinach, loc. cit., pp. 41 ff.
[3] Thierry, CCCLXXXVII, i, p. 219. There must have been Senones among these mercenaries, perhaps Senones of Italy. Cf. Steph. Byz., and also Domaszevski, p. 214.
[4] A. J. Reinach, in CXXXIV, 1910, pp. 55 ff.; Dittenberger, IV, 757.

But they did not think of writing in Gaulish; they wrote
in Greek. Their Greek is very straightforward and shows
no subtlety, but Greek it is, and the spelling is so correct as
to shame our troops who record the simple distractions of
a soldier's life on the walls of monuments in distant lands.
Greek was the language of the Gallic troops. I do not know
that they ever had Greek officers[1]; so it is not a military
question, but a question of civilization. Greek was likewise
the official language of the Gauls of Asia Minor. They have
not left a single inscription in Celtic. All their inscriptions
are in Greek.

But we must add that they had not, at least in general,
forgotten their own tongue. Strabo vouches for it.[2] In the
second century after Christ, Lucian[3] tells us of a sorcerer
from Paphlagonia who could give answers in Celtic to people
who asked him for consultations. Still later, in the fourth
century, St. Jerome,[4] while saying that the Galatians used
Greek, admits that they had kept a Celtic dialect. Moreover,
the Galatians of Asia Minor have left a few Celtic words in
Greek, such as λειούσματα or λελούσματα, a kind of body-
armour; ἔμβρεκτον, a kind of soup or porridge; ὅς, the
kermes-oak; τασκός, a stake; κάρνος, a trumpet.[5]

Another point to note is that none of the Gauls at Abydos
has a Celtic name, and many of those buried in the cemetery
of Hadra have Greek names. This would be easy to explain
if the corps of Galatians were recruited as the auxiliary corps
of the Roman army were afterwards recruited, being originally
formed of men of one race, the name of which was given to
the unit, but being filled up by men of all nationalities. But
we have no reason to suppose that this was so. The Gauls in
Greek lands assumed or gave to their children additional
names, Greek names, as a result of intermarriage, or simply
because they liked them.[6] In Galatia itself, such names

---

[1] On the other hand, there were Gallic leaders in command of troops of
other races (Polyb., v, 79, 11 ; 82, 11). The Galatian Lysimachos commanded
the Cardaces at the battle of Raphia.

[2] Strabo, xii, 567.

[3] Lucian, *Alexander*, 37.

[4] St. Jerome, *Prol.*, ii, *in Ep. ad Galatas* (Migne, *Patrologie latine*, xxvi, 382).

[5] And all the words which passed directly into Greek—*gaison, kartamera,
drouggos, karnyx*. A. J. Reinach, **CXL**, 1909, p. 65 ; Dottin, **CCCXVII**, p. 25.

[6] But even in Egypt the Gallic mercenaries had with them Gallic women
with Gallic names (Boudoris).

as Apaturios and Lysimachos appear as early as the events of 223–218.[1]

The Gauls of Asia and the mercenaries kept their own weapons,[2] at least the chief of them, certain peculiarities of armament, and certain military traditions. These were the marks of their units. They had the great sword with a central rib (this is what they kept most faithfully), the helmet, with or without horns, copied from the Italic helmet and derived by them from Cisalpine Gaul, the sword, worn on the right, the long sword of La Tène II,[3] besides Greek or Asiatic swords, and, finally, various types of javelin. Although they had body-armour, which is represented on the trophies, the historians describe them as fighting naked for choice. Some of the horsemen painted on the tombstones in the cemetery of Hadra are accompanied by their squires, so the system of the *trimarkisia* survived in the mercenary cavalry. The troops were always followed by women and children, who went with the baggage,[4] as with the Senegalese troops of France.

We have seen that those Gauls who formed political units adhered in a curious way to their national organization. If we are to believe the ancient anecdote-mongers, they remained true to their racial character and even to their manner of living. Plutarch depicts them in the bath with their children, emptying pots of porridge.[5] The one year's feast given to the Galatians by a noble called Ariamnes[6] (here is a man with a non-Gaulish name already) reminds one of the feasts of Luernius, King of the Arverni, or, in Celtic literature, of that prepared by Briccriu for the chief men of Ulster. It was a *potlatch*, as it would have been called in the north-west of America ; it was not a banquet of satraps. Among the settled populations of Asia with their urban civilization, the Gauls seem on the whole to have been not very strongly

---

[1] Polyb., v, 79. But Celtic names survived—Gaulotus, Cambolomarus, Epossognatus, Toredorix, Adiatorix, Bogodiatarus, Deijotarus. See the list in Stähelin, **DLIV**, p. 109 ; Bitorix, **CXXXIV**, 1912, 2, 290.

[2] P. Couissin, in **CXXXIX**, 1927, i, p. 138.

[3] Statuette found at Caere (in Berlin Museum), see ibid., pp. 148–157 ; statuette from Panticapaeon (in British Museum), see A. J. Reinach, in **CVII**, xviii, p. 97 ; Diod., xvi, 94, 9 (the Gallic sword used by the murderer of Philip).

[4] Just., xxvi, 2 ; Polyb., v, 78.

[5] Plut., *Symp.*, viii ; *Quæst.*, 9.

[6] Ath., iv, 34.

attached to one spot ; their chief wealth is pastoral.[1] But
excavation in Galatia has yielded nothing more than the
hope of finding a few portable objects of Gaulish origin—
a blue glass bracelet in a tumulas, a little pottery at Gordion,
and that is all.[2] In crafts and gear, as in language and the
habits of daily life, the Gauls borrowed largely from the
people among whom they lived, and indeed became merged
with them astonishingly quickly. They adopted their religion.
Plutarch twice tells us a story of a beautiful Gallic woman
named Camma who was priestess of Phrygian Artemis.[3] The
priest-kings of Pessinus were Celts ; the first of them is
mentioned in inscriptions of 153 and 139.[4]

In addition to the arts and crafts of material life, Greece or
the Hellenistic world had something to teach ·its guests
which was new to them, and that was, if not its moral culture,
at least its culture of the soul. For nearly three centuries
all Greece had been educated by the school of the rhetors
or the philosophers, who taught them to use their reason
and to use it about themselves, to analyse the motives of
human actions and to interpret the rules which govern
them. They were not more moral or more just than other
men—far from it—but there were in Greece men with more
lively and enlightened consciences than elsewhere. Greek
culture, grafted on the good instincts and solid morality of
the Gauls, produced excellent fruit. Plutarch tells us of
noble ladies who were not only beautiful but models of virtue.
Among the men, in the long list of chiefs of whom we do not
know much, two figures stand out—those of Cauaros, King
of Thrace, and Ortiagon, one of the four kings of the Tolistoagii who came into contact with the Romans a few years
after the date at which I stopped. Unfortunately, we only
see them in the summaries of the lost books of Polybios. But
the summaries tell us enough. Polybios had known Ortiagon.
He had conversed at Sardis with his wife Chiomara, who had
had, in the course of the war, an adventure which had certainly
lost nothing of its tragic character through her ; she was

[1] Strabo, xii, 6, 1 (the three hundred flocks of Amyntas in Lycaonia).
[2] A. J. Reinach, in **CXL**, 1909, p. 66 ; R. Zahn, in **XXX**, 1907, p. 87 ;
XX, 1907, p. 500 ; Stähelin, " Galatia," in **CCCLXVIII**, p. 534 ; Ebert,
CCCXXIV, iv, p. 284.
[3] Plut., *Amat.*, 22, p. 768 ; *De Mul. Virtut.*, 20, p. 257 ; Polyaen., *Strat.*,
viii, 39.
[4] Dittenberger, **IV**, No. 315 (i, p. 484).

a heroine by birth and by education.[1] Ortiagon doubtless inspired Polybios with equal enthusiasm. He aspired, the summary tells us, to the kingship of all Galatia. " He was well prepared for it by nature and by upbringing, for he was liberal and magnificent, full of charm in his personal dealings, and highly intelligent. Moreover, what the Galatians always hold in esteem, he was brave, and, in war, efficient ($\delta \nu \nu a \mu \iota \kappa \acute{o}s$)." So, then, he was a fine man, able and well educated, with distinguished manners and lively intelligence. He shows these qualities in history. As for Cauaros, Polybios depicts him acting successfully as arbiter between Byzantion and the king of Bithynia. He was, then, both a diplomatist and a just man. The summary tells us that he had a kingly nature, greatness of soul.[2] He had displayed his phil-Hellenism in assisting the Greek traders of the Black Sea. It follows from this that he had an economic policy and that he kept good order in his dominions, which extended to the Black Sea.

The Hellenization of the Galatians does not seem to have greatly benefited the Celtic world as a whole, not so much because they were cut off from it by the states of Western Asia Minor as because they looked in another direction. We have a conclusive proof of this.

One result of the Hellenization of the Gauls was that they entered into a world which had long made use of coinage. It is true that the Celts of the West might have known (though not for long) of coinage through Marseilles and its colonies. But these cities were on the fringe of the Celtic world and the coins of Marseilles do not seem to have spread there in the form of imitations so very quickly. The Gauls of Italy had likewise seen coins. The Roman *as* has been found in Celtic surroundings. But Italy was ill-provided with coins at that date. The Gauls in the East suddenly found themselves with fairly large masses of coin in their hands—the tribute of the cities and the payment of their services. Byzantion, for example, paid a tribute of eighty talents a year, for which it obtained a loan of four thousand gold pieces from Heracleia. The Gallic tribes taken on by Antigonos Gonatas received a gold piece per man.[3] So the

---

[1] Plut., *De Mul. Virtut.*, 22, p. 258 ; Polyb., xxi, 38 ; Livy, xxxviii, 24.
[2] Polyb., iv, 52 ; viii, 24.   [3] Cf. Polyaenos, iv, 6.

Gauls had coins, and they made coins themselves, copying those which came their way. These were Macedonian coinages and those of certain cities such as Thasos[1] and Larissa.

Now, the coins of the Galatians are not Macedonian; they are imitated from the coins of Tarsos.[2] The coins of Tarcanos of Tarsos, bearing a woman's head on the obverse and a helmeted warrior on the reverse, were copied in Galatia. Other Galatian coins are imitated from those of Euthydemos of Bactriana, with a portrait on the obverse and a seated Heracles on the reverse. The diffusion of the former is perhaps explained by the commercial relations of Galatia. The choice of the models may have been imposed by the mercenaries.

It seems to me that, while the colonization of Northern Italy had a great and beneficial influence on Celtic culture as a whole, the colonization of Asia Minor had no effect on it whatever. That colony was lost to the Celtic world. It was not so on the Danube.

IV

THE CELTS ON THE DANUBE

To the ancient historians, the Celtic Danube was still an unknown world at the time at which we have taken our stand in order to view it. A few proper names, a few archæological data, scanty but valuable, may help us to picture that ancient world, not without having resort to conjecture.

Behind the armies and the roving bands whose expansion we have followed, the middle valley of the Danube was becoming peopled and organized as a Celtic country. Northwest of the Scordisci, two main groups had formed. The Taurisci[3] had carved a domain out of the territories of the Veneti in Upper Austria, Carinthia, and Styria. They had taken their name, as the Scordisci had done, from the mountain on whose slopes they had settled, the Taurus, now the Tauern. Later the country was called Noricum, from its capital Noreia. This group comprised the Ambidravi,[4] who lived in Styria and Carinthia on both sides of the Upper

---

[1] Forrer, **DXLIII**, pp. 226 ff.
[2] Ibid., pp. 238-9.
[3] D'Arbois, **CCXCIX**, 129.
[4] Ibid.

Drave, and the Ambisontes,[1] who were settled north of the Tauern, astride of the Isonta (Saltzach).

The other group was that of the Pannonians, who had settled in the northern domain of the Antariatae[2] in Lower Austria, Western Hungary, and Croatia. Attached to this group were the Osi[3] on the left bank of the Danube and the Aravisci[4] on the other side, extending from the station of Carpi (Κάρπις),[5] at the point where the river turns south, to the border of the Scordisci, whose country lay between Mount Scordus and the Danube.

Apart from the Aravisci, about whose origin there is doubt,[6] and who may have come with the Boii when the latter invaded Noricum, these are certainly Celtic peoples, or at least bands in which the Celtic element predominated. Thirty years before Cæsar wrote his *Gallic War*, a Latin historian, Sempronius Asellio, observed that Noreia was in Gaul.[7] Indeed, a great Danubian Celtic domain had come into being between the Celts of Germany and those of Italy. The map is dotted with a great number of Celtic names of towns and villages, some old, some formed later, even in the time of the Roman Empire, according to habits of name-making which outlive languages.[8] Noreia is a Celtic name, formed on a stem *noro* which appears in the proper names Noromertus (in Britain) and Norus (the name of a potter). In Carinthia[9] Matucaium (Treibach) is also Celtic (*math* " pig ", *caion* " enclosure "), and so are Gabromagus, " the plain of goats " (Windisch-Garstein) and Lauriacum (Lorsch) in Upper Austria, Graviacae (*villa* understood) (Tamsweg) in the province of Salzburg, Cucullae, " the city of cowls " (Kuchl), and Masciacum, east of Innsbruck. In Pannonia[10] we have Vindobona (Vienna), Carnuntum (Petronell), Brigetio (Ószöny), Cornacum (Šotin) ; among the Scordisci there

---

[1] Pliny, iii, 137 ; cf. I, v, 7877 ; Ptol., ii, 13, 2.
[2] See above, p. 34.
[3] Or Onsi, *Ptol.*, ii, 2, 10 ; Ritterling, in **LXVII**, 1917, p. 132.
[4] *Ptol.*, xi, 15, 2 ; Tac., *Germ.*, 28 ; Pliny, iii, 148 (Eravisci). Cf. Tomaschek, in **CCCXXIV**, ii, p. 200.
[5] Kauffmann, **CCCXLVIII**, p. 221.
[6] Their coins are all Roman coins of the first century ; this suggests that they came later (Forrer, **DXLIII**, p. 120).
[7] Schol. on Virg., *Georg.*, iii, 47. Cf. d'Arbois, **CCXCIX**, p. 140.
[8] See d'Arbois, op. cit., pp. 121 ff. ; Kauffmann, op. cit., p. 219.
[9] D'Arbois, op. cit., p. 131 ; von Grimberger, in **LXXXI**, xl, pp. 135-9.
[10] Von Duhn, in Ebert, **CCCXXIV**, vi, p. 289.

are Singidunum (Belgrade), Capedunum (? Banostor), and Viminacium (Kostolatz). The Latin inscriptions of the country, especially in Pannonia,[1] present a great number of Celtic proper names—Enigenus " son of the Inn " ; Broccus " badger " (Irish *brocc*, Welsh *broch*) in Carniola ; Assedomarus, Excingomarus, Nertomarus, Ategnatus, and Devognata in Styria ; Iantumara in the province of Salzburg ; Ritumara and Ateboduus in Carinthia ; Atepomarus and Drogimarus in Austria ; Retimarus in Hungary. The inscriptions also speak of Teutates at Seckau in Styria and a Belinus at Klagenfurt in Carinthia.

We may reasonably imagine this great Celtic population of the Danube as a kind of hotch-potch in which the Celtic element predominated. What Strabo tells us of the country of the Iapodes [2] is very significant in this respect. They lived south of Pannonia, near the Adriatic ; the names of their towns, Metulum, Avendone, Monetium, are perhaps Celtic ; their weapons were those of the Celts and they tattooed themselves in the fashion of the other Illyrians and the Thracians. It is a mixed civilization and a mixed people. We may say the same of the Taurisci and the Pannonians, among whom the Venetian and Illyrian elements survived. The actual name of the Pannonians is an Illyrian racial name and, if we are to believe Tacitus,[3] the mixed people which they formed spoke a language which was not Celtic.

Given what we already know of the habits of the Celts at this time, we may suppose that the greater part of the country newly conquered by them was not of a kind to tempt them. They probably occupied the valley-bottoms and the lower slopes, which could be tilled ; they made for the bank of the Danube, where they had many settlements down to Pest. But these settlements were towns, crossing-points, between which the banks, being too low, were no doubt left unoccupied. Let us look at the map : Austria and what were until recently its southern provinces, with their mountains and their many valleys, offered the Gauls a very broken-up domain ; Hungary, too, was unsuitable, for other reasons, which are revealed in the fact that the river along

[1] Scholer, in **CLI**, x, 1923, p. 10.
[2] Strabo, vii, 5, 4.
[3] *Germ.*, 43.

its whole length in that country was occupied by the Aravisci, who may not have been Celts. Between the places held by the Celts the aborigines remained.

Everything, to the very names borne by these Gallic populations, shows that they were formed on the spot out of unrelated elements. We must imagine, with the ancient historians, a reflux of the great expeditions into Greece and a steady influx from early times of immigrants from Bavaria or Bohemia; in short, a series of complicated happenings, very different from a systematic conquest made by one organized people. Even more clearly, the Gallic peoples scattered about from the Adriatic to the Black Sea and from the Ægean to the Sea of Azov were unconnected groups in the midst of the Illyrians, the Thracians, and the Scythians.

Archæological finds add something to this picture. A certain number of cemeteries of the second La Tène period have been found in what was once the Austrian Empire.[1] The civilization of the same period is very well represented in the Budapest Museum by objects discovered in the western part of Hungary. But this culture extended a long way beyond the Danube. A cemetery of La Tène II has been excavated at Apahida in the old county of Kolozs.[2] In the Kluj Museum (Kolozsvár) there is a chariot-burial with brooches of La Tène II, found at Balsa, near Szabolcs.[3] Celtic remains have been discovered between the Danube and Theiss.[4] Were these left by isolated Gauls who had strayed far from their own territory, or by the Dacians imitating Celtic culture? The tombs at Apahida are indistinguishable from other Celtic tombs. It is quite conceivable that there was here a small body of Celts, lost in the midst of the Dacians and forgotten by history.

One thing is certain, and that is that the culture of the Danubian Celts came to be accepted by the Dacians, as it was by the Illyrians and Raetians. It would be extraordinary if the relics of the Celts alone had survived and those of their neighbours had disappeared, or the survival of native

[1] For La Tène civilization in Austria, see R. Pittioni, *La Tène in Nieder-österreich*, fasc. v of *Materialen zur Urgeschichte Œsterreichs*, Vienna, 1930.
[2] K. Itsvan, in **CLV**, ii, 1911, pp. 35 ff.
[3] Déchelette, ii, 3, p. 1082.
[4] L. Rödiger, in **XXI**, 1904, p. 351 (tomb at Hodsagh). For the archæology of La Tène in Hungary, see F. de Pulszky, in **CXXXIX**, 1879, pp. 158–172, 211–222, 265–275 ; Reinecke, in **LXXXIV**, ii, 1907, p. 45.

habits were represented only by objects of early date ; indeed it is quite impossible. In any case, the Dacians, who had been under the influence of the Scythian civilization before the Celts descended the valley of the Danube, came under that of the Celtic civilization when it reached them. This is what one gathers from the series of archæological finds made in Dacia.[1]

The little that we know of these settlements points to a sedentary people, which, at least for a time, had given up adventurous undertakings. But we still have to record a few expeditions on the part of the Danubian Celts. At the end of the second century, they seem to have invaded Macedon and Thessaly again [2] ; in 110 the Scordisci and Thracians menaced Delphi. The Balkan campaigns of the Romans Republic evidently woke up all the unsettled and unruly elements among them. But these were accidental episodes, and it would be wrong to regard these peoples, among which brigands were certainly to be found,[3] as a collection of freebooters. A passage in Livy [4] enables us to pass a fairer judgment on them. In the neighbourhood of Pella in Macedonia, the historian mentions Celts and Illyrians as being " indefatigable tillers of the soil ". These few words (which show, incidentally, that there were Gallic settlers outside the Gallic political formations) pick out of all the characteristics of the Celt one which distinguished him and won him the esteem of the Greeks and Latins ; he was a hard-working and efficient farmer. As we have already found him, so we find him here, more particularly in his own country —in Noricum, for example. It was a rich and peaceful country, anxious to have good relations with its neighbours, given up to its agriculture and its trade,[5] and, what is more, a mining country which produced an iron ore of some reputation.[6]

The Scordisci had the name of being rougher folk, more

---

[1] For the Celts in the Danube valley and their civilization, cf. Parvan, **DXLVIII**, pp. 459 ff. ; **DXLVII**, *passim*.

[2] Forrer, **DXLIII**, p. 142.

[3] Oros., v, 23, 17–18.

[4] Livy, xlv, 30, 5 ; *Permultos Gallos et Illyrios, impigros cultores.*

[5] Strabo, iv, 6, 10, 12 ; vi, 2, 2, ; 5, 2 ; 9, 21 ; Pliny, xxxix, 5, 1–4 xliii, 5, 2–9.

[6] Mines at Noreia, near Hallstatt. Rice Holmes, **CCCCXXXIII**, p. 231.

attached to the old ways of the Celts,[1] and readier to take up arms. What has been related of their partiality for silver seems to indicate that they worked the mines of the Drena.[2] Here they extracted the metal, which was beginning to spread among the Celts [3] and is still found in the region in the form of various objects. Political history shows them sometimes allied to Mithradates, sometimes combining with the Dacians,[4] in the capacity in which they must have constantly appeared, that of middlemen of civilization.

The archæological evidence of these exchanges is scanty— three small plaques of repoussé silver. One, which is said to have been discovered at Roermond in Dutch Limburg,[5] represents a human figure strangling a lion, crudely modelled in the style of the Gundestrup cauldron. All round are galloping animals, and above the man are two lions attacking a lamb, above which again are two confronted dogs with a bull's head between.

The two other plaques, which come from Asia Minor,[6] have the same arrangement : in the centre a wolf or a lion attacks a kid ; above it, the same beast is attacked by two winged monsters ; below is an ox's head flanked by two griffins ; the field is adorned with spirals and dotted lines representing foliage. They bear an inscription which was doubtless the same on both but is completely preserved on only one : $NAO\Sigma$ $APTEMIA$ EX $T\Omega N$ TOY BA $MI\Theta PAT$ . . . . . "Temple of Artemis, from the gifts of King Mithradates." We may suppose that this Artemis is she of Comana, and it is quite possible that the king is Mithradates Eupator, the ally of the Scordisci.[7] In any case, these two plaques are in quite a different style from that of Roermond ; they are more skilful, better drawn, and in higher relief. But the Dutch specimen was copied from a similar model. It is an imitation which might have been produced among a silver-producing people which had dealings with Pontus where its warriors took service, and exchanged gifts with

---

[1] Human sacrifices. Amm., xxvii, 4. D'Arbois, **CCXCIX**, p. 166.
[2] Reinecke, **CCCCVI**, p. 18 (silver treasures) ; Parvan, **DXLVIII**, 559 (list of finds of silver ware).
[3] Drexel, in **LXXII**, 1915, p. 24.
[4] Ibid., p. 23.
[5] Ibid. ; S. Reinach, **CCCLXXVII**, ii, p. 433.
[6] A. Odobesco, **DXLVI**, i, p. 513 ; in S. Reinach, op. cit., v, p. 239.
[7] App., *Mithr.*, iii, p. 107.

the kings of Pontus or traded with the Scythians, but was capable of getting models from them.[1] This description applies to the Scordisci.

The art of the Pontic medal-maker,[2] which recalls the very ancient art of the Hittites, is more truly like that of the Scythians. The kingdom of Pontus and Southern Russia were closely bound in civilization as in politics. Pontus was one of the stages through which the Scythian style would pass on its way to Celtic lands. At any rate, the Celts of the Danube must have passed it on. Déchelette[3] thought that the practice of wearing the torque as a sign of chieftainship had come to the Gauls from Scythia. But, while the torques of Southern France may be derived from the same region,[4] it is not at all likely that the Gauls waited until they were settled in the valley of the Danube, in contact with the Scythians, before they started wearing trousers.[5]

To a certain extent, the Gauls played the same part in the Danube valley as the Greeks round the Ægean Sea and in Asia Minor. Their racial origins were very mixed, and their cultures varied greatly in origin and in depth. The Greeks made one single world out of their motley world; the Celts did the same, except for the language, in the valley of the Danube. In the culture of these kingdoms there was a special element, which, however, only appears in a very few monuments. To their relations with Asia Minor and Scythia they owed certain new forms of art, and they handed on a certain number of these acquisitions to the rest of the Celts.

They owed to the Greeks, and they left for us, something

---

[1] Relations with Scythia, Parvan, **DXCVII**, pp. 606–629. Græco-Iranian influences, ibid., pp. 550–561.

[2] Rostovtsev, in **CLXXXVII**, i, p. 257.

[3] **CCCXVIII**, ii, 3, p. 1310.

[4] The torques discovered at Lasgraïsses (Tarn) and Aurillac (Cantal) (ibid., pp. 1342–4) are to be compared (O. Costa de Beauregard, Autun, in **LX**, 1907, p. 824) with similar objects found in Hungary, Bohemia, and the neighbouring regions (e.g. at Herczeg-Marok, in the county of Baranya). Messrs. Read and Smith likewise ascribe an Eastern origin to a bronze torque adorned with animals' heads found at Vieille-Toulouse, **CCCLXXXIV**, p. 55).

[5] This costume was common to the Northern peoples, who had had it since the Bronze Age. But one cannot help comparing it to that of the Scythian archers at Athens (cf. the soldier of Rhesos on a Lower Italian vase in the Naples Museum) and that of the warriors on the Hallstatt scabbard (Déchelette, ii, 2, p. 770).

more important—coins.[1] The gold and silver coins which they received are chiefly of Macedonian origin ; they are dated by the reigns of the rulers who issued them, and so they constitute a new source of information for the history of the Danubian Celts.

The oldest coins are gold staters and tetradrachms of Philip II of Macedon (359–336),[2] silver coins of Alexander (336–332),[3] Philip Anthidios,[4] and Lysimachos (d. 281),[5] and, lastly, coins of the kings of Paeonia, Patraos (340–335)[6] and Audoleon (315–306),[7] which were of the same type as the Macedonian pieces.

It is evident that the Danubian Celts got the coins of Philip at the very beginning of his reign, about 350,[8] and that they copied them before they had any very large supply of other current models; that is, in the reign of Alexander at the latest. They had, therefore, dealings with the Macedonians which brought a quantity of money into their hands long before they settled in the country of the Antariatae, either because the services which they rendered to Macedonian policy with regard to the Illyrians were not given for nothing, or because they exported goods into Macedonia. These models continued to be popular in the Danube region, perhaps in consequence of the release of depreciated coins, and the Celts remained faithful to them until the Roman province was erected.

All these coins are of silver. The gold staters of Philip and Alexander and those of Lysimachos were imported direct into the Danubian country, but they also travelled in other directions and seem to have gone to Raetia direct.[9] The reason was that in ancient Greek times gold coins were a kind of international coinage, and it was as such that they entered Celtic lands by other sides.

The Celts of the Danube faithfully maintained the types,

---

[1] See Parvan, **DXLVIII,** pp. 598 ff. ; Forrer, **DLIII** ; Déchelette, ii, 3, p. 1569.

[2] Coins with a bearded, laureate Zeus on the obverse and a horseman on the reverse. Forrer, **DXLIII,** p. 143.

[3] Head of Heracles and Zeus with an eagle. Ibid., p. 157.

[4] Ibid., p. 174.

[5] Ibid., pp. 200, 205.

[6] Ibid., pp. 153 ff.

[7] Ibid., p. 163.

[8] Ibid., p. 143.

[9] Ibid., p. 192

alloys, and weights of the Macedonian coins. They had the same standard. Beyond Vienna, large coins are found at greater intervals, the size decreases as one goes westwards,[1] the type, while remaining the same, degenerates, and the influence of another coinage and another standard makes itself felt. Noricum was definitely the boundary of the Danubian Celts, who were more closely attached to the Hellenistic world than their neighbours and acted as middlemen between that world and the other countries subject to them. The Illyrian groups [2] copied the local coinages of Damastium and Pelepia Illyriae, while those of the Lower Danube and Black Sea copied the money of Thasos exclusively.[3] This special coinage corresponds to the commercial relations which the lower valley of the river and the shores of the Black Sea must have had normally with the region of the Bosphorus and Dardanelles. It also shows that in these eastern regions the Celts of the Black Sea formed a distinct province, looking in other directions than their kinsmen of the Danube.

On the two sides of the Julian Alps, with the Celts of the Po and those living north of the Danube, the Gallic peoples were in political communication.[4] Coins of the Aravisci, which have been found in considerable quantities in the district of Mortara, point to a commercial intercourse which had doubtless been going on for some time.[5] On the Upper Danube, the Boii of Bohemia, who had furnished so many men for the Celtic expeditions, were still sufficiently powerful to extend their sway to the Theiss.[6] In their rage for conquest they disturbed the peace of the peoples of Noricum [7] and Pannonia,[8] a large part of which they occupied. This was, indeed, the only important event in the history of these peoples, which is brief, before the arrival of the Romans. The area over which their coins are discovered—concave

---

[1] Ibid., p. 189 ; Blanchet in **CXLII**, 1902, pp. 160 ff.
[2] Forrer, op. cit., p. 237.
[3] Ibid., pp. 211, 226.
[4] Livy, xxxix, 45, 6 ; 55, 1–3 ; xliv, 5 ; xlv, 1–2.
[5] Forrer, op. cit., p. 120.
[6] Strabo, vii, 313 ; cf. **CLXVIII**, xlii, 1898, pp. 153 ff. ; Reinecke, **CCCXCIX**, v, ix, pl. l, and p. 287 ; cf. **XV**, 1907, p. 397.
[7] Cæsar (*Gall. War*, i, 5) relates that the Boii invaded Noricum and besieged Noreia. Cf. Jullian, **CCCXLVII**, i, p. 299 ; Blanchet, **CCCVI**, pp. 458–463.
[8] Pliny, iv, 146.

pieces known as *Regenbogenschüsselchen*, or "rainbow saucers", the most distant and barbarous derivatives of the stater of Alexander—is evidence of their roving disposition.[1]

V

COMPOSITION OF THE CELTIC ARMIES

Unlike the great army which invaded Italy,[2] the warriors who fell on Macedon and Greece were not, for the most part, grouped in tribes. They were a collection of bands, recruited no one knows how from groups which were politically unassociated.[3] It is possible that some of them came from a great distance.[4] The Gallic bands contained more than one adventurer who was attracted by the prospect of loot and a mercenary's pay.

But you cannot make a great army out of rovers alone, and the great companies of Gallic mercenaries never numbered more than a few thousand men. To form the army of Brennus, recruiting of a more regular kind was needed, drawing largely on groups of neighbouring tribes. Men to train them were needed, and leading tribes to direct the others.

This time the lead was taken by the Belgæ. Historians who lay stress on the different names of Celt, Galatian, and Gaul have not failed to point out that the name of Galatian prevailed from this time onwards.[5] But this is merely a question of pronunciation; the word which was written

[1] Forrer, **DXLIII**, pp. 214–17 ; Déchelette, ii, 3, p. 1569.
[2] See above, pp. 9 ff.
[3] We have a piece of evidence about the way in which these bodies were recruited in a little romance by Aristodemos of Nysa, preserved in a collection of love stories compiled by Parthenios of Nicæa (d'Arbois, **CCXCIX**, p. 199). It tells of the misadventures of a Milesian named Xanthos, whose wife had been carried off by a Gaul. The Gaul was named Cauara, and he came from the neighbourhood of Marseilles. Cauara was doubtless not a personal name, but a racial name—the men belonged to the country of the Cauari, who were settled later about Avignon and Orange.
[4] Justin (xxxii, 3, 8–9) assigns a double origin to these Danubian and Gallic bands, but perhaps he confuses the Tectosages of Toulouse with those of Bavaria. The same information is found in Strabo, iv, 1, 13, following Timagenes. For peoples or tribes from the Danube, Πραῦσοι (Strabo, iv 1, 13) and Tolistoboii (Pliny, v, 141 ; Strabo, xii, 5, 1), cf. Jullian, **CCCXLVII**, i, p. 299, n. 1. These latter nations are unknown otherwise, and this information, even it it is correct, tells us nothing.
[5] Paus., i, 3, 6 ; d'Arbois, **CCCI**, i, p. 14.

down as Keltos ($K\epsilon\lambda\tau\delta\varsigma$) in Spain and the neighbourhood
of Marseilles sounded differently in the ears of the Greeks of
the Balkan Peninsula, who wrote it down Galates ($\Gamma\alpha\lambda\dot{\alpha}\tau\eta\varsigma$).
But it was the same name ; the Gallic mercenaries buried in
the cemetery of Hadra [1] were described on their tombstones
as Keltos or Galates without distinction. " Galatian,"
therefore, does not mean Belgic ; but there are certain facts
which indicate that there were Belgæ in the bands of
Galatians and that they were at the head of them.

First, there is the name of the leader of the expedition
of 281, Bolgios.[2] If Bolgios is a proper name, that in itself is
significant ; and it would be still more so if the Greek
historians had called the leader after the body which he led.
In Pannonia, Pliny mentions a town called Belgites.[3] So the
name of the Belgæ remained attached to these Danubian
expeditions and to the settlements left by the invaders.

The archæological remains, too, preserve the memory of
the descent of the Belgæ into the East. The statuette at
Naples representing the suicide of Brennus,[4] the statue of
a Gaul in the New York Museum,[5] and many other similar
works show the Gauls of the Danubian armies dressed in
wide, flapping trousers. Even the women wore them, and
are depicted in that costume ; there is a statuette in the
British Museum of a Gallic woman lying down, wearing
trousers and cloak.[6]

Other representations of Gauls, of a semi-realistic
character, namely the paintings on the tombstones at
Hadra, show Gallic mercenaries wearing trousers which
are not the wide *bracca*.[7] It is clear that this latter garment
was not, and never was, worn by all Celts. It was peculiar
to the northern Gauls, and more particularly to the Belgæ,
who, as has been said before, owed their name to it.[8]

Lastly, St. Jerome states that in his time these Galatians
still speak Gaulish, and he particularly compares their

---

[1] A. J. Reinach, in **CVII**, xviii, pp. 41 ff.
[2] D'Arbois, **CCXCIX**, p. 200.
[3] Pliny, iii, 148. There was a Belgida, a Celtiberian place whose site is
unknown, in Hispania Tarraconensis.
[4] A. J. Reinach, op. cit., xxi, pl. xviii.
[5] Ibid., p. 182 and figs. 6–7.
[6] Ibid., p. 85 ; Lang, in *Œsterr. Jahr.*, 1919, pp. 207–280.
[7] Ibid., p. 64.
[8] See *Rise*, p. 227.

language to that of the Treviri, who were Belgæ.[1] That, too, is perhaps of significance.

That there were Belgæ among the Gauls who invaded the Balkans and Asia Minor, and also among those who settled in the Danube valley, is a fact beyond dispute, and we find them in the position of leaders. Their rank makes up for their lack of numbers.

---

[1] *Comm. on Galatians*, ii, 3 : *Galatas, excepto sermone Græco, quo omnis Oriens loquitur, propriam linguam eandem pene habere quam Treviros, nec referre si aliqua exinde corruperint.*

CHAPTER III

THE CELTS IN THE WEST. ITALY AND SPAIN

I

THE BELGÆ IN ITALY

FROM the end of the third century onwards, the Belgæ are to be found taking a part in every movement which occurs in the Celtic world. The other Gauls seek their help for special purposes, defend themselves against them, or follow them. While they are trying to carve out an empire for themselves on the Danube and in the East, new bodies descend on Italy and Spain. The political events of the second century bring the Celts into contact with a great organized state, a creator of order in its own fashion, the Roman Republic. The history of these peoples is henceforward the story of their struggle with Rome, in which, from the west of the Mediterranean to the east, they are vanquished, and it is through the ups and downs of that story that we catch glimpses of their internal life.

Yet another danger threatens them. To the north, over an area of the same extent, the Celtic world has at the same time to suffer encroachments and advances on the part of men of inferior civilization, speaking another language and forming another group, who have begun to move in the wake of the Belgæ, a hundred years after them. These are the Germans, whose name has already turned up in the course of this history, in Ireland, then in Italy, and finally in Spain, though in this last country its meaning is uncertain.[1]

A century after the first invasion, the peace of the Gauls of the Po valley was disturbed by the arrival of a large body of men from over the Alps.[2] The Gauls treated with them, and succeeded in diverting their attention to Rome,

---

[1] Livy, x, 107 ; Polyb., ii, 19, 1.
[2] Homo, **CCCXLI**, English, pp. 191 ff.

which was then engaged in the fourth Samnite War.[1] The
Samnites had as allies the Etruscans, to whom the Gauls
offered their assistance and that of the newcomers, who
asked for land and a home in return.[2] The Gauls descended
into Etruria and slaughtered a legion at Clusium, on the usual
road taken by invaders. In 295 they found themselves
faced by a larger Roman army at Sentinum on the eastern
slope of the Apennines, near the source of the Æsis. In
spite of their valour and dash, they were crushed.[3]

Ten years later the Gauls appear again, this time alone.
They besieged Arretium [4] on the Clusium road. A Roman
army came to the relief of the town, and lost many prisoners.
Envoys, sent to obtain an exchange of captives, were ill
received. In 283 the Romans took the offensive and invaded
the country of the Senones,[5] whom they utterly defeated.
According to a family tradition of the Livii, the Consul
M. Livius Drusus found among them the thousand pounds
of gold which had been paid in ransom of the Capitol. In any
case, he was able to collect enough booty without that.
The Etruscans had meanwhile taken up arms again, and
while the Senones were getting beaten an army of Boii had
come down into Etruria. It passed Clusium and Volsinii
and was defeated on the shores of the small lake of Vadimo
(Bassano), close to the Tiber between Volsinii and Falerii.[6]
The Boii made peace, and it lasted for forty-five years,
giving the Romans time to finish the Samnite War, to
dispose of Pyrrhos, and to conduct the first Punic War without
having anything to fear from the Gauls.

They had considered it wise to keep a foothold in the
country. The colony of Sena Gallica [7] was probably founded
in 283. The circumstances which led to the establishment
of a colony at Ariminum [8] in the north of the Senonian
territory in 268 are unknown to us. This was the terminus
of the Via Flaminia, which was not finished until 221. Possibly

[1] Livy, x, 10, 10 ; Jullian, CCCXLVII, i, p. 285.
[2] Cf. d'Arbois, CCCI, ii, p. 389.
[3] Polyb., ii, 19, 7–8.
[4] Livy, xxi, 20, 6.
[5] Suet., *Tib.*, 8.
[6] Polyb., ii, 20, 1–5.
[7] Vell. Paterc., i, 14, 7.
[8] App., *Celt.*, ii ; Polyb., ii, 19, 12.

it was already planned. Meanwhile, the Senones did not recover anything like their former power in the district and the Romans were consolidating their positions. It was not until 232 that the Lex Flaminia ordered that this territory should be divided up.[1] This was a serious matter. The Gallic settlements might be able to suffer small losses of ground and the foundation of colonies in towns which were hardly Gallic, but the dividing-up of the country meant eviction, and evicted they were.

This incident produced the greatest indignation, if not among all the Gauls, at least among the Boii and the Insubres, who had already, in 238 or 236, begun to call upon the Transalpine peoples [2] whom they had received with mixed feelings in 299. An army had at that time entered the country, and had advanced as far as Ariminum. They do not seem to have been received with open arms by the greater part of the population, for there was a rising against the Boian kings Atis and Galatos,[3] who came with them. The two kings were slain and the expedition came to nothing. No doubt there was some question of a division of land, and the Gauls were not fond of such methods. But in 232 the alarm occasioned by another division of land was general. Once more appeal was made to the men beyond the Alps.

These latter took their time to prepare for their invasion. But they seem to have managed things well, and it was a large and well-armed force which was sent into the plain of the Po in 225, led by the kings Concolitanus, Aneroestus,[4] and Britomarus.[5] The report of this new Gallic incursion was not without influence on the negotiations which brought the first Punic War to an end.

One of the Consuls of that year, L. Æmilius Papus, awaited the Gauls at Ariminum.[6] The other, C. Attilius Regulus, was engaged in Sardinia. In Etruria there was a small army under the command of a Praetor. The Gauls, with a force of 50,000 foot and 20,000 horse and chariots, having struck right across the Apennines, once again came

[1] Id., ii, 21-2.
[2] Id., ii, 21, 5.
[3] Id., ii, 23, 1.
[4] Id., i, 10 = ii, 4-3.
[5] Id., ii, 21, 4-6 ; Cf. Homo, op. cit., English, pp. 281 ff.
[6] Polyb., ii, 25, 2.

down the central road of Etruria, again appeared before
Clusium, and surprised the small army of the Praetor in
a fashion which proves that their leader was not without
military skill.[1]   The return of L. Æmilius caused them to
change their route. They turned towards the coast, which
they reached at Telamon, north of Orbetello.[2] There they
were met by all the Roman forces and with them those of
the whole of Italy. This time the Gauls were not quite of
one mind. The Cenomani had stood apart, and the Romans
had obtained from them not only neutrality but an auxiliary
corps,[3] which marched with a body of Veneti, forming with
it a unit of about 20,000 men. This was one of the great
encounters between the Gauls and the peoples of Italy. The
Gauls were thoroughly worsted ; their army was destroyed.
Concolitanus was taken prisoner and Aneroestus killed
himself.[4] In memory of this battle a magnificent temple
was built at Telamon, containing a symbolic arsenal and
relics from the battlefield.[5] Excavation has yielded a bronze
statuette of a fallen Gallic chief and terra-cotta fragments
of pediments. One of these latter represented the two leaders
of the Transalpine tribes in the guise of Adrastos and
Amphiaraos, two of the Seven against Thebes, Adrastos
falling into an abyss made by a thunderbolt, and Amphiaraos
dragged away on his chariot by a Fury.

Next year the Roman army ravaged the country of the
Boii,[6] who begged for peace and submitted, as did the
Lingones. In 223 the Romans, supported by the Anamari,
attempted to cross the Po near the mouth of the Addua, but
they were beaten and secured their escape by negotiation.
They returned to the attack with the support of the Cenomani,
and drove the Insubres as far as Milan. The Insubres raised
50,000 men and brought out of the temple of their goddess
certain gold standards, which must have been the symbol
of their possession of the place. The Romans were victorious,
we are told, but they retired.

The Insubres took advantage of this to bring in, next

[1] Id., ii, 27–31 ; Cf. Homo, op. cit., English, pp. 282–3 and fig. 10.
[2] Polyb., ii, 22, 7–8 ; Dion, xii, 43. Cf. Jullian, CCCXLVII, i, p. 326.
[3] A. J. Reinach, in CVII, 19, p. 174.
[4] Milani, DXXXIII, i, pp. 125–143.
[5] Polyb., ii, 31, 8 ; 35, 2.
[6] Homo, op. cit., Eng., p. 284 ; Jullian. op. cit., i, pp. 449–450.

year, an army of 30,000 Transalpine warriors, led by a chief named Viridomar, who called himself a son of the Rhine. The collision took place on the right bank of the Po, at Clastidium, south-west of Comillomagus. The Consul M. Claudius Marcellus is said to have slain Viridomar with his own hand in single combat. The Gauls, flying with the Romans close at their heels, crossed the Po near the mouth of the Addua, abandoned Acerrae, and retreated to Milan, which was in its turn taken by the Consul. Peace was made, the Insubres surrendering part of their territory and giving hostages.

As they had done among the Senones, the Romans founded two colonies, one at Placentia on the right bank of the Po, among the Boii, and the other at Cremona on the left bank, among the Insubres. Mutina was held by a garrison, which commanded the road from Placentia to Ariminum, later the Via Æmilia.

In spite of the succession of reinforcements from across the Alps which they received during more than a hundred years, the Cisalpine Gauls did not succeed in extending their territory, and still less did they get the better of the Romans. On the contrary, they lost considerable ground to them, and above all lost their independence.[1] They were either allies or subjects of Rome. What independence they retained was precarious. They were to make a timid attempt to renew the struggle on the advent of Hannibal, only to fall still lower.

The newcomers who took part in the struggle of the Cisalpine Gauls against the Roman Republic are represented as Gauls of the Alps, the Rhone, or the region between them.[2] The contingents of 232 are said to have come from the remotest part of Gaul and from the Rhine district.[3] So they must have passed the Rhone and the Alps on their way, and their predecessors may have done so too.

According to the ancient historians, the Cisalpines regarded them as kinsmen of their own, being like them

---

[1] Polyb., ii, 15, 22.
[2] Id., ii, 34, 2. Cf. Jullian, op. cit., i, p. 450, n. 2.
[3] Polyb., ii, 22 ; Bertrand (CCCIII, p. 453) observes that Polybios seems to have used the name of Galatians to designate them, for choice, but not exclusively.

descended from the Gauls who took Rome.[1] They are described as a *Gaisatai*. This was a name which was known to have a meaning. Polybios [2] suggests an etymology : " They are called *Gaisatai* because they are mercenaries, for that is what the word means." We have no confirmation or explanation of this etymology. There is another interpretation of the term—that the *Gaisatai* are Germans armed with a spear or javelin, the *gaesum*. [3] It is perfectly true that the word *gaesum* 'is a transcription of a Gallic name, but the Latins used it with a wrong meaning. They confused the new weapon with other javelins, which had long been used by the Etruscans [4] and the Roman light infantry.[5] But they did not confuse it with the *pilum*—a mistake of which some modern archæologists have been guilty.

Other documents, mainly inscriptions, mention *Germani* and *Rheti Gaesati*.[6] These were probably bodies raised in the Alps or in Germany. The population of the Roman Germanies was for the greater part Belgic. The *Germani Gaesati* were Belgæ. Of this we have proof. Just as they introduced the name of *gaesum* into Italy, the Belgæ who went warring in Ireland took into that country the weapon which has exactly the same name.[7] They arrived with a better armament than that of the natives, and the thought of those terrible weapons (among which there was a special spear or javelin) [8] is bound up with the memory of them. So the Gaesati or *Gaisatai* were Belgæ, or at least there were a great many Belgæ among them.[9] Perhaps this is why the ancient writers, who so often confuse the Belgæ with the Germans, describe the Gaesati as *Semigermani* or *Germani*.[10] Moreover, the Gaesati had other characteristics of the Belgæ. Like them they wore baggy trousers.[11] The historians who describe the

[1] Polyb., ii, 22, 1 ; Oros., iv, 15, 5. Cf. **CXC**, 38, p. 324.
[2] Polyb., loc. cit. ; Virg., *Æn.*, viii, 661 ff. ; Polyaen., vii, 33, 156 Eustath., ii, 774 ; Cæs., *Gall. War*, iii, 4, 1.
[3] Livy, ix, 36, 6 ; xxviii, 45.
[4] Id., viii, 8, 5.
[5] **CVIII**, vi, p. 188.
[6] **II**, vii, 1092 ; **I**, viii, 2786 ; vii, 1002 ; xiii, 1041.
[7] Irish *gai*, *gae* ; Corn. *gwaw*.
[8] Rhys, **CCCCL**, ii, pp. 205, 207.
[9] Jullian, **CCCXLVII**, i, p. 315, n. 6.
[10] See *Rise*, p. 13.
[11] Like the Gaul of Alesia and other representations of Gauls of the Alexandrian age.

battle of Telamon describe them as fighting naked, that is to say, naked down to the waist but wearing trousers.[1]

But these were not the same Belgæ as those who invaded the Danube valley and the East. They were not confused with the Taurisci, who also figured in the army defeated at Telamon. Moreover, they still had the war-chariot, the *essedum*, which was no longer used by the army of Brennus or the Galatians of Asia. If there is one thing to remember in the battles in which the Gaesati engaged, it is the use of the large, heavy sword, made for cutting-strokes which were parried with the shield, and never bending save in the heat of funeral pyres, but less useful for hand-to-hand fighting than the *gladius* which the Romans had copied from their predecessors.

At all events, their expeditions in the south of the Celtic world contributed to the unification of Gallic civilization during the second La Tène period.

II

THE BELGÆ IN SPAIN. THE CELTIBERIANS

At the same time new bodies of Celts were entering Spain, which had for two centuries been separated from the rest of the Celtic world by the Iberian invasion of Languedoc and the valley of the Garonne.[2]

All through this period, the civilization of the Gallic settlements had developed on independent lines.[3] In the place of the La Tène I brooches, which are only found exceptionally, there are quantities of very curious types, transitional between Hallstatt and La Tène. The great sword of the first La Tène period is likewise absent. Down to the third century, its place is taken by small swords derived from the dagger with antennæ. All these objects can be dated fairly exactly by the Greek vases found with them in the same cemeteries.

This archaic civilization is succeeded immediately by that of La Tène II. The largest group of finds belongs to

---

[1] Polyb., ii, 28, 4.
[2] See *Rise*, pp. 298 ff.
[3] For post-Hallstatt civilization, see Bosch Gimpera, **DV** ; Pericot, **DXV**, pp. 51 ff. ; Schulten, **DXVII**, pp. 187-9 ; Siret, in **CXXXVI**, 1909.

the Castilian cemeteries of Aguilar de Anguita, Arcobriga, and Luzaga, some of the tombs in which contained brooches, swords, and shield-bosses of this period.[1] Some of the brooches and swords belong to earlier types. In Catalonia outside the old limit of Celtic settlements the cemetery of Cabrera de Mataro (Barcelona)[2] and in Andalusia that of Torre de Villaricos (Almeria)[3] have yielded many Campanian vases of the third century. But swords are still very rare. At that time the Celts used a kind of sabre with a hilt shaped like a horse's head, which archæologists call the Almedinilla sword.[4] This weapon is found in the graves, bent in the Celtic fashion, as are the small antenna-sword and that of La Tène II. It is shown on the Osuna relief[5] in the hands of a warrior who carries a great Celtic shield with a central rib. It has been suggested that this weapon is the κοπίς of the Thracians and Eastern peoples, imported into Spain by the Greeks. But it seems rather to have spread by the Celtic land-routes. The κοπίς is depicted in a caricature of a Galatian warrior on a crater of the third century found at Volterra[6] and in the Telamon statuette.[7] Sabres have been found in burials of La Tène II in Illyria and Germanic countries.[8] The κοπίς is the sister of the cutlass which takes the place of the sword in many Gallic tombs[9]; it is the result of an evolution of Hallstatt weapons parallel to that of the sword, and it came from Central Europe to Thrace, Greece, and Italy. Whether it originated in Celtic countries or was copied by the Celts on their Eastern expeditions, it was from the north that it entered Spain with the Celts of La Tène II.

In the Celtic place-names of Spain we can see a second stratum,[10] which appears to date from this second Celtic occupation. These are names of fortified towns ending in -*dunum*.[11] There are only four of these—Caladunum (Calahorra, near Monte Alegro in the Portuguese province of Tras-os-

[1] Déchelette, in LVIII, 1912, p. 433; Cerralbo, DVIII.
[2] Bosch, CCCCXCIX.
[3] L. Siret, in CXXXVI, Déchelette, DIX, p. 65.
[4] Paris, DXIV, ii, pp. 277 ff.
[5] Couissin, in CXXXIX, 1923, 2, p. 62.
[6] Déchelette, ii, 1, p. 435, fig. 178.
[7] See above, p. 72.
[8] Déchelette, ii, 2, 691.
[9] H. Hubert, in CXL, 1925, p. 259.
[10] D'Arbois, CCXCIX, p. 185.
[11] Ibid., pp. 111–112.

Montes) among the Callaici, who were Iberians ; Estledunum (Estola, near Luque, province of Cordova) in the country of the Turduli, who were not Gauls ; Sebeldunum (in Catalonia, south of Gerona) among the Ausetani ; and Arialdunum, the site of which is uncertain. We may also add Berdum in the province of Huesca and Verdu in that of Lerida, which were originally called Virodunum. The name of Cogos, in the province of Gerona, recalls that of Cucullae. There was a town of the Arevaci called Clunia. Lastly, a Gallic leader slain by the Romans in 179 bore the name of Moenicaptus, " Slave of the Main." [1]

There are names corresponding to this series at the other ends of the Celtic world. Most of those ending in -*dunum* have been discovered north of the Seine and east of the Cevennes.[2] There is a whole string of places called Virodunum from Tarn-et-Garonne to Germany. Kuchl in the province of Salzburg and Cogolo in the Tyrol were once Cucullae.[3]

These analogies suggest that it is in the north and in the east that we should seek the starting-point of the new body of invaders, and many of them were certainly Belgæ. In Hispania Tarraconensis there were a Belgida,[4] site unknown, and a Belgica, which is also written Vellica. A third city, Suessatium,[5] recalls the name of the Suessiones, who were a Belgic people.

Lastly, we find in Spain people called Germani,[6] and that among the Oretani, who were Celtiberians according to a statement of Pliny the Elder.[7] These again are Belgæ, whether they actually bore the name, which is clearly of Celtic origin, or it was given to them by analogy.

We may try to imagine the order of events. Of the portions of Celtic peoples which made for Italy in the fourth century, some stopped or were stopped along the Garonne towards the mouth—Bituriges Vivisci at Bordeaux [8] and probably Senones at Cenon, opposite the town on the other side of the river,[9] and Lingones at Langon, higher up.[10] At the

---

[1] Ibid., p. 16.   [2] Ibid., p. 110.   [3] Ibid., p. 123.
[4] Oros., v, 23, 2 ; Diod., xxxi, 39 ; App., *Hisp.*, 100 ; **II,** viii, 439.
[5] Schulten, **DXIX,** pp. 10, 106.
[6] Ibid., p. 124.   [7] Pliny, iii, 25.
[8] Strabo, xiv, 2, 1 ; Cf. Jullian, **CCCXLVII,** i, p. 309.
[9] Jullian, op. cit., p. 305. Cenon is written Senon in the Chartulary of St. Seurin (pp. 26, 93).
[10] Jullian, loc. cit. Langon is called Portus Alingonis in the *Letters* of

other end of the Pyrenees there were Volcae—Volcae Tectosages south of Narbonne and Volcae Arecomici (or Arecomii) between that town and the Rhone. These last, who took the place of the Iberians and Ligurians in Languedoc, came from the same regions as the first Celtic occupants of Aquitania. They did not enter Spain. But we may suppose that they were followed by Belgæ who managed to make their way to the Pass of Roncesvalles on the one side and into Catalonia on the other. These newcomers cannot have been very numerous.

All this doubtless happened between 350 and 250.[1] It may possibly have been some years before the irruption of the Gauls into the Balkan Peninsula and the later Italian expeditions.

In what condition did the arrival of the Belgæ leave the Celtic settlements in Spain ?

The Peninsula had been a Celtic land. Then it had become " Iberia ", and seems to have been given this name in Greek geography for the first time about 230 by Eratosthenes.[2] The peoples of the interior, roughly from the fourth century onwards, are called Celtiberians,[3] and this appellation probably goes back to Timaeos, about 260. It must have had a fairly precise meaning, for the Celtici of the south and west kept it, whereas the Berones are called simply Celts by Strabo.[4] What, then, were the Celtiberians ? A mere formation. But of what kind ? What proportion of Celtic elements did it contain ?

The most generally accepted notion, which is based on the sentiment of the ancient writers,[5] is that the Celtiberians were not very different from the Celts who were known to be in the Peninsula before the new name çame to prevail. They were Celts of Iberia, mixed in various degrees with Iberian elements. This is not the view of Herr Schulten.[6] He regards the Celtiberians as Iberians who had settled in the country

Sidonius Apollinaris (viii, 12, 3). This name may be derived from an ancient name *ad Lingones*.
  [1] Ephoros (*F.H.G.*, i, 245, fr. 43) includes the greater part of Spain in the Celtic world (341 B.C.).
  [2] Schulten, DXIX, i, p. 97. Cf. Eph., fr. 38.
  [3] Ibid.
  [4] Ibid., p. 111.
  [5] Pliny, xiv, 3, 13.
  [6] Schulten, op. cit., i, p. 19.

of the Celts and had then moved towards the Pyrenees from
350 onwards under the pressure of the Ligurians and Celts ;
these Iberians tried to extend their ground in Spain, and
established themselves on the plateau, going up the valleys.[1]
The new peoples whose names the historians then give—
Oretani, Carpetani, Lusitani, Vettones, Arevaci, Vaccaei,
Lusones, Belli, and Titti—are Iberian, not Celtic tribes.[2]
Polybios, too, describes the Celtiberian Oretani, Carpetani,
and Vaccaei as Iberians. The Celts, driven from their settlements on the central plateau, retreated westwards or were
reduced to subjection or assimilated by the conquerors.[3]

But why, then, the name Celtiberians, which cannot in
any way be taken as a national designation ? It is a Greek
ethnographic term formed like the word " Libyphoenicians ",
which obviously means Phoenicians settled on Libyan
territory.[4] In fact, even if these terms are fundamentally
ancient, their meaning is vague, and is intended to be so.

One thing at least is certain : the Iberian civilization
reached the plateau.[5] In their states in the south, where
they were in contact with the Greek colonies, the Iberians
in the fifth and fourth centuries developed a culture some
aspects of which are now well known—towns with stone
ramparts and stone houses, large temples inhabited by a host
of statues and statuettes, and painted pottery with geometric,
animal, and vegetable ornament.[6] This culture, which had
its birth in the south-eastern corner of the Peninsula, whence
it spread in the fifth century along the east coast to the Rhone,
makes its appearance in the fourth century in the upper
valley of the Ebro, and then, gradually advancing, arrives
a hundred years later in Castile, in the country which had
once belonged to the Celts. There it spread in the southern
part of the territory occupied by the Oretani, and further

[1] Id., **DXVII**, p. 80.
[2] Polybios (iii, 14) mentions only Celts in the south-west and north-west.
In Hannibal's time, the centre is occupied by Iberians only.
[3] One should add, to understand Herr Schulten's argument, that the
Celtic invaders of the fifth century had found the country in which they
settled occupied, not by Iberians, but by Ligurians. The Iberians were
strangers in Spain, colonists and conquerors from Africa.
[4] Schulten, **DXIX**, 19.
[5] Bosch, in **XIV**, vi, p. 671. For the excavation of Celtiberian sites on
the plateau see B. Taracena Aguirre, " Excavaciones en las provincias de
Soria y Logroño," in **XCIX**, No. 103 (1929).
[6] Paris, **DXIV** ; R. Lantier, **DXI** ; Bosch, **DI**.

north in that of the Carpetani. It also made its way into the northern parts of the domain of the Arevaci and into some of the groups established on the plateau. The scarcity of Iberian objects in the country of the Vaccaei, Vettones, and Lusitani seems to indicate that these peoples were less strongly Ibericized. The distinction made by the ancient historians between *Celtiberi citeriores* (closer to the coast) and *Celtiberi ulteriores* (further from the coast and wilder) may also have corresponded to a difference of race.[1]

Altogether, then, there is nothing against the supposition that the racial framework of the country was usually supplied by the Iberians. The Oretani and Carpetani have Iberian names similar to that of the Turdetani, for example, who are outside the Celtic area. The Lusitani are probably a branch of the Lusones which had advanced westwards, and we may by analogy suppose that the Arevaci and Vaccaei were likewise of Iberian origin,[2] But all these peoples allowed a considerable number of Celts to stay in the country and absorbed them. This is shown by the names which appear in the inscriptions of Celtiberian towns. Such Celtic names as Acco, Atto, Boutius, and Reburrus are frequent. They prove that Celtic elements lived on in the country and maintained their family organization.

But they did not live in a subordinate position. The leaders, the heroes in the Celtiberian war of independence are Celts—Rhetogenes (Rectugenos) Caraunios, Caros, Ambon (Ammo ?), Leukon, Megaravicus, and Auaros. Orosius[3] relates that after the fall of Numantia, Scipio asked a Celtic prince named Thyresius why the city had held out so long. Lastly, even if the Lusitani were Iberians, their chief Viriathus had a Celtic name.[4]

To explain this state of things, we may suppose that Celtic families which had been previously settled in the country entered the Iberian tribes or survived alongside of them. We may also suppose that the meeting of the Celts and the Belgæ who arrived on the Iberian plateau at the same time, moving in opposite directions, led to agreements by which the smaller body was incorporated in the larger.

The two hypotheses are equally reasonable and account

[1] Jullian, **CCCXLVII**, i, p. 307.
[2] Schulten, **DXIX**, i, pp. 247–8.
[3] v. 8, 1.
[4] Schulten, op. cit., i, p. 100.

for many features of Celtic civilization,[1] which are attested
by archæology and by the ancient writers, in the Celtiberian
tribes—the survival of cults such as that of Epona and that
of the Lugoves, the observation of Celtic funeral rites in the
cemeteries of Castile, the survival of Gallic armament, the
use of horse and foot together in tactical formation, the
use of standards and trumpets, the wearing of the *sagum*,
the drinking of beer.

But while something of Celtic civilization survived, there
were no vestiges of Celtic states (if they had ever existed)
in the centre of the Peninsula about the middle of the third
century. The coming of the Belgæ had neither revived
old political units nor created new ones.

III

THE CELTS IN THE PUNIC WARS

At the time when the Punic wars commenced, the races
of Spain were arranged as follows : in the centre on the
plateau there had grown up a group of peoples of great
military excellence which, though mainly Iberian, contained
a large number of Celts, who enjoyed a certain standing.
The collaboration of these two elements in Celtiberia was
not unlike that of the Arabs and the Berbers in Algeria and
Morocco before the European conquest.

In the first Punic War Carthage lost her Spanish colonies.
After the war, in 237, the first generation of the great generals
of the Barca family, Hamilcar and Hasdrubal, set out to
reconquer the country,[2] with the idea of extending the
Carthaginian domain and making it a base for the war which
they were preparing. The first operations among the Tar-
tessians brought them into conflict with bodies of Celts.[3]
They next crossed the Sierra Morena and attacked the
Celtiberians, whom Hannibal finally conquered in 221.[4] From
Cartagena to Burgos they had subdued the whole plateau.
It would doubtless be more correct to say that they had
concluded agreements with the Celtiberian tribes, which

[1] Ibid., pp. 246 ff.
[2] Polyb., ii, 1, 16.
[3] Diod., xxv, 10, 1.
[4] Schulten, op. cit., i, p. 99 ; Jullian, i, p. 460.

supplied them with mercenaries. In 218, the Lusitani are mentioned for the first time as soldiers of Hannibal.[1]

The second Punic War began. Hannibal resumed or started negotiations with the Volcae, who lived on the northern slope of the Pyrenees. The envoys of the Roman Senate, returning from Carthage, where war had been decided on, landed on the coast of Languedoc, likewise with a view to negotiation. Livy [2] describes them addressing the assembly of armed Volcae. There they had to listen to all the complaints of the Gauls of Italy, which were possibly a genuine expression of public discontent but may have spread by the emissaries of Hannibal preaching the cause of Celtic unity. The Volcae remained undecided. They went through the form of opposing the passage of the Carthaginian army at Ruscino, but they came to terms before there was any fighting. Hannibal passed without trouble through the land of the Volcae Tectosages, and then through that of the Arecomici. At the Rhone, the same undecidedness began again. An army of Volcae or Salyes was disposed along the east bank. Hannibal turned it and put it to flight, and then, instead of marching up the Durance and crossing by Mont Genèvre—perhaps in order to avoid observation by the army of Scipio, who had landed a body of cavalry by the mouth of the Rhone—he went up the east bank of the Rhone to the Isère, and passed without fighting through the country of the Allobroges, escorted by a king whose cause he had taken up. He probably took advantage of his march through these peoples to repair and renew the equipment of his force.[3] Leaving their territory, he entered the Maurienne, where another Gallic people, the Medulli, received him very ill. At Mont Cenis, yet another tribe, the Centrones, disputed his passage. After that there was Italy.

All this information about Hannibal's journey through Gaul is of the greatest interest. For the first time, it shows us Gallic peoples in Gaul, and places them. Although sometimes contradictory, it is all of good quality, and goes back to the Greek historians who accompanied the expedition, Silenos and others.[4] The Volcae occupied Languedoc [5] from the Pyrenees to the Rhone. Between that river and the

---

[1] Ibid., p. 109.   [2] xxi, 20. Cf. Jullian, op. cit., i, p. 460.
[3] Ibid., 4, i, p. 475.   [4] Ibid., p. 455.   [5] Ibid., p. 459.

Durance, Livy [1] mentions the Tricastini and the Vocontii. The valley of the Isère belonged to the Allobroges up to the Maurienne.[2] North of the Rhone, Polybios [3] places the Ardyes, who are probably the Ædui. These positions are permanent, and we must conclude from them that, if there were large shiftings of peoples in Gaul, first before the earliest invasions of Italy and then at the time when the Belgæ made their appearance on the borders of the Celtic world, these movements were for the main part over by 218. Behind the Ædui must have been the Belgæ.

It is possible that the Celts missed their opportunity in Hannibal. He seems to have counted on a general Celtic invasion, but he did not succeed in bringing it about. The Gauls of Gaul were cool or hostile. Those of Italy, one nation of whom, the Boii, had summoned him, were hardly more enthusiastic. They made up their minds when the game was lost.

There was no general rising. All that Hannibal managed to do was to recruit Gallic mercenaries, whom he used skilfully to spare his Spanish troops.[4] But the Romans also had Gallic mercenaries.[5] They were able to maintain garrisons at Mutina and a small army of observation in Cisalpine Gaul, and to preserve their colonies at Placentia, Cremona, and Ariminum.[6] It is true that in 216, after Cannae, the Boii seem to have been tempted to do something. They cut down the little army of the Praetor L. Postumius in the Litana Forest.[7] But that victory led to nothing.

Hasdrubal, Hannibal's younger brother, came very near to succeeding where his elder brother had failed. Being placed in charge of operations in Spain, he managed to recruit troops north of the Pyrenees.[8] In 214, at the battle of Jean, two Gallic chiefs named Moenicaptus and Vismarus, who may have been Belgæ, are mentioned among the slain.[9] On his defeat in 208 Hasdrubal eluded the Romans who were waiting for him in the gorges of Roussillon by going round the west of the range [10] and travelled through Aquitaine and Languedoc, gathering a new army. Then he descended into

[1] Ibid., ii, p. 515.
[2] Ibid., i, p. 475.
[3] iii, 42, 8.
[4] Jullian, op. cit., i, p. 492.
[5] Ibid.
[6] D'Arbois, CCXCIX, 182.
[7] Ibid.
[8] Jullian, op. cit., i, pp. 494 ff.
[9] Livy, xxiv, 42, 8.
[10] Jullian, op. cit., i, p. 496.

Italy, where, after being better received than Hannibal, he was defeated with his Gauls on the banks of the Metaurus in 207.[1] Two years later, another brother, Mago, renewed the attempt. He landed at Genoa and held the district for two years. Then, being driven back into Savoy, he re-embarked, taking with him part of his European troops. Hannibal took back others, so that at Zama half of his army was composed of Celts and Ligurians.[2]

In Cisalpine Gaul, the Barcas had left a Carthaginian officer, Hamilcar, who succeeded in rousing the Cenomani, who had so long been allies of the Romans, and in taking Placentia. But he was defeated and killed before Cremona in 200.[3]

The war went on with hard fighting and much bloodshed, and the Gallic peoples submitted one after another, the Cenomani in 197,[4] the Insubres in 196.[5] The Romans gave them a *foedus* on good terms, and they became *civitates foederatae*. The Boii held out until 191 ; to them surrender brought the total destruction of their political organization. They had to give up half of their territory and three of their cities, Bononia (Bologna), which was made into a colony in 189, and Mutina and Parma in 183. Livy relates that only old men and children were left.[6] It is also said that a body of Boii went back over the Alps into their old home.[7] Of the Lingones nothing more is heard.

In 186 a new Gallic tribe appears in the north of Venetia. This was the Carni,[8] coming from Noricum, who settled in the country and vowed that their intentions were peaceful. A Roman army was sent against them in 183. They were defeated, but they remained. A Roman colony was established at Aquileia in 187.

A story went about that Philip of Macedon intended to bring the Celts down on Italy. In 178 yet another small body of 3,000 Gauls appeared, asking for land.[9] They had to go. This was the last Celtic invasion of Italy down to the campaign of the Cimbri. Henceforward the Roman

[1] Ibid., p. 498.
[2] App., *Lib.*, 40, 44 ; Jullian, op. cit., i, p. 500.
[3] Ibid., i, p. 501.   [4] D'Arbois CCXCIX, p. 182.
[5] Cic., *Pro Balbo*, 32.   [6] Livy, xxxvi, 40, 5.
[7] Strabo, v, 1, 6, 10 ; Polyb., ii, 35, 4.
[8] I, p. 460.   [9] Livy, xl, 53, 5–6.

people regarded the Alps as the boundary of the Celtic world, and did not allow the Gauls to cross it.[1]

It was not long after these events that Polybios [2] visited Cisalpine Gaul, of which he has left a very attractive picture : " Words fail," he says, " to describe the fertility of the country. Corn is so abundant that in our own time a Sicilian medimnus of wheat has more than once been seen to fetch only four obols, a medimnus of barley two obols, and a metretes of wine no more than a measure of barley. Millet and panic produce enormous crops. A single fact may give an idea of the quality of the acorns furnished by the oaks which grow at intervals on the plain [3] : many pigs are slaughtered in Italy both for daily life and for the supply of camps, and it is from this district that most of them come.[4] Lastly, here is conclusive proof of the cheapness and plenty prevailing there. Travellers stopping at the inns do not make terms over each item separately, but ask what the rate is per head ; as a rule the innkeeper undertakes to give them all they want for a quarter of an obol,[5] and this price is seldom exceeded. Need I speak of the enormous population of the country, of the stature and good looks of the people, and of their warlike spirit ? "

The Gauls had their share in the prosperity of this bountiful land. Everything, down to the system of inns, can be put down to them, for there were inns in Ireland too.[6]

They had suffered much in the recent wars. In 197 and 196 alone the Insubres are said to have lost 75,000 men. These were great losses. But there were still Gauls left in Italy. The excavations at Ornavasso [7] and the neighbourhood of Como show that the Lepontii and Insubres remained distinct, with their civilization, down to Imperial times. This does not mean that they had given up their unruly ways for good.

The misfortunes of the Gauls were not yet quite at an

---

[1] Id., xxxix, 54, 11 : proclamation of the Senate forbidding the Gauls to enter Italy.
[2] ii, 15.
[3] This is a feature of the landscape which has vanished.
[4] Pig-breeding is still important in Emilia.
[5] Something under a halfpenny.
[6] The six Bruidne of Ireland. For inns in the Transpadane country, cf. Jullian, op. cit., i, p. 377.
[7] CXLV, 1907, 101 ; 1908, 22.

end.   But the Gallic wars were over, for one cannot describe the revolt of the slaves, chiefly Gauls, which embarrassed the Romans at the end of the century as a Gallic war.

Not only in Italy did the Celts retire before the Roman Republic, which henceforward was mixed up in everything that happened in the Mediterranean world.   In Spain and in the East the Celtiberians and Galatians presently lost their independence.

While Hannibal was carrying the war into Italy, a fleet commanded by Publius Scipio as Consul and his father Cneius was making for Spain.   Publius Scipio returned to Italy, to get beaten on the Ticinus, and Cneius continued on his way and landed at Emporion.[1]   At first he found allies among the Celtiberians.   But in 212 they returned to their alliance with Carthage.   The two Scipios, who had been in command since 217, were defeated separately and killed within a month of each other.   Young Publius Scipio, Africanus that was to be, quickly restored the situation in 211 and, having driven out Hasdrubal, made ready in Spain for the African campaign which brought the war to an end.

The Spanish campaigns of the Scipios form a parallel to that of the Barcas, and what the Barcas had done for Carthage the Scipios did for Rome.   But they went further.

In 197 they attacked the Celtiberian positions on the plateau [2] and commenced a stubborn war which went on until 133, with a few years of respite between 178 and 154. The fall of Numantia [3] brought the war to an end.   The whole of Spain, except the Pyrenees and the free or federated cities of the coast, was organized as a Roman province.

From the rapid conquest of Gaul and the long resistance of the Celtiberians some have argued that there is no such thing as a Celtic character.   The Gauls have left a name for quickly losing heart.   Arguments of this kind, which do not take into account the circumstances on either side, are a fruitful source of error.   Moreover, the Celts seem to have always had an idea of civilization which was quite opposed to their concern for their national independence, and led them to see a friend and guide where others saw an enemy.

[1] Jullian, op. cit., i, pp. 510 ff. ; Homo, **CCCXLI**, English, pp. 315 ff.
[2] Schulten, **DXVII**, p. 82.
[3] Id., **DXIX**.

But, for all their wavering, their resistance, even in Italy, lasted over a hundred years.

In the Eastern Mediterranean the Romans found it necessary to intervene in Macedon and Greece. They were constantly finding Gallic colonies on their way. They had to make terms with those in Noricum which were determined to be left in peace, to be wary with the Celts of Illyria, and to hold the balance between the Galatians and the Kings of Pergamon.

One of the first consequences of the Punic War was that the Romans came into contact with the Galatians. After Zama, Hannibal had taken refuge with Antiochos the Great, and finally with Prusias. Antiochos allowed himself to be won over. The Galatians took sides with him and shared his defeat at Magnesia on the Maeander. The Consul Manlius Vulso marched against them.[1] The first to be attacked, the Tolistoboii, retired to a fortified position on Mount Olympos, where the Romans blockaded them and took over 40,000 prisoners. The Tectosages and Trocmi were likewise compelled to take up their position in another stronghold on Mount Magaba. It was taken by storm. Manlius's campaign was memorable for disgraceful pillage,[2] but on the whole he dealt fairly generously with the vanquished, who were included in the general peace-treaty and allowed to keep their territory provided they did not come out of it. But the King of Pergamon seems to have now obtained a sort of protectorate, which had rather a disturbed history. The Galatians revolted several times. They were crushed in 166. But now the Romans intervened in their favour, and established their independence as a permanency. In 152 Attalos III of Pergamon bequeathed his kingdom to the Romans. The situation changed, though it is not possible to say exactly how, save that the Galatians were drawn into the wars against Mithradates [3] and that they thereby at first lost their independence. In 73 they succeeded in recovering it, and until the death of Mithradates they were faithful allies of Rome. At the end of the war, in 63, Pompey reorganized the Galatians in three principalities, one of which, reaching to the sea and including Trapezus, went to the famous Deiotarus. Deiotarus

---

[1] Jullian, op. cit., i, p. 514.
[2] Livy, 45, 7.
[3] T. Reinach, DLI, p. 74.

was not satisfied, and took advantage of the Civil War to intrigue between Pompey and Cæsar. He had to go to Rome to defend his conduct before Cæsar, and was defended by Cicero in 45 so successfully that he returned to Galatia as a king. By the favour of the Romans, the kingdom of his successors, Castor and Amyntas, was still further extended. But in 25 the whole kingdom was declared a Roman province.

The kingdom of Deiotarus had already ceased to be Celtic; it was a kind of large satrapy, devoid of any racial or national character. The fact was that the Galatians had merged into the population of Anatolia, just as, at the other end of the world, the Celts of Spain had merged into the Iberian peoples. The most conspicuous trace of themselves which they seem to have left in Asia Minor was their blood. Travellers have noted in the country a considerable number of blond types, in which some of the physical characteristics of the Celts doubtless reappear.

In Thrace the little kingdom of Cauaros had disappeared in 193. In 171 the Romans entered Illyria to defend the colony of Aquileia, which was threatened by the Iapodes. An army marched through their country, and probably also that of the Scordisci, to attack Perseus in Macedonia. It seems to have behaved very badly there, for the Consul C. Cassius on his return found an embassy of Istrians and Iapodes who had come to complain to the Senate. From the middle of the second century onwards, the Scordisci were constantly at war with the Romans, and twelve expeditions were sent against them. In 135 they were severely beaten south of Haemos,[1] and they remained quiet for a time. In 110, in alliance with the Thracians, they threatened the Temple of Delphi, and they doubtless took part in the looting of 90. They were crushed by L. Scipio in 83 and planted on the other side of the Danube; nevertheless, we find them again, about 78, in Macedonia, allied with Mithradates and supplying him with most of his Gallic mercenaries, and also plotting with the Dacians.

On the Adriatic the Illyro-Celtic pirates were driven back into the interior in 135. With 129 began a series of small expeditions against the Iapodes, ending in a treaty in 56. They started again in 52, and only ended with the

[1] Jullian, op. cit., i, p. 515.

subjection of the country. In A.D. 8 the whole Celtic region
on the Danube, including the territory of the Scordisci, was
made into a Roman province.

At the end of this stage in history, we have to note that
the Belgic contingents had no real success save in the East.
In Spain they established themselves, but did not last. In Italy
their appearance was transitory. Their advance to the south
of the Mediterranean was stopped in the first half of the third
century, and after that the settlements founded or reinforced
by them declined. Decisive defeats in the first half of the second
century set the seal on those of the third. The Celts in Spain
began by yielding ground to the Iberians, and those of the
East to the Thracians and Pergamenes. All, one after another,
were crushed, or wiped out, or subdued by the Romans.
Those who suffered least were still the Galatians. But, as
we have seen, Galatia was by that time no more than an
island, lost to the Celtic world. The kingdom of Deiotarus
and his successors was Galatian in name alone. The Celtic
states and tribes lost all their dominions, one after another.
But everywhere they left traces, stocks of men. Nor does it
seem that these lands which they had conquered were in any
great danger while they held them.

Moreover, the Gallic conquerors, old and new, do not
seem to have declined in quality. During those two hundred
years they were defeated often and thoroughly, and won
the esteem of their opponents. Also, they fought more
often for others than on their own account, like the bodies of
mercenaries which they lent on every hand. This is
especially true of the Belgæ.

This account would, therefore, not be complete if it did
not once more mention the Gallic mercenaries, those roving
bands which enormously extended the area covered by the
Celts. As early as 307, Agathocles had taken Celts to Africa.[1]
To the history of the Celts they added that of heroic,
picturesque lands and they gained a great sum of individual
experiences, which cannot all have been lost, in spite of the
great slaughter of men involved.

Polybios [2] tells a story of 3,000 Gauls who were enlisted
by the Carthaginians in Italy in 263 and transported to

[1] Diod., xx, 64, 2.
[2] ii, 7, 6 ; Jullian, op. cit., i, p. 327.

Sicily.   They were a difficult body to keep in hand ; they
looted Agrigentum and finally betrayed their employers.
The Romans got rid of them as best they could. We find them
later in Epeiros, about 800 in number, in the service of the
city of Phoenice against the Illyrians, when they delivered
up the city to the brigands. Thus we can follow them for
thirty years.

Carthage had larger bodies of Gallic mercenaries in her
service during the first Punic War, and it was one of their
leaders, named Antarios (who, by the way, spoke Punic
excellently, according to Polybios), who was responsible for
the great mutiny of the mercenaries in 241–237.[1]

Mercenary service was a regular Celtic industry, and
a well paid one.[2]   The 10,000 horse and 10,000 foot enlisted
by Perseus was commanded by a *regulus* and had all the
appearance of a tribal army.   It is, indeed, often very difficult
in the Gallic wars to distinguish between large companies
of mercenaries and belligerent armies.

<hr/>

[1] Ibid., i, p. 326.   [2] Ibid., p. 328.

CHAPTER IV

THE CELTS IN THE WEST. GERMANY AND GAUL

I

CELTS AND GERMANS

IN the middle valley of the Danube the development of the Celtic settlements had been checked by the Getae and Dacians. The Boii advanced to the Theiss, but their sway extended no further. Beyond that there were doubtless Gauls in Transylvania, just as there were Saxons later. Celtic culture spread in this region, and the Dacians became Celticized.

On the Black Sea, an inscription from Olbia [1] records the appearance of the Sciri, who were probably Germans, in the company of the Galatians. But they were soon absorbed, In the same parts, at the same date, we find a much more important people, though of uncertain origin, the Bastarnae.[2] They are mentioned for the first time at the beginning of the second century, as newcomers on the Lower Danube. All these barbarians were employed as auxiliaries down to the time of the collision. In 182 Philip of Macedon sent them against the Dardanians.[3] In 179 there was a great drive of the Bastarnae, with which the Macedonians had great difficulty in dealing.

Some ancient writers, particularly Polybios,[4] who lived at the time of these events, regard the Bastarnae as Galatians.[5] Ptolemy,[6] on the other hand, makes them Germans, and in this he is justified by the names found among them.[7] It is possible that the Bastarnae were a confederation

---

[1] C.I.G., 2058. Cf. LXX, 3, pp. 441 ff. ; CXLIX, 34, pp. 56–61 ; Pliny, iv, 97 ; Müllenhoff, CCCLXII, ii, pp. 110 ff.

[2] A. Bauer, in CXLIX, clxxxv, 2, 1918.

[3] Livy, 40, 57.

[4] Polyb., 26, 9 ; 29 ff.

[5] Müllenhoff, op. cit., ii, p. 104.

[6] Ptol., i, 3, 5, 19.

[7] The leaders' names are Germanic : Clondicus, O. Sax. Indico ; Cotto, O. Sax. Goddo ; and indeed Alemannic names, Talto (Müllenhoff, op. cit.,

of Celtic and Germanic bands, like the army of the Cimbri and Teutones later.[1] However it may have been, whether they were associated with the Celts or not, the Germans broke through the Gallic barrier and joined them at the furthest limit of their expansion. Even more clearly than the example of the Sciri, the arrival of the Bastarnae tells of the vast Germanic drive which was beginning to bear down on the Celtic world. While the Celts were moving to the south of Europe, important things were about to happen on their north-eastern borders.

However far back we go, the original habitat of the Celts in Western Germany does not reach to the Elbe. On the west, the frontier, always fluctuating, takes in an increasing part of the future Gaul; south and north, the boundary is marked by Switzerland and the North Sea.[2] The emigration of the Goidels [3] left the northern part of this region empty, but down to the first centuries of the La Tène period the Brythonic Celts kept their part of it. The expedition of Sigovesus,[4] forming a pendant to the great Celtic invasion of Italy, must represent an advance from the old positions in Bohemia to more northern or eastern ground and inroads from Thuringia into other parts of Germany, all somewhat different from the descents into Italy, Spain, and the East in character and in results.[5]

It is certain that in Bohemia the area of Celtic occupation increased from the first La Tène period onwards. This is attested in the centre and north of those regions by large cemeteries of that date. Further north, in Thuringia—where the crests of the Thüringerwald had in the Iron Age formed a frontier between two civilizations which must have been the racial frontier between Celts and Germans—the peoples of the southern slope moved forward at the end of the Hallstatt period.[6] At the beginning of La Tène, the Celts still extended

---

ii, 109). The name of the Qvenen, one of the Bastarnian peoples, reminds one of that of the Sitones, a nation of the Baltic coast (ibid.). Lastly, the suffix of *Bastarnae* or *Basternae* is found in the form -*erno-* in some Germanic derivatives, e.g. in Gothic *widuwairna*, " orphan."

[1] See below, pp. 108 ff.   [2] See *Rise*, pp. 178 ff.
[3] See *Rise*, p. 176.   [4] Livy, v, 34. See above, p. 33.
[5] This is not the opinion of Herr Schumacher (in LXVII, 1918, pp. 98–9), who explains it by an advance of the Celts of the region of Metz on Thuringia.
[6] This advance is revealed by a group of flat burial-graves discovered on the northern slope (Götze, CCCXCII, xxi).

beyond the Thuringian mountains eastwards in the upper valley of the Saale, in the Kreise of Saalfeld and Ziegenrück. Brooches of La Tène I are found in the Elbe valley, where it leaves Bohemia, and up to the river and beyond it at the level of the confluence of the Saale. They have been picked up, less frequently, all the way down to the mouth of the Elbe and in Mecklenburg, close to the Baltic coast.[1] But these do not come from recognizably Celtic tombs or cemeteries, and we must therefore conclude that outside the limits which we have already drawn there is no trace of a settlement of the Celts, permanent or otherwise.

But it is beyond doubt that the Celts had a very great political and military influence on the Germans at this date. This is shown by the words borrowed by Germanic from Celtic [2]—words connected with politics, law, warfare, and civilization in general. On the whole, the Celts seem to have been for hundreds of years, and in every matter, the educators of the Germanic peoples. But their influence was not due to their mere neighbourhood, and we may take it that it was enforced. There were in Germanic countries Celtic *kings*, or kings after the Celtic fashion, and where there was no king or kingdom we find Celtic *officials* or ambassadors. Celts and Germans strike treaties, exchange oaths and hostages, do business, and make contracts of marriage or friendship. In some instances the two races formed what may be regarded as a single society; they combined in political associations and their tribes formed a confederation or confederations in which the Celts were the larger and predominant element. These relations did not always develop in peace, for we must suppose that they engaged in wars, sometimes against each other and sometimes on the same side.

Another proof of the intimacy of the Celts and Germans at this time is afforded by certain names of Germanic peoples which are Celtic in form or are like Celtic names Germanized. The name of the Hessi, for instance, seems to be the same as that of the Cassi. The Burgondiones correspond to the Brigantes. The Nemetes, the Triboci, and the Marcomanni,

---

[1] Cf. Herr Beltz's map of the distribution of brooches in **CLXIX**, 1911; cf. id., in **LXXXV**, 1913, p. 117.
[2] See *Rise*, pp. 62 ff.

who lived next door to the Gauls, had Gallic names.[1] Yet
there is no doubt that these are Germanic peoples.

One should note that the borrowed words are found in
the eastern dialects of Germanic no less than in those of the
west and north. This diffusion enables us to judge how far
Celtic influence reached. It even went beyond German
regions and affected the Slavs and Finns.

To estimate how deep it went, we must turn to the
ancient authors. The association of the Celts and Germans
and its effects lasted long enough for these writers to bear
witness to it. If there was a difference between the languages
there was not much between the men. Cæsar [2] was the first
to make a great distinction between them. Poseidonios,[3]
before him, who was perhaps the first man to speak expressly
of the Germans, laid weight on their points of resemblance.
Strabo, who came after Cæsar, regarded the Germans as
Gauls in their original pure state ($\gamma\nu\eta\sigma\acute{\iota}o\nu\varsigma$ $\Gamma\alpha\lambda\acute{\alpha}\tau\alpha\varsigma$) and
suggests that this was what their name meant (" germane ").[4]
Their speech was different, but their institutions, manners,
costume, and arms were the same, and the Greek geographer
drew his picture of the early Celts from the Germans of his
own day.

But the Celtic domination of the Germans was a thing of
the past in Cæsar's time. The Germans now stood along the
Rhine from the Lake of Constance downwards, and about
sixty years before, the catastrophe of the expedition of the
Cimbri and Teutones had taken place. Can one determine
the stages of the retreat of the Celts and the date at which
it began ?

That retreat was long in coming, and was sudden when
it came. It was in the second La Tène period that Celtic
influence extended furthest. It is perfectly true that the
Germans followed close on the heels of the Celts. They
occupied every piece of country as it was left vacant, and
for every Celtic retreat there was a Germanic advance.

These movements began very early. About 400, and
probably long before, the Germans had reached the Rhine,[5]

---

[1] Dottin, **CCCXXII**, p. 452 ; Kluge, **CCXI**, i, p. 327 ; Müllenhoff, **CCCXLII**,
ii, p. 23, n. 7.
[2] Mommsen, **CCCLIX**, i, 47.   [3] Ibid.
[4] vii, i, 2.
[5] The Germanic name of the Rhine, Rinos, is not derived from the

but only on its lower course.[1] Moreover, the character of the Celtic sites in Western Germany suggests that the country between Thuringia and the Rhine was contested every foot of the way. The Thüringerwald was a first frontier, with its line of forts. The Rhön was a second, likewise with its fortresses, the redoubt being the Steinsburg near Römhild.[2] Further west, the Vogelsberg and beyond it the Westerwald and Taunus had their strongholds.[3] There were yet others south of the Main and in the valley of the Neckar.[4]

The great number of these forts is surprising, contrasted with the peaceful aspect which Gaul must have presented at that time. The Celts do not seem to have been fond of shutting themselves up in citadels. The fortified sites of Germany point to hard necessity.

One would like to be able to picture the resistance of the Celts on their different lines of defence. Unfortunately, their forts do not run in chronological order from Thuringia to the Rhine. Also, they are found on heights and in woods, like the Hallstatt defensive settlements in Gaul. Habitats changed with the population. Nor do the finds enable us to follow the steps of the Celtic retreat. At the beginning of the La Tène period we can define the limit of their settlements and those of the Germans in Thuringia and Saxony, and at the end of the period we can recognize the Germanic forts and villages of the Rhine valley, but we cannot trace the shifting frontiers intermediate between these two positions and dates.

Some have described the distant colonizing expeditions of the Celts as having been made at the expense of the peoples established in Germany. Instead of supposing an extension of their frontiers on this side as on the other borders of their domain, they have depicted the reservoir of men as emptying on this side and leaving vacancies, which were

---

Celtic name Renos but from Reinos. Otherwise the *e* would have survived. The change from *ei* to *e* occurred at the same time in Goidelic and Brythonic, and therefore cannot be much later than the separation of the dialects (d'Arbois, **CCCI**, ii, p. 326).

[1] Aristotle (*De Mirac. Auscult.*, clxxxii) says that the Rhine flows through the country of the Germans and is covered with ice in winter.

[2] A. Götze, " Die vorgeschichtlichen Burgen der Rhön und die Steinsburg auf dem kleinen Gleichberge bei Römhild," in **LXXXV**, ii ; id., **CCCXXXV**.

[3] **LXXXV**, 1912, pp. 115 ff. ; **LXVII**, 1919, p. 23 ff. ; 1923, p. 8 ; **CXVIII**, 1921–2, p. 212 ; 1916, pp. 145 ff.

[4] Schumacher, **CCCCIX**, pp. 138 ff.

soon filled up by neighbouring folk of an equally adventurous spirit and equally greedy for land whereon to spread themselves.

But that is not what happened. Among the Celtic peoples of Germany there were two whose habitats are perfectly well known, the Volcae and the Boii.[1] They furnished contingents to every Celtic expedition, no doubt to the very earliest. Yet not only did they not vacate their old home, but the Boii even advanced their frontier eastwards and maintained it for a very long time. We may take it as certain that, so long as the Celtic peoples did not emigrate *en masse*, they kept their positions in Germany. It was the surplus population, the marching forces, that emigrated ; the central portion stayed where it was and spread out. The Turoni, a section of whom (perhaps the majority) had settled on the Loire, are mentioned in Ptolemy's time in the upper valley of the Main, south of the Chatti.[2] They had become Germanized, like the Volcae later.

Two prejudices, one archæological and one historical, keep alive the very widespread opinion that the Celts abandoned a large part of Germany in the second La Tène period, their decline beginning about 250.[3] The truth is that, even if they had at that date lost ground in Italy, they were still fighting there with considerable success, while they were holding their own in the Celtiberian tribes in Spain and were establishing themselves in Asia Minor. The supporters of this view are obviously not thinking of the general halt and retirement of the Celts which occurred soon after, but of a decline in civilization which they see in the second La Tène period, a decline which appears in a weaker resistance to outside influences, and especially in Germany.

It is true that the archæological finds of this period are not so brilliant as those of the first. The grave-goods are not so rich. In Germany and in Gaul the beautiful Greek objects, the earthenware vases and the bronze vessels, have gone. From this, it has been concluded that communications between the Mediterranean world and the Celtic interior were interrupted. This view is incorrect. The culture of La Tène III was indebted to the civilizations of the South

---

[1] See *Rise*, pp. 140–1.   [2] Ptol., ii, 11, 22.
[3] Déchelette, ii, 3, p. 918.

for many things—technical devices, domestic usages, methods of construction. These benefits were diffused in the course of the second period or as a result of relations commenced at that time. It was, too, at this date that coinage began to spread in the Celtic world,[1] and it cannot be said that the adoption of coinage and of copies of coins corresponds to a falling-off of relations with the peoples which supplied the models.

It is, moreover, very hazardous to try to show a decay in skill and taste in the Celtic craftsmen of this period. The fine swords with engraved scabbards, the most beautiful belts, and the richest bracelets date from La Tène II.

Besides, one would have to be very sure of being able to tell all the objects belonging to each of these two periods before speaking of a weakening of the Celtic societies and of depopulation. Archæology is often a deceptive mirror of the past, and usually it is a broken one.

Lastly, there is no constant relation between the civilization of a people and the extent of its political power. When the Celts finally bowed before Rome and her culture, they were by no means decadent. They were a strong, healthy social body, which benefited the Roman Empire by its healthiness and lived on in that Empire.

The second prejudice is that the Belgæ were Germans or semi-Germans. If so, the Germans encroached on the domain of the Celts a hundred or two hundred years before the date at which they appear in history under their own name.

In Cæsar's time [2] the Belgæ were all settled between the Seine and the Rhine. We have several lists of the peoples composing this nation, but they agree in the main.[3] They were : the Treviri, Mediomatrici, and Leuci in the east ; the Remi and Suessiones in the west, with the Catuvellauni, Meldi, Parisii, and Silvanectes ; and in the west again and north, the Veliocasses, Bellovaci, Caleti, Ambiani, Atrebates, and Morini, and after them the Aduatuci, Eburones, Nervii, and Menapii. Strabo included the Armorici and, although

---

[1] Livy (xxxvi, 40, 12 ; xxxiii, 3, 13), speaking of the triumph over the Boii in 196 and 191, says that among the booty there were 1,471 torques and 2,340 pounds *argenti infecti factique in Gallicis vasis.*
[2] Cf. for the Belgæ, Rademacher, in Ebert, **CCCXXIV,** s.v. " Belgen ".
[3] Cæs., ii, 3, 4, 11 ; iv, 19 ; viii, 6 ; Pliny, iv, 105 ; Ptol., ii, 9 ; Strabo, iv, 196, 15.

he is alone in doing so, his opinion is not to be despised. They
formed a mass something like that of the Brythons of Gaul.
The large scale of their movements suggests that their number
was great. Like the Goidels and Brythons, the Belgæ were
a family of kindred or associated peoples ; they were a group
in which natural relationships were cemented by political
ties. They were distinguished from other peoples by the
affinities which they found between themselves and the
strangers across the Rhine.

For part of the Belgic peoples, including some of the
most important of them, called themselves Germans or
were so called by the ethnographers.[1] First, there were the
Aduatuci or Tungri.[2] But these had been left behind by
the expedition of the Cimbri. Along the Meuse and the
Sambre, the Eburones of Limburg, the Condrusi of Condroz,
and the Paemani of the valley of the Lesse are classed together
as Germans.[3] To them we must add the Segni [4] of the upper
valley of the Ourthe. These peoples, which were grouped
round the Treviri, called themselves their clients. Now,
the Treviri and the Nervii, who surrounded them on the
north, claimed to be of Germanic origin and were proud of
it.[5] Lastly, the Menapii on the North Sea shore are placed
by Cæsar with the Nervii under the description, " Germans
from this side of the Rhine," *Cisrhenani*.[6] It is a term which
is used by Cæsar several times, and always to designate
the peoples of the Belgic group, and not the remnants of the
expedition of Ariovistus.[7]

A good half of the Belgæ then, if we are to accept con-
cordant evidence based on the traditions of the tribes themselves, should be regarded as Germans. Should one go further
and do the same with the Remi, Suessiones, Bellovaci,
and other Belgæ ? Or should one not go so far, but try to
interpret the evidence ? Usually it is accepted literally.[8]
It is agreed that there were among the Belgæ at least a great

[1] Cæs., ii, 4 ; Tac., *Germ.*, 2.
[2] Tac., loc. cit.
[3] Cæs., loc. cit. : *uno nomine Germani appellantur.*
[4] Id., vi, 32.
[5] Tac., *Germ.*, 28.
[6] Cæs., vi, 2, 3 ; ii, 3. Cf. Jullian, CCCXLVII, ii, p. 10.
[7] Cæs., v, 27, 8 ; vii, 63, 7 ; Jullian, op. cit., ii, p. 467.
[8] e.g. by Mr. MacNeill (CCCCXLI, p. 18), who regards the Belgæ as a
product of this community formed by the Celts and Germans on their boundary.

many Germans, and that in any case they all came from *Germania*, from beyond the Rhine, from the region bounded on the south by the Main. If we are to believe Pomponius Mela,[1] they came from still further, from the Cimbric Peninsula and the shores of the Baltic ; they were a branch of the Scythians or Celto-Scythians mentioned by Pytheas in that region, and their shores were opposite Thule, that is, Scandinavia. But Pomponius Mela may perhaps be confusing them with the Cimbri and Teutones, whom Pytheas had certainly met in Jutland.[2]

We may ask when these Belgic peoples, which we find on the edge of the Celtic world in the second La Tène period, crossed from the east to the west of the Rhine. Their preponderance explains the new development which appears at this time in the civilization of the Western barbarians. They are supposed to have acted during this period in the same way as the Brythonic Gauls at the beginning of La Tène, their settlements in Gaul, like that of the Celts of the Danube, being founded by their rear-guard. But at the same time there reappears in the Celtic world a practice which, during the first La Tène period, seems on the whole to have been confined within the probable frontier of the Germans— burning of the dead. Here is another reason for calling the Belgians Germanic. Cæsar,[3] too, says that their culture was different from that of Gaul and more like that of the peoples beyond the Rhine—municipal life less highly developed than in Gaul, merchants fewer and trade more rudimentary, a character wilder and more warlike.

As a matter of fact, the evidence of the historians is not so definite or so clear as it seems, for the name of *Germani* which they give to the Belgæ may not have the meaning which it is usually given. It is a late word,[4] perhaps a Belgic word like *Gaesati*,[5] used to designate different groups or elements of tribes, which, being applied by the Latins to

---

[1] iii, 36 and 57. Cf. Jullian, op. cit., i, p. 242.
[2] Strabo, i, 2, 27 ; xi, 6, 2 ; Plut., *Mar.*, ii.
[3] I, 1. Cf. Jullian, op. cit., ii, p. 469.
[4] Tac., *Germ.*, 2 : *vocabulum recens et nuper additum.* Various etymologies have for a long time been suggested for the word *Germani*—*garm, gairm* " place ", or *ger* " neighbour ", both Celtic. The latter is perhaps the better. It is supported by a gloss of Bede, v, 9 : *Garmani (a vicina gente Brittonum).*
[5] See above, p. 74.

the new family of strangers, took on a new meaning and was used again by the historians to define the Belgæ.

While the Belgians claimed kinship with the peoples beyond the Rhine, they also had public ties with the Celtic peoples which were outside their confederation. The Remi were the patrons of the Carnutes,[1] and the Bellovaci had from time immemorial been friends of the Ædui.[2] Although the peoples in question are only the Remi and Bellovaci, and not the Treviri or Nervii, these facts are of no less account, for the whole of Belgica or its various tribal bodies several times combined with the rest of Gaul.

Besides, even if the Eburones, Nervii, and Treviri were Germans, their chiefs had Gallic names. Doubtless this was true of more than one Germanic king, but we should note that there is never any word of the language of these supposedly Germanic tribes of Belgica. This silence means that they spoke Gaulish,[3] as might be inferred from the names of places and men which they have left.[4]

A passage in Ausonius [5] enables us, to some extent, to determine the place held by the Belgæ among the other Gallic peoples. When he says that the Volcae Tectosages called themselves *Belcae Tectosagi*, the poet seems to suggest that the two names were closely related.[6] It is of no consequence whether the word is spelt *Belcas* or *Belgas*.[7] Their identity is undeniable, and recalls that of Κελτός and Γαλάτης.[8] From that identity, we may reasonably suppose that this is one of those generic terms by which the Celts designated themselves. A difference in pronunciation aggravated by a false etymology would lead to the name of Belgæ being given to the folk north of the Main.

So, though the Belgæ called themselves Germans, they

---

[1] Cæs., v, 4, 5.

[2] Id., ii, 14, 2. Cf. Jullian, op. cit., ii, p. 442.

[3] Strabo (iv, 176) says that the Gaulish of Belgica was not greatly different from the Gaulish of the Ædui (Cic., *De Div.*, i, 41).

[4] We know an Æduan Diviciacus and a Diviciacus among the Suessiones (Cæs., ii, 4).

[5] *Ordo Urbium Nobilium*, xiii, 7–10 :—

Qua rapitur præceps Rhodanus genitore Lemanno,
interiusque premunt Aquitanica rura Cebennæ,
usque in Tectosagos paganaque nomine Belcas,
totum Narbo fuit.

[6] Belcæ = Volcæ. Cf. Pauly, **CCCLXVIII**, iii, cols. 198–9.

[7] Pomp. Mela, 36, 57 : *Belcæ*.

[8] See *Rise*, pp. 21 ff.

were not Germans at all ; they were Gauls, who had come from the district north of the Main and other places as well.

The archæological evidence also tends to prove that no great movement of population can have occurred in Central Germany and Gaul during the second La Tène period.[1] In those Hallstatt sites in Western Germany which can, by the different types of the pottery,[2] be assigned to various tribes or groups of tribes, one finds a definite continuity of population. Two of these groups, the Helvetii in the south and the Treviri in the north, did not move in the La Tène period. In Cæsar's time, the Treviri were still in their old country on the west bank of the Rhine.[3]

There is yet another place where the settlements of the Belgæ were already fixed in the second La Tène period. In Champagne and Soissonnais there is no sign of the popu- lation changing at that time. The same cemeteries contain tombs of La Tène I and II, and in general the centres of population remained the same. Although few cremations of the third period happen to have been discovered, we may conclude that the Romans there found the Gauls in the places where they had settled in 400.[4] It would, moreover, be very hard to find a place on the map for the peoples which the Belgæ would have driven out of Champagne and Soissonnais about 300. Nor should we forget that in the time of Pytheas the Armorici, who may have been Belgæ, were already established in the west of Gaul.[5]

From their original home in the middle valley of the Rhine and on the right bank north of the Main, the Belgæ probably spread at the very beginning of this history over Belgium and Northern France, just as the Brythons or Volcae of the south of Germany spread over central and southern Gaul. It is true that they were not all established by 400,[6] but, since they were beginning to appear in Illyria,

[1] Herr Schumacher (**CCCCIX**, pp. 196 ff.) has very happily laid stress on the continuity of the population of the Rhine Valley from one age to another.
[2] The pottery of Salem, Koberstadt, and Mehren. Cf. Schumacher, in **CXVIII**, 1914, pp. 257 ff. ; H. Horning, in **LXVIII**, 1921, pp. 19 ff.
[3] Müllenhoff, **CCCXLII**, ii, pp. 201–2.
[4] In Cæsar, whenever the Remi and Suessiones come into question, these peoples appear as having been always established, and rather different from the peoples recently settled in the north of Belgica. Jullian, in **CXXXIV**, 1915, pp. 218 ff.
[5] Jullian, **CCCXLVII**, i, p. 323.
[6] The Menapii did not reach the neighbourhood of Tournai till 54. Before that, they were still on the two banks of the Rhine.

Italy, Spain, and probably Britain somewhere about 300, it is hard to believe that they were not permanently settled in the Gallic domain until some 150 years later. Since the point from which they started at the end of the fourth century was no longer the east bank of the Rhine, but the whole region between the Seine and the Harz, one must suppose that they had spread into the western part of that vast area while the earliest Gauls were wandering into Italy and the valley of the Danube. The settlements which they then founded must have been about a century later than the cemeteries of the first Gauls. Setting forth later, they expanded in the same manner all round their domain, including what is now Germany.

The distribution of the brooches of La Tène II, which have been found right up to the Oder and lower Vistula, the Magdeburg district, and the shores of the North Sea and Baltic,[1] points to the age when Celtic civilization in Germany spread widest and sank deepest, and the reciprocal penetration of Celts and Germans was most complete. It was also at this time that the German workers started to alter the types of objects, especially arms, furnished to them by their Gallic brother-craftsmen. The Germanic swords and spears are derived from those of La Tène II and III, not La Tène I.

The most important object in Celtic archæology, the silver vessel found at Gundestrup in Jutland, outside the true domain of the Celts, in the country of the Cimbri, comes from just about the end of the La Tène period. It is generally agreed that it was made about the beginning of the first century B.C. [2] among the Danubian Celts, in the country of the Scordisci, who were rich in silver.[3] It must have been used for religious purposes by the people who had charge of it among the Cimbri, for they left it in the brush, in a place which was probably forbidden ground, where no one set foot until the cauldron was completely covered over and the heath had become bog. It is of some importance that a sacred vessel, made by Celts and covered with Celtic mythological subjects, should have been used for religious ceremonies by a Cimbric tribe about a hundred years before Christ.

[1] Beltz, in **LXXXV**, 1913, pp. 117 ff.
[2] F. Drexel, in **LXXII**, 1915, pp. 1 ff.   [3] See above, p. 62.

So the civilizing and political influence of the Celts in Germany was in full swing during the third and second centuries.

But if we examine the facts more closely, looking not so much for signs of events as for evidence of the conditions which must have led to events which occurred later, we find two contrary processes taking place : a process of assimilation of the German world on the one hand, but on the other, as a result of that very assimilation, a process of penetration by the Germans into the Celtic world. Then there happened what would happen again to the Roman Empire. The Celts had auxiliaries, some of whom settled down among them, and, being the more occupied on the outer edge of their domains, they squandered the reserves of men which had fed their expeditions. The result was that one fine day a body of Germanic peoples grew restless, as the Belgæ had done, and led the Celtic tribes of the east bank of the Rhine off to new adventures which were to take them beyond the Celtic world. Then, and not till then, the Celts abandoned the east bank of the Rhine to the Germans. But the charm was not broken, for fifty years later, when Ariovistus appears in Gaul, it is not as a foreigner. He speaks Gaulish like a man who knows it and is used to speaking it.[1]

II

THE CIMBRI AND TEUTONES

Comparative calm had been restored for over a century in the region from which the chief expeditions of the Belgæ had started, when another mass of peoples began to move. These were the Cimbri and Teutones. They were probably Germans, but the story of their exodus is none the less linked with that of the Celtic migrations.

The expedition which Augustus afterwards sent along the coasts of Germany [2] came upon Cimbri, but these were only the tiny remnant of a great nation. They were then in Jutland, the Cimbric Peninsula.[3] We may suppose that

[1] Cæs., i, 47.
[2] Mon. Anc., 26.
[3] Strabo, vii, 2, 1–4 ; Pomp. Mela, iii, 32 ; Pliny, ii, 167 ; iv, 95–7, 99 ; Tac., Germ., 37 ; Ptol., ii, 11, 2, 7, 16. Cf. Müllenhoff, CCCLXII, ii, pp. 285 ff.

these had stayed at home when the rest went in search of adventure.

Pytheas had encountered the Teutones.[1] They held the trade in amber, which they got from the people of the island of Abalum (Œsel),[2] off the east coast of the Baltic, and sold to the merchants of the west. They doubtless lived on the Danish islands in what the ancient geographers called the Sinus Codanus.[3] It is very likely that they were neighbours of the Cimbri, since they combined with them, and it is certain that both extended to the seaboard between the Elbe and the Oder.[4]

Contemporaries regarded them as Celts.[5] But it was only after the Cimbric invasion, and probably as a result of the many prisoners left in the hands of the Romans, that the Romans and Greeks learned to distinguish between Celts and Germans. Their names do not help us to place them. That of the Teutones is Celtic in form. Germanic, Celtic, and Italic all have the root; it is an old word meaning " tribe ", " town ", " people ".[6] The name of the Cimbri led Poseidonios to connect them with the Cimmerians,[7] and has led modern writers to connect them with the Cymry. The ancients had an etymology for the word which was Celtic, *Cimber* meaning " brigand ".[8]

The names of Teuton and Cimbric leaders given by the historians are Celtic or of Celtic form.[9] A Teuton chief is called Teutoboduus, and a Cimbrian Claodicus. Both of these names may have been Celticized; but there are also a Boiorix, " King of the Boii," a Caesorix or Gaesorix, probably

---

[1] Pliny, xxxviii, 35. Cf. Müllenhoff, op. cit., ii, pp. 476, 479 ; d'Arbois, **CCCI**, i, p. 19.

[2] There is on it a village named Aboul. It is a town of apple-trees, and the island was an island of apples ; cf. the old Italic Abella—*Abella malifera.*

[3] Pomp. Mela, ii, 32, 54. After the Elbe comes the Sinus Codanus, full of islands ; *in ea sunt Cimbri et Teutoni.* Cf. Jullian, **CCCXLVII**, iii, p. 45.

[4] Pomp. Mela, iii, 32, 54 ; Pliny, iv, 99 ; xxxvii, 35.

[5] Cic., *De Orat.*, ii, 66 ; *De Prov. Cos.*, 266 ; Sall., *Jug.*, 114 ; App., *Celt.*, i, 2. Cf. Jullian, op. cit., i, p. 243, n. 3 ; Mommsen, **CCCLIX**, ii, p. 172 ; Holder, **CCVII**, s.v. " Cimbri ".

[6] Müllenhoff, op. cit., i, p. 113 ; d'Arbois **CCXCIX**, p. 170.

[7] Müllenhoff, op. cit., ii, pp. 167 ff. ; Poseid., in Strabo, vii, 293 ; cf. Diod., v, 32 ; Plut., *Mar.*, ii.

[8] *Cimbri lingua Gallica latrones dicuntur.* Festus, *Epit.*, 43. Müllenhoff (ii, pp. 116 ff.) supposes that they got their Celtic name in Gaul. Old Irish has a word *cimb* " tribute ", " ransom", and a word *cimbid* " prisoner ". D'Arbois (**CCXCIX**, pp. 205 ff.) supposes an active formation, *Cimb-r-os*, from the same root, meaning one who takes prisoner.

[9] Müllenhoff, op. cit., ii, p. 118 ; Jullian, op. cit., iii, p. 53.

" King of the Gaesati," and a Lugius, whose name, if it has been correctly recorded, contains that of one of the great Celtic deities, Lugh. All these names are Celtic, and they cannot be anything else ; but that alone is not enough.

Most of the historians of the Empire speak of these peoples as Germans,[1] and Tacitus,[2] who was an authority on the subject, places them in the group of the Ingaevones, one of the three great groups of Germanic tribes. So, too, the archæology of Hanover, Holstein, and Schleswig [3] in the Hallstatt and La Tène periods is utterly different from that of regions where Celtic names are frequent. Cremation of the dead was the usual practice, whereas further south burial continued to prevail for a long time. The characteristic objects of the southern culture, brooches and pottery, are found there only sporadically.

So it was down to about 300. After that, the doors were opened and Celtic influence and fashions gained ground northwards, predominating more and more until the time when Gallic industry became Roman industry. It was about now that the Cimbri ordered from the Scordisci or perhaps in Gaul the sacred vessels, of which the Gundestrup cauldron, found in their country, may be regarded as the chief specimen.[4] The Cimbri were Germans, Celticized by the trade or policy of the Celts in the third and second centuries. Just as the Galatians took Greek names, and the Scots and Welsh later took Anglo-Saxon names, they took Celtic names, and spoke Celtic, at least in their dealings with other peoples. Marius's intelligence service, run by Sertorius, took the trouble to learn Celtic, and found that language sufficient.[5] Needless to say, these peoples were armed in the Celtic manner, and indeed the throwing-axe of the Celts, the *cateia*, was called the *teutonus*.[6]

It is possible that there were Celtic elements among the Cimbri and Teutones. Names like Boiorix and Gaesorix, which have a racial meaning, were perhaps not bestowed

---

[1] Dottin, **CCCXXI**, p. 21 ; Müllenhoff, op. cit., ii, p. 154.
[2] *Germ.*, 2. Cf. Jullian, op. cit., iii, p. 50.
[3] Schwantes, in **CXVIII**, 1909, pp. 140 ff.
[4] See above, p. 102.
[5] Mommsen, **CCCLIX**, ii, p. 172.
[6] Isid. Sev., *Orig.*, 18, 7, 7 ; Müllenhoff, op. cit., ii, p. 115. For helmets and body-armour among the Cimbri, see Plut., *Mar.*, 25. Cf. Jullian, op. cit., iii, p. 55. For the white shield of the Cimbri, Plut., loc. cit.

lightly.   Certainly they were followed by peoples, some of
which were doubtless not Germans, while others were
undoubtedly Celts.

The historians mention the Ambrones as being [1] a crack
corps of the Teuton army.   The origin of the name may
perhaps be geographical.[2]   Festus [3] calls them a *gens Gallica*.
The Ligurians of the Genoese coast had the same name, and
formed an auxiliary corps in the army of Marius.[4]

If there is any doubt about them, there is none about the
Helvetii, who followed the Cimbri or were carried along by
them.   Tribes of this nation, the Tigurini and the Tugeni,[5]
took part in these campaigns.

The history of the invasion of the Cimbri and Teutones [6]
gives a fuller and more correct idea than does that of the
expeditions of the fourth and third centuries of the great
hordes which from time to time fell on the good lands of
Europe—sometimes timid, sometimes furious, encumbered
with baggage and spoil, inclined to straggle but also capable
of a rapid, orderly march, sometimes led by extraordinarily
clear-headed chiefs and sometimes apparently drifting under
the guidance of chance and instinct alone.

In 113 the Cimbri started to move, possibly driven from
their country by a tidal wave, like the Celts, and advanced
to the south, where they came up against the Boii and were
thrown back by them on to the Volcae.   The Volcae drove
them on to the Taurisci of Noricum.   They went on into
Pannonia, to the country of the Scordisci, but there they were
compelled to turn in their tracks, and re-entered Noricum by
the Save or Drave, till they reached Noreia (Neumarkt),
the capital.   The Romans were already interested in Noricum.[7]
The Cimbri found in front of them the army of the Consul
Cn. Papirius Carbo, which, after an attempt at negotiation,
they routed.   Nevertheless, they continued their retreat

---

[1] Plut., *Mar.*, 19 ; Müllenhoff, op. cit., ii, p. 114 ; Jullian, in **CXXXIV**,
N. GR., lxxii.
[2] Several rivers in Celtic country were called Ambra. One is a tributary
of the Weser in its upper course, the Emmer.
[3] *Epit.*, p. 17, 2 M.
[4] Plut., *Mar.*, 19.
[5] Jullian, op. cit., ii, p. 61.
[6] For the expedition of the Cimbri and Teutones, see Müllenhoff, ii, pp.
112–189. Jullian, **CCCXLVII**, iii, pp. 39 ff. ; Chapot, **CCCXI**, English, pp. 12 ff.
[7] See above, p. 65.

into Germany, where, in the region of the Main, they were joined by the Teutones.

There they remained from 113 to 109. They had wandered about for a whole year without stopping, living on the country—that is ravaging it. We must now picture them on the Main, founding colonies, sowing crops, and reaping them. In these four obscure years they probably achieved more than in their whole career. They occupied a country which had been Celtic and now ceased to be so. It was at this time, too, that they pushed forward the Helvetii, whose departure made a desert of the Gallic country south of the Main.

When the Cimbri and Teutones set off again in 109, they probably left rear-guards or colonies behind them.[1] Their name still survived in the Roman period in that region of the Limes which they occupied, and the memory of the great exodus, which had made a strong impression, had supplied a legend to the great fortified enclosures of the Taunus and Westerwald.[2]

In the same year the Teutones and Helvetii crossed the Rhine, and met the Consul Silanus and his army somewhere in Gaul. They must have remained facing each other for several weeks, for the Cimbri had time to send an embassy to Rome. They asked for lands, as they had already asked them of Carbo, but Rome had no land to give them. The conversations were broken off, and Silanus was defeated. But the barbarians did not advance. They changed their route, and for two years we lose track of them. In 107 the Tigurini, operating on their own account, descended into Provence and in the Roman province joined up with the Volcae Tectosages of Toulouse, who had revolted and were besieging the garrison. One of the Consuls of the year, L. Cassius Longinus, pursued them, but they escaped down the Garonne. Cassius made contact with them in the country of the Nitiobriges near Agen. He was defeated and killed, and his army had to capitulate. In this affair the Tigurini were commanded

---

[1] On the Greinberg, near Miltenberg, on the Main in Franconia, text regarding the boundaries of a Teutonic territory (I, xii, 6610) ; cf. J. Quilling, in **LXXXV**, 1914, p. 334).

[2] Dedications addressed *Mercurio Cimbriano*, on the Greinberg (I, xiii, 6604–5) ; *Mercurio Cimbrio* on the Heiligenberg near Heidelberg (ibid., 6402). Cf. Schumacher, **CCCLIX**, p. 159.

by a capable man named Divico, whom Cæsar knew. The other Consul, Servilius Cæpio, succeeded not only in saving the garrison of Toulouse, but in obtaining the surrender of the treasure of the Tectosages, estimated at 200,000 pounds of gold. It was sent to Marseilles but never arrived there, and the Consul was accused, not unreasonably, of being himself responsible for the theft. It was said that the gold of Toulouse was the gold of Delphi. It brought bad luck to Cæpio.

It seems very likely that the treasure of coins, ingots, and a torque found at Taillac-Libourne [1] in 1893 had something to do with this campaign of the Tigurini in south-western Gaul. It may have been their war-chest. The coins can be divided into a few fairly large groups, which can be distributed on the map along the route taken by the Cimbri and Teutones. Sixty-five are gold staters of the Bellovaci, a hundred and ninety-five others belong to the Ambarri or the Arverni, and seventy-five are *Regenbogen-schüsselchen*. These coins would, then, be shares or remains of tribute collected by the Tigurini on the road. After the battle of Agen the Tigurini would have reached the Atlantic coast, leaving a post to guard the treasure, which was buried in some emergency.[2]

In 105 Cimbri, Teutones, Ambrones, and Helvetii were reunited, and went down the Rhone. At Orange they came on the two Roman armies of Cæpio, now Proconsul, and Cn. Mallius Maximus, a Consul, and crushed them. Then once again Cimbri, Teutones, and allies went their different ·ways. The first reached Spain, where all trace of them is lost. The second went through Gaul from south to north, ravaging like wild beasts, and Cæsar more than once gives a picture of the terrible distress which they created. Only the Belgæ were able to stop them. Still, they left 6,000 men in Belgium, on the Sambre at Namur, to guard the baggage and protect their lines of communication. From this band was formed, fifty years later, the important, more than half Celtic tribe of the Aduatuci.

[1] Forrer, **DXLIII**, p. 316 ; Cartailhac, in **XV**, 1897.
[2] This hypothesis has not been accepted by M. Blanchet (in **CXXIV**, xii, pp. 21 ff.), who holds that the treasure of Taillac represents the movable property of a private individual. That would give us a high notion of Gallic capitalism. But I am much attracted by Herr Forrer's ingenious explanation.

Two years later, in 103, the Cimbri, sorely tried by the
resistance of the Celtiberians, reappeared north of the
Pyrenees, and were joined by the Teutones somewhere in
Gaul. Their leaders agreed on an ambitious and well thought
out plan, which was in part very well executed.

They had not found what they wanted in Gaul. They
had not been allowed to settle down, or were incapable of
doing so. The country was too full or too completely assigned
to existing proprietors, except perhaps in the district of the
Belgæ, who do not seem to have been inconvenienced by
the colony of the Aduatuci. For ten years they had been
hovering round Italy and beating Roman armies, but after
each victory they had stopped. At last they decided to make
a serious effort to force their way into the country ; they
would attack it from two sides. The Teutones were to cross
the Western Alps by the southern passes, following the
Durance ; the Cimbri should move eastwards along the north
of the Alps and then over the Brenner ; the Tigurini, on the
left wing, should go yet further east, into Noricum, either as
a reserve or to bring reinforcements from the direction of
the Julian Alps.

Marius defeated the Teutones at Aquae Sextiae (Aix).
The Cimbri crushed his colleague Catulus on the Adige, but
once again they hesitated or dispersed in Venetia and
Lombardy, and in the end lost time, which Marius gained.
The two Consuls joined forces, and at Vercellae in Piedmont
they put an end to the Cimbric danger. The Tigurini had
remained in Noricum. Sulla was sent there and seems to
have had no great difficulty in getting them to join the
other Helvetii in Switzerland.

The battles of Aquae Sextiae and Vercellae were frightful
slaughters. The dead and prisoners ran to thousands. Whole
armies were wiped out, and with them all their following of
women, children, old men, and the non-fighting people.
After Aquae Sextiae, a small body of horse managed to
escape and to reach the land of the Sequani, who gave them
up. At Vercellae no one escaped.

What remained of the great hosts brought by the Cimbri
and Teutones was in reality transplanted. The sequel to
this destruction of peoples was that strange Servile War which
broke out thirty years later. It was a class-war, no doubt,

but it was also a national war, conducted by Gallic, German, and Thracian leaders, and for the Rome of Sulla it was as terrible a danger as the invasion of the Cimbri in the days of Marius.

The Servile War is interesting as guaranteeing the likelihood of the number of prisoners, and also of the generally different figures given by the historians. We hear of 300,000 Teutones at Aquae Sextiæ and as many Cimbri. This is the fighting strength, not the whole people including women, children, and a great many other non-combatants. They were tribes, whole social units and probably groups of units or large political units. The expedition of the Cimbri and Teutones involved the peoples concerned almost in their entirety. The Cimbri left at home only the small remnant which was afterwards found there by the expedition of Augustus.[1] They sent an embassy to the Emperor, and presented him with a cauldron ; one thinks of that of Gundestrup. Shortly afterwards they disappeared.

Of the Teutones, there is no more question in their old home.[2] The Ambrones disappeared likewise. As for the Helvetii, the country which they had occupied is called " the Desert of the Helvetii " ; they left it empty and for a time nobody came to occupy it.

There are many interesting things about this half-Celtic half-Germanic adventure—the uncertain advance, the way in which peoples crossed each other's paths, without always fighting, the heterogeneous mass which followed it, and the anxiety for a permanent home which appears to have ruled these barbarians, although they seem to have had a notion that their settlement would send other peoples wandering off. But it left no settlement, save that of the Aduatuci and perhaps that of the Teutones of the Taunus. Gaul must have been populated to saturation point, and Rome was growing steadily. The depopulation and weakness of the Empire of five centuries later were needed before similar expeditions could lead to conquest and the creation of new states. The adventure of the Cimbri and Teutones was doubtless a perfect replica of the great earlier invasions, except in

[1] Tac., *Germ.*, 37.
[2] When geographers like Strabo and encyclopædists like Pliny speak of the Teutones on the coast of the Baltic and their share in the amber-trade, they are merely copying previous Greek historians.

that it failed. But we can judge of the alarm and the destruction which it created. The memory of it lasted long, for, although the Ambrones had vanished, the Latin grammarians of the Late Empire say that their name survived as a word of abuse.

III

RESULTS OF THE INVASION

The expedition of the Cimbri and Teutones had a great effect on the Celtic world and, indeed, turned it upside down. In 103 it was no longer what it had been in 113.

For nearly four hundred years the Gauls had lived as agriculturists, scattered in farms and open villages,[1] deserting the citadels in which the Hallstatt men and those of the Bronze and Neolithic Ages had shut themselves up, at least for long periods.[2] From the end of the second century onwards, Gaul bristled with fortresses, large and small,[3] and its people returned to the abandoned *oppida*, for example to Fort-Harrouard.[4] Except on the east bank of the Rhine and the Celto-Ligurian marches in the south of France, objects of La Tène III come directly after those of Hallstatt in the prehistoric forts.

Behind those ramparts the Gauls endured long and severe sieges, to which eloquent allusion is made in the speech which Cæsar places in the mouth of the Arvernian Cintognatus during the blockade of Alesia.[5] A process then took place in Gaul which was repeated four centuries later in the first Germanic invasions. The Gallo-Roman towns, sprawling wide over the plains, were in a very few years surrounded by walls hastily built with the materials of the demolished suburbs. In each case, a long period of peace and prosperity followed times of insecurity and distress. But Gaul had more vitality in the first century before Christ than in the third of our era.

To the same circumstances as these *oppida*, which are fortresses, not fortified cities, we may attribute the underground refuges which are usually some distance away from a

[1] See above, p. 7.   [2] See above, p. 8.
[3] Déchelette, in **CXXXIX**, 1912, i, pp. 101 ff.
[4] Philippe, **CCCCLXVII**.   [5] vii, 77.

group of dwellings and have two or more entrances, stairs, and passages barred by doors.[1]   They were used in several epochs, and are not all contemporary. But the Gauls certainly had them—witness the story of the Lingonian Sabinus, who lived in one with his wife Eponina after the failure of the revolt of A.D. 70.[2]

Another consequence of the Cimbro-Teutonic invasion was that the Celts retreated to the Rhine. In the middle valley of that river, north of the Main, the villages of La Tène III are Germanic settlements, whose culture, though reminding one that the Celts were near, is only an imitation of theirs.[3] The Helvetii had cleared out completely, and it was to Switzerland that Divico returned to live. It was no doubt the same with the Celts north of the Main. The Germans advanced in their track between the Rhine and Bohemia. A fairly large Celtic population remained in and round Bohemia for some time yet, but it spread in the direction of the Danube and did not retreat to Gaul. The eastern frontier of the rest of the Celts, which had so long been fixed in Thuringia, was suddenly withdrawn to the Rhine.

It seems to have happened strangely easily, and in any case very quickly, between 113 and 109. The whole system of forts appears to have been abandoned without a blow. It was the result of causes which had long lain in the very nature of Celtic societies. This was the region from which all the thousands had set forth to settle or fight in Gaul, Spain, Italy, the Danube valley, and the East. However prolific these nations of the original Celtic country may have been, they were clearly much reduced in numbers. In that quarter, especially north of the Main and in Thuringia, there were now only the phantoms of peoples which had vanished, scattered, retired before the effective force of nations hitherto kept back by their prestige. These Gauls who lived north of the Main must have been very insignificant to have left no trace of themselves either among the Celts of the west bank who may have taken them in or among the Cimbri who may have absorbed them. There must have been some movements of peoples inside Gaul, and it has been

---

[1] Blanchet, CCCLXV ; CXXIV, 1910, ii, p. 265 ; CXX, 1924, p. 63.
[2] See below, p. 150.
[3] Schumacher, in CXVIII, 1914, pp. 277 ff.

suggested that one took place in the valley of the Garonne as a result of the expedition of the Tigurini. The name of Vevey in the canton of Vaud (*Viviscus*), may possibly indicate that a body of Bituriges *Vivisci*, whom we find established at the mouth of the Garonne, had followed the Helvetii in their wanderings. This is mere hypothesis, for the name may equally well record an earlier settlement of the same people. There is no archæological evidence to help us.

Still more important is the succession of great movements which were set going for over a century by the descent of the Cimbri and Teutones on Western Europe. When those peoples started, they must have gone up the valley of the Elbe, which the Boii blocked. The country was populous, and they probably did not create a void before them. They went through the tribes and came out on the other side.

These peoples of Central Germany, the Lombards, Hermunduri, and Semnones, whom the ancient authors [1] place in the group of the Herminones, were then united in a confederation whose members called themselves by the common name of Suevi.[2] To this adhered, but as a separate body, the Marcomanni,[3] the Marchmen, from the frontier strip which the Germans regarded as a kind of desert.[4] But the Marcomanni were not an old existing people ; they were probably a combination of the scattered bodies of Cimbri and Teutones which had remained in or returned to the old territory of the Helvetii. The Black Forest, which formed a backbone to their country, was called Abnoba in Celtic ; under the Empire, it was given the Germanic name of Silva Marciana, when the only inhabitants of the country were new settlers.

The Suevi were settled, since they remained. But perhaps they were not settled quite in the same way as the Celts.[5] The passage of the Cimbri and Teutones may have introduced

---

[1] Tac., *Germ.*, 38–9 ; Pliny, iv, 28 ; Strabo, vii, p. 290.
[2] Jullian, CCCXLVII, iii, p. 49.
[3] Müllenhoff, CCCLXII, ii, p. 300.
[4] Cæsar (iv, 3, 2) had heard say that the Suevi had on one side a desert march about 600 Roman miles wide.
[5] Speaking of the Suevi, Cæsar (i, 37, 3) mentions an annual redistribution of land. But we must not treat this information too seriously. Cæsar, even if his information is correct, does not always interpret correctly the social facts which he describes.

some disturbance into their social life. Indeed, they started
moving in their turn, and forty years after the defeat of the
Cimbri we find them on the Rhine and in Gaul.

They then formed a mass like that of the preceding
invasion,[1] but, unlike their predecessors, they had a method.
Their king, Ariovistus,[2] does not seem to have had any
trouble at home. He co-ordinated all the unconnected operations of his people, and all the acts of the Suevi appear to be
the result of a deliberate political purpose. They formed
a state which methodically extended its frontiers and made
settlements which lasted. Their leader, too, seems to have
been an exceptional man. Cæsar, who defeated Ariovistus,
gives him his due in ascribing to him acts and speeches,
which look as if they were genuine, displaying clear-sighted-
ness and great qualities as a leader of men. He was neither
a barbarian nor a particularly simple soul.[3] He has rather
the air of a statesman, and of one with large conceptions.
His success tempted him to dreams of an overlordship of the
whole of Gaul which, had it not been for Cæsar, might have
become a Germanic state now instead of waiting till the
sixth century.

If we suppose that the Suevi followed the lead of Ariovistus
we must imagine them crossing from the valley of the Elbe
to that of the Main about 75 B.C., and descending the Main
unopposed to the great meeting of ways at Mainz.[4]   On
coming into contact with Gaul, they were induced, between
72 and 62, to take sides in one of those squabbles for hegemony in which the Sequani and Ædui engaged. The
Sequani, being the weaker, looked for auxiliaries in Germany,
and brought in Ariovistus with 15,000 Suevi.[5] But when their
combined forces had won the day, Ariovistus began to talk
as a master, demanding one-third of the territory of the
Sequani, and taking it. We find, indeed, that from this
date Alsace ceases to be part of Sequania, and further north

---

[1] One hundred *pagi* for the Suevi (Cæs., loc. cit. ; iv, 1, 4) and as many
for the Semnones alone (Tac., *Germ.*, 39).

[2] Jullian, op. cit., iii, p. 153.

[3] Cæs., i, 44, 9 : *non se tam barbarum neque tam imperitum esse rerum.*

[4] Schumacher, in **CXVIII**, 1914, p. 273.

[5] Jullian, op. cit., iii, p. 154. Strabo (p. 192) says that the Romans bore
a grudge against the Sequani because they had helped the Germans to invade
Italy. This passage perhaps refers to the beginning of the expeditions of
Ariovistus, if not to some unknown episode in the Cimbric war.

the Triboci, who are settled on the territory of the Mediomatrici, are probably some of Ariovistus's Suevi.[1] Further north still, the villages of the Nemetes round Spire and those of the Vangiones round Worms made with those mentioned a continuous chain of Germanic possessions on both banks of the Rhine from Mainz to above Strasburg.[2]

Ariovistus' demands united the Gauls against him. He defeated their great army at Admagetobriga and made them give him hostages and pay tribute.

About the same time another people, the Dacians,[3] repeated the Cimbric attack against another front of the Celts, on the Danube. They were not Germans, but Getae and perhaps Thracians too. Their origin and the extent of their possessions are unknown. In the first century they were in Hungary, east of the Theiss. Gradually they began to assert themselves. Then, about 82, they, like the Suevi, got a chief of wide vision in Boerebistas, who was a moral as well as a political leader.[4] Their history is obscure. They probably conquered the Bastarnae, for they took Olbia about 63. With the Scordisci they had previously had friendly relations,[5] and that people does not appear to have resisted them. But further north they came into conflict with the Boii and the people of Noricum.

The Boii had advanced their frontiers to the Theiss [6] and now formed a kind of large composite state, governed by a king named Critasirus. They went to war with the Dacians over the question of the Theiss frontier. Critasirus was defeated and the Boii were pursued to the south bank of the Danube. They then vanished from the neighbourhood of Bohemia, as the Helvetii had vanished from Wurtemberg, leaving behind them the " Desert of the Boii ".[7]

According to Jordanes,[8] the Dacians carried the war still further, to the country afterwards occupied by the Franks. In any case, they did not join forces with the Suevi.[9]

[1] Strabo, iv, 3, 4 ; Pliny, iv, 106 ; Tac., *Germ.*, 27.
[2] Schumacher, in **CXVIII**, 1914, p. 269 ; Müllenhoff, op. cit., ii, p. 301.
[3] Brandis, in **CCCLXVII**, iv, col. 1948 ; Jullian, op. cit., iii, p. 144.
[4] **CCCCXVII**, vii, col. 626 ; Jullian, op. cit., iii, p. 152.
[5] See above, pp. 60–1.
[6] Ibid.
[7] Strabo, vii, 1, 5 ; v, 2 ; Pliny, iii, 146. Cf. Jullian, op. cit., iii, p. 145.
[8] xi, 67. Cf. Jullian, op. cit., iii, p. 154.
[9] Ariovistus had married the sister of a king of Noricum named Voccio (Cæs., i, 53, 4).

The encroachments of the Suevi and Dacians on the frontiers, old or new, of the Celts, by creating a pressure in the border districts, caused the last migration of the Continental Celts, that of the Helvetii and Boii.

The Helvetii suffered from the inroads and forays of the Suevi quite as directly as the Sequani had done and the Ædui were now doing.[1] Moreover, some of their tribes had not yet taken root in Switzerland, and one can easily imagine that they were not satisfied with their new country. In Germany they had occupied a fertile region, hilly, certainly, but with rich belts of loess surrounding the hills, and their villages had been bound to the earth which fed them. Switzerland was less kindly.

Cæsar's account [2] presents a very vivid picture, and certainly gives an idea of the typical way in which great migrations were planned and carried out—the problems, the aims, the collective phantoms which arose, the powwows in which the programme was fixed and the exodus organized. A clan chieftain, Orgetorix, took the lead. He was a powerful man, who could bring 10,000 clients to the assembly of the Ædui. But the matter was not altogether simple. Orgetorix embarked on political intrigues for a condominium of three peoples, the Sequani, Ædui, and Helvetii, over the whole of Gaul, and aimed at the kingship for himself. He broke himself over these schemes, and finally committed suicide. The Helvetii returned to the original plan of simply emigrating.

They had laid it down as their object to reach the country of the Santones ; perhaps they knew it already.[3] They first entered into negotiations with their neighbours for reinforcements, and succeeded in winning over the Raurici of Basle, the Tulingi, and the Latovici or Latobrigi.[4] A large part of the Boii of Noricum, doubtless those driven out by the Dacians, also joined them. They treated with the Ædui and Sequani for the passage through their country and, after burning their own villages and what corn they did not

---

[1] Cæs., i, 40, 7.
[2] Cæs., i, 2 ff. ; Cic., *Ad Att.*, i, 19, 2. Cf. Jullian, op. cit., iii, p. 160.
[3] See *Rise*, pp. 153–4.
[4] These were fairly small peoples, which were not reckoned among the Helvetii and should doubtless be placed somewhere near the Raurici, along the Rhine. They may have been remnants of the Celtic population of Germany.

take with them, all the different bodies united on the 24th March, 58, to the number of 368,000 souls, of whom 263,000 were Helvetii, 36,000 Tulingi, 14,000 Latobrigi, 23,000 Raurici, and 32,000 Boii, or 92,000 combatants in all.[1] These figures are interesting, for they give one an idea of the relative forces of the various members of the combination. In the case of the Helvetii, however, they probably do not give a true ïdea of the size of the people.

There was no room in Gaul, where the various tribes, already crowded, had had to close in yet more to admit the Belgæ. Those most immediately exposed to attack grew disturbed and prepared to resist.

An unexpected event, the intervention of a foreign force to maintain the existing order and stability, wrecked the enterprise of the Helvetii. Cæsar marched against them. They were defeated in the country of the Ædui and driven home, being reduced to 110,000 in number.[2] The Ædui intervened on behalf of the Boii, with whom they were always on friendly terms.[3] They were allowed to settle on the triangle at the junction of the Allier and the Loire as a free part of the Æduan people.[4]

Cæsar, having decided to remain in Gaul, turned against Ariovistus, who had in 59 obtained from the Senate the recognition of his kingship and the title of Friend of the Roman people.[5] He summoned an assembly of Gaul at Bibracte, that it might ask him to intervene.[6] After some marching and counter-marching in the north of Sequania, he defeated Ariovistus in Upper Alsace and drove him with his forces across the Rhine, where they looked for a settlement, except the Triboci, Nemetes, and Vangiones, who remained on the west of the river.

North of Mainz some Germanic tribes, hard pressed by the Suevi, tried to cross the Rhine during the years in which Cæsar was campaigning in Gaul. At the level of Cologne the Ubii, who had long had relations with Gaul, were attacked

[1] From the census-tablets, written in Greek, which fell into Cæsar's hands (i, 29, 2–3).
[2] Jullian, op. cit., iii, p. 194.
[3] Coins from Gaul at Stradonitz. Cf. Déchelette, iii, 2, p. 1579.
[4] Cæs., i, 28, 5.
[5] Cæs., i, 35, 2. Cf. Jullian, op. cit., iii, p. 163.
[6] Cæs., i, 30 ff. Cf. Müllenhoff, op. cit., ii, p. 301 ; Jullian, op. cit., ii, p. 467.

by the Suevi, but they made terms and paid tribute. Further south the Usipetes and Tencteri were compelled to give up their country, and wandered away looking for land,[1] first in Germany and then on the Rhine, which they crossed. They were wiped out in 55.

So Cæsar introduced the Romans to the Rhine in that character of policemen which they maintained for 500 years. He was the first to make this line the provisional frontier of the Celts.

East of the river, the Boii still occupied Bohemia, but not for long. They were in the centre of a group of peoples which remained distinct until the times of Tacitus and Ptolemy. There were Cotini in Silesia or Galicia,[2] who spoke a Celtic dialect but were subordinate to the Quadi and Sarmatians. To the south, along the Danube, the Carpi and Rhacatae [3] were perhaps Celtic peoples,[4] remnants, with the Tulingi and Latobrigi, of the Volcae, who are mentioned by Cæsar for the last time,[5] and perhaps also of the Vindelici of the Bavarian plateau. The Danube had stopped the Germans and, as on the Rhine, the frontier was permanently laid down by the Romans in the upper valley of the river.

All these expeditions and migrations have added little to our picture of the Celtic world but losses. Apart from the small settlement of the Boii on the Bec d'Allier and the Germano-Celtic foundations of the Aduatuci, Triboci, Nemetes, and Vangiones, these great movements of peoples left no colonies. They failed, and these later movements were on a far smaller scale than the earlier. Rome, too, was making ready to conquer Gaul, and Britain shortly after.

IV

THE CHARACTER OF THE CELTIC EXPEDITIONS

The migrations of the end of the second century and the beginning of the first take a great place in history because

---

[1] Cæs., iv, 1 ; 4 ; Müllenhoff, op. cit., iv, pp. 419 ff.

[2] Tac., *Germ.*, 43 ; Ptol., ii, 11, 12, 13, 14, 15 ; Jullian, op. cit., i, p. 198.

[3] Ptol., ii, 2, 11. Cf. Much, in Hoops, **CCCXLII**, iv, p. 424.

[4] The name of the Κάρποι may come from that of the Chamb, a sub-tributary of the Regen, in which we may see Celtic *kambos* " curving, winding ". The name of the 'Ρακάται reminds one of Welsh *rhagawd* (**racat*), which expresses the idea of opposition, battle.

[5] vi, 24. Cf. Jullian, op. cit., iii, p. 297, n. 3 ; Much, in op. cit., iv, p. 425; Müllenhoff, op. cit., ii, p. 300.

they are fairly well known, having been described by contemporaries. But they have a special interest for us, in that they give a picture of what the earlier great invasions were probably like.[1]

Except for the last move of the Boii, the migration of the Atrebates from Gaul to Britain, the inroads and conquests of the Goidels in these islands, and the settlement of the people of Cornwall in Brittany, most of the Celtic peoples were now in the last stage of their wanderings. The Celtic world now assumed the face under which it was last known to antiquity, and it was a face of death. What was to revive later would be quite different, and much smaller. At this moment of time, suddenly, just when it was about to be completely conquered and absorbed, its features, hitherto obscure, appear in broad daylight, and that thanks to its conqueror. We are told the names of its peoples and the places where they lived.

However far we go back in the history of the Celts, we find them distributed in great racial units or confederations of neighbouring peoples, bound by alliance, kinship, and every tie which makes for the stabilization and permanence of a group of tribes. Goidels, Picts, Brythons, and Belgæ all had their age of growth. Each race in succession spread out from its original home. Each movement gave rise to a series of expeditions, roughly contemporaneous and sometimes ensuing one from another.

These migrations have been explained by sudden catastrophes,[2] by attacks.[3] The most likely reason is an excess of power, resulting from the growth of the population and a stronger political organization of its forces.[4]

When the great movements took place, the nations which led them seem to have divided up and sent out swarms in quite an organized fashion. The ancients compared this regular dispersion to the *ver sacrum* of the Samnites,[5] the great invasions of Italy. The Sacred Spring was an Italic institution, but we may legitimately suppose that it existed

---

[1] The German historian Niese thought that the expedition of the Cimbri was the source of the legend of the first Celtic migration (**CCCXXIV**, vii, p. 613). Cf. Z. f. d. Alt., 1898, 133 ff.

[2] See *Rise*, p. 141.

[3] e.g. the Helvetii. See above, p. 116.

[4] See below, pp. 122-3.

[5] Just., xxiv, 4, 1-3.

also among the Celts, some of whose prehistoric customs may have had the same effects.[1]

Moreover, the Celtic migrations and their causes varied greatly. From the trek of a whole people to the emigration, often temporary, of a single band of mercenaries, the wandering of the Celts took many forms ; the emigrants might be a social unit or part of one, a people making an exodus *en masse* like the Cimbri and Teutones, or a composite host made up from various groups of tribes.[2]

Those units which were not broken up on the way appear at their journey's end as homogeneous groups, whatever they may have been when they started ; in a word, they were colonies. Those which were broken up re-formed in new units. So each new wave altered not only the racial structure of the widening Celtic world, but its political geography ; frontiers shifted and new dominions were acquired. Each wave left a separate deposit. In Ireland, where the various elements were most mixed of all, the tribes of Goidels, Picts, Gauls, and Belgæ kept their own status well into the Middle Ages. As for the masses, properly so called, they fell into large political and racial divisions, the most conspicuous of which were Belgica, Lugdunensis, and Aquitania, each corresponding to a new migration of the Celts. So the map of the Celtic world presents areas which reflect the original divisions of the Celts.

[1] See above, p. 11.
[2] See above, pp. 103 ff.

CHAPTER V

CELTIC GAUL

I

THE FORMATION OF THE GALLIC PEOPLES

IN the last years of life which were left to it, the Celtic world shows the most complete picture of itself within the frontiers of Gaul. Its curiously shifting peoples are condemned, at least in the great mass, to an almost definitely fixed abode. It is now time to inquire into the positions held by the chief peoples and the date at which their frontiers were permanently fixed.

Positive information about the settlement of the peoples of Gaul is almost entirely lacking. The evidence of archæology is also too uncertain. The exploration of what was once Gaul is deplorably incomplete, and we are still very far from having recovered the traces of every Gallic settlement. Their history is almost always impossible to follow. Moreover, the civilization of the Celtic countries in the Hallstatt and La Tène periods is in the main highly homogeneous, so that it is difficult to study local variations. Only at a few points are the finds continuous down to the time of Cæsar; we may conclude that these areas of uninterrupted occupation correspond to settled peoples. Elsewhere finds are discontinuous, and it is very likely that the population itself changed greatly. Archæology by itself cannot furnish a picture of Gaul at the time of the conquest, and it is to the names of places and men and to the map of Roman Gaul that we must turn for the information which we need in order to study the population.

In a document presented to the Roman Senate after the death of Augustus, 305 Gallic peoples are mentioned.[1] But the historians do not tell us the date of their settlement in the country except in the case of a few—the Aduatuci about 105,

---

[1] Joseph, ii, 16, 4. In Cæsar's time there were said to be about 330 peoples in Gaul (Plut., *Cæs.*, 15). Cf. Bloch, in Lavisse, **CCCCLXVII**, i, 2, p. 191.

but they were Germans ; part of the Helvetii about 103 ; the Menapii in 54. At the time of Hannibal's expedition, about 218, the Volcae Tectosages and Arecomici were already in the country in which they remained. Hasdrubal passed through the territory of the Arverni. We must come down to about 125 before we know for certain that the Ædui are in their place. At the time of the Cimbric invasion, the Sequani and Nitiobriges appear. The rest of the political map of Gaul is a large blank.

The 305 Gallic peoples officially recorded at the death of Augustus were very different in size and rank. Many were or had been subdivisions of larger groups. In reality, there were about sixty peoples in Gaul, some small and others large, which could call themselves independent. In the centre and in south-eastern Belgica there were large nations whose territory corresponded to that of several modern French departments ; the political map was divided into smaller districts on the shores of the Channel and in the Pyrenees and Alps.

The relationship of the sub-group to the group, either at the time of which we are speaking or at the beginning, is in some useful cases marked by a double name. The Tectosages and Arecomici are Volcae, but they are inserted among the Volcae as independent bodies. The Eburovices, Cenomani, Andecavi, Diablintes, and Brannovices are Aulerci. The first four still compose the people of the Aulerci, while the last have broken away. We find Bituriges Cubi and Bituriges Vivisci. These sub-groups are fractions broken off from their parent-group recently or long ago. Sometimes they have become independent, like the Arecomici and Tectosages, the Cubi and Vivisci, and the Cenomani of Cisalpine Gaul ; or they have become attached to other groups, as the Brannovices to the Ædui. But normally the Gallic people is divided into sub-groups.

In the geographical terminology of Roman Gaul, the sub-group is called a *pagus*, whereas the whole people, unless it is the principal people, is called a *civitas*. The group may have been originally formed by conquest, vassalage, the voluntary union of citizens,[1] or kinship. Independent but

---

[1] Cæsar (v, 39) gives a list of the peoples under the sway of the Nervii— Centrones, Grudii, Levaci, Pleumoxii, Geidumni.

neighbouring peoples, such as the Ambarri and Ædui [1] or the Remi and Suessiones,[2] are related by blood. Have we in these various cases peoples which have gone on organizing their internal divisions to a point at which they have split up, or which have amalgamated ? We find the Gallic nations arranged in composite groups which are perpetually in process of formation and dissolution. However, as within other Celtic societies, we may reasonably suppose that political association at first took the form of kinship.

An examination of the names of peoples shows that Celtic colonization was the work of a fairly few nations which split up and sent out swarms. Some of these names are unintelligible, but the meaning of the rest is plain enough. Some come from the geography of the country occupied— Taurisci from Tauern ; Scordisci from the Shar-Dagh ; Ambiani, people of the river Amb ; Nantuates, people of the valley. The unintelligible names are obviously ancient ; the others are new, adopted names. With this second class is allied a whole series of geographical names which no longer correspond to the last habitat of their bearers (Raurici, people of the Ruhr ; Sequani, people of the Seine), names referring to numbers (Remi, the First [3]; Vocontii, the Twenty Clans),[4] and nicknames or warnames (Ruteni, the Fair-haired [5]; Leuci, the Lightners ; Medulli, the Mead-drinkers).

It is obvious that there are several strata of names of different dates. Some are assuredly very old, such as Bituriges, Kings of the World, Ædui, Burning,[6] and Mediomatrici, the people between the Matrona and the Matra. The antiquity of some others is proved by their corruption, such as that of the Osismii of Finistère, which is explained by the name Uxisama, the Furthest Island.[7] A good number are not perfectly clear, but this very fact is certain proof of their great age. Of these there is a small series grouped in a most interesting way—the names of the Boii, Volcae, Helvetii,

---

[1] Cæs., i, 11.
[2] Cæs., ii, 3.
[3] Irish *riam* " before " ; Welsh *rhwyf* " king ". Cf. *primi*, with the *p* dropped.
[4] CCCXXIV, 1911, p. 351.
[5] Jullian, CCCXLVII, ii, p. 500, n. 5.
[6] *Aedh* " fire ".
[7] *Uchel* " high ".

and perhaps Turoni, the peoples which remained longest in the original cradle of the Celts. Among the Belgæ we have the names of the Nervii, Suessiones, and perhaps Remi ; in the west, the Veneti, Aulerci, Unelli, Pictones, and Centrones ; in the south, the Cadurci, Gabali, and Vellavi. This is only a provisional list, which may be extended or cut down. Of these ancient peoples, some remained first-class nations, while others attached themselves now to one neighbour and now to another, such as the Parisii, oscillating between the Suessiones and the Senones.[1]

Having sorted out these few, we need not attempt to form hypotheses to make the sixty *civitates* of the Gauls come as full-blown nations from the Celtic cradle or the west bank of the Rhine. The Volcae, Boii, Helvetii, Lemovices, Menapii, Turoni, and perhaps Aulerci and Pictones stayed there and came from there. The other peoples were formed on the western and southern edge of the old Celtic domain, and perhaps sprang from these parent peoples.

So the great nations of the beginning dispersed themselves over the Celtic world, where many portions of them are to be found disguised under new names. They seem to have preserved a definite memory of their origins, since in some cases they kept their name. The peoples which formed later proceeded in the same manner. If we bring together all these names and certain names of towns and of sections of the population showing fairly close resemblances, we can complete our picture of that dispersion. We find Boii in Bohemia, in the basin of Arcachon, in Italy, and in Galatia ; Tectosages at Toulouse and in Galatia ; Brigantes in Britain and at Bregenz ; Parisii and Atrebates in England. From the Aulerci there broke off the Brannovices [2] between the Loire and Rhone, the Cenomani in Italy, other Cenomani [3] among the Volcæ Arecomici, and Andes in Italy. The Senones, who moved about much, founded little settlements here and there in Gaul—Cenon near Bordeaux, Senon in Vienne, Sénonnes in Mayenne. They passed some time in Belgica. In the Pas-de-Calais,

[1] D'Arbois, **CCXCIX**, p. 24.
[2] Jullian, op. cit., i, p. 313.
[3] D'Arbois, op. cit., pp. 153 ff. ; Jullian, in **CXXXIV**, 1913, p. 50.

Sainz-lez-Hautecloque was once Senonis, and Senon in the Meuse has the same origin.

The Caturiges,[1] who must originally have been one single people, were scattered in the valleys of the Ornain and Nòro and in Italy, in the form of tribes of peoples which had formed more compact groups.

The Medulli [2] of Médoc and Basse-Maurienne may be of the same extraction, and so may the Centrones of the Nervian country. The Carnutes had sent off a colony to Brittany [3]; the Helvetii had colonies on the west bank of the Rhine, where we find three places called Helvetum in Alsace. It is also quite possible that the Helvii of Ardèche were an off-shoot of them.

In Noricum there dwelt a tribe of Alauni [4] who had goddesses called Alounæ. On the west coast of Brittany are a town named Alauna and a river Alaunus, and in south-eastern Gaul there is an Alaunium. These names doubtless survive in the modern Alleaume and Allonnes.

This wide distribution makes it reasonable to associate, as one is tempted to do, names having only slight differences, such as those of the Picts and Pictones. We may suppose that the names and the peoples are the same.

In Calvados we find the Esuvii. Like their neighbours, the Atesuii of the Orne, they worshipped the god Esus and were descended from him. They were portions of the same people, and their proximity corroborates the likeness of name. A whole series of names of peoples and places contains the word *eburos*, the yew, the most sacred of all trees, and all must be connected. There were Eburones between the Main and Rhine, Eburovices at Évreux, an Eburobriga in Yonne (Aurolles), an Eburomagus in Aude (Bram), an Eburodunum in Switzerland (Yverdon), and another in the Hautes-Alpes (Embrun). The Eburovices were Aulerci or Belgæ associated with them, or else Brythons who had remained in the midst of the Belgæ.

Inscriptions from the neighbourhood of Mainz, two of them from the marches of the Belgæ and Brythons, mention

[1] Jullian, ibid.
[2] Strabo, iv, 6, 8; i, 11; i, 7; Pliny, iii, 137; Ptol., ii, 10, 7; Vitruv., viii, 3, 20.
[3] Ptol., ii, 13, 2.
[4] D'Arbois, CCC, p. 49.

the Dii Casses. There are a few peoples whose names contain this element—the Tricasses at Troyes, the Veliocasses in Vexin, the Viducasses on the Orne and in Calvados, and the Baiocasses somewhat lower down.

All these facts call for two remarks. The first is that the names are spread in the direction of the advance of the Celtic tribes, and fanwise. They show that the settlements to which they correspond were the result of more than one expedition, carried out in different directions. The second observation is that in the midst of the territories occupied by the great Celtic peoples there were dozens and perhaps hundreds of little colonies of various origin dotted about. The great swarms founded settlements of their own, while the small ones attached themselves as sub-groups to their larger neighbours. So the unity of the latter comprised heterogeneous elements, of which history had preserved the memory. The various regions of the Celtic world were peopled by groups arriving at different dates and mixing. Their amalgamation contributed to the formation of the great peoples.

II

THE CONSTITUTION OF ROMAN GAUL [1]

The map of Gaul in the Roman period almost exactly represents the political condition of the country at the time of the conquest. That condition was largely a result of the manner in which the population had come into the country.

The political units of Gaul were not destroyed ; only two peoples, the Aduatuci and Eburones, were not Celts. These two, or what remained of them, were placed together under the name and in the administrative district of the Tungri, probably forming a sub-group. This exception confirms the rule. The political divisions of Roman Gaul were those of independent Gaul. So, too, the relationships of the various units with one another were almost always maintained. South of the Garonne, where the population was distributed rather differently from elsewhere, some autonomous groups were founded and the number of *civitates* reduced to five,

[1] Bloch, in **CCCCLXVII,** 1, 2, pp. 126 ff.

to be raised later to nine. In the Rhine Valley, the settlements of the Triboci, Nemetes, Vangiones, and Batavians
were made into *civitates*. In the rest of Gaul, a certain number
of *clientelæ* were abolished ; the Morini were detached from
the Atrebates, the Silvanectes and Meldi from the Suessiones,
the Abrincatui from the Unelli, the Viducasses from the
Lexovii, the Tricasses from the Lingones, the Segusiavi
from the Ædui, and the Vellavi and Gabali from the Arverni.
This dismembering process was developed throughout the
Imperial period.

Conquered Gaul was at first an extension of the Roman
Province,[1] but in 49 B.C. it was separated from it. Under
Augustus, Gallia Comata became the Tres Galliae, and this
distinction, which was maintained after various experiments
and with occasional subdivision as long as the Empire
lasted, certainly existed before the Roman Government
made use of it. This is plain from Cæsar's words,[2] *Gallia
est omnis divisa in partes tres*, save that Cæsar's Aquitania
was bounded by the Garonne, whereas that of Augustus
reached to the Loire, but the eleven peoples of the greater
Aquitania, living between the Garonne and Loire, the
Pictones, Santones, Bituriges Cubi, Lemovices, Cadurci,
Petrucorii, Nitiobriges, Arverni, Vellavi, Gabali, and Ruteni,
formed in certain respects a group distinct from the Province
as a whole.[3] Evidence of this is provided by the method of
recruiting troops, for under the Empire these peoples had
a special *dilectator*.[4] The five or nine peoples north of the
Garonne formed another unit, and their territories in the
third century were a separate district from the Gallic
provinces.[5] In these two cases, as in that of the Belgæ,
we have pre-existing relationships between the natives taken
into consideration by the Roman Government and finally
compelling its attention when they had been neglected.
They were like those which made Belgica and Aquitania
south of the Garonne separate regions from the rest of Gaul ;
they were associations which were political in some cases
and racial at bottom, and therein different from true political

[1] Jullian, **CCCXLVII**, iv, pp. 28 ff.
[2] i, 1.
[3] **I**, xiii, 1808.
[4] **I**, xiii, 412. Inscription from Hasparren.
[5] Hirschfeld, "Aquitania in röm. Zeit," in **CXLVIII**, 1896, p. 452.

associations created simply by the alliance of two nations or the subordination of one to another. The same considerations may explain why certain neighbouring *civitates* are placed together in small groups, for example for the collection of taxes, and also the subdivisions of the provinces introduced under Diocletian.

In short, the political map of Roman Gaul shows the structure of the Gallic colonization, and inversely the history of that colonization should explain it.

Some historians [1] have gone further, and have held that the whole political life of the peoples of Gaul was governed by racial traditions. According to their view, at the time when Cæsar commenced operations there were two groups of allies, two factions, namely that of the Ædui and that of the Arverni and Sequani, and while the former represented the true Gauls, the latter represented the " Celticans ", that is to say, men who were originally Goidels. This is a mistake. It would be equally erroneous to suppose that the Gallic peoples were disposed on the map in the order of their coming. The Belgæ, who were the last to take part in the great Gallic expansion, had main settlements, in relation to the old Celtic domain in Germany, behind the Brythonic Gauls. The Gallic peoples of Italy settled, each in front of that which preceded it, and that is what happened in many other cases. The Celtic peoples, advancing one after another, did not necessarily push their predecessors in front of them ; more often they passed over their heads.

III

THE POSITIONS OF THE GALLIC PEOPLES

In our inquiry, all these dates are interdependent, for the position of one people affects that of a certain number of others, and all depend on the time when the Belgæ settled in the north of Gaul. We may, therefore, suppose two chronological systems, according as we say that they arrived about 300, coming from the east bank of the Rhine and driving the Gauls before them, or that they settled in Belgica, in their own country, about 500.

[1] Rhys, CCXXX, p. 58.

The latter supposition seems to be confirmed by the facts. In the Marne, Aisne, and Seine-Inférieure [1] we find areas of population belonging to the beginning of the La Tène period and corresponding to the settlements of the Remi, Suessiones, and Caleti and their sub groups, Catuvellauni, Meldi, Veliocasses of Vexin. It is the same in Lorraine and the valley of the Rhine,[2] where districts inhabited since the Hallstatt period can be attributed to the Treviri and the Mediomatrici.[3] One naturally asks, too, where all the mass of Gallic peoples which from the third century onwards poured into the Danube valley and the East, into Italy and France, could have found room in Germany between the Lippe, Rhine, Main, and Upper Weser.

It appears to me that the Belgæ were from the very beginning astride of the Rhine, and occupied from Neolithic times the whole schistous Rhenish *massif*. On the French side, they had a wide frontier zone extending over the Ardennes, the plains of Belgium, and the northern rim of the Paris basin.[4] It was because they had plenty of elbow-room here that they were the last to expend their energies on distant expeditions.

The Treviri [5] and Leuci [6] had been in the same place since the Bronze Age. The Remi and Suessiones, breaking off from the main Belgic body, formed independent settlements in Marne and Aisne at the beginning of the La Tène period, absorbing or driving away the scanty Hallstatt population of the country. At the same time the Caleti probably took shape as a people, having received contingents from Hessen.[7] The Bellovaci must have come later, for their district is a blank on the archæological map of this period. The Morini, Ambiani, and Atrebates form a compact group which may have been undivided. Under the Empire, they compose a small province for fiscal purposes.[8] They, too, arrived comparatively late. The Eburones, Nervii, and other peoples

[1] Jullian, op. cit., ii, p. 471.
[2] Schumacher, CCCCIX, pp. 126 ff. ; Jullian, op. cit., p. 477.
[3] Schumacher, op. cit., pp. 130 ff. ; Fuchs, in CXVIII, 1915, p. 227.
[4] Jullian, op. cit., ii, pp. 472 ff., 479 ff.
[5] Ibid., p. 477.
[6] Ibid., p. 476.
[7] Peoples whose names contain the element *casse*—Velicasses. Vendryès, in CXL, 1923, p. 172.
[8] *Procurator ad census accipiendos trium civitatum Ambianorum, Murinorum, Atrevatum.* Inscription from Ostia. Héron de Villefosse, in XCIV, lxxiii, p. 249.

of the Meuse and northern Ardennes existed as peoples and were settled before the invasion of the Cimbri.

If Strabo [1] is correct in saying that the Armorici were Belgæ, the dispersion of the latter must have been still earlier. Pytheas,[2] who knew the Osismii, called them Ὠστίωνες. It is tempting to compare this form with the name *Œstrymnis*, which Avienus [3] in the sixth century uses of the western promontories of Europe and the islands lying off them.

Three points may be urged in support of this opinion, though they have no great force. The first is the relations which we find during the Brittany campaign subsisting between the Armorici, Menapii, and Morini.[4] They have the same relations with the inhabitants of the valleys of the Orne and Touques, who are certainly not described as Belgæ. The second is the discovery of objects in a Belgic district, the valleys of the Rhine and Moselle—columns with giants and horsemen, and drums and bases of columns bearing representations of gods, the seasons, etc.[5]—and of similar objects in Brittany.[6] The third point is a passage in Ausonius, in which the Belgian Viridomar, defeated and slain by Marcellus, has the epithet *Armoricus*.[7]

The Armorici form a compact group, quite distinct from the other peoples of Celtic Gaul. The Hallstatt culture in Brittany presents rather a peculiar appearance.[8] One thing is certain : Brittany contributed from the end of the Hallstatt period to the peopling of Britain.[9] If the Belgæ held the coasts of the Channel in the second Iron Age, the Brythons can have entered the island only from the coast west of the mouth of the Seine.

From the occupation of Belgica by the Belgæ at the beginning of La Tène, one must conclude that the Brythonic Gauls were established, then and much earlier, in the districts

[1] iv, 1, 4. Cf. Jullian, op. cit., ii, p. 488, n. 1.
[2] Holder, **CCVII**, s.v. " Osismi ".
[3] v, 90-3.
[4] Cæs., iii, 9, 10. Cf. Jullian, op. cit., pp. 113, 227, n. 9.
[5] Espérandieu, **CCCXXV**, vi–viii *passim*.
[6] Monuments at St. Maho, Kerlot, Guelen. Espérandieu, op. cit., 3036, 3038–9.
[7] *Technopaegnion*, 10, 83.
[8] Déchelette, ii, 2, pp. 681–2 ; Bénard le Pontois, **CCCCLXIII**, pp. 148 ff.
[9] Jullian, op. cit., ii, p. 386, n. 2 ; Allen, **CCXCVIII**, pp. 148 ff.

which they still held in Cæsar's time. In the region north of the Seine, which was a kind of " Debatable Land " of the Belgæ, the Hallstatt population, which was probably sparse, received but little of the industries and fashions of the districts south of that river. The new culture of La Tène was brought in here, not by great movements of tribes, but rather by small groups which went about in this vague belt between the Belgæ and the Celts, passing through peoples already settled, which sometimes counted as Belgæ and some-times as Gauls or Britons.[1] There were conflicts, and above all, conflicts of influence. At the time when this history ends, the influence of the Belgæ is on the decline.

There were, however, peoples which were driven back from the frontier zone or forced to emigrate. In the first La Tène period one big people, the Sequani, changed its abode in the north of Gaul, and another, the Helvetii, started off on wanderings which were not to end for a long time.

In Franche-Comté, which had been thickly populated at the end of Hallstatt, we have already followed the imperceptible change from the civilization of the first Iron Age to that of the second.[2] For some time there was no change in settlements or funeral rites. The La Tène graves were dug in the tumuli. One notes, however, that the latest are really charnel-houses, and that means a radical change of race. Moreover, all these tombs are earlier than 375, and later cemeteries are almost unknown. What had happened was that the population had moved. The old settlements on the plateau were abandoned, given back to the forest, and the people descended into the valley-bottoms and the plains of northern Bresse, which they cultivated. These newcomers hailed from the country on the banks of the Seine between the domains of the Lingones and Senones, and they were Sequani. This was doubtless not the first time that such a thing had happened in Franche-Comté since there had been Celts there. The invaders of the end of the Hallstatt period formed two groups, which were distinguished by their fashions and also by their way of building tumuli[3] ; both advanced

---

[1] Cæsar (ii, 4, 9 ; v, 5, 2 ; viii, 7, 4) assigns the Veliocasses, Caleti, and Meldi to Belgica. Afterwards they are in Lugdunensis. Cf. the Parisii, above, p. 124.

[2] See above, p. 8.

[3] The groups at Moidons and that at Alaise. See *Rise*, pp. 253 ff.

beyond the line of the Saône.[1]   The valleys of the Doubs and the longitudinal corridors of the Jura were the way into central and southern Gaul for wandering tribes from beyond the Gap of Belfort.[2]

We see a similar change in Switzerland, but the problem is different.   A sparse, comparatively nomadic Hallstatt population is succeeded by a fairly dense, concentrated, settled population.[3]   Opinions differ about the origin of the newcomers, and many will not call them Helvetii before the third La Tène period.[4]   But this is a mistake.[5]   Strabo,[6] in other words Poseidonios, mentions three tribes among the Helvetii, and Cæsar[7] four, excluding the Raurici and other peoples already named.   Now, whenever the Helvetii of the east bank of the Rhine are mentioned, we only hear of the Tigurini and Tugeni.   So before the invasion of the Cimbri there was at least one Helvetian tribe, that which Cæsar[8] calls the *pagus Verbigenus*, and perhaps there was another.   The Tigurini must have had one foot on the left bank of the Rhine north of Zurich, and that explains their return to Switzerland after their adventures in company with the Cimbri.[9]   The Raurici must have been in their place near Basle by La Tène II.[10]   We must accept this as fairly certain if we regard the station of La Tène itself as a toll-post.[11]   A line of similar posts, or at any rate military posts, at Port-sur-la-Thiele near the lake of Bienne, at Tiefenau on the Aar, and at Wipfingen on the Limmatt marks a frontier, in all probability that of the Raurici.[12]   It is hard to believe that that people, which barred the important crossing of the Rhine and the way along the Aar, was settled there before the Helvetii.

Nor do the finds of the second Iron Age give any grounds

[1] The Ædui and Sequani fought each other for the line of the Saône. Strabo, iv, 3, 2.
[2] Jullian, op. cit., i, p. 315, n. 5.
[3] Viollier, CCCCXCI.
[4] Déchelette, ii, 3, p. 941 ; Jullian (ii, pp. 520 ff.) is disinclined to place them in Switzerland before the expedition of the Cimbri.
[5] Schumacher, in CXVIII, 1914, pp. 230 ff.
[6] iv, 2, 3 ; vii, 2, 2.
[7] i, 12, 4, 6 ; 27, 4.
[8] i, 27, 4.
[9] See above, p. 106.
[10] Viollier, op. cit., p. 92.
[11] See *Rise*, pp. 85-6.
[12] Viollier, loc. cit.

for making a distinction between the populations of the two Helvetic areas. At the very most, we see in the northern part some influence of their northerly neighbours.

It should be remembered that the Helvetii did not occupy the whole of Switzerland, but only the plateau north of the Bernese Oberland. In the upper valley of the Rhine there were other Celtic peoples, the Nantuates round Saint-Maurice, the Veragri round Martigny, the Seduni round Sion, the Uberi in Haut-Valais.[1] Throughout the Iron Age, the civilization of this valley was quite different from that of the plateau. We have, therefore, very distinct peoples, but we cannot say that any of them were the Gaesati. There is nothing specifically Belgic about the crafts of the Alpine valleys. They developed among peoples in which the native element was doubtless still considerable and the Celtic admixture was reduced to small isolated groups, whose civilizing influence, however, continually increased.

Can we conclude from these movements that there were similar migrations on the part of the Ædui, Senones, Carnutes, and Aulerci?[2] The fact that the Sequani and Helvetii seem to have formed a separate body among the other Celtic peoples is against this view. None of the reasons given[3] is sufficient to make one regard them as Belgæ, among whom Cæsar did not include them. The settlement of the Sequani and Helvetii coincided with very large movements of population on the fringes of the Celtic world. It happened at the time of the great invasion of Italy. But their predecessors did not appear among those who took part in that expedition.[4] The invaders of Italy buried their dead in cemeteries similar to those of the Marne, whereas the inhabitants of the Sequanian and Helvetian regions at the beginning of La Tène buried them in tumuli. It is on the other side of the Rhine, perhaps among the Allobroges, that we should look for their remnants, if they can still be identified.

There does not seem to have been any great movement among the peoples which had occupied Aquitania north of

---

[1] Jullian, op. cit., ii, p. 463, n. 5.
[2] Ibid., p. 463.
[3] Pliny (iv, 106) includes them among the Belgæ. They were detached from Lugdunensis to enter the organization of the German border, where, in the fourth century, they formed a special province, the Maxima Sequanorum. See above for the explanation of their partiality for the Germans.
[4] Jullian, op. cit., i, p. 315.

the Garonne.   For one thing, this group comprised the
Pictones, whose very name and position on the coast are
sufficient evidence that their settlement was very old, being
contemporaneous with the Pictish migrations.[1]   Secondly,
archæological exploration has brought to light certain nuclei
of Hallstatt population which did not disappear.   The groups
of tumuli in Indre and Cher correspond to the main mass of
the Bituriges Cubi,[2] a third belongs to the Cadurci, and in
Cantal a fourth is evidence of the settlement of the Arverni.
Tumuli have also been found among the Gabali and in the
north of the country of the Ruteni (Lozère and Aveyron).[3]
These are good evidence of population, which, unfortunately,
is lacking for the greater part of the country of the Arverni
and for that of the Lemovices [4] and Santones.[5]   Nor do we
know more about the cemeteries of the people who occupied
these districts in the La Tène period.   It was, then, in the two
first Hallstatt periods that this part of Aquitania must have
received the bulk of its population.

Some of the elements which had taken part in the descent
of the northern peoples on the Pyrenean region and Spain
at the end of the first Iron Age [6] likewise contributed to the
making of the population of Aquitania.   A very large group
on the plateaus south of Albi and another about Agen correspond to the Ruteni and Nitiobriges.   Later on, some Senones
and Lingones took up their abode on the Garonne, not to
mention the Bituriges Vivisci.   So the occupation of the
country was finally made complete by bodies which passed
through it at the end of the Hallstatt period and during La
Tène, entering the existing political formations or setting
up new ones.

Between the Loire and Seine the country was held by the
Ædui and their kinsfolk, Ambarri of Lugdunensis and Sequani
of Forez, Lingones, Senones, Aulerci, and the peoples of
Normandy ; to these we must add the Carnutes and Turoni,
whose position astride of the Loire well shows that the constitution given by the Roman Government was not made

[1] See *Rise*, pp. 202 ff.
[2] The groups at St.-Aoustrille and Prunay.   Déchelette, ii, 2, p. 679.
[3] Ibid., p. 671.
[4] Jullian, op. cit., ii, p. 495.
[5] Ibid., p. 490.
[6] See *Rise*, chap. v.

by geographers, with their eye on natural frontiers, but was inspired by the wish to conform to a pre-existing grouping of the peoples.[1]

Some of these were among the oldest in the Celtic world. But it is very difficult to establish their original position, for too often archæology tells us nothing about them. Even here, however, we find some centres of Hallstatt habitation. The bronze swords discovered in the bed of the Seine bear witness to the passage of armed men [2]—the Parisii? In the Côte-d'Or the great iron sword remained in use far longer [3] than in Franche-Comté and, what is more, when the sword with antennæ was adopted its length was immediately increased. We have, therefore, a very different population, and one which remained in its place in the La Tène period, using the same tumuli. These may then be regarded as the tombs of a portion of the Ædui. Unfortunately neither Nièvre nor Saône-et-Loire furnishes any equivalent.

In the north, in Yonne, Aube, and Haute-Marne, there appears at the end of the second Iron Age a fashion which barely touched the Æduan country. The women wore hollow, gadrooned, turban-shaped anklets or thigh-rings of thin bronze. It was not a local fashion. Such objects have been found in Germany, in Vendée (introduced by traders or roving bands among the Caturiges, who, however, passed by the Meuse and Haute-Marne), in the environs of Paris, and on the borders of the country of the Senones.[4] The great number of these finds perhaps indicates that there were already groups, distinct from the Ædui, on the territory of the Lingones and Sequani.

Apart from the Boii, it was in this group of peoples that the bands were levied which invaded Italy—Insubres (that is, Ædui), Cenomani and Andes, Lingones and Senones. With the Bituriges and Arverni, they formed the kingdom of Ambicatus, King of Bourges.

The route which Livy [5] describes the Insubres as taking on their march into Italy, though it may have been the shortest way for a people massed between Dijon and Nevers,

[1] Déchelette, ii, 2, pp. 680, 725, 728.
[2] Ibid., list of swords, app. iv, Villeneuve-St.-Georges and Paris.
[3] Piroutet, in XV, xxix, p. 425.
[4] Déchelette, ii, 2, p. 835.
[5] v, 35. See above, pp. 14 ff.

does not correspond to the position of the Gallic settlements
at the exit from the mountains. Their position indicates
that their founders had entered the plain of Lombardy
by the eastern shore of Lake Maggiore.

We must not credit the Gauls of the fourth century with
too great powers of organization. It would be more reasonable
to explain such a concentration of forces from Anjou to
Bohemia by a deep-seated intimacy between the Boii and
their allies the Lingones, Senones, and Ædui, which had
survived all separations. Grouped at the foot of the Gap
of Belfort, these last could easily have reached the valley
of the Reuss. We can also, if necessary, suppose that the
Insubres, who organized the expedition and were the first
to march, had remained detached from the body of the Ædui
in Germany, like the Cenomani and Andes. The main body
of the Aulerci in its move to the west left a few fragments
in Germany, which joined in the expeditions of the Volcæ
and Boii.

In brief, between the Loire and the Saône the Celtic
peoples were less ancient than between the Loire and the
Garonne. They date at earliest from the second Hallstatt
period. They were reinforced during the third period, and
at the beginning of the second Iron Age, just when the
Suessiones and Remi were settling in Aisne and Marne, they
received a large new admixture, in which there may have
been some Belgæ.[1]

When the colonies composed of these various peoples
were established east of the Ticino, other Gauls descended
into Italy over the French Alps, working up the tributaries
of the Rhine to their sources. On the other side of the Alps
the corresponding valleys were presently occupied by tribes
with Gallic names, which, although they mixed with the
Ligurians of Piedmont, kept some trace of their old selves.

At the beginning of the Hallstatt period Gauls had begun
to travel down the Rhone. Between Valence and Avignon,
on both banks, tumuli have yielded large bronze swords [2]
or somewhat later Hallstatt objects, which are dated by
Greek objects.[3] These tombs represent a fairly large Celtic

---

[1] A place near Orleans is called Belia in the *Antonine Itinerary*.
[2] Déchelette, ii, 2, pp. 660 ff.
[3] Ibid., p. 661, fig. 252, a proto-Corinthian vase from the tumulus of
Trois-Quartiers, at Le Perthuis, Vaucluse.

population in the country of the Vocontii and Cavares, who perhaps already existed as peoples.[1] The area over which these weapons are discovered is a continuation of Franche-Comté and Dombes, and so enables us to connect the Celtic settlements of the Rhone with the old Hallstatt groups between the Saône and the Jura.

The furniture of the tumuli of the Alpine valleys [2] in Late Hallstatt contains, side by side with objects peculiar to the region, types copied from Franche-Comté and beyond. The Celtic infiltration, which was complete in the fourth century, made itself felt among the Ligurians even at this early date. It is the same with the contemporary tumuli of Chablis and Faucigny, which are probably Gallic.

The retreat of the Iberians in Languedoc in the fifth century shows that a new military power was predominant there. It can only have been the Volcae. A hundred years later everything was Gallic or Celticized, except on the coast east of Marseilles.

Of these Gauls, some came from very far or fairly far, like the Volcae, their allies the Cenomani, the Caturiges, the Medulli, and the Centrones. Others had come down from the Cevennes, such as the Sigovellauni of Valentinois, who were a sub-group of the Cavares, or else from the west bank of the Rhone, such as the Allobroges. But the Allobroges, Vocontii, Tricastini, Tritolli, Tricorii, and Cavares are groups of peoples whose names give no indication as to their origin. We may suspect that there were Belgic contingents among them, for the Cavares seem to have taken part in the expeditions of the third century.

The peoples of the Alps were a body apart. Under the Empire they formed three small provinces, the Maritime, Cottian, and Pennine Alps, the last comprising Tarentaise and Valais. The Cottian Alps corresponded in part to the kingdom of Cottiris, the last ruler of the country, Susa being the capital. The peoples of the mountains seem never to have shared the fortunes of those of the plains and the wider valleys, but remained independent between Cisalpine Gaul and the Province. Celtic civilization reached them, changing somewhat as it did so, and it is possible that the Gallic tribes

---

[1] Jullian, **CCCXLVII**, ii, pp. 517, 514.
[2] Déchelette, ii, 2, p. 658.

which entered the higher valleys were absorbed by them.
The racial mixture here cannot have been quite like that of
Dauphiné or Provence. Political relations, types of culture,
and racial character lie at the bottom of this distinction of
the Alpine provinces.

IV

THE GENERAL ASPECT OF CELTIC GAUL

The political face of Gaul, which was still undergoing
variations in Cæsar's time, had been almost fixed since 400 ;
it had taken ten centuries to make it. Of the first Celtic
settlements of the Bronze Age, hardly anything survived.
The Picts were probably the sole representatives of those
heroic days. The Hallstatt period had left definite traces,
and some of the settlements created at that time still existed.
During the first period of La Tène Gaul received a considerable
number of new colonists, who established themselves in the
deserted or little-populated border zones, squeezed their
way into spaces between older settlements, and sometimes
even took the land of the earlier Gallic occupants. The
successive waves—whole peoples or sub-groups associated
with groups already settled—went all over Gaul in search
of a home, intermingling, but to different degrees. Later,
with a few exceptions, all the room was taken up.

It has been supposed that the Celts formed a kind of
military aristocracy, small in numbers compared with the
rest of the population. This view rests on a serious sociological
error about the nature of the Celtic family.

Down to the fifth century the Gallic occupation looks
like a fairly loose network. Gaul had been occupied by
Ligurians and invaded in the south by the Iberians, who
remained where they were in the extreme south-east and
south-west, mingled with the Celts to various extents. The
place-names which can be connected with these two peoples
with certainty are extremely few.[1] The great majority of
place-names which are not Latin or Germanic in origin are
Gaulish. The names of peoples are Gaulish, and they have
endured. That means that between the Garonne, the Durance,

[1] Longnon, CCXII ; Jullian, op. cit., i, p. 247.

and the Rhine not only the mass of the population was Celtic but the whole social structure was Celtic. The Celts were the creators of the immense majority of markets, meeting-places, villages, and towns. They took possession of the country, but they altered it. It is very possible that many Ligurians remained among them, but, with a few exceptions, they formed no distinct organized groups. As slaves, isolated farmers, *coloni*, they adopted Celtic customs and speech wholesale. Only in Provence and in the Alps could native tribes find a place within Celtic groups, like the Salyes of Marseilles. Certainly there were foreigners in the Celtic communities. The blood in these was not very pure, and the ancient writers have no illusions on the point. They noted the racial differences between the Gauls of the Continent and those of Britain.[1] But in Gaul itself only the blood was mixed; society was purely Gallic.

Attempts have been made to reckon the size of the Gallic population,[2] based chiefly on the figures of effectives given by Cæsar for the levy of 52.[3] Since this was not a levy *en masse*, some historians have placed the total number of the population too low. But we have other data. Thus, the Bellovaci were able to put 100,000 men into the line, so that the total population must have been at least 400,000 souls, that is, the present population of their country.

To get a correct idea of the population of Gaul, it is to modern statistics that we must turn, taking into account the number of units of all sizes and multiplying the average ones. According to Poseidonios,[4] the biggest nations of Gaul could raise 200,000 men and the smallest 50,000. That gives an average of 100,000 inhabitants to a people, or thirty million altogether. This figure is still too low, for it seems to allow for too large a proportion of combatants. If we start from the strength of the *pagi*, we must count about 500 of them, and we get the same population. It certainly seems that Gaul must have had, including slaves, at least as many inhabitants as France under Louis XIV. At a time when Greece and Italy were suffering from depopulation, we can well understand that it gave the ancients an impression of

---

[1] Strabo, iv, 5, 2. Cf. Lucan, *Phars.*, ii, 77.
[2] Jullian, op. cit., ii, pp. 4 ff.
[3] For the censuses taken by the Gauls, see above, p. 117, n. 1.
[4] In Diodoros, v, 25, 1.

inexhaustible fruitfulness and seemed like a brimming reservoir of men who poured out to terrorize the whole world.

Thus constituted, Gaul turned towards poles of attraction outside the country. For some little time Germany, in which new powers were arising, educated by Gaul, attracted chiefly the Belgæ, Sequani, and Helvetii, who were in immediate touch with it. For centuries Greece had exercised its civilizing influence on Gaul and the Gauls had looked to Greece by preference. As early as the fourth century they had been regarded as phil-Hellenes, but this reputation had occasionally been clouded. In the third century they were considered very wild, and perhaps they were better known. But the phil-Hellenism was real enough. While continuing to be themselves, the Gauls who settled in Greek lands borrowed much from their teachers, and the others were influenced by Hellenism in inverse ratio to their distance from its centre. Their coins, copied from Greek types, and their decorative art both show this, and there are still remnants of the Greek articles which were in demand among the Gauls—vessels of bronze and earthenware for holding oil and wine.

Greek influence was followed by that of Rome. Negotiations, intrigues, and wars all contributed to it, but it was particularly the prestige of a higher organization and culture that appealed to these peoples who were so eager for everything that was not Celtic. This trait of the racial character explains their sudden metamorphosis and the continuity of their rôle as civilizers in Europe.

The stranger from the Mediterranean always had a special charm for them.[1] The civilization of La Tène III, which was contemporaneous with the conquest, reveals the growing influence of the arts and industries of the south. Bronze statuettes appear, enamel-working is developed, the technique of pottery is changed, Celtic characteristics disappear from the decoration of vases and jewel-work. New ways of life come in. At Mont Beuvray square houses of the Roman type with a heating-system arise in the midst of the Gallic huts. City life begins and develops under the influence of Rome and Greece. The forts reoccupied or built during the Cimbric War gradually turn into towns. These, it should be noted, grow less frequent as one leaves the coasts of the

[1] Cæs., vi, 24, 5.

Mediterranean. They are dense in the valley of the Rhone. There were some among the Ædui and the Remi, but the Bellovaci had no longer anything but temporary refuges. These towns, such as Bibracte or Gergovia, perched on stony plateaus, with rough, narrow little lanes running up and down, cramped, badly built, full of mud and dung, were certainly not marvels of town-planning.[1] But the Gauls were proud of them, or of some of them, such as Avaricum, the finest city in Gaul,[2] the jewel of the Bituriges. We already find that municipal patriotism was one of the most deep-seated characteristics of Roman Gaul.

But as time went on, Gaul modelled itself on its patterns more and more diligently. The magnificence of Luernius and Bituitus is still mere barbaric splendour. Cæsar shows us nothing of that kind in the Druid Diviciacus, who lived a long time in Rome and talked philosophy with Cicero, or in Orgetorix the Helvetian, or in Ambiorix the Eburonian, the wildest and most picturesque of guerrilla leaders, or in Vercingetorix. These men are very different from those whom Diodoros and Poseidonios met about 100 B.C., uneducated, bragging, noisy, and quarrelsome.[3] The great nobles of whom Cæsar has left many very lively portraits display the fine, gracious manners which the Welsh chieftains may have had later. They were men of taste, too, fond of beautiful things, which they ordered from great distances and even kept in their baggage when at war.[4] That is how the leaders of the war of independence are portrayed by their conqueror.

[1] Cic., *De Prov. Cos.*, 12, 29. Cf. Jullian, op. cit., ii, pp. 240 ff.
[2] Cæs., vii, 15, 4.
[3] Jullian, op. cit., ii, pp. 420 ff.
[4] The silver bowl found in the trenches of Alesia bears a Gallic inscription, perhaps the name of the owner. S. Reinach, CCCLXXII, ii, p. 283.

PART TWO

THE END OF THE CELTIC WORLD

CHAPTER I

The Romans in Italy, Spain, and Gaul

I

THE COMPLETION OF THE ROMAN CONQUEST OF ITALY AND SPAIN

THE independence of the Celtic world was nearing its end. In addition to the Germanic danger, one yet more urgent appeared. The Roman Republic was preparing to complete its domination of the Gallic countries. In Italy [1] something still remained to be done. The four great Gallic peoples had been crushed, and what remained of them had been reduced to the status of *civitates fœderatœ*. But the condition of the Celtic or Ligurian peoples on the outskirts was very uncertain, and remained so for a long time.

In the first century the peasant culture of the Cisalpine country was still entirely Gallic and no change seems to have occurred there when the Cimbri came in. After the end of the Cimbric invasion the policy of founding colonies was at once resumed. In 100 one was erected at Eporedia (Ivrea), to keep watch on the country of the Salassi. As a result of the Social War, the towns of the Insubres and Cenomani obtained Latin rights by the Lex Pompeia of 80. This privilege, which was of certain advantage to the towns, which were incorporated in the Italian municipal system, but of doubtful benefit to people living in the country, completed the breaking-up of the old nations. A few years later Sulla made the Cisalpine region a province, Gallia Cisalpina, which was attached to Italy in 42 and broken up. Colonization was carried on after the Civil War by expropriations and the distribution of land to veterans. The Gallic peasant was the sufferer.

[1] Chapot, **CCCXI**, English pp. 122 ff.

In Spain [1] the fall of Numantia marks the end of the country's independence. The Celtiberians, though exhausted, had found the strength to oppose the Cimbri successfully. But soon afterwards revolts against Rome began again. In 90 the Arevaci rose, and from 81 to 73 Sertorius had all Spain behind him. But the people concerned were Celtiberians, not Celts. And these spurts of independence are no more than episodes in the political history of Rome.

II

THE CONQUEST OF GAUL [2]

The establishment of the Romans in Cisalpine Gaul and Spain after the first Punic War was bound to lead them to take heed to their communications with these provinces by the Provençal coast and Languedoc. In spite of its determination to limit its ambitions by the Alps and the Pyrenees, the Senate was compelled to intervene in Gaul. Its ancient ally Marseilles needed help. Besides, at the end of the second century Rome had discovered new ways of solving her social problems. The thing to do was to distribute lands, to found cities, to colonize.

In 154 and 125, the Salyes having attacked Marseilles, two expeditions were sent against them, the second commanded by the Consul M. Fulvius Flaccus, the friend of the Gracchi. The Romans established themselves in the country and the district was made into a province. The Proconsul C. Sextius Calvinus founded the city of Aquæ Sextiae on the Rhone, if not as a colony, at least as a garrison.

The chiefs of the Salyes took refuge among the Allobroges, who were allied with the king of the Arverni, Bituitus, son of Luernius. This was probably enough to make the Ædui seek an alliance with Rome.

Going on from the Salyes to the Allobroges, Cn. Domitius Ahenobarbus, one of the Consuls of 122, led a small army up the Rhone, treating all the way. At Vindalum, at the confluence of the Sorgue, he fell on the Allobroges. But Bituitus had raised 20,000 men. He crossed the Rhone by a bridge and pontoons and descended the river in pursuit

[1] Ibid., English, p. 154.
[2] Jullian, CCCXLVII, iii ; Chapot, op. cit., English pp. 12 ff., 293 ff.

of the Romans, who were joined by C. Fabius Maximus with new troops. Bituitus was defeated and Fabius carried the war into the country of the Allobroges. Domitius doubtless succeeded in excluding the influence of the Arverni from the country of the Cavares, Helvii, and Arecomici and part of Albigeois, which were reunited to the Province. The Volcae Tectosages of Toulouse were included, under the euphemistic name of " allies ". Toulouse had a Roman garrison when the Helvetii appeared in the neighbourhood.

Bituitus desired to treat in person in the name of the Arverni and Allobroges. Domitius sent him to the Senate, which interned him at Alba, where he was joined by his son, Congentiatus or Comm. The Tour Magne at Nîmes represents the trophy set up by Domitius after his victory. But its most lasting monument was the Province itself, transformed. The Domitii and Fabii were its patrons and the Allobroges were the guests and friends of Domitius. Great public works, such as the Via Domitia, were carried out.

Shortly afterwards the Cimbri arrived and central Gaul, after the destruction of the empire of the Arverni, was powerless to stop them. Small risings procured further easy triumphs, and then the story of the Province becomes part of that of the Roman Republic.

In 75 Pompey passed through the country on his way to fighting Sertorius in Spain. He was followed by M. Fonteius, who restored order among the Vocontii and Volcae. Literature has made Fonteius the type of the oppressive, unscrupulous governor. But did he act differently from Claudius in 64 and Murena in 63 ? However that may be, the Allobroges, who in this case seem to have had the most life left in them, brought an action against him before the Senate in 63. In Rome their envoys became mixed up in the conspiracy of Catiline, whom they betrayed in return for his failure to keep his golden promises. Then the Allobroges rose and fell on Vienne. C. Pomptinus put down the revolt so effectively that they did not move during Cæsar's campaigns.

The case of Fonteius is a very familiar story.[1] First of all there were expropriations. Colonies and garrisons were planted at Vienne and at Toulouse in the Gallic town. Then the things happened which always happen when two economic

[1] Cic., *Pro Font.*, i, 2.

systems and two political organizations come into contact, the stronger of which is based on money. The financier comes on the scene. The Gauls had money, but not enough for the Roman fiscal system to be anything but a burden. They borrowed, and got into debt. The worst of it was that the governors became involved. Money was to be made quickly in Gaul. But the Province was not really impoverished. It was one of those agricultural countries in which a good harvest at once restores the financial situation. Profitable crops, vine and olive, were being introduced just now. The Romans forbade them, so they must have been prosperous. Besides, Rome, which seems to have been so oppressive in some things, was easy in others. It allowed the Gauls to keep their political organization and their usages. This was the time when the envoys of the Allobroges in their trousers and smocks filled the Forum with their exuberance. For fifty years Gallia Narbonensis was distinguished from Gallia Braccata; it wore the toga and talked Latin. In 83 the Helvii were admitted to Roman citizenship. The Roman leaders found among these provincials agents, and also friends, such as the Helvetian C. Valerius Pocillus, to whom Cæsar pays an interesting tribute of friendship. Finally, Narbonensis furnished troops and remained loyal.

Outside the Province the Romans had friends among the Ædui and Nitiobriges. From all over Gaul exiled sons of good families came flocking to Rome. There were even treaties with some Gallic nations in which it was provided that the Republic should not receive exiles.[1]

Of what went on in the interior at that time we know nothing save a few names, such as those of Celtillus, father of Vercingetorix, who was put to death for aiming at tyranny, and of Diviciacus, King of the Suessiones, who invaded Britain at least once and seems to have ruled over a kind of Belgic confederation.

The adventure of Celtillus is in itself characteristic of the political crisis in which Cæsar found Gaul involved when he arrived in the country. The old Celtic kingships were breaking up, and doubtless the influence of the Roman Senate had something to do with it. At the same time other kingships were on the point of reviving in virtue of the same

[1] Id., *Pro Balbo*, 14.

rights, though inevitably different in essence. The political conflict was violent. Moreover, after the destruction of the kingdom of the Arverni, Gaul had entered on a period of political dissolution which was not yet ended. One group formed round the Arverni, another round the Ædui, re-forming later round the Sequani ; but everything was fluid and chaotic. The great peoples pursued a policy of prestige. Cæsar profited by the weaknesses resulting from that policy and, indeed, it was one of his favourite instruments, of which he made as much use as of military operations. If he succeeded, with 60,000 men, in carrying through the difficult task of conquering a large country, rich in men and owning a glorious past, it was because he had in Gaul allies, friends, spies, who were also traitors, like the Æduan Dumnorix. He always had sources of information among the enemy, an intelligence service which rarely failed him ; but he also had friends like the Pictones, the Lingones, and, above all, the Remi.

All these political weaknesses, all these defects, shine out from the pages of the *Commentaries*. But we see something else there as well. Gallic society had latent powers of co-ordination which came into play with great vigour, but too late, and with some success, but too brief. The assembling of the army of relief during the siege of Alesia, with all the deliberations, sending of messages, and movement of troops entailed, was a remarkably well-conducted operation, which pre-supposes a habit and rules.[1] Vercingetorix used these institutions in a masterly fashion, and Cæsar the historian has given him full credit. He has set him up at the beginning of the history of France and at the end of the history of the Gauls as a wonderful symbol of patriotism—young, good-looking, eloquent, modest, able to learn, expressing himself like an old soldier, interested, no doubt, in everything about the new civilization, but conscious of his own country and jealous of it to the point of sacrifice. Cæsar very nearly failed, and he does not disguise the fact. As the greater Celtic world had, in the time of Hannibal, missed its chance of becoming a kind of great, loose confederation in the world of its day, so the smaller Celtic world of Gaul missed, in Vercingetorix, the opportunity of becoming, side by side with

[1] Jullian, **CCCXLVII,** iii, pp. 415 ff.

the Roman Republic, the prototype of the modern great nation.

The conquest took eight years. After the first year,[1] which was taken up with containing the Helvetii and driving Ariovistus across the Rhine, there were four years of partial affairs—unconnected risings and attacks on the part of the Gauls and attempts to conquer territory and military promenades on that of the Romans. At the end of 54 the first concerted rising broke out, and from 53 to 51, the hardest years of the war, the Gauls waged a real national war with great successes in 52. The fall of Alesia brought this series of operations to a close, but it was not the end. The campaign of 51 consisted of scattered but constantly renewed attempts on the part of the Gauls, and at the end of the year the country was subjugated.

It is a commonplace of history to marvel at the rapidity of the conquest. But Gaul had at that time not acquired the rudiments of a state structure, without which a nation cannot be made. Neither their few common institutions nor their more or less connected attempts at collaboration could give the Gallic people a sense that they must regard themselves as one and that they owed duties of love and sacrifice towards the fatherland of which we now speak, but of which they assuredly knew nothing. Gaul had not had time to make the long, painful experiments in common which are necessary to develop the patriotism of a nation.

For Vercingetorix and his friends there probably was a Gaul, a Gallic fatherland. They also had a great love of political freedom, supported by faith in their country. It was the glory of Gaul to have produced such men. The rest were content to try to reconcile the interests of their small nation, their own small fatherland, with foreign rule. The great mass of the Gauls had not the faith which makes nations ; they had no faith in the language which they gave up, or in the religion which they disguised, or in the institutions which they hastened to Romanize. But they had faith in civilization, which meant that of Rome, and in the prestige of their conqueror. The Roman Empire did more to make Gaul a fatherland than the Republic and Cæsar did to destroy it.

[1] Ibid., iv, p. 21.

For about a hundred years, however, the submission of Gaul might seem uncertain, and minor incidents arose from time to time. It is true that the most serious of these was the work of a Roman army and was connected with the Imperial succession, but none the less the word of " freedom " was spoken.

Even before the death of Cæsar, in the year 46, the Bellovaci revolted ; in 44, the Allobroges ; in 33 and 30, the Aquitani and Morini. Little is known of these affairs— a few dates and a few allusions, no certain history at all. Between 25 and 7 B.C. a series of small campaigns achieved the reduction of the Alpine tribes.[1] Then incidents are fewer and further between, and when they occur they are more serious and of a different character.

The Roman administration, particularly in fiscal matters, did not continue to be so easy as in the early years. The survey operations, commenced in 27, while laying down the rights of ownership in detail, did injury to many. It happened in the new province just as it had happened in Narbonensis over the collection of taxes ; there were outbursts of rage, plots, and risings, even military risings. In A.D. 21, under Tiberius, there was a revolt. Among those involved in it were found two Roman citizens, both Julii, one a Treviran named Florus, and the other an Æduan named Sacrovir, and both officers of cohorts of the regular army.[2]

Graver incidents occurred at the end of Nero's reign in 68. At that time the governor of Lugdunensis was C. Julius Vindex, an Aquitanian of royal descent, recently made a citizen. He declared himself for Galba, the Legate of Spain, and against Nero. Was he acting as the Roman he had become or as the Gaul he still was ? In any case, he had the Gauls with him. He was defeated at Besançon by the troops of Germany, which remained loyal to Nero, and killed himself. During the military anarchy which followed Nero's death, there were Gauls in all the different parties. When Vitellius was holding his court at Lugdunum a rising of a new kind broke out in the Boian country. The leader was a peasant named Mariccus, who assumed the manner of a prophet and proclaimed himself the champion of the Gauls and a god.

[1] Ibid., pp. 69 ff.
[2] For all the following, see Jullian, op. cit., iv, pp. 153–200.

Is this a first specimen of those upheavals from the depths which recur in the history of France—Crusades of the Poor, *Jacqueries* ? In Gaul, as in the Cisalpine country, the poor had grievances enough ; they were slow to be Romanized, and it is possible, things being so, that the national spirit took shape in that social stratum. The movement failed deplorably.

It was only the second act. In Rome the Capitol was burned down. The news was exploited as an omen by the Druids, who formed a religious opposition and now proceeded to preach a Holy War. All that remained to be done was to get the malcontents together. There followed the revolt of Civilis, the Treviri Tutor and Classicus, and the Lugdunensian Sabinus. Civilis had at his side a prophetess named Velleda, who lived among the Bructeri. She must have been a German, but her name seems quite Celtic— curious evidence of the intercrossing of Celticism and Germanism. These four associates were all regular officers commanding cohorts, soldiers by profession. Classicus donned the purple and had himself proclaimed *Imperator Galliarum*. Sabinus declared himself a descendant of Cæsar.

But then something happened of far greater importance than the foundation of the Gallic Empire. The *civitas* of the Remi seems to have taken upon itself to convoke, as in old days, an assembly of the *civitates* of Gaul. It met as a completely autonomous body, apparently, and discussed the question of independence, which was urged by Tullius Valentinus, a Treviran, as against peace and submission, defended by Julius Auspex of the Remi. If Gaul now, through the mouths of its delegates, declared itself content with the condition to which Cæsar had brought it, it was because it did not yet exist. The assembly sent to the Treviri, in the name of the Gauls, orders to lay down arms and offers of intercession. The wisdom of Cerealis did the rest. Classicus and Tutor vanished. Sabinus hid with his wife Eponina in an underground place of refuge, but they were eventually taken and both put to death.

This time, the old independent Gaul was really finished. Something new was beginning.

III

THE ROMANIZATION OF GAUL [1]

At the time when the assembly organized by the Remi met, Gaul was already three-quarters Romanized. Dress, utensils, furniture, and jewellery were Roman in style. Latin was spoken. Henceforth the culture of the country was Latin.

No doubt, many Italians came to Gaul, settling chiefly in Narbonensis, on the Rhine, and at Lugdunum, and there must have been a few merchants from Greece and Syria. But all these would not be sufficient to account for the rapidity with which the country was assimilated, and we must suppose that Gaul was spontaneously eager to become Romanized. The sudden development of city life favoured the transformation. All through the first century there was an expenditure on building which may be compared to what went on in France from the twelfth century to the seventeenth. The Gallic peoples became *civitates*, and identified themselves with them. The cities took the names of the peoples whose capitals they were. And there was no model of city life and municipal organization available but the Roman model.

The general extension of the citizenship had the same effects as in Narbonensis on a larger scale. Under Claudius Gallic senators, already Roman citizens, were admitted to the Roman Senate. Later, the Edict of Caracalla made the assimilation complete by extending the citizenship to the lower classes of the population.

Now, at this time when the whole world contained nothing but Roman citizens, jurisprudence shows by repeated declarations that provincial customs based on ancient rights were respected.[2] Yet we have only three evidences of any kind of survival of a Gallic legal custom. This is very little, for the Gauls had a law of their own.

The national religion was never abolished or persecuted. Indeed, the Gallic gods continued to be worshipped under the ægis of the worship of the Emperor. But they gradually

[1] Ibid., iv–vi ; Chapot, op. cit., English pp. 314 ff.
[2] Ulpian, in the *Digest* ; Jullian, op. cit., iv, p. 278.

assumed a Roman disguise ; even the household gods, those of the hearth and the flame, took the names of Roman gods, and often their figures, except for some native effigies. Of all the vast mass of Gallic tradition of which Cæsar speaks, what remained ?   Nothing was done like the endeavour of the Irish to collect and catalogue their old poems.   Of Gallic history and theology we know nothing but what the Greeks and Latins happen to tell us—what survives of Trogus Pompeius and a few culinary and magical recipes picked up by Pliny and Marcellus of Bordeaux. That is all. It is true that the Empire persecuted the Druids. They were attacked (partly, doubtless, for political reasons) under the laws regarding human sacrifice, murder, and magic (Lex Cornelia de Sicariis) by Tiberius and Claudius. At that time, if we are to take a passage in Pomponius Mela literally,[1] they continued to teach the young in secret. They too must have come round, for there is no question of their giving trouble in the second century, and in the time of Ausonius we find their descendants among the teachers at the school of Bordeaux. In the only cases in which the Romans struck, they evidently struck rightly, for the Druids alone were in a position to try to stem the general rush of Gaul to Latinism.

To sum up, all the upper parts of Gallic civilization, those which make a people other than an amorphous mass of peasants, fell. All that remained was the lower parts and, in addition to a good many habits and some handicrafts of importance, the superstitions and magic of the people. Higher activities were monopolized by the civilization of the upper classes. This tradition was reinforced by teaching in the great schools which succeeded those of the Druids but were quite different, the first of which we have seen at work at Autun under Tiberius. The Gaulish language survived only in the dialect of the peasant, which steadily declined and did not make much resistance to the Roman domination.

The Gaul which was taking shape under the wing of Roman institutions was very different from the Gaul which had gone down with Vercingetorix. It no longer had the same popular soul. It went on changing very fast. It has a quite different appearance from what it had worn at the time of the assembly of the Remi, when it suddenly finds

[1] *Pomp. Mela*, iii, 2, 19,

itself, in the later third century, mistress of its destinies for sixteen years.

The episode is worth telling.

After the death of Alexander Severus the Roman Empire relapsed into the dynastic chaos which it had already experienced more than once. Between 253 and 255 bands of Alemanni and Franks broke through the frontier and perhaps penetrated, even at this early date, into Auvergne. These inroads of barbarians, even in small numbers, destroyed for a long time the peace in which Gaul throve. Measures of protection had to be taken. The towns drew themselves in and girt themselves with fortifications within a few years as in the days of the Cimbri. In 258 the Emperor Gallienus had sent his son Valerian to Germany, but the real command of the frontier lay with the Gaul Marcus Cassianus Latinius Postumus. The legions of the Rhine did what they had done before—wanted an emperor of their own and chose Postumus. Young Valerian was made prisoner at Cologne. Gallienus attempted two or three attacks, but in vain. Postumus systematically made Gaul his object. He does not seem to have had any aspiration to the Empire as a whole; he does not even seem to have tried to break away from the rest of the Roman world. Gaul was apparently quite unchanged; above all, there was no question of independence. Postumus set up a fortuitous combination similar to the division of the Empire which was afterwards effected under Diocletian. This combination proved good and salutary. Order and security were restored. There are innumerable coins of this period, and they are of better weight. That is a sign of good, honest government and economic healthiness.

But Postumus's legions grew tired of him and murdered him. His successors, Lælianus and Victorinus, disappeared in their turn. The Germans crossed the frontier. The wife of Victorinus, named Victoria, escaped the slaughter. She was probably a Gallo-Roman of good family. In the little that we know of these events, she makes rather a good impression. She was compared to her contemporary, Zenobia. She was popular with the troops. It is said that she might have been Empress, but she gave the throne to a relation, C. Pius Esuvius Tetricus, who kept it from 268 to 274. He had been governor of Aquitania; he was not a soldier, but must have

been a first-rate administrator. After a disgraceful affair
in the army of the Rhine, all was restored to order. Victoria
died, and Tetricus continued to reign in peace until Aurelian
was free to attend to the West. Tetricus did nothing to
defend himself. When his army was defeated, he entered
the Imperial army. His career gives a very clear idea of what
that Roman Empire of Gaul was like—an essentially
transitory regime, which was not destined to survive the
circumstances in which it had its birth.

It may be asked, however, whether something of it did
not survive—a memory—in the insurrections of the
Bagaudæ,[1] which began ten years later, in 283. Bagaudæ
is a Gallic name, the first part of which is similar to Irish
baga, meaning " battle ". They were peasants. Their
movements were local and disconnected ; they did not
form an army. They belonged to the lower strata of the population, those which had remained most Celtic and in which
even the language was still used, as we know from contemporaries. We can imagine what the countryside of Gaul
had become like in those successive years of invasion and
pillage. The tax-collector took turns with the barbarian.
We can understand why they revolted. In 283 they even
elected emperors, Ælianus and Amandus. They held out
until 285. It should be noted that, when defeated by
Maximian, Ælianus and Amandus became martyrs and
a kind of saints (in the *Life of St. Babolinus*). This throws
a faint gleam of light on the size and popular nature of the
movement, which, moreover, went on. Brigandage continued,
and the name of Bagaudæ remained attached to it.
Reinforced by all the discontented (and these were many),
they even came to form small states, like those which the
Germans were beginning to set up in Gaul.

But what emerges in clear and convincing fashion, not
from the chronicle of events as they occur but from the
institutions and opinions of the Gaul of the time, is that,
over the municipal life and the habits which it had created,
the Roman organization had given Gaul provincial formations
and habits of normal life based on large units. The three, or

---

[1] Bagaudæ is a Gallic name, with a termination like *auda* in Alauda,
following a first element which is similar to Irish *baga*. Cf. Jullian, in **CXXXIV**,
1920, pp. 107 ff.

the four, provinces were divisions of Gallia. There were fixed frontiers with custom-houses on them and an army to defend the most exposed of them. There was a system of roads. Above all, there were an order of rank, capitals, subordination, stability, and agreement. This was everything that the Gauls had lacked. The country took on what it could not have had in old days—the air of an individual. In the fourth century Gaul begins to present this aspect, with its new features, in literature, in Rutilius Numatianus, in Ausonius, in Avitus. Sidonius Apollinaris even speaks of *patria nostra*, and after that it is always so, down to the day when *France dulce* in the popular tongue takes the place of *Gallia* in Latin.[1] Perhaps those very misfortunes of the third century began to complete the political education of the people by the sufferings of their country. They gave it the venerable wrinkles which men have always loved to see on the face of their motherland.

IV

THE CELTS OF THE DANUBE

So much for Gaul proper. There was another Gaul, that of the Danube, which was connected with the province of Illyricum as Gaul proper with Narbonensis. Cæsar had got Illyricum in his province just as he had got Gaul, and had kept an eye on the country. He had, for example, been in Dalmatia for part of the winter of 57–56. Things might happen on this side as in Gaul. Troops might pass through on the way to Macedonia as they could through Gaul on the way to Spain. Roman policy had sources of intelligence in Noricum, and Roman influence was active there ; the consular coinages were imitated, a sign that Latin traders were travelling and doing business in the country.[2]

Augustus inherited the programme which Cæsar had not carried out completely. The death of Bœrebistas, the break-up of the sort of empire which he had set up, and a series of campaigns conducted by the best generals of Augustus,

[1] CCCLVII, *Poetæ Latini Ævi Karolini*, pp. 367–8, hymns *de martyribus Agennensibus*.
[2] Roman denarii and copies of consular coins. Forrer, DXLIII, pp. 120, 124, 127.

Agrippa, Drusus, and Tiberius, from 35 to 9 B.C. carried
the frontiers of the Empire to the Danube,[1] thus placing
a broad buffer-zone between Italy and Germany and securing
for the Empire a good line of communication. Just at this
time the Germans were arriving among the Gauls who were
still settled on the northern bank of the Danube. It was now,
in my opinion, that the Marcomanni moved into Bohemia
in the place of the Boii.[2] The information which we have
about the campaigns of Augustus's generals between the
Danube and the Elbe confirms this view. Drusus came
upon the Marcomanni on the upper Main and defeated them
in 10 B.C. In 8 B.C. L. Domitius Ahenobarbus[3] marched
out from the Danube in order to reach the Elbe, and
established in their country, at that time unoccupied, a body
of Hermunduri, come from no one knows where and perhaps
themselves dislodged by the migrating Marcomanni.

The Marcomanni must have moved in 9, and settled
after that date in Bohemia, under a famous leader, Marbod
(Maroboduus). The Boii who remained gradually depleted
themselves by migrations and vanished, the remnant being
perhaps absorbed by the Marcomanni, leaving only a name,
which is that of the country at this day. Thus the Celts
were completing the movement which brought them to
a position along the Danube, as on the Rhine, at the time
when the Danubian colonies were finally submitting to
Rome. In the north they left only lost elements. On both
sides the Roman Empire defended the frontier.

On both sides the generals of Augustus crossed it. We
find Marbod again, in A.D. 6, opposing Tiberius, who is
trying to attack Bohemia from the south. But Illyricum
was uncertain. When it was cleared of troops a revolt broke
out, and Tiberius judged it wise to make terms with Marbod.
Marbod suffered for this, and was driven out by the

---

[1] Jullian, **CCCXLVII**, iv, pp. 100 ff.

[2] The question of this date is important from an archæological standpoint,
for it makes it possible to date the finds of the Hradischt of Stradonitz and
the La Tène III civilization which is there represented as brilliantly as at
Mont Beuvray. It is very clear from Cæsar's words (i, 5) that the Boii of
Noricum who joined forces with the Helvetii and ended up in Gaul were
only a fraction of the people, the greater part of which had remained in
Bohemia and did not emigrate till about the year 8. Almgren, in **LXXXV**,
1913, p. 265 ff. ; d'Arbois, **CCXCIX**, ii, p. 11.

[3] Müllenhoff, **CCCLXII**, iv, p. 44.

Marcomanni. He took refuge with the Romans, who established him at Forum Julii.

Strabo,[1] who wrote shortly after, speaks of Pannonia as a ruined country. It had not yet repaired the damages of the conquest when Gaul had long obliterated them. It did recover later, and the Roman ruins of the Danube valley do not give an impression of poverty.

In any case, there was nothing in the way of social organization in this region comparable to what we have seen in Gaul. The reason may be that the native society of the Danube was so much Romanized that it could not become aware of its unity.

[1] vii, 3, 5, 11.

CHAPTER II

The Romans in Britain

I

BRITAIN BEFORE ITS ROMANIZATION

THE historians tell us that Comm, the chieftain of the Atrebates already mentioned, who was one of the most remarkable figures of the Gallic War, after serving Cæsar became a deadly enemy of Rome in consequence of a quarrel with an officer of the Roman army, who had betrayed him. In 51 he withdrew into Britain with some of his people, continuing the work of colonization done by the Belgæ in the south of the island. He struck coins with Latin characters. He had three sons, who reigned in Britain.[1]

Britain had not yet been conquered by Rome. Celtic civilization held its own there ; Celtic art prevailed [2] ; ornament developed with taste, particularly enamel-work, with its combinations of colours. This art, indeed, quickly travelled far from the classic models of Celtic art ; decorative fancy had free rein, while the workmanship continued to be admirable. The centre of this art, and of all the civilization of Britain, was in the south of England, in a region bounded on the north by a line drawn from the Bristol Channel to the Wash. Only here do we find Celtic coins.

There were a few towns in Britain, open towns or *oppida*, such as Londinium (London), the port of the Cantii, Camulodunum (Colchester), the stronghold of the Trinovantes, Eboracum (York), the capital of the Brigantes. Ptolemy mentions only about sixty, and many of these were doubtless only refuges or markets. Britain does not seem to have been so advanced as Gaul in the organization of city life.

There is never any mention of British shipping. Cæsar's

---

[1] MacNeill, **CCCCXLI**, p. 168 ; Jullian, **CCCXLVII**, ii, p. 470.
[2] Parkyn, **CCCCXLVI**, p. 101 ; Reginald A. Smith, " On Late Celtic Antiquities discovered at Welwyn," in **CXXII** ; S. Reinach, in **CXXXIX**, 1925, 172. Cf. Collingwood, **CCCCXX** ; Bushe Fox, *Excavation of the Late-Celtic Urn-field at Swarling, Kent,* **CXXVI**, 1925.

two expeditions would have been at the mercy of any such fleet. But the monopoly of the Veneti probably extended to Britain.[1]

II

THE ROMAN CONQUEST

Britain lived in peace until the time of Caligula, when the Romans made an expedition. The resistance was headed, as in Cæsar's time, by the King of the Trinovantes and by Cassivelaunus's successor Cunobelinus, Shakespeare's Cymbeline.[2] The Romans returned under Claudius in 43, for the first time with the fixed intention of remaining. Gradually they had learned to know Britain better. Aulus Plautius, the commander-in-chief of the expedition, was remarkably well informed. The pretext of the expedition was a refusal to deliver up deserters.[3] Cunobelinus's two sons, Togidumnus and Caratacus (Caractacus) led the opponents of the Romans. Camulodunum was taken, and the south of the island reduced to a province. In this campaign the future Vespasian conquered the Isle of Wight (Vectis).[4] The first successors of Plautius, in a series of campaigns of which Tacitus gives a mere summary, tried to extend the new province northwards in the direction of the Brigantes, and westwards in that of the Irish Sea and the Silures. Caratacus took refuge with the Queen of the Brigantes, who gave him up. He was taken to Rome, where he defended his conduct so eloquently that he was restored to liberty.

The Romans established a colony at Camulodunum and a system of small forts in the west facing Cornwall and the Silures, on the last spurs of the chalky uplands.

A serious set-back led to the appointment in 57 of a capable general, Suetonius Paulinus. He organized an expedition against the Druid sanctuary on Anglesey, which is described as a refuge of deserters. The Druids had been

---

[1] Lloyd, CCCCXXXVIII, 41.
[2] Ibid., 47.
[3] Windisch, *Das keltische Britannien bis zu Kaiser Arthur*, p. 14 ; Tac., *Agr.*, 14.
[4] Dion Cass., ix, 210 ; Suet., *Vesp.*, 4 ; Eutrop., vii, 19. Cf. Bruton, CCCCXVI, 208–210 ; Windisch, p. 15.

an element of opposition in Britain.[1]   Suetonius Paulinus
was recalled by a general rising; the Trinovantes had
retaken Camulodunum and massacred the colony, and
a legion had been wiped out.   The general, after evacuating
London and Verulamium (near St. Albans), gained a decisive
victory which saved the Roman settlements.[2]

After some years of uncertainty, Vespasian, who knew
the country, revived the attempt to conquer it.   The Brigantes
and the Silures were defeated in turn.[3]   Then the famous
Agricola arrived, who governed Britain from 78 to 86.   Thanks
to him and to his son-in-law Tacitus, the story of the conquest
of the island has become classic, almost as much so as that
of Gaul.   He had served under Suetonius Paulinus, and made
Anglesey his objective.   Then he advanced north, gaining
ground every year.   In his third year in the field he reached
the Firth of Tay, *æstuarium Tanaum*.   Subsequently, he
erected a first edition of the *vallum* of Antoninus between
the Clyde and the Firth of Forth.   In his sixth and seventh
campaigns he went beyond his *vallum* either with his
fleet or with his land-forces, but did not establish himself
permanently.[4]

After that, Hadrian and Antoninus built each a *vallum*.
Under Commodus the future Emperor Pertinax put down
a rebellion.   Later, Septimius Severus made an expedition
into Caledonia, of which we know nothing.[5]

Britain was conquered, except that mysterious Caledonia
and the central portion of Wales, occupied by the Ordovices
and Demetæ, who were to be reinforced by Irish colonies.

The Roman government carried on the same policy of
assimilation in Britain as in Gaul, but with some differences
and less success.   Tacitus gives the credit of this policy to
Agricola, who won over the people with the conveniences of
Roman civilization and city life.   He advanced money for
building, set up schools, and instituted fashions.   The
archæological finds show us a Britain living partly in buildings
of Roman type.   Towns sprang up (the remains of about
thirty are known), but less spontaneously than in Gaul,

[1] Tac., *Ann.*, xiv, 29–30 ; cf. Windisch, p. 17.
[2] Tac., *Ann.*, xiv, 32 ; Windisch, pp. 18–19.
[3] Windisch, pp. 19–20.
[4] Tac., CCCCXXVII.   Cf. Macdonald, CCCCXL, pp. 111–138.
[5] Windisch, pp. 42–3.   Cf. Paus., vii, 31.

since the legionary camps constituted towns in Britain. The
IInd Legion was quartered at Isca Silurum, or Cærleon,
" Camp of the Legion " ; the VIth at Eboracum, or York ;
the XIVth at Uriconium (Shrewsbury) ; the XXth at Deva
(Chester). In the seventh century the *Historia Brittonum*
of Nennius gives a list of twenty-six towns whose names
begin with *Caer*, derived from *castrum*. These are garrison
towns, in which the soldiers seem to have been more
intermingled with the population than in Gaul.[1]

In these towns Latin was spoken. It was the official
language, that in which the inscriptions are written. But
whereas in Gaul it outlasted the Roman rule, in Britain it
vanished with it ; much of it lingers in the Welsh vocabulary,
but it was British that survived. We may consider the
reasons for this.[2]

The chief reason was that in Britain Romanization was
far less general and less deep than in Gaul. It is true that
the remains of a large number of very luxurious Roman
villas have been found, which confirm what Tacitus tells us
of the Romanization of the British nobility. In fact it is to
this nobility that we must ascribe the permanent buildings
rather than to the Roman officials, whose stay was transitory,
or to the men planted in the colonies, who must have been
chiefly small folk. But the evidences of Roman culture are
very definitely confined to certain districts—the neighbourhood of the northern garrisons, the south coast (Kent, Sussex,
the Isle of Wight), and the agricultural areas of Gloucester-
shire and Lincolnshire, which seem to have been supply-
centres of the Roman army.[3]

About the towns, one point is to be noted—the absence
of municipal inscriptions of any importance. The fact is
that the country continued to be military and the
administration was purely military until the time of Diocletian.
The names of peoples disappeared ; the small nations were
not, as in Gaul, made the basis of the political and territorial

[1] Windisch, pp. 46-8 ; Sagot, CCCCLIV. Cf. Loth, in CXL, 1914, p. 109 ;
Drexel, " Denkmäler der Brittonen am Limes," in LXVII, 1922, p. 31 ;
Haverfield and Macdonald, CCCCXXXI ; Lethaby, CCCCXXXVIII ; Collinge,
CCCCXIX ; Fabricius, " Neuere Arbeiten über die britannischen Limites,"
in LXVIII, 1923, p. 79.
[2] Budinsky, CXCII.
[3] Collingwood, CCCCXX ; Taylor, CCCCLX ; Macdonald, " The Building
of the Antonine Wall," in LXXVIII, 1921 ; Miller, CCCCXLII.

organization of the country. At any rate each was not centred on a town, as in Gaul, and held together by its town. In Diocletian's time each province corresponds to a group of little nations; for example Flavia Cæsarensis consists of the Iceni, Trinovantes, Cantii, Regni, and Atrebates.

III

THE ARMY OF BRITAIN. ARTHUR

At the end of the second century, in the *Notitia Dignitatum*, we find in Britain four chief officials, two of whom are military. One commands the fleet, and is called Count of the Saxon Shore (*comes littoris Saxonici*). This proves that the Saxon invasions started nearly two hundred years before Hengist and Horsa. He had the IInd Legion under his orders. The other military official is called Duke of the Britains (*dux Britanniarum*), with the VIth Legion under him. It was his duty to resist the repeated attacks of the northerners, who were no longer held back by the ramparts of Hadrian and Antoninus—Caledonians, Picts or Scots, and also people from the west. The military forces of Britain were caught between these two groups of enemies, and faced now one, now the other, and sometimes both.[1]

These officials, stranded on the very edge of the Empire, beyond the Channel, and left to their own resources, gradually became independent in practice. They also tried to obtain complete independence, and there were revolts. Some sought the Imperial throne, and crossed the sea. The story becomes mixed with legend. The attitude of chroniclers like the pseudo-Nennius and Geoffrey of Monmouth after him is very interesting. The usurper and the rebel are to them the heroes of the story, and in their eyes they are not Romans, but Britons. In the curious work of Gildas entitled *De excidio et conquestu Britanniae* [2] we already find signs of

---

[1] Lloyd, **CCCCXXXVIII**, 59 ; Windisch, *Das keltische Britannien*, pp. 43 ff., 57. Cf. Ridgeway, " Nial of the Nine Hostages," in Phil. Soc. Cambridge, 1924, p. 14 ; R. G. Collingwood, " The Roman Evacuation of Britain," in **LXXIX**, xii, 1922, pp. 74–98.

[2] Published by Mommsen in **CCCLVIII**, xiii, *Chronica Minora*, iii, pp. 1 ff. See Faral, **CCCCXXVI**, i, p. 39. For the sources for the life of Gildas, see Lot, *Mélanges d'histoire bretonne : études et documents*, Paris, 1907. Gildas died in 569 or 570.

the same state of mind, and the *Historia Brittonum* of Nennius, in repeating a passage from Gildas, alters and further amplifies its character in this respect.[1]

In the time of Diocletian, in 286, the Count of the Saxon Shore, Carausius, revolted and assumed the purple, and was killed by one of his lieutenants.[2] A little later Constantius Chlorus took the field in Britain against the Picts and died at York in 306. The attacks of the Picts were repeated; they came down as far as London; and Ammianus Marcellinus, the great historian of this period, shows us Theodosius the Great fighting them from 364 to 366. Some years later Britain produced another pretender, Maximus, who must have been the Duke of the Britains. In 387 he left Britain with his army, which was scattered and annihilated by Theodosius. This Maximus is doubtless the hero of the legend which tells of an Emperor of Rome of that name who was attracted to Britain by a wonderful beauty whom he had seen in a dream; he there forgot his duties. Rome revolted, he reconquered it, and his British troops returned to their country no more. It is the subject of a Mabinogi, the *Dream of Macsen Wledig*.[3]

A line of Claudian suggests that Stilicho defended Britain against the Picts and Saxons. In any case, there were still troops in the country under Honorius,[4] and they there set up three emperors in succession—Marcus, Gratian, and Constantine III. This last, like Maximus, left the island and

---

[1] The question of the composition of the compilation known as the *Historia Britonnum*, ascribed to Nennius, and of the identity of its supposed author, has given rise to a series of important controversial works. The latest is that of M. Faral, op. cit., ii, pp. 56-224 ; in his third volume he has attempted a critical restoration of the text. Mommsen published the text, op. cit., xiii, *Chronica Minora*, iii, pp. iii, 59. Mgr. Duchesne had, in **CXL**, xvii, p. 15, made a preliminary classification of versions which is still a very remarkable piece of work. Zimmer has devoted an important work to Nennius, in which he says that he really existed and ascribes the whole of the original version of the history to him. According to M. Faral, this text is later than 687 and earlier than 801. In any case it contains traditions of older origin, which probably refer to the south of Britain.

For Geoffrey of Monmouth, who wrote about the second quarter of the twelfth century, see Faral, op. cit., ii, and the critical restoration of his *Historia Britanniæ* in the third volume of that work. At the same time as M. Faral's work, Messrs. Griscom and Jones brought out an edition of Geoffrey's text, with a translation and an essay on the author (London, 1929). Cf., too, the important work of Bruce, *The Evolution of Arthurian Romance*, Göttingen, 1923, two vols. Cf. below, p. 266.

[2] Eutr., ix, 22 ; Oros., vii, 25 ; Windisch, op. cit., p. 43.

[3] Windisch, op. cit., p. 44 ; cf. Loth, **CCLXX**, i, p. 219.

[4] Windisch, op. cit., p. 45.

fought Stilicho in Gaul. He had a detachment in Spain, commanded by his son Constans. During this time, the towns of Britain seem to have succeeded in running the affairs of Britain independently. The historian Zosimus quotes a curious circular letter written to them by Honorius, asking them to provide for their own defence.[1] But the loosening bonds were not yet broken, and it appears that in 446 the Britons came into Gaul to help Aëtius. Britain was still theoretically part of the Empire in 537, when Belisarius ceded it to the Goths who had been driven out of Aquitania by Clovis.

During the period of the first Saxon invasions, the office of Duke of the Britains does not seem to have lapsed. We know of two historical Dukes, and there are two others who are chiefly legendary. In Nennius these officials are called *reges*. In Welsh they bear the same title as Maxen Wledig.

The two historical Dukes are Guortigernus or Vortigern, who was certainly a Briton, and Aurelius Ambrosius, who came of a Roman or very much Romanized family and whose father is said to have been a Consul. He is the hero of the story for Gildas and the Latin and Welsh chroniclers.[2]

The two legendary Dukes are Uther Pendragon, the father of Arthur, and Arthur himself. The Triads of the *Red Book of Hergest* make Uther Pendragon the brother of Emreis, that is Ambrosius, and the son of Kustennin Vychan, that is Constantine the Small, the usurper Constantine III. The conquest of Rome is one of the main episodes in the legend of Arthur, which symbolizes and depicts not only the fight of Britain against the northerners and Saxons but also the revolt of Britain against Rome and its defeat of the Roman power.[3]

---

[1] Zosim., vi, 10, 2.
[2] Windisch, op. cit., p. 38 ; cf. Gildas, xiv.
[3] Windisch, op. cit., p. 52. Cf. Faral and Bruce, opp. citt.

CHAPTER III

The End of Celtic Britain and Ireland. Saxons, Scots, and Norsemen

I

THE GERMANIC INVASIONS

THE historians lay the blame of bringing the Saxons into Britain on Vortigern,[1] who is said to have called them in to help him against the Picts in 449. Once again we see the Celts playing the weak man's game of putting yourself in the hands of one enemy to save yourself from another. According to the story, Vortigern married a daughter of Hengist and gave him the isle of Thanet and the Kentish coast in exchange, and the alliance between Vortigern and the Saxons came to an end when the latter treacherously massacred a number of Britons at a banquet.

Vortigern fled to Wales, to the Ordovices, whose country was then called Venedotia (Gwynedd). They were ruled by a line of warlike princes who had their capital at Aberffraw in Anglesey. These kings of Gwynedd, trained by uninterrupted fighting against the Irish and the Picts, seem to have taken on the work of the Dukes of the Britains after Ambrosius or Arthur, and to have been regarded as kings in Britain as a whole.[2]

It was apparently at this time that the name of Cymry, which became the national name of the Britons, came to prevail. The Cymry are the tribes who fight side by side, under the command of a chief called the *Gwledig*, against the Irish, Picts, or Saxons. The country of these Cymry is called Combrog in the British of that day, or Cambria.[3]

A hundred years after this first settlement in Kent, the

[1] Lloyd, **CCCCXXXVIII**, 79. Cf. A. W. W. Evans, " Les Saxons dans *l'Excidium Britanniæ* ", in **LVI**, 1916, p. 322. Cf. *R.C.*, 1917–1919, p. 283 ; F.Lot, " Hangist, Horsa, Vortigern, et la conquête de la Gde.-Bretagne par les Saxons," in **CLXXIX**.
[2] Lloyd, op. cit., p. 102.
[3] Ibid., pp. 79, 84.

Saxons advanced rapidly. In 577 they reached the Severn, and cut off Wales from Cornwall for good. About 600 the foundation of a kingdom of Mercia shut the Britons up in the mountains of Wales, where they held their ground.[1] Other kingdoms were founded in the north, which, united in the kingdom of Northumberland, reached the Irish Sea and from 613 onwards separated Wales from a group of Britons who hung on in the north on the borders of the Pictish country. These latter continued to form a kingdom, that of Strathclyde or Cumbria, and its citadel of Dumbarton on the Clyde was not destroyed until the attack of the Norsemen of Ireland in later years.[2]

The introduction of Christianity contributed greatly to the denationalizing of the Celts in Britain. It is true that the Saxons were not Christians when they settled in the island, and in Bede's time the Britons found it difficult to regard them as Christians. But the reforming mission of Augustine, sent to Britain in 596 by St. Gregory, had already shocked British opinion by the sympathetic impartiality which it showed to the newly converted Saxons. In Britain, on account of the rapid conversion of the Saxons and the way in which they were welcomed by the Church, the Celtic resistance could hope for nothing from Christianity.[3]

By the end of the sixth century the game was lost. Celtic Britain had fallen to pieces and only a few fragments remained.

II

THE OCCUPATION OF BRITTANY

The emigration to Brittany or Armorica had begun very early. According to Gildas, who was one of the emigrants and ended his days on the shores of Morbihan, it occurred immediately after the settlement of the first Saxon invaders. Indeed, a bishop of the Britons, Mansuetus, appears at the Council of Tours of 461, and one may wonder whether the Britons who fought on the Loire against the Visigoths in 468 and 472, for Aëtius under a leader named Riotimus,

[1] Ibid., p. 93. Cf. Windisch, p. 62.
[2] Ibid., p. 103.
[3] Ibid., pp. 86, 96.

belonged to Britain or Brittany. The latter was, according to Procopius, one of the most deserted parts of Gaul, and there was plenty of room there for occupation.[1]

The Britons were not contented to fit themselves into a country left empty for them. They really colonized it and founded states, into which they remained divided. One part of Armorica was called Domnonea, and was occupied by Dumnonii of Cornwall ; another was called Cornavia, being settled by Cornavii from Lancashire. They had kings. The story of Cædwalla, the last King of Gwynedd, who was still of some consequence at the beginning of the seventh century, is blended with that of one Salomo, *Rex Armoricanorum Brittonum*, a contemporary of Dagobert (who died in 638).[2]

There were probably more than one emigration. Geoffrey of Monmouth places one in 664. After years of defeat, famine, and plague, Cadwaladr, son of Cædwalla, flees to Armorica, and history adds that his flight marks the end of the British kings and the triumph of the English.

The history of Celtic Brittany is even vaguer than that of the emigration. Legend tells more about it than history, for it is inexhaustible on the subject of the kinships and common endeavours of the heroes and knights of Britain and Brittany. Tristram is a Briton ; Lancelot has come from France to Arthur's court ; Arthur has destroyed the demon of Mont St. Michel ; Merlin flits to and fro between the two countries. This tradition is not without significance. Brittany never ceased to look towards Britain, bound to it by its resuscitated shipping, until the day when it found itself in contact with the very body of France, a France which was no longer Germanic or Celtic but was France and absorbed Brittany naturally and without a struggle.

III

THE INDEPENDENT CELTS OF SCOTLAND AND IRELAND

The unceasing inroads of the Picts which disturbed Britain in the fourth and fifth centuries seem to point to

[1] Loth, **CCCCLXXX**. Cf. Loth, " La Vie la plus ancienne de St.-Samson," in **CXL**, 1923, pp. 1, 8. Cf. Windisch, p. 57.

[2] Loth, op. cit. For Celtic Armorica see Loth, *Mélanges d'histoire bretonne*, Paris, 1907.

a renewal of vitality. But, though we know the dates of their expeditions, we have no information about the Picts themselves or the Caledonians of Scotland. We only know that the Picts had been founding settlements in Ulster since the fourth century, and that they were formidable fighters.[1]

In Ireland, on the other hand, a series of political events occurred which gave a kind of organization, still very patchy, to the racial medley of natives, Goidels, Picts, Britons, and Belgæ,[2] of which I have given some idea in the previous volume. About the time of St. Patrick this organization culminated in the institution of the High Kingship of Ireland, the Kingship of Tara. The strength and health which it gave to Ireland were utilized in expeditions abroad and expressed in civilization at home. All that is historical in the epic Cycles of Ulster and Leinster lies in this period of history.

For these events we have no direct evidence, and contemporary Greek and Latin writers say almost nothing of Ireland. We must be content with two useful pieces of information which we owe to them. One-half of the sixteen peoples of the coast named by Ptolemy are identified anew, and a passage in the polygrapher Solinus, stating that there are no snakes in Ireland, is based on an authentic Irish tradition. For the Irish give to St. Patrick or to Finn mac Coul, as the case may be, the glory of having rid the island of snakes.[3] There were Irish exiles who kept the Roman commanders or governors with whom they happened to come into contact well supplied with information. We have only fragments of what they may have told.

On the other hand, we have a considerable mass of indirect information, furnished by the epics, local legends, laws, and, lastly, the Annals. These last can only be used in the most cautious and critical spirit. The older parts of the dynastic lists and pedigrees are composite, and we should note in general that the Annals hardly mention anything but exceptional occurrences, outside the normal course of life, and so give a false impression of the course of events. All these data have been utilized with great skill by Mr. Eoin MacNeill in the last chapters of his *Phases of Irish History*.[4]

[1] MacNeill, CCCCXLI, p. 141.   [2] Ibid., p. 109.
[3] Joyce, CCCCXXXIV, ii, p. 514.   [4] MacNeill, op. cit., pp. 178, 190.

Although the Romans did not know Ireland, they were known there and their influence was felt there. Ireland had more or less continuous commercial dealings with Britain and with Gaul, which sent it wine. One curious witness to this influence is the alphabet. The Irish invented an alphabet of their own, in which the letters are represented by strokes drawn above or below or across a chief line, or obliquely to it. It has twenty letters—A, B, C, D, E, F, G, H, I, L, M, N, O, QU, R, S, T, U, V, NG. There was no sign for X or for Y. It has only one letter, NG, which the Latin alphabet lacks. If the Irish had evolved their alphabet entirely out of their own heads, they would obviously have invented signs for the aspirated forms of their dentals, labials, and gutturals. But they did not even adopt those of Greek. It was, therefore, the Latin alphabet which they used when analysing sounds, though they did so in an original fashion—distinction of vowel *u* from consonant *u*, classification of sounds. The ogham inscriptions cover the same area as the Irish language of the time just before the earliest Christian phases of Ireland and the earliest manuscripts. Moreover, some ogham inscriptions are Christian. The use of oghams must be placed between an end, somewhere about the sixth century, and a beginning, doubtless about the second or third century.[1]

Yet another feature presented by Ireland in the first centuries of our era may, according to Mr. MacNeill, be due to imitation of the Romans. That is the troops of Fianna, the standing force of professional soldiers, who have their epic in the Leinster Cycle or the Cycle of Finn and failed Ireland so badly in after years. These troops have nothing to do with the early military organization of the Celts, and must have been levied in imitation of Roman military institutions.[2] In any case, it was they who supplied the source of the power which we shall see at work.

The political development of Ireland lies between two terms—the existence of five equal, independent kingdoms in the time of Conchobar mac Nessa, King of Ulster, the king in the epic of Ulster whom the Annals with more or less truth make a contemporary of Christ, and the foundation of the kingdom of Meath as the realm of a High King, with

[1] Ibid., pp. 171 ff.   [2] Ibid., p. 150.

his capital at Tara, in 483. An intermediate date emerges from the Annals, namely that of the reign of Cormac mac Airt, King of Connacht about 275, who conquers Tara. With the conquest of Tara by Cormac is connected the idea of the foundation of a High Kingship held by the Kings of Connacht.

The time of Conchobar is called *Aimser na Cóicedach*, the Time of the Five Fifths. Ireland was divided between the kingdoms of Ulster, Connacht, North Leinster, South Leinster, and Munster. Tara belonged to North Leinster, and Ulster stretched a long way westwards. The frontiers of Munster towards Connacht and Leinster varied a little, but it is not in that direction that one must look for great changes, but in the frontiers of Ulster and Leinster towards Connacht.[1]

The epic of Ulster shows us all Ireland united against that luckless region, under the leadership of the Kings of Connacht. Gradually Connacht gains ground to the east at the expense of Ulster, which it reduces to Counties Down and Antrim, and of North Leinster, which in the end it absorbs entirely. These enlargements are the foundations of its hegemony; eventually it embraces half Ireland.[2]

For, about 150, the people of Connacht occupy Uisnech. The Kingdom of Conchobar is by this time unrecognizable; moreover, it is almost entirely Pictish. A second stage is marked by the occupation of Tara by King Cormac; a third, by the destruction of the Kingdom of Ulster by exiles from Connacht, whose dramatic history is known to us. The single kingdom of Ulster is divided in two—the kingdom of Airgialla and Ulster properly so called. About 400, at the time of Niall of the Nine Hostages, Ulster is still further reduced in the south-west, and the sons of Niall take all that is still left to it in the north-west in County Donegal. The year 483 is marked by the battle of Ocha, which leads to the separation of the kingship of Connacht from the High Kingship, which is attached to the possession of the kingship of Meath with Tara.

There are now not five but seven kingdoms in Ireland,[3] namely Meath, Connacht, Ailech, Airgialla or Oriel, Ulster,

[1] Ibid., pp. 100 ff.   [2] Ibid., p. 129.
[3] Ibid., pp. 113–117.

Leinster, and Munster. The last six are subordinate to Meath. This is the organization which St. Patrick finds in Ireland some years later. The kingship of Tara was still not firmly established, and the Saint took up his abode not there, but at Armagh.[1] Leinster was not yet, after hundreds of years, resigned to its fallen estate, for it still occasionally attacked Connacht and the kingdom of Meath. But unity was practically an accomplished fact. The Irish represented Ireland or its kingship as a sublime princess, the mythical or metaphysical bride of the King of Tara, and this conception was expressed in poems which are sometimes wonderfully beautiful. Moreover, the distinction between the Goidels and the Aithech-thuatha, the rent-paying clans of which I have spoken, in which all non-Goidelic groups were lumped together, was gradually obliterated; in fact, an Ivernian, Eterscél, appears in the list of the great pre-historic kings. Yet it was at the end of the first century that the famous, if ephemeral, revolt of the Rent-payers took place, which drove the Connacht line out of the country to Britain, perhaps shortly after the time of Agricola. But the banished house returned with Tuathal Teachtmar, more powerful than ever.

A tendency towards unity, the sense of which became ever deeper, and a fusion of races—these were the results of the political development of Ireland which we have just surveyed.

IV

THE INROADS OF THE SCOTS

The Irish had been fighting for four hundred years, and so were well trained to warfare and daring. Also, some of them had been defeated. Groups had been driven out of their homes. The Desi, who lived about Tara, were reduced to vagabondage by the conquerors of Connacht. So Ireland seems to have had surplus men and energy to spend abroad.[2]

From the third century, the Romans in Britain had to

---

[1] Ibid., p. 160.   [2] Ibid., p. 188.

be on their guard against Irish incursions. The invaders are designated by the historians of the Later Empire under the names of Hiberni, Attecotti, Scotti. *Scotti* became one of the usual names of the Goidels of Ireland. *Attecotti* does not appear outside the documents of that time. Scottus is a Gaulish name, and seems to mean " skirmisher ", " runner ".[1]

The Irish did not halt in Britain, but went on to the Continent. St. Jerome [2] speaks of inroads of the Attecotti, barbarous men with cruel habits and abominable morals. They cut off the breasts of women and ate them, he says, and they lived in promiscuity. They landed at the mouth of the Loire and engaged in brigandage in the country. Sometimes they came in large numbers, and Stilicho had to meet a real invasion of Irish. Sometimes they took service under Rome ; the *Notitia Dignitatum* gives Attecotti Juniores and Seniores. Ammianus Marcellinus speaks of a body of scouts or spies called Areani.[3] These were Irish *vigiles* (in Irish, *aire* means ." guard ", " watcher "). The Scots settled down in colonies ; the village of Écuisses in Saône-et-Loire was originally Scotiæ.[4]

The Irish Annals and other documents show us the other side of these adventures. We are told, not of bands of pillagers, but of military expeditions led by kings. The earliest of these expeditions is ascribed to King Crimthann Nia Nair, who is said to have reigned over the whole of Ireland between 74 and 90. The conquests attributed to Crimthann the Great, who is supposed to have reigned from 366 to 379, coincide in a curious way with the command and victories of Theodosius, the father of Theodosius the Great.[5] The campaigns of Stilicho in Britain and Gaul have a counterpart in the expeditions of the famous King Niall of the Nine Hostages. He ravaged the north of Britain, unpeopled the country, and took thousands of captives, among whom may have been St. Patrick, who, as we know was a slave in Ireland. In 405 Niall was killed by a king

---

[1] Haverfield, "Ancient Rome and Ireland," in **LXII**, xxviii, 1913, p. 8. Cf. Zimmer, in **CXLVIII**, 1891, p. 280 ; Lloyd, **CCCCXXXVIII**, 51 ; MacNeill, op. cit., p. 148.
[2] Jerome, *In Jovin.*, ii. Cf. Müllenhoff, **CCCLXII**, ii, p. 183.
[3] Amm. Marc., xxviii, 3, 8 ; MacNeill, op. cit., p. 151.
[4] For these settlements, cf. MacNeill, op. cit., p. 144.
[5] Joyce, op. cit., i, 73–4.

of Leinster while fighting in Gaul, and his successor is likewise said to have warred in that country.[1]

At the same time the Irish were establishing themselves in Britain and on all the projecting parts of the west coast. Between 250 and 000 the Desi occupied the country of Dyfed.[2] Then the Ui Liatháin, one of the chief branches of the Eoganachta of Munster, settled in Cornwall.[3] In the north, the Dal Riada of Ulster took possession of Argyll and the neighbouring islands.[4] In Wales, the Goidels also occupied Anglesey and almost the whole of Gwynedd. The district held by them is dotted with ogham inscriptions and such names as Cerrig y Gwyddell (Rocks of the Goidels).[5] They installed themselves and came to terms with the natives who remained. There were intermarriages and associations. This common life is perpetuated in the complete intermingling of Irish and British traditions, of which the Mabinogion and the legend of Tristram afford striking evidence.

Moreover, the Britons occasionally paid back the Irish in their own coin.[6] In 250 we see an army of Britons led into Ireland by a claimant of the High Kingship, Lugaidh mac Conn. St. Patrick speaks of one Coroticus, who raided Ireland for captives. Now, Coroticus is the same as Ceredig ap Cunedda, the son and successor of the Cunedda who reconquered Gwynedd from the Irish about 400. A descendant of Cunedda, Maelgwyn, who died in 547, recovered Dyfed. At all events, by the middle of the fifth century the Irish kings seem to have given up expeditions on a big scale. The Britons had recovered ground in Wales and Cornwall.

V

THE SCOTS IN SCOTLAND

Of their conquests of those days, the Goidels kept the Isle of Man and Scotland. In Man they left their Goidelic

---

[1] MacNeill, op. cit., p. 157 ; Joyce, op. cit., i, p. 77.
[2] Joyce, op. cit., i, p. 79 ; MacNeill, op. cit., p. 155. Cf. Windisch, *Das keltische Britannien*, p. 27 ; "Les Irlandais (Desi) en Dyfed," in **CXL**, 1917–1919, p. 315 ; Kuno Meyer, " Early Relations between Gaels and Brythons," in **CLIV**, 1897, pp. 59–195.
[3] MacNeill, op. cit., p. 156.   [4] Ibid.
[5] Joyce, op. cit., i, p. 78. Cf. J. Rhys, " Three Ancient Inscriptions from Wales," in **CCCLVI**, p. 227. Cf. Windisch, p. 27.
[6] Joyce, loc. cit. ; Loth, in **CXL**, xviii, p. 304.

dialect, which was kept up by constant intercourse with the Irish coast. In Scotland they founded a state which grew steadily, and finally absorbed the Picts and Caledonians (if, indeed, these last two were distinct).

The first landing seems to have been in the first half of the third century. Conaire II, who was a king of Munster but appears in the list of High Kings of Ireland from 212 to 220, had a son Cairbre Riada, who, on a famine breaking out in Munster, set off with his men to settle in the north of Ireland, in Ulster. Some of the Dal Riada remained there, in County Antrim. Another body crossed the sea and settled in Argyll. That, according to tradition, is the origin of the double kingdom of Dal Riada. In 470 Fergus mac Eirc, King of the Ulster Dal Riada and a descendent of Cairbre Riada, crossed into Scotland with his brothers. It was doubtless an attempt to reunite the two halves of the tribe. This is the official date of the foundation of the kingdom of the Scots and its royal line. The attempt succeeded, and a double kingdom was thus founded, the Isle of Man being attached to it.

This double kingdom furnished an interesting case for Irish public law, and the question was not settled until the famous Assembly of Druim Ceata, under the presidency of St. Columba, disposed of this and other like problems in 575. The King of the Scots in Britain was made independent of the authority of the High King of Ireland, and a mixed solution was adopted for the Irish kingdom of the Dal Riada, which had to serve the High King with its land forces and the King of the Scots with its sea forces.[1]

For a long time the Scottish colony of the Dal Riada was inconsiderable. At the end of the seventh century it was still confined to Argyll and the adjoining isles. On the east, the Picts extended southwards to the Firth of Forth. To the south, the Britons held the west coast to beyond Dumbarton, leaving a small group of Picts cut off from the rest in Galloway. But at this date the Scottish kingdom began to grow. By the time of Bede, the Scots had supplanted the Picts in the neighbourhood of the Firth of Forth.

[1] MacNeill, op. cit., pp. 194, 599. Cf. CXL, xxxix, 888 ; Ore, CCCCXIII ; Joyce, op. cit., i, p. 79.

Ireland identified itself with Christianity to such an extent and so successfully that it set it up in the place of its own heroes to express its national soul. St. Patrick became the true national hero of Ireland.[1]

Christianity had certainly reached the country before his time. If we are to believe St. Jerome, Pelagius, who flourished in the fourth century, was an Irishman, swollen with Irish porridge. The Chronicle of Prosper of Aquitaine says that in 431 Pope Celestinus I sent a certain Palladius to the Scots who believed in God. St. Patrick arrived in Ireland in 432 at the earliest.[2] Zimmer, in a work of which I have spoken in connection with the relations of Gaul and Ireland, ingeniously suggests that from 419 to 507, between the date of the settlement of the Visigoths in · northern Aquitania and the time when Clovis restored a little order in Gaul after the troublous years of the fifth century, the educated men of Gaul, and especially of Aquitania, found a refuge in Ireland. It is possible, but not proved.[3] As a fact, neither the Latin of St. Patrick nor that of St. Columba, who adorned the Irish Church in the following century, shows any sign that they were disciples of the learned men of Aquitania and their preciosity.[4] In any case, while it is almost certain that St. Patrick was not the first apostle of the Irish, it is beyond all doubt that Christianity was triumphant after his time.

Certain important things are to be observed immediately afterwards. There is no longer the least question of racial diversity in Ireland except in the legendary past. All are Gædhil, whether they be Ivernians, Picts, Gauls, or Belgæ by origin. Mr. MacNeill, who rightly lays stress on the question of the subject tribes, *Aithech-thuatha*, thinks that at this date the distinction expressed by the opposition of the words *soer*, free, and *doer*, unfree, corresponds chiefly to the difference of status between the skilled craftsman, who is likewise called *soer*, and the peasant—a distinction similar to that maintained on the Continent between burgher and villain. These are social, not racial, differences.[5]

[1] MacNeill, op. cit., p. 159.   Cf. Czarnowski, **CCCCXXXIII**; White, **CCCCXLII**.
[2] MacNeill, op. cit., p. 162.   [3] Ibid., p. 165.
[4] Ibid., p. 166.   [5] Ibid., p. 229.

Secondly, St. Patrick seems to have made a special fight against slavery, and particularly against the enslavement of prisoners of war and against war itself. He preached, for example, in favour of Christian brotherhood. He had been a slave in Ireland, and had been summoned back to the country by voices. The success of his preaching is attested by the stoppage of the slave-trade. There were no more expeditions, and, therefore, no more standing armies, and the institution of the Fianna became obsolete. Two hundred years later, the Venerable Bede, in telling of a raid made in Ireland by the Northumbrians in 684, describes them as falling on an inoffensive people.[1]

Lastly, the superabundant energy of which I have spoken found a new outlet—the preaching of the Gospel. St. Columba and the monks of Iona went to the Continent, where they founded monasteries—Luxeuil and St. Gall—in which valuable Irish MSS. are preserved.[2]

From the sixth century onwards Ireland became a centre of Christian culture, a school of theology and morals. The substance of the earliest Penitentials is Irish. Bede tells us that a crowd of young Englishmen followed the teaching of St. Colman. Later, Alcuin corresponded with the monastery of Clonmacnoise.[3]

But the Christian culture of Ireland was now as it were the flower of the national civilization. St. Patrick had attracted one of the intellectual classes to his side—the poets. Christianity gave them a better script than the oghams. In St. Patrick's time they already began to make written collections of the ancient epics. We shall see later that the honour of ordering these collections to be made is ascribed to Loegaire, King of Ireland in St. Patrick's time. It is a fact in the history of the Celts to be compared to the putting of the Homeric poems into writing in the history of the Greeks. In the seventh century, too, the Irish grammarians began to extol and cultivate their language. All this movement likewise was originally started by St. Patrick.[4]

[1] Ibid., p. 159.
[2] See Gougaud, CCCCXXVIII; Lloyd, op. cit., p. 109.
[3] MacNeill, op. cit., p. 242.
[4] Ibid., p. 167.

VI

CHRISTIAN IRELAND TO THE SCANDINAVIAN INVASIONS

It was truly the Golden Age of Ireland that commenced with Christianity and lasted about three hundred years ; three hundred years of continuity, peace, prosperity, and unity, things which no other Celtic people had ever had. The result was that Ireland had time to complete herself and to-day there is an Irish nationality, or rather an Irish nation, which, alone of the Celtic nationalities, has survived persecutions and disasters.

Not that all was golden in that Age of Gold. Ireland suffered by the disappearance of the mercenary militia which gave her a kind of army for defence and attack. She suffered also by her laws of succession. She suffered, lastly, by the rivalry of the ecclesiastical power and the state. There were internal wars, competitions between Leinstermen and men of Connacht and between the families descended from the Kings of Connacht, for the High Kingship. But these conflicts were not more than small incidents. Moreover, there is no history for this period but mere anecdotes.

One anecdote tells of the abandonment of Tara, the seat of the High Kingship, in the reign of Diarmait mac Cearbhail, a great-grandson of Niall, in circumstances which seem to be quite legendary, the city being cursed and abandoned in 545. In reality Tara was not destroyed at all, and probably not cursed, for a council was held there in 780. But it was really a gathering-place for festivals and a military camp rather than a city, and times were changed. Cruachain in Connacht and Ailinn in Leinster, which were likewise great camps, were likewise abandoned. The military organization was disappearing. Besides, although Irish Christianity was of such a national character, it could not do otherwise than change the old system of festivals and secularize the places in which they were held, unless it consecrated them. Now, St. Patrick had not established himself at Tara, but at Armagh. It seems, too, that the High Kingship was no longer absolutely bound up with the possession of Tara.[1]

[1] Ibid.

VII

THE SCANDINAVIAN INVASIONS

The development of Ireland and its civilization in an evangelical and monastic peace along the lines laid down by St. Patrick was cut short at the end of the eighth century by a new movement of peoples. It was at this time that the peoples of the Scandinavian peninsula, followed soon after by those of Denmark, began to migrate. In reality the operations of the Norseman were more systematic and better organized than is usually imagined. They were expeditions of conquest and colonization, in the course of which true states were founded, and these states formed federations with each other and united with the mother-country. Magnificent plans of vast sea-empires for a moment came very near realization.

The Norsemen appeared about 790 in the northern archipelagos of the British Isles and on the coasts of Ireland. Some time after their first piratical raids, they occupied islands and peninsulas, establishing a fortified post at Dublin in 841 and another at Annagassan in County Louth about the same time. At Dublin they were between Leinster and Meath, and took advantage of the enmity of the two districts. Having thus succeeded in interfering in the internal affairs of Ireland, they got a foothold in the country, and in the tenth century a number of agreements and inter-marriages established their position permanently. From time to time they received reinforcements or new leaders, or a Norwegian fleet would come and establish or restore the authority of some distant king. From 863 Harold Fairhair was able, in the course of a long reign lasting three-quarters of a century, to form and consolidate his empire.[1]

The enterprise of the Scandinavians was destroyed by the rivalry of the Norwegians and the Danes. The latter first appear in Ireland in 851, being described in the Annals as black heathen. Ireland, which had been taken by surprise by the Scandinavian invaders when it was without any military organization, had great difficulty in making a recovery. But by 870 the whole north of the country seems to have rid itself of the Norsemen. From that date, the

[1] Ibid., pp. 248–253.

struggle is mainly concentrated in the southern provinces, the Kings of Cashel playing an important part with varying success.

It seems that the Irish never mixed up their civil wars with these national conflicts. Leinster is at war with Munster, and Cormac, the good King-Bishop of Cashel, is slain in 908. In Munster, the rival families of the Eoganachta and the Dal Cais contend for the kingship. About 1000 the Dal Cais are in power, under Brian Bóramha (Brian Boru). He is one of the outstanding figures of Irish history. A shrewd politician and a temporizer, he aimed at the High Kingship, but was content with exercising a real hegemony. It was the whole of Ireland that followed him in 1014 to the victorious battle of Clontarf. Sigtrygg, King of Dublin, had called in Sigurd, Count of Orkney. The battle was decisive ; Brian won the day but was killed. The prestige of the Norsemen was destroyed. An attempt on the part of Magnus, King of Norway, to restore it in 1103 was a failure.[1]

In Scotland, the Scandinavian inroads benefited the small kingdom of the Dal Riada, which successfully opposed them, while they weakened the Picts in the north and the Angles in the south. The Scots, having now a good foothold in the interior, concentrated there, fortified their positions, and made ready to step into the shoes of their neighbours. In the middle of the ninth century the kingdom of the Picts came to an end and was absorbed by that of the Dal Riada. In 870 Olaf and Ivar, the Scandinavian Kings of Dublin, took Dumbarton. But at the end of that century the Scottish kingdom was extending at the expense of the Angles in the old domain of the Britons in the south of the present Scotland. The colonization which followed the conquest is attested by the diffusion of Gaelic place-names all over Scotland. Gaelic also gained ground in the Scandinavian settlements of the west coast and the Isles. Here small states had grown up— the earldom of Orkney, the kingdom of the Isles (the Hebrides), the kingdom of Man—all subject to the King of Norway in varying degrees.[2] The Danes who came after the Norwegians had set up in 980 a Danish kingdom of the Hebrides, which seems to have come to an end in 1005.

[1] Ibid., pp. 253–280. Cf. Vendryès, in **CXL**, 1920–1, p. 348.
[2] MacNeill, op. cit., pp. 211, 216.

Some of these small kingdoms remained in the allegiance of the Kings of Norway, such as that founded by Sumarlidi in Argyll and the Isles, which did not break off from that allegiance until 1269. Orkney was Norwegian until 1470, when James III of Scotland acquired it by marriage. It was still long before the Hebrides and Orkney became Scottish for good.

Wales, too, was touched by the Scandinavians, but they made no settlements there. The Welsh did not take advantage of this comparative tranquillity, nor of the stronger pressure to which the Scandinavians were subjecting the Anglo-Saxons, to reconquer the ground which they had lost. Sometimes, notably in the reign of Alfred the Great, they fought against the Danes by the side of the Anglo-Saxons. A certain amount of assimilation had eventually taken place. The Kings of Wales entered into the allegiance of the Anglo-Saxon Kings. In the tenth century, in time of peace, they appeared at their councils ; Howel the Good called one of his sons Edwin. So Wales did not succeed in forming a strong and really lasting state, in spite of occasional attempts like that of Howel the Good to unify the country.[1]

We must, however, recognize that they were the Celts who best resisted the Scandinavian assault on the Western world, and that their resistance did more than that of any other people to break it. That was a great achievement.

VIII

THE WARS OF INDEPENDENCE

1. *Wales*

The Norman followers of William the Conqueror who took the place of the Anglo-Saxons in 1066 showed themselves more capable than they of reducing and absorbing the Celtic states of the British Isles. The fact was, they had become French in two generations. Their undertaking bears no resemblance to the movements of the Scandinavians described above. It was an act of policy, served by the self-interest

[1] Lloyd, op. cit., pp. 112–129.

of a crowd of adventurers.   The object was to enlarge possessions, to obtain feudal lands.   The island Celts were the dissenters of the West, and they had against them the Pope, that is the head of the society which was created by the amalgamation of Germanic elements in the now Christian Roman Empire.   The Normans conquered the country permanently, and very soon transformed it.   The change was not at all unlike that which so surprised us in Roman Gaul. The Normans were great builders, in an age of lavish building. Wherever they set foot, they built churches, castles, and towns, and everywhere they were imitated, until the face of the country was utterly changed.

The Welsh, having committed themselves to resistance, brought the Conqueror down on them.   He operated along the Marches in 1070, and left it to the Earls of Chester and Shrewsbury to subjugate them gradually.   At the beginning of the twelfth century the Welsh still held the mountains, while the Normans were on the coasts and in the valleys. On the death of Henry I, the Welsh took sides with Matilda, the late King's daughter, against Stephen of Blois.   They took sides against King John, and in 1258 with Simon de Montfort against Henry III.   Really, the Welsh kings and princes of the twelfth and thirteenth centuries recognized the overlordship of the Norman kings; but they revolted often.   In 1282 Edward III, having put down one of these revolts, reserved the title of Prince of Wales for the heir to the English crown.[1]

The historical development is rather well symbolized by the figure of Giraldus Cambrensis, Gerald of Wales. He was the son of a Norman baron and a Welsh mother, studied in France, and became an official of Henry II.   He has left a series of books, including the *Itinerary of Cambria* and the *Conquest of Ireland*, which show a real knowledge of Celtic matters and an interest in them not always friendly.

It was in the days of the Plantagenet kings, perhaps at the court of Henry II, in the circle of Giraldus and Walter Map, that the Arthurian legend developed,[2] based partly on a Welsh narrative which, according to Giraldus, was composed by one Bledri, *famosus ille fabulator Bledhericus*, and partly on the traditions of Glastonbury Abbey.

[1] Ibid., pp. 150–199.   [2] Cf. Faral, Bruce, opp. citt.

The Britons submitted quickly, the Normans and they seem to have taken to each other fairly easily.

2. *Scotland*

The Gaelic kingdoms of Scotland and Ireland did not fall into the arms of the Normans so quickly. In Scotland, King Malcolm had received and taken under his protection the Anglo-Saxon royal family, and married Margaret, grand-daughter of King Edmund, in 1067. She, who afterwards became St. Margaret of Scotland, exercised great influence, and it was not in favour of Celticism. Thanks to her and to most of Malcolm's successors, the Anglo-Saxon element gained in Scotland, in language and in institutions. But neither William the Conqueror nor his successors made any progress in Scotland. In spite of the extinction of the royal line and the rivalries of claimants to the succession, neither Edward I nor Edward II managed to conquer the country, and Robert Bruce made a victorious resistance at Bannockburn. But Scotland was increasingly won over by contact, growing less and less Celtic, until the process culminated when the Stewart line ascended the throne of England in the person of James VI and I.[1]

This does not mean that the spirit of independence disappeared wholly in Wales and Scotland. The peoples kept their native character. But the capacity and the desire to form an independent national body had gone.

3. *Ireland* [2]

The case of Ireland was quite different.[3] It was free of the Scandinavians, but was in a condition of moral and material distress of which we hear from St. Bernard, the friend of the Irish St. Malachy. There was a movement of Cistercian reform at the beginning of the twelfth century, but it came into conflict with an independent movement of reform in the Irish monasteries, which went with a revival of the schools. The Cistercian circle of Henry II took offence, and the King suggested to Pope Adrian IV that he should

[1] MacNeill, op. cit., pp. 203 ff.   [2] Ibid., pp. 300–322.
[3] Ibid., p. 309.

conquer and reform Ireland. The Pope claimed rights over Ireland in virtue of the famous but apocryphal Donation of Constantine. He gave the King of England *carte blanche*. Once again Norman conquest was to bring the Western dissenters into the fold.

An army of Normans, Flemings, and Welsh landed in Ireland in 1169. Henry II arrived in person in 1171. There was still a High King in Ireland, Rory O'Connor. He was the last of the High Kings, for he was compelled to acknowledge the overlordship of the King of England. But only the edge of Ireland had as yet been touched. The invaders had made hardly any real conquest outside Counties Dublin, Meath, Kildare, and Louth. Henry II left the task of completing the conquest to a few great feudal magnates, the FitzGeralds, the De Courcis, the De Burghs, who had to secure real possession of their fiefs. They took advantage of dynastic rivalries and civil wars, always had Irish supporters on their side, and succeeded in concluding agreements and matrimonial alliances with the families of Irish chiefs. They built castles, and sometimes, as at Downpatrick, transformed fortified monasteries into castles.

After 1255 comes a series of setbacks for the conquerors. A national reaction arises and lasts until Tudor times. The de Burghs, having tried to secure a real hold on the districts in Ulster and Connacht which had been assigned to them, found themselves confronted by an Irish coalition, formed by the Kings of Thomond and Connacht and Brian O'Neill, King of Tir Eoghain (Tyrone), who led the resistance. The Gall-Ghaedhil of the Hebrides supplied a nucleus of permanent troops. The Irish then started looking for allies and leaders abroad ; in 1263 they applied to Hakon, King of Norway, then in the Hebrides, and in 1314 to Robert Bruce, who sent them his brother Edward.[1]

At the beginning of the fourteenth century the son of Brian O'Neill wrote to a successor of Adrian IV, repudiating the Plantagenet overlordship of Ireland and claiming the right of the country to choose its own sovereign. At the same time, the feudal lords established in Ireland sometimes became Irish. The conquerors conformed to the Irish practice of sending children away from home to be brought up by

[1] Ibid., pp. 323 ff.

foster-parents, placing them with Irish people, and so real bonds were created, which were reinforced by matrimonial alliances.   The old Irish families restored the kingdoms. Truly national feasts were held—in 1351 by O'Kelly, to celebrate the restoration of his kingdom, and in 1433 by Margaret, daughter of O'Carroll, King of Eile, and wife of O'Connor, King of Offaly.[1]

This state of things went on to the end of the sixteenth century, to the time of Elizabeth and James VI and I, or rather to that of Cromwell and William of Orange. Ireland took up the Stewart cause; it was conquered, but not absorbed, and was always ready to revive. Then began the endless succession of brutalities and extensive expropriations under the ignorant and unskilful direction of legislators, which led to the revival of Ireland at this day.

IX

CONCLUSION OF THIS HISTORY

Such was the history of the Celts, those groups of Aryan tribes which had become aware of their native character and covered half Europe in their migrations. There they were conquered and merged in new nations. In the islands, they resisted. Then they retired. They were turned back on themselves; they were partly absorbed by the Roman Empire. What survived the fall of the Celtic states in Britain was absorbed by the Normans, the last Germanic people to emigrate. There remains nothing but one small, indomitable nation, full of vigour, on the outermost edge of their earliest conquests, and, behind that front, in Scotland, in Wales, in Brittany, Celtic-speaking communities which are no longer nations.

[1] Ibid., p. 344.

PART THREE

THE CIVILIZATION OF THE CELTS

CHAPTER I

THE OBJECTS AND METHOD OF A SOCIOLOGICAL STUDY OF THE CELTS

WE have tried to set forth the main features of the history of the Celts. But another question arises regarding the Celtic peoples; we must inquire what were the bonds which held men together in social organization, how families and clans were constituted, how land was owned (in whole or in part, in precarious possession or in permanent, absolute ownership, in common or individually, in fairly distributed lots or in aristocratic tenures), what was their law, what were their gods, and their priests, how they traded, and travelled, and built. The structure of society; private law; public law and political institutions; religion; economic life; craftsmanship; morphology; art and literature—these are the headings for a description of Celtic society.

I

THE BASES OF A COMPARATIVE STUDY OF CELTIC CIVILIZATION

We shall, of course, deal with the Celts of antiquity, but not only with those of Gaul. We shall look at Gauls, Irish, and British all together, comparing them.

Before starting on an inquiry of this kind, we must first of all reply to an objection which naturally occurs to the mind. In order to make a description such as we are going to attempt, we must look to literary documents, the Irish and Welsh epics, or summaries of epics, which have come down to us and the Welsh and Irish laws, for light on the little which the classical writers tell us about the institutions and life of Gaul. It will then be objected (such was the opinion of Fustel de Coulanges) that these two sets of information come from very different dates. The Irish documents cannot materially have been put down in writing before the conversion of Ireland in the fifth century. A preface to the *Senchus Mor*, the most important of the Irish legal treatises, states that it was composed by a commission called by King Loegaire on which St. Patrick sat. The anonymous author of the *Book of Acaill*, which comes next in importance, says that it is of the third century, but it was certainly not written down then ; besides, the ancient text is so concise that it cannot be understood without the glossary, which must have been written in the ninth or tenth century at earliest, since it implies the use of the penny, which was not introduced into Ireland before then. Nor can the oldest of the Irish epics have been put together any earlier. It is much the same with the Welsh texts. The compilation of the laws is ascribed in the prefaces to King Howel the Good, who reigned in the first half of the tenth century. The Mabinogion were not compiled later than the first half of the twelfth century, but certainly after the Norman Conquest.[1] Roughly, then, there is an interval of about a thousand years between the information given us about the Continental Celts and that which the island Celts have themselves furnished.

But what was the nature of these documents ? For the mythology and hero-tales of Ireland, there was a tradition preserved orally, like the poems of the Druids of Gaul, which was put into writing because it was beginning to be forgotten, just at the time when the introduction of a new tradition, that of Christianity, threatened to hasten its disappearance. It was said that for the most important of these epics, the *Táin Bó Chuailgné*, the *Cattle-lifting of Cooley*, the ghosts of the dead had to be called in to assist the editor ; Fergus, one of the actors in the story, arose from his grave to relate it.[2] The Welsh Mabinogion consist of mythological material which had long lost its original character, being transformed to a greater or less extent into tales and romances. But in each case the substance of the stories is several centuries older than the literary version.

The same is true of the laws. Neither in Ireland nor in

---

[1] Loth, **CCLXX**, i, p. 44.
[2] Windisch, **CCXCV** ; *Táin*, introd., p. liii. Cf. d'Arbois, in **XXXII**, xl, p. 152 ; Zimmer, in **LXXXIII**, xxviii, pp. 426 ff.

Wales are they legislative texts. They are customs. Now, a custom necessarily has no date in itself. The date is that of the state of society to which it corresponds.

That is why there is no reason for refraining from using the Irish and Welsh documents because they were written late. With their aid, we can make up a picture of much earlier times. We only need to keep our critical faculty awake in dealing with them, as, indeed, we must do with the classical authors, who did not understand the institutions which they described.

II

THE SOLIDARITY OF THE CELTIC SOCIETIES. THE ACTION OF THE DRUIDS

On the other hand, there are good reasons for studying all parts of the Celtic world together. They were in communication, they were inter-connected, they must have had resemblances. Here is one fact which gives food for thought. It was at the time of the first Roman campaigns in Asia Minor after the Punic Wars. In 197-196 the city of Lampsacos sent envoys to Rome. They landed at Marseilles, which was allied to the Romans, doubtless expecting to receive recommendations and information there. The Senate of Marseilles gave them, among other things for their return journey, a public letter of recommendation to the Galatian Tolistoagii, who lived west of the Tectosages in the valley of the Sangarios, separated from Lampsacos by the kingdom of Pergamon, with which, as we know, they were on friendly terms. The people of Marseilles had relations with the Gauls of Gaul, and they probably made the most of the fact in writing to the Tolistoagii, whose good offices the Lampsacenians must have desired, with a view either to recruiting mercenaries or to persuading them not to supply any to Antiochos III. These facts are related in an inscription in honour of the envoys, which M. Holleaux has recently edited. They show that the Greeks of Marseilles and of Lampsacos knew that they would find among Celtic peoples living very far apart a sense of oneness of which the Romans had been aware some years earlier when they had sent ambassadors to ask the Volcae to be neutral when Hannibal passed through the country.[1]

This solidarity of the Celtic peoples, even when distant from one another, is sufficiently explained by the sense of kinship, of common origin, acting in a fairly restricted world, all the parts of which were in communication. But the Celts had at least one institution which could effectively bind them together, namely the Druids, a priestly class expressly entrusted with the preservation of traditions. The Druids were not an institution of the small Celtic peoples, of the tribes, of the *civitates* ; they were a kind of international institution within the Celtic world, with provinces corresponding to the great racial or territorial groups constituted by Ireland, Britain, and Gaul. Cæsar tells us that the Druids of Gaul were in touch with those of Britain, and Irish tradition gives evidence of the relations of the Druids of Britain and Ireland. It is certain that this priesthood, provided, as we shall see later,[2] with a legal doctrine, a moral doctrine, a doctrine of the immortality of the soul, and an authority recognized by all, covered the greater part of the Celtic world, and it is almost unthinkable that it did not cover it all. The bonds which united the Celtic peoples were made secure by the spread of Druidism, and we can be sure that those peoples owed to those professional teachers moral ideas, conceptions about the future life, mythological traditions, ritual practices, and legal solutions which they all had in common—that is, that similar principles everywhere governed or reformed the structure and working of society.

III

CELTIC SOCIETIES AND INDO-EUROPEAN SOCIETIES. THE CELTS AND THE INDO-EUROPEAN WORLD

In the course of this account we shall have occasion to compare the various Celtic peoples in respect of their institutions, not only with one another, but with various Mediterranean and Germanic peoples with which they had relations, which gave them something or received something

[1] Holleaux, **CCCXL**, ii, " Lampsaque et les Galates en 197/6."
[2] Cf. below, ch. iii.

from them. I have already spoken twice of the influence exercised by the Celts, and particularly the Gauls, in Germany. Germanic took from Celtic important terms in the language of politics, law, and economics—the words for king, office, hostage, value.

The peoples of Italy, which once formed with the Celts a single group which, in its undivided state, I made the starting-point of this history, developed rapidly. They took a host of words from their Mediterranean neighbours, and they became city-dwellers like the Greeks and Etruscans. On the whole, they were to the Celts in respect of institutions much what the Gauls of Gaul were to the Irish. For example, they invented the State ; they had a clear notion of the *respublica*, of which the most progressive of the Celts certainly had no more than a rather vague idea. Their institutions give the impression of a term of social development at which the Celts would have arrived if only they had remained independent. But there are many things in the civilization of the Celts and the Italici which recall the times when the two peoples were one. The Latin word for a king, *rex*, is the same as the Celtic *rix*, but the Romans confined it to the religious side of the office. The name of the Latin tribe, *tribus*, another institution becoming fossilized, is probably the same as Welsh *tref* (Irish *treb*), which appears in the name Atrebates.

There is another Indo-European group with which the Celtic group is connected by verbal relations and analogies of a particular type—the Indo-Iranian group. The analogies appear especially in the religous and political vocabulary, as M. Vendryès has pointed out.[1]

There are, moreover, religious scruples and practices which are identical in the two groups, though not designated by the same names. At Kildare, for example, the nuns of St. Brigid (who took the place of a previous goddess) were as careful as the Persian Magi not to soil with their breath the flame of the sacred fire which they kept alight.[2]

So, too, in Irish law the pursuer cannot demand the seizure of the goods of a person who is superior to him, who is *nemed* in regard to him, that is sacred (a noble, a *filè*,

---

[1] XCIII, 1918, xxi, pp. 265–285.
[2] *R.E.G.*, 1915, p. 189.

a clerk). He sits down before his door and patiently proceeds to fast. The person against whom he fasts must, under pain of disqualification, give the pledge desired. This process of coercion by mystical methods is simply the Hindu *dhârṇa*, which was regularly practised all over India as late as the end of the eighteenth century. *Dhârṇa* seems to mean the same as Latin *capio*, " taking possession." In *dhârṇa* the Brahmin sits and fasts at the defender's door until the pursuer has obtained satisfaction, and he has poison, a dagger, or some other means of suicide by him in case violence should be attempted against him. A man who allowed the faster to die would bring down a capital crime on his head for all eternity. *Dhârṇa* seems to have been used like the old *pignoris capio* of Roman law. One may reasonably suppose that it is very ancient, even if the written formulas regarding it are comparatively recent.[1]

A still more striking resemblance is furnished by the very existence of the Druids. Nothing could be liker to the Druids than the Brahmins of India and the Magi of Iran, except perhaps the College of Pontifices at Rome and the Flamens attached to it. The Flamen has the same name as the Brahmin, and M. Vendryès has shown the similarity between the terms relating to priests and sacrifices. The priesthoods are not merely very similar, but exactly the same, and they are preserved nowhere so completely as at the two opposite ends of the Indo-European world. Between the two, the remnants of similar priesthoods once survived, as in Thrace and among the Getae.

All these similarities prove that institutions mentioned even in late texts are of very great antiquity. This will be confirmed by our further analysis.

IV

CELTIC SOCIETIES AND MORE PRIMITIVE SOCIETIES. PRACTICES DATING FROM BEFORE THE FORMATION OF THE INDO-EUROPEAN GROUP

In addition to these survivals from a past common to all the different branches of the Indo-European stock,

[1] Maine, **CCCLII**, pp. 40, 291, 297. Cf. **CCXLVII**, *Senchus Mor*, 113 ; d'Arbois **CCXLVII** (Droit), i, 269 ; ii, 46 ; Joyce, **CCCCXXXIV**, i, p. 205.

Celtic institutions present some strangely preserved relics of a past lying in the depths of prehistory. The Indo-European societies, so far as one can attempt to imagine them in the remote time when the members of the race were beginning to part company, were already societies of a high type. They had chiefs, priests, and a formal law, and their organization of the family implies development through a long past. But these societies had evidently gone through the stage at which men are grouped in clans, which are politico-domestic groups of kinsmen, in which kinship is constituted by the notion of a common origin and often by participation in the nature of a living species or some inanimate thing. That stage is known as totemism. The species or thing is regarded as akin to the men, and provides them with their mythical ancestors, their name, and their heraldic device. In this condition of society, the whole of social life is concentrated, as it were, without political, religious, or even economic differentiation, in the life of the clan and the ceremonies which it entails.[1] As a fact, European societies had long advanced beyond this stage.

Yet we can see, among the Celts, in a state of remarkable preservation, three systems of institutions or rites which correspond to certain forms of early life—head-hunting, the blood-covenant, and the gift.

1. *Head-hunting*

What is head-hunting ? The Gauls [2] cut off the heads of their slain enemies. Poseidonios, who travelled in Gaul, says that horsemen hung them at the necks of their horses, or nailed them to the timbers of their houses like trophies of the chase,[3] or dressed and embalmed them. He adds that his hosts showed him these trophies with pleasure and boasted of the great sums offered by the families of the victims to buy them back. In the Celtiberian *oppidum* of Puig-Castelar, near Barcelona, human skulls have been found, pierced by a nail,[4] and cut-off heads are depicted on Gallic

---

[1] See **CCCLX**.
[2] **CXL**, 1919, p. 274. Cf. A. Reinach, in **CXL**. Cf. Amm. Marc., xxvii, 4, on the Scordisci using skulls as drinking-cups ; Livy, xxiii, 24, on the Boii.
[3] Diod., v, 29, 4 ; Strabo, iv, 4, 5.
[4] Déchelette, ii, 3, p. 946.

coins and monuments (for example, at Entremont in Bouches-du-Rhône). The Irish had the same custom [1]; a battle was a " head-harvest " (*árcenn*). The Annals of the Four Masters relate that Aed Finnliath, King of Ireland, having defeated the Danes in 864, caused the heads of the slain to be piled in a heap. When the famous Bishop-King Cormac was killed in 908, somebody cut off his head and presented it to the victorious King Flann Sina, who, as a matter of fact, restored it with honour to Cormac's party. This collecting of trophies might be an obligatory ritual matter connected with the period when a youth arrived at man's age and left his school of military training. When a young Ulsterman went to war for the first time, he had to cross the border into Connacht and try to kill a man there. This was what the hero Cuchulainn did.[2]

We find an exact parallel to this custom in one which is quite general all over the Austro-Asiatic world, from Assam to Papuasia. Among the Dyaks of Borneo, for instance, head-hunting is the consecration of the initiation of the young men, who are grouped in classes according to age like *hetairiai* of *epheboi* and live in the Men's House. They go off hunting, and when they have brought back their trophies they have proved their worth and can enter on the life of grown men and marry, just as Cuchulainn, having proved his worth, could marry Emer.

2. *Blood-covenant*

Another institution which survived among the Celts was the blood-covenant. Giraldus Cambrensis says that the Irish sealed their leagues by a rite of this kind, each party drinking some drops of blood of the other. In spite of assertions to the contrary, that this custom really existed is attested by other documents. St. Cairnech, having succeeded in bringing the Hy Neill and the Cian Nachta to form an alliance, caused blood of the two tribes to be mixed in a vessel, that the treaty might be written with it and so be inviolable.[3] Similar incidents are told of the Scottish islesmen, but we have no evidence about the Gauls.

[1] Joyce, op. cit., i, p. 150. Cf. Hull, **CCLXII**, 75.
[2] Joyce, i, p. 99. Cf. *Coir Anmann*, in **CCXCV**, iii, p. 405.
[3] Giraldus Cambrensis, *De Conquestu*, iii, xxii. Cf. *Silva Gadelica*, 413 ; *R.C.*, xiii, 73 ; Joyce, **CCLXVI**, ii, 463 ; Martin, **CCLXXI**, p. 109.

Now, the blood-covenant is a well-known institution. It was one of the first things to be studied and interpreted by science dealing with the materials furnished by ethnography. Robertson Smith [1] was calling attention to it fifty years ago. The object is, however small the quantity of blood used, to make the same blood run in the veins of the parties concerned and so to create or confirm kinship between them. In Ireland the rite serves to confirm a contract, making it more solemn and giving it a mystical sense. But it is a relic of an earlier condition, the segmentary condition of society, in which there was no express contract and legal relationships were not distinguishable from those of kinship.

3. *Potlatch.*

A third system of facts and rites preserved in Celtic institutions was what we call the system of the gift. It belongs to an order of facts to which attention has only recently been drawn, by M. Mauss [2] in *Mémoires de l'Année sociologique* and in a certain number of articles. These are designated by the name of *potlatch.*

In the Romances of the Round Table, we find that a number of episodes begin in this way. A knight or damsel appears at Arthur's court, goes to the King, and asks for a boon, without saying what, and the King promises it and has to keep his word. What is usually requested is some adventurous or dangerous service on the part of the King or of a knight. Arthur is liberal and anxious to maintain his repute ; his table is free to all, and he heaps those about him with munificent gifts.

Similar episodes are found in Irish and Welsh literature, for example the *Tochmarc Etaine* [3] (the *Wooing of Etain*), one of the finest Irish stories. Etain is a goddess, the wife of the god Mider, and has become mortal and married King

---

[1] CCCLXXXV ; CCCLXXXVa.

[2] See Mauss, " Le Don," in **XIII**, N.S., ii ; id., " Une forme ancienne de contrats chez les Thraces," in **CXXXV**, 1921, p. 988. Cf. also Davy, in **CCCXVI**. All these practices are collected under the name of *potlatch*, taken from the Chinook vocabulary of north-western America, where these phenomena are especially developed. Cf. H. Hubert, " Le Système des prestations totales dans les littératures celtiques," in **CXL**, xliii, 1925, pp. 330–5 ; Hubert and Mauss, in **CXL**, 1926.

[3] Windisch, **CCXCV**, i, p. 127. Cf. d'Arbois, **CCL**, pp. 218 ff.

Eochaid Airem. One day Mider appears, and challenges the King to a game of chess. The King accepts. They speak of stakes ; Mider offers fifty horses, and the King offers whatever his opponent wishes. He loses, and the god asks for Etain. The King claims a revenge game, which is arranged for a year later. Mider returns punctually and, having won again, takes away his stake at the end of a month.

In the Mabinogion the story of Pwyll turns on a similar episode. Pwyll, the god of the Underworld, is about to marry the goddess Rhiannon. In the midst of the banquet, Gwawl, a god of light, stands up and asks for a boon. Pwyll grants it, and Gwawl demands Rhiannon herself. Here again a future date is fixed, but this time, after a year, Pwyll appears at his rival's wedding and demands a gift. He only asks to be allowed to fill a small bag which he has in his hand, but everything goes into it, including Gwawl, who gets a beating.[1]

The fact is that the gift implies a return. The gift is compulsory, but it places an obligation on the asker, and the whole fairy world which revolves round Arthur—knights of the Round Table, squires, ladies, even demons—is involved in an extraordinary round of gifts and services in which all vie in generosity or malice, often by arms. The tourney certainly forms part of this vast system of competition and outbidding, which we also find in the Irish stories grouped round the person of Finn and in what has been called the Leinster or Ossianic Cycle.[2]

But, if the boon depends on the person of whom it is asked, it cannot be just anything ; it must be proportionate to his condition, and a little above it. The donor is challenged to be generous or to be able to be so, and he takes up the challenge. A third feature to note is the sanction of obligations which are granted ; a man who does not fulfil his undertaking loses countenance and falls in rank. Rhiannon says as much to Pwyll when he hesitates to keep his promise. The injured or disappointed party has a hold on the other, on his liberty and his life.

For these subjects of romances and myths there were actual practices, of which something survived in all Celtic

---

[1] Loth, **CCLXX**, i, pp. 26–63.
[2] Cf. below, ch. v.

countries. In Ireland homage is expressed by an exchange of gifts between superior and inferior.[1] The superior chief gives a present called *tuarastal*, to accept which is a sign of allegiance, and the inferior chief gives a present of cattle. Moreover, there is usually some outbidding in the exchange of gifts which constitutes these ties in Gaul, Britain, and Ireland. The whole of Ireland is involved in an unending cycle of obligatory loans and borrowings of cattle at a high rate of interest, which affect the condition of individuals in causing their social position to change.

These practises are explained if they are taken in connection with the state of society in which they first arose. Societies on a clan basis are divided into opposing groups which are, however, united because they exchange wives. This division is as fundamental as the law of exogamy. Often the clans are distributed in two groups, doubtless the two old original clans, which are usually called phratries. The phratries, already united one with the other by the constant exchange of gifts constituted by each supplying the other with wives, are still further united by many other means, but always in the form of gifts, service, both in secular, daily life and in mystical, social, and religious life. In this system of exchanges, the presenting of objects develops, but without prejudice to the furnishing of services. The ceremonial exchange of gifts is so important in these societies that it comes to be performed for its own sake, and by itself to give occasion for feasting, outbidding, challenge, ostentation, and competition on the part of individuals and of groups. We must picture these societies as coming together in winter and concentrating their liturgy on that period, spending a large part of the bad season in the exchange of ostentatious entertainments, prepared beforehand, and in a series of operations as speculative as those of a stock exchange, in which gains and losses are paid in social advantages—consideration, rank, the possession of heraldic insignia.

Of this institution of potlatch we find indisputable traces in two Celtic tales, one Irish and the other Welsh. The *Feast of Briccriu* relates how that individual invited King Conchobar and his people to a feast (*fled*).[2] The feast was

---

[1] Cf. Joyce, **CCCCXXXIV**.

[2] D'Arbois, **CCXLVIII**, v, pp. 80–147 ; Windisch, op. cit., i, pp. 235–311.

passed in competitions, mingled with challenges, for the place of honour and the " hero's share " among the heroes and their wives. At the end, the place of honour fell to Cuchulainn and the men of Emain Macha. In the Mabinogion we have the story of Kulhwch and Olwen, the daughter of the giant Yspaddaden. Kulhwch learns that his foredestined bride is Olwen. He goes to Arthur's court and asks for a boon, which is granted, namely assistance in making his suit. Accompanied by the comrades of Arthur, Kulhwch goes to Yspaddaden, who states his terms : a certain number of things must be brought to him for the bride-feast. The things are brought, and Kulhwch kills Yspaddaden and marries Olwen.[1]

So it is evident that our sources, the literature and law of the Celts, even though they were compiled very late, contain distinct and quite authentic traces of the law and institutions of a state of society far earlier than the Celtic societies themselves. There is, therefore, no reason for doubting the quality and authority of the Welsh and Irish sources, and we can use them to make up a picture, composite no doubt, but fairly accurate, of the social system of the Celts.

[1] Loth, op. cit., i, pp. 175–283.

CHAPTER II

The Structure of Society. Legal and Political Institutions

I

THE SEGMENTARY CHARACTER OF CELTIC SOCIETY AND THE POLITICO-DOMESTIC CHARACTER OF ITS INSTITUTIONS

IN a Celtic society, the state usually remains rudimentary and almost undifferentiated. The King was never more than the direct head of a small unit, with definite powers, limited and personal, over the other elements in his kingdom. When the kings disappeared in Gaul, their place was taken by aristocratic bodies of magistrates which did not constitute republics.

The cells of the Celtic societies are of the politico-domestic order ; their political functions are of the same nature as those of the family. There is no state to interfere in their administration or in their dealings with one another ; there is no public ministry to punish offences.[1] The Celtic societies are at the tribal stage, and have only a private law. Disputes can lead only to arbitration. It is for the injured party to compel the injurer to accept arbitration. Wrongs can be corrected only by private vengeance or compensation. Celtic law is based on arbitration, compensation, and seizure. The system of compensation was to a great extent codified and developed by the establishment of a scale of fines, fixed and co-ordinated according to the quality of the person entitled to damages and the nature of the offence. This scale of compensation-fines as it were stereotyped the inequalities of Celtic society.[2]

Inequalities were introduced from above by the action of the chiefs and the families of chiefs, who embodied all the public power of which these societies were capable. Other

---

[1] Cf. Sophie Bryant, *Liberty, Order, and Law under Native Irish Rule : a study in the Book of the Ancient Laws of Ireland.* London, 1923.
[2] D'Arbois, **CCXLVIII**, viii, ch. i, pp. 1 ff. ; Joyce **CCCCXXXIV**.

inequalities came from below, partly as a result of the round game of private vengeance and the ruinous rates of compensation. So a class of men outside the law grew up. Outlaws established themselves somewhere in the service and under the protection of wealthy and powerful chiefs. Debtors were dependent on their creditors. In the institutions of the Celtic world there were internal causes of evolution which led it, after creating aristocracies, to create plebeian classes which tended to become democracies.

II

THE DIVISIONS OF SOCIETY

1. *The Tribe*

In a Celtic society, the tribe is the group of cells which constitutes the first self-sufficing social unit. For neither clans nor families are self-sufficing ; one clan needs another to supply it with wives and do other indispensable services, and the same is true of the family. In Ireland, the unit is called *tuath*, plural *tuatha*.[1] Its equivalent existed in Gaul ; this is attested by the name of the god Teutates, who is probably the *genius* of the *tuath* ; by the word *toutio* in an inscription from Briona, apparently meaning " citizen " ; and by the word *toutiorix*, apparently meaning " king of the *tuath* ". The word also exists in Oscan and Umbrian, and evidently belongs to the Western Indo-European vocabulary.[2]

The members of the *tuath* are putatively kinsmen, united, fed on the same milk, living on the same soil. They are descended from the same ancestor, and that descent is indicated by the name, which is a gentile, collective, or composite name, indicating the ancestry. If the ancestor, as is more frequently the case, is a historical personage, the history to which he belongs borders on legend.

Mr. MacNeill[3] disagrees with this conception of the *tuath*. He holds that all we have is an onomastic method,

---

[1] Joyce, op. cit., i, p. 39. Cf. Czarnowski, **CCCCXXIII**.
[2] Czarnowski, op. cit., p. 231, n. 1.
[3] MacNeill, **CCCCXLI**, pp. 350, 353. Cf. ibid., pp. 293, 297.

designating by the name of the ruling family a whole territory and the people living on it.   He shows that, for example, the Ui Maine comprised people of different race and unequal condition, grouped under the rule of kings descended from Maine Mor.   But he fails to see that If, even in the case of a highly developed *tuath* like the Ui Maine, territories with the groups of men on them are still designated by gentile names, it is because they have in theory been populated by groups of kinsmen which were once true tribes.

The equivalent of the *tuath* in Gaul is probably the *pagus* of the *Commentaries* and Roman Gaul.   The Greek writers call these *pagi* φῦλα or φυλαί, in contrast to the *civitates*, which they call ἔθνη.   The *pagi* are still managing their own affairs under the Roman Empire.   In independent Gaul, the citizens may pursue the policy of the *civitas*, but they remain grouped by *pagi*.   The army of the Helvetii marches in *pagi*, like the army of Queen Medb in Ireland.[1]   The corresponding unit in Wales is called *cantref*, that is the hundred *trefs* or units of agriculture and economic activity in general. The notion of a tribe, in the sociological sense, implies a limitation ; the members of the tribe must not be too many, nor its territory too large, for them to be able to live together to some extent and to meet periodically.   The Welsh word *cantref* likewise implies a limitation on the territory and the proximity of other *cantrefs*.   Irish seems to have, in addition to *tuath*, an equivalent to *cantref*, namely *tricha ced*, thirty hundreds, thirty groups of a hundred hearths.[2]

In general, we may reasonably suppose that the settlement of a population in a district and its accumulation must have tightened up the rather loose organization of the tribe and favoured the territorial aspects of the term at the expense of the aspect of kinship.

2.   *The Clan*

By some chance, ethnographers and sociologists have taken from the Celtic vocabulary the word *clan* ; it is a Goidelic word which does not designate a type of unit of a definable shape or size.   It means " descendant "

[1] Czarnowski, op. cit., p. 232, nn. 3–4.
[2] Ibid., p. 232.

or " descent ".   In the plural, for instance, in Irish, *clanna Morna* means the descendants of Morann, but the *clanna Morna* may equally well constitute what sociologists would call a tribe, a family, or perhaps a clan. So, too, in Welsh, the equivalent word *cenedl* means a nation, tribe, or family.

Now, it so happens that the clan, in the sense in which the word is used by modern sociology,[1] does not exist—or does so no longer—as an institution in Celtic countries. A somewhat vague term taken from the Celtic vocabulary has been used to designate an institution which had already almost entirely vanished in the Celtic civilizations. The result is that there has been some confusion in the accounts of the societies which we are considering.[2]

So the clan, in the Celtic sense of the word, is something very different from the normal clan, and in particular the totemic clan. A fair number of Irish *tuatha* were formed round historical families which were collateral branches of royal lines. This is the case with the whole series of the Ui Neill, where one family, perpetuated and growing greater, formed the nucleus of the tribe. The Celtic clans are families, or tribes regarded as families or from the point of view of families, and therefore not at all the same thing as the totemic clan.

Nevertheless, certain facts seem to suggest that it was not always so. The *tuath* or tribe of Erainn comprised twenty-four *forslointe* or denominations, grouped in pairs in twelve *aicme* or stocks.[3] The Soghan tribe, in the territory of the Ui Maine, comprised six clans.[4] There must, therefore, have been clans within the tribe, but it must be admitted that in Celtic society no clan-law survives outside tribal law and family law.

Yet there are some relics of the totemic clan in Celtic institutions.   M. Salomon Reinach[5] has endeavoured to trace remains of early totemism in the food-taboos and animal worships still in force among the Celts. Thus a Connacht tribe, Clanna Coneely, might not eat seals (*coneely*

---

[1] See Davy and Moret, **CCCLX**.
[2] As in Vinogradoff's, **CCCXC**.
[3] Windisch, **CCXCVI**, p. 832, n. 3.
[4] O'Donovan, *Hy Many*, p. 70. Cf. Czarnowski, op. cit., p. 248 ; Joyce, **CCCCXXXIV**, i, p. 167.
[5] In his article on survivals of totemism among the Celts, in **CXL**, xxi, repr. in **CCCLXXIV**, i.

meaning " seal "), and it was said that the forbears of the tribe had been turned into seals.[1]

But, above all, there survived in the Celtic societies (and this argument is far more important) remnants of the normal organization of the clan. In the history of Munster two royal houses appear, Clanna Deirgthene and Clanna Dairenne, which hold the power generation about, intermarry, and put their children out to board with each other. These two lines stand in the relation of two exogamous clans belonging to different phratries, especially if we suppose that descent went by the distaff side.[2] This method of reckoning descent, moreover, presented a difficult problem in regard to the education of the children and their preparation for initiation. For the child belonged to his mother's clan, but she lived in the clan of his father ; he was sent to his mother's clan, at least for some considerable time. The children of a clan were also often placed together under qualified persons in a large house, the Men's House. This institution had another object too : to keep these growing youths under supervision and away from women whom they should not marry.

This institution, which is usually called by the Anglo-Norman name of " fosterage ", was kept up in Celtic countries. We find children entrusted to foster-parents, with whom they form real bonds of kinship, as is shown by the fact that some individuals mention their foster-father in declaring their descent, and that mutual legal obligations, comparable to those of kinship, bind the foster-father to his ward. In Ireland the institution is called *altram*.[3] It takes different forms, according to the choice of the *aite* or foster-father. Men were selected for this trust from the members of the mother's family, or else from the intellectual classes, Druids or *fili*.[4] There are many instances of children brought up by the mother's family. King Muirchertach mac Erca spent his childhood in Scotland with his maternal grandfather, and I have already spoken of the two royal families of Munster. There are still more examples of children educated by Druids or *fili*—Cuchulainn, and the two daughters of King Loegaire

[1] Joyce, op. cit., ii, p. 129. Cf. Conrady, CCCCXXI.
[2] Czarnowski, op. cit., p. 255.
[3] D'Arbois, CCXLVIII (Droit), i, pp. 112, 187 ; ii, p. 36. Cf. Czarnowski, op. cit., p. 257 ; Maine, CCCLIII, p. 242.
[4] Joyce, op. cit., ii, p. 18.

who were converted by St. Patrick. In this case the institution tended to take on the form of a school; the Druid Cathbad teaches a hundred pupils besides Cuchulainn. Conn of the Hundred Fights, King of Ireland, has a guard of fifty foster-brothers, who are evidently the companions of his childhood and school-days. So, too, Cæsar and Pomponius Mela remark on the way young men flock round the Druids. Now, the Druidical priesthood, whose civilizing and educative influence was so great, was, as we shall see presently, a clan or group of clans transformed into a secret society.[1]

It can, therefore, be proved that Celtic institutions contained many relics of organization in clans. The mentality which has elsewhere manifested itself in totemism still survived among the Celts; it contributed to giving to the tribe on the one hand and to the family on the other features so like those of the old clans as to be hard to distinguish from them, and it gave them that love of emblems, colours, and heraldic devices for which the Celtic clans have always been conspicuous.

3. *The Family*

A family is a group of men having certain forbears, known or remembered, but usually fairly recent, from whom they are descended direct. In Irish the family is called *fine*. The proper name Venicarius shows that a corresponding word existed in Gaulish. It was replaced in Welsh by *teulu*, which properly means "the occupants of the house" (*ty* "house"; *llu* "guest"). The word belongs to the Western Indo-European group; in Germanic *Wini* means "friend". In Ireland *fine* designates both the big family of several households and the small family or household; it contains the idea of legal solidarity which constitutes the essence of these kinship-groups. This family, while presenting the general characteristics of the agnatic, undivided family and the patriarchal Indo-European family, also presents in some points interesting relics of the uterine family.[2]

---

[1] Cf. below, ch. iii.
[2] See d'Arbois, op. cit. (Droit), i, p. 185; Joyce, op. cit., i.

4. *Marriage and Descent*

The ancient writers went to the Gauls for heroes embodying the virtues, particularly in respect of the family and marriage.[1] They have left us a fine conception of marital fidelity and dignity among the Gauls. But the passages in which they speak of the island Celts and their matrimonial ways give a very different picture. The literature of Ireland and Wales leaves one with rather mixed impressions. There is a magnificent song of love and married faithfulness in the Irish *Exile of the Sons of Usnach*.[2] But on the whole sexual morals seem to have been fairly lax. The true explanation, as we shall see, lies in the survival of old institutions which had lost their meaning and often conflicted one with another.

Strabo[3] tells us that the Irish boasted of their licence and that they recognized neither mothers nor sisters, and for Northern Europe Strabo copies Pytheas, whose information often comes from good sources. But Pytheas may very well have heard some story related like that of Conchobar and his sister Dechtiré, or that of Clothru.[4] Clothru, who was the sister of Medb, Queen of Connacht, had three brothers, who fought their father for the kingship of Ireland, and before the battle she bore to the three of them a son, whom she married.[5]

Cæsar[6] gives us more detailed information. According to his account, among the Celts of Britain one wife was owned by ten or twelve men, the husbands being each other's brothers, fathers, and sons and the children belonging to a nominal father who had contracted the marriage and taken the woman into his house. One might at first sight suppose that we have here a group of clan kinsmen, sharing wives as the women share husbands. But probably it is really a form of polyandry suited to a fairly large group, living together in one large house, not deriving enough from its common

[1] Ibid., i, pp. 219–229. Cf. A. Bayet, *La Morale des Gaulois*, Paris, 1930.
[2] D'Arbois, op. cit., i, pp. 217–319.
[3] Strabo, iv, 5, 4. Cf. Jerome, *Adv. Jovinian.*, ii, 7 ; Dion. Cass., lxii, 6, 3 ; lxxvi, 12, 2.
[4] These events are placed nearer our own time by the Irish annalists. Really they go back to a very ancient foundation.
[5] CCL, English pp. 206, 212. Cf. Vendryès, in *IFA.*, 21st June, 1923.
[6] Cæs., *Gall. War*, v, 14.

labour to support many wives and perhaps not needing female labour because it does little agriculture. Similar phenomena are reported in Northern India and among the Southern Slavs. Cæsar's description, which is quite credible, does not reveal the survival of a very ancient phase of marriage, but a rather peculiar manner of applying the rules of the Celtic family.

But the epics, history, and law of the Celts contain memories or important remnants of the uterine family.

The descent of heroes like Cuchulainn and Conchobar is indicated by their mother's name. Moreover, they were of irregular birth, and Irish law assigned children born out of wedlock to the mother's family. When, too, the husband was a foreigner, having no family in Ireland, the small family which he founded was attached to that of his wife, being called the " blue family ", *glasfine*, because the man was supposed to have come over the sea.[1] In that case the " marriage " was said to be " of the man " and the " property " " of the woman ". We have instances of succession in the female line and even of matriarchy in the legendary ruling houses of Ireland [2] and the historical ruling houses of Britain.[3] Celtic law implied that women had some political competence. Plutarch, in his essay *On the Virtues of Women*, describes them smoothing over quarrels, taking part in the discussions of assemblies, and being appointed arbiters by a treaty between Hannibal and the Volcæ.[4] Strabo, following Poseidonios, says that the Armorican priestesses were very independent of their husbands.[5]

It has been observed that the Celtic women wore trousers. Those of Gaul certainly did, witness a statue in the British Museum.[6] The Gallic women accompanied their husbands in war, and those of Ireland had military duties proportionate to their rights to landed property. They were only relieved of them by Christianity, and stage by stage. One stage was the purchase of exemption from service by giving up half

---

[1] D'Arbois, op. cit. (Droit), i, 187.
[2] Ibid., i, 237.
[3] Joyce, op. cit., i, 41, cites the instance of Macha Mongruad, the legendary foundress of Emain.
[4] Plut., *De Mul. Virtut.*, 24, 66.
[5] Strabo, iv, 4, 6.
[6] A. J. Reinach, in CVII, xviii.

one's property to the family.[1] This was one episode in the process of depriving woman of her powers which everywhere accompanied her loss of the privilege of conveying descent.

Apart from these exceptional cases and relics of the past, the normal Celtic family was an almost entirely agnatic family. The woman was the instrument of natural parentage but not of legal parentage. The son of a daughter did not belong to his grandfather's line save in one single case: a man without male issue might give his daughter in marriage, reserving to himself any child which should be born, and that child became legally, not his grandson, but his son.[2]

This family was gathered round a hearth, which was the centre of its worship and never ceased to hold a central place in the representation of its essence and unity. It worshipped its dead and its ancestors, like the Latin family, but no trace of that worship survives. The father of the family was master in his own house, master of the house and of his folk.[3] Cæsar and the jurist Gaius [4] observed that *patria potestas* of the Roman kind was exercised in Gaul. The father had, according to Cæsar, the right of life and death over his children. The laws of Ireland and Wales bear witness to the same powers. They differ on the age of emancipation. In Ireland, *patria potestas* could be terminated only by the death or incapacity of the father. In Northern Welsh law emancipation came at the age of military service, namely fourteen. But we should note that in this case the youth escaped from the tutelage of his father only to enter into dependence on the chief to whom he had been presented.[5]

According to Cæsar the Gaul had the same power over his wife as over his children. In the noble families, on the death of the paterfamilias, the women fell into the power of his relations, who could, if the death was suspicious, have them tortured or slain.[6] It could be a method of settling the inheritance of the childless widow. But in fact the situation was not so simple. Married women might have property; accounts had to be rendered to them. Cæsar himself in the

[1] Joyce, op. cit., ii, N.
[2] Czarnowski, op. cit., p. 239.
[3] **CCXLVI**, vii, pp. 244–7. Cf. Havet, " Les Institutions et le droit spéciaux aux Italo-Celtes," in **CXL**, xxviii, pp. 113 ff.
[4] Cæs., *Gall. War*, vi, 19 ; Gaius, *Instit. Comm.* i, 51–2, 55.
[5] D'Arbois, op. cit., i, pp. 242, 245, 247.
[6] Cæs., vi, 19.

same passage indicates that the wife was far from being completely in the *manus* of her husband. She brought a dowry, in the form of property, *pecunia* ; the amount of it was reckoned and the husband doubled it, and this constituted a stock ; accounts of it were kept and the *fructus*, the profits, were retained. The survivor became the owner of both halves and of the sum total of previous profits. Whatever may have been the nature of the property to which Cæsar here refers, the passage proves that it was possible for these common goods to be managed jointly or in some other equitable fashion.[1]

Now this account agrees with the Irish and Welsh laws, in which we again find the dowry and the wife's jointure. The woman whose marriage is the occasion of these patrimonial arrangements is of the same rank as her husband.[2] On general principle, a woman is incapable, under Irish law, of making a contract without her husband's consent, except where their properties are exactly equal. The *Táin* begins with a long discussion between Queen Medb and her husband Ailill about the amount of their wealth and therefore of their rights.[3] The Celtic family, then, included the position of matron, *cet muinter*, the chief woman of the family. Her position was, however, more independent than that of the matron who had married again. In this respect the Celtic family is at an earlier stage in the development of the paternal family than the Roman.

The Celtic societies were evidently moving towards monogamy, but polygamy was allowed.[4] Normally there was only one matron in a family, but there were other women, slaves or wives. The marriage of the matron involved purchase, but the rites of purchase were simpler for women of lower condition. Concubines (in Irish *ben urnadma*) were bought at the great annual fairs for the term of a year. By this time-limit the woman was saved from coming under the *manus* of the man. But in practice this marriage often lasted more than one year.[5]

[1] Cf. Jullian, **CCCXLVII**, ii, p. 407.
[2] D'Arbois, op. cit. (Droit), i, p. 231 ; Joyce, ii, p. 8.
[3] Ibid., i, p. 229.
[4] D'Arbois, op. cit. (Droit), i, p. 216. Cf. Stokes, **CCLXXXVIII**, pp. 52–6 ; **CCLXIX**, pp. 35–6 ; Joyce, ii, 7.
[5] D'Arbois, op. cit. (Droit), i, p. 227 ; **CCXLVI**, ii, p. 380, 390.

As in Rome, the purely civil forms of marriage had superseded the ancient religious forms among the Celts. Giraldus Cambrensis declares that a similar kind of marriage was in force among the Welsh, where the purchase was no more than a lease, and it was really a trial marriage, since it did not become permanent until children were born.[1] This type of marriage was practised in the families of Scottish chiefs down to the end of the Middle Ages. Divorce was allowed even by mutual consent, and Canon Law itself had to accept it. In Ireland, under the ancient law, a woman leaving her husband kept even the products of her domestic labour.[2]

For the children, *altram* made up for the weakness of the marriage tie. The mother's rank did not affect that of the children; the consequences of descent by the father were absolute.

5. *Extension of the Family*

Among the Celts, the family is a large family, tracing kinship fairly far back in the ancestral line and forming a considerable group of agnates. This is true of Ireland, Wales, and Gaul. The Irish family, in particular, comprises four groups of relations named *gelfine*, the family of the hand (*geil*), *derbfine*, the certain family, *iarfine*, the distant family, and *indfine*, the final family.[3] The *gelfine* includes the man himself with his father, son, grandson, great-grandson, and great-great-grandson. The *derbfine* adds the grandfather in the direct line and, in the collateral line, the uncle, first cousin, and first cousin's son. The *iarfine* takes in, in the direct line, the great-grandfather and, in the collateral line, the great-uncle and two degrees of cousinship, namely his sons and grandsons. The *indfine* includes, in the direct line, the great-great-grandfather and, in the collateral, the great-great-uncle and two degrees of cousinship, namely his sons and grandsons. All these kinsmen are agnates, but of these concentric circles of kinship only the *gelfine* and *derbfine* constitute the family in the strict sense.[4]

[1] Girald. Cambr., *Descriptio Kambriæ*, ii, 6. Cf. Vinogradoff, CCCXC, i, p. 246.
[2] D'Arbois, op. cit.. (Droit), i, p. 228.
[3] Ibid., i, pp. 185 ff.
[4] Ibid. (Droit), i, 188. Cf. Maine, CCCLII, p. 216; Vinogradoff, op. cit., i, p. 305.

In the Gaelic clans of Scotland kinship is still wider, being traced further up in the ancestral line and down into the collateral branches.[1] It is extremely probable that the Gaulish family was organized in some similar fashion.

The family tie is expressed or revealed in the sense which all members of the family have that they are one and have certain rights and duties in respect of each other.[2] The whole family is responsible for the crimes committed by one member, and shares according to the positions of its members in the payment of fines.[3] But the tie is strongest within the *derbfine*. Murder is forbidden inside that smaller family ; the murderer in such a case loses the advantages of kinship while remaining subject to some of its burdens. In fact, the *gelfine* and *derbfine* constitute the normal family.[4]

6. *Inheritance*

The manner in which the succession was conferred and property was inherited is explained by this organization of the family. This is true, in particular, in the case of something which could not be divided—the kingship. As a rule, a king was not succeeded by his son. The reason is that the son was not designated by the system of descent of the *derbfine* to be his heir. He may have been his natural next-of-kin, but not his civil next-of-kin. That civil next-of-kin was his younger brother or some representative of his own or an earlier generation in the *derbfine*. Moreover, while the kingship was hereditary, the heir was chosen from among a number of kinsmen presumed equal, comprising the living agnates of the late king, that is, his uncles and cousins.[5] Irish history contains many tragedies which show how the royal families tried to evade these rules.

To secure a regular succession, pains were taken in Ireland to name the heir beforehand—from among the agnates, of course. He was called the *tanaiste* or tanist—a title difficult to explain—and acted as lieutenant to his predecessor. There were tanists for every degree of royalty, from the

[1] Meitzen, **CCCLIII**, p. 205.
[2] D'Arbois, op. cit. (Droit), i, p. 181. Cf. *Domesday Book*, i, 179.
[3] D'Arbois, ibid., p. 66.
[4] Ibid., p. 67. Cf. *Senchus Mor*, i, 182, 260 ; **CCXLVII**, iv, p. 284.
[5] See, e.g., the order of succession in the royal family of Eochaid between 398 and 533. Cf. MacNeill, **CCCCXLI**, pp. 230, 294.

chieftainship of a tribe to the High Kingship, and even in certain noble families ; in short, wherever a succession was indivisible. This system is called tanistry.[1]

Divisible goods were apportioned so as to take the agnates into account on a system designated by the English word *gavelkind*[2] ; they were divided into gavels, or portions, which were based on a count of the heirs by heads (*per capita*) or by lines (*per stirpes*). The right to make a will existed in Celtic law ; but it seems to have been brought in chiefly by Christianity and under the influence of Roman law.[3] In this respect the power of the Irish or Welsh father seems to be far less than that of the Roman paterfamilias. He only enjoys the usufruct of the family property ; he must render account of the latter to the family and in theory he cannot dispose of it. But this last right he gradually obtained.

The head of a family makes a line of nobles.[4] The head of the Irish *fine* is a noble ; it is not so certain that the head of a Welsh family is. The head of the *fine* has political, judicial, and military functions ; he represents the family, speaks for it, leads it in war. In Gaul the head of a family, to judge from the Æduan Dumnorix, seems to have had the guardianship of such women of the family as were not in the power of husbands.[5] But in Ireland and Wales he was chosen from among all eligible members of the family, his wealth, popularity, and strength being taken into account. Perhaps he suffered by the lack of that mystical predestination which a stricter succession would have given him.

To sum up, the Celtic family is in essence a fairly undivided group of agnates, much more clearly defined as such than the Roman group of agnates, since in it the succession devolves on the agnates and not on the sons, and, apart from the constitution of property, the agnates are ranked in it by generation and age-class. This explains, but does not justify, the confusion sometimes made between the Celtic clan and the totemic clan.

But this family was evolving, and natural kinship was

---

[1] Maine, op. cit., 201. Cf. Spencer, **CCCCLVIII**.
[2] Mackay, " Notes on the Custom of Gavelkind in Kent, Ireland, Wales, and Scotland," in **CXXIV**, xxxii, 1898, pp. 133 ff. Cf. **CCXLVII**, iv, pp. 284–295 ; i, p. 250 ; iii, p. 331.
[3] Vinogradoff, op. cit., i, 289.
[4] **CCXLVII**, iv, pp. 346, 348. Cf. Czarnowski, p. 246.
[5] Jullian, **CCCXLVII**, ii, 407. Cf. Cæs., i, 18, 6, 7.

becoming more important.   Even in the case of the royal families of Ireland, we see kings working for the future of their sons or grandsons, and gradually becoming more successful, and more frequently so, in securing for them the direct succession to the crown.[1]   The same change was taking place in Gaul, where, for example, Comm of the Atrebates was succeeded by his own sons.[2]

7.   Floating Elements

There is no society without floating elements.   By the side of the Celts there were native populations—few in Gaul outside Aquitania and the Provençal coast, very few in Wales, regarding which our texts are very precise on the conquest of the Cymry in the sixth century, and not many in Ireland.   There were slaves, also few, for the Gauls did not take many prisoners.   Above all, there were the outcasts, men who had left their family, and then their tribe, after committing a crime, or to avoid responsibility for a debt, or for some other reason.   Cæsar indicates that they were numerous in Gaul, and they played an important part in Ireland.[3]   Lastly, there were the intellectual men—Druids, poets, bards.

Some of these elements, slaves and freedmen, had become absorbed in the organization of the families, which, besides, could legally adopt members.[4]   Some of them had succeeded in forming families of the same type as the Irish or Welsh families, and enjoyed a legal status after passing a certain stage.   Some constituted tribes living in dependence on free tribes.   But most gathered round the chiefs and nobles ; these *hetairiai*, these bodies of companions, impressed the first Greek writers who came into contact with the Gauls.[5] The Gallic chief was surrounded by shield-bearers and spear-bearers, and Cæsar speaks of the devotion of the *soldurii*.   The chiefs with whom he had dealings had hosts

---

[1] MacNeill, op. cit., pp. 114, 238, 290.
[2] D'Arbois, op. cit. (Droit), i, 97.
[3] Maine, op. cit., p. 173.
[4] Joyce, CCCCXXXIV, i, 166.   Cf. Maine, op. cit., p. 231 ; and, for emancipation, Cæs., v, 45.
[5] Polyb., ii, xviii ; Diod., v, 29, 2.   Cf. d'Arbois, op. cit., p. 62.

of dependents, forming small armies.[1] So, too, in Ireland
the nobles were surrounded by dependents.[2]

All these floating elements had their place in the plebs of
which Cæsar speaks in connection with the Celtic societies.
He distinguishes between three orders—Druids, *equites*, and
plebs—but in that plebs he confuses the free families (except
their chiefs and the families founded by them) with another
stratum of families. This second stratum had formed in
consequence of an evolution which took place through
contact with the soil.

III

THE LAND AND OWNERSHIP

The Celts had always been very mobile, and therefore
not very strongly rooted in the places where they stopped.[3]
But the soil had its place in their social conceptions. I have
already pointed out a word common to the Italo-Celtic
languages, represented by Latin *tribus*, Welsh *tref* " portion
of the tribe ", and Irish *treb* " house ". This word stands in
essence for a group of men who clear and work a certain
tract of ground, and also designates the ground which they
occupy. In Old Slavonic, *trèbiti* means " he clears "
(ground). The tribe lives in a clearing and is surrounded
by a line of boundary-marks. At an early date the Celts on
the whole, and particularly in Britain and Ireland, were at
pains to mark their frontiers by ditches, hedges, and walls.[4]
In Gaul the frontier was marked by custom-posts, watch-
houses, and boundary-lines.[5] The Roman government
took over these limits, which continued to bound bishoprics
and bailiwicks until recent times.

We can now see how the elements of which the tribe was
composed, namely the families, established themselves on
the land, how the soil was appropriated by men, as

---

[1] Fustel de Coulanges, **CCCXXXIV**, pp. 27, 195 ; Cæs., vi, 15 ; cf. Cæs.,
vii, 40 ; iii, 22 ; i, 18 ; Diod., v, 29.

[2] Maine, op. cit., p. 273.

[3] See the account of the migration of the Helvetii in Cæsar.

[4] Joyce, op. cit., ii, p. 266. Cf. MacNeill, op. cit., p. 131 ; **CXL**, xxxvii,
p. 367.

[5] **I**, xiii, 6127. Cf. Jullian, op. cit., ii, p. 53, n. 2.

individuals or in families.   There was a long controversy once between Fustel de Coulanges and d'Arbois de Jubainville,[1] who, interpreting Cæsar's remarks and working down to the Middle Ages, discussed whether there was individual appropriation or collective ownership.   The fact is that both types existed, as they do to-day.   It is also true that the land was divided into the estates of large families, which were afterwards grabbed by individual chiefs of those families.   Among the island Celts and in Gaul before Cæsar's time most property was collective.   An Irish law-treatise declares that the observance of common rules in agriculture is one of the fundamental institutions of Ireland.[2]   It is also plain from the laws of Ireland and Wales that ploughing with the large eight-ox plough required the co-operation of several persons interested.[3]   But as a rule among the Celts the village is not the effective owner of the land on which it stands.

In Ireland it is the tribe which has the eminent ownership of the land.   It was only later, it seems, that the country became covered with hedges.   We can imagine a tribe of stock-raisers, on finding itself in possession of a vast territory, grouping the flocks and herds of its families, and the families installing themselves as they pleased on ground which no other claimed.   That is how the ancient writers depict the Gauls of Italy, and all the Celts must have been the same at first.[4]

But this condition of undivided property implies an unlimited extent of available ground and an almost entirely pastoral life Now, the Celts were great husbandmen.   After saying that the Cisalpine Gauls lived solely on meat, Polybios [5] describes a country abounding in corn, which

---

[1] D'Arbois, op. cit. (Propr.), p. 104.
[2] Maine, op. cit., p. 101.
[3] Cf. Dottin, **CCCXXII**, p. 185.
[4] Polyb., ii, 17. Cf. d'Arbois, op. cit., pp. 61, 69, 100 ; Joyce, op. cit., i, p. 184 ; Lloyd, **CCCCXXXVIII**, p. 138. See MacNiell, op. cit., p. 351 ; the annalists place the first erection of the hedges dividing estates in the reign of Aodh Sláine, about A.D. 600. A passage in the story of Cuchulainn indicates that in ancient times horsemen could ride about freely without being held up by hedges. See the text entitled *Compert Conculaind*, in Windisch, **CCXCV**, i, p. 136.
[5] See above, p. 23.

was what he had seen ; the rest was tradition. Gaul was a corn-country. The army at Alesia starved for lack of corn. Ireland must always have eaten as much barley as meat. A developed agriculture means some fixity. Besides, stock-raisers in all ages must have known that a cow needs a certain amount of fodder daily, summer and winter, and this must have led them to make the area of the ground proportionate to the number of beasts and, therefore, to distribute it. As a fact, we find the land of the Celts divided into the estates of families. Let us see what these families were like.

Family property in Irish is called *baile*.[1] It is an old word of the common Celtic, which, through Gaulish, has left a descendant in French *bailliage*. There were 30 *baile* in a tribe, and a *baile* normally corresponded to 300 cows and between 2,500 and 3,500 acres. It was divided into four quarters, which were subdivided into four households each.[2] While the *baile* tends to become an administrative unit, the quarter keeps its character as landed property. Ireland is a chess-board, on which the squares are quarters, measuring from 160 to 320 acres. They have been subdivided and amalgamated, but they are fixed.

The *Senchus Mor* tells us that the members of the *fine* have one house and one bed.[3] Strabo [4] says that the Britons lived in enclosures like round kraals, in which the cattle also were kept. The topographical accounts of Ireland show circles inside the quarters, which may have been the common dwelling of the people of the *baile* or of the quarter. Often the great families had *duns* and *raths*, fortified houses or collections of houses with a stone wall round them.[5] The roof of the house was borne on two rows of three columns (Irish *gabhal*, Welsh *gafl* " fork " or " branch "). The centre was a common hall, with the hearth. The two sides formed four divisions, which were again subdivided into four ; here the beds were. The house sheltered sixteen *ménages* ; it was a replica of the family. The Welsh, indeed, took from the house

[1] CXL, xxxix, p. 57. Cf. Joyce, op. cit., ii, p. 372.
[2] Meitzen, CCCLIII, i, p. 175.
[3] Czarnowski, CCCCXXXIII, p. 246. Cf. *Senchus Mor*, i, pp. 122, 130, 132 ; CCXLVII, iv, p. 374.
[4] Strabo, iv, 5.
[5] D'Arbois, op. cit. (Droit), ii, 71.

the various terms designating the divisions of territorial property.[1]   These family estates were the collective properties of the large family.   On the extinction of each generation, the land was redistributed.   The free Welshman seems to have had an inviolable right to a share of the tribal land in the portion of the family, and it seems that there was a legal obligation that each member of the family should receive a *trev* of land (about five acres) on reaching manhood.

This system seems to have gone on working, fairly successfully, in Wales until the fourteenth century.   The chief inconvenience was the practice of a father of a family giving part of his land to the Church on condition that it reserved the working of it for his own descendants.[2]   There was plenty of available land in the Welsh mountains ; it was not so in Ireland, where the system of dividing landed property proved less elastic, and it was the large family that altered until it was no more than a kind of territorial division of the *tuath*.[3]

The family broke up.   In some cases, to fill gaps, it had to call in strangers[4] ; or else it had to multiply shares so that they became too small.   The number of *bailes* increased. The result was much emigration and transplanting of groups, which contributed to transforming the character of the *tuath*.[5]

1.   *Causes of the Formation of a Landed Aristocracy*

The working of the institutions described above might have produced a society of equally poor persons.   But there developed in the Celtic societies an aristocracy, a plutocracy, while the freeman was reduced to the position of tenant farmer and even servile tenant.[6]   There were four reasons for this : (i) the custom of giving appanages to kings, heads of families, and tanists of the various classes[7] ; (ii) the

---

[1] Ibid. (Propr.), xxv ; Joyce, op. cit., i, pp. 39, 196 ; Meitzen, op. cit., i, p. 184 ; Vinogradoff, CCCXC, i, p. 309.
[2] Meitzen, op. cit., i, p. 196.
[3] Czarnowski, op. cit., p 248.
[4] Meitzen, op. cit., pp. 187, 202.
[5] Ibid., p. 196.
[6] *Senchus Mor*, iii, p. 52 ; cf. ii, p. 282 ; iii, p. 303 ; Czarnowski, op. cit., p. 242 ; Joyce, op. cit., i, p. 186 ; d'Arbois, op. cit. (Droit), ii, 78 (cf. ibid., p. 2) ; CCXLVII, iv, pp. 68, 159.
[7] *Senchus Mor*, in CCCXLVIII, ii, p. 280 ; cf. Czarnowski, p. 235, n. 5 ; Joyce, op. cit., i, p. 147.

grabbing of unappropriated land by chiefs ; (iii) the development of movable wealth ; (iv) the substitution of contractual relations of feudal type for the statutory relations of men within groups. The tribe's eminent right to the land was seized by individuals. In consequence, landed property ceased to be collective and became individual, but aristocratic.

1. The territory of a tribe comprised the chief's mensal land, the portions appropriated by families and divided into *bailes*, a proportion of available pasturage, and, lastly, moorland, swamps, and rocky tracts. The freemen had the limited enjoyment of part of these commons. Now, not only kings but nobles carved out private estates from the tribal territory and added them to their share of the family property. The tenants who established themselves there for a limited period were really tenants of the king and nobles.

2. Inequality in movable fortune also contributed to the creation of an aristocracy. Wealth was wealth in cattle, which the rich man grazed on the commons, which he tended to appropriate.[1] But as his stock increased he lent cattle, and his debtors became a *clientela*. You could lend *free* cattle, that is without change in the condition of the borrower, or *serf* cattle, which entailed a change in his condition. Debtors preferred serf cattle, at the cost of their freedom, for in that case the loan was economically more advantageous. So there grew up in Ireland a class of persons known as *bo-aire*, cattle-nobles.[2] At the same time the practice of compensation, with its heavy fines, in a society involved in a maze of interconnected feuds and the contracting of debts to pay blood-prices created further inequalities. The whole of society gradually became arranged in a scale of vassalage and clientship.[3] In Cæsar's time the heads of families must have had their large family among their debtors and clients, and they alone formed the knightly class of the *equites*.[4] As in Gaul, so in Wales, the head of the family

[1] Cæs., vi, 22, 3 ; 11, 4 ; i, 4, 2. Cf. Maine, p. 159 ; d'Arbois, op. cit. (Droit), i, p. 119 ; **CCXLVII**, ii, pp. 126, 206, 222 ; Joyce, op. cit., i, p. 188.
[2] Joyce, op. cit., i, p. 158.
[3] D'Arbois, op. cit. (Droit), i, p. 105. Cf. Joyce, op. cit., i, p. 157 ; Maine, **CCCLVIII**, pp. 131, 136.
[4] Cæs., vi, 15. Cf. d'Arbois, op. cit. (Propr.), p. 52 ; Jullian, **CCXLVII**, ii, p. 69.

alone fought on horseback. His kinsmen, dispossessed of their collective rights by mortgage of otherwise, usually remained on the family estate. A number of the villages of France were once the estates of Celtic nobles, the Gallo-Roman *fundi*.

So the tribal system of the Celts gradually became an aristocratic feudal system. But the aristocracy sprang from the Celts themselves.

2. *The System of Agriculture*

Irish and Welsh family properties and their subdivisions were surrounded by hedges, ditches, or earth banks. There were only the rudiments of villages where roads crossed.[1] This is still the case in Brittany and Vendée, and in varying degrees in Central France. In the north and east of France, on the other hand, we find large villages, few isolated farms, and few hedges, and the fields run down the slopes in parallel bands. This disposition comes from a past age in which the village had common land, with alternate fields which were not appropriated but merely allotted. The same arrangement of the fields is found in Ireland and Wales around the towns and large villages ; in Scotland it is called *runrig*, division into elongated fields. These towns and villages are later creations, as we have seen.

Both methods of occupation are of Celtic origin, and both correspond to a distribution of the tribal soil into family estates. But the park system corresponds to a pastoral life and the field system to an agricultural.

IV

PENAL LAW

As I said at the beginning of this chapter, the Celtic state had no magistrates, but only arbiters—originally Druids, *fili*, *prud'hommes*, or Brehons. These did not intervene unless called in by both parties, or at least one. Normally, the man who had suffered by the infraction of the law had a right to exact justice himself.[2]

[1] Meitzen, op. cit., i, p. 214. Cf. Joyce, ii, p. 264.
[2] S. Bryant, *Liberty, Order, and Law under Native Irish Rule*, London, 1923, p. 259.

The payment of compensation was at the very foundation of Celtic penal law. It was also a method of avoiding bloodshed. The amount was determined by the victim's rank, whether the crime was murder, wounding, or injustice. If he was a free man of superior class, there was added to the price of the body the price of honour, proportionate to his dignity.[1] As late as the sixteenth century, when a man was murdered in Ireland, the brehon made the murderer and the kinsfolk of the victim effect a transaction whereby, on payment of an indemnity (*eric*, meaning compensation-fine), the crime was extinguished.[2] In Gaul, in Cæsar's time, the Druids fixed the *poenas*, that is, apparently, the fine paid by the defender, if he lost the case and was solvent, or by his family in his default, if it was itself solvent. At the same time they laid down the punishment which he should receive if insolvent. The Druids also fixed what the Latins called the *prœmia*, the sum to be shared by the family of a murdered man or to be received by one wounded or treated with injustice. The fine not only repaired the damage done, but paid for the outrage on honour and enriched the injured individual or family.[3] To escape the payment of it, which fell on all members of the family, as has been said already, the guilty man or even part or the whole of the family would go into exile. We have already seen the importance of the exile in Celtic society.[4]

For the murder of a free man the body-price (Irish *dire*) was seven female slaves.[5] To this was added the price of honour (*enechlann* or *log eneich*), which was graded according to the rank of the victim. That of the king of a *tuath* in Ireland was fixed at seven female slaves, or twenty-one cows, or thirty-five horned cattle of medium value.[6] In legend this figure appears among the teachings of the famous King Cormac mac Airt. According to the *Senchus Mor* the price of the honour of the king of a province is twenty-one slave-women or sixty-three cows or a hundred and five horned cattle of medium value. Lastly, the price of the honour of the High King rises to twenty-eight slave-women or eighty-three cows or a hundred and forty horned cattle

---

[1] D'Arbois, i, pp. 76, 199.   [2] *R.C.*, ix, p. 143.
[3] D'Arbois, pp. 82 ff.   [4] Ibid., p. 83.
[5] In *Ancient Laws of Ireland*, iii, p. 70.
[6] Ibid., iv, p. 346.

of medium value.[1] Tariffs of compensation are laid down for the price of the honour of the various categories of *aire* or free men.

Similar conceptions are found in Wales, where the *gwyneb garth* or " price of the face " seems to correspond fairly exactly to the Irish *enechlann*.[2]

From the date of summons before the arbiter to the date of appearing there are forty days. When that time has passed, the pursuer can proceed to seize the immovable property after fulfilling certain formalities.

The fine is fixed by the arbiters. We shall see how this function was performed by the Druids, and by the *fili*, who were attached to the Druids as subordinates, became their rivals, and finally superseded them in their capacity of arbiters and judges.

The payment of the fine fell on the family in the strict sense, the *gelfine*, and if it could not meet it by itself, the responsibility was extended to the wider family, the *derbfine*, and so on to the *iarfine,*

By the side of the private penal law based on compensation and dispensed by arbitration, there were some rudiments of a public penal law, marked by the increasing intervention of the great assemblies, which tended to form a kind of supreme court of conciliation, and to judge offences against the state or what took the place of a state.

V

POLITICAL INSTITUTIONS

1. *The King and the Evolution of Kingship*

To designate chiefs of a certain dignity, the Celts had inherited from their Indo-European past the word *rix*, corresponding to the Latin *rex* and the *râja* of the Hindus. They had, therefore, had kings before they had been long parted from their Indo-European kinsfolk.[3] In Ireland there was a whole scale of kings, ranging from the king of

---

[1] Ibid., ii, pp. 224, 226. Cf. i, p. 230 ; iv, p. 236 ; iii, p. 42.
[2] J. Loth, *Les Mabinogion du Livre Rouge de Hergest*, Paris, 1913, i, p. 127, n. 2. Cf. d'Arbois, *Etudes sur le droit celtique* i, pp. 134–5, 153.
[3] D'Arbois, op. cit., i, p. 192.

the *tuath* to the High King of Ireland.[1] Among the Gauls of the Continent the Latin writers mention *reges* and *reguli*. These latter were doubtless the petty kings of the *pagi*, in other words of the *tuatha*, or tribes.[2]

The Irish kings [3] have all the appearance of sacred kings, endowed with mystical powers far exceeding their real political power. In the reign of Cormac mac Airt, says an Irish poem, the world was happy and pleasant ; there were nine nuts on every branch and nine branches on every bough. The king is a chief, embodying the mystical powers of the clans. A good king makes the land fruitful and is a guarantee of plenty, prosperity, and security.[4] He is in relations with the order of nature ; his movements are connected with the movement of the sun.[5] His mystical virtues are protected by taboos, *geasa*. He must not do any work, any slavish labour ; he must not rear pigs, although the domestication of that animal is one of the gifts of the heroes ; he must not till the soil, although he is the great creator of fertility.[6] His physical perfection is the guarantee of his virtues ; when Cormac mac Airt lost an eye he was deposed.[7] He answers on his head for the victories expected of him.

It was the same among the Continental Gauls. The suicide of Brennus after Delphi corresponds to that of Ailill Inbanna, King of Connacht, after his defeat.[8] Deiotarus, the soothsayer king of the Galatians, is a king of the same type.[9]

The relationship of these kings to their subjects was certainly originally conceived on the model of that of the head of a family or clan to his family or clan. In Ireland, the king appears in his capacity of father of a family when he collects a tax, called the maiden's ring, for the marriage of the girls of the tribe.[10] In Irish law the chief acts as family to those who have none.[11]

---

[1] Joyce, op. cit., i, pp. 41, 599. Cf. d'Arbois, **CCXLVIII** (Droit), i, p. 105
[2] Polyb., iii, 50 ; Jullian, **CCCXLVII**, ii, p. 39.
[3] MacNeill, **CCCCXLI**, p. 26. Cf. **CXL**, xxix, p. 5.
[4] **CXL**, xxxix, p. 21. Cf. Joyce, op. cit., i, pp. 55–6.
[5] **CXXXIV**, 1917, p. 37.
[6] Joyce, op. cit., i, p. 60 ; cf. p. 55.
[7] Maine, **CCCLII**, p. 37.   [8] Joyce, op. cit., ii, p. 532.
[9] Jullian, op. cit., ii, p. 44. Cf. **XI**, vi, p. 168.
[10] Joyce, op. cit., ii, p. 7.   [11] D'Arbois, op. cit., i, p. 63.

The king is the head of a royal line in a society composed of lines. In Ireland and Wales at least he seems to have ruled his kingdom in the manner of the father of a family. He is elected by the *aire*, the nobles. In Ireland and Gaul the election did not always go off peacefully. The kingship was conferred, then, both by right divine and by election.[1]

The existence of several royal houses, of the same origin or rivals, complicated the problem of the succession. Sometimes, particularly in the case of the High Kings of Ireland, the kingship went to the paternal and the maternal family alternately. At other times (there are five instances in the list of High Kings from 565 to 664), rival ambitions were satisfied by the association of both kings in the sovereignty.[2] The election was attended by ceremonies of divination which gave the gods a part in the proceedings, and was complicated by ceremonies of inauguration. There was a stone of inauguration—a stone seat or a stone with an impression on which the king set his feet. The new king, unarmed and holding a white rod, turned round several times, listened to the royal *file* reading the laws, and took the oath.[3]

Once appointed, the king possessed all power, religious, judicial, and military ; he had certain subsidies in addition to the revenues of the royal land,[4] and lived at his subjects' expense on his official tours. He had a regular retinue, a court [5]; he was hospitable by tradition and kept open table.[6] He travelled often and was the guest of his vassals.

Ireland had a very high ideal of kingship,[7] an ideal of loyalty, fairness, fidelity to the laws, knowledge, and judgment. The legendary instructions of King Cormac mac Airt to his son Cairbre are an exposition of this ideal.[8]

At the time when Cæsar conquered Gaul, royalty was passing through the same crisis in that country as it had undergone centuries before in Italy and Greece. There

[1] Jullian, op. cit., ii, p. 44. Cf. Joyce, op. cit., i, p. 44 ; MacNeill, op. cit., p. 353.

[2] Ibid., i, p. 45.

[3] Ibid., i, p. 46.

[4] Ibid., i, p. 50. See Cæs., vi, 15.

[5] Ibid., i, p. 61.

[6] Ibid., i, p. 48.

[7] CCXLVII, iv, p. 51.

[8] Cf. Maine, op. cit., p. 184 ; Joyce, op. cit., i, p. 57. See, in Kuno Meyer's ed. and trans., *Tecosca Cormaic*, CCXCI, ser. xv (1909) (the *Instructions of Cormac*). Cf. MacNeill, op. cit., p. 320.

were no kings left except among the Nitiobriges and the Senones.[1] In Britain, on the other hand, the institution was still untouched.[2] The men who destroyed the kingships of Gaul were the heads of the great families, the patricians, as is plain in the case of the Arverni and Ædui. The royal families took part in the government with the other aristocratic houses. About Cæsar's time attempts were made to create monarchies of a new type. Among the Arverni, Vercingetorix succeeded where his father Celtillus had failed ; he relied on the numerous outcasts, who formed the body of companions enlisted by a rich and powerful chief. These might be called democratic kingships.[3] At first Cæsar favoured the re-establishment of monarchies, until the success of Vercingetorix revealed the latent power of the masses, to which a king could give unity.[4]

The royal authority seems to have remained stronger among the island Celts than in Gaul, where many states, such as the republic of the Ædui, presented a spectacle of anarchy. The Gauls made an effort to set up constitutions [5] and magistrates, who bore the title of *vergobret* [6] (*vergo*, effective ; *breto*, judgment) and exercised the executive power among the Ædui, Santones, and Lexovii. Among some peoples there was a military leader besides.[7] Among the Ædui, the *vergobret* became military leader when his office expired.

2.   *Public Bodies and Assemblies*

The assembly of free men still took some share in the sovereignty in the Gaul which Cæsar knew.[8] He speaks of the *publicum concilium*, which in some cases becomes the *armatum concilium* when the leader in war has to be appointed. The Irish texts are less definite, and speak chiefly of assemblies for feasting.

[1] Jullian, in **XXXIV**, 1919, p. 104. See the passages on the Gallic kings in Just., xliii, 3, 8, and Cæs., v, 24, 26 ; iii, 22.
[2] Diod., v, 21 (following Pytheas).
[3] Fustel de Coulanges, **CCCCLXV**, p. 42.
[4] For Vercingetorix, see Jullian, **CCCXLVII**, iii, 45, 197 ; Cæs., vii, 4, 1. Cf. Jullian, op. cit., iii, pp. 138, 315.
[5] Cæs., vii, 32–3.
[6] Cæs., vii, 20 ; i, 16. Cf. Jullian, ii, p. 46.
[7] Cæs., vii, 4 ; 6 ; 57, 3 ; iv, 17, 2. Cf. Jullian, ii, p. 203.
[8] Dottin, **CCCXXII**, pp. 173 ff. ; Cæs., v, 27, 3. Cf. Jullian, ii, p. 57.

In Gaul there were restricted councils which the Romans likened to their own Senate.[1] Were these assemblies of the chiefs of tribes or of former magistrates ? In any case, they were administrative councils of the patricians, which saw to it that the Gallic republics maintained a continuous policy. For anarchic as they may appear, they had given up none of their national ambitions. They had a policy of expansion and prestige or one of security, and they had a diplomacy. Cæsar gives us a detailed account of the ups and downs of that policy, and introduces us to men who were not lacking in talent, ideas, or character.

3. *The Nation*

The elements which made up the nation, whether individuals or secondary groups, were held together by very loose ties. An Irish law says, " He is no king who has no hostages in his chains." There was a House of the Hostages at Tara. These hostages were a pledge for the loyalty of the groups associated and united under the High King.[2] Their loyalty must have been a precarious thing. The Celts had nothing like our notion of the definite, permanent character of the union of men in a state or nation. The hero Fergus leaves Ulster and settles in Connacht without becoming discredited. The state does not embrace men from their birth to their death.

Cæsar represents all the peoples as devoured by political activity and divided by factions.[3] Ireland shows nothing of that kind. The reason is that Gaul had advanced much further in the direction of aristocracy. Tribes and clans had disappeared in *pagi* and *fundi* ; *civitates* arose over the *pagi* ; the body of companions and territorial situation were the principles of the new organizations. A veritable revolution, social and political, had levelled all the lower ranks of the communities living together on the same territory and created a wide gap between them and the higher stages of the social scale.[4] In Ireland and Wales groups of foreigners survived unassimilated, subject tribes or clans, vassals, who

---

[1] D'Arbois, **CCXLVIII** (Propr.), p. 57. Cf. Dottin, op. cit., p. 172 ; Jullian, ii, p. 48.
[2] Joyce, **CCCCXXXIV**, i, 53.
[3] Cæs., vi, 11.
[4] Ibid., i, 4, 18. Cf. Jullian, iii, p. 120 ; Dottin, op. cit., p. 175.

remained outside the political society formed by the true Celts and Welsh.

4. *The Army*

There was no standing army in Gaul. A levy was made in time of war, in virtue of the statutory obligations of certain members of society. The cavalry was an aristocratic body. The noble who serves does so on horseback, and fights with his servants attending him on foot.[1] By his side we find paid horsemen, enlisting individually.[2] The rest of the army marches in *pagi* under the leadership of its natural chiefs.[3] Among the Welsh and Irish, on the other hand, the chiefs fight on chariots or horseback, but among their own men ; they do not form a separate body of cavalry. So the Celts of the islands march in tribes or clans with their signs and emblems.[4] In tribes, too, march the permanent mercenary troops of Ireland, the Fianna.[5]

5. *The Nation: Relations of the Celtic Peoples. The Celtic Empire*

The grouping or subdivision of social units does not take place haphazard, but according to a sort of rhythm or numerical law. Hence comes the wholly ideal conception of the five kingdoms of Ireland, that is the four kingdoms of Ulster, Connacht, Leinster, and Munster, with the central kingdom of Meath, containing the *omphalos*, or navel, the central country, the point of divergence of the great roads.[6] Ireland dreamed of a quadripartite organization of the state and the nation corresponding to the similar organization of the family. In Wales this organization was brought about by the grouping of the people in four tribes—Gwynedd, Powys, Deheubarth, and Morganwy.[7] In Gaul it is revealed by the name of the Petrucorii.[8] This division, which the Celts seem to have regarded as the ideal form of society (four is the perfect number), seems to come from a more distant

---

[1] Jullian, iii, p. 352.
[2] Cæs., i, 18, 5.
[3] Cæs., ii, 28, 2. Cf. Jullian, ii, p. 50.
[4] Joyce, op. cit., i, p. 91.
[5] Ibid., i, pp. 87 ff.
[6] Loth, in **CXXXIV**, xvii, pp. 198–206. Cf. **CXL**, xxvii, 1917, p. 142.
[7] Lloyd, **CCCCXXXVIII**, p. 131. This division corresponded to that of the four bishoprics.
[8] Loth, in **CXXXIV**, 1916, p. 280.

age. For it is the theoretical division of a society composed of two phratries containing two clans each, inter-connected by marriage and the exchange of gifts or services.

The political societies of the Celts were composed of autonomous elements standing in juxtaposition ; in practice these heterogeneous elements often amalgamated. In Cæsar we see the peoples of Gaul, which are themselves agglomerations of *pagi*, agglomerating into compact groups. For example in the relief-army at Alesia we find the Cadurci, Gabali, and Vellavi combining their contingents with those of the Arverni,[1] and the Segusiavi, Ambivareti, and Aulerci Brannovices with those of the Ædui. This combination was not merely made to meet the occasion, but was the result of long-standing, deep-rooted associations. Cæsar describes these associations of Gallic peoples as kinships or *clientelæ*. The notion of *clientela* is defined in a certain number of cases by that of *imperium*[2] ; the client peoples were the subjects of the patron peoples, and *clientela* was a natural relationship and one of blood.[3] In this way there was a perfect network of ties among the peoples of Gaul. In addition, there were hierarchies, hegemonies,[4] assemblies.[5] So, too, in Ireland the four great kingdoms were subordinate to the High King, though rather loosely so. But their union was always conceived of on the same principle of kinship and *clientela*. The northern and western kingdoms were called Milesian, that is, kin ; Leinster was tributary,[6] and so a client kingdom.

The Celts seem to have risen to the notion of empire. When they first come into Roman history, Livy depicts a sort of great kingdom, the sovereign of which was a Biturix, that is, a King of the World, namely Ambicatus. He sent his two nephews on two great imperial expeditions, one to Germany and the other to Italy. It is idle to ask whether the empire of Ambicatus ever existed.[7] It is certain that the

[1] Bloch, **CCCCLXVII**, p. 79. Cf. Rhys, **CCXXX**, p. 60.
[2] Fustel de Coulanges, op. cit., p. 69. See Cæs., vii, 75, 2.
[3] Jullian, op. cit., ii, p. 442 ; Cæs., ii, 14, 2 ; vii, 5, 2 ; vi, 4, 2 ; vii, 75, 2.
[4] Jullian, op. cit., ii, p. 543 ; Cæs., v, 3, 1 ; vii, 64, 8 ; iii, 8, 1.
[5] Livy, xxi, 20, 3 ; Jullian, op. cit., iii, p. 223. The first general assembly of Gaul was held at Bibracte in 58 B.C., after the departure of the Helvetii.
[6] MacNeill, **CCCCXLI**, p. 238.
[7] D'Arbois, " L'Empire celtique au IVe siècle avant notre ère," in **CXLI**, xxx (1886), pp. 35–41, maintains that Ambicatus was a real person. M. Jullian has shown that this tradition is unlikely (op. cit., ii, p. 544).

idea of it was conceived by the Celts, for Livy's account comes from a Celtic tradition. Of that tradition Ireland presents an equivalent. It regards itself as a microcosm, an image of the greater universe. It enthusiastically adopts the Idea of the King of the World, introduced by a St. Jerome or an Orosius.[1] But the Celts, while they failed to create an empire themselves, readily rallied to the imperial idea.

[1] MacNeill, op. cit., p. 270.

CHAPTER III

The Structure of Society (*continued*)

The Religion of the Celts and the Druidic Priesthood

I

THE DRUIDIC PRIESTHOOD A PAN-CELTIC INSTITUTION

RELIGION is yet another element of social organization. Celtic religion in particular has the appearance of being such, for its most interesting and striking aspect was the constitution of the priesthood of the Druids, the organization of a religious society which made the whole series of Celtic peoples into one cohesive people.

First of all, this priesthood is a pan-Celtic institution, cementing Celtic society. There were Druids in Ireland. The modern Welsh Druids are only an archæological revival, but there were Druids in Britain, of whose power Cæsar gives evidence.[1] Gaul, too, had them. If we hear nothing of Druids in the Celtic settlements in Spain, Italy, the Danube valley, and Galatia, that seems to be no reason for denying that they existed among those branches of the race. If, moreover, it is true that the Latin word *vates* is borrowed from Celtic, the Gauls of Italy had among them persons described as *vates*, who were like the Druids, and organized like them.

Cæsar tells us that Druidism first started in Britain, and that the Druids of Gaul used to go to Britain to visit famous schools and sanctuaries. British Druidism had an equally high reputation in Ireland, and the Irish Druids went to Britain to complete their education. Does this mean that Druidism was unknown to the Celts as a whole and took shape among the Britons of Britain ?[2] We have no ground for saying that.

Some students, starting from this idea that Druidism had its origin in the west of the Celtic counties, have said that

---

[1] Cæs., vi, 13. Cf. d'Arbois, **CCXLVIII**, i, and Dottin, **CCCXXIII**, p. 38.
[2] Desjardins, in **CCCCLXXIV**, ii, p. 519, notes the absence of references to the Druids in Aquitania, Narbonensis, and the country near the Rhine.

it was not Celtic at all.[1] They have tried to attach it to the peoples which the Celts found established in the west of Europe, the builders of the megalithic monuments. But an analytical, comparative study of the institution shows that it is an essential part of the organization of the Celtic societies. History, moreover, shows clearly enough that it was an element of resistance to the Romans in Gaul and Britain and to Christianity in Ireland, and that it was attacked as such by persecution in Gaul, by the campaigns of the Roman generals against the sanctuaries in Britain, and by a kind of degradation in Ireland.[2] It was an element of resistance because it was an element of cohesion. The travels and meetings of the Druids cemented the union of the Celtic peoples and encouraged that sense of kinship which might have given birth to unity.

II

THE CHARACTER AND WORKING OF THE DRUIDIC PRIESTHOOD

The Druids are known to us by long passages in the Greek and Latin historians and polygraphers—Cæsar,[3] Diodoros,[4] Strabo,[5] Ammianus Marcellinus [6]—who all owe their information to Poseidonios and Timagenes. These writers enumerated the functions and powers of the Druids.

For Ireland, a great number of epic texts speak of the Druids. There are also many legal texts regarding the functions and powers of the *fili* (the poets and men of letters), who formed a corporation parallel and to some extent rival to that of the Druids and were spared by Christianity, whereas it wrought havoc with the Druids.[7] But the two bodies lived side by side and were complementary to each other, and in earlier times had been associated in their

[1] Rhys, **CCCCLI**, fourth ed., 1908, p. 9. Cf. id., **CCLXXXII**, p. 216. A similar theory is maintained by Pokorny, " Der Ursprung des Druidenthums," in **C**, 38, 1 (Vortrag), translated in **CXXIX**, 1910, pp. 589 ff.

[2] Tac., *Ann.*, xiv, 30, account of the expedition of Suetonius Paulinus against Anglesey. But Fustel, **CCCCLV**, p. 103, denies that the Druids were persecuted in Gaul. D'Arbois has proved the contrary, **CCXLVIII** (Droit), i, pp. 172 ff.

[3] vi, 13–14.

[4] vii, 31.

[5] iv, 197.

[6] xv, 9, 8 (following Timagenes).

[7] See a discussion of the question in Joyce, **CCCCXXXIV**, i, 222.

organizations and privileges. The literature and laws of Ireland were not written down until after the introduction of Christianity, and the work was done by *fili*, who therefore appear in a more favourable light than the Druids. But if we boldly fill in the gaps in our knowledge of the Druids from what we know about the *fili*, we get a picture of the Druids of Ireland which corresponds at every point to that of the Druids of Gaul. So we obtain a check on the accuracy of both portraits and a strong presumption that we are dealing with a common institution dating from the most distant past of the two peoples. The Latin variants of the name take one back to a declension identical with that of the Irish name of the Druids (*drui, druad*). The ancients connected this name with that of the oak,[1] regarding the Druids as dryads, priests of the oak (δρύς). In Wales, the late name of the Druids, *derwydd*, is a restoration based on the name of the oak, *derw*. But now, following Thurneysen and d'Arbois, Celticists prefer to connect *drúi* with *súi* " wise ", on the ground that these words are composed of a qualifing element, *su* " well " or *dru* " strong," and a verb-root, *uid* " know," which also comes into priestly names in Germanic, Slavonic, and the Baltic languages. So the Druids would be the very wise men, soothsayers.[2]

However that may be, it is certain that in Gaul the Druids were connected with the oak, plucking the mistletoe and eating the acorns to acquire their prophetic powers. In Ireland, the walnut and rowan are their trees, and certain nuts reveal the future. The Irish Druids have wands cut from their favourite tree, with the aid of which they exercise their powers, or silver branches representing the boughs of a sacred tree or of a Tree of Life in the next world. They are attached to these trees as totemic clans are to their totems.[3]

There are certain priests, called *gutuatri*, attached to a sanctuary.[4] But these may very well have been Druids, for Ausonius, in speaking of one of them, says that he was of a Druid family—*stirpe Druidarum satus*. The Druids

---

[1] A. W. Bird, "A Note on Druidism," in **XIX**, 1922, p. 152, 4. Cf. ibid., p. 155.

[2] MacBain, p. 141. Cf. Pedersen, i, 175; d'Arbois, **CCC**, p. 1.

[3] Luc., *Phars.*, i, 53; Tac., *Ann.*, xiv, 30; Pliny, xvi, xliii, 249.

[4] Loth, in **CXL**, xxviii, 118 Cf. Holder, i, col. 2046; d'Arbois, **CCXCIX**, p. 32.

formed a large clergy, which could have many special functions.[1]

In most Indo-European peoples functions were divided between the king and specialists. In Rome the *rex* and the *flamen* had each his own duties. The Irish King had his Druid, who probably received his powers from him in delegation.[2] M. Jullian has, I think wrongly, described the Druids of Gaul as priest-kings and the Assembly of Druids as a convention of kings of the *pagi*.[3]

In Gaul the Druids took part in sacrifices, public and private ; they ordered the ceremony and perhaps acted as sacrificers or ministers, at least in certain exceptional cases, where human beings were sacrificed, or white bulls at the plucking of the mistletoe.[4]

But their chief religious function was divination. The Druids were diviners, seers. Cicero in his *De Divinatione* introduces Diviciacus (although he was, rather, a statesman), on the ground of his augural science, served by his knowledge of man.[5] Some of the human sacrifices in Gaul and those sacrifices in Ireland in which the sacrificing was done by Druids were of a mantic character. The Irish texts show us the Druids at work, prophesying, interpreting omens, using the divining-wheel. The Druids are men of science, but they are also men of God, enjoying direct intercourse with the deities and able to speak in their name. They can also influence fate by making those who consult them observe positive rules or ritual taboos (the *geasa* which figure so largely in the Irish epics) or by determining the days to be chosen or avoided for an action which is contemplated.[6]

Between these religious functions and magic the distinction is vague. The Druids of Gaul certainly slipped into magic, and those of Ireland always practised it, with methods which are very obscurely described.[7]

[1] Livy, xxiii, 24.
[2] See Joyce, op. cit., i, p. 238.
[3] Cf. Jullian, CCCLXVII, ii ; Cæs., vi, 16, 5 ; iv, 4, 4.
[4] Cæs., vi, 16 ; Strabo, iv, 4, 5 ; Diod., v, 31, 4 ; 32, 6 ; Poseid., in *F.H.G.*, i, 261. Cf. d'Arbois, CCXLVIII, i, p. 151 ; Frazer, CCCXXXII, p. 234.
[5] Cic., *De Div.*, i, 41, 90 ; Cæs., vi, 13 ; Tac., *Hist.*, iv, 54 ; cf. Dion. Chrys., *Or.*, 49 ; Mela, iii, 19.
[6] Diod., v, xxxi, 4 ; Strabo, iv, 198. Cf. Joyce, op. cit., i, p. 229 ; d'Arbois, CCCI, p. 99 ; Windisch, CCXCV, pp. 69–70 ; Czarnowski, CCCCXIII, p. 95 ; *Táin*, i, 10, 70.
[7] Pliny, xvi, 249 ; xxiv, 62–3 ; xvi, 95 ; xxix, 12 and 52 ; Joyce, op. cit., i, pp. 245, 227, 247. Cf. *Silva Gadelica*, ii, pp. 85, 516.

The Druids also had judicial powers, for Cæsar tells us that they had to give judgment on almost all suits, public and private. In private law they dealt with matters of murder and inheritance and disputes about property. In international law (which is probably what Cæsar means by public suits) they acted as arbiters in disputes between political groups. In Ireland the same judicial powers, those of the Brehons, were exercised by *fili*, and we may fairly suppose that these took them over from the Druids. We find the Brehons at their work in the law-books which they compiled. They are jurisconsults, arbiters, and advocates rather than judges. They give consultations, based on precedents interpreted in the light of equity. They act as arbiters in matters of private law; for instance, they lay down compensation to settle suits arising from injuries which call for private vengeance. In the evolution of Celtic law, the public powers of the state eventually exceeded those of the Druids and the Brehons. The king and the assembly give judgment; the Brehon proposes the sentence, gives an opinion. But the Druids and Brehons seem, both in Gaul and in Ireland, to have been able to pronounce some kind of ban against those who did not accept their decision, and to this the *fili* added a magical enforcement.[1]

The Druids also had privileges and an authority of a political nature. Cæsar tells us that they were exempt from military service and taxation. We find Druids, such as Diviciacus and Cathbad, the Druid of King Conchobar, fighting; but they do so of their free will and not by obligation.

In Ireland, moreover, the *fili* had a sort of permanent safe-conduct pass, even during the intestine wars which ravaged the country; and this gave them an inter-tribal function. Every king in Ireland, great or small, had a Druid who was his political adviser. Cæsar gives evidence of the authority and social position of the Druids, whom he places in the same rank as the *equites*. Many sprang from royal or aristocratic families. In the order of precedence observed

---

[1] Cæs., vi, 13 ; Diod., v, 31 ; Strabo, iv, 4, 4 ; *Senchus Mor*, CCXLVII, i, pp. 22, 80, 86. Cf. O'Curry, CCCCXXXII, ii, p. 20 ; d'Arbois, CCXLVIII (Droit), i, pp. 271, 279, 294, 315 ; id., CCC, Druides, p. 103 ; Maine, CCCLII, i, pp. 4, 21, 25 ; id., CCCLIII, pp. 51 ff. ; CCXLVII, i, pp. 788, 250.

at Tara, the *fili*, who took the place of the Druids, appear
in the same ranks as the nobles.[1]

I have said above that the Druids acted as teachers
of the young. Cæsar shows that they sometimes raised their
pupils to power. Education was one of their essential functions
and perhaps it was the only one of a constitutional kind
in the organization of the Celtic society. The Druids lingered
on in Gaul as the teachers of higher schools ; in Ireland the
fili, who succeeded them as educators, founded schools
which, handed over to Christianity, survived all through
the Middle Ages. So the Druids and their successors were
a permanent element of civilization in Celtic societies.[2]
But before they taught classical learning, they diffused
ideas which must be defined.

Their teaching was purely oral, both in Ireland down to
Christian times and in Gaul, and seems to have consisted
in the setting forth of a tradition, recorded in innumerable
poems which were learned by heart. These doubtless included
epico-historical accounts of the origin of the race, as
a specimen of which we may take the *Leabhar Gabhála* ;
perhaps some cosmological digressions, such as are found
in the *Senchus Mor* ; certainly travels into the next world,
like the literature of the *Imrama* (Voyages).[3] And in all this
a doctrine was expounded. The ancient writers, who on the
whole were fairly well informed by good observers, have
given us an idea of this doctrine in a few brief words which
are full of sense. They placed the Druids among the mystic
philosophers associated with the ancient Greek philosophers
who evolved the doctrine of the immortality of the soul.

The Druids had a complete doctrine of that immortality,
with a moral system, general view of the world, mythology,
ritual, and funerary practice to match.[4] They taught that
death is only a changing of place and that life goes on with

---

[1] Cæs., vi, 14 ; d'Arbois, **CCCCXLVIII**, i, pp. 126, 342. Cf. *Book of Leinster*,
p. 29 ; *Táin*, i, 47, 23 ; ibid., 93 ; Dion. Chrys., *Or.*, 49 ; Joyce, op. cit.,
i, p. 237.
[2] Cæs., vi, 14, 2–3 ; Mela, iii, 18 ; Tac., *Ann.*, iii, 43 ; *Táin* ; *L. na
hUidhre*, p. 61, 1, 21, 23 ; ib., 64, 2, 10, 13 ; K. Meyer, in **CXL**, xi, pp. 442–453.
Cf. d'Arbois, **CCC**, Druides, p. 115 ; **CCXLVIII** (Droit), i, p. 339 ; **CCXLVII**,
ii, pp. 150–5 ; Czarnowski, **CCCCXXIII**, pp. 291, 294.
[3] Diod., iv, 56. See above, ch. vi.
[4] Cæs., vi, 14, 5–6 ; 16 ; Strabo, iv, 4, 4 ; Amm. Marc., xv, 9, 8 ; Diog.
Laërt., *Prooem.*, 5 ; Diod., vi, 27, 6 ; Luc., i, 450 ; Mela, iii, 19 ; iii, 2, 19 ;
Val. Max., ii, 6, 10.

its forms and its goods in another world, the world of the dead, which rules the dead and gives up living men. It is a world of life, forming a reservoir of available souls. A constant, floating capital of souls is distributed between the two counterpart worlds, and exchanges take place between them, life for life and soul for soul. But, what is more, this stock of souls is apparently not confined to the human species ; souls pass from one species to another. The Druids seem to have held a belief in metempsychosis, traces of which are found in the myths and stories.[1] With some notions of physics and astronomy, applied in the construction of calendars, some knowledge of plants and their properties (which was passed on to the physicians), and a few magical prescriptions, this stock of philosophical ideas seems to have formed the bulk of the wisdom of the Druids, which contributed in no small degree to the spiritual education of the Celts.[2]

The Druids formed an *order* in Celtic society, but that order was a brotherhood (*sodaliciis adstricti consortiis*), a society of individuals collectively exercising a social function. Their organization cut across the divisions of tribes and states ; the Druids of Ireland were one single body, those of Britain turned their eyes to the sanctuary of Mona (Anglesey), and those of Gaul turned to the shrine among the Carnutes.[3] All these groups communicated with one another. The Druidical colleges obtained new members by training and co-option, but there were also Druid families. There must have been initiations, a preparation, and stages, of which we find traces among the *fili*. There seem to have been Druidesses in Gaul and Ireland, but we cannot be sure whether they really belonged to the college of Druids, or merely got the name by analogy, on account of their gifts in magic. In any case, the Druids formed a widespread college, the members of which, distributed about the political framework of the nation, performed the most varied functions. The college asserted its unity in its sanctuaries, its schools,

[1] Czarnowski, op. cit., pp. 156 ff. Cf. Windisch, **CCXCV**, i, p. 117 ; Nutt, in **CCLXXIV**, ii, p. 96.

[2] Pomp. Mela, ii, 2 ; Strabo, iv, 197 ; 4, 4 ; **CCXLVII**, i, p. 22 ; Pliny, xvi, p. 250 ; Cæs., vi, 18 ; Windisch, op. cit., i, p. 215 ; d'Arbois, **CCXLVIII**, i, p. 141. Cf. Maine, **CCCLII**, p. 34 ; Joyce, op. cit., i, 230.

[3] Joyce, op. cit., i, p. 223 ; O. Curry, **CCCCXXXII**, ii, 182 ; Jullian, *R.E.A.*, 1919, p. 109.

and its assemblies, like the assembly of the country of the Carnutes, held in Gaul, which was at once a council and a guild-congress of the Druids.

By the side of the Druids, the ancient authors, following Poscidonios and Timagonos, mention the bards, who were popular poets with less refined methods, and the *vates*, who were seer-poets and ἱεροποίοι.[1] In Ireland we hear of bards and singers (*cainte*), *fili*, and Druids. The *fili* and their Welsh equivalents are much the same as the *vates* of Gaul. Several corporations were lumped together under this title.[2] They were at first subordinate to the Druids, but eclipsed them when Christianity came in.

III

THE DRUIDS AND OTHER INDO-EUROPEAN BROTHERHOODS

This account of the college of Druids naturally brings to mind the similar colleges of the ancient world, and first of all those of the Romans [3]—Flamens, Augurs, Vestals, Arval Brothers, Luperci. But the Roman priesthood had a larger number of brotherhoods, with fewer members in each. Moreover, the ancients were struck by the resemblance of the doctrine of the Druids to that of the Pythagorean *syssitiai* which had developed among the Dorians of Southern Italy.[4] It is highly probable that the Dorians, before moving down into Greece and then over to Italy, had been quite near the Celts in Central Europe. What is more, the country extending from the Middle Danube to the Ægean, from which the Dorians came, had been a nursery of institutions like the Pythagorean communities. It was there that Orphicism, which the ancients likened to Pythagoreanism,

---

[1] Cæs., vi, 13 ; Amm. Marc., xv, 9 ; ii, 8 ; Stokes, *Tripartite Life*, pp. 235, 326. Cf. Dottin, **CCCXXII**, p. 54 ; Czarnowski, op. cit., pp. 287, 278 ; d'Arbois, **CCXLVIII**, i, p. 234.

[2] Diod., v, 31 ; Strabo, iv, 4, 4 ; Cæs., vi, 13 ; Amm. Marc., xv, 98 ; Ath., iv, 37 ; vi, 49 ; Luc., i, 44, 7 ; Joyce, op. cit., i, pp. 223, 230 ; Czarnowski, op. cit., pp. 227, 278 ; d'Arbois, **CCXLVIII**, i, p. 196.

[3] D'Arbois, **CCC**, p. 9 ; Schrader, "Aryan Religion," in **CCCXXXVI**, ii, p. 43.

[4] Pliny, xxx, 5 ; Clem., *Strom.*, i, 15, in *F.H.G.* (following Alexander Polyhistor, a historian of the first century), iii, 233 ; Amm. Marc., xv, 9, 8 ; Val. Maz., vi, 6, 10. Cf. Delatte, "Études sur la littérature pythagoricienne," in *Bibl. de l'Éc. des Htes. Études*, 1915, p. 217.

came into being.[1] Orphicism comprised the worship of the Getic god or hero Zalmoxis, a brotherhood of priests, a doctrine of immortality, a myth of the descent into the underworld, and, like the ritual of the Druids, human sacrifice.[2]   In Thrace, among the Satrae, there was a brotherhood of priests called Bessi, who ran an oracle of Dionysos, a Thracian god.[3] Here we have one same family of cults, in which the societies in which they were observed were merely onlookers and the active part was played by brotherhoods of initiates.

Moreover, in the east of the Indo-European region we find societies of priests very like the Druids in the credit which they enjoy and the area over which they are spread— the Iranian Magi and the Brahmins of India.   The Druids seem to differ from the latter only in that they do not form a closed caste.   We have previously seen the analogies in religious vocabulary between the two most widely separated branches of the Indo-European family, the Italo-Celts and the Indo-Iranians.[4]   This series of similarities proves that Druidism was an Indo-European institution, and that its origins went back to the most distant past of the Indo-European societies.   But we can go back yet further.

Sir James Frazer and M. Jullian after him have supposed that Druidism was derived from the kind of sacrifice described in the *Golden Bough*, the sacrifice of god-priest-kings like the Priest of Nemi whom Sir James makes the central example in his great work.[5]   Really, Druidism is something quite different.   In the various types of priestly society which we have been considering, the collective exercise of spiritual functions is essential to the nature of the institution.   We must, therefore, go back to a type of collective body, not to one of individuals.   The god-priest-kings are individuals.

But the forms of these collective bodies, these brotherhoods, which we have been surveying are as different from one another as the societies in which they appear.   Some are mere colleges, others are colleges of initiates, others are societies on a basis of kinship (castes or priestly families).

[1] Diod., iii, 65, 6. Cf. d'Arbois, **CCCI**, i, p. 296.
[2] Hdt., iv, 94 ; Strabo, vii, 35. Cf. Dottin, **CCCXXII**, p. 58.
[3] Hdt., vii, iii ; Strabo, vii, 3, 3 ; Dion Cass., 51, 25 ; 54, 34 ; Apollod., iii, 5, 1–2 ; Macrob., i, 18, 11 ; *F.H.G.*, iii, 641, 20. Cf. d'Arbois, **CCCI**, i, pp. 292–6 ; Farnell, v, p. 102.
[4] See above, pt. iii, ch. i ; Vendryès, in **XCIII**, xx, 6, 265.
[5] Frazer, **CCCXXXII**, pp. 82, 129, 218, 225–6 ; Jullian, in **CXXXIV**.

Now, comparison with non-Indo-European phenomena will give us the key to these institutions, showing us collective bodies which are just like those of the Druids and Brahmins and have a perfectly clear place in the evolution of totemism. These are the so-called secret societies of British Columbia and Melanesia, which are really brotherhoods.[1] These brotherhoods are constituted alongside of totemic clans, and are copied from them. Each secret society has originated in a revelation which is represented in myths similar to those of Zalmoxis or Pythagoras. They are recruited by co-option, and members, belonging to successive generations, qualify themselves by initiations. Their activity centres on the periods of feasts in which the members of the brotherhood are the actors. Thus they assume functions which fall to them by escheat in communities where totemism is breaking up. It is brotherhoods of this kind that lie at the source of Brahminism and Druidism.

The influence of the Druids was always meeting opposition, in Gaul from the jealousy of the *equites*, which partly explains the rapid decline of Druidism, and in Ireland from the hostility of certain kings. Thus, some of the texts tell us of the incredulity of Cormac mac Airt. The elevation of the *fili* at the expense of the Druids was doubtless favoured by such opposition. It was only through the intervention of St. Columba at the Assembly of Druim Ceata in 574 that the *fili* themselves were allowed to maintain some of their prerogatives, which they had inherited from Druidism.[2]

IV

WHAT CELTIC RELIGION OWED TO DRUIDISM

One thing strikes us at the very first in the religion of the Celts, and that is the supreme importance of agrarian rites, which, with their myths, play the chief part in religious life. Fruitfulness, fertility, and life have always been the chief concern of these orgiastic brotherhoods, and they have always

---

[1] Hutton Webster, *Primitive Secret Societies* ; Boas, *Social Organization and Secret Societies of the Kwakiutl* (for North American practices). Cf. Frazer, op. cit., iii, pp. 449, 459, 490. For interpretation, see Durkheim, in **XIII**, iii, p. 336 ; Davy, **CCCXVI**, pp. 201, 328 ; **CCCLX**, English, p. 102.
[2] Joyce, op. cit, i, p. 456.

stretched out their hand, over the head of the state religion, to the herdsman and the husbandman. Secondly, we see a metaphysical and moral system developed in religion. Interest in the soul, its origin and destiny, the world of souls and the dead, and the myth of the Beyond stand in the forefront of representations, as agrarian rites stand in the forefront of ritual.

V

THE UNITY OF THE CELTIC RELIGIONS

The existence of a pan-Celtic priesthood, dating from the origin of the race, must have ensured a certain unity for the religions of the various Celtic peoples. It is true that such unity is far from obvious. The reason is that the various Celtic religions are not known to us from documents of the same kind, and the different branches of the Celts did not develop equally and at one time everywhere. In Cæsar's time Gaul was ahead of Ireland. Moreover, for Gaul, about which our evidence comes from the Greek geographers, we know a good deal about ritual, but nothing at all of mythology, whereas for Ireland, where our sources are epic and lyric poems collected after the Celtic religion was dead, we have a body of tales and legends and know nothing definite about ritual. As for Welsh literature, it is a miracle that it contains any traces of British religion at all, for it was created in a Christian country, first Romanized and then colonized by Irishmen.

In spite of these difficulties, we find signs of a deep-lying identity. The Brythonic Celts of Gaul, Britain, and the Danube, being of the same family and united by a thousand different bonds, had the same gods, or gods of the same name, and they were many. But the Goidels and Brythons of the island and the Continent shared them too. They may not have been so many, but they were important gods. There was Lugh, the great sun-god, who gave Lugdunun its name and was represented in Spain by the Lugoves.[1] There was Taranis, the god of lightning,[2] represented in

---

[1] Loth, *Le Dieu Lug, la Terre Mère et les Lugoves*, in **CXXXIX**, ii, 1914, pp. 205–210. Cf. **XL**, xii, p. 52.
[2] Luc, *Phars.*, i, 444. See MacCulloch, **CCCXIV**, pp. 20–48.

Ireland by a little-known hero, Tornà. Esus, a Gallic god, appears in the Irish name Eogan (= Esugenos). Goibniu, the smith-god of the Goidels, had a Brythonic counterpart whose name appears in that of Gobannitio, the uncle of Vercingetorix. Corresponding to the name of the Gallic and British god Camulos we have that of the Irish hero Cumhal, father of Finn. For the Goidelic goddess Brigid there was a Brythonic Brigantia.[1] It is better not to look for homonyms of the Irish deities among the characters of the Welsh Mabinogion, since the Welsh may have borrowed from Irish tradition. Manawyddan is the same as the sea-god Manannán. All these facts taken together enable one to picture an ancient stock of common cults and myths, preserved better in one place than another.

VI

STAGES OF THE CELTIC RELIGIONS

Attempts have often been made to distinguish in the Celtic religions the elements of Aryan origin and those belonging to the earlier inhabitants of Ireland. Mr. Cook holds that the Aryan gods were the gods of the sky, light, the sun, the stormy sky (like Tanaris) or the sunny sky (like Lugh), and that the worship of the oak and mistletoe were likewise Aryan.[2] The non-Aryan gods, he believes, were the dark gods (and, more especially, goddesses) and those of vegetation. That would explain why the gods of the underworld and those of light are engaged in furious strife in the mythology of Ireland and Wales. But such theories fail to observe that these mythological conflicts are imposed on the gods by the dramatic parts which they play in the seasonal festivals. These cults are not the memory of historical wars, but the mythological version of a ritual. One might say that the conflicts of the gods are syntheses of various functions which are antithetic or successive. The racial ingredients of the Celtic peoples were fused together at an early date, and the differences presented

[1] Caes, vi, 17 ; Cormac, 23 ; Holder, **CCVII**, s.v. ; d'Arbois, **CCXLVIII**, ii, p. 273.
[2] A. B. Cook, in **LXIV**, xvii, p. 30. Cf. id. *Zeus : a study in ancient religion*, London, 3 vol., 1914–1925 ; Rhys, in **CCCLXXXII**.

by the lists of gods drawn up for the various parts of Ireland have told us nothing so far. It must, too, be remembered that the study of these local pantheons is still in its infancy.

Certainly the Celts owed much to their predecessors. They made use of the megalithic monuments. The great tumuli or funerary chambers of New Grange in Ireland (Brugh-na-Boyne) were regarded as the dwelling-place of gods and revered as sanctuaries. The twelve stones which formed the satellites of the Irish idol Cromm Crúaich were the pillars of a cromlech. In Britain, and doubtless in Gaul, the Celts likewise took over the megalithic monuments, but we do not know what they really borrowed from the predecessors of their civilizations.[1]

The most interesting trace of the old stock is, as we have seen, Druidism itself. Can one go still further back, to totemism ? The Gauls had beast-gods, such as the horse of Neuvy-en-Sullias, Rudiobos, the mule of Nuits,[2] and Segomo, the ram-headed serpent represented on monuments at Mavilly, Paris, and Rheims ; anthropomorphic gods with some touch of a beast-god, such as Cernunnos with his antlers and March (Mark) of the Britons with his horse's ears [3] ;   and sacred animals attached to certain gods, like the horse of Epona,[4] the dog of the hammer-god,[5] the bear of the goddess Artio,[6] and the boar of Diana Arduinna.[7] But a beast-god is not necessarily a totem. Often the animals portrayed on the monuments represent the popular elements of the myths, and though these may be derived from totemism we cannot say by what road. In Irish literature there are several heroes with animal affinities, including the most famous of all, Cuchulainn, the Dog of Culann, who was forbidden to eat dog, and Oisin, whose mother was changed into a doe and who was himself a fawn. We find traces of animal emblems of clans, food-taboos. But in any case these are only survivals of a long-superseded past. In the course

[1] Squire, CCCCLIX, p. 38 ; cf. K. Meyer, CCLXXIV, app. B. to *The Voyage of Bran*.
[2] Loth, *Le Dieu gaulois Rudiobos, Rudianos*, in CXXXIX, p. 195, 2, 210.
[3] Squire, op. cit., p. 327.
[4] Espérandieu, CCCXXV. Cf., for Epona, H. Hubert, in XV, xxxii, 1922, pp. 291–2 ; id. *Le Mythe d'Epona* in CLXXXIV, 1925, pp. 187–191, repr. in CCXLIV.
[5] Id., in CXXXIX, 1915.
[6] Reinach, CCCLXXIII.
[7] Kruger, *Diana Arduinna*, in LXXXI, i, 1917, p. 4.

of the evolution which took place, heroes took shape, civilizers or founders of social groups, some of whom may have once been totems while others may have been provided with totemic emblems.   One thing is certain—in Celtic societies, in the place of the totem of the clan we find the hero of the clan, of the tribe, of the nation.

VII

POLITICO-DOMESTIC ORGANIZATION AND HERO-WORSHIP

This worship of hero-gods corresponds very closely to the extremely loose organization of political and family life in Ireland. We know that Gaul at the time of the Roman conquest was moving towards a different state of things, but in Ireland society was far less centralized, and religion was of the same character.   The great seasonal feasts of agricultural life marked a momentary concentration.[1]

Not only does Irish mythology take the form of a history in which several generations of invaders [2] (the chief being the Fomorians [3] and the Tuatha Dé Danann) [4] disappear one after the other, but these Fomorians and Tuatha Dé Danann are always represented as men who have lived on earth and retired into death.   Now, these spirits include the gods, and indeed the great gods—Ler,[5] Nuadu,[6] Manannán,[7] Dagda,[8] Brigid,[9] and Ogma [10] among the Tuatha Dé Danann and others among the Fomorians,[11] Lugh belonging to both sides.   They dwell in tombs, which are actual megalithic tombs.[12]   So the gods are superhuman beings, not supernatural, and this is true of them all, especially the local gods attached to a district or a natural feature ; they are

[1] See Hubert, **CCCXLIII**, and *Le Culte des héros et ses conditions sociales*, introd. to Czarnowski, **CCCCXXIII**, *Rev. de l'hist. des religions*, lxx, pp. 1–20, and lxxi, pp. 195–247.

[2] See Squire, op. cit. ; d'Arbois, **CCXLVIII** and **CCC**. Cf. above, ch. iv.

[3] Squire, op. cit., pp. 48 ff.

[4] Ibid., pp. 70, 140, etc. ; cf. d'Arbois, **CCXLVIII**, ii, p. 155.

[5] Ibid., p. 136.

[6] D'Arbois, ii, p. 155.   Cf. Rhys, **CCLXXXI**, p. 122.

[7] Squire, op. cit., pp. 60–1.

[8] Ibid., pp. 54, 78.

[9] D'Arbois, op. cit., ii, p. 373.

[10] Squire, op. cit., p. 122.

[11] Ibid., p. 140.

[12] Ibid.

bound to it by their tomb, by the memory of their death. The Celts liked this funereal aspect of their gods ; their pantheon might be described as a cemetery.[1]

These gods and their myths were subjected to a general process of rejuvenation which placed their date later and later and brought them closer to existing human communities. This rejuvenation of myths is very characteristic. A famous Irish story tells how the god Mider, one of the Tuatha Dé Danann, dwelling in the tomb of Bri Leith, tried to recover his wife Etain from the King of Ireland, Eochaid Airem, who is contemporaneous with Cæsar in the *Annals*. The name Etain is found again in the south of Ulster.[2] The god Nuadu is brought into recent times by the legend which makes him a grandfather of Finn.[3] Gods produce sons and grandsons ; Cuchulainn is descended from Lugh [4] and Mongan from Manannán. Others are reincarnated ; according to one tradition Mongan was reincarnated in Finn. The mythico-heroic literature of Ireland is full of gods returning to human life and men visiting the world of gods and the dead, and both are merged in the form of heroes.

The gods appear in the genealogies. The whole race claims descent from the great god Bile, father of Mile, the ancestor of the latest conquerors, who was a kind of god of the dead.[5] Similarly the Gauls, according to Cæsar, claimed descent from Dispater.[6] The forts, the rallying-places of tribes and families, were built on heights which were tombs. The residence of the Kings of Leinster stood on the tumulus of Slanga the Fir Bolg.[7]

The religion of Ireland was that of the politico-domestic groups of which society was composed. These centred on their ancestors, who were heroes and gods ; their cults were ancestor-worships and their feasts were commemorations. The type of the hero absorbs the whole of mythology, and is succeeded by that of the saint. M. Czarnowski has demonstrated that the immense popularity of St. Patrick, who is

[1] Joyce, CCCCXXXIV.
[2] Squire, op. cit., p. 332.
[3] K. Meyer, OOOXXXIV, ii.   Cf. E. McNeill, *Duanaire Finn*, vol. vii of CCLXV, introd., pp xliii ff.
[4] Windisch, op. cit.
[5] Squire, op. cit., pp. 121–2, 153.
[6] Rhys, CCLXXXII, pp. 90–1 ; cf. Caes, vi, 17, 18.
[7] Joyce, op. cit.

a national hero in Ireland, completed the evolution of the ancient religion of the nation.

VIII

FESTIVALS

The Irish tribes normally lived in a dispersed manner, and the sanctuaries were also fair-grounds, without anything implying permanent worship. The population met at the political and religious centre of the tribes, which was the place where the tombs of its ancestors stood, and it did this on feast-days.[1]

There were four chief feasts. Samhain [2] (1st November) marked the end of summer (*samos*) and probably the beginning of the year. Six months later, on the 1st May, at the beginning of summer (*cèt-saman*), came Beltane, the feast of the fire (*tein*) of Bel or Bile.[3] Between these two, at intervals of three months, there were the feasts of Lugnassad,[4] the marriage of Lugh, which is the best described of all, on the 1st August, and Oimelc or Imbolc, on the 1st February, which survived in the feast of St. Brigid. Samhain was held chiefly at Tara,[5] Beltane at Uisnech,[6] and Lugnassad at Tailtiu (these three towns were in the central kingdom of Meath). But Lugnassad was also celebrated at Emain Macha in Ulster and at Carman in Leinster.[7] These four festivals divided the year into four seasons of three months or eighty-five days, which seem to have been subdivided by other feasts each into two periods of forty-five days. There is no record of these other feasts save in those of certain great Irish saints, which sometimes fall on the same dates—St. Finnian's in December and, above all, St. Patrick's on the 15th, 16th, and 17th March.

These feasts stood in the very forefront of the life and thoughts of the Irish. We are always coming upon them

[1] Ibid., ii, pp. 389, 447–9.
[2] D'Arbois, op. cit. (Droit), i, p. 317.
[3] Ibid., p. 297 ; cf. Henderson, CCCCXXXIII, p. 187.
[4] Joyce, op. cit., ii, p. 441 ; Rhys, VIII.
[5] Joyce, ii, p. 436.
[6] D'Arbois, op. cit. (Droit), i, 302. Cf. Loth, " L'Omphalos chez les Celtes," in CXXXIV, 1915, p. 192.
[7] Rhys, CCLXXXII, p. 414 ; Loth, in *R.A.*, ii, 1914, p. 216 ; *Metrical Dindsenchas*, iii, 57 ; Joyce, op. cit., ii, p. 439 ; Rhys, VIII, pp. 17, 27, 55, 57.

in their tradition, which is very historical, and in their epic literature. Moreover, all legend or mythology revolves round the dates of festivals and a large number of the myths are festival-myths. These feasts were fairs, political or judicial assemblies, and also an occasion for amusement and games, some of which, such as the races, were of religious origin (the horse-races at Tailtiu and Emain Macha, the races of women at Carman). Above all, they were religious assemblies.

They were conducted in an atmosphere of myth and legend. The day of Beltane commemorated the landing of the first invaders of Ireland, the sons of Partholon; the first fire, that of Uisnech, was lit by their latest successors. Later on, about the middle of the sixth century, in the plain of Uisnech, King Diarmait mac Cearbhail laid siege to the house of one Flann, who drowned himself in a vat while his house was burning; the feast was a commemoration and expiation of his death.[1] At Lugnassad the wives of Lugh or his foster-mother Tailtiu died. Carman the sorceress, who came from Greece like the Fomorians, the people of the other world, also perished on this day, a captive of the Goidels, and in Conchobar's time the goddess Macha, who had beaten the King's horses at the races, died in giving birth to two children.[2] At Samhain the great battle of the gods was fought at Moytura, between the Fomorians and the Tuatha Dé Danann. On this day, too, King Muirchertach mac Erca, having broken the prohibitions laid on him by a fairy whom he had married, was attacked by the ghosts and while the fairy set fire to his palace drowned himself in a barrel like Flann.[3] Cuchulainn himself died on the first day of autumn. The times of the feasts were times when spirits were let loose and wonders were expected and normally happened.

In Wales the year was divided in the same way as in Ireland, at the Calends of May and of November. It was the same in Gaul; in the Coligny Calendar we can distinguish

---

[1] D'Arbois, op. cit. (Droit), pp. 299 ff. Cf. Joyce, op. cit.
[2] Loth, in CXXXIX, ii, 1914, pp. 217, 220; Rhys, VIII, pp. 19, 55; CCLXXXII, p. 414.
[3] Rhys, CCLXXXII, p. 396. Cf. d'Arbois, op. cit. (Droit), i, p. 317; at the end of the feast these temporary sanctuaries were doubtless set on fire. This rite is recalled in the stories of Flann and Muirchertach.

the two great seasons Samonos and Giamonos.[1] The great solitary sanctuaries in the mountains, those of the Donon and the Puy-de-Dôme, show that similar festivals were held in Gaul at one period in its history. For a long time there were no permanent shrines in Gaul.

IX

HOW RELIGION DEVELOPED

Gaul had already advanced a long way, starting from the common Celtic stock.

Doubtless it already had temples, and many of them. In any case, Roman civilization covered it with religious buildings [2] But the native character of the Gallic temple is proved by the fact that among these temples of the Roman period some are of such a peculiar type that they can be explained only by the assumption of a Gallic inheritance. The Temple of Vesona at Périgueux and that of Janus at Autun have nothing in common with classical architecture. They have been compared to the little square *fana* surrounded by a peristyle which have been found in the Rhine valley and Normandy.   We must picture two-storied buildings, with a roofed peristyle below (that is, the side-aisles) and a central roofed portion (or nave) rising above it.

Ancient writers who treat of the religion of the Celts always begin by giving the names of their gods.   Lucan mentions a triad of Gallic gods, Teutates, Esus, and Taranis.[3] We know that the literatures of Ireland and Wales give the gods and heroes in threes.   Cæsar gives us a valuable piece of information when he enumerates the gods of Gaul not under their Celtic names but under Roman names, Mercury, Apollo, Mars, Jupiter, and Minerva, to whom we must add Dispater, whom he mentions elsewhere.   These are the very gods whom we find represented in the archæology of Roman Gaul by monuments of every sort, inscriptions, bronze statuettes, sculptures in stone.   It appears to me that Cæsar set the seal on a process of identification which had

[1] Rhys, **VIII**.
[2] De Vesly, **CCCCLXXXIX** ; Wheeler, " A Romano-Celtic Temple near Harlow, and a note on the type," in **XVI**, 1928, p. 301.
[3] *Phars.*, i, 444.

already taken place to some extent in the mind of the Gauls. Moreover, the names of the Gallic gods survived in the form of epithets attached to their Latin names,[1] Mercurius Cissonius, Mars Camulus, Mars Caturix, etc. In any case, after the conquest there was a kind of classification of the deities in types, which were furnished by the Roman pantheon. Sometimes there has been doubt about the label ; one same god may have become Mercury, Mars, and Dispater in turn. Also, the gods became vulgarized. Who would recognize the noble Lugh, the victor of Moytura, in the little Mercury with the heavy purse, or the god of the dead, the brewer of mystic beer, in the hammer-god, the genial, homely patron of the coopers, married to a peaceable, colourless Fortuna ?[2] These are commonplace, harmless figures, like modern village saints. In Gaul the hero was supplanted by the household genius, who assumed a classical appearance for which Rome supplied the type and the means of reproduction. The breaking-up of the politico-domestic groups and the formation of territorial groups in their place did away with the reason for the existence of the god-hero.

X

RITUAL

The Celtic religions were sacrificial religions, of the ritual of which we unfortunately know very little. There were blood-sacrifices and others, which were offerings of first-fruits. The ancient authors speak of human sacrifices among the Gauls, and massacres of prisoners which had a sacrificial character.[3] In Ireland there are very few allusions to human sacrifice ; one might mention the sacrifice of newborn infants to the idol Cromm Crúaich.[4] The ritual of Celtic sacrifice allowed the substitute-victim, as we see in the story of the goddess Becuma. She was married to a king of Ireland, and her ill-luck brought sterility upon the country. Expiation had to be made by the sacrifice of the young son of a virgin, but the sacrifice of a cow was accepted

---

[1] Toutain, in *Rev. hist. des. relig.*, lxxiv, 1916, p. 373.
[2] H. Hubert, " Une Nouvelle Figure de dieu au maillet," in **CXXXIX**, 1915, i, pp. 26-39.
[3] **CXXXIV**, 1913, p. 482 ; *R.P.*, 1908, p. 343 ; d'Arbois, i, 154 ; Joyce, op. cit., i, 239. Cf. Ériu, ii, 86 ; iii, 155.
[4] Squire, **CCCCLIX**, p. 38.

instead, and was effective.[1]   There is reason for believing that the blood-sacrifices for which the Celts have been blamed were not so very bloody ; the victim was a divine victim, who died transcendentally.   When one reads the long series of deaths of heroes commemorated by the festivals, one cannot help thinking that these legends are derived from myths of divine sacrifices renewed in the form of human, animal, and vegetable victims.   The stories of houses burnt down and heroes burnt in their houses on feast-days belong to the same order of facts.   These sacrifices at feasts, which appear also in other forms, such as games and races in which the victor perishes and is the victim, were agrarian sacrifices, the sole object of which was to maintain the life of nature and to secure the fertility of the land.

Sacrifice was the foremost thing in Celtic religion.   But the power of the formula, the spell, even a mere poem uttered by a man of power, a Druid or *file*, grew as time went on.   The wizard plays a particularly large part in the religions of the Celts of the British Isles.   Among the Britons, Merlin and Taliesin are famous heroes.   With them, religious power becomes magic.

XI

REPRESENTATIONS OF THE GODS

Very few purely Celtic portraits of gods survive.   A few bronzes, some coins, and the Gundestrup cauldron in the Copenhagen Museum give us some divine types—the horned god, the god with the wheel, the god with the hammer, the three-headed god, the ram-headed serpent, the matron Epona, etc.

On the other hand, there are a good many sculptures of the Gallo-Roman period representing the same gods and some others, which have been identified with varying success.

XII

MYTHOLOGY

The Celts had a rich and colourful mythology, much better preserved among the Gaels and Welsh than in Gaul.

[1] Czarnowski, **CCCCXXIII**, p. 123.

It has come down to us in the form of epics built up out of materials which were the common stock of the professional reciters, local traditions of a more special interest which in Ireland make up the literature of the *Dinnshenchas*,[1] and the allusions made in the Welsh triads, which enumerate and classify gods or heroes. Almost all these elements are incorporated in cycles—the mythological cycle, the Cycle of Ulster, and the Cycle of Finn or the heroes of Leinster in Ireland and the mythological and Arthurian cycles in Wales. In these various cycles the story of divine families is unfolded—Fomorians and Tuatha Dé Danann in Ireland and the families of Pwyll, Don, and Beli in Wales. Many of these traditions relate the origin of the great festivals, and the number of variants shows that they were still living. A whole series of myths of origin are connected with holy places and feasts.[2]

One large group consists of stories of a voyage to the country of the blest or the dead. A hero—Bran, son of Febal, or Cuchulainn, or Connla, or Oisin—is drawn by a mysterious beauty. He puts out on a magic boat, often made of bronze. He meets Manannán, god of the sea and the dead, either on the way or on his arrival in a wonderful country, where he is welcomed with open arms. After staying there a while, he grows weary and wants to return. In the end he does so, only to die.[3] This type of story reappears in the Christian stories of the voyages of Maeldune [4] and St. Brendan [5] to marvellous islands.

A second type of story describes the descent of heroes underground ; for example, Conn goes into a *sidh* or mound at Tara and visits the god Lugh, in the *Champion's Prophecy*.[6] A similar adventure at Cruachain is related in a prologue to the *Táin* entitled the *Journey of Nera to the Other World*.[7]

A third series of stories is preserved in St. Patrick's accounts of Purgatory.[8]   The hero goes down into a cave,

[1] Gwynn, **CCLXI**.
[2] See below, ch. v.
[3] See, in particular, the admirable *Voyage of Bran*, **CCLXXIV**, edited and translated by Kuno Meyer, with commentaries by Nutt.
[4] D'Arbois and Loth, in **CCXLVIII**, vol. v, " L'Épopée celtique en Irlande," i, pp. 449–500.
[5] Ibid., Cf. Schirmer, **CCLXXXVI**, pp. 17–26.
[6] Squire, op. cit., p. 201. Cf. O. Curry, **CCLXXVIII**, app. cxxviii.
[7] Thurneysen, **CCLXXXIX**, pp. 311–17.
[8] *De Felice*, **CCCXXVII**.

which is a holy place, he falls asleep, and the pains of Purgatory are revealed to him. An initiation-myth probably underlies these legends.

Lastly, a fourth series tells of attacks on the other world, forays with the object of capturing wonderful things like the inexhaustible cauldron which Cuchulainn took twice. A similar cauldron is captured by Pwyll and Arthur in the Welsh legends [1]; Pwyll at the same time brings back the art of pig-breeding, and another family of gods, that of Gwyn fights him for his herd. Here we have myths of civilizing heroes who are at the same time agrarian gods and kings of the dead.

All these stories form part of a larger cycle which might be called that of myths of death, in which the very origin of the race is connected with the world of the dead by a perpetual process of exchanges between that world and the world of the living.

All this Celtic mythology is a heroic mythology. The Celts made their gods into heroes and the typical ancestors of their clans and families. In the lives of these heroes they represented the state of their people and the essence of their religious traditions. Whatever certain modern scholars who have applied their analytical methods to the Arthurian cycle may think,[2] that cycle has its roots in the same circumstances and tradition as the other heroic cycles of the Celtic world. Arthur has the same adventures and his companions perform the same feats and carry out the same quests as Finn and his Fianna and the other Celtic heroes. So through the heroes the tradition of the Celtic gods has been kept alive and handed down.

[1] For Pwyll, see Loth, **CCLXX,** i, pp. 81–117. Cf. ibid., p. 307, and for the magic cauldron, Squire, op. cit., p. 273. I am of opinion that these legends may contain the Celtic prototype of the stories of the quest of the Grail.
[2] Particularly Bruce, Faral, and Wilmotte, in the works quoted. Cf. below, p. 266.

CHAPTER IV

The Setting of Social Life

CELTIC societies lived in a setting which they had in part made themselves—time, space, and number.

I

SPACE : FIELDS, DWELLINGS, AND DISTRIBUTION OF THE POPULATION

We can get an idea of the space, the landscape in which our Celtic societies moved, if we interpret the features presented by the same regions to-day. Gaul had none of the long curtains of poplars which give such unity to the aspect of modern France. But the look of a cultivated country—and the Celtic lands were cultivated—is chiefly due to the shape of the fields, which in its turn is due to the conception of the ownership of land. The law is written down on the soil. The Celts of both Ireland and Gaul had a system of land-measurement.[1] The French still have the Gallic *arpent* (*arepennum*) and the Gallic league (*leuga*) [2] ; the servants of the Roman Fiscus who made the survey took over the Gaulish names. In France there are still two types of field, the closed field and the long, open field. The first type makes a landscape of hedges, the second a landscape of plains or hillsides whose unbroken surface is patched with variously coloured strips of crop. As we have already seen, the first type is found in Ireland, Wales, England, Brittany, Vendée, Western France, and part of North-Western Germany ; the second predominates north of the Seine to the Rhine. The first corresponds to family groups settled in isolation and to family property, the second to village communities working common property under common rules, particularly as regards fallow, with possible partitions. Both systems existed among the Celts. The

---

[1] Jullian, **CCCXLVII**, ii, 394 ; iv, 283.
[2] **CXXXIX**, 1914, ii, p. 137, on the Gallic league.

first covers a region corresponding to their earliest settlements in Gaul and the British Isles, the second to their
later settlements in Gaul and their settlements on the Rhine.

Traces of prehistoric cultivation have been found in the
forests round the Hallstatt settlements. These consist of
parallel depressions, which were once fields with raised edges
like garden beds, probably worked with the mattock or hoe.
German archæologists call them *Hochäcker*, " high fields." [1]
In general cultivation moved downwards towards the plains,
encroaching on the swamp and swampy forest. Clearing
extended in the valleys, and the forest gained ground on the
heights. But the general aspect has changed little since
Cæsar's time. The Gallic population, as described by
Polybios,[2] lived dispersed about the cultivated land, being
particularly scattered in districts where the park system
obtained and everywhere in the grazing season. Some
French villages, which get their names from estates (*fundi*),
have their origin in Gallo-Roman villas ; and so we must
imagine the Gallic village as a small collection of huts in
which the remoter relations or servants of a great man
lived round his house ; that was what a villa was.[3] There
were quite large rural communities in Gaul, to judge from
the size of their cemeteries.[4]

As well as these open settlements, the Celts had fortified
settlements. Ireland bristled with little forts built on hills,
called raths or duns, to which the names of the heroic families
of the epics were attached. As we have seen, these were
private strongholds, and they were also refuges.[5] In the
plains in which the assemblies of Ireland were held the raths
were occupied only temporarily. But in Gaul, a more highly
developed country, they tended to be used as permanent
abodes. At Gergovia the Arvernian nobility had their
residences just as the later French provincial nobles had
their mansions in the towns in which their interests lay.[6]
In Gaul the town grew up round the *oppidum*, and even

---

[1] Weber, "Neue Beobachtungen zur Alterfrage der Hochäcker," in **LXXXIII**,
xxix, 1908, p. 17. Cf. id., " Das Verhalten der Hochäcker," in **XX**, 1906 ;
CXXXI, xxvii ; *Pr. Z.*, 1911, p. 189.

[2] See above, p. 210.

[3] **LXXX**, 1911, p. 118.

[4] D'Arbois, **CCXCIX**, p. 96.

[5] **LXXX**, loc. cit.

[6] Jullian, **CCCXLVII**, ii, p. 62.

had its suburbs. In theory, the Gallic *oppidum* was the capital of a *civitas* or a *pagus*[1]; but some *oppida* continued to be strongholds. An *oppidum* usually stood on an isolated height with a distant view, and sometimes (e.g. Lutetia and Melun) on an easily-defended island. In their demand for security, at the end of the La Tène period the Celts revived the tradition of building palafittes; an example is the lake-village of Glastonbury, where much excavation has been done.[2] These were sometimes built on piles and sometimes on an artificial island consisting of a timber framework filled with stones.

Apart from some stone houses of Roman type excavated at Mont Beuvray, town and country buildings were usually made of wood and roofed with thatch.[3] There were round huts and rectangular houses. In the first century B.C. the timbers were nailed together and the walls of woven branches were coated with clay. A farm was a group of huts rather than one big house. The Celts stored their provisions in silos, which developed into cellars of masonry. At the same time they erected drystone buildings, of which there are many specimens in Ireland and Scotland; they had walls composed of two faces filled with rubble, and roofs consisting of false vaults. In this way they built small round huts like bee-hives, rectangular chapels, galleries, and guardrooms in the Irish duns, and in Scotland they erected brochs. These brochs were round towers with a central court, with stairs and vaulted galleries and chambers in the thickness of the wall.[4]

The sites of these settlements were determined by the crossings of roads. Peoples established themselves along a river, and when they had done so they made arrangements together for free transit or the collection of tolls, as the Senones did with the Parisii and Ædui.[5] Forts were placed

[1] D'Arbois, **CCCXLVII** (Propr.). Cf. **CIX**, 1910, p. 723; **CXXIV**, 1912, p. 205; and, for the excavation of Sos, an *oppidum* in Lot-et-Garonne, **CXXXIV**, 1913. Cf. Thompson, **CCCCLXI**; **CCCLXXXIV**, p. 122; Philipon, "Le Gaulois Duros," in **CXL**, 1909, p. 73; Dottin, **CCCXXII**, p. 332.
[2] **CXXXIV**, 1912. Cf. "The Glastonbury Lake-village", in *Gl. Antiquarian Society*, 1911; Déchelette, iii, pp. 974–7.
[3] Joyce, **CCCCXXXIV**, ii, p. 65; Caes, v, 43, and viii, 5. Cf. Macleod, "Further Notes on the Antiquities of Skye," in **CXXIV**, xlvi, 1911–12, p. 202.
[4] E. Sloat, "Some Shetland Brochs," ibid., p. 94.
[5] Strabo, iv, 3, 5, ; 1, 14. Cf. Jullian, **CCCXLVII**, ii, p. 223.

on peninsulas. Natural roads, some of which were international routes, like the tin route, received very little
engineering.[1] There were fords, bridges, and ports to which
tracks ran, and these tracks were raised on causeways in
swampy parts.[2] So life developed in the Celtic communities
on the chess-board of the land-survey, along ways of communication which formed the veins and nerves of the settlements.[3]

II

TIME AND NUMBER

The movements of this life were set in the year, divided
up by seasonal occupations, assembly-days, and the cycle
of the months. The Coligny Calendar shows that on the top
of the calendar of the seasons, which seems to have been
the popular calendar of Northern Europe, the Celts had
superposed a calendar which was at first purely lunar and
was afterwards brought into agreement with the course of
the sun by means of intercalations. The months continued
to be lunations, but not of a strict kind. The interior of the
month seems to have been arranged on another principle,
that by which the year is divided into half-years and the
season into half-seasons. The Celts adopted the fortnight,
and it has survived in the British Isles and in France. They
divided the month into two halves, originally marked
roughly by the full moon. In the Coligny Calendar the
second half is called *atenoux* (perhaps cf. Irish *athnugud*,
renewal). The Irish expression " the three fortnights "
shows for one thing that the fortnight is a unit and
for another that the system of half-seasons of forty-five
days was maintained side by side with the system of
months.

The Celts reckoned time by moons and nights. It seems,
too, that the Irish year began with its dark half, at the feast
of Samhain (1st November). The Coligny Calendar would
seem to indicate that the year began between May and June.
But it is known that all over Northern Europe the beginning

[1] Jullian, op. cit., iii, p. 17. Cf. Caes., ii, 5, 6.
[2] **CIX**, 1911, pp. 55–6.
[3] Polyb., iii, 42, 2 ; Strabo, iv, 1, 11. Cf. Jullian, op. cit., ii, p. 228 ;
Joyce, op. cit., ii, pp. 393, 399.

of the year wavered between the spring festival and that of harvest.

In general, all reckoning in social life, all repetition and division, was governed by a numerical law and favourite numbers—periods of three and of nine nights, cycles of three and of seven years, and divisions into two, three, twelve and, above all, four.

CHAPTER V

SOCIAL ACTIVITIES

THIS is not the place to reproduce the picture of the social life of the Celts which has already been drawn for two Celtic peoples by M. Jullian in the third volume of his *Histoire des Gaules* and by Mr. Joyce in his admirable *Social History of Ancient Ireland*. We have not to describe, but to bring out, the essential features which give Celtic societies their pecular character, to show how far they had progressed when their independent evolution was arrested, and in particular to determine the native characteristics of their economic and industrial activity.

Some of these activities, namely law and religion, I have described in speaking of the structure of society. Another, warfare, we have considered in dealing with the history of the Celts. The Celts were fond of fighting, and war held a very great place in their social life. Peace was precarious, and was disturbed by feuds and rivalries, between families and inside them. Here we have to speak of economic and industrial activity.

I

ECONOMIC LIFE

The Coins of Gaul [1]

Before making regular use of coin struck in the Greek fashion the Celtic peoples tried various kinds of money. In Cæsar's time [2] the Britons still used bars or rings of copper or silver of a determined weight. A good deal of iron currency has been found, in hoards or scattered about, in the shape of bars weighing multiples of a pound of 309 grammes (11 oz.) with an average weight of a mina of 618 grammes (22 oz.).[3]

---

[1] For Gallic coinage in general, see Blanchet, **CCCVI**; Forrer, **DXLIII**; Déchelette, ii, 3, pp. 1557 ff.

[2] Caes., v, 12 ; iii, 21.

[3] Déchelette, ii, 3, p. 1558, fig. 720.

Déchelette held that he had proved that the Gauls used a currency of spits,[1] as the Greeks did at one time.

Coined money did not come into use among the Celts before the third century B.C. From then onwards they were amply furnished with coins of Greek origin, and they copied them extensively for their own use. The Celts of the Danube and the East copied the tetradrachms and silver staters of Tarsos, Thasos, Byzantion, the Pæonian ruling houses, and, above all, the Kings of Macedonia. Those of the West imitated the drachmæ of Marseilles, Rhoda, and Emporion. A gold coinage also appeared, based chiefly on the famous " Philips ", which came through Marseilles and were copied as far as Britain, while staters of Alexander reached Celtic lands by way of Raetia. Roman models furnished new types, and gold and silver were supplemented at an early date, but always on the same models, by a very abundant and plentiful coinage of bronze or tin.

The Celts copied not only the types but also the sizes and weights of their models. In general, silver coins were based on the tetradrachm in the East and on the drachma in the West, and gold coins on the gold stater. So Gallic coinage is an extension of Greek coinage. It is indeed a counterfeit of it in every respect. Execution, weight, and quality of the metal deteriorated, and depreciation took place so fast that it is obvious that there was no regular control of issues. It is very possible that the right of striking coin was not reserved by the state ; yet peoples certainly seem to have exercised this right. Certain late coins of the Meldi, Mediomatrici, and Lexovii bear the word *Arcantodan*, which must designate some mint official.[2]

Meanwhile, either because coin was still rare or because its bad quality made it unpopular, the old way of reckoning values did not go out completely. We find the connection between *pecunia* and *pecus* reappearing in Low Breton, where *saout* " cow " comes from *soldus*,[3] although the relationship is here reversed and it is the coin which has given its name to the animal used as a standard of value. The trade which we may suppose to have taken place between Gaul and Ireland did not bring coinage into the latter country.

[1] Id., in CXLIII, 1911, pp. 1 ff.   [3] Loth, in CXXXIV, 1919, p. 263.
[2] Id., in CXXXIV, 1916, p. 281.

No stamped coins are found there before the seventh century, and the name by which they are called, *pinginn*, is of Anglo-Saxon origin.[1]   For money there were " standard values "— gold pins weighing an ounce (*briar*), gold rings or necklaces, open rings (now often called *fibulæ*), also having a determined weight and being used as ingots.   But in the practice of law and probably of trade, prices were reckoned in cattle or slaves.

It must have been the same in Gaul, although there was coin in the country.   For coin ceases to exist in trade as soon as the standard and weight have to be checked every time, and it is evident that the Gallic financier must often have had his scales in his hand.[2]   Yet money circulated actively.   The spread of types in Gallic copies is a proof of this ; but the composition of treasures, in which four-fifths are local types, shows that they were used only to a limited extent in payments between one district and another.[3] It is also unlikely that the bad coinage of the Celts was ever used for settling commercial accounts between Celtic and foreign countries.[4]   But the only exchanges of money between Celts and non-Celts of which we hear are the payment of mercenaries and political subsidies ; and certain Gallic issues known to us, coins of Vercingetorix, of the league against Ariovistus or the Helvetii, were definitely struck for political purposes.

Even though confined to these services, money had, and from the very beginning, a place in general economic life, by the mere fact of its accumulation.   It certainly did not constitute capital, though it was the best measure of it, but it was the instrument of the formation of the movable capital which is in part made of credit, of belief in a power. In all phases of its history, money has been a sign of power, of which its purchasing capacity is only one manifestation. If Gaul fairly quickly became a country of movable capital after the conquest, it was because the development which

[1] Joyce, **CCCCXXXIV**, ii, p. 381.   Cf. Ridgeway, *The Origin of Metallic Currency and Weight Standards*, 1892.
[2] Scales from Beuvray and Gergovia.   Déchelette, ii, 3, p. 1573, n. 2.
[3] Forrer, op. cit. (list giving provenance of Celtic coins).   This list indicates that some of the purchases made by Mediterranean merchants among the Celts were paid for in Greek coin, and that the native middlemen paid gold for the goods which they were commissioned to buy from those merchants.
[4] Blanchet, op. cit., ii, p. 517.

at once took form under the Roman Empire had begun in the days of independence.

One must not picture the Celtic societies as groups of specialized warriors leaving their wives to look after the cattle and the crops with the aid of captives. In Ireland the king was forbidden to touch the plough or oversee his byres; but that was only because he was the king. All other men took their share in the work of their farms; only the king had to stand aloof. So the economic life of the Celts was chiefly rural [1]—mainly pastoral in Ireland, part of Britain, and Spain, and mainly agricultural among the Gauls and Belgæ. It is probable that agriculture began to gain ground in the Hallstatt period. The Celts practised fallow and invented the great two-wheeled plough, drawn by several span of oxen (Pliny calls it *ploum*), which made it possible to work heavy land. [2]

Rural activities aimed at the market [3] and were not confined to production. Exchange and sale were the object as well as exploitation of the soil. Gallic bacon filled the pickle-tubs of Italy in the time of Cato, and in the days of Cæsar and Varro Gaul was famous for its hams. The rapid development of the culture of the vine and olive in Provence shows that Gallic agriculture could adapt itself to the requirements of an international market. [4] Once wine-growing was introduced in Gaul, Gallic wine travelled to Britain and Ireland. The organs of rural trade were the markets and fairs. [5]

This development of marketing introduced into Celtic society specialists in trade and in industry [6]; it was the development in trade which gave birth to industry. The Celts of the Bronze Age had already advanced beyond the stage of household economy. A Celtic household made part of its material and repaired its tools, but it bought them outside. And Celtic artisans had spread in foreign countries, like the smith Elico, who was established in Rome and summoned Brennus. [7] With the rise of town life, professional crafts increased at the expense of household

[1] See the evidence of Pytheas in Diod., v, 21.
[2] Pliny, 18, p. 172, Roth's ed., p. 288.
[3] Jullian, CCCXLVII, ii, p. 239.
[4] Pliny, x, 53; xix, 8; xi, 240.
[5] Caes, iv, 2, 1.
[6] Jullian, op. cit., ii, p. 237. Cf. Strabo, iv, 2, 1.
[7] Pliny, xii, 5.

industry, and the town population was formed of the waste material of the tribal organization. Among this material there were slaves, who were a large part of the industrial labouring class. But there were also free workers who hired themselves out. Strabo, following Poseidonios, tells us of a man at Marseilles who hired out men and women for navvy work.[1] In Gaul the crafts were chiefly pursued by free workers, masters and men. In Ireland the craftsmen formed groups [2] which aspired to imitate the college of *fili*. A large part of society, perhaps the greater part of that amorphous plebs of which Cæsar speaks, became reconstituted on the basis of the crafts. Economic life had become an organizing principle for Celtic society.

The state then stepped into the organization of trade and industry, by means of taxes and tolls and by creating markets and policing them. The holding of the great fairs necessitated truces. Here we see the outlines of a market-law which must have been fairly complex.

We know little about the internal trade of the Celtic world before the Middle Ages,[3] when we have definite evidence of the commercial relations connecting Ireland with a no longer Celtic Gaul. On the other hand, the trade of Gaul with the Mediterranean countries is attested by many discoveries of Greek or Italian objects in Celtic tombs or settlements.[4] Déchelette gives a list of these objects, gold wreaths, mirrors, bronze hydriæ, and cups of painted ware. The Greek, Italian, or Gallic traders went up the Rhone and its tributaries, bringing, in particular, amphoræ of wine and other requisites of the drinker to the fairs of Franche-Comté, Burgundy, and the Rhineland. The Celts appreciated wine.[5] They paid for their purchases with a great variety of articles, such as textiles, particularly woollen garments. We know, too, of the trade and traffic in British tin, which was landed at the mouth of the Loire and taken by a portage to the valley of the Rhone.[6] Slaves, too, were doubtless offered by the Celts in payment for goods.[7]

---

[1] Strabo, iii, 4, 7.
[2] MacNeill, **CCCCXLI**, pp. 75, 82.
[3] Zimmer, in **CXLVIII**, 1909, pp. 363–400. Cf. Tac., *Agr.*, 24.
[4] See *Rise*, pp. 162–4.
[5] Müllenhoff, ii, p. 137 ; Jullian, op. cit., ii, p. 225 ; Caes, xi, 22, 3.
[6] Lloyd, **CCCCXXXVIII**, p. 41.
[7] Diod., v, 26.

The Celtic countries were also rich in gold[1]; the Helvetii had an established reputation in this respect.[2] The gold which the Celts gave in exchange was not money, but it did the work of money.

II

CRAFTS

The literatures of the Celts give a lively picture of their industrial activity. The Mabinogi of Manawyddan, son of Llyr,[3] is particularly rich in information about the trades plied in towns and villages. Manawyddan, a sea-god, and Pryderi, son of Pwyll, the sole survivors of a massacre of gods, fled into Dyfed, but one day the country was turned by enchantment into a wilderness, and they were compelled to leave it. They then settled at Hereford, where they opened a saddlery and did so well that they took all the custom from the saddlers of the town. The latter plotted to kill them, and the two heroes went off to seek their fortune elsewhere. They established themselves as shield-makers and the same thing happened again. In a third town they started as cordwainers and joined a goldsmith, whose trade Manawyddan learned, but once again they had to fly. The Celtic mythologies tell of other working gods,[4] and people who own or make marvellous tools.[5] In religion these great artisans are the protectors of the crafts, which are grouped in guilds like those of the Middle Ages, equally exclusive and unfriendly to outsiders.[6]

Manawyddan learned the trades of goldsmith and cordwainer in the course of his wanderings, Now, enamelling and leather-work were just the arts in which the Celts excelled, and the former is perhaps the best-known of all the industries

---

[1] Déchelette, ii, 3, p. 1207.

[2] Strabo, iv, 3, 3 ; vii, 2, 2.

[3] Loth, CCLXX, i, pp. 151, 599.

[4] Thus Goibniu, the smith or cooper, became one of the most popular figures in Irish folklore, the Gobhan Saer, the all-round craftsman.

[5] Cf. the Welsh romance Kulhwch and Olwen. Loth, op. cit., i, pp. 243, 599.

[6] In the Mabinogion these heroes live in the midst of craftsmen. But the state of society described in this work is not that of the Middle Ages ; it takes us back to the time of the Roman conquest of Britain. For instance, Manawyddan adorns the metal parts of the saddles which he makes with blue enamel (Loth, op. cit., p. 46) which is the Celtic enamel of Britain rather than French enamel of the twelfth century.

of Gaul.[1] At Mont Beuvray [2] enamellers and blacksmiths had their workshops in humble buildings of drystone with thatched roofs. But if their premises were wretched, their stock of tools was quite good. They seem to have specialized in the manufacture of buttons of enamelled bronze,[3] which must have had a respectable market and been sold largely at the fairs of Bibracte.

In the mining areas we find industrial establishments of another kind, isolated but grouped in districts. These were the ironworks, which were fortified workshops, with their heaps of slag.[4]

The manufacture and decoration of metal articles seem to have been practised industrially. The story of Elico the Helvetian [5] shows that at an early date they had a reputation as past-masters. They exported pigs of raw iron to Germany.[6] For the treatment of ore [7] and the preparation of the various qualities of the metal they seem to have had processes as scientific and highly developed as those of the other metal-workers of antiquity. Irish literature contains magnificent descriptions of the arms of its warriors,[8] and excavations have yielded specimens which reveal extraordinary skill and taste—the helmets of Amfreville, La Gorge-Meillet, and Berru, and the Battersea and Thames shields.[9] Every technical method which can be used for the decoration of metal—gilding, enamelling, engraving with the point and with acid [10]—was employed by the Celts. These processes, which a god like Manawyddan could learn in no time, imply professional training and trade traditions in mere mortals.

Leather-work seems to have been another craft which appealed to the Celtic imagination, since the gods excelled in it. The Gallic shoemakers who made the *caliga* or Celtic

---

[1] Déchelette, ii, 3, pp. 1547 ff.   [2] Bulliot, **CCCLXIX**.

[3] Buttons were a part of Gallic costume. One type of blouse in use was buttoned down the front from top to bottom ; and, since the sleeves are represented as open, these too were probably buttoned. Cf. a relief from Dijon ; Espérandieu, **CCCXV**, 3473, 3475.

[4] These settlements have not yet been studied except in the valleys running into the lower Loire (L. Maitre, in **CXXXIX**, i, 1919, pp. 234 ff. ; cf. id. in *B.A.C.*, 1905, p. xliv).

[5] Pliny, xii, 11.   [6] Kossinna, in **LXXXV**, 1915, p. 117.

[7] Refining-furnace. Bushe-Fox, **CCCVIII**, p. 72. Déchelette, ii, 3, pp. 1539 ff.

[8] *Táin*, ed. Windisch, p. 17.

[9] See *Rise*, p. 95, fig. 4 ; p. 125, fig. 31.

[10] Déchelette, ii, 3, p. 1148.

boot fashionable in the Roman world [1] were doubtless better than others. The goods produced by the weavers were equally in demand, but we do not yet know what was the nature of the woollens and linens which the Gauls sold to Italy.[2]

By the side of these industries of metal, leather, wool, and linen, we must allow a large place to the manufacture of metal vessels and coopering in estimating the position of the Celtic crafts in ancient industry as a whole. The Gauls were not only expert horsemen, keenly interested in the harness and trappings of their mounts [3]; they contributed more than any other people in Europe to the use of the horse as a draught-animal. They invented a war-chariot, the *essedum*,[4] and their various types of vehicle, the *carpentum* or heavy travelling-waggon, the *rheda*, and the *cissum* or two-wheeled gig were adopted, name and all, by the Latins. Of all these vehicles nothing remains but some representations [5] and great quantities of ironwork,[6] the complexity of which bears witness to great inventiveness.

The Gallic coopers, of whom we have some complete barrels, and the makers of wooden utensils, who have left only a few fragments, plied trades which had thriven from the earliest times in the countries of Northern Europe, where men had abundant raw material at their disposal and could study it and choose it according to its qualities. The share of the Celts in the progress of these industries is attested by the name of the *tun*, which seems to have been taken from the Celtic languages.[7]

Inventors in coopering, coach-building, and enamel-work, the Celts were also inventors in the manufacture of various tools, the more complicated of which are unknown to us.[8] They introduced some new agricultural implements—

[1] Jullian, op. cit., ii.

[2] Textiles of the Cadurci ; Jullian, op. cit., ii, pp. 272, 525, n. 5.

[3] Bits peculiar to the Celts ; Arr., *Ind.*, 16, 10 ; Hor., *Odes*, i, 8, 6. Cf. Déchelette, ii, 3, pp. 1199–202.

[4] Jullian, op. cit., ii, pp. 187, 234.

[5] Expérandieu, op. cit.

[6] Déchelette, ii, 3, pp. 1197–9.

[7] *Tunna* (Low Lat.).   MacBain, **CLXXXIX**, p. 382.   Barrels of the Roman period found in Holland (**CXXXIX**, 1918, p. 249).

[8] E.g. the *terebra Gallica*, an auger with a spiral bit (Pliny, xvii, 15). The great quantity of tools found in tombs and *oppida* bears witness to the skill of the Gallic metal-worker (cf. Déchelette, ii, 3, pp. 1352 ff.).

the large hay-sickle, types of harrow, the great plough, and even a reaper.[1] We must not forget the riddle in cooperage nor the coat of mail in metal-work.[2] So the Celts not only practised most of the industrial arts of the ancients with skill but brought to them an originality and inventiveness which can be explained only by the great place held by industry in social life, whether through the needs which it had to meet or through the quality of the men engaged in it.

III

ART

On the whole the art of the Celts is entirely decorative.[3] The kind of decoration which the Celtic artist put on his works usually has no meaning, except in some objects used for religious purposes. We find neither representations nor symbols. Ornament generally consists of geometrical patterns without ritual significance, stylized foliage, scrolls, and the like. Except in a few religious objects like the Gundestrup cauldron and the gods of Bouray and Stuttgart, art has added nothing but beauty. The Celts made works of art in almost every class of manufactured article, even the humblest brooch, for example. The plainest sword had a handsome chape ; shields, helmets, and vases were decorated. The Celtic craftsman liked beauty, and he had taste. He was particularly drawn to curvilinear decoration, the elements of which he took from the Greek palmette.

In their decoration the Celts broke up the model selected and conventionalized it. The artists of Gaul and Ireland were not given to realism.[4] On the stela of Entremont, on which, of all the monuments of independent Gaul, human and animal forms are treated with the most freedom (and that under Greek influence), the horsemen are framed in a decorative scroll. The outer figures of the Gundestrup cauldron are treated as pure decoration. Celtic art went in for broad planes in relief, maintaining a right balance between broad and delicate features in decoration and a right

---

[1] Four-wheeled plough (Pliny, xviii, 48) ; reaper (ibid., 72) ; harrow (Jullian, op. cit., ii, p. 276).
[2] Sieve (Jullian, op. cit., p. 277) ; coat of mail (Déchelette, ii, 3, p. 1155).
[3] Cf. Allen, CCXCVIII ; Verworn, CCCLXXXIX.
[4] CXL, 1911, p. 245.

balance between the field and the ornament standing against it. In Roman Gaul, human figures of the Roman type were cast in bronze or carved in stone ; it was an art full of homely geniality and facility. The Celts were always addicted to fine weapons, beautiful jewellery, and rich, brightly-coloured garments. The decorative art of the Celts is art of good quality, but not a strong art. The Celtic genius was to expand more in another form of æsthetic activity—literature.

IV

LITERATURE

It is very difficult to obtain an idea of Celtic literature as a whole, for what remains of it comes entirely from the British Isles. Literature so much depends on changing tastes and fashions that it would be very rash to try to picture one literature from what one knows of another some hundreds of years later, even though it belongs to a people of the same stock.

First, we are faced with a complete absence of any definite information about the literature of the Continental Gauls. They were great talkers, and interested in things of the mind.[1] Men like Deiotarus and Diviciacus impressed Roman intellectuals by their culture. The Druids had a reputation as philosophers. Gauls like Vercingetorix displayed a broad and elevated intelligence in the political domain. Lastly, when Gaul was Romanized it at once produced such a crop of teachers, great advocates, and distinguished administrators that we must suppose that the people was already prepared. It had had the literature of its *vates*, epic traditions such as the story of Ambicatus which Livy has transmitted to us ; this fragment of a history of the beginnings of the race must have been something corresponding to the histories of origins incorporated in the *Leabhar Gabhála*.[2] But these were the traditions of a society, and, as we have seen, that society was disappearing when the Roman conquest intervened. Gallic society was already divided into two parts, a nobility which was above tradition and a popular

[1] Diod., v, 31, 1. Cf. Jullian, op. cit., ii, p. 360.
[2] See d'Arbois, CCL.

class which was beneath it. This revolution hastened the neglect and loss of the national tradition.

Ireland, too, underwent a rather similar development. By the seventh century its ancient literature was becoming forgotten, being perhaps discredited or superseded by Christianity. The great ecclesiastical histories and, above all, the stories of the saints offered the newly converted Irish novel and attractive matter. But an effort was made to save tradition. This was done chiefly by the corporation of *fili*, who were interested in the preservation of the old tales. Their chief, Senchan Torpeist, who lived in the time of Guaire Aidne, King of Connacht (died 659), endeavoured to collect the fragments of the *Táin*.[1] The difficulty of the undertaking is shown by the legend that his son Muirgen had to call up the soul of the hero Fergus from the dead.[2] But tradition, once revived, was not lost again, and Christianity, which had made an alliance with the *fili*, kept it up.

The Britons had thrown all their literary traditions overboard and become Romanized. Only scraps of the Mabinogion, which form the oldest part of Welsh tradition, can be older than the Irish conquest of the west coast of Britain, and they contain a mass of Irish traditions. The rest of the tradition, which centres on Arthur, dates from the Saxon conquest, if it is true that Arthur was a historical personage who developed into a national hero. It is true that this new cycle of traditions contains some remains of an older tradition in the form of allusions, isolated names, and mythical subjects. But here Celtic tradition was saved by the conquerors, especially the Normans, who by adopting the history of the hero of the conquered in this way caused it to pass into literature.[3] The Welsh reconstructed their literature, the Irish rediscovered theirs, but that of the Gauls is lost. We lack the essential portion, and the most ancient.

We meet a second blank in regard to what may be called dramatic literature. Festivals in Gaul must have included dramatic performances, as is shown by the erection of a great number of theatres and arenas in the country in the very first years of the Empire. Some stood at places which

---

[1] Thurneysen, **CCLXXXIX**.   [2] See above, pt. iii, ch. i.
[3] Cf. Rhys, **CCLXXXI**.

were the scene of great pilgrimages, such as Saint Cybard of Aixe and Champlieu ; others were too large for the towns by which they stood and can only have been filled by crowds drawn from outside by the games.

It is certain, too, that the Irish feasts comprised dramatic representations, since they comprised games which are a kind of drama. Legends of heroes were attached to them and commemorated. But of these performances we have not the barest scenario. It is a whole side of the creative activity of the Celts of which we know nothing.

Let us, then, be content with what we have, namely, the written literature of Ireland and Wales. This literature, particularly that of Ireland, although it cannot have assumed its written form earlier than the seventh century, contains ancient elements which are often hard to understand. It may be able to give us an idea of its own past.[1]

It is composed mainly of *chansons de geste* in prose mixed with verse on epic and mythological subjects. In Ireland they are classified and catalogued under titles which describe them by class. There were Takings of Cities or Houses, Feasts (like that of Briccriu), and series of Battles (*Cath Muighe Tured*), Wooings (*Tochmarc Emire, Tochmarc Etaine*), Forays (*Táin*), Rapes (such as the story of Grainne), and Journeys to the Other World (like the *Journey of Bran*). These stories were arranged in three cycles, a Mythological Cycle and the two heroic cycles of Ulster and Leinster.[2]

The Mythological Cycle is the history of the successive gods and invasions of Ireland. The versions which have come down to us have undergone many transformations. One of them is the *Leabhar Gabhála*, the Book of Invasions, in which a great many narratives are linked together ; it was recast by O'Clery as late as 1631.[3]

The Ulster Cycle is that which has Cuchulainn and King Conchobar for its principal heroes. The chief epic in the cycle is the *Táin Bó Chuailgné*, which is over six thousand lines

---

[1] See O'Curry, **CCLXXVIII**; d'Arbois, **CCXLVIII**, and esp. **CCXLIX**; Best, **CCLII**; K. Meyer, " Addenda to the *Essai d'un catalogue de la littérature épique de l'Irlande*," in **CXL**; D. Hyde, *Story of Early Gaelic Literature*, Dublin, 1920.

[2] Squire, **CCCCLIX**; Hyde, **CCLXIV**. Cf. K. Meyer, " The Death-tales of the Ulster Heroes," in **CXXII**, xiv; d'Arbois, op. cit.

[3] Squire, op. cit., pp. 61–135; d'Arbois, op. cit., ii, p. 155; Rhys, **CCLXXXII**, p. 146.

long. It tells of a great war waged upon the heroes of Ulster by the rest of Ireland, led by Queen Medb, for the sake of a wonderful bull. Many famous passages which have come down to us separately are connected with this central theme, such as the stories of the birth of Conchobar, the conception of Cuchulainn, his sickness, his love of the goddess Fand, and the intoxication of the Ultonians, which compelled Cuchulainn to defend Ulster single-handed for several days. That is the most ancient part of this epic literature. But the whole cycle was modernized by the men who recast it, just as the annalists place King Conchobar about the beginning of the Christian era.[1]

The Leinster Cycle is known as the Fenian or Ossianic Cycle. It tells of Finn, his son Oisin or Ossian, and their kinsmen and comrades, the Fianna. It is represented in the ancient manuscripts by a not very large number of complete stories, and there are allusions and lists of subjects for recitation which show that its main elements were in existence about the seventh century. The annalists place Finn in 200 B.C. These datings, done long afterwards, are of no great importance, but the cycle in its original form seems to correspond to a state of civilization and society obtaining about that time. It developed later than the Ulster Cycle, but lived on in the folklore of Ireland and Gælic Scotland. Its origins are very ancient. Finn is probably a hunter-god, particularly a hunter of the boar, like the typical Celtic hero. He is designated by the epithet Fair-haired, springs from the family of the gods of death, and is the same as the Welsh Gwyn. This cycle never attained the cohesion of the Ulster cycle,[2] although it was

[1] The chief texts regarding Ulster are collected in Windisch, CCXCV. A translation of the more important ones will be found in d'Arbois, CCXLVIII, v, " L'Épopée celtique en Irlande." For the Ulster cycle, see Hull, CCLXIII ; Thurneysen, CCXC ; Nutt, CCLXXVI ; Lady Gregory, CCLIX ; Faraday, CCLVIII ; Windisch, CCXCVI ; E. MacNeill, "Relation of the Ulster Epics to History," in CXI, Feb., 1907 ; Joseph Dunn, *The Ancient Irish Epic Tale Tain Bo Cuailnge*, London, 1914 ; and above all Thurneysen's admirable work CCLXXXIX, which deals with the constitution, text, and interpretation of the whole cycle.

[2] The chief ancient texts of this cycle will be found dated and in part translated in K. Meyer's excellent *Fianaigecht*, in CXII, xvi, 1910. Many texts, usually later, are collected and translated by O'Grady in CCLXXIX. Lastly, a large number of valuable texts have been published, often somewhat hastily and from late versions, in the six volumes of CCXCII. Mr. Mac-Neill has edited, with an important introduction, a collection of poems related to this cycle in his *Duanaire Finn*, in CCCXV, vii. A great many

the cycle of the Fianna or mercenary troops of Ireland and was taken up by the poets and popular story-tellers.

The principal and most valuable portion of Welsh literature consists of the collection of plots of epic narratives called the Mabinogion, the plural of *Mabinogi*, meaning " literary apprentice ".[1] Four of these stories intended for " literary apprenticeship " deserve the name more particularly ; the Red Book of Hergest calls them the Four Branches of Mabinogi. They are mythology heroicized, based on legends of South Wales. The first tells the story of Pwyll, Prince of Dyfed and god of the dead ; the second, of the marriage of Bronwen, the daughter of the sea-god Llyr, to a King of Ireland ; the third, the hero of which is Manawyddan, son of Llyr, is a continuation of the first two ; the fourth is about Math, son of Mathonwy. Five other stories belong to the Arthurian cycle, but behind three of these lie the earliest French poems of the Round Table.[2] Another, entitled *Kulhwch and Olwen*, is of genuine Welsh inspiration. Two others are closely associated with them, namely the *Dream of Macsen Wledig* and a mythological story called *Lludd and Llevelys*, a doublet of the story of Manawyddan.

The great Welsh manuscripts also contain poems, many

---

stories linked with this cycle have been collected in the chief collections of tales of the Gaelic countries, particularly in three volumes published under the name *Waifs and Strays of Celtic Tradition, Argyllshire Series* (**CCXCIII**) : MacInnes and Nutt, *Folk and Hero Tales* ; Macdougall and Nutt, *Folk and Hero Tales* ; J. F. Campbell and Nutt, *The Fians*, all three volumes containing interesting commentaries by Nutt. Consult also Campbell, **CCLIV** ; Curting, **CCLV** ; Croker, **CCLVII**. One should also mention the collections of popular ballads and poems in Gaelic in Campbell, **CCLIII**, and in the *Book of the Dean of Lismore*, a sixteenth century collection edited by Skene (Edin., 1862). For these ballads and the use made of them by Macpherson, see Stern, in **CLXXIII**, vii, pp. 51 ff. Certain texts connected with the Leinster cycle are translated in d'Arbois, *L'Epopée celtique en Irlande*. Some of the finest stories in this cycle are adapted rather than translated, but on the whole delightfully and faithfully, by Joyce in his *Old Celtic Romances*.

For the interpretation of the whole cycle, see Nutt in the appendices to the collection of tales cited above ; Rhys, **CCCXXXII**, pp. 355, 553 ; Squire, pp. 201–216. These writers believe that the cycle is ancient and its origin mythological. MacNeill, in his introduction to the *Duanaire Finn* quoted above and **CCCCXLI**, favours a later date. Zimmer connects the cycle with the time of the Scandinavian invasions, particularly in **CCXLVI**.

[1] **CCLXXXIV**; Loth, **CCLXX**. Cf. Lady Guest, **CCLX**; Skene, **CCLXXXVII**; Rhys, **CCLXXXI–CCLXXXIII**.

[2] Weston, **CCXCIV**; Nutt, **CCLXXVII**. Cf. Faral, **CCCCXXVI**; Bruce, *The Evolution of Arthurian Romance*, Göttingen, 1923 ; Wilmotte, *Le Poème du Gral et ses auteurs*, Paris, 1930.

of them very ancient, which are ascribed to four bards, Aneurin, Taliesin, Myrddin (Merlin), and Llywarch Hen. They seem to represent the tradition of the north of British lands.

To all this romantic and poetic literature we must add a literature which might be called gnomic. In Ireland it consists of the *acallamh*, dialogues or colloquies,[1] such as the dialogue of Oisin and St. Patrick, dialogues of old men, and of the two wise men, which are connected with the romantic cycles. In Wales the literature of the Triads gives lists of allusions in gnomic form.

In both countries annals flourished. In Ireland a whole literature of antiquarianism, of dictionaries, of collections of local traditions and etymologies (*Dinnshenchas*) grew up.[2] We need not, of course, touch upon Christian literature.

One thing should be noted. The Cycles of Ulster and Leinster, which have survived, are composed of the traditions of those Irish kingdoms which were least successful politically, at whose expense the others expanded, and which were sometimes regarded by them as being peopled by foreigners. The truth is that what has come down to us is an inter-tribal tradition, which forgets internal conflicts. The subjects are selected on their æsthetic merits. It is the same in Wales, where the traditions of Dyfed, a conquered country, are preserved best. In other words, these literatures are already national literatures.

Starting from these data, we can recover in some measure the common characteristics of the ancient literatures of the Celts and the distinctive features of their intellectual activity.

The literature of the Gauls was an oral literature, and so were those of the Welsh and Irish. Every oral literature is a paraphrase of known themes and centos. Since the most powerful memory has its limitations, these themes are few. Popular literature is poor, although there are so many collections of folklore ; oral literature partakes of the nature of popular literature. It is not very varied. In Ireland the *ollamh*, or chief of the *fili*, had to know three hundred and

---

[1] See esp. **CCLXXIX**, i, ii.
[2] See Squire, **CCCCLIX** ; D. Hyde, op. cit. ; Loth, op. cit. ; Gwynn, **CCLXI**.

fifty stories, two hundred and fifty long and a hundred short. We have catalogues of the resources of the *fili*. The prose parts of the Irish romances seem to have been a foundation on which all kinds of fancies could be built up. The metrical parts were those which had acquired more permanence ; they were usually *bravura* passages. The oral tradition went on long after the form of the story had been fixed by erudition. Some of the most famous and affecting passages in the heroic legends and even in the Mythological Cycle, to which the ancient texts merely allude, were only developed in late poems of the seventeenth or eighteenth century—for example, the story of the sons of Ler being turned into swans by their stepmother. From this point of view we may say that " Ossian " Macpherson remained in the Celtic tradition ; only he took greater liberties than the ordinary arrangers of these themes.

Celtic literature was essentially a poetic literature. The Irish probably invented rhyme cn their own account.[1] The Celtic reciter added music to verse, like the minstrel of the Middle Ages. The harp was the tool of his trade. The literary profession was exercised by clans of specialists, who had their order of rank. We must not think of Celtic poetry as lyrical outpourings, but as elaborately ingenious exercises on the part of rather pedantic literary men. Yet Celtic literature was popular as no other was. The whole nation entered the field, not as specialists, and some of the best modern Celtic poets have been men sprung from the people. Romance literature also became popular. Nowhere else do oral tales contain more memories of heroic literature. In Celtic lands there is constant interchange between literature and folk-tale.

This literature [2] has a remarkably dramatic quality. Not only are the epics extremely interesting, lively, and full if movement, but the actors in them are real characters. Cuchulainn, Emer, King Conchobar, and Cathbad the Druid are living people. The Celts gave to the literature of the world Tristram and Yseult, to say nothing of Arthur and his companions. *Tristram and Yseult* is a Cornish tale, the

---

[1] Joyce, **CCCCXXXIV**, ii, pp. 499–501.

[2] For the general character of Celtic literature, see Arnold, **CCLI** ; Renan, **CCLXXX** ; Magnus MacLean, *The Literature of the Celts*, London, 1902 ; Nutt, **CCLXXV**.

Irish pendant to which is that of Diarmait and Grainne.[1]
These last are passionate lovers who fly to the forest, whither
they are pursued by Finn, Grainne's husband. It is hard
to imagine that the story-tellers of Gaul had less aptitude
for dramatic narrative than their brethren in the British
Isles. And one thinks of the men who were probably carrying on their work in French or Franco-Latin literature, and
more especially of the long succession of chroniclers who,
from Gregory of Tours and the monks of Saint-Denis, have
made the history of France the finest historical narrative
in the world.

Moreover, even if the Celtic literatures are not alone
in presenting heroes who are on the one hand dipped in the
marvellous and on the other bound to a chain of fates and
responsibilites which can never be broken, at least they have
obtained incomparable æsthetic effects from these two
elements. The fantastic is always there. Gods or fairies
are behind the door. You never know whether you are
dealing with a man or a spirit. A man is often a reincarnation
and sometimes he remembers it. The mysterious world
which makes the setting of the story is the world of the dead ;
the idea of death dominates everything, and everything
reveals it. All Celtic literature suggests mystery with a rare
power of evocation. And it is also because that literature
carries a hidden meaning that it turns readily to humour.
There is in Celtic literature a humorous vein we find even in
the finest of its early products, the *Feast of Briccriu* [2] and
Kulhwch and Olwen.[3]

V

A PICTURE OF CELTIC LIFE. THE MORALITY OF HONOUR

Let us end by trying to picture the Celts in peace and
ease, for example at one of the banquets described for Ireland
in the *Feast of Briccriu* and for Gaul in Athenaeos. Luckily

---

[1] Joyce, **CCLXVII**, pp. 274–350. Cf. **CCXCII**, iii.
[2] For editions of this text and its composition, see Thurneysen, **CCLXXXIX**,
pp. 445 ff. It is edited by Windisch in **CCXCV**, i, p. 235. Stern has published
an edition from another manuscript in Z.C.P., iv, 143, there is a complete
edition by Henderson in **CCLXV**, ii, 1899, and it is translated by d'Arbois in
L'Epopée celtique en Irlande, p. 81.
[3] See Loth, **CCLXX**, i, pp. 243–599.

the ancients found the Gauls picturesque enough to be worth describing or portraying.

The Gauls sit in a circle in a round building, with the chief or host in the middle, at an equal distance from all men of equal rank. If they are nobles, the guests have with them, behind them, some seated and some standing, according to their degree and office, their squires or servants. In Ireland the arrangement is different. The building is rectangular and divided into compartments, and every man has his proper place according to his station. The women are apart, but they appear when the time comes. Strangers are welcomed, for we are hospitable.[1]

All are clean and well dressed. The Celt is very particular about his person, and is not afraid of a bath. They are clean-shaven save for the moustache, and their hair, which they wear at half-length, is drawn back from the brow and is sometimes dyed, or rather bleached ; soap (*sapo*) is a Celtic invention, used for this purpose.[2] Tattooing or painting of the body completes the adornment.[3] The men wear trousers or breeches which vary according to the country, smocks, and cloaks fastened with brooches ; their footgear is hose not sandals. The colours of the clothes are bright and varied. The Gaul even had tartan, and the colours may have been governed by tribal rules, as at the present day. The men carry arms.

The furniture is meagre.[4] The party sit on bundles of reeds on the ground.[5] Seats, if not unknown, are rare. The meat and bread are laid out on low tables. Meals consist mainly of butcher-meat and venison ; there is plenty of this latter, for game is abundant, and the Celts are keen and well-equipped hunters, with famous hounds. Fish also appears on the table. Meat is either roasted and taken off the spit on the table or boiled and lifted out of the pot with iron hooks.[6] It is also baked on hot stones in holes dug in the ground. In addition there is porridge made of oats or barley. Poseidonios says that the Celts ate their meat in their fingers, occasionally using a small knife to cut stringy bits and to separate bones. The meal is washed down

---

[1] Diod., v, 28.   [2] Ibid., p. 270 ; Pliny, xxviii.
[3] Déchelette, ii, 3, p. 1206 ; Isid. Sev., 19, 23. Cf. **XIII**, xii, 1913, p. 73.
[4] Pliny, viii, 73 ; xix, 2. Cf. Girald. Cambr., i, 3.
[5] Diod., vi, 28.
[6] Déchelette, ii, 3, p. 1028. Cf. Joyce, **CCCCXXXIV**, ii, p. 123.

with beer or wine.[1] At first wine came from Italy or Greece in amphoræ, and it was drunk in the Greek fashion with all the complicated apparatus of the Greek drinker. Later on the Gauls produced their own wine and exported it. Beer was made with wheat or barley and seems to have been flavoured with herbs. It was drunk when new-brewed. Mead was also made.

Festive parties drank deep and heads grew hot.[2] Drunkenness was a failing of the Celts, and things often ended ill, since all were armed. But causes of strife arose at the very beginning of a meal. Various portions of the food had their order of superiority, corresponding to the order of rank among men, and nobody would have deigned to accept anything but what was his due. An inferior portion offered to the wrong man might be a serious insult. But many might have a claim to the best portions, and it was not easy to satisfy them all. In the *Feast of Briccriu*, Briccriu wants to lead the heroes on to kill one another. He invites them to a banquet. There was a " hero's bit ", the best portion. To whom is it to be given ? All rise up, ready to fight. The women join in. They agree to undergo trials, from which Cuchulainn emerges victorious. The Celts were a touchy race, and this sensitiveness was easily exasperated in company. In addition, there were memories of old quarrels, some of which had not been properly settled.

I have chosen this example rather than others because the feasters here afford an illustration of the very principle of social and moral life among the Celts, namely honour. The moral tales which the Greek writers relate of the Celts, that of Chiomara throwing down at her husband's feet the head of the centurion who had violated her, and that of Camma poisoning herself with her persecutor before the altar of Artemis, are all based on this morality of honour. The Celts did not excel as citizens, and that was one great source of their weakness. But in this refinement of the morality of honour there was a principle of civilization which did not cease to develop on the political collapse of the Celtic societies. The Celts bequeathed it to their descendants.

[1] Ath., iv, 152 ; Dioscorid., ii, p. 110. Cf. Windisch, **CCXCV**, i, pp. 319–320 ; Vendryès, "Les Vins de Gaule en Irlande," in **CXL**, xxxviii, 1920, p. 19.
[2] D'Arbois, **CCXLVIII**, i, p. 297.

CONCLUSION

The Heritage of the Celts

THE peculiar destiny of the Celts had carried them in a few centuries over the greater part of Europe, of which they had conquered and colonized a good third—the British Isles, France, Spain, the plain of the Po, Illyria, Thrace, Galatia, and the Danube valley, in addition to Germany, almost to the Elbe, which was their cradle. In a still shorter time they had lost all their Continental domain and part of the British Isles, being reduced to subjection in one place, driven out of another, and everywhere deprived of all political power. Then there had been a respite. But from the sixth century onwards the independent states in the British Isles were subjected to unceasing attacks, to which they succumbed. Only one is reviving, Ireland. The political creations of the Celts are among the great failures of the ancient history of Europe. The historical role of the Celtic peoples, except the Irish, for whom the future is opening again, is a thing of the past. I have tried to suggest that that role was once a large one, and that much of it remained. Certainly this was the feeling of their opponents. One has only to try to imagine what the history of the Celts would have been if Cæsar had not described the resistance of Vercingetorix and the Anglo-Normans had not adopted Arthur. But also how little evidence the Celts have left of themselves, compared with what we know of the Egyptians, the Greeks, the Romans, even the Germans! Even now, there may be some who fear, when confronted with this history, which has left so few monuments but which we are none the less tempted to regard as great, that they are the victims of a mirage produced by the imagination of Greek and Latin writers and the fancy of Celtic archæologists. One last check is needed, that of language.

There are still Celtic languages in existence, but they are no longer, as it were, languages working full time, completely sufficient for the social life of a whole society and, what is more, sufficient to themselves. Irish, it is true,

273

has once more become an official language, now that Ireland is once more a political community. But many Irish patriots have had to learn their language anew. The example of Breton is still more striking; it is the mother-tongue of a dwindling part of the population and a learned or rather a poetic language for a few lovers of the past. In different degrees, all Celtic languages were in this state. The difference which we see in the case of Irish and Welsh is due to the existence in both countries of an older and richer literary tradition. These various languages borrowed largely from all those which brought them into contact with a new life, particularly Latin. The degree of their independence is proportionate to the extent to which the peoples who spoke them resisted those who sought to assimilate them. They did not maintain themselves in their original independence and dignity.

But the Celtic languages are no longer spoken save in a very small part of the regions in which the Celts have left descendants. Great numbers of Britons remained in Britain after the Roman, Anglo-Saxon, and Norman conquests. Celts also remained in Gaul, where they formed the basis of the population. Many certainly remained in Spain and Northern Italy. But it is interesting to note how many remnants of Gaulish were preserved in Low Latin and French.

For Gaulish did not vanish as if by magic, quickly though Latin spread in Gaul.[1] A preacher like St. Irenaeus still had to learn it at the end of the second century,[2] and the Emperor Alexander Severus seems to have understood it.[3] In the time of Ulpian, the beginning of the third century, it was possible to draft certain acts in Celtic.[4] In the fourth century, St. Jerome could compare the speech of Treves and that of the Galatians. Sulpicius Severus in the fifth century perhaps knew a little Celtic,[5] and Ausonius, Gregory of Tours, Fortunatus, and Marcellus of Bordeaux [6] knew a few words each. This evidence is confirmed by inscriptions. Celtic continued in use for a long time, but in circles which grew ever smaller. Still, in abandoning their

---

[1] Loth, in **LVIII**, 1916, p. 169 ; Babut, " Le Celtique en Gaule au début du Ve siècle," in **CXLI**, 1910, pp. 287–292.
[2] Iren., *Contra Haereses*, i, pref.   [3] *Life of Alex. Severus*, p. 60.
[4] Ulp., *Digest*, xxxii, 11.   [5] Sulp. Sev., *Dial.*, i, p. 27, 1–4·
[6] *R.C.*, 1904, p. 351. See **CXXXIV**.

language, the vast majority of Gauls kept their manner of speaking and a great number of words for which Latin gave no equivalent.

Thus, Gaulish had lost u; the Gauls did not take up the Latin u, pronouncing it u.[1] In the syllable um in the genitive plural and accusative singular masculine of stems in u or in the nominative and accusative singular neuter of the same stems, they gave it a sound rather like o, which assimilated these terminations to Celtic terminations in om. They said *dominom*. So, too, they kept certain methods of noun-formation which were peculiar to their language, which formed adjectives in *-acos*. Names of *fundi* and some other words were formed in *-acus*.[2] Certain words passed into the Latin vocabulary, such as *cantus*, the iron felloe of a wheel, from Gaulish *cantos*[3] (Welsh *cant* " circle ").[4] Others survived in the Latin of Gaul, such as *esox* " salmon " (Welsh *ehawk*, Irish *eo*), *cavannus* " owl " (Welsh *cuan*). A large number of these relics remained in the Romance languages and some in French, in addition to the geographical names, proper or common nouns, which remain in languages as fossils. Gaulish left to the Romance languages names of plants like *verveine* (verbena), beasts like *alouette* (lark), and others. *Clock* and *cloche* (bell) are Celtic (Low Latin *clocca*, Old Irish *cloc*); bells were worn by animals, but in Ireland only by those of *nemed* or holy men. *Cruche* (jug) is of Celtic origin (Irish *crocan*, Welsh *crochan*). *Bar*, *tringle*, *barque*, *beret*, *chimney*, and *biretta*, and their French equivalents all come from Gaulish, and so do *chemin* and *bief* (mill-race). M. Dottin has made as full a list of these words as possible but it is not yet complete, and research among local *patois* will increase it.

On the whole, a great deal of Gaulish has survived in the Romance tongues. When one people progressively adopts the language of civilization of another people which rules it, it never completely gives up its own; the two languages become blended. Latin must have been spoken in Gaul in the same way as French in Périgord. First people go over from one language to another; then a time comes

[1] Meillet, in **XLVII**, 1922, 5. Cf. ibid., xxi, i, 1918, p. 40.
[2] MacNeill, **CCCCXLI**, p. 152.
[3] Schoell, " Zur lateinischen Wortforschung," in **LXXI**, xxxi, p. 319.
[4] **CXL**, 1913, p. 240.

when a mixed tongue comes into being. To a certain extent, French stands in the same relation to Gaulish as the English dialect of the Lowlands to Gælic.

So the Celtic languages survive in two ways, in structure (but with the admission of many foreign elements) or in the shape of single elements embedded in languages of other structures. Everywhere there is something left of them, but they were only the remnants of a vanishing life until the revival of Irish, because the Celtic societies had not lasted as Celtic nations and states. The language will be saved by the Irish Free State.

Such, as I said, has been the pecular fate of the Celts ; they were unable to create lasting states, and their languages have survived only in a partial and diminished condition. But that original, vigorous race, although it failed politically, chiefly through having no sense of the state or an insufficient sense of discipline, made very great contributions to civilization, to industry, art and, above all, literature. The La Tène craftsmen were masters in the arts and industries in general, and particularly in jewellery, and the earliest tellers of the Celtic epics showed a feeling for heroic poetry, a sense of the marvellous, mingled with humour, and a dramatic conception of fatality which truly belong to the Celts alone. Gaston Paris made the profound observation that the romance of Tristram and Yseult has a particular sound, which is hardly found elsewhere in Mediæval literature, and he explained it by the Celtic origin of these poems. It was through Tristram and Arthur that all that was clearest and most valuable in the Celtic genius was incorporated in the mind of Europe. And that tradition has been kept up by the unending line of poets and prose-writers of Ireland, Scotland, Wales, and Brittany who have adorned English and French literature by bringing to it the genius of their race.

I said above that the historians of France, who wrote such a peculiarly fine history, had in them the spirit of the Celtic race. But the very story which they were telling, the history of that undestroyable people of peasants, warriors, and artists, with its glories and tumults, its hopes and enthusiasms, its discords and rebirths, is surely the story of a nation whose blood and bones are mainly composed of Celtic elements.

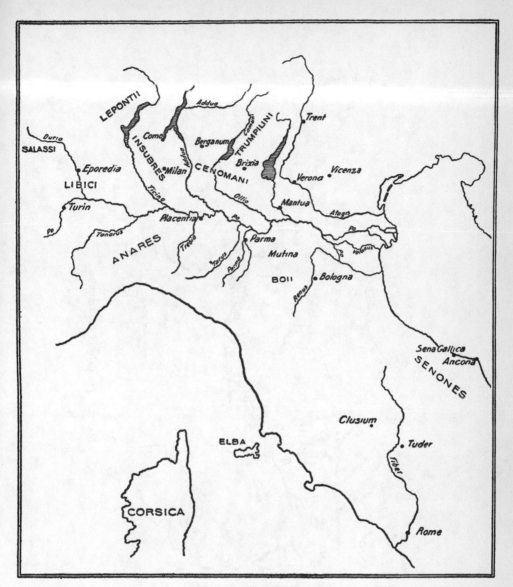

MAP 1.   Cisalpine Gaul.

[*Page* 277.

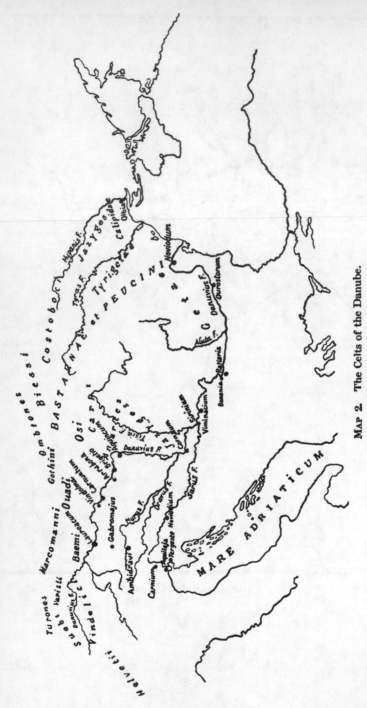

Map 2   The Celts of the Danube.

Helvetii
Vindelic.
Suebi Varisti
Danuvius
Turones
Marcomanni Ouadi Gothini Ombrones Biessi
Baemiseum
Osi
Costoboci
Carpi Tyrigetae
Hyanis F.
Jazygasidae
Tyras F.
Calipidae
Olbia
Vindobona
BASTARNAE et PEDCINI
Carnuntum
Arrabona
Brigetio
Aquincum
Bastarnae
Cabromajus
Ambid Favi
Flua F.
Danuvius R.
Tisia
Marisus F.
Drauus F.
Noviodum F.
Savus F.
Carnium
Aemona
Tergeste
Noviodum
Partiscus
Singidum
Viminacium
Bononia
Ratiaria
Alata F.
Danuvius F.
Novidunum
Durostorum
MARE ADRIATICUM

Page 278.]

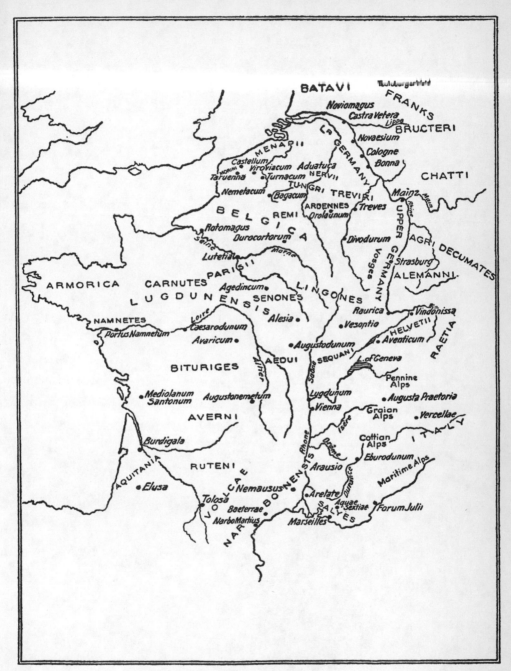

BATAVI
Teutoburgerwald
FRANKS
Noviomagus
Castra Vetera
Lippe
BRUCTERI
Novaesium
Cologne
Bonna
CHATTI
LOWER GERMANY
MENAPII
Castellum
MORINI
Viroviacum
Aduatuca
Tarvenna
Turnacum
NERVII
Mainz
Main
Nemetacum
TUNGRI
TREVIRI
Bagacum
ARDENNES
Treves
REMI
Orolaunum
UPPER GERMANY
Rhine
BELGICA
AGRI DECUMATES
Ratomagus
Durocortorum
Divodurum
Strasburg
Seine
Lutetia
Marne
Vosges
ALEMANNI
PARISII
ARMORICA
CARNUTES
LINGONES
LUGDUNENSIS
Agedincum
SENONES
Raurica
Vindonissa
NAMNETES
Loire
Alesia
Vesontio
HELVETII
Portus Namnetum
Caesarodunum
Aventicum
RAETIA
Avaricum
Augustodunum
Saône
SEQUANI
L. of Geneva
AEDUI
Allier
Pennine
Alps
BITURIGES
Lugdunum
Augusta Praetoria
Mediolanum
Santonum
Augustonemetum
Vienna
Graian
Alps
Vercellae
AVERNI
Isère
ITALY
Burdigala
Cottian
Alps
Rhone
Eburodunum
AQUITANIA
RUTENI
Arausio
Maritime Alps
Elusa
VOLCAE
Nemausus
Arelate
Tolosa
Baeterrae
NARBONENSIS
Aquae
Sextiae
Forum Julii
NarboMartius
Marseilles
SALYES
Drôme
Durance

MAP 3.   Gaul.

[Page 279.

INDEX

BIBLIOGRAPHY

I. SOURCES

Greek and Latin authors are indicated by the usual abbreviations. *F.H.G.* stands for Carolus Müller, *Fragmenta Historicorum Græcorum*, in the Collection Didot.

[Certain English editions have been added in square brackets, but the footnotes do not refer to the pages of these editions unless it is so stated.—Trs.]

II. INSCRIPTIONS

Corpus Inscriptionum Latinarum, consilio et auctoritate Academiæ Regiæ Borussicæ, Berlin, 1863, etc. . **I**
Ephemeris Epigraphica . . . . . **II**
Allmer (A.), *Inscriptions antiques de Vienne*, Viennc, 1875–8 . . . . . . **III**
Dittenberger (G.), *Sylloge Inscriptionum Græcarum*, 2nd ed., Leipzig, 1898 ; 3rd ed., 1915–1923 . **IV**
Durrbach (F.), *Choix d'inscriptions de Délos*, Paris, 1921 . . . . **V**
Rhys (Sir John), *The Celtic Inscriptions of Gaul and Italy*, London, 1910 . . . . . **VI**
—— *Gleanings in the Italian Field of Celtic Epigraphy*, repr. from **CXXI**, London, 1915 . . . **VII**
—— *Notes on the Coligny Calendar*, London, 1910 . **VIII**

III. PERIODICALS

Abhandlungen der königlichen preussischen Akademie der Wissenschaften, phil. hist. Klasse, Berlin . **IX**
Abhandlungen der naturhistorischen Gesellschaft zu Nürnberg, Nuremberg . . . . **X**
Annales de la Faculté des sciences de Marseille . . **XI**
Annales de la Société Éduenne, Autun . . . **XII**
Année sociologique, Paris . . . . . **XIII**
Anuari de l'Institut d'Estudis catalans, Barcelona . **XIV**
Anthropologie, Paris . . . . . **XV**
Antiquaries' Journal, London . . . . **XVI**
Anzeiger für schweizerische Altertumskunde (Indicateur d'antiquités suisses), Zurich . . . . **XVII**
Archæologia, or miscellaneous tracts relating to antiquity, published by the Society of Antiquaries of London, London . . . . . **XVIII**
Archæologia Cambrensis, Cambridge . . . . **XIX**
Archaeologischer Anzeiger, Berlin . . . . **XX**
Archaelogiai értesitö, Budapest . . . . **XXI**
Archeologo portugues, Lisbon . . . . **XXII**

Archiv für Anthropologie, Brunswick . . .   **XXIII**
Archiv für slavische Philologie, Berlin . .   **XXIV**
Archives suisses d'anthropologie générale, Geneva .   **XXV**
Association française pour l'avancement des sciences.
     Comptes rendus des Congrès annuels, Paris . .   **XXVI**
Atti della reale Accademia dei Lincei, scienze morali,
     Rome . . . .   **XXVII**
Atti della Soc. arch. e B. Arti di Torino, Turin .   **XXVIII**
Bericht der römisch-germanischen Kommission des
     kaiserlichen archäologischen Instituts, afterwards
     deutschen Arch. Instit., Frankfort on Main . .   **XXIX**
Berliner philologische Wochenschrift, Berlin . .   **XXX**
Berliner Monatschrift, Berlin . . . . .   **XXXI**
Bibliothèque de l'École des Chartes, Paris . . .   **XXXII**
Biblos . . . .   **XXXIII**
Boletín de la Academia de la Historia, Madrid . .   **XXXIV**
Boletín de la Sociedad Española de Excursiones,
     Madrid . . . .   **XXXV**
Boletín de la Sociedad geográfica, Madrid . . .   **XXXVI**
Bonner Jahrbücher, Jahrbücher des Vereins von Alter-
     tumsfreunden im Rheinlande, Bonn . . .   **XXXVII**
Bulletin archéologique du Comité des travaux
     historiques, Paris . . . . . .   **XXXVIII**
Bulletin de correspondance hellénique, Athens . .   **XXXIX**
Bulletín de la Commission archéologique de Narbonne   **XL**
Bulletin de la Société d'anthropologie, Paris . .   **XLI**
Bulletin de la Société anthropologique de Bruxelles .   **XLII**
Bulletin de la Société archéologique du Finistère,
     Quimper . . . .   **XLIII**
Bulletin de la Société archéologique de Provence,
     Marseilles . . . .   **XLIV**
Bulletin de la Société d'émulation du Doubs, Besançon   **XLV**
Bulletin de la Société Jersiaise, Jersey . . .   **XLVI**
Bulletin de la Société de linguistique, Paris . .   **XLVII**
Bulletin de la Société préhistorique française, Paris .   **XLVIII**
Bulletin de la Société des sciences historiques et
     naturelles de l'Yonne, Auxerre . . .   **XLIX**
Bulletin anthropologique et biologique de Lyon . .   **L**
Bulletin hispanique, Bordeaux . . . . .   **LI**
Bullettino dell'Instituto di correspondenza archeologica,
     Rome . . . .   **LII**
Bullettino di paletnologia italiana, Parma . . .   **LIII**
Cahiers d'histoire et d'archéologie d'Alsace, Strasburg.   **LIV**
Cechiset Revue, Prague . . . . . .   **LV**
Celtic Review . . . .   **LVI**
Classical Review, London . . . . .   **LVII**
Comptes rendus de l'Académie des Inscriptions et
     Belles-Lettres, Paris . . . . . .   **LVIII**
Congrès international d'anthropologie et d'archéologie
     préhistoriques . . . .   **LIX**
Congrès préhistorique de France, C. R. des sessions,
     Paris . . . .   **LX**
Congrès archéologique de France . . . .   **LXI**
English historical Review, London . . . .   **LXII**
Erin, Dublin . . . .   **LXIII**

Folklore LXIV
Fundberichte aus Schwaben LXV
Geographical Journal LXVI
Germania. Korrespondenzblatt der römisch-germani-
    schen Kommission des deutschen archäologischen
    Instituts, Frankfort on Main . . . LXVII
Giornale storico e letterario della Liguria . . . LXVIII
Globus, Brunswick LXIX
Hermes, Berlin LXX
Indogermanische Forschungen, Strasburg . . . LXXI
Jahrbuch des deutschen archäologischen Instituts,
    Berlin LXXII
Jahrbuch der Gesellschaft für lothring. Geschichte und
    Altertumskunde, Metz LXXIII
Jahrbuch des städtischen Museums für Völkerkunde zu
    Leipzig LXXIV
Journal Asiatique, Paris LXXV
Journal of the Anthropological Institute of Great
    Britain, London LXXVI
Journal of Committee Studies (see CXXVI) . . LXXVII
Journal of Hellenic Studies, London LXXVIII
Journal of Roman Studies, London LXXIX
Journal of the Royal Society of Antiquaries of Ireland,
    Dublin LXXX
Korrespondenzblatt der deutschen Gesellschaft für
    Anthropologie und Urgeschichte, Brunswick and
    Munich LXXXII
[For LXXXIII, see below, CLXXIV]
Mainzer Zeitschrift, Mainz LXXXIV
Mannus, Berlin LXXXV
Matériaux pour l'histoire primitive et naturelle de
    l'Homme, Paris LXXXVI
Mémoires de l'Académie des sciences, Paris . . LXXXVII
Mémoires de la Société d'anthropologie, Paris . . LXXXVIII
Mémoires de la Société d'émulation du Jura, Lons-le-
    Saunier LXXXIX
Mémoires de la Société archéologique de Montpellier . XC
Mémoires de la Société archéologique du Midi de la
    France, Toulouse XCI
Mémoires de la Société archéologique de Bretagne,
    Rennes XCII
Mémoires de la Société de linguistique, Paris . . XCIII
Mémoires de la Société nationale des Antiquaires de
    France, Paris XCIV
Mémoires de la Société archéologique lorraine et du
    Musée historique lorrain, Nancy . . . XCV
Mémoires de la Société préhistorique suisse, Zurich
    (see CI) XCVI
Memorias de la Sociedad española de antropología,
    etnografía y prehistoria, Madrid . . . XCVII
Memoirs of the Anthropological Society, London . XCVIII
Memorias de la Junta superior de Excavaciones y
    Antigüedades, Madrid XCIX
Mitteilungen der Anthropologischen Gesellschaft in
    Wien C

Mitteilungen der Anthropologischen Gesellschaft, Zurich CI
Mitteilungen des deutschen archäologischen Instituts, Athenische Abteilung, Athens CII
—— —— Römische Abteilung, Rome . . . CIII
Mitteilungen der prähistorischen Commission der kais. Akademie der Wissenschaften, Vienna . . CIV
Mitteilungen (wissenschaftliche) aus Bosnien und Herzegowina, Vienna CV
Monumenti antichi pubblicati per cura della R. Academia dei Lincei, Milan CVI
Monuments Piot, Paris CVII
Musée Belge, Liége and Paris CVIII
Musée Neuchâtelois, Neuchâtel CIX
Nassauische Annalen CX
New Ireland Review, Dublin CXI
Notizie degli scavi di antichità, Rome . . . CXII
Nouvelles Archives des missions scientifiques, Paris . CXIII
Orientalische Literaturzeitung, Berlin . . . CXIV
Památky archœologické, Prague CXV
Philologica, Journal of Comparative Philology, London CXVI
Portugalia, Oporto (1899–1908) CXVII
Prähistorische Zeitschrift, Berlin CXVIII
Pro Alesia, Paris CXIX
Pro Nervia, Bavay CXX
Proceedings of the British Academy, London . . CXXI
Proceedings of the Royal Irish Academy, Dublin . CXXII
Proceedings of the Society of Antiquaries of London . CXXIII
Proceedings of the Society of Antiquaries of Scotland, Edinburgh CXXIV
Rassegna delle scienze geologiche, Rome . . . CXXV
Reports of the Research Committee of the Society of Antiquaries of London CXXVI
Report of . . . the British Association, London . . CXXVII
Rendiconti della R. Accademia dei Lincei, classe di scienze morali, storiche e filologiche, Rome . CXXVIII
Reports of the Smithsonian Institute, Washington . CXXIX
Revue d'anthropologie, Paris CXXX
Revue de l'Instruction publique en Belgique, Bruges . CXXXI
Revue de Nîmes CXXXII
Revue de phonétique, Paris CXXXIII
Revue des Études anciennes, Bordeaux . . . CXXXIV
Revue des Études grecques, Paris CXXXV
Revue des questions scientifiques, Paris . . . CXXXVI
Revue du Mois, Paris CXXXVII
Revue anthropologique, Paris CXXXVIII
Revue archéologique, Paris CXXXIX
Revue celtique, Paris CXL
Revue historique, Paris CXLI
Revue numismatique, Paris CXLII
Revue préhistorique. Annales de palethnologie, Paris CXLIII
Rheinisches Museum für Philologie, Frankfort on Main CXLIV
Rivista archeologica della provincia di Como . . CXLV
Rhodania, Vienne CXLVI
Scottish Review, Edinburgh CXLVII

Sitzungsberichte der koenig. preussischen Akademie der
    Wissenschaften, Berlin . . . . .   **CXLVIII**
Sitzungsberichte der kais. Akademie der Wissenschaften
    zu Wien, philos. hist. Klasse, Vienna . . .   **CXLIX**
Société de statistique, d'histoire et d'archéologie de
    Marseille et de la Provence. Volume du
    Centenaire . . . .   **CL**
Sonderhefte des österr. arch. Institut, Vienna . .   **CLI**
Symbolæ Osloenses, Oslo . . . . .   **CLII**
Syria, Paris . . . .   **CLIII**
Transactions of the Honourable Society of
    Cymmrodorion . . . . . .   **CLIV**
Travaux de la section numismatique et archéologique
    du musée de Koloszvar . . . . .   **CLV**
Trabalhos da Sociedade portugueza de Antropologia e
    Etnologia, Oporto . . . . . .   **CLVI**
Trierer Jahresberichte, Treves . . . .   **CLVII**
Verhandlungen der Berliner Gesellschaft für Anthro-
    pologie, Ethnologie und Urgeschichte, Berlin .   **CLVIII**
Veröffentlichungen des oberhessischen Museums und der
    galischen Sammlungen zu Giessen, Abteilung für
    Vorgeschichte . . . .   **CLIX**
Westdeutsche Zeitschrift für Geschichte und Kunst,
    Bonn . . . .   **CLX**
Wiener Studien, Vienna . . . . . .   **CLXI**
Indogermanisches Jahrbuch . . . . .   **CLXII**
Wochenschrift für klassische Philologie, Berlin . .   **CLXIII**
Wörter und Sachen . . . . . .   **CLXIV**
Würtembergische Vierteljahrsschriften für Landes-
    geschichte, Stuttgart . . . . .   **CLXV**
Zeitschrift der deutsch. Morgenländischen Gesellschaft,
    Leipzig . . . .   **CLXVI**
Zeitschrift der Savigny-Stiftung für Rechtsgeschichte,
    Berlin . . . .   **CLXVII**
Zeitschrift für deutsche Altertumskunde . . .   **CLXVIII**
Zeitschrift für Ethnologie, Berlin . . . .   **CLXIX**
Zeitschrift für romanische Philologie, Halle . .   **CLXX**
Zeitschrift für celtische Philologie . . . .   **CLXXI**
Zeitschrift für Sozialwissenschaft . . . .   **CLXXII**
Zeitschrift für vergleichende Literaturgeschichte, Berlin   **CLXXIII**
Zeitschrift für vergleichende Sprachforschung, auf dem
    Gebiete der indogermanischen Sprachen, Berlin .   **CLXXIV**

IV. MISCELLANIES

Festgabe für Hugo Blümner, Zurich, 1914 . . .   **CLXXV**
Festschrift W. Stokes, Leipzig, 1900 . . . .   **CLXXVI**
Festschrift zur Feier des fünfundsiebzigjährigen
    Bestehens des röm.-germ. Centralmuseums zu
    Mainz, 1902 . . . .   **CLXXVII**
Heilbronner Festschrift . . . . .   **CLXXVIII**
Mélanges Ch. Bémont, Paris, 1913 . . . .   **CLXXIX**
Mélanges R. Cagnat, Paris, 1912 . . . .   **CLXXX**
Mélanges L. Havet, Paris, 1909 . . . .   **CLXXXI**

Essays and Studies presented to William Ridgeway,
Cambridge, 1913 CLXXXII
Mélanges de Saussure, Paris, 1908 CLXXXIII
Mélanges Vendryès, Paris, 1925 . . . CLXXXIV
Opuscula archaeologicà Oscari Montelio dedicata,
Stockholm, 1913 CLXXXV
Recueil d'études égyptologiques dédiées à la mémoire
de J.-F. Champollion, Paris, 1922 . . . CLXXXVI
Recueil Kondakow, Prague, 1926 . . . . CLXXXVII.

V. LANGUAGE

ARBOIS DE JUBAINVILLE (H. d'), *Éléments de la grammaire celtique*, Paris, 1903 CLXXXVIII
MACBAIN (Alexander), *An Etymological Dictionary of the Gaelic Language*, 2nd ed., Inverness, 1911 . CLXXXIX, CXC
BERNEKER (E.), *Slavisches etymologisches Wörterbuch*, Heidelberg, 1908–1913 CXC
BUDINSZKY (A.), *Die Ausbreitung der lateinischen Sprache*, Berlin, 1881 CXCII
CLINTON (O. H. Fynes), *The Welsh Vocabulary of the Bangor District*, Oxford, 1913 . . . CXCIII
Corpus Glossariorum Latinorum, Leipzig, 1888–1901 . CXCIV
CRAMER, *Rheinische Ortsnamen*, Düsseldorf, 1901 . CXCV
DOTTIN (Georges), *La Langue gauloise*, Paris, 1920 . CXCVI
—— *Manuel d'irlandais moyen*, vol. i (grammar), Paris, 1913 CXCVII
ERNAULT (E.), *Glossaire moyen-breton*, Paris, 1895–6 . CXCVIII
FINCK (F. N.), *Die Araner Mundart*, Marburg, 1899 . CXCIX
FISCHER (F. T. T. A.), *Die Lehnwörter des Altwest-nordischen* (Palaestra, lxxxv), Berlin, 1909 . . CC
FRASER (John), *History and Etymology*, Oxford, 1923 . CCI
GILES (Peter), *A Short Manual of Comparative Philology*, London, 1901 CCII
GILLIES (H. C.), *Elements of Gaelic Grammar, based on the work of the Rev. Alexander Stewart*, London, 1902 CCIII
GINNEKEN (van), *Principes de linguistique psychologique*, Paris, etc., 1907 CCIV
HENEBRY (Richard), *Contribution to the Phonology of Desi-Irish*, Greifswald, 1901 CCV
HERMET (Abbé F.), *Les Grafittes de la Graufesenque*, Rodez, 1923 CCVI
HOLDER (A. T.), *Alt-celtischer Sprachschatz*, 3 vols., Leipzig, 1896–1913 CCVII
JONES (Sir John Morris), *A Welsh Grammar, historical and comparative*, Oxford, 1913 . . . CCVIII
KEIL (Heinrich), *Grammatici Latini*, Leipzig, 1857–80 . CCIX
KLUGE (F.), *Etymologisches Wörterbuch der deutschen Sprache*, 6th ed., Strasburg, 1899 [*An Etymological Dictionary of the German Language*, London, 1891] CCX
—— *Vorgeschichte der altgermanischen Dialekte*, in H. PAUL, *Grundriss der germanischen Philologie*, vol. i, 1901 CCXI

LONGNON (A.), *Noms de lieux anciens de la France*,
Paris, 1926   CCXII

LOTH (J.), *Chrestomathie bretonne*, Paris, 1890 . .   CCXIII

—— *Vocabulaire vieux-breton* (Bibl. É.H.É., vi), Paris,
1884   CCXIV

MACALISTER (Robert A. Stewart), *Studies in Irish
Epigraphy*, 3 vols., London, 1897–1907 . .   CCXV

MEILLET (A.), *Les Dialectes indo-européens*, Paris, 1922   CCXVI

—— *Introduction à l'étude comparative des langues
indo-européennes*, 3rd ed., Paris, 1912 . . .   CCXVII

—— and COHEN (M.), *Les Langues du monde*, Paris,
1924   CCXVIII

MOLLOY (John H.), *A Grammar of the Irish Language*,
Dublin, 1867   CCXIX

MORRIS (Meredith), *A Glossary of the Demetian Dialect*,
Tonypandy, 1910   CCXX

MOULTON (James H.), *Two Lectures on the Science of
Language*, Cambridge, 1903   CCXXI

MEYER (W.), *Fragmenta Burana*, Berlin, 1901 . .   CCXXII

NICHOLSON (Edward W. Byron), *Keltic Researches:
studies in the history and distribution of the ancient
Goidelic language and peoples*, London, 1904 . .   CCXXIII

—— *Sequanian: first steps in the investigation of a
newly discovered ancient European language*,
London, 1898   CCXXIV

O'DONOVAN (John), *A Grammar of the Irish Language*,
Dublin, 1845   CCXXV

O'NOLAN (Rev. Gerald), *Studies in Modern Irish*,
Dublin, 1919   CCXXVI

PEDERSEN (Holger), *Vergleichende Grammatik der
keltischen Sprachen*, Göttingen, 1909–13 . .   CCXXVII

QUIGGIN (Edmund C.), *A Dialect of Donegal*, Cambridge, 1906   CCXXVIII

REID (Duncan), *A Course of Gaelic Grammar*, Glasgow,
1902 [3rd ed., 1908]   CCXXIX

RHYS (Sir John), *Celtæ and Galli*, London, 1905 .   CCXXX

ROWLAND (T.), *A Grammar of the Welsh Language*
Wrexham, n.d., 4th ed.   CCXXXI

[For CCXXXII, see below, STOKES, CCXXXVI]

SOMMERFELT (A.), *Dē en Italo-celtique: son rôle dans
l'évolution morphologique des langues italo-celtiques*,
Oslo, 1920   CCXXXIII

—— *The Dialect of Torr, Co. Donegal*, Oslo, 1922 .   CCXXXIV

STOKES (Whitley) and STRACHAN (J.), *Thesaurus
Palæohibernicus*, 2 vols., Cambridge, 1901–3 .   CCXXXV

—— *Three Irish Glossaries*, London, 1862 . .   CCXXXVI

—— *Urkeltischer Sprachschatz*, trans. BEZZENBERGER,
Göttingen, 1894 [pt. iii of A. FICK, *Wörterbuch der
indogermanischen Grundsprache*, 4th ed., 1890–1909)   CCXXXVII

Beiträge zur Kunde der indogermanischen Sprachen,
Göttingen, 1877–1900   CCXXXVIII

[For CCXXXIX, see above, STOKES, CCXXXVII]

THURNEYSEN (Rudolf), *Keltoromanisches*, Halle, 1884 .   CCXL

VALLÉE (F.), *La Langue bretonne et le français*, 4th ed.,
Saint-Brieuc, 1916   CCXLI

302   BIBLIOGRAPHY

VENDRYÈS (Joseph), *Grammaire du vieil irlandais*, Paris,
1908   CCXLII
WALDE (A.), *Lateinisches etymologisches Wörterbuch*,
2nd ed., Heidelberg, 1910   CCXLIII
—— *Über älteste sprachliche Beziehungen zwischen
Kelten und Italikern*, Innsbruck, 1917   .   .   CCXLIV
WINDISCH (E.), in GROEBER, *Grundriss der romanischen
Philologie*, 2nd ed., Strasburg, 1905, pp. 390–4 .   CCXLV
ZIMMER (H.), *Keltische Beiträge, Studien*, in CLXXIV,
1888   CCXLVI

VI. LITERATURE

Ancient Laws of Ireland, 6 vols., Dublin, 1865–79 .   CCXLVII
ARBOIS DE JUBAINVILLE (H. d'), *Cours de littérature
celtique*, 12 vols., Paris, 1883–1902   .   .   .   CCXLVIII
—— *Essai d'un catalogue de la littérature épique de
l'Irlande*, Paris, 1883.   CCXLIX
—— *Le cycle mythologique irlandais et la mythologie
celtique*, Paris, 1884 [*The Irish Mythological Cycle
and Celtic Mythology*, Dublin, 1903]   .   .   .   CCL
ARNOLD (Matthew), *The Study of Celtic Literature*,
London, 1891 [new ed., 1910]   CCLI
BEST (R. I.), *Bibliography of Irish Philology and
Literature*, Dublin, 1913   CCLII
CAMPBELL (John F.), *Leabhar na Feinne*, London, 1872   CCLIII
—— *Popular Tales of the West Highlands*, Edinburgh,
1890   CCLIV
CURTIN (Jeremiah), *Hero-tales of Ireland*, London, 1894   CCLV
Domesday Book   CCLVI
CROKER (Thomas Crofton), *Fairy Legends and Traditions
of the South of Ireland*, London, 1882 .   .   .   CCLVII
FARADAY (Winifred), *The Cattle Raid of Cuailnge*,
London, 1901   CCLVIII
GREGORY (Isabella A.), Lady Gregory, *Cuchulain of
Muirthemne*, London, 1902   CCLIX
GUEST (Lady Charlotte), *The Mabinogion* .   .   .   CCLX
GWYNN (Edward), *The Metrical Dindsenchas* (Todd
Lectures, viii, ix, x), 3 vols., Dublin, 1908–13   .   CCLXI
HULL (Eleanor), *A Text-book of Irish Literature*, 2 pts.,
Dublin, 1906   CCLXII
—— *The Cuchullin Saga in Irish Literature*, London,
1898   CCLXIII
HYDE (Douglas), *A Literary History of Ireland*, London,
1899   CCLXIV
Irish Texts Society, *Publications*, London, 1899, etc. .   CCLXV
JOYCE (P. W.), *The Origin and History of Irish Names
of Places*, 2 ser., Dublin, 1869–75   .   .   .   CCLXVI
—— *Old Celtic Romances*, London, 1879 [2nd ed., 1894]   CCLXVII
MACALISTER (Robert A. Stewart) and MACNEILL (John),
ed., *Leabhar Gabhála. The Book of Conquests of
Ireland*, 1917   CCLXVIII
Lives of Saints, from the Book of Lismore, ed. W. STOKES,
Oxford, 1890   CCLXIX

LOTH (J.), *Les Mabinogion*, 2 vols., Paris, 1913 . . CCLXX
MARTIN (Martin), *A Description of the Islands of Scotland*, London, 1703 CCLXXI
MEYER (Kuno), *Fianaigecht*, Dublin, 1910 . . . CCLXXII
—— *Totenklage um König Niall Noigiallach*, in CLXXVI CCLXXIII
—— and NUTT (Alfred), *The Voyage of Bran*, 2 vols., London, 1895–7 CCLXXIV
NUTT (Alfred), *Celtic and Medieval Romance*, London, 1899 CCLXXV
—— *Cuchulain, the Irish Achilles*, London, 1900 . CCLXXVI
—— *Legends of the Holy Grail*, London, 1902 . . CCLXXVII
O'CURRY (Eugene), *Lectures on the Manuscript Materials of Ancient Irish History*, 8 vols., Dublin, 1861 . CCLXXVIII
O'GRADY (Standish), *Silva Gadelica*. 2 vols., London, 1892 CCLXXIX
RENAN (Ernest), *La Poésie des races celtiques*, Paris [*The Poetry of the Celtic Races*, London, 1896] . CCLXXX
RHYS (Sir John), *Studies in the Arthurian Legend*, Oxford and New York, 1891 CCLXXXI
—— *Lectures on the Origin and Growth of Religion as illustrated by Celtic Heathendom* (Hibbert Lectures), London, 1888 CCLXXXII
—— *The Mabinogion*, London, 1901 . . . CCLXXXIII
—— and EVANS (J. G.), ed., *Mabinogion*, Oxford, 1887 CCLXXXIV
Sanas Cormaic, ed. K. MEYER, Halle, 1912 . . CCLXXXV
SCHIRMER (G.), *Zur Brendanus-Legende*, Leipzig, 1888 . CCLXXXVI
SKENE (William F.), *Four Ancient Books of Wales*, 2 vols., Edinburgh, 1868 CCLXXXVII
STOKES (Whitley), *Three Middle Irish Homilies*, Calcutta, 1877 CCLXXXVIII
THURNEYSEN (Rudolf), *Die irische Helden- und Königssage bis zum siebzehnten Jahrhundert*, Halle, 1921 CCLXXXIX
—— *Sagen aus dem Alten Irland*, Berlin, 1901 . . CCXC
Todd Lectures, Dublin, 1885–1924 . . . CCXCI
Transactions of the Ossianic Society, Dublin, 1855–61 . CCXCII
Waifs and Strays of Celtic Tradition, Argyllshire series, 3 vols., London, edited by Lord Archibald CAMPBELL and others CCXCII
WESTON (Jessie L.), *King Arthur and his Knights*, London, 1899 CCXCIV
WINDISCH (E.), *Irische Texte*, Leipzig, 1880 . . CCXCV
—— *Die altirischen Heldensage, Táin Bo Cuailnge, nach dem Buch von Leinster*, Leipzig, 1905 . . CCXCVI

VII. GENERAL WORKS

ÅBERG (Nils), *Das nordische Kulturgebiet in Mitteleuropa während der jüngeren Steinzeit*, 2 vols., Upsala, 1918 CCXCVII
ALLEN (John Romilly), *Celtic Art in Pagan and Christian Times*, 2nd ed., London, 1912 . . . CCXCVIII
ARBOIS DE JUBAINVILLE (H. d'), *Les Celtes depuis les temps les plus reculés jusqu'en l'an 100 avant notre ère*, Paris, 1904. CCXCIX

ARBOIS DE JUBAINVILLE (H. d'), *Les Druides et les dieux celtiques à forme d'animaux*, Paris, 1906 CCC

—— *Les Premiers Habitants de l'Europe*, 2nd ed., 2 vols., Paris, 1889–94 CCCI

ARMSTRONG (E. C. R.), *Guide to the Collection of Irish Antiquities. Catalogue of Irish Gold Ornaments in the Collection of the Royal Irish Academy*, Dublin, 1920 CCCII

BERTRAND (A.), *Archéologie celtique et gauloise*, Paris, 1876 CCCIII

BIENKOWSKI (P.), *Les Celts dans les arts mineurs gréco-romains*, Cracow, 1928 CCCIV

BIENKOWSKI (P. R. von), *Die Darstellungen der Gallier in der hellenischen Kunst*, Vienna, 1908 . . CCCV

BLANCHET (A.), *Traité des monnaies gauloises*, Paris, 1905 CCCVI

BOAS, *The Social Organization and the Secret Societies of the Kwakiutl Indians*, Washington, n.d. . . CCCVII

BUSHE-FOX (J. P.), *Excavations at Hengistbury Head*, in **CXXVI** 1915, ... CCCVIII

CASTILLO YURRITA (A. del), *La Cultura del vaso campani-forme*, Barcelona, 1928 CCCIX

CAVAIGNAC (E.), *Histoire du Monde*, Paris . . . CCCX

CHAPOT (V.), *Le Monde romain*, Paris, 1927 [*The Roman World*, in this series, London and New York, 1928] CCCXI

COOK (A. B.), *The European Sky-god*, repr. from **LXIV**, 1904 CCCXII

Corpus Vasorum Antiquorum CCCXIII

MacCULLOCH (Rev. John A.), *The Religion of the Ancient Celts*, Edinburgh, 1911 CCCXIV

DAREMBERG and SAGLIO, *Dictionnaire des antiquités grecques et romaines*, Paris, 1877–1919 . . . CCCXV

DAVY (G.), *La foi jurée*, Paris, 1922 CCCXVI

DÉCHELETTE (J.), *La Collection Millon. Antiquités préhistoriques et gallo-romaines*, Paris, 1913 . . CCCXVII

—— *Manuel d'archéologie préhistorique, celtique, et gallo-romaine*, 4 vols., Paris, 1908–14 . . . CCCXVIII

DELATTE (A.), *Études sur la littérature pythagoricienne*, Bibl. É.H.É., Paris, 1915 CCCXIX

DENIKER (J.), *Les Races et les peuples de la terre*, Paris, 1900 [*The Races of Man*, London, 1900] . . CCCXX

DOTTIN (G.), *Les Anciens Peuples de l'Europe*, Paris, 1916 CCCXXI

—— *Manuel pour servir à l'étude de l'antiquité celtique*, 2nd ed., Paris, 1915 CCCXXII

—— *La Religion des Celtes*, Paris, 1904 . . . CCCXXIII

EBERT (M.), *Reallexikon der Vorgeschichte*, 15 vols., Berlin, 1924–32 CCCXXIV

ESPÉRANDIEU (E.), *Recueil général des bas-reliefs de la Gaule*, Paris, 1907–30 CCCXXV

FEIST (S.), *Kultur, Ausbreitung, und Herkunft der Indo-germanen*, Berlin, 1913 CCCXXVI

FELICE (P. de), *L'Autre Monde : mythes et légendes. Le purgatoire de Saint Patrice*, Paris 1906 . . CCCXXVII

BIBLIOGRAPHY 305

FLEURE (Herbert J.), *The Races of England and Wales*, London, 1923 CCCXXVIII

FÖHR (Julius von), *Hügelgräber auf der Schwäbischen Alb*, ed. L. MAYER, Stuttgart, 1892 . . . CCCXXIX

FORRER (R.), *Reallexikon der prähistorischen, klassischen, und frühchristlichen Altertümer*, Berlin, 1907 . CCCXXX

FOUGÈRES (G.), GROUSSET (R.), JOUGUET (P.), and LESQUIER (J.), *Les Premières Civilisations*, vol. i of *Peuples et civilisations*, Paris, 1926 . . . CCCXXXI

FRAZER (Sir James G.), *Les Origines magiques de la royauté*, Paris, 1920 [*Lectures on the Early History of the Kingship*, London, 1905] CCCXXXII

—— *Le Totémisme*, Paris, 1898 [*Totemism*, Edinburgh, 1887] CCCXXXIII

FUSTEL DE COULANGES (N.-D.), *Histoire des institutions politiques de l'ancienne France*, 2nd ed., 5 vols., Paris, 1900–7 CCCXXXIV

GÖTZE (Alfred), *Führer auf die Steinsburg bei Römhild*, in CXVIII, 1921–2 CCCXXXV

HASTINGS (James), *Encyclopædia of Religion and Ethics*, Edinburgh, 1908–18 CCCXXXVI

HIRSCHFELD (H. O.), *Timagenes und die gallische Wandersage* (*Kleine Schriften*, Berlin, 1913) . . CCCXXXVII

HIRT (H. A.), *Die Indogermanen, ihre Verbreitung, ihre Urheimat, und ihre Kultur*, 2 vols., Strasburg, 1905–7 CCCXXXVIII

HÖRNES (Moriz), Yr., *Urgeschichte der bildenden Kunst*, ed. O. MENGHIN, 3rd ed., Vienna, 1925 . . CCCXXXIX

HOLLEAUX (M.), *Rome, la Grèce et les monarchies hellénistiques au IIIᵉ siècle avant J.-C.*, Paris, 1921 CCCXL

HOMO (Léon), *L'Italie primitive et les débuts de l'impérialisme romain*, Paris, 1925 [*Primitive Italy*, in this series, London and New York, 1927] . . CCCXLI

HOOPS (J.), ed., *Reallexikon der germanischen Altertumskunde*, Strasburg, 1911–12 CCCXLII

HUBERT (Henri), *Le Culte des héros et ses conditions sociales*, Paris, n.d. CCCXLIII

—— *Divinités gauloises. Sucelus et Nantosuelta, Epona, dieux de l'autre monde*, Mâcon, 1925 . . CCCXLIV

JARDÉ (A.), *La Formation du peuple grec*, Paris, 1923 [*The Formation of the Greek People*, in this series, London and New York, 1926] CCCXLV

JULLIAN (Camille), *De la Gaule à la France*, Paris, 1922 CCCXLVI

—— *Histoire de la Gaule*, 3rd ed., Paris, 1920, etc. . CCCXLVII

KAUFMANN (F.), *Deutsche Altertumskunde*, 2 vols., Munich, 1913–23 CCCXLVIII

KEANE (Augustus H.), *Man, Past and Present*, Cambridge, 1899 [revised ed., 1920] CCCXLIX

KEMBLE (John M.), *Horae Ferales ; or, Studies in the Archæology of the Northern Nations*, London, 1863 CCCL

LEUZE (O.), *Die römische Jahrzahlung*, 1909 . . CCCLI

MAINE (Sir Henry J. Sumner), *Lectures on the Early History of Institutions*, 8 vols., London, 1875 . CCCLII

MEITZEN, *Siedelung und Agrarwesen der Westgermanen und Ostgermanen*, Berlin, 1895 CCCLIII

MEYER (Éduard), *Geschichte des Altertums*, 1st and 3rd
eds., Stuttgart, 1893–1913 CCCLIV
—— *Histoire de l'Antiquité*, vol. i, *Introduction à l'étude
des Sociétés anciennes*, Paris, 1912 . . CCCLV
MEYER (Kuno), *Miscellanea Hibernica*, Urbana, 1916 . CCCLVI
MONTELIUS (O.), *Die älteren Kulturperioden in Orient
und Europa*. i. *Die Methode*, Stockholm, 1913 . CCCLVII
MOMMSEN (Theodor), *Monumenta Germaniæ historica*,
Berlin CCCLVIII
—— *Histoire romaine*, translation, 8 vols., Paris,
1863–72 [English translation, London and New
York, 1911] CCCLIX
MORET (A.) and DAVY (G.), *Des clans aux empires*, Paris,
1923 [*From Tribe to Empire*, in this series,
London and New York, 1926] . . . CCCLX
MUCH (A.), *Kunsthistorischer Atlas*, Vienna, 1889 CCCLXI
MÜLLENHOFF (K. V.), *Deutsche Altertumskunde*, 2nd ed.,
Berlin, 1890, etc. CCCLXII
MUNRO (Robért), *Les Stations lacustres de l'Europe aux
âges de la Pierre et du Bronze*, Paris, 1907 [*The
Lake Dwellings of Europe*, London, 1890] . . CCCLXIII
NIEDERLÉ (Lubor), *Manuel de l'antiquité slave*, 2 vols.,
Paris, 1923–6 CCCLXIV
NIESE (B.), *Geschichte der griechischen und makedonischen
Staaten*, 2 vols., Gotha, 1893–1908 . . CCCLXV
PARKYN (E. A.), *An Introduction to the Study of Pre-
historic Art*, London, 1915 CCCLXVI
PAUL (H.), *Grundriss der germanischen Philologie*,
3 vols., 2nd ed., Strasburg, 1901, etc. . . CCCLXVII
PAULY and WISSOWA, *Real-Encyclopädie der klass.
Altertumswissenschaft*, Stuttgart, 1894, etc. . CCCLXVIII
PHILIPON (E.), *Les Peuples primitifs de l'Europe
méridionale*, Paris, 1925 CCCLXIX
RANKE (J.), *Der Mensch*, 2 vols., 2nd ed., Leipzig, 1890 CCCLXX
RIDGEWAY (Sir William), *The Origin of Tragedy*, Cam-
bridge, 1910 CCCLXXI
REINACH (Salomon), *Description raisonnée du Musée
des Antiquités nationales*. ii. *Bronzes figurés*,
Paris, 1895 CCCLXXII
—— *Catalogue illustré du Musée des Antiquités
nationales au Château de Saint-Germain-en-Laye*,
vol. i, 2nd ed., Paris, 1926 ; vol. ii, 1924 . . CCCLXXIII
—— *Cultes, mythes et religions*, 4 vols., Paris, 1905–12
[*Cults, Myths, and Religions*, London, 1912] . CCCLXXIV
—— *Les Gaulois dans l'art antique et le sarcophage de
la vigne Ammendola*, Paris, 1889 . . . CCCLXXV
—— *Répertoire de peintures grecques et romaines*, Paris,
1922 CCCLXXVI
—— *Répertoire de la statuaire grecque et romaine*,
7 vols., Paris, 1897, etc. CCCLXXVII
RIPLEY (William Z.), *The Races of Europe*, London, 1900 CCCLXXVIII
ROGET DE BELLOGUET (D. F. L.), *Baron, Ethnogénie
gauloise*, 2nd ed., 4 pts., Paris, 1872 . . CCCLXXIX
ROSCHER (W. H.), *Ausführliches Lexikon der griechischen
und römischen Mythologie*, Leipzig, 1884, etc. . CCCLXXX

SCHRADER, *Die Indogermanen*, 1911 . . . . **CCCLXXXI**

—— *Reallexikon der indogermanischen Altertumskunde*,
2nd ed., Berlin, 1917–28 . . . . . . **CCCLXXXII**

SCHUCHARDT (C.), *Alt-Europa*, Strasburg and Berlin,
1919 . . . . **CCCLXXXIII**

SMITH (Reginald A.), *Guide to Early Iron Age
Antiquities* (British Museum), 2nd ed., London, 1925 **CCCLXXXIV**

SMITH (William Robertson), *Kinship and Marriage in
Early Arabia*, Cambridge, 1885 [New ed., London,
1903] . . . . **CCCLXXXV**

—— *Lectures on the Religion of the Semites*, Edinburgh,
1889 [3rd ed., London, 1927] . . . . . **CCCLXXXVa**

TAYLOR (Isaac), [*The Origin of the Aryans*, London,
1890] *L'Origine des Aryens*, Paris, 1895 . . **CCCLXXXVI**

THIERRY (Amédée), *Histoire des Gaulois*, 10th ed.,
Paris, 1877 . . . . **CCCLXXXVII**

TOUTAÏN (J.), *Les Cultes païens dans l'Empire romain*,
3 vols., Paris, 1907–20 . . . . . **CCCLXXXVIII**

VERWORN (M.), *Keltische Kunst*, Berlin, 1919 . . **CCCLXXXIX**

VINOGRADOFF (Sir Paul), *Historical Jurisprudence*,
Oxford, 1920 . . . . **CCCXC**

VIII. GERMANY

BEHRENS (G.), *Bronzezeit Süddeutschlands* (*Katalog d.
röm.-germ. Central-Museums*, 6), Mainz, 1916 . **CCCXCI**

GÖTZE, HÖFER, and ZSCHIESCHE, *Die vor- und früh-
geschichtliche Altertümer Thuringens*, Würzburg,
1909 . . . . **CCCXCII**

GROSS (V.), *La Tène. Un oppidum helvète*, Paris, 1886 **CCCXCIII**

GRUPP (G.), *Kultur der alten Kelten und Germanen*,
Munich, 1905 . . . . **CCCXCIV**

KOSSINNA (G.), *Die deutsche Vorgeschichte* (Mannus-
Bibliothek, 9), 2nd ed., Berlin, 1925 . . . **CCCXCV**

—— *Ursprung und Verbreitung der Germanen in vor-
und frühgeschichtlicher Zeit* (Mannus-Bibliothek, 6),
Leipzig, 1926 . . . . **CCCXCVI**

KRAUSE (W.), *Die keltische Urbevölkerung Deutschlands*,
Leipzig, 1906 . . . . **CCCXCVII**

KROPP (P.), *La-Tènezeitliche Funde an der keltisch-
germanischen Völkergrenze zwischen Saale und
Weisser Elster* (Mannus-Bibliothek, 5), Würzburg,
1911 . . . . **CCCXCVIII**

LINDENSCHMIT (L.), *Die Altertümer unserer heidnischen
Vorzeit*, Mainz, 1858–1911 . . . . . **CCCXCIX**

MONTELIUS (O.), *Chronologie der ältesten Bronzezeit in
Nord-Deutschland und Skandinavien*, Brunswick,
1900 . . . . **CCCC**

Nationalmuseet : Bogspœndefund fra de Seneste, Copenhagen, 1925 . . . . **CCCCI**

NAUE (J.), *Die Bronzezeit in Oberbayern*, Munich, 1894 **CCCCII**

—— *Die Hügelgräber zwischen Ammer- und Staffelsee*,
Stuttgart, 1887 . . . . **CCCCIII**

NORDEN (E.), *Die germanische Urgeschichte in Tacitus
Germania*, Berlin, 1922 . . . . . **CCCCIV**

NORDEN (A.), *Kivike graven och andra fornminnen i Kivikstrakten*, Stockholm, 1926   CCCCV

REINECKE (P.), *Zur Kenntniss der La Tène Denkmäler der Zone nordwärts der Alpen*, in *Festschrift des röm.-germ. Central-museums zu Mainz*, Mainz, 1902   CCCCVI

SCHAEFFER (F. A.), *Les Tertres funéraires préhistoriques dans la forêt de Haguenau*, 2 vols., Hagenau, 1926–30   CCCCVII

SCHUMACHER (N.), *Materialen zur Besiedelungs-Geschichte Deutschlands (Katalog des röm.-germ. Centralmuseums*, 5), Mainz, 1918 . . .   CCCCVIII

—— *Siedelungs- und Kulturgeschichte der Rheinlande.* i. *Die vorrömische Zeit*, Mainz, 1922 . . .   CCCCIX

—— *Verzeichniss der Abgüsse und wichtigere Photographien mit Gallier Darstellungen*, Mainz, 1911 .   CCCCX

WAGNER (E.), *Hügelgräber und Urnenfriedhöfe in Baden*, Carlsruhe, 1895   CCCCXI

IX. BRITISH ISLES

ABERCROMBY (Hon. John), *A Study of the Bronze Age Pottery of Great Britain and Ireland and its Associated Grave-Goods*, Oxford, 1912 . .   CCCCXII

ANDERSON (Alan Orr), *Early Sources of Scottish History*, A.D. 500 *to* 1286, 2 vols., Edinburgh, 1922 .   CCCCXIII

ANDERSON (Joseph), *Scotland in Pagan Times*, 2 vols., Edinburgh, 1886   CCCCXIV

ARMSTRONG (L. A.), *Archæological Notes from Ireland*, 1909–1910   CCCCXV

BRUTON, *The Caratacus Stone on Exmoor* . .   CCCCXVI

BULLEID (Arthur) and GRAY (H. St. G.), *The Glastonbury Lake Village*, 2 vols., Taunton, 1911–17   CCCCXVII

COFFEY (George), *The Bronze Age in Ireland*, Dublin, 1913   CCCCXVIII

COLLINGE, *Roman York*, Oxford, 1927 . . .   CCCCXIX

COLLINGWOOD (R.), *Roman Britain*, London, 1923 .   CCCCXX

CONRADY (Alexander), *Geschichte der Clanverfassung in dem schottischen Hochlande*, Leipzig, 1898 .   CCCCXXI

O'CURRY (Eugene), *On the Manners and Customs of the Ancient Irish*, 3 vols., London, 1873 . .   CCCCXXII

CZARNOWSKI (S.), *Saint Patrick et le culte des héros en Irlande*, Paris, 1919   CCCCXXIII

EVANS (John), *Ancient Stone Implements*, London, 1897   CCCCXXIV

—— *Ancient Bronze Implements*, London, 1898 . .   CCCCXXV

FARAL (Edmond), *La Légende arthurienne*, 3 vols., Paris, 1929   CCCCXXVI

FURNEAUX and ANDERSON, ed., TACITUS, *Agricola*, Oxford, 1923   CCCCXXVII

GOUGAUD (L.), *Les Chrétientés celtiques*, Paris, 1911 [*Christianity in Celtic Lands*, London, 1932] .   CCCCXXVIII

GREENWELL (William), *British Barrows*, Oxford, 1877.   CCCCXXIX

GUEST (Edwin), *Origines Celticæ*, London, 1883 .   CCCCXXX

HAVERFIELD (Francis J.), *The Roman Occupation of Britain*, revised by Sir George MACDONALD, Oxford, 1924   CCCCXXXI

HENDERSON (George), *Survivals in Belief among the Celts*, Glasgow, 1911 CCCCXXXII

HOLMES (T. Rice), *Ancient Britain and the Invasions of Julius Cæsar*, Oxford, 1907 CCCCXXXIII

JOYCE (P. W.), *A Social History of Ancient Ireland*, 2 vols., London, 1003 CCCCXXXIV

KEATING (Geoffrey), *The History of Ireland*, New York, 1866 [London, 1902–14] CCCCXXXV

KEITH (Sir Arthur), *The Antiquity of Man*, London, 1915 [new ed., 1925] CCCCXXXVI

LETHABY, *Roman London*, London, 1924 . . CCCCXXXVII

LLOYD (John E.), *A History of Wales*, London, 1911 . CCCCXXXVIII

MACALISTER (Robert A. S.), *Ireland in Pre-Celtic Times*, Dublin and London, 1921 . . . CCCCXXXIX

MACDONALD (Sir George), " The Agricolan Occupation of North Britain " in **LXXIX**, ix (1919) . . CCCCXL

MACNEILL (Eoin), *Phases of Irish History*, Dublin, 1919 CCCCXLI

MILLER (S. N.), *The Roman Fort at Balmuildy on the Antonine Wall*, Glasgow, 1922 . . . CCCCXLII

WHITE (Newport J. D.), *St. Patrick, his Writings and Life*, London, 1920 CCCCXLIII

MONTGOMERY (William E.), *The History of Land Tenure In Ireland*, Cambridge, 1889 . . . CCCCXLIV

O'DONOVAN, *The Tribes and Customs of Hy Many*, Dublin, 1843 CCCCXLV

PARKYN (E. A.), *An Introduction to the Study of Pre-historic Art*, London, 1915 . . . CCCCXLVI

PEAKE (Harold), *The Bronze Age and the Celtic World*, London, 1922 CCCCXLVII

POKORNY (J.), *The Origin of Druidism (Ann. Report of Smithsonian Institute*, 1911) . . . CCCCXLVIII

RHYS (Sir John), *Lectures on Welsh Philology*, 2nd ed., London, 1879 CCCCXLIX

—— *Celtic Folk-Lore*, 2 vols., Oxford, 1901 . . CCCCL

—— *Early Britain, Celtic Britain*, 3rd ed., London, 1904 CCCCLI

—— and JONES (David Brynnor), *The Welsh People*, 4th ed., London, 1906 CCCCLII

LEROUX (H.), *L'Armée romaine de Bretagne*, Paris, 1911 CCCCLIII

SAGOT (François), *La Bretagne romaine*, Paris, 1911 . CCCCLIV

SKENE (William F.), *Celtic Scotland*, 3 vols., Edinburgh, 1876–80 CCCCLV

—— *Chronicles of the Picts, Chronicles of the Scots, etc.*, Edinburgh, 1867 CCCCLVI

—— *The Highlanders of Scotland*, 2 vols., Edinburgh, 1836 [new ed., 1902] CCCCLVII

SPENSER (Edmund), *View of the State of Ireland*, Dublin, 1713 CCCCLVIII

SQUIRE (Charles), *The Mythology of the British Islands*, London, 1905 [new ed., 1910] . . . CCCCLIX

TAYLOR (M. V.), *The Roman Villa at North Leigh*, Oxford, 1923 CCCCLX

THOMPSON (A. Hamilton), *Military Architecture in England during the Middle Ages*, Oxford, 1913 . CCCCLXI

X. GAUL

BEAUPRÉ (J.), *Les Études préhistoriques en Lorraine de 1889 à 1902*, Nancy, 1902   CCCCLXII

BÉNARD LEPONTOIS, *Le Finistère préhistorique*, Paris, 1929   CCCCLXIII

BLANCHET (A.), *Les Enceintes romaines de la Gaule*, Paris, 1907   CCCCLXIV

—— *Les Souterrains-refuges de la France*, Paris, 1927   CCCCLXV

BLEICHER (G.) and BEAUPRÉ (J.), *Guide pour les recherches archéologiques . . . dans l'Est de la France*, Nancy, 1896   CCCCLXVI

BLOCH (G.), *La Gaule romaine* (E. LAVISSE, *Histoire de France*, vol. i, 2), Paris, 1901   CCCCLXVII

BONSTETTEN (G. de), Baron, *Notice sur des armes et chariots de guerre découverts à Tiefenau, près de Berne, en 1851*, Lausanne, 1852 . . .   CCCCLXVIII

BULLIOT (J. G.), *Mémoire sur l'émaillerie gauloise à l'oppidum du Mont-Beuvray*, Paris, 1872 . .   CCCCLXIX

CHATELLIER (P. du), *Les Époques préhistorique et gauloise dans le Finistère*, Rennes and Quimper, 2nd ed., 1907   CCCCLXX

—— *La Poterie aux époques préhistorique et gauloise en Armorique*, Paris, 1897   CCCCLXXI

DÉCHELETTE (J.), *Les Fouilles du Mont-Beuvray de 1897 a 1901*, Paris, 1904   CCCCLXXII

—— *Les Vases céramiques ornés de la Gaule romaine*, 2 vols., Paris, 1904   CCCCLXXIII

DESJARDINS (E.), *Géographie historique et administrative de la Gaule romaine*, 4 vols., Paris, 1876–93 .   CCCCLXXIV

FUSTEL DE COULANGES (Numa D.), *La Gaule romaine*, Paris, 1891   CCCCLXXV

GERIN-RICARD (H. de), *Le Sanctuaire pré-romain de Roquepertune*, Marseilles, 1928 . . .   CCCCLXXVI

GOURY (G.), *Les Étapes de l'Humanité*, 2 vols., Nancy, 1911   CCCCLXXVII

GRENIER (A.), *Les Gaulois*, Paris, 1924 . .   CCCCLXXVIII

ISCHER (T.), *Die Pfahlbauten des Bielersees*, Biel, 1928   CCCCLXXIX

LOTH (J.), *L'Émigration bretonne en Armorique du Ve au VIIe siècle*, Paris, 1883   CCCCLXXX

LOT (F.), *Mélanges d'histoire bretonne*, Paris, 1907 .   CCCCLXXXI

MARTEAUX and LEROUX, *Les Fins d'Annecy*, Annecy, 1913   CCCCLXXXII

MOREAU (F.), *Collection Caranda aux époques préhistorique, gauloise, romaine, et franque*, St. Quentin, 1877, 1881, 1887   CCCCLXXXIII

MOREL (L.), *La Champagne souterraine*, Rheims, 1898   CCCCLXXXIV

NICAISE (A.), *L'Époque gauloise dans le Département de la Marne*, Paris, 1866   CCCCLXXXV

PEYNAU (B.), *Découvertes archéologiques dans le Pays de Buch*, Bordeaux, 1926   CCCCLXXXVI

PHILIPPE (Abbé), *Cinq ans de fouilles au Fort-Harrouard*, Rouen, 1927   CCCCLXXXVII

POTHIER (General), *Les Tombes du Plateau de Ger*, Paris, 1900   CCCCLXXXVIII

VESLY (L. de), *Les Fana*, Rouen, 1910 CCCCLXXXIX

VIOLLIER (D.), *Essai sur les fibules de l'âge du fer trouvées en Suisse. Essai de typologie et de chronologie*, Zurich, 1907 CCCCXC

—— *Le Cimetière gallo-helvète d'Andelfingen*, Zurich, 1912 CCCCXCI

—— *Essai sur les rites funéraires en Suisse des origines à la conquête romaine (Bibl. de l'Éc. des H.-Études, sciences relig., vol. xxiv, 1)*, Paris, 1911 . . CCCCXCII

—— *Les Civilisations primitives de la Suisse. Sépultures du IIe âge du fer sur le plateau suisse*, Geneva, 1916 CCCCXCIII

VOUGA (P.), *La Tène*, Leipzig, 1923 CCCCXCIV

XI. SPAIN AND PORTUGAL

ÅBERG (N.), *La Civilisation énéolithique dans la péninsule ibérique*, Upsala, 1921 CCCCXCV

BONSOR (G.), *Les Colonies agricoles préromaines dans la vallée du Bétis*, Paris, 1899 CCCCXCVI

—— and THOUVENOT, *Nécropole ibérique de Setefilla*, Paris and Bordeaux, 1929 CCCCXCVII

BOSCH-GIMPERA (P.), *La Arqueologia pre-romana hispanica*, Barcelona, 1920 . . . CCCCXCVIII

—— *Los Celtas y la civilización celtica en la peninsula iberica*, Madrid, 1923 CCCCXCIX

—— *Els Celtes y la cultura de la primera edat del ferro a Catalunya*, Barcelona, 1924 . . . D

—— *La Ceramica iberica*, Madrid, 1915 . . . DI

—— *Ensayo de una reconstruccion de la etnologia prehistorica de la peninsula iberica*, Santander, 1923 DII

—— *El problema etnologico vasco y la arqueologia*, St. Sebastian, 1923 . . . . . DIII

—— *La Prehistoria de los Iberos y la etnologia vasca*, Santander, 1926 . . . . . DIV

—— *Prehistoria catalana*, Barcelona, 1919 . . DV

BOUDARD (P. A.), *Essai sur la numismatique ibérienne*, Paris, 1859 . . . . . . DVI

CARTAILHAC (E.), *Les Âges préhistoriques de l'Espagne et du Portugal*, Paris, 1886 . . . . DVII

CERRALBO (Marquis de), *El Alto Jalon*, Madrid, 1909 . DVIII

DÉCHELETTE (J.), *Essai sur la chronologie préhistorique de la péninsule ibérique*, Paris, 1909 . . DIX

Fontes Hispaniæ antiquæ. Avieni Ora Maritima, ed. A. SCHULTEN and P. BOSCH, Barcelona and Berlin, 1922 . . . . DX

LANTIER (R.), *El Santuario iberico de Castellar de Santisteban*, Madrid, 1917 . . . . DXI

LEITE DE VASCONCELLOS (J.), *Religiões da Lusitania*, 4 vols., Lisbon, 1904, etc. . . . . DXII

MENDEZ-CORREA (A. A.), *Os Povos primitivos da Lusitania*, Oporto, 1924 . . . . DXIII

PARIS (P.), *Essai sur l'art et l'industrie de l'Espagne primitive*, 2 vols., Paris, 1902–04 . . . DXIV

PERICOT (L.), *La Prehistoria de la peninsula iberica*, Barcelona, 1923 . . . . . DXV
PHILIPON (E.), *Les Ibères*, Paris, 1909 . . . DXVI
SCHULTEN (A.), *Hispania*, Barcelona, 1920 . . DXVII
—— *Numantia : eine topographisch-historische Untersuchung (Abhandl. d. Göttinger Ges. d. Wiss.*, 1905) DXVIII
—— *Numantia.* i. *Die Keltiberer und ihre Kriege mit Rom*, Munich, 1914 . . . . . DXIX
—— *Tartessos*, Hamburg, 1922 . . . . DXX
SIRET (H.) and (L.), *Les Premiers Âges du Métal dans le sud-est de l'Espagne*, Antwerp, 1887 . . DXXI
SIRET (L.), *Questions de chronologie et d'ethnographie ibérique*, Paris, 1913 . . . . DXXII
—— *Villaricos y Herrerias*, Madrid, 1908 . . . DXXIII
VEGA (Estacio da), *Antiguedades monumentaes do Algarve*, 4 vols., Lisbon, 1886–91 . . . DXXIV

XII. ITALY

BRIZIO (E.), *Il Sepolcreto gallico di Montefortino*, Rome, 1901 . . . . DXXV
CASTELFRANCO (P.), *Cimeli del museo Ponti nell' Isola Virginia (Lago di Varese)*, Milan, 1913 . . DXXVI
DUHN (F. von), *Italische Gräberkunde*, Heidelberg, 1924 DXXVII
DUCATI (P.), *Storia di Bologna.* i. *I Tempi antichi*, Bologna, 1928 . . . . . . DXXVIII
GRENIER (A.), *Bologne villanovienne et étrusque*, Paris, 1912 . . . . DXXIX
ISSEL (A.), *Liguria preistorica*, Genoa, 1908 . . DXXX
MAGNI (A.), *Le Necropoli ligure-gallice di Pianezzo nel canton Ticino*, Milan, 1907 . . . . DXXXI
MARCHESETTI (C.), *La Necropoli di S. Lucia presso Tolmino*, Trieste, 1886 . . . . DXXXII
MILANI, *Studi e materiali di archeologia e numismatica*. DXXXIII
MONTELIUS (O.), *La Civilisation primitive en Italie depuis l'introduction des métaux.* i. *Italie septentrionale*, Stockholm, 1904 . . . DXXXIV
—— —— ii. *Italie centrale*, 1910 . . . . DXXXV
MODESTOW (B.), *Introduction à l'histoire romaine*, Paris, 1907 . . . . DXXXVI
NISSEN (H.), *Italische Landeskunde*, Berlin, 1902 . DXXXVII
PAULY (C.), *Altitalische Forschungen*, 3 vols., Leipzig, 1885–91 . . . . DXXXVIII
PEET (T. E.), *The Stone and Bronze Ages in Italy and Sicily*, Oxford, 1909 . . . . DXXXIX
SERGI (G.), *Arii e Italici*, Turin, 1898 . . . DXL
ULRICH, *Graberfeld Bellinzona* . . . . DXLI

XIII. DANUBIAN CELTS

BERTRAND (A.) and REINACH (S.), *Les Celtes dans les vallées du Pô et du Danube*, Paris, 1894 . DXLII
FORRER (R.), *Keltische Numismatik der Rhein- und Donaulande*, Strasburg, 1908 . . . . DXLIII

JOUGUET (P.), *L'Impérialisme macédonien et l'hellénisation de l'Orient*, Paris, 1926, [*Macédonian Imperialism*, in this series, London and New York, 1928] . . . . DXLIV

MEHLIS, *Raetia* . . . . DXLV

ODOBESCO (A.), *Le Trésor de Petrossa*, Paris, 1889 . DXLVI

PARVAN (Vasile), *Dacia*, Cambridge, 1928 . . . DXLVII

—— *Getica*, Bukarest, 1926 . . . . . DXLVIII

PIČ, *Le Hradischt de Stradonitz en Bohême*, Leipzig, 1906 . . . . DXLIX

RADIMSKY (W.), *Nekropola na Jezerinama u Pritoci cid Bisca*, repr. from *Glasnik Zemaljskog museja u Bosni i Hercegovini*, Sarajevo, v, 1893 . . DL

REINACH (T.), *Mithridate Eupator, roi de Pont*, Paris, 1890 . . . . DLI

RICHLY (H.), *Bronzezeit in Böhmen*, Vienna, 1891 . DLII

RIDGEWAY (Sir William), *Early Age of Greece*, Cambridge, 1901 . . . . DLIII

STAEHELIN (P.), *Geschichte der kleinasiatischen Galater*, Leipzig, 1907 . . . . DLIV

STOCKY (A.), *La Bohême à l'âge de la pierre*, Prague, 1924 DLV